THE TYRANNY OF TASTE

THE
TYRANNY OF TASTE

*The Politics of Architecture and Design
in Britain 1550–1960*

Jules Lubbock

Published for the
Paul Mellon Centre for British Art by
Yale University Press
New Haven and London
1995

Endpapers: detail of wallpaper showing False Principles of Design from *c.* 1850, exhibited in the Chamber of Horrors, Marlborough House, 1852.

Set in Bembo by Best-set Typesetters Co., Hong Kong
Printed and bound through World Print Ltd., Hong Kong

Designed by Mary Carruthers

Library of Congress Cataloging-in-Publication Data
Lubbock, Jules.
    The tyranny of taste: the politics of architecture and
design in Britain 1550–1960 / Jules Lubbock.
        p.   cm.
    Includes bibliographical references (p.   ) and index.
    ISBN 0-300-05889-6
    1. Design—Political aspects—Great Britain.   2. Design—Economic
aspects—Great Britain.   3. Aesthetics, British.   4. Art and
society—Great Britain.   5. Architecture—Great Britain.   6. City
planning—Great Britain.   I. Title.
NK1443.A1L8   1995
720′.1′030942—dc20   94-26853
                                                                CIP

CONTENTS

ACKNOWLEDGEMENTS

BOOKS ARE COLLABORATIVE. I feel the warmest gratitude to my university, the University of Essex, for its extremely generous study leave and for granting me an additional two years of unpaid leave between 1986 and 1988, which was munificently funded by fellowships from the Nuffield Foundation and the Economic and Social Research Council, enabling me to complete my research. Books like this take a long time to write and are hugely expensive – this cost £250,000 at 1995 prices over fifteen years – and could not be written without public and private funding. My immense gratitude to the Higher Education Funding Council for England and its predecessor, the UGC, is, however, tinged with regret. Under their current form of research assessment, which allocates research funding on the basis of the collective 'output' of each department, requiring, in effect, the equivalent of a short book from each academic every four or five years, I could not have written a book like this without penalising my departmental colleagues and my university. It is right for the taxpayer to know whether public money is being well spent, but a system which measures and rewards crude productivity and thus encourages the output of so many of books (irrespective of quality) that few people will ever have time to read them is bad. It smacks of the excesses of the Soviet command economy. It is Stalinist. That cannot properly reflect the policies of a government which set its course by the two books published during his lifetime by Adam Smith, whose theories I discuss at length in a subsequent chapter.

My long-suffering colleagues in the Department of Art History and Theory at Essex have waited very patiently, as well as providing a most fertile intellectual environment in which to work. Sad to say, few academic writers nowadays mention their students; mine, undergraduates and postgraduates, were true collaborators whom it would be invidious to name individually.

Among individuals no one could have been more liberal with his time than Andrew Saint whose enthusiasm for an early draft encouraged me to persevere. He later read the whole manuscript more than once and his detailed comments have made it a shorter and I hope better book. John Nicoll, almost unique amongst publishers, gave me a (light) lunch once a year over ten years and quietly waited. Michael Podro, an inspiration over many years, aroused my interest in Hogarth and eighteenth-century aesthetics. Mark Crinson, my co-author on a related history of architectural education, read and commented upon the manuscript, as did my brother Richard Lubbock. Louise Durning persuaded me of the need for an extended period of study leave if I were ever to finish, and Tim Dalton kept waiting.

Sir Ernst Gombrich, Professor Joe Trapp, Charles Saumarez-Smith, Paul Thompson and Leonora Davidoff invited me to give papers. Joe Trapp kindly pointed me in the direction of the right funding bodies. Peter Davey, Jessica Rutherford, Colin Amery and Keith Middlemas were editors of journals who provided opportunities, and extra-special thanks are due to Gillian Wilce and Harriett Gilbert who were the literary editors of the *New Statesman* where much of my preliminary thinking was explored. Robert Thorne, Clive

Wainwright, Tony Seldon, Madeleine Mainstone, René Marcousé, Steve Couling, Thomas Puttfarken, Dawn Ades, Sheila Lee, Margaret Iversen, Ludmilla Jordanova, Jessica Lubbock, Sue Lubbock and Margaret Puxon all assisted in different ways. Other personal thanks are recorded in footnotes. Jennifer Iles, Maureen Reid, Barry Woodcock and Tim Laughton helped in the production of the manuscript. I thank the staffs of Essex University Library, the London Library, the British Library, the Victoria and Albert Museum and the Public Record Office for their help. David Woodcock of the Science Museum and both Timothy Stevens and Charlotte Orrell-Jones of the Victoria and Albert Museum helped beyond the call of duty.

Finally I have greatly enjoyed working with all the staff of Yale University Press and particularly my editor, Mary Carruthers.

In loving memory of my father
Isaac Lubbock

INTRODUCTION
The Political Economy of Design

WHY DID THE 'Good Design' of essentially *private*, often domestic possessions become an important issue of public policy and debate from the mid-nineteenth century onwards? This was the very simple question on which I started work almost fifteen years ago.

Originally I had intended it to be international in scope, covering Europe and the United States as well as Britain. But as my work proceeded it expanded unexpectedly in several different dimensions, into economic theory and policy, social history and into architecture and town planning as well as design – all of which I now regard as constituting a tradition of thought and practice which can be referred to collectively as the Political Economy of Design.

As the breadth of the subject matter expanded so did the timescale – instead of concentrating upon the last century and a half it covered the past four centuries – 'la longue durée'. It therefore seemed to make for coherence to restrict myself to Britain which, because of its leading role in the Industrial Revolution, had made a major contribution to this tradition, a contribution which was readily acknowledged by leading continental and American figures from the late nineteenth century onwards such as Louis Sullivan, Thorsten Veblen, Adolf Loos, Walter Gropius and Le Corbusier.

I think one can, moreover, take a genuine and far from chauvinistic pride in this tradition forged by such major figures as Elizabeth I and Lord Burghley, Adam Smith and William Hogarth, David Hume, Ruskin and more recent figures in our own century including Adólf Loos and Le Corbusier – who were inspired by the British tradition. Their concerns while centring upon the housekeeping or economy of a nation are not narrow or parochial, and the tradition does possess a certain narrative coherence arising from the fact that they were largely arguing with one another. I believe that their topic of discussion possesses an interest as universal as other topics which likewise arose and were debated within a particular national culture such as those of the Italian Renaissance or the eighteenth-century French Enlightenment.

As a result of this concentration the book has also come to serve another purpose – that of explaining why Britain has come to look the way it does. Why terrace houses, London squares, country houses, ribbon development, English comfort, chintz, nineteenth-century design reform and post-war slab blocks? Other countries have developed differently and my narrow focus will, I hope, be compensated for by greater explanatory force and a general framework of analysis which others might find fruitful in applying to other national situations.

I have also been narrow in another respect: this is not a continuous narrative history of the Arts of Design in Britain since 1550, but an attempt to study some of the factors involved in the formation of ideas and policies. Hence my chief concern has been with certain key periods when ideas were in flux, when debate was keen and when policy was being formed. These were: the early seventeenth century, the mid-eighteenth century, the

1   Cream Jug, 1868, by Minton. Design Reformers of the 1850s attacked such designs for making a handle look like a butterfly's wing.

mid-nineteenth century and the mid-twentieth century. English Palladianism does not receive much of a mention nor does the Greek Revival because my interest lay in the broad sweep of the classical tradition in Britain and particularly its inception. Likewise I have not discussed William Morris and the Arts and Crafts Movement because I was more concerned with the formation of their leading ideas in the work of Pugin and Ruskin, for example, than to add another, inevitably abbreviated account of their work to the many that exist.

I will also, inevitably, be held to task for the fact that I have crossed several disciplinary boundaries, particularly into the history of economic thought and social history which, as an art historian, I am not professionally qualified to discuss. But it is fundamental to the tradition of thought which this book reconstructs that it is holistic. Indeed, it must be holistic because it claims that the pattern of a butterfly on a teacup can have serious and extensive ramifications for society as a whole. The whole bent of the tradition is against narrow specialisation, whether in the arts or in economics. As an art historian, therefore, I had to do my best to cope with the economic theory. Had I been an economist I would have had to do my best with the architecture and design. So I make a modest plea for tolerance both from the specialist and from the general reader.

A few words seem warranted to explain how the subject opened itself up as I worked upon it, which will also help readers to find their bearings.

From 1835, when the parliamentary enquiry into improving the standards of design of British manufactures published its report, through the Great Exhibition of 1851 and its aftermath in the foundation of the Victoria and Albert Museum (or Museum of Ornamental Manufactures as it was initially called), to the 1940s Utility Scheme and its surviving progeny, the Council for Industrial Design, 'Good Design' has occupied a succession of brilliant and diverse talents. Was it not faintly ridiculous, this exaggerated concern with the appearance of such ordinary, everyday things?

An obvious answer is that 'Good Design' became important for commercial reasons: British manufacturers had to compete with France and, increasingly, with other European countries in the trade of textiles, cutlery, pottery and other items whose shape and appearance were clearly important attractions for customers. But such an answer would be convincing only if the energies of the design pundits, and the institutions associated with them, had indeed been directed towards improving the competitiveness of British manufacturers, with making their products more commercial, more popular, more fashionable. This was not the case. Instead, their efforts were directed *against* the prevalent fashions, the tastes of the public, both at home and abroad: in short, against the market. In the mid-nineteenth century, much ink was spilt attacking the popular three-dimensional and illusionist floral patterns on carpets, wallpapers and all manner of decorative goods, while an alternative system of Good Design in ornament and construction was formulated as a basis for training students of design at the government schools and, simultaneously, for re-educating the public.

Those who devised this system were associated with the government Museum of Ornamental Manufactures and the Department of Practical Art. Their principles of conventionalised, or simplified, ornament continued to provide the basis for design training, even for art teaching in schools, until the First World War and probably long after; generations of schoolchildren were brought up on geometric pattern-making and outline drawing. But long before the introduction of compulsory elementary education, in 1876, the design reformers had convinced government of the value of design education and this involved considerable public expenditure over a long period. To this very day Britain continues to train more designers at public expense than any comparable state, in institutions which have, until the very recent past, cheerfully continued their search for principles of design in headlong opposition to fashion and markets and popular taste, teaching them without any demonstrable benefit to the competitiveness of British goods or the fortunes of our manufacturing industry.

There must, therefore, have been other reasons than the purely commercial why the design of *private* possessions became a *public* issue. Most historians of design, particularly Sir Nikolaus Pevsner in his seminal *Pioneers of Modern Design* of 1936, have dodged this question. As passionate partisans for the continuing campaign for design reform, they took it for granted that those naturalistic floral patterns condemned in the 1840s were indeed of no merit. Their own publications a century later simply repeated the original criticisms of three-dimensional illusions, endorsed the efforts of their nineteenth-century predecessors and presented the modern movement as its evolutionary successor. We are faced here with the Whig interpretation of history, literally so, insofar as several of the nineteenth-century design reformers had strong links with political reform. It is this Whig interpretation of design history that I am challenging.

I began with a couple of assumptions. The first, concerning the relation between trade and Good Design, was that one was dealing with economic *perceptions* rather than *facts*. As early as the seventeenth century there was certainly a perceived threat to British industry from French goods, which were supposed to affect the British balance of trade adversely. In spite of Adam Smith's attempt to demythologise the balance of trade statistic as an index of production and the health of the economy, it remained, until 1855, the only available one. Besides this, goods for private and domestic consumption were perceived by some to be of great importance in the total economy, to be its growth sector. Private consumer goods were highly conspicuous, particularly amongst the middle and upper classes in London, as were the shops in which they were sold, and 'clothes, equipage and state' remained a major area of expenditure for those with disposable income. In fact, however, food still remained the largest item of consumption and agriculture was accordingly the largest sector of production, as well as an important area of growth, while heavy industry was to become of major importance.

My second and very important assumption was that the underlying concern of the design reformers was not with the competitiveness of British goods but with their moral and social influences.

By going back more than a century, to the Luxury Debate of the early 1700s and its sixteenth-century antecedents, I found the first explicit airing of the issues implicit in the nineteenth-century debates on design reform: the balance of trade; the importation of luxury goods (particularly from France); the questions of whether such goods were the growth sector of the economy; the moral effects of the consumption of such goods upon individuals, upon different social classes and upon the moral fibre and military strength of the nation. Above all, I found that the issue of 'taste' was central to that debate.

On one side stood Bernard de Mandeville, author of *The Fable of the Bees* (1714), who favoured unbridled luxury consumption as the means by which the prosperity and power of the nation could be increased and who considered that taste was relative, fluctuating, at the mercy of markets and of fashion. In a slightly different position was Adam Smith who, in an early paper 'On the Nature of that Imitation which Takes Place in what are called The Imitative Arts'[1] expressed an interest in the *nature* of taste on the grounds that anyone who uncovered the rules by which taste changed would enjoy a commercial advantage. On the other side, however, were those who believed that 'good taste' was an absolute, immutable quality and that, if the luxury market could be made to conform to its standards, the nation would benefit aesthetically, morally and socially as well as economically. Although their arguments differed in detail, such men as Joseph Addison and Richard Steele (who wrote in *The Spectator*), Bishop Berkeley, Alexander Pope, Francis Hutcheson and, above all perhaps, David Hume were in search of a recipe for tempered consumption and, hence, a temperate and civilised life-style.

One important focus for this luxury debate in the early eighteenth century was the building, furnishing and equipping of aristocratic country houses. Mandeville saw the aristocrats as men in the grip of a relentless passion to indulge in ostentatious extravagance in order to outshine their neighbours. They themselves and their apologists, however, believed that they were acting for the public good: fulfilling their aristocratic duty to set an example, maintain social stability and stimulate trade. In their eyes too, in other words, the consumption of luxury goods could indeed have a moral and social, as distinct from purely economic, dimension. In their eyes luxury consumption was an onerous form of taxation rather than a pleasure.

Instead of dismissing their arguments as pure hypocrisy, as Mandeville did, I took the view that the conventions of an age so unlike our own deserved more careful consideration and study. This led me back yet another century, to the early 1600s, where we find proclaimed by king and council, as well as by country gentlemen themselves, the very ideal of the gentry and nobility dutifully keeping house on their country estates and sustaining the rural economy of the provinces through their employment of servants, feasting, alms-giving and hospitality, building and rebuilding mansions, laying out costly gardens, keeping good stables: all of which was to be done in order to provide a bulwark against the explosive growth of London at the supposed expense of the rest of the country.

This added a new dimension. Here, in the early seventeenth century, were two broadly opposing conceptions of how the economic problems of the time were to be solved. On the one hand was the kind of solution that Mandeville was subsequently to espouse, with foreign trade, growing cities, increased personal consumption – in short a considerable measure of economic freedom – seen as the answer. On the other side, what was proposed was a stable but prosperous rural society, with a magnificent but far from colossal capital city, with the provinces ruled from the country seats of a hierarchy of country gentlemen and members of the nobility. A crucial component of this latter policy, moreover, was the importance accorded to town planning, aesthetic control of the design of buildings and the arts of design as well. While landowners were being encouraged, or indeed ordered, to live on their country estates, proclamations were issued which either prevented new building in London or else ensured that any rebuilding conformed to a disciplined Italianate style.

In addition to this, in its search for solutions to the perennial problems of under-employment and the ailing fortunes of the cloth industry, the court took the view that the answer was to encourage activities in which the value-added or, what is approximately the same thing the profit' was greater than it was in the manufacture of unfinished cloth. One example of this was James I's attempt to domesticate silk production; another was Alderman Cockayne's scheme of 1615 for cloth dyeing and finishing. Yet another, more significant in the context of design, was the foundation of the Mortlake Tapestry Works, which imported the skills of Flemish tapestry weavers as well as Flemish artists to make designs, and which also purchased as stock-in-trade the Raphael Cartoons, originally drawn for tapestries to hang in the Sistine Chapel.

In studying this earlier phase, the answer to my original question became clearer. In the early seventeenth century the issue of private possessions, of fashion, mattered because of the view that the great city was a market place for such things. It was argued that the gentry and nobility flocked there on their shopping sprees, and lived there *privately*, neglecting their *public* duties, draining their districts of the benefit of their expenditure and, insofar as the luxuries that they bought were foreign, the whole country as well. In addition they were condemned for deserting the communities of which they were the leaders, whether they were Justices of the Peace or ordinary squires. Luxury goods were thus seen to be the solvent of the whole social structure (something which Adam Smith, however, positively welcomed) and the Good Design of cities, of buildings, ultimately of personal possessions, the means to reverse or control this dissolution.

Here then was a 'lost discourse' which once connected personal consumption to issues of style, design and urbanism. These in turn were related to morality, social order and political economy. Those active in the fields of architecture, urbanism and design between the late sixteenth and the late nineteenth centuries could take this discourse for granted without having to spell out all the broader implications of their ideas and actions. Here too was the answer to my question: the reason why the design of ordinary everyday things became a major public issue was because their private consumption was seen to have public effects. And this pointed the way to another relationship which is a major theme in this book – between the design of domestic objects and the planning and design of towns and cities, and indeed of society as a whole. Because it was believed that personal consumption caused cities to increase in size, those who were opposed to this trend hoped that legal restrictions upon urban expansion, combined with the encouragement given to landowners to stay put in the country, might contribute to curing the problem. Hand in hand with these straight-forward restrictions went aesthetic controls upon building. Therefore there seemed to be an intimate relationship between good design at all levels from teapots to cities, founded not merely upon some general aesthetic 'good taste' but upon a more profound and far-reaching political will to control and direct the development of society.

It would be wrong, however, to give the impression that this desire to control social and economic change through design has been itself impervious to change over the four hundred years covered in this book. While it has been, and remains, a continuous theme in British domestic policy it has also been debated with great heat, and policy has veered from efforts at total restriction at all levels – consumption, building and the planning of towns, during the Elizabethan and early Stuart period and more recently during and after the Second World War – to a more liberal laissez-faire; while there have also been periods when the design of towns has been publicly controlled but the design of goods has been free from official interference, as it was throughout the eighteenth century. In every period, however, the issue has been furiously discussed and debated, and continues to be not only in Britain but in every developed and developing country in the world.

There remains the question of whether in the Conclusion I should present my own views on the subject. But I decided that it was enough, in an already lengthy book, to have reconstructed this tradition of thought and I hope to make its framework available to others to think out the urgent problems facing our physical environment.

Part One

THE
CONSUMER
SOCIETY

2 A great street of London shops, Cheapside, *c*.1750, part of London's great shopping line stretching from Oxford Street to Shoreditch. London was indeed the capital of a nation of shopkeepers.

LONDON – THE FIRST MODERN CITY

> Did men content themselves with bare
> necessities we should have a poor
> world.
>
> Sir Dudley North[1]

The most prosperous trading nation on earth, Britain in the eighteenth century was a land where aristocrats lived like princes and the middling classes lived better than many chief ministers of foreign states. Prosperity was not manifested in magnificent public buildings, but in the neat unornamented brick houses with their white sash windows, in London's immense streets of shops where rare merchandise from the four corners of the globe was sumptuously displayed, in the fine roads, in the clean and comfortable inns serving plain but delicious meals and, finally, in the cleanliness and relative wealth of the well-dressed working classes.[2]

The growth of towns and cities all over the country testified to the bustle of commerce. But to people of the period, particularly visitors from abroad, it was London that was the most astonishing phenomenon, both on account of the 'bub, noise and bustle' of the international trade which was conducted there – an American merchant was 'surprised whenever I think on it that England could furnish the quantity of goods that is exported; it is beyond my conception, the demand for them to all parts of the world'[3] – and on account of the prodigious, uncontrolled expansion and the luxurious way of life of the city itself, daily increasing in a seemingly unlimited fashion.

In *The Prelude*, Wordsworth recounted how, as a schoolboy in Cumberland in the 1780s, his vision of the London he had never seen for himself far exceeded the marvels of Rome or Babylon, so much so that when a school-friend returned physically unchanged from visiting the capital, Wordsworth was bitterly disappointed

> to behold the same
> Appearance, the same body, not to find
> Some change, some beams of glory brought away
> From that new region.[4]

The physical expansion of the city, which by 1700 had a population of 500,000 and had already out-distanced all the other cities of Western Europe, Paris included, most vividly symbolised the growth of the British economy and was widely regarded as the harbinger of a new way of life which would rival and even surpass the ancient world. In the whole world only Constantinople, with a population of 700,000, Peking and Edo were bigger.[5]

For Daniel Defoe, writing in 1725, London was the new Rome, the great centre of England and of a new Empire: 'How much further it may spread, who knows? New Squares, and new streets rising up every Day to such a prodigy of Buildings, that nothing in the World does or ever did, equal it, except Old Rome in Trajan's Time, when the Walls were Fifty Miles in Compass, and the Number of Inhabitants Six Millions Eight hundred thousand souls.'[6]

Defoe was an old man of sixty-five when he wrote these words, marvelling at the changes that had taken place in his native city during his lifetime. When he was a child London had still been a largely mediaeval city of wood houses, narrow lanes, and gothic churches which had not spread too far beyond the circuit of its walls and was surrounded by open fields and meadows. Now, following two great building booms – one after the Restoration, spurred on by the rebuilding of the City of London after the Great Fire of 1666; the second after the Peace of Utrecht in 1713 – much of London had been built or rebuilt in brick and stone in a style of architecture deriving from the classicism of the Italian Renaissance (Plate 2).

From Westminster to Wapping London was now, in effect, a new-built city, almost half as large again as it had been in the seventeenth century. The notable exceptions to this were the royal Palace of Whitehall, which Defoe called 'really mean', now deserted by the court for St James's, and the parliament building at Westminster which he was at a loss to describe – was it a barn, or a house, a church, or indeed, a heap of churches?[7] But in glorious contrast to this Defoe placed St Paul's, whose dome rivalled that of St Peter's in Rome;[8] the hospitals which he regarded as testimony to the philanthropy of the age; the wharfs and shipbuilding yards on the river where one could count the masts of more vessels than at Amsterdam, carrying the great import and export business on which the wealth of the city was founded; and down on the quayside the stately Custom House, also designed by Wren, in which all this trade had to be entered and recorded (Plate 3). There were, in addition, the offices of the institutions associated with this trade – the Navy Office, the Bank of England and trading companies like the South Sea Company 'whose stock supported that prodigious paper commerce, called Stock-Jobbing; a trade which once bewitched the nation almost to its ruin'.[9]

An immense wealth was being created in 'the smoke and dirt, sin and seacoal' of the City, and the proceeds were used to build the villas or the 'South Sea Seats' of the merchants and nobility. These encircled London like jewels in a rich coronet shining among the trees of their fine gardens and the fertile countryside in a ring ten miles across the fields. From there – Hampstead, Edgware, Wanstead, Richmond, Kew and Hampton Court, it was possible to have a glorious prospect of the city itself, St Paul's at its centre – one which rivalled Rome or Jerusalem in their heyday.[10]

Finally, back in London itself, there was what Defoe and many others correctly regarded as the most significant portent of the future: the West End; a completely new town of squares and streets built to a uniform design for people of quality and lying to the west of St Martin's Lane, bounded by St James's Park, Green Park and Hyde Park on two sides, but just beginning to extend on the fields to the north side of Oxford Street. It was this 'monster' which opened the prospect of seemingly unlimited growth. As we shall see, the economic demand for household goods, the consumption created by the inhabitants of this square mile, was considered by some people to be the dynamo of the British economy.[11] But the West End was more than a dynamo, or a symbol of prosperity: it was also topographically the battleground upon which the conflicting interests shaping the future political economy of England were being fought out, and the very appearance and design of these streets and squares reflected this.

For the squares of the West End – Covent Garden, Leicester Square, Lincoln's Inn Fields, St James's Square and the rest, with their public open space and subdued Renaissance style architecture – were not the spontaneous creation of public-spirited aristocrats in an Age of Taste as some historians would have us believe, but a compromise solution imposed by the

3 'The Imports of Great Britain from France', by L.P. Boitard, 1757. The busy scene by the Custom House, but it is also an attack by the Antigallican Society on French imports.

monarch, from Elizabeth I onwards, to a long-running battle between the citizens of London and Westminster and the building speculators. The citizens wished to preserve their common fields on the outskirts for recreation, grazing and fresh air to prevent the plague from returning, whereas the developers wished to make as much money as possible by building streets of houses.[12] By insisting that when development took place the London Square be laid out with paths, trees and benches the sovereign, James I and Charles I in particular, acted to preserve some of the citizens' rights to the common land and open air while permitting building on condition that it was clothed in the grand Renaissance style which accorded with their ambition for a magnificent capital to impress foreign ambassadors and make 'a memorable work of our time to all posterity'.[13]

This was not simply vainglory. In that age of imperfect statistics, foreign rulers and policy makers estimated the power of neighbours and rivals as much from what they saw as from what they knew. Thus the magnificence of a nation's capital city was eloquent testimony to its prosperity and power, particularly if that magnificence were invested in things useful and beautiful which also formed the wheels that drove the trade.[14]

Not only ambassadors but all kinds of foreigners visited London in their droves from the late seventeenth century and throughout the eighteenth century and, on the evidence of dozens of accounts that they wrote about their experiences, they generally were agreed that the Stuart kings had indeed succeeded in making their capital a memorable city. This did not mean that they found it magnificent in the traditional manner. Although the foreigners all remarked upon the size and number of the squares in the West End, upon the rapid growth of buildings in London, upon its size and population, they were dismissive of its claims to *architectural* grandeur.[15] What impressed them most, what indeed they were looking for, was something different. For these foreign visitors were not ordinary tourists; they included government officials, diplomats, politicians, writers, philosophers and scientists who came in order to report upon and analyse the *economic* miracle that was taking place in England, much as journalists today report upon the economic miracles of China, Japan

5

or Germany. Their books were intended to mould public opinion in France, the German States and Scandinavia – from where most visitors came. In addition official diplomatic reports, written in similar style and on similar topics, were the most accurate guide that foreign governments had to English economic developments.

For, in Europe, Britain was regarded with a mixture of fear and admiration as the major political experiment of the age, in which a new kind of constitution guaranteed individual rights and liberties against the arbitrary power of the state and seemed capable of yielding an untold growth in national wealth. The French feared that Britain would monopolise world trade. There were important lessons in political economy to be learnt from this fascinating and dangerous competitor.

The underlying form of the visitors' accounts was the panegyric, a type of essay in praise of a city or a country which dated back to classical times.[16] The writer of a traditional panegyric made observations about the form of government, the laws and the character of the different classes of citizen, after which he would convey his sense of the magnificence of the country by describing the palace of the king, the layout of his capital city, the mansions of its leading citizens or nobility and its great public buildings and monuments.

For London, the writers of panegyrics were forced to adapt the formula. As we have already seen, the king's palace, whether in Whitehall or St James's, was a motley huddle of gothic buildings; so too were the Parliament buildings. Greenwich Hospital, the only truly palatial building in the vicinity of London, turned out to be a hospital for sailors rather than the palace of the king.[17] By and large, it seemed as if the nobility, when they were in London, inhabited ordinary houses rather than mansions or palaces – though there were, in fact, several such mansions. The only classical public edifices to compare with those of Paris or Rome were St Paul's, the Custom House and the Monument to the Fire of London. Almost all the travellers were agreed that in terms of architectural taste London did not compare with Paris or Rome. But they were also agreed that this was not so much a criticism as evidence of the total novelty of the society that was being created. A French Huguenot refugee, Souligné, writing as early as 1706, was quite explicit about this. He granted that Old Imperial Rome had many magnificent temples, theatres, porticos and palaces, all of them the product of the ambition of each successive emperor to out-do his predecessors, and that London had none of these. His design, therefore, was not to compare London to Old Rome in that point. 'But I dare aver, that all the beauties of Old Rome, taken altogether, were not comparable to the noble sight of so many hundreds of ships and boats that swam upon our Thames . . . a beauty not only useful and lasting, but also comfortable and delighting; producing daily new profits and delights . . . whereas all the fine structures of Rome were most expensive, but barren and useless things, subject to decay, and empty shows of human impotent pride.'[18]

According to this widely accepted view, the novelty and greatness of London lay in the fact that it was a great city of commerce, the heart and capital of a country where the arts, sciences, trades and manufactures flourished and where all the people were gainfully employed; whereas in Old Imperial Rome (or contemporary papal Rome for that matter) there was only vice, debauchery and superstition and the streets were full of beggars. So it was no longer appropriate to measure the greatness of a nation purely in terms of the noble taste of the architecture of its principal edifices, for these only signified the ambitions of the princes. The yardstick for this new kind of city was its number of streets, houses, markets, slaughterhouses, size of population, sense of order, ships in port and above all the number of shops. 'The great admirers of old Rome', wrote Souligné 'must be very much to seek, before they can find in it so many thousands of large and rich shops, adorned with handsome costly signs, and stocked with all sorts of goods both foreign and domestic as we have in London'.[19]

Long before Adam Smith in 1776 called Britain 'a nation of shopkeepers', this observation was being made by people who had never seen or heard of a city with so many shops as London. Retail shops, as distinct from craftsmen's workshops from which goods were sold, were themselves a relatively new phenomenon in Europe, but where besides London were they to be found so richly stocked and in such profusion? For the first time in the history of mankind the size and quality of the shopkeeper's stock – textiles for clothing, furniture for houses – had become the yardstick of a country's greatness. It is only a slight exaggeration to say that the candlestick had supplanted the triumphal column and the armchair the imperial palace.[20]

Indeed the following passage from Adam Smith's *Wealth of Nations* makes precisely this point: that the true measure of a country's greatness and civilisation lay not in the monuments of the nobility but in the humble possessions and accommodation of 'the most common artificer or day labourer', in

> . . . all the different parts of his dress and household furniture, the coarse linen shirt which he wears next to his skin, the shoes which cover his feet, the bed which he lies on, and all the different parts which compose it, the kitchen-grate at which he prepares his victuals, the coals which he makes use of for that purpose dug from the bowels of the earth, and brought to him perhaps by a long sea and a long land carriage, all the other utensils of his kitchen, all the furniture of his table, the knives and forks, the earthen or pewter plates upon which he serves up and divides his victuals, the different hands employed in preparing his bread and his beer, the glass window which lets in the heat and the light, and keeps out the wind and the rain . . . Compared, indeed, with the more extravagant luxury of the great, his accommodation must no doubt appear extremely simple and easy; and yet it may be true, perhaps, that the accommodation of a European prince does not always so much exceed that of an industrious and frugal peasant as the accommodation of the latter exceeds that of many an African king, the absolute master of the lives and liberties of ten thousand naked savages.[21]

It is also interesting that Souligné's comparison of London and Old Rome referred to another favourite debate of the period: the controversy of the ancients and the moderns. Had Roman civilisation attained the highest pinnacle or could mankind either surpass it or strike out in totally new directions? The answer, for Souligné and for many commentators on Britain, was that London not only proved the superiority of the moderns over the ancients, but also demonstrated that the creativity of mankind had not been exhausted. London was the first modern city.

PORTRAIT OF AN ECONOMY

From contemporary comments on eighteenth-century London we can assemble a composite portrait of what were considered the most modern features of this most inventive and creative of societies. It will be something more than a simple portrait; it will also be a model of the working mechanism of the new society and its economic relations, with the shops at the heart of the capital as the mainspring, the market place by means of which the wants and desires of the inhabitants of the new houses in the West End, or of the villas and country houses further afield, created a demand for the work of craftsmen in the manufactories of London and Britain as a whole, as well as for the commodities that poured into the Port of London from the four corners of the globe.

With this model we can follow the chain of consumption and production back from the suburbs and West End to the workshops and warehouses in the east of London, conveying a broad sense of the way in which this new economy was, however misguidedly, seen to operate. We can also begin to see how private, domestic furniture, ornaments and clothes assumed their aura of public importance.[22]

Since most foreign visitors arrived in London through the counties of Kent or Essex their first impression of England was of a well kept garden in which the grass was greener than anywhere else, where apple and cherry trees were weighed down with fruit and where herds of deer and cattle grazed in picturesque parkland. The brick-built villages were kept in the most exact order and their inhabitants were well-fed, well-clothed and in a perpetual state of the greatest prosperity and plenty.[23] Nearer to London, especially at weekends, the smooth roads bordered with flowering hedgerows were covered with a cavalcade of shining carriages conveying prosperous merchants and members of the professional classes to and from their suburban retreats. Yet even this 'impetuous whirlwind' was so orderly and harmonious that it reminded one normally sober French geologist of the happy fields of Elysium.[24]

The countryside round London was thick with the villas and gardens of the wealthiest and most successful Londoners of the eighteenth century: Pope and Horace Walpole lived at Twickenham, Hogarth and the Earl of Burlington at Chiswick, Sir Joseph Banks, President of the Royal Society, at Kew, Hallett the upholsterer at Edgware, Warren Hastings at Beaumont Lodge. The profits from international trade, landed wealth, property in London, politics, slavery, India, house decorating and the liberal professions financed the creation of these luxurious retreats.

One of the most notable was Osterley Park in Middlesex. Osterley's succession of owners had all played major roles in the saga of England's commercial development. The Elizabethan house had been built by Sir Thomas Gresham, the great wool merchant, financier and economist, and brother-in-law of Elizabeth I's chief minister Lord Burghley. Gresham had founded Gresham's College, an ancestor of the Royal Society of London, where the practical application of mathematics to commerce and technology, which was to prove so important in the Industrial Revolution, had been cultivated. He had also built the Royal Exchange at his own expense – as a speculation but also as a great public building. In 1683 Osterley Park was acquired by Dr Nicholas Barbon, a property speculator and builder of somewhat unsavoury business practices who played an important part in creating Defoe's 'flourishing metropolis'. He was also the author of two treatises on economics, to which we shall return, one of which justified the growth of London on the grounds of its contribution to economic growth generally, the other of which extolled the economic benefits of extravagance and free trade. He was one of the pioneers of fire insurance. Osterley's next owner was Sir Francis Child (1642–1713), director of the East India Company, goldsmith and another pioneer of modern banking. His grandchildren had employed Robert Adam to remodel the house within and without and, in 1786, shortly after the work had been completed, the house was visited by a German novelist from Hanover, a friend of Goethe – Sophie von La Roche.[25]

Her account of Osterley conveys far better than the world-weary description of Horace Walpole, who disapproved of nouveau-riche ostentation, the cumulative effect of proceeding in growing admiration from one inventive room to another. At last, after the Gobelin Tapestry Room, and the Etruscan Room with its Wedgwood-style painted decorations, Sophie von La Roche reached the dairy. There, at its entrance 'milk and milking pails and butter-tubs stood in splendid array, all white and with brass rings gleaming like gold; the milk was standing in large, flat china pans, especially made with broad spouts for pouring off the milk, around the four walls on grey marble tables. The fresh butter lay in large Chinese tumblers and butter saucers were strewn all around on marble slabs; it is impossible to imagine anything nicer and more attractive. Greater sweetness or neatness are impossible, and, to make the picture perfect in its way, the sweetest prettiest girl in the world entered, wearing a grey frock, white apron and collar, with a small straw hat upon her lovely brown tresses, and brought us each a glass of cream and bread and butter with it.' This dairymaid's rustic simplicity and shyness reminded Sophie von La Roche of a scene from Arcadia, and her own description is indeed a vision of the Promised Land, flowing with milk and honey.[26]

Sophie von La Roche was by no means unique in regarding the countryside round London studded with these pleasure houses as a paradise, in sharp contrast to the country round Paris and to the Compagna of Rome which Smollett in 1765 described as 'nothing but a naked withered down, desolate and dreary, almost without inclosure, cow-field, hedge, tree, shrub, hut, or habitation'. The dirt, the rags, the clogs, the misery and the mendacity of the French and Italian peasants were simply not in evidence, though they did of course exist in lanes and alleys into which these eighteenth-century travellers did not penetrate, unlike their nineteenth-century successors.[27] It goes without saying that their portrait of England and its economy was highly idealised.

Once again, the significance of these pleasure gardens and of the landscape in the Home Counties that seemed like one great garden to foreigners was far from being entirely aesthetic. They were testimony to the immense success of the new agricultural improvements that were taking place in England, and which to some commentators and economists were the *real* basis of England's new prosperity and power. To the French Foreign Office of 1781, preparing contingency plans for an invasion, this meant that there would be no problem of food supply for the invading forces, but also that England, self-sufficient in food, could without difficulty survive a blockade.

If England's countryside was described as a paradise, London, as we have seen, was far from being regarded as an inferno – blackened though it already was by the smoke from the coal fires of a hundred and fifty thousand hearths.[28] Besides being brilliantly lit at night, having better pavements than anywhere in Europe and numerous squares laid out with lakes, gardens, trees and statues, its new town houses – whose design one observer considered to be of the barest and most niggardly simplicity, and uniform to the point of boredom – concealed the most opulent and comfortable interiors.[29] 'Nothing can exceed the luxury and magnificence displayed in the decorations of the inside of the English houses. Staircases covered with the richest carpets, are adorned with rails of mahogany most exquisitely carved, and illuminated with lamps enclosed in vases of crystal; the walls of the superb staircases are generally covered with pictures, busts and medallions; the ceilings and wainscoting of the apartments are laid over with the finest varnish, and decorated with bas-reliefs, gilding and other admirable performances in painting and sculpture; the chimneys are of marble, with figures, flowers and fruits in excellent taste carved upon them, and the locks of the doors are of brass, lacquered with gold; carpets which often cost three thousand pounds, and which one is almost ashamed to tread on, are spread on the floors; the window curtains are made of the finest Indian silk, and watches and clocks of the most ingenious and costly workmanship, add to the conveniency and magnificence of the scene.'[30]

Of course this writer was referring to one of the grand houses of Portland Place, or to a house like Home House, decorated by Robert Adam, in Portman Square. Eminent foreigners as a rule did not have the opportunity to visit more ordinary houses, except for inns and lodging houses, yet even these were remarkable for the carpeting, the papering of the walls, the chintz curtains, the soft mattresses, the spotless bed-linen and the efficiency of the mahogany furniture – commodes and chests of drawers whose drawers were truly commodious.[31]

This was a constant theme in writings about England throughout the eighteenth and nineteenth centuries – this new standard of private domesticity and English comfort which,

4 Staircase, Home House, Portman Square by Robert Adam, 1773–6. Foreign visitors were dazzled by the luxury of such interiors concealed behind plain facades.

at least in the West End, went with a new manner of life, with one family to a house instead of many families living in rooms and apartments.

It generated a high demand for household goods. Dr Johnson's friend, Mrs Thrale, the widow of a wealthy brewer, found that the furnishing of her Streatham villa by Gillows in 1794 cost her so much more than she had expected – £2,380, or perhaps as much as £150,000 in today's money – that she was forced to economise by taking lodgings in Bath. Sir Lawrence Dundas spent £10,000 in 1763 furnishing his house in Arlington Street and one can only guess at the cost of remodelling Osterley – £50,000, or £3,000,000 in today's money? Certainly Lord Stanhope spent £1,200 merely upon a set of gilt chairs and love-seats for his country house, Chevening.[32] At the other end of the spectrum of wealth a class 3 or 4 house in the West End might have cost two or three hundred pounds to furnish (£12,000–£18,000 in 1994 money).[33] Since the most conservative estimate of the number of houses being completed between 1680 and 1800 is an average of 600 houses a year, London alone must have generated a minimum demand for new household goods in excess of £150,000 a year. And London shops did not only supply London houses. The most acute and least rosy-tinted observers, the German pastor Wendeborn, who had lived twenty years in London, remarked that anyone who came to London and saw the thousands of well-fitted shops must be all the more amazed when he noticed that hardly any customers entered. 'But it is not the chance-customer that drops in, who supports shops that betray such opulence.' It was inland trade that was served by the multitude of waggons setting out daily from the capital carrying these goods into the various parts of the kingdom, and

5 Eighteenth-century bow-fronted silk merchant's shop, Artillery Lane, E1. Bow windows were used to make goods visible to strolling window-shoppers.

abroad to the East and West Indies, to America and to Europe. A printseller had told him that he did an annual trade of £25,000 in this way, with barely a single passing customer. If so the estimate of £150,000 a year in sales of household goods must underestimate total demand by a very large factor.[34]

London was not the only city in Europe in which there had been an astonishing increase in the numbers of shops. As early as 1606 a Spaniard was complaining that in Madrid everything had turned into shops. Paris had shops in the Rue St Honoré whose stock competed in taste and expense with those of London. But the infinite multitude of shops in London defied comparison with other cities. By the end of the eighteenth century they stretched in two great lines, each continuing unbroken for three or four miles from one end of the town to the other. The northern line ran from Oxford Street through Holborn, Cheapside to Bishopsgate and Shoreditch; the southern line ran from the Strand through Fleet Street to Leadenhall Street and Whitechapel. Defoe remarked upon the monstrous growth of shops. In 1663 there had only been 50–60 mercers in London, by 1700 there were 300–400. In 1759 there were 21,603 shops in London alone – one shop for every thirty people.[35]

It was not only the sheer number of shops that was so breathtaking, but the spectacle they offered. Their windows were glazed with very fine glass, frequently in bow-windows so that the merchandise could be seen as one walked down the street (Plate 5). The doors were of glass and the shop-fronts were 'all adorned on the outside with pieces of ancient architecture, the more absurd as they are likable to be spoilt by constant use; all brilliant and gay, as well as an amount of things sold in them, as the exact order in which they are kept; so that they make a most splendid show, greatly superior to anything of the kind at Paris.'[36]

All this splendour gave rise to a new recreation – window-shopping. Ladies particularly were in the habit of daily promenading along the new broad pavements not to buy but simply to stand and stare, or to make assignations with lovers whom they could not invite to their homes.[37] Sophie von La Roche, writing home to Frankfurt, provides us with a vivid description of one section of this dazzling parade:

> We strolled up and down lovely Oxford Street this evening, for some goods look more attractive by artificial light. Just imagine dear children, a street taking half an hour to cover from end to end, with double rows of brightly shining lamps, in the middle of which stands an equally long row of beautifully lacquered coaches, and on either side of these there is room for two coaches to pass one another; and the pavement, inlaid with flagstones can stand six people deep and allows one to gaze at the splendidly lit shop fronts in comfort. First one passes a watchmaker's, then a silk or fan store, now a silversmith's, a china or glass shop. The spirit booths are particularly tempting, for the English are in any case fond of strong drink. Here crystal flasks of every shape and form are exhibited: each one has a light behind it which makes all the different coloured spirits sparkle . . . Most of all we admired a stall with Argand and other lamps, situated in a corner house, and forming a really dazzling spectacle; every variety of lamp, crystal lacquer and metal ones, silver and brass in every possible shade; large and small lamps arranged so artistically and so beautifully lit, that each one was visible as in broad daylight. There were reflecting lamps inside, which intensified the glare to such an extent that my eyes could scarce stand it a moment.

Shops did not close at 5.30 p.m. 'Up to eleven o'clock at night there were as many people along this street as at Frankfurt during the fair, not to mention the eternal stream of coaches.'[38]

A NEW ECONOMIC THEORY

Contemporaries were aware that London's shops were a symptom of a new kind of society, and of a new kind of economic order in which consumption was beginning to be centred around the family houses of the moderately well-to-do rather than the royal palace or the great households of the nobility. Not everyone believed this to be beneficial. The West End might applaud it, but some merchants and traders in the City were of a different opinion as were many landowners.

The City, in contrast to the West End, was seen as being 'more severe and more exact, where the love of order and of labour is also greater', and where the shops and counting houses were open at eight in the morning, while the inhabitants of the West End lay abed.[39] In spite of the total rebuilding of the City after the Great Fire, the streets remained narrow and dark. The 'staid cits' ('pert low townsmen' as Samuel Johnson defined them) reproached 'them of the other end for their idleness, luxury, manner of living, and desire to imitate everything that is French: these in their turn never mention an inhabitant of the City but as an animal gross and barbarous, whose only merit is his strongbox.' Here, in the layout of the capital, the conflict of the landed and the moneyed interest was reflected. An American merchant, Joshua Johnson, justifying the expense of his house in the City to his partners back home, assured them that 'it has added all the consequence to us that I wished, as it has stripped me of the appearance of a transient person. If you'll permit me, without thinking me vain, I will add that the very different step pursued by most of my countrymen

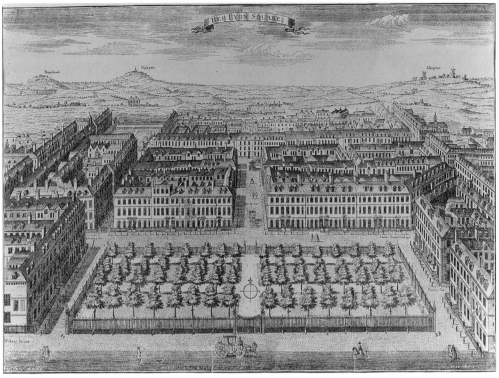

6   Red Lion Square from Nicholls, *London Described*, 1731, developed by Nicholas Barbon, 1684. Barbon was an early advocate of free-market economics, but his developments nonetheless obeyed planning regulations.

and me, in their running to the other end of the town to lodge and my fixing here, has not been without its good effects with the staid cits.'[40]

So, as we shall see in more detail, the 'cits' by no means held the view that profligate personal consumption enriched the kingdom. On the contrary, they believed that Britain's foreign trade was being destroyed by it. Like Joshua Johnson, they took the view that one's reputation as a good and reliable merchant was better served by a restrained consumption which would indicate that one's credit was not in danger of being overdrawn by luxury.[41]

But, for others, the phenomenon of the physical growth of the town and of the retail trade which it supported was in the process of being transformed from a mere spectacle into a fundamental principle of a revolutionary economic theory and, eventually, of state policy itself. This process had started in the seventeenth century. Dr Nicholas Barbon, the Leyden-trained doctor who owned Osterley, was one of the most ingenious and unscrupulous of the property developers who pioneered the building of the West End.[42] In 1684 his designs to build upon the open fields to the north of Holborn, now Red Lion Square (Plate 6), had so aroused the gentlemen of Gray's Inn, who objected to the loss of open air and feared that more houses would bring back the plague, that two hundred of them challenged Barbon and his workmen to a battle, a challenge which Barbon took up, taunting them to do their damnedest. 'A sharp action ensued' in which brickbats were thrown and in which the gentlemen had the better of Barbon and his men. The Privy Council instructed the attorney general to prosecute Barbon for inciting a riot; but the action got nowhere.[43]

Barbon's response to community objections to development were even more vigorous than those of his modern successors, and the next year he published his *Apology for the*

13

Builder, a pamphlet to prove conclusively the causes and the good effects of building in London. His argument was simple. New houses were required because the population was rapidly increasing, as naturally it must and as it had ever since Adam and Eve. In a civilised society, unlike a primitive one, a division of labour obtained whereby rich men no more built their own houses than they butchered their own meat or made their own clothes. Builders and developers supplied these houses in response to the demands of the market; 'by the quick selling of the commodities that are ready to be sold'[44] the market enabled the builder to estimate how many houses he needed to build in a year. The market alone was the true test, whereas the wishes of the local parishioners for open fields and fresh air ignored the needs of the growing population for one thousand houses a year in which to shelter their families.[45] Only if the market were oversupplied or if statutory building restrictions were enforced by the Privy Council would the rate of building drop. Indeed Barbon argued that the effect of the Elizabethan and Stuart restrictions on building in London, the subject of the next chapter, had been to limit the growth of the city's population by driving people overseas to the colonies, thereby impoverishing London itself.[46]

The effects of so much building were to provide work for everyone from the bricklayers and joiners to 'all those trades that belong to the furnishing of an house . . . as upholsterers, chairmakers, etc.'[47] and further afield to the 'vast number of people that are employed in digging and making the materials, the bricks, stone, iron, lead'. Thus the metropolis was 'the heart of a nation, through which the trade and commodities . . . circulated like the blood through the heart, which by its motion giveth life and growth to the rest of the body . . . and it is the only symptom to know the health, and thriving of a country by the inlarging of its metropolis.' One might add that houses constituted the fibres of the heart.[48]

Barbon's picture of an economy centred upon providing for the comforts of the home had become a commonplace by the middle of the next century. Campbell's *The London Tradesman* of 1747, published to advise parents upon an occupation for their children, arranged London's trades in the order of processes required in building and furnishing a house. First the architect drew the plan and superintended the work of the building tradesmen who constructed it; next it was 'time for the glazier to keep out the cold and damp';[49] then, as Campbell intended this house should be finished tastefully, so he must have a blacksmith to make and adorn 'iron rails without, and iron bannisters in the grand staircase'. And once the house had been completed it was necessary to think of 'furnishing it with fashionable furniture. The upholder is chief agent in this case: he is the man upon whose judgement I rely in the choice of goods; and I suppose he has not only judgement in the materials, but taste in the fashions, and skill in the workmanship. This tradesman's genius must be universal in every branch of furniture; though his proper craft is to fit up beds, window-curtains, hangings, and to cover chairs that have stuffed bottoms: he was originally a species of the tailor; but, by degrees, has crept over his head, and set up as a connoisseur in every article that belongs to a house. He employs journeymen in his own proper calling, cabinet-makers, glass-grinders, looking-glass frame-makers, carvers for chairs, testers, and posts of bed, the woollen-draper, the mercer, the linen-draper, several species of smiths, and a vast many tradesmen of the other mechanic branches.' Finally, when the house had been furnished 'with every thing that can come properly under the cognizance of the upholder', it was time to look for utensils for the kitchen, pottery and porcelain for the dining room. Only when his house had been fully equipped did Campbell turn to look at the trades which would clothe, transport and feed its inhabitants.

It was therefore understandable for people at this period, especially the up-to-date people of new London, to regard domestic goods as the growth sector of the economy, products for which demand was increasing most rapidly. The requirement for food was, in their view, limited by the size of the population and the size of the human belly, limited by necessity in short; but for creature comforts and articles of taste and fashion there could be no limit. What had been fit for a king a hundred years earlier was by the mid-eighteenth century the ordinary standard of living for a linen-draper or tallow-chandler whose expectations were continuously rising from his desire, as Barbon saw it, to emulate and out-vye his neighbours in the increasingly populous cities.[50] Moreover the range of consumer products upon which people were able to spend their money was far more limited then than it has become in the twentieth century. Today prosperous people can enjoy the most ephemeral and costly pleasures, travelling in luxury and dining in expensive restaurants. Then, even the wealthiest ventured abroad only once and rarely more than twice in a lifetime. Finally, the full complexity of our modern industrial economy had not yet developed to provide the whole range of what are called intermediate goods like machine tools, financial and other services all of which require plant and equipment; not to speak of all the services of modern government. So the consumption of domestic goods, many of them luxuries rather than necessities, designed to entice the window-shopping public and highly conspicuous as signs of wealth and status, assumed an overwhelming importance for the progress of the nation's wealth, and hence for all those who were involved in public affairs – politicians, political theorists and moralists.

The suppliers of such goods prospered. William Hallett, the leading London furniture maker and upholder of the reign of George II, died leaving £20,000, or over a million pounds in today's money.[51] His fortune offers an ironic reflection upon our theme since, in 1745 or thereabouts, it was he who bought the estate and house of the first Duke of Chandos at Edgware in Middlesex, Canons, which had served Defoe in his *Tour of England* as a major example of that princely magnificence which symbolised the boom. Canons was also considered to be one of the models for Timon's Villa in Pope's essay 'On the Use of Riches' in which he satirised the ostentatious luxury of his age:

At Timon's villa let us pass a day,
Where all cry out, 'What sums are thrown away!'

There, using the materials from the demolition of the older house, Hallett built a villa for himself. His grandson fulfilled his ambitions for the family by entering the ranks of the landed gentry and was painted with his wife by Gainsborough in *The Morning Walk* now in the National Gallery.

Hallett, like other large cabinet-makers, was far more than a manufacturer of furniture, he also drove the more extensive trade of upholder which Campbell defined as 'a connoisseur in every article that belongs to a house'. In other words he was a cross between a modern furnishing department store and interior decorator as well as a manufacturer.

Just how large such firms as his could be is indicated by the records of stock taken at the firm of George Seddon, the leading upholder of the later eighteenth century who left a fortune of £250,000 (£10 million) at his death in 1801. His stock grew from £3,000 in the 1750s, to about £7,000 in the late 1760s, to £153,000 in 1791. These were enormous sums in the era before giant corporations, equal to the fortunes made by early industrialists such as Wedgwood and Arkwright.[52]

In the late eighteenth century Seddon's purpose-built furniture showrooms in Aldersgate became one of the spectacles of modern London, ranked with the British Museum, Wedgwood's showroom, Bedlam Hospital, the Towneley Gallery of classical sculpture, Pope's Villa and Osterley Park. And although little furniture attributable to him survives, for much of it was inexpensive and plain in style, the character of his business lives for us as that of no other 'upholder' of the period in another description by Sophie von La Roche.

We drove first to Mr. Seddon's, a cabinet-maker . . . he employs four hundred apprentices on any work connected with the making of household furniture – joiners, carvers, gilders, mirror-workers, upholsterers, girdlers – who mould the bronze into graceful patterns – and locksmiths. All these are housed in a building with six wings. In the basement mirrors are cast and cut. Some other department contains nothing but chairs, sofas and stools of every description, some quite simple, others exquisitely carved and made of all varieties of wood, and one large room full up with all the finished articles in this line, while others are occupied by writing tables, cupboards, chests of drawers, charmingly finished desks, chests, both large and small, work and toilet tables in all manner of woods and patterns, from the simplest and cheapest to the most elegant and expensive.

But not all Seddon's wares were displayed so routinely. One floor was taken up with beds fully draped in fine hanging, and like his contemporary Josiah Wedgwood, in whose London showroom dinner tables were fully laid out with place settings, he aimed both to guide and to entice his customers with room settings (Plate 7). La Roche tells us how his scheme 'of a dining room designed both for practical use and ornament took my fancy most. It contains a mahogany table some feet in breadth, of which a third on either side is reserved for drawers, and with an opening in the middle like most writing tables have. Attached to the wall is a bracket on which to stand glasses and salvers. And by pressing a spring in the place where the drawers are indicated by attractive fittings, a lead-lined compartment flies open with shelves, where wine-bottles are kept cool in water, with the monteith fixed on the other side.'[53]

Sophie von La Roche considered that Seddon was a new species of businessman, almost a public benefactor, supplanting the nobility in that role. 'Seddon, foster-father to four hundred employees', she called him, and when one realises that the average size of a furniture factory in Britain today is 200 workers it is possible to appreciate the scale of his

Mary & Ann Hogarth

from the old Frock-shop the corner of the Long Walk facing the Cloysters, Removed to ÿ Kings Arms joyning to ÿ Little Britain gate, near Long Walk. Sells ÿ best & most Fashionable Ready Made Frocks, sutes of Fustian, Ticken & Holland, stript Dimmity & Flanel, Wastcoats, blue & canvas Frocks, & blue coat Boys Dra Likewise Fustians, Tickens, Hollands, white stript Dimitys, white & stript Flanels in ÿ piece:
By Wholesale or Retale at Reasonable Rates.

7 Wedgwood's Showroom, 1809, was one of the sights of London.

8 Mary and Ann Hogarth's ready-made clothes shop by W. Hogarth, 1730. Off-the-peg goods were one of the innovations of eighteenth-century London retailing.

operations. His firm was the largest in the country, but the conditions that enabled it to grow to such a size are even more significant.

Sophie von La Roche notices one feature to which both Barbon and another German traveller, von Archenholz, drew particular attention: namely the considerable division of labour involved in the production of goods, so that a mirror, for example, passed through the hands of glass makers, silverers, joiners, carvers and gilders before it was ready. Not least amongst these craftsmen was the pattern drawer, or, as we would now call him, designer. Campbell stresses that a youth ambitious to succeed as a cabinet-maker 'must learn to draw, for upon this depends the invention of new fashions, and on that the success of his business'.[54]

Associated with this division of labour was the totally new practice of being able to buy all kinds of goods ready-made and off-the-peg, instead of having to order them. Von Archenholz, also writing no doubt about Seddon's showrooms, observed that the ease of buying things off-the-peg 'gives great activity and industry to internal commerce. There is for instance a sort of people in London, called cabinet-makers, who have always a warehouse filled with every kind of new furniture ready for use . . . This custom is exceedingly convenient for strangers who come to London with the intention to settle. In a few hours a house may be hired and in a day or two completely furnished.' It was not only furniture that could be bought in this way that is so familiar to us today – coats, shirts, handkerchiefs, ready-bound books and even over-ready poultry 'hung in a very neat manner in their shops' could be thus acquired 'ready for the spit' (Plate 8). Of course a critical point about this development was that it facilitated the large inland and overseas trade driven by shops like Seddon's and Wedgwood's, which would more properly be called showrooms. Whether it was a small shopkeeper in a market town in Westmoreland, or a dry-goods store in Annapolis in Maryland, or a potential Nabob setting out to make his fortune in India, all the equipment they required was available from such emporia, in a fashion not very different to the modern mail-order firm or wholesale warehouse.[55]

It was indeed a cradle-to-grave economy, and it was difficult if not impossible for those who had not seen London for themselves to appreciate just how far inventions of this kind had been carried. 'The relations of a person newly dead are spared the melancholy duty of laying him in the earth. An undertaker is sent for' and the deceased was laid in his grave without his family being put to any inconvenience. The undertaker, moreover, was frequently the same person as the upholder who had furnished his house while he was alive.[56]

The whole trade flourished upon a further English convenience that the natives took for granted, but which foreigners found remarkable and somewhat shocking – credit. Only the poor paid for goods with ready money, the well-to-do were allowed to run up debts for a whole year or more by the shopkeepers, for which they paid in higher prices. The shopkeepers and tradesmen used an extensive system of credit in their dealings with one another. If London was the heart of British trade, then credit as well as consumer goods was its life blood. 'Many a man of principle, and of substance, is jostled in the streets by a person better dressed than himself . . . whose draper's, tailor's, shoemaker's, and other tradesman's bills, he in part discharges, because the other does not.'[57] And of course this whole system of credit was associated with the development of the modern system of banking, whereby private citizens deposited their money in private banks, who were free to lend it out to finance trade, manufactures and government debt. Although banking had been developing since the late middle ages in Italy, nowhere else had it developed to the same sophistication as in London. In Paris, for example, debts still had to be settled in coin, and on quarter days, when debts were due, merchants could be seen rushing from place to place carrying around bags of money.

The importance of the new banking to the growth of the economy has been widely recognised by historians; less so the importance of taste, fashion and design. But by many in the eighteenth century these were assumed to be crucial matters – even if, for the most part, 'taste' was seen as describing what customers wanted, or could be tempted to want, as distinct from an absolute quality. What Campbell said of the tailor can be applied more or less to all the other trades in this home-centred economy – builders, upholders, potters and silversmiths: 'His fancy must always be upon the wing, and his wit not a wool-gathering, but a fashion-hunting; he must be perfect Proteus, change shapes as often as the Moon, and still find something new'.[58]

It was as a result of the activities of these tradespeople that, to quote that brilliant quack and mountebank Dr Nicholas Barbon once more, London has 'caused England's monarch to be acknowledged Lord of all the navigable cities and sea-port towns in the world; to have made a universal monarchy over the seas, an Empire no less glorious, and of more profit, than of the land; and of larger extent than either Caesar's or Alexander's'.[59]

We have seen that both Englishmen and foreign visitors regarded the character of London – with its plain, domestic facades and lavish, luxurious interiors, its paved and well-lit shopping streets, its numerous attractive squares – as a symptom, an expression and indeed a consequence of the new kind of economy that flourished under the protection of English Liberty. But were they right? Was it really the relatively greater trading freedom and other political liberties that had given London, or rather its West End, that special neatness, trimness and sense of efficiency? Or had this character developed despite the commercial bustle; even in reaction to it? This is the question we shall examine in the following chapters.

———Part Two———

THE
STABLE
SOCIETY

PREFACE

EXACTLY WHAT WAS the connection between this thriving modern city and industrial design? On one level it was straightforwardly instrumental. In the words of Campbell's *London Tradesman* the invention of new fashions was the key to business success, and fashion depended upon turning out new designs and patterns to tempt sophisticated metropolitan customers into buying, simply because they were bored by the appearance of the old and enticed by the novelty of the new. 'How whimsical is the Florist in his Choice! Sometimes the Tulip, sometimes the Auricula, and at other times the Carnation shall engross his Esteem, and every Year a new Flower in his Judgment beats all the old ones, tho' it is much inferior to them both in Colour and Shape', wrote Bernard de Mandeville,[1] who was the most important of Barbon's successors in the early eighteenth century and whose theories justifying this world of changing fashions we shall examine later. 'Experience has taught us', he subsequently observed, 'that these Modes seldom last above Ten or Twelve Years, and a Man of Threescore must have observed five or six revolutions of 'em at least.'

Design as a fashion parade of different styles is not the primary subject of this book, but rather the kind of Good Design that emerged in reaction to fashion and which engaged the interest of figures like Ruskin or William Morris. Why did the design of commonplace domestic articles, chairs, tables, teacups and textiles become something both serious and fascinating for the moralist on one side and for the aesthete on the other, as well as for the businessman?

First, as we have seen, because these things became symbols of the new consumerist civilisation of this 'First Modern City' and they began to take the place that magnificent public buildings had held for ancient cities. As a result, these humble objects also came to be seen as yardsticks for the state of the nation – economic, social, moral and spiritual. As a corollary, it became an article of faith for some people that only if these artefacts were correctly designed would the nation be set upon a correct course. In short, luxury goods, that were offered for sale in the sparkling shops of modern London became the focus for the most important public debate about the economy and society of the eighteenth century – the Luxury Debate – which we will examine in the third section. The issues raised in this debate formed the context for a great deal of the detailed discussion of design theory in the eighteenth and nineteenth centuries when the very notion of Good Design was being formulated. Because an awareness and understanding of these wider issues could be taken for granted at the time, they were referred to implicitly rather than explicitly stated in the discussions about design. The context of the luxury debate needs to be reconstructed if the meaning of design is to be fully intelligible to us today.

As we have remarked, there are in fact two very different kinds of activity both called design, which should be distinguished from one another. Both involve making drawings from which an article can be manufactured. But that is about the only thing they have in common. The first, connected with fashion, is sometimes referred to as pattern-making in the eighteenth century and as styling in the twentieth, and is part of a business strategy to sell more goods; the other came to be known as Good Design and was a reaction against the first. Whereas the function of the first species of design was to serve merely as a blueprint for production, Good Design owed its very existence from the start to ideological reactions to the most important issues arising from the new economy, aired in the luxury debate.

Good Design, therefore, is nothing without its accompanying ideology or theory. A 'well-designed' object is in some sense quite unlike an ordinary object, merely intended to answer the needs of its user; a well-designed object must, in addition, function as the tool of its ideology. It must be in some way improved and improving. Where we expect any ordinary chair to support us in a sitting position, a chair of Good Design must do much more than this: it must support us in a posture which accords with certain ideals of good deportment and it must be assembled from ideologically sound materials in accordance with ideologically sound principles of construction.

Good Design is improving, reforming and coercive. In reaction to the baubles and vanities of fashion and the luxuries of the modern metropolitan phenomenon, in opposition to kitsch, Good Design claims to stand for the permanent verities of human nature and to be a regulator of manners, social behaviour and domestic life generally. It could even be regarded sometimes as a regulator of society as a whole. Concerned though it is with commonplace things it has acquired its authority and reforming power because those things were seen as the crucial link between the affairs of the individual and the family and the affairs of the nation – the equipment of domestic life with a formative influence upon social behaviour – while their manufacture and sale constitutes a large sector of the modern economy. Domestic equipment and the economy devised to serve such desires were subject to heated debate.

In practice, of course, the dividing line between ordinary industrial design or pattern-making and Good Design has not been and cannot ever be an absolute one. Any object or service is probably 'good' in the eyes of its consumer. On the other hand, Good Design itself can sometimes become the fashion. Certainly it can influence fashion, as it is intended to do; moreover certain fashions may be approved of and admired by Good Designers and incorporated in their work. Indeed, at crucial junctures what had previously passed for Good Design may come to be seen as positively bad in its influence on society, and a revolutionary school of design theorists might advocate principles of design which are less Olympian in their ideals and more in touch with contemporary fashion and popular taste. More generally there has not been simply one type or tradition of Good Design, but many conflicting ones. Furthermore, since the establishment in the nineteenth century of schools for training industrial designers perhaps the majority have been trained in principles of Good Design, which they have brought to their commercial work even though they have had to compromise with the demands of the marketplace. So there has been, in practice, constant interaction between the two species of design, and not merely outright opposition. The important point to bear in mind is that beyond the apparently narrow concerns about the shape, function, style and construction of an object, be it a chair or a candlestick, the debates about Good Design have focused an enormous range of very serious social, economic, moral, religious, political and even cosmological issues – paradoxical though this may seem, and absurd though some of the manifestations may appear.

So behind the conflict between Good Design and fashion then, there has been a division on bigger and broader issues. On the one hand fashion was associated with the London that has been portrayed in the preceding chapter, with that city of private one-family houses, comfortably and even elegantly furnished off-the-peg with the latest fashions from the large number of retail shops. This London was a major centre of world trade and therefore open to the influence of all kinds of exotic novelties in domestic consumption from China tea to

Indian chintz. Those who, like Barbon or Mandeville, were in favour of fashion and the goods of the imagination championed London's unrestricted growth, and credited it with the increasing prosperity of the whole country. They saw no need for any measures either to restrict London or to assist provincial towns, ports or regions. But they also entertained important assumptions about human nature, which they conceived of as essentially malleable, according to the nature of society at a particular time, fluctuating in its tastes, and always in search of novelty. This fickle creature was also constantly engaged in a competition to rival and outdo his neighbours in his personal possessions. To be successful a businessman needed to be something of a psychologist both to predict new fashions and indeed to create them so as to seduce customers with his wares – hence Mandeville's 'whimsical florist'.

Against this point of view were ranged those who regretted the fact that this prosperous city was lacking in magnificent public architecture which could rival the great capitals of past empires, people who consequently wished to reassert the traditional hierarchy of the fine arts and architecture over the 'fribbling' applied arts, who in the case of painting, favoured history painting in the grand style of Michelangelo or Poussin to still life and genre by the modern Dutch painters. They would prefer a nation which had a grand public presence to a comfortable, commercial and unheroic one and were not averse to the institution of sumptuary laws to regulate people's dress, nor to measures to restrict the importation of foreign goods, both to protect British manufacturers and agriculturists as well as to stop the influx of all those foreign fashions, foreign people and foreign ideas which came with them. Above all they would restrict the growth of London which they believed to be throttling the economic life of the rest of the country and they would be in favour of positive measures to help the provinces to prosper.

Their conception of human nature was correspondingly at odds with that of the free traders. While they acknowledged that novelty had a psychological appeal they argued that it was unimportant in comparison to the fundamental and unchanging principles upon which the mind operated and the fundamental rules of good taste. It is from the ranks of these essentially conservative people that the ideologies of Good Design have arisen.

Once again in reality, of course, the dichotomy between these two camps was by no means so clear-cut nor so simple. For one thing English trade was free of restrictions to a remarkable degree compared to other nations, and this was true both for the internal trade between different parts of the country which enjoyed good communications and was not obstructed by any tariffs, as well as for foreign trade. Thus England was open to new fashions in consumption arriving from abroad, and once these had caught on in London they spread rapidly to the rest of the country. Short of imposing an absolute ban upon all foreign importations it was impossible to control this process.

This posed, as I think it continues to do, major difficulties for those who have sought to 'improve' the design of manufactured goods, difficulties that were not experienced by more self-contained and protected economies like France, the German States or Italy. In Britain the Good Designers and protectionists have never had it their own way, and in most spheres the result has been a hybrid of market forces and protection, of fashion and Good Design.

Between the two extremes of those who were altogether opposed to economic growth and change and those who were totally in favour of unrestricted free trade there were any number of intermediate points of view. There were, for instance, those who believed that it was only necessary to intervene insofar as the benefits of growth ought to be better distributed between different areas of the country; there were those who believed that control, regulation and Good Design because of its appeal to the unchanging truths of the mind actually sold more goods, thereby increasing trade and prosperity more effectively than free trade itself. But it is helpful nonetheless to identify these two extremes so as to establish a scale of values upon which to plot the profusion of intermediate points of view which we shall encounter.

In this section, however, I do not yet wish to enter into these minute distinctions nor, in contrast to the first chapter, to present a corresponding pictorial diagram of the social economy seen through the eyes of the opponents of fashion and free trade; rather, I should like to discuss three spheres where they attempted, with some success, to stem the tide of the new order and to make their mark in very substantial ways upon both the visual appearance and the social character of Britain. First there was the campaign to control both the physical expansion and the growth of London's population through town planning and aesthetic controls; then, as we have seen, there was the corresponding regional policy of encouraging and at times ordering aristocrats and landowners to reside on their country estates rather than in London, for at least part of the year, building and rebuilding their country houses and spending their incomes to the benefit of provincial businesses, trades and employment rather than those of London; third, there were the efforts made by governments of the day as well as by public spirited noblemen to encourage the formation or the settlement of new manufacturing industries, and to improve agriculture through their direct patronage in order to provide employment, to diversify the economy and supply substitutes for imported goods and commodities. Since many of the goods in question were luxury goods, Good Design was central to their manufacture.

CHAPTER 1

The Control of London's Expansion

IT IS NOW important to understand that the physical appearance of eighteenth-century London was not – whatever foreigners or the English themselves believed – the result of Barbon's unfettered market forces. And to see why, we need to go back as far as the late sixteenth century.

Between 1580 and 1630 over a dozen royal proclamations were issued and two acts of parliament were passed to prohibit the building of new London houses, except for redevelopments on old foundations. Promoted by the government at the request of the City of London, their initial object was to stop any further growth in London's population. But as soon as James I became king in 1603 a secondary objective, that of controlling the appearance of new buildings and of encouraging public magnificence, became increasingly important; and after 1607 the proclamations made allowance for the granting of special licences 'in some rare cases' for completely new buildings. The regulations which had originally been designed to stop the influx of immigrants to London by restricting the supply of lodgings, dwelt more and more upon issues of design and town planning.[1]

London's population was growing so fast, and for reasons so deep-rooted and complicated that it is hard, in retrospect, to see how anyone could have had the slightest faith that the proclamations would be effective. Before the first national census of 1801 figures for the population of greater London are no more than guesstimates. Contemporaries themselves often wildly over-estimated – one visiting clergyman in 1689 believed the total population to be about 1,500,000 when it was no more than a third of that size.[2] But the following table represents the best modern estimates:

GREATER LONDON

Year	Estimated population	Increase/year in previous 50 years	Proportional increase in population over previous 50 years
1500	50,000		
1550	70,000	400	1.4 ×
1600	200,000	2,600	2.9 ×
1650	400,000	4,000	2.0 ×
1700	575,000	3,500	1.4 ×
1750	675,000	4,000	1.2 ×
1800	900,000	4,500	1.3 ×
1861	2,800,000	31,000	2.9 ×

Derived from R. Finlay, *Population and Metropolis: the Demography of London, 1580–1650*, Cambridge, 1981, Table 3.1

9 Overhanging house fronts in Leadenhall Street (engr. J.T. Smith 1796) were forbidden after the Royal Proclamation of 1618.

These figures show that in the century from 1550–1650, whilst the proclamations were in force, the population grew as fast, proportional to its size, as during the first half of the nineteenth century. However, contrary to what Barbon believed, not even this was a natural increase. So unhealthy were living conditions that more people died in London than were born there, and in 1600 the population would have been diminishing by 2,000 a year had there not been an influx of something like 6,000 a year.[3]

The restrictions upon new buildings had been imposed by the crown and Privy Council at the request of the Lord Mayor and Aldermen of the City of London, to prevent what both regarded as the disastrous effects of this immigration. The newcomers were believed to be the rural poor 'of the worst sort', living in overcrowded wooden shanties, subdivided tenements or in cellars where the plague and other infections would spread rapidly, endangering not only their own lives but, more important, the lives of the sovereign, the courtiers and foreign ambassadors as well as the existing citizens.[4] Thirty thousand died from the plague in 1603. This rabble was disorderly and somewhat difficult to police; its presence placed enormous strains upon the supply of food to the capital which rose in price and caused riots both in London and the country. In addition, the shortage of building land within the boundaries led to building upon the private gardens within the city and, when they were exhausted, to enclosure and building upon the common fields around London which had traditionally been used for recreation, grazing and the drying of washing. Moreover the city whose former beauties and amenities had been so lovingly described by John Stow, a tailor turned antiquarian, in his *Survey of London* of 1598, was now blemished by 'filthy cottages' and its outskirts were rapidly turning into a shanty town. In the eastern suburbs and elsewhere houses, inns, sheds, even a hayloft were subdivided and converted into dwellings to meet the housing shortage.[5] In the ringing words of Charles I's proclamation of 1625: London 'the Seat Imperiall of this Kingdom', the residence of the court and of foreign ambassadors, had become 'the greatest, or next the greatest Citie of the Christian World' and *only* the 'increase of Honour, Liberty, Health and Safety' should be permitted in it.[6] London, as the heart of the Commonwealth should be a model of harmony and good order. Finally, and perhaps most decisive for the City of London, was the fear that newcomers would depress wages, and that workshops set up in the suburbs, outside the jurisdiction of the City companies, would undercut established businesses.

Thus it was the threat to public health, public order, the food supply, the beauty of the city and the amenity of its public open spaces as well as its economy which led to the ban on new building.

Such were the dangers to London itself. Of equal if not greater concern to the government was the effect of its uncontrolled growth upon the rest of England. In the words of James I, London was grown so great that it threatened to 'devour the kingdom'. One fear was that London was consuming the natural resources of the rest of the country – both food and timber for building. But far more serious was the fear that the expansion of London's working population was causing a corresponding depopulation and loss of trade to the provincial towns, ports and regions. The misfortunes of Southampton in the sixteenth century vividly illustrate this. Southampton had been a major port for the wool and cloth trade to Italy, whence imported goods were sent by road to London for distribution. Initially as a result of improvements in the design of ships and in navigation through the Channel and along the Thames, and then because of the increasing tendency for England to restrict the export of wool and to weave it into cloth herself, it became more convenient for the Italian traders to use the port of London. Southampton sailors migrated to London in search of work, and her merchants and shipmasters followed, even her mayors and other elected officers, leaving the once prosperous port in a woeful state. People believed that London was not only becoming ungovernable itself but that its growth was undermining the economy and hence the public order of the whole kingdom.[7]

The government also believed that this situation had been exacerbated by 'the too frequent resort and ordinary residence of Lords Spirituall and Temporall, Knights and Gentlemen of quality' to London. Some of these landowners were believed to be spending in London a considerable part of the incomes they derived from the rents of their country estates, estimated in the late seventeenth century at as much as two-thirds of their income. This was believed to cause even greater unemployment and destitution in the provinces and a greater influx of people to London to seek work. The presence in London of the gentry made civil unrest even more difficult to control since it was they, as JPs, who were responsible for 'a great and principall part of the subordinate government of this Realme'. Thus, alongside the proclamations forbidding new building in London, others were issued at regular intervals commanding landowners to reside in their 'Mansion Houses in the Country', there to exercise 'the ancient and laudable custom' of housekeeping and hospitality for the economic and political well-being of the provincial regions. This parallel policy had major implications for country house building, as we shall see in the next chapter.[8]

Such were the most commonly mentioned effects of the growth of London's population. But people were less clear about the causes, which was not surprising in view of their complexity. Because they confused the effects for the causes many of the proposed remedies were unworkable. The residence of the gentry in London was considered to be a cause of expansion, but what was the cause of their being there? Even though the proclamation of 1607 stated that the 'manifest cause of the greater concourse of people' to London was the presence of the court and the law courts, few were prepared to consider the possibility of decentralising the administration of justice, or moving the court permanently out of London. Nonetheless, James I in his Charge to the Assize Judges in Star Chamber, 1616, observed that 'It is an ancient and laudable custome in this Kingdome, that the Judges goe thorow the Kingdome in Circuits, easing the people thereby of great charges, who cannot otherwise come from all the remote parts of the Kingdome to Westminster Hall, for the finding out and punishing of offences past and preventing the offences that may arise.' On another occasion James I threatened to ruin the City by removing parliament and the law courts to Oxford. The City's arrogant response was given by an alderman who wondered whether the king also intended to divert the Thames, otherwise 'we shall by God's grace do well enough at London whatever become of the Courts and Parliament'.[9]

The alderman was, of course, referring to that other major factor in London's expansion: the port of London's increasing share of England's foreign and domestic trade and the consequent rise of trade-related industries and services such as shipping, shipbuilding, banking and insurance.[10]

However strongly London merchants may have called for restrictions upon the growth of the city, it was not in their interests to tackle the root causes of the immigration by restoring trade to the provincial ports, even if that had been possible, any more than it was in the interests of the lawyers or of the court itself to decentralise. As is so often the case, the authorities were attempting to prohibit, without tackling the causes, what were in part the symptoms of their own actions and policies. Moreover many people connected with the court and with the City benefited from the building speculations. Even the city companies themselves were profiting from their speculative interests in the housing market following the first proclamation, and the crown also benefited increasingly from the sale of building licences. In any case, neither the government nor the City possessed the bureaucracy to police all new buildings in the area of about thirty square miles around London which lay within the three mile radius.[11]

As a means of preventing the growth of London's population the proclamations were a complete failure. However, the secondary objective of the regulations, that of regulating the appearance and materials of new building, was enormously successful, at least in the West End, for they effectively determined the typical facade of the London terrace house, derived (for reasons which will be made clear subsequently – Part IV, chapter 1, ii) from the Italian Renaissance palazzo, and the pattern of regular squares, streets and gardens which governed its appearance and that of other major cities in Britain until late into the nineteenth century.

As soon as James I came to the throne he wrote to the lord mayor and aldermen 'congratulating them upon the care bestowed upon the walks of Moorfields, the re-edifying of Aldgate' and offering £500 towards restoring the steeple of St Paul's, destroyed by fire in 1561. The king's strong personal involvement was still manifest when, towards the end of his reign, he complained to the Commissioners for Buildings in London that he could see with his own eyes the effects of people's attempts to frustrate 'so glorious a work of building so well begun and so honourable to himself and beneficial to his peoples'.[12]

The objective of regulating the appearance of building first became prominent in the proclamation of 1607. This prohibited any new building at all within two miles of the gates of the City of London except in very rare cases when a special licence had to be granted. Builders and workmen who broke the prohibition were to be tried and punished by the Star Chamber, and any building demolished. The only new building to be allowed was the redevelopment of existing buildings 'such as shall both adorne and beautifie' the king's city. Redevelopment would only be permitted on condition that the facades were constructed in brick or stone and of a 'uniforme sort and order' prescribed by the local authority. Once again offenders would be punished by being fined and imprisoned after a trial in the Star

Chamber.[13] There were additional regulations to prevent any increase in the total number of dwellings in and around London which might occur as a result of permitted redevelopment or through the subdivision of existing buildings.

In 1611 a new regulation governing appearance and construction was added prohibiting any jutties or overhanging stories. Apart from oriel or bay windows 18 inches deep the walls of new buildings henceforth had to be sheer.[14]

In 1615 King James I appointed a special Commission the better to enforce the proclamations. This consisted of the entire Privy Council and others including Sir Henry Wotton. The Earl of Arundel was reputed to have been instrumental in establishing it – one of the first fruits of his major inquiry into the state of the arts in Italy undertaken between 1612 and 1614 with Inigo Jones, who had been designated successor to the Surveyor of the King's Works in 1613. The Commission was established in April and in July a new proclamation was issued, not in order to add any fresh regulations, but to affirm the king's policy that he wished to transform London into a truly magnificent city comparable to the Rome of the Emperor Augustus. In this document particular emphasis was placed upon works of a public nature as opposed to private building, a theme which was inherent in all the manifestations of the policy to control the country's economic growth, as we shall see. Public works such as the paving of Smithfield and the planting of Moorfields were specifically cited as models of good practice.[15]

The next proclamation, of July 1618, was the first to bear the stamp of Jones and Arundel. To the previous regulations this added new ones to ensure that all new or redeveloped buildings would indeed be uniform in appearance. All full storeys had to be a minimum of 10 feet and windows had to be taller than they were broad. Not only were no jutties allowed but bay windows were entirely prohibited (see Plate 9). Such a simple code set down the broad specification for the London terraced house which was followed until the late nineteenth century.[16]

Subsequent proclamations in 1620, 1622, 1624, 1625 and 1630 did little more than reaffirm the rules of 1618. The 1620 proclamation tried to extend the zone to five miles from London almost trebling the area. In 1622 a special proclamation was devoted to specifying the size, quality and price of bricks to be used in the rebuilding. The size, $9 \times 4\frac{3}{8} \times 2\frac{1}{4}$ inches, has remained the British Standard ever since, give or take a fraction of an inch. This proclamation was subsequently incorporated in the later general proclamations.

The theory behind the operation of these regulations was simple. Within the radius of two or three miles from London owners were deprived of the development rights to their own property. These had been, so to speak, nationalised, so that, in theory, the king could have total control over the character of the redevelopment of his capital even though he owned little of the land. After the Restoration the proclamations fell into disuse. It was not until the 1947 Town and Country Planning Act that development rights, for the whole country this time, were nationalised again in an attempt to control urban expansion, particularly in London, as well as the appearance of buildings.[17]

In practice, however, things did not run to plan. In spite of the proclamations, the population of London was still growing on average by 4,000 people a year. In other words, a population the size of the larger towns in the rest of the country, towns like Salisbury, Ipswich or Nottingham, was being added to London each year. These people could not be accommodated simply by splitting up existing buildings or converting farm buildings, sheds and cellars. Furthermore, the area under control was far too large to be policed effectively either by JPs and parish officers, all of whom were voluntary and unpaid, nor even by the Commission and the Surveyor after 1615. On top of this it seems clear that the system of licences was used by the crown as a tax upon new development rather than a prohibition, in spite of a vigorous denial in the 1615 proclamation.

For the code to be effective in regulating the appearance of the capital it was not sufficient to rely upon enforcement. The assent of landowners and developers to the underlying principles had to be obtained, and for that a model of good practice had to be achieved which could set an example and show that it was not financially disadvantageous to observe the rules.

The accepted explanation of how this happened is that given by Sir John Summerson in his *Georgian London* of 1945. In his view the model which set that standard was the new Covent Garden. He argued that when the entrepreneurial Earl of Bedford wanted to develop the property behind his mansion on the Strand in about 1630 Charles I struck a deal: the crown was only prepared to release the development rights on the property in return for a £2,000 fee and the condition that the development should be an ornament to the capital. Summerson summed it up in a well-turned sentence:

> . . . it is pretty clear that we owe Covent Garden to three parties: Charles I, with his fine taste and would-be autocratic control of London's architecture; Jones with his perfectly mature understanding of Italian design; and the Earl of Bedford with his business-like aptitude for speculative building.

Here was 'the first great contribution to English urbanism' as a result of which open spaces became characteristic of new developments and the houses were arrayed in a show of trim discipline with uniform, ungabled facades.[18]

It is a very neat story which, published as it was by a powerful advocate of town planning at the very time that the 1947 Town and Country Planning Act began its journey to the statute book, divides the credit between the state and a great architect-planner. But although Covent Garden was certainly a success for the policy initiated by James I and continued by Charles I, Summerson's account is misleading. Covent Garden was not the first square. Even the architectural uniformity of its facades were to be the exception and not the rule. The London square as a form of land use arose not from an alliance between the state and the nascent profession of architect-planners but from community action against development in favour of common rights to common fields. Finally, in the case of Covent Garden itself, the deal between Charles I and Bedford was infinitely more complicated than Summerson suggested.

The first square and the model for this peculiarly London approach to maintaining open space within the built-up areas of a rapidly growing city was not Covent Garden but Moorfields, now called Finsbury Circus, then just to the north of the city walls (Plate 10). It was one of the great public works to which James I referred in his 1615 proclamation, and it came about as a result of his support for the citizens' opposition to building development. Foremost amongst the objections that Londoners had to new buildings was the loss of green fields. Stow wrote that Hog Lane, forty years earlier, had had 'On both sides fair hedgerows of elm trees, with bridges and easy stiles to pass over into the pleasant fields, very commodious for citizens therein to walk, shoot, and otherwise to recreate and refresh their dulled spirits in the sweet and wholesome air.' But now these had become totally built up:

> And where there were hedges and ditches and ponds of water
> Now we have nothing but bricks and mortar.

This process had been taking place throughout the sixteenth century but it is often forgotten that many of the fields around London were *common* fields in which the parishioners enjoyed legal rights of grazing and on which they could walk, play and lay out their washing 'as of right'.[19]

One such field was Moorfields to the north-east of the City, which had been given in trust to the City of London 'for the ease of the citizens' by two nuns before the Norman Conquest and, as Fitzstephen vividly described in 1173, was used for ice skating in winter.

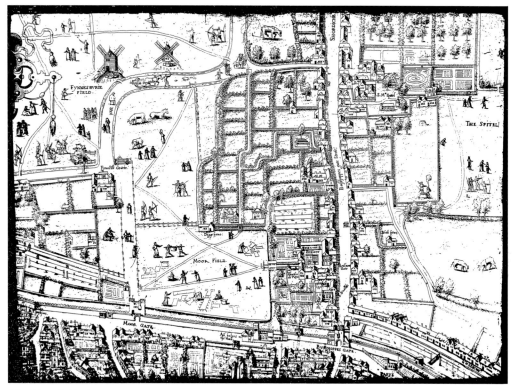

10 Moorfields in 1559, attrib. A. van den Wyngaerde. They had been publically owned recreation grounds since the eleventh century.

Illegal enclosures were effected for market gardens until, in 1515, so the chronicler Hall tells us, the London levellers led an anti-enclosure riot to reclaim their playing and recreation fields: 'a great number of the city assembled themselves in a morning, and a turner in a fool's coat, came crying through the city, "shovels and spades! shovels and spades!" So many of the people followed that it was a wonder to behold; and within a short space all the hedges about the city were cast down, and the ditches filled up, and everything made plain.'

Subsequently enclosures once again encroached upon this common land, not for gardens but 'summer houses . . . like Midsummer pageants, with towers, turrets and chimney-pots . . . betraying the vanity of men's minds, much unlike the disposition of the ancient citizens' who 'spent their wealths in preferment of the common commodity of this our city'.

In the wake of the 1580 Royal Proclamation against new buildings within a three mile radins of the City of London, the Corporation itself prepared a plan to level the enclosures, and one of James I's earliest acts as king was to write to the lord mayor commending the citizens for their energy and generosity 'in things that doe concern the ornament of that our Cittie in the walks of Moorefields a matter both of grace and greete use for the recreation of our people'. By 1607 the fields had been laid out as a park 'in the fashion of a cross' with fences, benches and no fewer than three hundred trees subscribed by and named after individual citizens. Even a porter had subscribed a tree appropriately labelled 'Stubbs – His Tree'. This was a popular undertaking, supported by the crown. And it was in embodying this concept – of a laid-out public open space in which common rights were preserved in

31

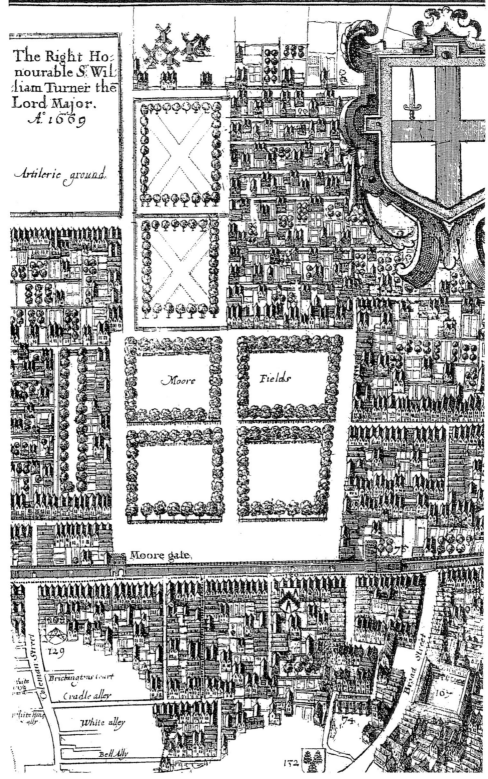

The Right Honourable S.ᵣ William Turner the Lord Major. A.º 1669

Artilerie ground.

Moore Fields

Moore gate

Coleman Street

Brickington Court

Cradle alley

White Hind alley

White alley

Bell Ally

Broad Street

11   Moorfields, London's first square showing the gardens laid out in 1607, from John Leake's *Exact Surveigh*, 1667.

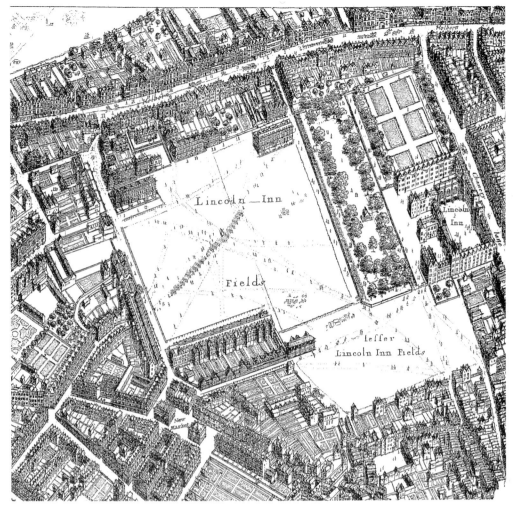

12 Lincoln's Inn Fields, London's fourth square laid out after 1639 'in the manner of Moorfields', by Hollar, 1658.

the centre of a building development – that Moorfields was the chief model and prototype of the London square (Plate 11).[20]

When, for instance, after 1613, development began to encroach upon the great common fields owned by the crown near Lincoln's Inn objectors cited Moorfields in their petitions. In 1617 they petitioned that 'the fields commonly called Lincoln's Inn Fields . . . might for their generall Commoditie and health be converted into walkes after the same manner as Morefieldes'. James I, in 1618, responded through the Privy Council by setting up a commission, including Inigo Jones, then the Royal Surveyor, to survey the fields and draw a 'mapp' showing how the fields could be laid out in 'faire and goodlie walkes' to provide 'a grate ornament to the Citie, pleasure and freshness for the health and recreation of the Inhabitants thereabout . . . and a memorable worke of our tyme to all posteritie'.

Unfortunately nothing came of this. Building continued and it was only finally in 1639 that the developer William Newton came to an agreement with Lincoln's Inn that the great open space remaining in the centre be left unbuilt – almost ten acres, the same size as Moorfields (Plate 12).[21]

The next site where the issue arose, ten years later, was to the west of St Martin's Lane on Lammas Lands – that is to say, common fields where rights were transformed into a

13 Leicester Fields or Square, London's second square, laid out in 1630, commuting public time rights over the land into public space; by T. Bowles, 1750.

14 Covent Garden, from Hollar's *Great Map of 1658*, was London's third square laid out after 1631.

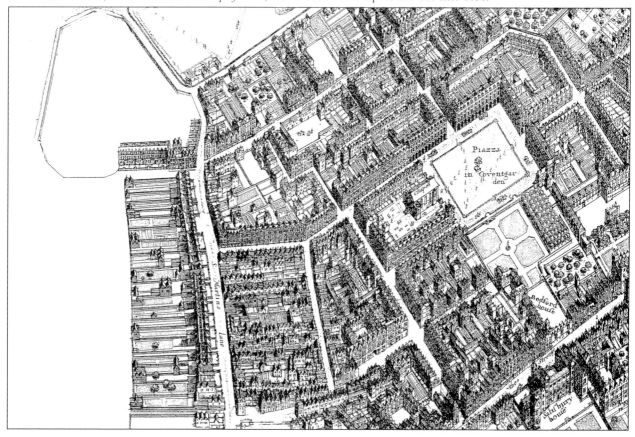

form of timesharing, being open for grazing from Lammas tide (1 August) till 1 April. Some time in 1629 or 1630 the Earl of Leicester wanted to build a mansion on what is now Leicester Square. The parishioners of St Martin's in the Fields had been vigorous defenders of their common fields. Green Park is a section of their common fields whose survival we owe to the parish vestry, the local authority as it were, as much as to the crown who owned the land. For example, on Lammas Day, 1 August 1592, a large group of parishioners marched on to the Lammas Fields with shovels and pickaxes and pulled down the fences in order to lay claim to their common rights. The enclosers were committed to the Marshalsea Prison by the order of Elizabeth I.[22]

It was these doughty parishioners who in 1630 petitioned the Privy Council against the Earl of Leicester's plans. A sub-committee, including the Earl of Arundel, recommended sometime in 1630 that a portion of the field 'shall be turned into walks, and planted with trees along the walkes, and fit spaces left for the inhabitants to dry their clothes there as they were wont, and to have free use of the place, but not to depasture it . . . All this likewise to be done at the earl's cost'. It was, in other words, a layout 'in the manner of Moorfields' (Plate 13). And in August 1631 the earl received permission to build.

What in the meantime was happening at Covent Garden? In March 1630 the Privy Council ordered the Earl of Bedford to pave Long Acre. He replied defiantly that because of the prohibitions on building it was unprofitable for him to do so. Only if the king gave him permission to build would he pave the street.[23]

There were no common rights attached to the site of Covent Garden, a walled garden belonging to the earl's mansion. So the vestry of St Martin's had no rights of petition as they had in the case of Leicester Square. But ever-vigilant as they were this does not seem to have deterred them. For in 1638, when building was nearing completion, eighty-seven parishioners did petition the council complaining that the earl had broken several promises given to the king and the inhabitants, when he had proposed building, namely that he would pave the piazza and widen the roads entering it; that he would erect a statue of the king; that he would build a proper chapel with a steeple and bells; and that he would endow a preacher at £100 a year. The king, meanwhile, obtained a guarantee that a uniform facade would be observed, even though Bedford only observed this on the piazza itself. Elsewhere in the development, as early engravings show, houses were gabled in the London vernacular, which the Commissioners in 1637 complained were contrary to the proclamations. Nonetheless permission was granted in January 1631 (Plate 14).[24]

Permission for Covent Garden was more or less contemporaneous with Leicester Square and although the legal framework was very different the local residents influenced the terms of the building licence, without obtaining all that they asked for. It was yet another solution 'in the manner of Moorfields' with the additional architectural advantage of a uniform Italianate frontage. Seeing that there were no common rights attached to the land, it was an even greater victory for regulation than Leicester Fields.

The deal under which the development was permitted was very curious. In November 1629 Bedford had been arrested alongside John Selden and Sir Robert Cotton for 'seditious libel' in publishing a pamphlet accusing the king of tyranny. Bedford apologised but remained under house arrest to stand trial. Yet only four months later in March 1630, as we have seen, Bedford was seeking permission to build on Covent Garden; in May 1630 he received a pardon on the birth of the future Charles II; and on 10 January 1631 the licence for Covent Garden was authorised. Later that year, in December, as a result of negotiations which had been proceeding throughout 1630, the earl promised to give the king 12,000 acres out of the 95,000 acres of fenland which his consortium had been awarded for draining at the King's Lynn Court of Sewers held on 13 January 1631, three days after the Covent Garden development had been approved.[25]

In other words we actually owe Covent Garden in part to a complicated political and

15 and 16   Street frontage, Church Row, Hampstead, 1720 and, opposite, the backs of the same houses. Regulations forbidding bay and oriel windows on the street drove these favourite English features round the back until the late nineteenth century when they were permitted again.

financial deal between the king and a mighty and potentially rebellious magnate, in which, in return for his pardon, permission to drain the fens and to develop Covent Garden, the magnate had to pay the king £2,000 for a licence, 12,000 acres of drained fenland, and agree to follow the model of Moorfields by leaving a public square at the centre of the development and building in a uniform Italianate style in addition.

Moorfields, therefore, created through community action in defence of common rights and supported by the king, set the model for the concept of the London square, which was followed at Leicester Square and Covent Garden in 1630–1 and in 1639 at Lincoln's Inn. In addition Covent Garden set the standard for the uniform architectural frontage specified in the 1618 proclamation, although in practice it was not often followed.

These model developments of the reigns of James I and Charles I subsequently established the pattern of squares and regular streets by demonstrating that it was both attractive and commercially viable to develop and build in such a manner. Following the Restoration a fresh proclamation reiterating the same regulations as its predecessors was issued. But from now on the general principle seems to have been accepted as the common custom and practice for new developments on both private and public land in the suburbs of London and Westminster, though access to the gardens in the squares was almost always restricted to householders. Bloomsbury Square and St James's Square were begun in 1661, Golden Square in 1675, Soho Square in 1681 and Red Lion Square in 1684. The last of these was developed by none other than Dr Nicholas Barbon himself and was the occasion for the battle between Barbon's builders and the local benchers of Grays Inn which has already been mentioned. Nonetheless when the great free-trading Dr Barbon came to build he did so in the specified form surrounded by houses which conformed to the regulations. On the great aristocratic London estates such as the Bedford estate, to which the Bloomsbury estate of the Earl of Southampton had been added by a marriage in 1669, the spirit of the proclamations was incorporated in varying degrees at different periods into the leases granted to builders. The leases granted up to 1776 imposed a bare minimum of uniformity,

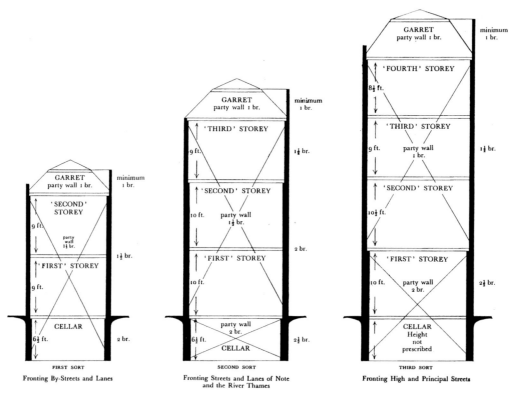

17 Diagrams showing the relationship between the height of houses and width of streets under the Rebuilding Act of 1667.

establishing a master plan but allowing builders to build houses of different widths and frontages although all houses in a street or square shared a common height and alignment (Plates 15 and 16). (Although in 1776 the building contract for Bedford Square specified 'one uniform row of houses' on each side with detailed instructions for every aspect of appearance, building materials and construction, this was fairly unusual, both at the time and later.) On the Foundling Hospital Estate Donald Olsen claims that the surveyor, S.P. Cockerell, made 'no attempt to impose a formal architectural pattern' although he did insist upon a general uniformity.[26]

In the City of London, in the aftermath of the Great Fire of 1666, the 1667 Act for Rebuilding the City of London was the first of a long series of statutes which regulated building within the City and after 1774 in greater London as well.[27]

Thus, under sections 5, 12, and 43 of the Act of 1667 it was ordained that there could be only four different types or classes of house in the City, each adapted to the width of the street and of a fixed number of stories of specified height. On by-lanes one could build only two storeys with a garret, about 25 feet; on streets or lanes of note, three storeys and a garret, about 35 feet; and on high and principal streets, four storeys and a garret, or about 45 feet. Finally the fourth class of house was that of mansion houses for 'citizens of extraordinary quality', which could be constructed to a maximum of four storeys, each of any height whatsoever. As a result, in the course of the rebuilding each street would be uniform in height in relation to its width against which grander buildings would stand out (Plate 17).

This remained in force until the Act of 1774 which covered the Cities of London, Westminster and the parishes of St Mary le bon, Paddington, St Pancras and St Luke Chelsea. This Act dispensed with any relationship between the width of streets and the

18   High Holborn showing the effect of the 100 feet height limit imposed in 1890 and lasting till 1947, which also permitted purely ornamental features to exceed the limit.

heights of building. It seems basically to have been designed to increase the number of building classes from four to seven to accommodate warehouses and industrial and commercial buildings of one sort or another. Nonetheless anarchy did not result, presumably because the spirit of the earlier acts had become so much a matter of custom and practice and because it was in the interests of property owners to maintain the standards of their developments. In addition this Act was the first to have been policed by District Surveyors rather than JPs.[28]

However this experiment in deregulation was short-lived. An Act of 1844 reintroduced the four classes of dwelling with limits upon height. It also specified a minimum width of 40 feet for all new streets and prescribed that streets must be at least as wide as they were high if the buildings were higher than 40 feet.[29] But such rules as these applied only to new streets, and not to redevelopment upon existing streets; not until the late 1880s when the house of the editor of the *Nineteenth Century*, James Knowles, an architect by training, in Queen Anne's Gate was being overtowered by the 150 feet high Queen Anne's Mansions, did the danger of anarchy become real enough for new legislation to be passed. Acts of 1890 and 1894 created a maximum limit of 100 feet for buildings on either old or new streets and remained actively in force until 1947 (Plate 18).[30]

Thus the general principles of the Jacobean regulations remained in force in London for over three centuries, and it is somewhat ironic that, far from inhibiting development as originally intended, the orderly pattern of facades, streets and above all the amenity of all those well-planted squares, about which so many of the foreign visitors to London in the eighteenth century enthused, actually increased the attractions of living in London and have remained a sound investment in environmental planning which continues to pay dividends three centuries later.

19   Charlotte Square, Edinburgh New Town, which was laid out after 1766 in imitation of London's West End.

Indeed, no sooner had the new town begun to take shape than interested observers began to attribute London's economic prosperity to its orderly layout and design, the result in fact of an original intention to *prevent* its growth.

Among the several Causes to which the prosperity of a nation may be ascribed, the situation, conveniency, and beauty of its capital are surely not the least considerable. A capital where these circumstances happen fortunately to concur, should naturally become the centre of trade and commerce, of learning and the arts, of politeness, and of refinement of every kind.

In the opinion of this writer of 1752 London was the most striking example of this rule.

40

20 Charlotte Square, Edinburgh New Town.

The neatness and accommodation of its private houses, the beauty and conveniency of its numerous streets and open spaces, its large parks and extensive walks, buildings, bridges, Royal Exchange and other major public buildings, the magnificence of its court and the pleasures of its theatres, were features responsible for attracting a 'mighty concourse of people . . . within so narrow a compass', and for animating a spirit of industry and improvement 'in every art and profession which had spread over the greatest part of South Britain', and had inspired 'the whole people with the greatest ardour and emulation'.[31]

The writer was Gilbert Elliott of Edinburgh, and these were the opening lines of his *Proposals for carrying on certain Public Works in the City of Edinburgh*, published in the summer of 1752 to justify and explain the passing of a resolution of the Royal Burghs on 8 July to purchase land at the Cross of Edinburgh, for the creation of a public forum or exchange and a records office. For while Elliott ascribed to a flourishing capital the same positive affects for the national economy as Barbon had done, his prescription was exactly opposite. His view was that God helped those who helped themselves, and that those European countries whose trade had expanded most rapidly since the late sixteenth century were the very ones whose governments had done most to encourage it by their active intervention in the economy. As examples of this he instanced England under Elizabeth I and France under Louis XIV and his minister Colbert. Scotland, in contrast, had suffered both from its peculiar political circumstances after James VI became King of England in 1603 when it became 'little better than a conquered nation', but also from both the inertia of her leading public figures amongst the nobility and gentry and from the archaic fabric of her capital city, Edinburgh. Not until after the rebellion of 1745 had things improved and then as a result of 'that spirit, liberality and application with which our nobility and landed gentlemen have of late engaged in every useful project ... chief adventurers in our fisheries, manufactures and trading companies'.

He argued that 'the meanness of Edinburgh has been too long an obstruction to our improvement, and a reproach to Scotland'. In contrast to London it was built upon the ridge of a hill, it had only one good street, its lanes were narrow, steep and dirty, and because of the restricted compass of the walls its 'houses stand more crowded than in any other town in Europe and are built to a height that is almost incredible'. Hence people were forced to live in flats or tenements, ten or twelve families on top of one another sharing a dirty common stair.

For Edinburgh, therefore, to compete with London as a magnet to the gentry and as a centre for consumption, and for Scotland to enjoy the benefit of the increased personal expenditure that great cities stimulated, Edinburgh had to be systematically improved and provided with a Royal Exchange, new Courts of Justice, a Council Chamber, and an Advocates' Library. In addition, an Act of Parliament should be obtained to extend the royalty to North and South so as to enlarge and beautify the town – what was to become the New Town (Plates 19 and 20). The expense of these projects, moreover, should be covered by subscriptions and by state contributions.

As we know, these proposals were executed almost to the letter under the direction of the Lord Provost, George Drummond (1687–1766), surely one of the most formidable city bosses of all time. And thus just as Moorfields and subsequently Covent Garden had earlier been established as models for the expansion of London, so the West End of London as a whole became a model for town planning in the rest of Britain and indeed farther afield.

CHAPTER 2
Seating the Gentry

COMPETITIVE CONSUMPTION OR NOBLESSE OBLIGE?

The decay of Hospitalitie in all the parts of this Our Kingdome, so much the more increaseth, by reason that Noblemen, Knights, and Gentlemen of qualitie, doe rather fall to a more private and delicate course of life, after the manner of forreine Countreys, by living in Cities and Townes, then continue the ancient and laudable custome of this Realme in housekeeping upon the principall Seates and Mansions in the Countrey, whereby there was wont to be more mutuall comfort between the Nobles and Gentlemen, and the inferiour sort of Commons in this Our Kingdome, (to the great strength and renowne thereof,) then in any other Kingdome of Europe, which course of alteration to the worse, We hold to be a disorder and inconvenience by all good pollicie to be remedied.

from *His Majesties Proclamation, requiring the Residencie of Noblemen, Gentlemen, Lieutenants, and Justices of the Peace, upon their chiefe Mansions in the Countrey, for the better maintenance of Hospitalitie, and discharge of their duties.* Newmarket, 9 December 1615.[1]

This extract from the proclamation of 1615 clearly expresses the contrast between the fashionable life in town, with all its private and luxurious attractions, and the public duties of a country landowner dispensing 'Olde Englisshe Hospitalitie' from his homely mansion. This ideal and the practice which it governed had, as we are about to see, as great a part to play in subsequent arguments about design as the battles over urban planning.

One must admit from the start that it is very hard for us today to grasp the idea of the English country house as the embodiment of public service and a bulwark against fashion and cosmopolitan extravagance. Even if we are able to grasp it we find it very hard to believe; it contradicts all our preconceptions. Over and over again we have been told that country houses are the very epitome of competitive consumption, the most ostentatious of status symbols and the most blatant displays of power and wealth. But competitive consumption is one of those catch-all historical explanations, 'a *deus ex machina* to be called upon when no other explanation is available', similar to 'the rise of the middle classes' and 'the rise of the money economy' that historians use to bridge over problems that have not been properly examined or resolved.[2]

I shall argue, on the contrary, that it is our modern idea of the country house that is incorrect and that the ideal expressed in the proclamations was actually followed to a considerable degree. But before pursuing a detailed examination of the evidence we should consider in more detail the objections that are held against it.

One of the most popular and authoritative of recent country house historians, Mark Girouard, dismisses the very existence at that time of the concept of duty: 'The concept of a great nobleman serving the public for duty rather than gain is a nineteenth century one. Both Elizabethan statesmen and Whig magnates expected to do well out of their country.'[3] He points to the example of Elizabeth I's Lord Treasurer, Lord Burghley, who made so much money out of his offices of state that he was able to build two huge country houses, Burghley House and Theobalds as well as Exeter House in London, all of them on the scale of palaces, as well as to buy vast estates to go with them (Plate 21). Then there was the eighteenth-century Prime Minister, Sir Robert Walpole, who built 'Houghton Hall, the most sumptuous house of its day, out of the proceeds of public service'.

In answer to this one can show that the *concept* of duty certainly did exist at the time. The proclamations and other documents are evidence. It may or it may not have been widely practised, but that is another matter. Second, there is no reason why public duty and private gain must be mutually exclusive; people can, without dishonour, be motivated by both.

Another recent leading social historian, Lawrence Stone, has explained country house building directly in terms of twentieth-century theories of competitive consumption: the 'unacknowledged reason for extravagant building' was 'to satisfy a lust for power, a thirst for admiration, an ambition to outstrip all rivals, and a wish to create a home suitable for the residence of a nobleman'. These reasons were particularly urgent for social parvenus.[4]

The distinguished architectural historian, Sir John Summerson, has referred directly to Thorstein Veblen's influential *Theory of the Leisure Classes* of 1899 in support of his expla-nation of the motives for building what he has called 'prodigy houses': 'Like so much great architecture, these country houses were what an economist has grossly called "conspicuous waste". Both Burghley and Hatton confessed to having spent more than even they could afford on houses which they did not need . . . And country gentlemen, of little account outside their own counties, copied the spirit of their betters and built as arrogantly as they could.'[5] Finally the great historian R.H. Tawney, who did acknowledge the reality of the practices of housekeeping and hospitality, argued that they had had to be sacrificed by aristocrats caught in a financial squeeze between static incomes from rent and huge social pressures upon them to spend extravagantly.[6]

It is difficult at times, reading mid-twentieth-century explanations such as these side by side with the early seventeenth-century proclamations and other evidence of the period, to recognise that they are referring to the same thing. Which is correct? I shall argue that we should put aside our twentieth-century notions of competitive consumption and our modern moral view that politicians ought not to profit from office, and take very seriously the ideals and justifications advanced during the period. According to these, country houses were built and maintained as theatres of a gentleman's hospitality out of a sense of duty incumbent upon status and, indeed, as a bulwark to preserve a stable gentry against fashion, competitive consumption and social change.[7]

Of course the arguments against this interpretation are powerful. One does not deny that ambition and self-interest were also involved, while it is of course true that the ideal was not always achieved in reality. There is no doubt whatsoever that some of these justifica-tions sound like special pleading and whitewashing to twentieth-century ears. Here is a test case. What should a twentieth-century reader make of the following passage from a panegyrical biography or obituary of Lord Burghley, Queen Elizabeth's chief minister, written shortly after his death? This defends him against accusations that he profited corruptly from his public offices on the grounds that any grasping miserliness and corrup-tion (covetousness, as the writer calls it) was really quite modest for someone in his position:

> . . . he was neither covetous nor miserable; for to be covetous is to desire more than he hath, but he might have had farre more than he had; *ergo* he was not covetous; for where he had a shillinge he might have had a pound, if that vile humor had possessed him. And to be in so great favour of his prince, so great a Counsellor in so great offices, so long

21 Lord Burghley on a donkey. To create employment Burghley encouraged landowners to spend liberally on housekeeping, housebuilding and hospitality.

tyme together, carrieing the whole swaie of the State, what wealth might he not have gathered if he had coveted to gather more.

But the writer goes on to argue that if any element of graft had actually been involved in obtaining his fortune this was justified by the *uses* to which the money was put, by the fact that Burghley was not a miser with his money, was not 'miserable' to use the writer's own adjective, but a lavish spender. It is a bit like justifying large robberies on the grounds that the robbers who escape enjoyed spending all their money. But it amounts to more than that; read carefully it must be interpreted as praise for a man whose behaviour was exemplary for someone of his status.

> . . . to be miserable, is he that can find in his hart to spend nothing; but I can prove he spent liberally, and therefore he cold not be miserable. Look upon his huge expences, and the truth will then shyne out; he spent infinite somes in building, hospitality, and in maintenance of his honorable port; he gave £500 a yere to the poore; he spent more in interteynements of his Prince then anie subject; he kept as faire a stable of horse as anie Nobleman; he made as costlie gardaines, walks, and places of pleasure, as are to be seene: Put thes and the like somes together, and you will confesse them to be greater then cold proceed from a miserable man. Neither spared he any cost for the maintenaunce of his

honor pleasure and reputation; then must his ennemyes confesse, and his frends approve, he cold never be miserable, that could spend so liberally; for a miser will spend nothinge.[8]

Clearly this was assuming a very different climate of ideas and social practices from our own. Obviously the end should not be used to justify the means; however, the writer's logic is less important than the fact that he extolled Burghley as the very model of a rich and powerful man: his behaviour in spending on an epic scale would have been admirable whatever the source of his wealth and it was a model of imitation for others of his status. Lord Burghley himself was aware that as chief minister of the crown he had to set an example for others according to their own station and means. In short, this kind of behaviour was not the result of an obsessive involuntary urge to emulate others competitively; but it self-consciously and dutifully aimed to set a standard for others to imitate – a different matter.

Burghley's own *Precepts*, written for his son, were published in 1617, twenty years after his death, and went through several editions. His advice on hospitality reiterated the injunction against excessive frugality, though it placed a greater and less hyperbolic emphasis than the obituary upon living within one's income and observing a temperate mean between the extremes of prodigality and niggardliness. Burghley's precepts were themselves the model for the advice given by other fathers, and for other published exhortations. He may well have had a hand in drafting the two Elizabethan proclamations ordering gentlemen back to their estates; certainly, as a leading member of the Privy Council during the great dearth, or famine, of 1596, he would have instituted measures that were dependent upon the gentry for the relief of the people's hardship through the exercise of traditional hospitality. He personally 'bought greate quantities of corne in tymes of dearth, to furnishe markets about the houses at underprices, to pull downe the price to relieve the poor'.[9]

Moreover Burghley's example was still being used well over a century later to justify the expenditure of the then first minister, Sir Robert Walpole, against charges of corruption in building Houghton Hall out of the fruits of high office. The Burghley obituary was first published only in 1732 when Walpole was under heavy attack from the opposition writers in *The Craftsman* for his gross corruption, and the passage in question would have been seen by contemporaries as a vindication not only of Burghley but also of Walpole with whom he was often compared.[10] Pasted inside the back cover of my personal copy of the 1732 publication is a cutting from a contemporary magazine which concludes 'Now, Mr. Printer, I want to know where we shall find a Cecil in our times'. In 1738 a new biography of Burghley was published which drew upon the obituary explicitly to exonerate Walpole on the grounds that expenditure on a country house must be considered as an act of public generosity, not of avarice: 'The personal Character of Lord Burghley, and his Conduct in private Life, shew that Beneficence towards those who are about a great Minister, and a proper degree of Magnificence in his Household, were not in Queen Elizabeth's Days held to be ill Qualities, or Things which the Friends of a Minister ought studiously to conceal; but the contrary rather . . . If three magnificent Houses be allowed to one Minister, shall we refuse another a single House? or while we admire the Generosity of a Great Man, who lived two Ages before us, shall we be angry with Marks of the same Virtue in a Minister living in the same Age with us?'[11] We will return to Houghton in a later chapter.

But by the age of Walpole this kind of justification was beginning to sound a little hollow, for the climate of opinion concerning the expenditure of the rich and the great was under attack and people were beginning to challenge its efficacy as the driving force of the economy, or even as a means of relieving the poor. Indeed, our modern idea that we consume in order to compete with and to outshine our neighbours and that this, however morally indefensible, makes the economy go round, comes from precisely this period – the early eighteenth century. Those modern historians who use the theory of competitive consumption to explain both the building of country houses in the seventeenth century, and the way of life that went with them, are simply repeating the ideological attacks upon their Tory opponents by early eighteenth-century Whig propagandists and critics, people like Bernard de Mandeville. Recognising the origin of our received ideas, we should set them to one side and look at the evidence in its own terms.[12]

High-living such as Burghley's was the very opposite of competitive, market-style consumption: it was not the product of some uncontrollable lust to surpass others in magnificence, but the proper behaviour for the members of a certain rank or station – behaviour that others were expected to imitate consciously according to their degree. It was their duty. It was even a kind of self-imposed taxation. In 1633 Lord Wentworth, the future Earl of Strafford, then President of the Council of the North, informed his nephew, Sir William Saville of Thornhill in the West Riding, that 'your Houses in my judgement are not suitable to your Quality, nor yet your Plate and Furniture'. He recommended that to pay for the appropriate improvements 'your Expence ought to be reduced to two Thirds of your Estate, the rest saved to the accommodating of you in that kind'. It was not intended that the gentry should bankrupt themselves in order to live in appropriate style, though sometimes, of course, they did.[13]

Such commands as these, and those of the proclamations were reinforced by powerful peer group pressures to conform to the pattern of bountiful open-handedness. Those who kept open house, who were convivial and hospitable to their fellow squires and towards the poor were popular and hence influential. Those who practised excessive frugality like Sir John Hotham, the richest squire in Yorkshire, earned disrespect for 'very narrow living'. Sir John Wyndham of Orchard Wyndham, who lived 'privately', was described as striving 'rather to please his affection then to suit himself according to his rank'.[14]

In fact, these values survived well into the eighteenth century and beyond. Peter Walter, the 'dextrous attorney' and land agent to the aristocracy, who assembled a large landed estate in the early eighteenth century, was a favourite target for the social satire of Alexander Pope and of Fielding on account of the fact that his 'wealth was never seen and his bounty never heard of'. He was the archetypal 'miserable man'. Pope asked, where on his estate were

> to be found
> Those ancient woods that shaded all the ground?
> We see no new-built palaces aspire,
> No kitchens emulate the vestal fire.
> Where are those troops of Poor, that throng'd of yore
> The good old landlord's hospitable door?
> Well, I could wish, that still in lordly domes
> Some beasts were kill'd, tho' not whole hecatombs;[15]

In the seventeenth century, however, these norms were reinforced by government, both through the kind of persuasion which Strafford used in his role as Viceroy of the North of England and through the proclamations which explicitly contrasted private pleasures with public duties. The proclamations condemned the 'more private and delicate course of life . . . by living in Cities and Towns' as well as the selfishness of those members of the gentry and aristocracy who lived as if they were private citizens 'born for themselves, and their families alone'. On the other hand those who believed themselves born 'for the publique good and comfort of their Countrey' were extolled. The public-spirited were assured by the king that their conduct would be rewarded, that it would be 'a meanes for them to purchase our good opinion and favour, as the contrary shall not pass without our note and dislike'.[16]

There can be no doubting James I's (Plate 22) personal commitment to the campaign to defend the tradition of gentry and nobility keeping house on their estates. This was not the policy of some faceless bureaucrat, some Jacobean town planner, some faction on the Privy Council. It was the king's own policy based upon his deep convictions about government and kingship. At the same time, as Felicity Heal has observed, the elaborate language of the proclamations characterises them as 'royal polemics'.

The strength of his feelings is illustrated by the following incident. When he learnt that the Privy Council had withheld the fifth of the eight proclamations of his reign, 'because they found it needless', James 'broke into a great choler, saying that he was contemned and his commandments rejected . . . that he would never endure that a matter so solemnly determined by him in the presence of his council and by them approved, should as soon as his back was turned be changed without his privity'.[17] The very tone and wording of the final two proclamations of his reign vividly express the rage of an old man who felt that his personal will had been defied. In 1623 he accused Lords Spirituall and Temperall of deliberately frustrating his intention of reviving and settling 'Hospitalitie and good Government in all the parts of this our Kingdome'.[18] And in the final 1624 proclamation he broke into such a raging 'choler' at disobedient landowners that it is impossible to believe that the words were drafted by anyone but himself. On that occasion he wrote: 'finding by experience, that such as are addicted unto that course, of withdrawing themselves from their countries, are prone to flatter themselves in their vaine humour; we have thought good (for once) to publish our absolute and peremptorie command, That Our said proclamations be in all parts dutifully obeyed.'[19] Indeed we know that James drafted some of his own proclamations, and that on one occasion he strongly resisted the advice of senior Privy Councillors to tone down his more colourful language.[20]

Speaking in the Star Chamber in 1616 in his charge to the Assize Judges before they departed on circuit, a speech delivered without notes, he expanded upon the causal connection between the growth of London, spending on fashion, women's pride and luxury and the gentry deserting the country for the town, to which he had alluded in the proclamation of only a few months earlier. 'Another thing to be cared for, is, the new buildings here about the Citie of London: concerning which my Proclamations have gone forth . . . And this is that, which is like the Spleene in the body, which in measure as it ouergrowes, the body wastes. For is it possible but the Countrey must diminish, if London doe so increase, and all sorts of people doe come to London?'

James believed that the cause lay in the desire of the idle rich to dwell in London, and in turn the cause of that was female personal consumption: 'the pride of the women: For if they bee wiues, then their husbands; and if they be maydes, then their fathers must bring them vp to London; because the new fashion is to bee had no where but in London: and here, if they be vnmarried, they marre their marriages, and if they be married, they loose their reputations, and rob their husbands purses.'

Worse still in James's opinion, the practice of living in town was profoundly un-English. In a passage which echoes John of Gaunt's dying speech from Shakespeare's *Richard II* he compared the English fashion for French clothes with the Italian fashion for living in cities: 'It is the fashion of Italy, especially of Naples (which is one of the richest parts of it), that all the Gentry dwell in the principall Townes, and so the whole countrey is emptie: . . . For as wee now doe imitate the French fashion, in fashion of Clothes, and Lackeys to follow euery man; So haue wee got vp the Italian fashion, in liuing miserably in our houses and dwelling all in the Citie.' In other words, living like a private citizen in a small lodging in town was to live 'miserably', to behave like a miser.

Therefore, the king went on to exhort his hearers, 'let vs in Gods Name leaue these idle

22   James I also believed fervently in the duty of landowners towards the poor.

forreine toyes, and keepe the old fashion of England'. His speech, he declared, was to have the force of yet another proclamation commanding the gentry to depart to their own houses in the country, and it was to be understood that his proclamations were not intended to last only during the Christmas season but permanently.[21]

James's own view was that competitive consumption of ephemeral female fashions and 'idle forreine toys' was something that went on in cities. He did not want these to contain markets and shops catering for all purses. In 1623 he was disgusted to find that the goldsmith's row in Cheapside which had formerly contained 'faire and flourishing' jewellers and goldsmiths had now been 'overrun and blemished with porre pettie trades which he wold have removed'.[22] He desired a none too populous but magnificent capital city, rebuilt on Augustan principles, with parks and squares and fine houses and a limited number of grand shops selling real luxuries. He loathed the idea both of a new town of lodging houses for the gentry and of suburban shanty towns for the poor. He did not want the nobility and gentry to live privately and 'miserably' – a point taken up by several of his subjects who specifically censured rural landlords for taking lodgings in 'some cabbine in a towne or city'.

James wanted nobility and gentry to live with due decorum, in a manner that neither demeaned nor aspired above their status. As public figures they should live publicly on a grand, even a heroic scale housed in their country mansion – the nobility in magnificent palaces, the gentry in more modest piles. For James, as for Burghley, it was a virtue to consume conspicuously on a princely scale, to possess and display symbols befitting one's status. And moreover, unlike Elizabeth I, the new king was prepared to set an example himself. No sooner did he succeed to the throne than expenditure on royal building, which under Elizabeth had been largely a matter of maintenance, rapidly increased from about £5,000 a year in 1603 to £35,000 a year in 1610.[23]

We get the impression of an unruly group of prefects always rushing off to enjoy the bright lights, and of a headmaster waging an unending battle to make them carry out their duties. But is this picture correct? Was it in fact true that the gentry were deserting their estates for London and other towns? Was the king's point of view entirely his own and one which he had to impose from the centre, or was there common ground between the gentry and the crown? Finally, why did it all matter so much where the landowners lived?

In answer to the first question it is very difficult to judge whether the gentry were actually abandoning their country seats for a private life in town. We lack sufficient systematic information. Of the great landowners of Somerset in 1600 only five actually possessed a London home as opposed to renting lodgings. Lord Poulett returned home because he couldn't 'abide the incommodities' of his hired lodging in London. None of them spent more than one month in the year away. Sir Richard Grosvenor, the leading JP in Cheshire, went to London but rarely and believed that his duty lay in his own county. Another 'godly magistrate', Sir John Newdigate, expressed strong disapproval of the fashionable frivolities of London but while he spent most of his time in Warwickshire he nonetheless 'regularly spent time and money in London'. The Earl of Clarendon's father, Henry Hyde of Dainton in Wiltshire, never came to London in the thirty years he survived after the death of Elizabeth I. His wife never came to London at all.[24]

On the other hand, in Devonshire, during the famine of 1596, the lord lieutenant complained that the gentry had left their homes for Exeter.[25] In Yorkshire, unlike Somerset, quite a large number of the gentry owned houses in the city of York, and several of them, having found the cost of housekeeping in the traditional style recommended by the king too expensive, went to live in York in order to retrench.[26] The father of Sir Hugh Chomley of Whitby had fallen into debt and went to live in York on an annuity, having turned his estates over to his son. Sir Hugh and his family spent three years in London from 1620 to 1623 when they returned to Yorkshire in obedience to the proclamations; they spent a whole year in London in 1630–1, another period in 1633; six months in 1637; the whole winter in 1639, and when Sir Hugh was elected to the Long Parliament in 1640 he was back and forth between London and Yorkshire over a period of three years. Over a period of twenty-three years he spent almost a third of his time in London. All the same, when he was at the height of prosperity again, in 1636, he wrote proudly that 'having mastered my debts I lived in as handsome and plentiful a fashion at home as any gentleman in all the country, of my rank'. Thus the evidence from different parts of England is inconclusive, but it does not indicate very severe absenteeism.[27]

But looked at from London the situation would have seemed far more serious. Seven thousand families, that is, between 30,000 and 70,000 people depending upon the number of relatives and servants in each family, were said to have left London as a result of the 1622 proclamation – the only one of James I to be stringently enforced.[28] This may well have been exaggerated but, even so, at a time when the total number of gentry families in England must have been about 16,000 it represented a large proportion.[29] And when the population of London was something over 200,000 it amounted to between one third and one sixth of that. This does not mean that the gentry were permanent absentees from their estates. It simply means that they spent some time, at the very most a month or two in a year, living in a large town or city. It points to the beginnings of the Season. London must have been a very strange capital city in the seventeenth and eighteenth centuries, a bit like a spa or holiday town, with a large floating population of visitors.

The effect of this upon the growth in the population of London is more important. Whereas there were few *permanent* absentees from the country, there was in numerical terms a more or less permanent influx of visitors to London, even though the individuals who composed it changed all the time. These visitors created employment in London and other major towns which was of a very precarious nature. When townspeople were thrown out of work either because of trade depression or the departure of visitors for the country they had no other work to turn to, which was not the case in the country.

Nonetheless the drift of absentee landlords into the cities does not seem to be anything like so serious in its effect upon rural areas as the proclamations made out.

What about people's attitudes? Were the sovereign and his immediate councillors alone in their view of the responsibilities which accompanied gentle and noble rank? It is sometimes argued that the evidence of all those proclamations, of Books of Orders, of continual correspondence from the Privy Council to the local JPs exercising a 'minute, constant and overbearing control' over local life only goes to show that the gentry were indeed a recalcitrant lot who needed to be spurred into action; that the hand of the Privy Council 'was never taken off, its attention never flagged'.[30]

Certainly it must be granted that there were some who found the life of a country gentleman extremely irksome. Lord Pembroke wrote from Wilton House in 1601, 'I have not yet been a day in the country, and I am as weary of it as if I had been a prisoner there seven year'. But the Earls of Pembroke were hardly typical of the gentry; they were grandees, Privy Councillors, lords lieutenant of much of the West Country and of Wales. Such people 'of the best condition who have been constantly used to much converse', as the fourth Lord North put it, inevitably found country life tedious, to be taken in small dutiful doses. They were not representative, and in any case the proclamations expressly exempted Privy Councillors from having to leave London.[31]

On the other hand there were several substantial gentlemen whose views and principles are well documented, who were fervently committed to the country life on terms very similar to those of the royal proclamations. Sir Richard Grosvenor, one of the leading landowners in Cheshire, MP in 1621, 1625 and 1628 and the senior JP in the 1620s and '30s, believed that the local magistrate acted as a crucial link in the chain between the monarch, parliament and the provinces: 'every man owes his countrey [i.e. his county] a tribute of action'. His social horizons were exclusively local and all his friends came from his immediate circle of neighbours. He believed that not only JPs but also gentlemen of less exalted rank such as the jurors at Quarter Sessions and presumably the even humbler householders who served as village constables and overseers of the poor had an obligation to be involved in local government.[32]

Sir John Newdigate, a Warwickshire magistrate who flourished in the first two decades of the same century, also believed strongly in the local duties: 'Absence of a good magistrate doth great harm', and he enjoined the jurors 'not to be lookers on but actors in the public service'. In the parliamentary debates on the great Elizabethan Poor Law of 1597–8 it was the landowners who moved with 'enlightened and determined vigour to lay great responsibilities on themselves and on their land'.[33]

While men like Newdigate and Grosvenor wrote down their principles for the benefit of jurors and as precepts for their sons, members of the succeeding generation, men like John Evelyn, the diarist, and the Earl of Clarendon, commemorated the communal piety of their fathers in corresponding terms. Evelyn's father was 'a lover of hospitality; and in briefe, of a singular Christian moderation in all his actions, not illiterate, nor obscure; as having continued Justice of the Peace, and of the Quorum; and served his Country in the Charge of high-Sheriff'.[34]

The father of Edward Hyde, the later Earl of Clarendon, had studied at Oxford and must have been one of the earliest to tour Europe; even so he settled down to the life of a country gentleman on his estate at Dinton in Wiltshire, with occasional visits to London on parliamentary business. 'The wisdom and frugality of that time being such', Clarendon explained, 'that few gentlemen made journeys to London, or any other expensive journeys, but upon important business and their wives never; by which providence they enjoyed and improved their estates in the country, and kept good hospitality in their houses, brought up their children well, and were beloved by their neighbours.'[35]

It is arguable that this picture of a Golden Age of kindly and paternalistic country gentlemen, sharply contrasted to the hard-hearted and dissolute present, must be treated with great scepticism on the grounds that it was a convention always described as existing in the past before the rise of modern corruption and luxury.[36] But this is to misunderstand the rhetorical and homiletic purpose of evoking these images of worthy forefathers, explained by Izaak Walton in this passage from his biography of Sir Henry Wotton concerning the achievements of his ancestors: 'such a kindred as left a Stock of Reputation to their Posterity, such Reputation, as might kindle a generous emulation in Strangers, and preserve a noble ambition in those of his Name and Family, to perform Actions worthy of their Ancestors'.[37] Camden described Sir Philip Sidney as 'that Sidney whom Providence raised as an example of our ancestors to our age'. The design of Fuller's *Worthies* was, inter alia: 'to present examples to the living, having here precedents of all sorts and sizes; of men famous for valour, wealth, wisdom, learning, religion and bounty to the public, on which last we most largely insist.'[38] These descriptions of the men of the past were not therefore false, but they were idealised and moralised to some extent in order to bind 'the gentry to their own countryside' and to set the ideals and the standards for succeeding generations.[39]

And there was another reason for setting a good example, even more foreign to our way of thinking today. That was magic – as this quotation taken from, of all places, a treatise on economics, demonstrates:

In the next place it hath beene observed in some places, where the poore for want of abilities cannot trade, and where the great or rich have not will, or dare not adventure their Estates in forraigne Traffike, that the examples onely of the Prince hath throughly effected it, and proved a maine Furtherer of the generall Commerce and Traffike of his Countrey; which doth not only hold in this matter of Trade, but in all other state matters whatsoever; for then it will be impossible for the rich Subjects to forbeare, when they see their Soveraigne bend his mind, and addict himselfe therunto. For the wise have observed, that *Princes cannot frame an Age unlike unto themselves* [my italics]; and that it is easier (as one said) for Nature to erre, then that a Prince should form a Common-wealth unlike himselfe: Just if they be wicked, regular if they be dissolute, chaste if they be immodest, and religious if they bee impious . . . Therefore, for conclusion, if the Prince love the Sea, his Subjects will be all Sea-men; and if he be a Lover of trade and traffike, the rich and powerfull of his Kingdomes, will be all Merchants.[40]

James I, then, was not alone in his convictions concerning the responsibilities of the gentry and nobility to their own estates and localities. His patriarchal principles and theirs were in many respects identical. Each gave support to the other. Indeed one can identify a propaganda campaign aiming to advocate and uphold the values of country life against the dangers of erosion, and to present that way of life in the best possible light. It was a campaign to which royal proclamations, Privy Council chivvying, sermons, pamphlets, the charges delivered by magistrates to the members of juries, the memoirs and precepts they wrote for their sons, conduct books and many other forms of writing all contributed. But it was not restricted even to these: literature, both poems and plays, biography, architectural theory and the design of buildings themselves all helped to present a rich and attractive picture of country life, its duties, pleasures and recreations.

If the gentry did continue, by and large, to reside at home rather than deserting their estates in droves for London and the provincial capitals, if there were this measure of mutual agreement, if the king's point of view did receive such strong and practical support from so many gentlemen around the country, then why was a campaign necessary?

One of the reasons is given in the proclamations. The system of local government, 'the great and principall part of the subordinate government of this Realme', depended upon the appointment of the nobility, country gentlemen and clergy as voluntary and unpaid lords lieutenant of the counties, deputy lieutenants, sheriffs and JPs. These officers were, in effect, the local councillors and administrators of their day, their duties including the implementation of national policy at local level, responsibility for military service and the local administration of everything from road maintenance to the relief of poverty. The ideals which governed their conduct are reflected in their memorials in the parish churches where they rest. Sir Henry Poole (d. 1616) of Sapperton in Gloucestershire was 'Much given to Hospitality, he was always faithful to his Prince, and loving to his country, true to his friends and bounteous to his servants'.[41]

The lord lieutenant was the most powerful personage, the representative in the county of the monarch and governor of the county. He was almost without exception a nobleman, frequently a duke or earl and often a member of the Privy Council. In 1716 almost half of the Privy Council were also lords lieutenant. These were the Arundels, Bedfords, Pembrokes, Devonshires and Derbys.[42] On the other hand, the JP did most of the work. His duties cannot be neatly divided, for he exercised judicial as well as administrative functions so intertwined that no one tried to separate them. He also had quasi-legislative and political functions, for the bench decided amongst themselves which of their many duties should be given special emphasis and they even had discretion to determine policies where they were not bound by statute – for example, the evangelical justices under the influence of Wilberforce in the late eighteenth century imposed the Sunday closing of the alehouses of their own free accord. In addition, the Chairman of the Bench opened the Quarter Sessions with a charge to the jury which could take on the character of a political homily. The godly magistrate, Sir Richard Grosvenor, to whom we have already referred, was doing just this when in 1625 he charged the jurors to be actively involved in the government of their districts and to fight the evils of popery, vagrancy and the alehouse.[43]

Administratively the JPs were responsible for the maintenance of roads and bridges, for the supervision of trade and commerce, for consumer protection such as weights and measures, and even checking the quality of cloth. They also enforced wage and price control and apprenticeship legislation and, above all, were responsible for the relief of poverty, unemployment and famine.

Obviously it mattered that these offices should be filled, but as only about one fifth of the gentry served in such posts at any one time there needed to be a second reason why *all* the gentry were required to repair home. And the second reason was that the country faced severe and intractable problems of unemployment, poverty and famine.

Poverty was an overwhelming problem in Tudor and Stuart England. Between 1550 and 1640 England, in common with the rest of Europe, suffered simultaneously from a population explosion and the longest period of price inflation until the Second World War, during which prices rose sixfold, accompanied by a sharp decline in the real value of wages. According to one rough estimate the population of England rose from about 3 million to about 5.5 million; according to a more precise one it grew from 4.1 to 4.8 million in the thirty years 1570–1600. Accurate or not such figures indicate the scale of the problem and the general trend. In addition real wages did not keep pace with the rise of prices, falling by about a third in value. Then there were serious harvest failures which occurred at disastrously regular intervals approximately every ten or twenty years: in 1595–8, 1622–3, 1630, 1645–6, 1661, 1673–4, 1696–7, and 1709. Finally, on top of all these other problems, the cycle of industrial boom and slump began to make its presence felt for the first time.[44]

There were some sensible, some bizarre and some horrifying solutions to these problems. Sir Walter Raleigh looked to the carnage of war as the means for reducing the surplus population; like others he also favoured colonisation and emigration. Some urged the development of foreign trade, new industries and improved agriculture. But these latter were long term solutions; in the short term there was the urgent necessity to cope with the immediate threat of civil disorder arising from poverty, vagrancy, periodic urban unemployment and the spectre of famine.[45]

These immediate remedies were socially and economically conservative, as they had to be; they attempted to slow down and even to halt the changes that were taking place by propping up the traditional rural society whose institutions were in fair working order and susceptible of improvement to take the strain. Although *under*-employment was widespread in the countryside 'starvation was scarcely possible or tolerated in the still uncomplicated and amazingly stable society which rural England remained'. This was not true of the cities, particularly not of London, growing as it was to an unprecedented size.[46]

There, if people were thrown out of work they would not be able to find other employment; if there were dearth they must starve; if there were plague it spread rapidly threatening the court itself, whereas in the country it spread more slowly. Therefore, anything that stimulated the drift of people to the cities in search of work had to be stopped. Clearly the presence there of several thousand gentry families at any one time, even if intermittently, had the effect of creating employment, and the effect was all the worse because the employment it did create was largely seasonal, throwing those people into destitution when the gentry departed – which is just what did happen. This continued so long as the London Season lasted. A London seamstress recently recalled the unemployment caused by the end of the Season before the First World War: 'The races, the Derby and Ascot, were very important, then it faded out because London became empty in August and they didn't want us, so they sacked the work crew . . . People would say "Oh we'll have to live off air pie now".'[47]

Correspondingly everything needed to be done to preserve the rural economy and its way of life as a stable counterweight to the attractions of London. The injunction to live there had to apply to all the gentry and not just to the small proportion of heads of families who held office as JPs.[48]

At the centre of the new policy to deal with poverty was the Poor Law of 1597–8, administered by the JPs, which introduced for the first time the power when necessary to levy a direct and compulsory poor rate on every householder in the parish in place of the previous voluntary system.[49] It might be thought that this would have superseded the two older methods that are explicitly mentioned in the proclamations and elsewhere.[50] The first of these was hospitality, which did not merely mean entertaining one's family and friends, but also had the precise meaning of providing a regular soup kitchen for the poor of the district at the gatehouse or in the buttery. Besides this, housekeeping meant living in the style appropriate to one's status, with a large household of servants, thereby creating employment or what economists call 'concealed unemployment' and keeping poverty at bay. Additional duties of the squire were the giving of alms and the endowment of almshouses and other charities, as well as providing local employment by spending his income in his own locality rather than in towns.[51]

The *compulsory* levy instituted by the new Poor Law was not intended to supersede or displace the voluntary exercise of charity on the part of the rich, nor to remove from them the burden of providing a measure of stable employment through housekeeping, but simply to provide a basic minimum level of assistance to which all the other means would be supplementary.

The Stuart proclamations therefore were part and parcel of a package of measures, no single one of which was intended to be sufficient in itself but which, taken together, could make an impact upon a thoroughly bewildering and complex set of problems. And at the centre of this stood the Country Seat as an economic and social counterweight to the cities, intended to set a model for all to emulate and to provide a stable fulcrum for this patriarchal if somewhat ramshackle welfare state. Indeed it can be argued that it was part of a grand design for a humanist Common Weal, initiated by Thomas Cromwell and prudently carried forward by his proteges, Burghley, Sir Thomas Gresham and Sir Nathaniel Bacon amongst others, after the accession of Elizabeth I, whose overriding aim was stability and 'tranquillity, wherein people prosper and the welfare of nations is preserved'.[52]

BOTH RULER AND RULED

The Country Seat, as we have seen, was more than simply a building, a residence that happened to be located outside the big towns. It was the physical manifestation of a complex political and economic theory and policy, one which belonged to a definite historical period.

Between 1570 and 1640 a substantial number of country seats were built or rebuilt in the course of the 'Great Rebuilding of England' – to use W.G. Hoskins's ringing phrase.[53] More precisely, this began in the 1560s and reached its peak between 1575 and 1625. Although Hoskins derived his concept from somewhat impressionist evidence, such as dated houses and the observations of county historians, there seems no reason to doubt his inspired guess. Counting manor and country houses listed in Pevsner's *Buildings of England* for the counties of Dorset, Kent, Wiltshire and Northamptonshire, and including only those houses either newly built or substantially rebuilt which are firmly dated or assigned to a decade or quarter century, broadly confirms Hoskins's picture, as the block graph on the next page (Plate 23) shows.[54]

This can only give a rough idea, and because demolished, unrecorded and undated houses are excluded, these figures can only indicate trends and *relative* magnitudes, but there indeed appears to have been a peak between 1580 and 1620 and, more specifically, about double the number of houses in the sample were built in the first two decades of the seventeenth century than in the last two decades of the sixteenth century – 103 compared to 56. These levels were never achieved again till a century later, when, between 1690 and 1710, some 99 houses were constructed or substantially rebuilt. Never again did country house building

Light grey blocks represent smaller country houses, black blocks prodigy houses.

Houses per decade

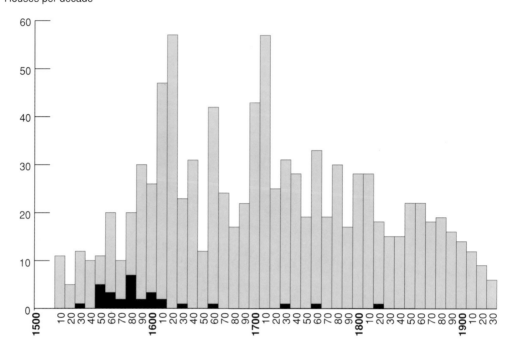

23   This graph indicates the approximate levels of country house building for each decade from 1500 to 1900 in Dorset, Kent, Wiltshire and Northamptonshire. Figures derived from Pevsner's *Buildings of England.*

in those counties reach such levels. The picture is very much the same when we only include new buildings or very substantial rebuilding of existing houses.

Looked at another way the figures tell an even more curious tale. Almost all the largest and grandest houses in these counties, houses like Wilton, Burghley, Longleat, Knole and Althorp, those that have been dubbed the 'prodigy houses', were established or initially constructed between 1540 and 1610, many in the 1540s following the dissolution of the monasteries and many more in the 1570s when the Protestant Succession was re-established. 'The Great Rebuilding' of country and manor houses, therefore, fell into two distinct phases: that of the prodigy house starting in the middle of the sixteenth century, and in full swing in the 1570s when Elizabeth was firmly established on the throne, and that of the smaller houses which followed in the early seventeenth century.

Conventional explanations exist for this 'Great Rebuilding' in the countryside and for the two distinct phases in which it occurred. Most of these explanations hinge upon 'competitive consumption', and will be critically examined in the following pages. Hoskins argued that a necessary precondition was the increasing prosperity of the yeomen and farmers who benefited from the inflation in the prices of their produce without a corresponding increase in the wages of their labourers or their rents.[55] There was, however, no reason why they should have spent this money upon houses and furnishings, nor is the 'cause' to which Hoskins attributed the phenomenon more convincing. According to him, this was the filtering down to the bulk of the population of that taste for privacy which the upper classes had enjoyed in the previous two centuries: splitting the old common hall, sub-dividing it into two floors and creating more small specialised rooms so that the master could withdraw from the common life.[56] Here, in short, is the conventional trickle-down and upward emulation explanation for changes in the way that people spend their money.

But most squires, according to Hoskins, had already rebuilt their houses on this new pattern by the early sixteenth century. The wealthy yeomen did likewise in the 1560s and by the turn of the seventeenth century 'a considerable part of the rural population, above the cottager level, were following suit'. So why, if the squires had already rebuilt their houses once to accommodate their new style of living, were they doing it again for the same reason in the early seventeenth century?

A few years after Hoskins's article Eric Mercer observed that the prodigy houses were distinct both in size and plan from the houses of the gentry. The prodigy houses were built by the Tudor administrative elite, men like Lord Burghley whose main income came from office and crown grants. The heyday of the construction of those houses, with their double courtyards, external display and formal symmetry, was in the 1580s. By the early seventeenth century very few were still under construction. Besides Hatfield House (1608–12) for Sir Robert Cecil, Earl of Salisbury, the second son of Lord Burghley and his successor as Lord High Treasurer, there was New Hall, Essex for the Earl of Buckingham and Audley End for the Earl of Suffolk (1605–14). But Audley End, according to Mercer, was a throwback, a freak; he explained the decline in construction of prodigy houses in terms of the 'crisis of the aristocracy' theory invented by Tawney and developed by Lawrence Stone. The wealth of the courtiers at the start of the seventeenth century was supposed to have become more directly dependent on the court, less upon their own resources, and the court itself was becoming increasingly impoverished. The flow of royal bounty was drying up, and the royal progresses that had occasioned so much extravagant building under Elizabeth gradually decreased as the finances of the crown got into deeper and deeper difficulties. According to this theory, by the reign of Charles I we were to find only the remodelling and extension of great houses that were already in existence, like Castle Ashby, Rushton and Temple Newsam rather than the construction of new ones.[57]

While the pheonomenon remarked upon by Mercer certainly seems to be supported by my rough-and-ready sample, his explanation seems to ignore the obvious: once the great country palaces of the newly established Tudor dynasties such as Burghley, Longleat and Wilton had been completed there was no need for more, except when new magnates rose to power, men such as the Earl of Dorset, the Earl of Salisbury and the Earl of Suffolk or Walpole in the eighteenth century. The building of Audley End was not a freak but normal practice for the highest officers of state, if they had not inherited such a place.[58] It was not that there were fewer men around with the funds to build on such a scale but that of those who would be encouraged to do so, most already possessed or had prospects of possessing a splendid building and therefore needed to do nothing other than some remodelling or extension.

This, rather than the crisis of the aristocracy or the trickle-down effect, seems a better explanation for the increase in the construction of more compact 'courtier' type houses and gentry houses in the early seventeenth century. For it is vital to understand that, when the court encouraged the lesser nobility and country squires to build in 'generous emulation' of their social superiors, it was certainly not encouraging a hell-for-leather competitiveness which would have disturbed the social hierarchy which the government wished to preserve. One legislative proposal at the beginning of Elizabeth's reign, for example, was to forbid a yeoman or artificer from purchasing land worth more than £5 a year, a clothier land worth more than £10 a year, and a merchant land worth more than £50 a year. Prodigy houses were, above all, an example of *appropriate* living for the magnates.[59]

Take the example of Lulworth Castle. This was built by Viscount Bindon as a hunting

24   Burghley House, Stamford, 1556–63 and 1575–87. Far from ruining himself through extravagance Burghley budgeted prudently and maintained a force of perhaps 140 builders throughout most of his lifetime.

lodge 'well seated for prospect and pleasure; but of little other use'.[60] A letter written in 1608 by Lord Bindon to the Earl of Salisbury – who was himself rebuilding Cranbourne Court also as a hunting lodge, also in Dorset – indicates that Salisbury had exerted some pressure upon him to build. 'If the little pile in Lulworth Park', wrote Bindon, 'shall prove pretty or worth the labour bestowed in the erecting of it, I will acknowledge as the truth is, that your Lordship's powerful speech to me at Bindon, to have laid the first foundations of the pile in my mind.'[61]

Bindon was lord lieutenant of Dorset in 1601, so maybe he was being persuaded to turn Lulworth into a pretty large place. This tallies with the Earl of Strafford's later injunction to Sir William Saville that his 'houses in my judgement are not suitable to your Quality' and that Saville should remedy the situation by building.

Again and again we see this pressure being exerted upon landowners to build appropriately. Take Lord Burghley's two major country mansions, that feature so much in accounts of prodigy house building: Burghley House near Stamford in Northamptonshire (Plate 24) and Theobalds at Cheshunt in Hertfordshire. Burghley's motives are conventionally explained in terms of competitive consumption, conspicuous waste and competing for the queen's favours. According to this explanation, 'building for the queen, building in rivalry with others, building to the limit of their resources and beyond' had become a major outlet for the ambitions of the established and now peaceful nobility; prowess on the battlefield had been replaced by prowess in building. Related to this, Burghley House and Theobalds, like the other prodigy houses, were 'an expression – conscious and deliberate – of a cult of sovereignty . . . built or enlarged specifically as places in which to receive the queen, as tributes and as monuments to loyalty'.[62] After the queen's visit to Theobalds on her progress in 1571, for instance, when the building works were in full swing, the house became,

58

according to this theory, 'an offering to his royal mistress' for which 'no magnificence could be in excess'. Indeed, Burghley is quoted to support the contention that she instigated this excess by finding fault with the size of her chamber.[63]

A similar tale is told of Sir Nicholas Bacon's house at Gorhambury nearby, on which the queen is said to have commented only a year later, 'My Lord, what a little house you have gotten'. Bacon is supposed to have replied, 'Madam, my house is well, but it is you that have made me too great for my house'.[64] This is generally interpreted to mean that those who were ambitious to reap or to preserve the rewards of office and royal patronage had to speculate by building on a scale appropriate to the proper entertainment of the sovereign so as to ingratiate themselves with the ultimate source of those rewards.[65] But there is surely all the difference in the world between social obsession to compete by conspicuous consumption and a deliberate policy to spur landowners into grand building projects?

But what this kind of explanation does not answer is the question: why did the queen wish her dues to be paid in the form of lavish buildings?

First of all the royal progresses, for whose reception these palaces were partly designed and constructed, must be better understood. They were 'part of the great effort to identify the queen with the nation at a time when communication, in every sense, was poor. It was a great display of monarchy: queen, ministers, servants, hundreds strong, moving slowly through the countryside, staying a few days in the various great houses on the way. Often the full splendours of the masque would be brought into play with its heavy symbolism of monarchy and nation.'[66]

Also, since it was government policy to rule the provinces through the gentry and nobility on their country seats, progresses must be seen in part as a form of royal visitation. They were an inspection of the greater seats, with the aim of ensuring that the greater nobility were obeying government policy. Once built, their palaces would not only fill their permanent function as the seats of the lords lieutenant, whose administration and organis-ation was being systematised at the very time of the progresses, they would also ensure that their owners and their heirs would retain their substantial local interests in perpetuity – which is exactly what has happened in the case of Burghley and many other surviving family owners of prodigy houses.[67] The progresses did not last the whole of Elizabeth's reign, but were concentrated in the years from 1565 to 1580, the very years during which the building of the prodigy seats was at its height, certainly in the four chosen counties, and which the progresses were intended to stimulate. James I progressed every year except 1610, 1611 and 1622 but by this time few prodigy houses were being constructed, though this was the boom period for all other types of house.[68]

Once the prodigy houses were completed, the 'progresses' of their own noble masters could be relied upon to perform the same function for the lower ranks of the country hierarchy as the progresses of the monarch had done for the greater; the gentry and lesser nobility had to possess houses large enough and in good enough repair to be fit for the reception of the lord lieutenant. Similarly the lesser gentry invited *their* superiors to feasts and celebrations. When Sir John Strode celebrated the consecration of the chapel attached to his new home at Chantmarle in Dorset in 1619 he was able to record proudly in his journal that the Bishop of Bristol had officiated and that two of the county magnates, Sir John Strangeways of Melbury House and Sir Thomas Trenchard of Wolfeton, had attended alongside many other leading gentry all of whom 'were feasted in the house'.[69]

In this light the great prodigy houses were indeed monuments in the precise sense of commemorating, reminding and warning. They represented the traces of the great cere-monial progresses; they were, in a sense, the chivalric castles of the Faery Queen's Arthurian knights; they were the palaces of the great officers of state and the viceregal residences of the lords lieutenant acting as reminders of the glory of the monarchy. In the words of Francis Bacon in 1594, 'the plain and approved Way that is safe, and yet proportionate to the

Greatness of a Monarch, to present himself to Posterity, is . . . the Magnificence of goodly and Royal Buildings and Foundations . . . that your Coin be stamped with your own Image; so in every part of your State there may be somewhat new; which, by Continuance, may make the Founder and Author remembered.' In an age without television, film or news-papers, in an agrarian society, monumental buildings set in the countryside and covering every single county played an indispensable role in mass communication and state propaganda. The attendance of ambassadors gave them international significance. Especially when they were unoccupied they would have been a potent and stern reminder to the local populace, particularly in areas remote from London surrounded as it was by royal palaces, of the political power of the state manifested in the bounty it dispensed to the chief servants of the crown. To quote the Earl of Strafford once again, writing this time to Archbishop Laud in 1637 as Lord Deputy of Ireland about the house he was building there. 'They say I build unto the sky. I acknowledge that were myself only considered in what I build it were not only to excess but even to folly . . . but his Majesty will justify me that, at my last being in England, I acquainted him with a purpose I had to build him a house at the Naas, it being uncomely that his Majesty should not have one there of his own, capable to lodge him with moderated conveniency (which in truth he has not) in case he might be pleased sometime hereafter to look upon this kingdom.'[70] Thus, even though built by a minister, these buildings were emblems of the sovereign.

Far from being the product of compulsive extravagance and rivalry, then, country houses were, quite simply, one of the major things upon which an office-holder was expected to spend his receipts from office. Indeed, within this ideology, competition and social mobility were actively discouraged because of the social strains they created. Moreover, far from extravagance being the norm, members of the nobility and gentry were expected to build within their means. Burghley himself who was, as we have seen, one of the greatest builders of the age, and whose projects continued throughout his whole lifetime, not only counselled his son to be prudent but, within his considerable means, was exceptionally prudent himself. Like Kalender in Arcadia he 'knew that provision is the foundation of hospitalitie, and thrift the fewel of magnificence'.[71] Like Henry, Prince of Wales, 'He was frugally bountiful, which is true liberality'. Thus the rebuilding between 1556 and 1563 of his ancestral seat outside Stamford, Burghley House, was deferred when he bought Theobalds near Totteridge in Hertfordshire in 1564 and not returned to until he had finished his new house, fourteen years later.

It is doubtful whether he spent on average much more than £1,000 a year on building during the half century that he was in office. The total amount was huge but it was spread over a very long period and was well within his means, perhaps less than 2 per cent of his annual income. A century later Sir William Petty recommended that 'A man of estate ought not in England to build an house [out] of above 1½ years revenue (in Ireland but of one) and to bestow ⅔ in the furniture'. Burghley spent a good deal less than this even though he built two houses.[72] Indeed he had a very decorous sense of the expenditure appropriate to rank, a man's 'port' as it was called. His annual household expenses in the 1570s after he had been made a baron were half as large again as they had been in the years when he was a plain knight. When in 1589 the Queen offered to raise him to the rank and title of Earl of Northampton he refused on the grounds that his income did not allow him to carry the port of an earl, particularly in view of his desire to provide for his younger son Robert, for whose seat Theobalds was originally constructed.[73]

Burghley's various building enterprises were also carefully phased to accompany the progress of his career. Building operations on Theobalds reached a peak in 1571–2, the year in which he was made a member of the Order of the Garter, raised to the peerage and appointed Lord Treasurer and de facto first minister. In the following decade the newly constructed Conduit Court was actually rebuilt to serve, in effect, as a royal palace which the queen visited some thirteen times, and from which affairs of state were conducted, where foreign ambassadors came to conduct business. After all, there was no civil service as such and its function was fulfilled by the household of high ranking ministers like Burghley. Burghley in turn was a servant of his queen's household. Palaces like Theobalds were like modern ministry buildings.

In 1585 defending himself against various charges, including that of covetousness, made against him by his enemy the Earl of Leicester and others, Burghley wrote as follows: 'If my buildings mislike them, I confess my folly in the expences, because some of my houses are to come, if God so please, to them that shall not have land to match them (i.e. his second son Robert). I mean my house at Theobalds; which was begun by me with a mean mesure; but encrease by occasion of her Majesty's often coming: whom to please, I never would omit to strain myself to more charges than building it. And yet not without some especial direction of her Majesty. Upon fault found with the smal mesure of her Chamber, which was in good mesure for me; I was forced to enlarge a room for a larger chamber: which need not be envied of any for riches in it, more than the shew of old oaks, and such trees with painted leaves and fruit.' Since this vindication was written as a letter to William Herle, who advised Burghley on industrial projects, and was intended to reach the ears both of his enemies at court and of the queen it is only reasonable to assume that she would not have quarrelled with the intentions he attributed to her.[74]

In fact Theobalds did indeed prove to be a palace on a scale too great even for a man of Robert Cecil's means, and it does not seem unlikely that he breathed a sigh of relief when James I asked him to swap Theobalds in exchange for the royal palace of Hatfield and some sixteen other manors. Cecil was able to sell part of the land for £25,000, which contributed towards the £40,000 that it cost him to build Hatfield House, and the remainder of those lands returned a rental of £1,500 a year by 1640 compared to the £500 that Theobalds' land returned in 1607. Also tied up in the deal was the renewal of the farm on the customs on imported silk which were worth £7,000 to him by 1612. So he profited handsomely by being able to switch the capital tied up in what was effectively a royal palace back into revenue yielding assets and a 'smaller' house. At the same time it ought not to be forgotten that Theobalds set an effective upper limit of sumptuousness that no other subject could surpass.[75]

Thus far we have identified four inter-related functions which were fulfilled by the building of the prodigy houses. First, they served as regional centres of government, rural town halls and centres of authority. Second, the many splendid mansions of the queen's servants dotted around the realm served the purpose of state propaganda as potent reminders to the populace and to foreign ambassadors of the power of the crown and its capacity to reward those who were loyal and to punish the disloyal. Third, the houses were monuments to the queen's progresses. Finally the chief magnates of the court initiated a 'generous emulation' amongst the lesser nobility and the squirearchy, encouraging them to seat themselves according to their status.

An additional contemporary explanation for the size of Theobalds was provided by Burghley's anonymous memorialist. Besides being forced to 'inlardg it . . . for the Quene and her great traine', Burghley also did so in order 'to sett poore on worke'.[76] Obviously building on such a scale did indeed provide a great deal of employment, but that does not prove that the demands of economic policy, such as the creation of employment, were a *conscious* motive for building. What is the evidence either way for taking this claim seriously?

First of all we need to know how much work Burghley's buildings provided. He is recorded as having spent something like £14,000 over the twelve years between 1566 and 1578 at Theobalds, about £1,200 a year, and he may have spent an average of £1,000 a year building both Burghley and Theobalds together between 1556 and 1587. These recorded sums certainly understate the total cost since building materials like stone, brick and timber were provided from the estate. Nonetheless £1,000 a year was enough to employ 140 builders a year at an average daily wage of 9d. for 190 days in the year. Some kind of confirmation of this is provided by the fact that at the beginning of the eighteenth century some 200 men were annually at work on Castle Howard between 1700 and 1724.[77] Trentham Hall, Staffordshire, built by Sir Richard Leveson employed 156 workmen for the middle three years, and numbers fell to less than 100 in the final three years. At Wollaton Hall in Nottinghamshire at the height of the building campaign between October 1584 and November 1585, 77 masons and carpenters were employed, which points to a total workforce of 115 assuming that labourers constituted about a third.[78]

It seems then reasonably certain that Burghley maintained a building workforce of about 140 during the greater part of his career. But was the creation of employment his chief motive for building or merely a moral justification for his ostentation?

There is no shortage of evidence that people at the time were very much aware of the effects of certain activities in creating employment, and that some activities were encouraged directly for that reason. For example, housekeeping or maintaining a household commensurate with one's status was an obligation upon the gentry and nobility, specifically mentioned in the royal proclamations, partly on account of its contribution to reducing under- and unemployment. Harrison, for instance, refers to 'the decaie of house-keeping whereby the pore have been relieved'.[79] Sir Henry Slingsby of Scriven observed proudly in his diary for 1638 that 'the number we are at this time in household is 30 persons whereof 16 are men servants and 8 women, besides ourselves. Our charge is such every year . . . being well accommodated with good faithfull diligent servants, so that at least I spend every year in housekeeping £500'.[80] Even in the following century people were so very aware of the economic benefits of housekeeping that its withdrawal could be used as a punishment for political misdemeanours. Such a case was reported by a visitor to Norwich in 1731: 'The Duke of Norfolk had a fine House in this Town of 50 years standing, but not finished; this the present Duke pulled down 20 years ago upon a quarrel with a Whiggish Mayor; the Latter refused to give some Players leave to act in the City, though they had his Grace's licence; upon which the Duke let 'em act in his own House and afterwards pulled it down. This was very much to the Town's loss, the Duke's family laying out a great deal of money in Norwich. His Grace has now no grand Seat.'[81] It seems almost certain that at this time the nobility and the gentry regarded their expenditure on housekeeping as a form of voluntary taxation – one which they were under a strong obligation to honour – and continued to do so well into the eighteenth century, if not later, contrary to Bernard de Mandeville's scornful dismissal of this justification.[82]

But even this underestimates the importance of housekeeping both in practical economic policy and in the economic theory of this period and subsequent centuries. It is no exaggeration to claim that the housekeeping of the country house and its estate was central to the polity of the nation. Thomas Fuller in his preface to *The Worthies of England* compiled in the 1640s and '50s wrote that: 'England may not unfitly be compared to an house, not very great, but convenient; and the several shires may properly be resembled to the *rooms* thereof. Now, as learned Master Camden and painful Master Speed, with others, have described the rooms themselves, so it is our intention, God willing, to describe the *furniture* of these rooms; such eminent commodities which every country doth produce, with the persons of quality bred therein, and some other observables coincident with the same subject.'[83]

Correspondingly a country house could be regarded as a microcosm of the kingdom. Sir Henry Wotton in his *Elements of Architecture* of 1624 compared 'Every Mans proper Mansion House and Home' to 'a kinde of private Princedome; Nay, to the Possessors thereof, an Epitomie of the Whole World'.[84] Consequently the management of the finances of the household of a private estate was the model for that of the nation as a whole. The word economy, indeed, has the original meaning of household financial management and writers on national economic policy of the period readily made this identification. Gerard de Malynes, an early writer on economics, asserted that: 'As a commonwealth is nothing else but a great household or family . . . the Prince (being as it were the father of the family) ought to keep a certaine equalitie in the trade or trafficke betwixt his realme and other countries, not suffering an ouerbalancing of forreine commodities with his home commodities, or in buying more then he selleth. For thereby his treasure and the wealth of the realme doth increase, and as it were his expences become greater, or do surmount his incomes or revenues.'[85]

His contemporary Thomas Mun expressed similar sentiments on the opening page of his *Discourse of Trade* of 1621: 'For as in the estates of priuate persons, we may accompt that man to prosper and growe rich, who being possessed of reuenues more or lesse, doth accordingly proportion his expences; whereby he may yearely aduance some maintenance of his posterity. So doth it come to passe in those Kingdomes, which with great care and warinesse doe euer vent out more of their home commodities, than they import and vse of forraine wares; for so vndoubtedly the remainder must returne to them in treasure. But where a contrary course is taken, through wantonnesse and riot, to ouerwaste both forren and domesticke wares, there must the money of necessity be exported, as the meanes to helpe to furnish such excesses, and so by the corruption of mens conditions and manners, many rich countries are made exceeding poore.'[86]

It was natural, therefore, to think of the economic management of the nation directly in terms of the budget and housekeeping of the greater landowners. Their housekeeping was only another word for economics, and the economic well-being of the nation as a whole could only flourish if that of all the households of the gentry and aristocracy did so too.

There is good reason to believe that building was considered within the category of housekeeping, both as one of the means by which the wealthy could dutifully exercise their bounty and maintain the stability of the realm by providing employment, and as a means of providing the very 'plant', in the form of mansion houses, through which bounty could be dispensed. In the *Life of Burghley* the size of his household and its cost as well as the cost of building are listed amongst his virtuous actions alongside his charitable works and hospitality. 'Look upon his huge expenses, and the truth will then shyne out; he spent infinite somes in building, hospitallity, and in maintenaunce of his honorable port . . . he made as costlie gardaines, walks, and places of pleasure, as are to be seene.'[87] The estimate that Burghley maintained 140 building operatives over and above a permanent household establishment of about 240 people gives substance to these eulogistic statements.

A century later Sir William Petty proposed building pyramids on Salisbury Plain or, better still, bringing 'the stones at Stonehenge to Tower Hill' in order to get the poor to work. A few years later *The Spectator* reflected upon the economic virtues of building the Tower of Babel: 'There were indeed many greater advantages for building in those times, and in that part of the world, than have been met with ever since. The earth was extremely fruitful, men lived generally on pasturage, which requires a much smaller number of hands than agriculture. There were very few trades to employ the busy part of mankind, and fewer arts and sciences to give work to men of speculative tempers.'[88]

But there is, in addition, very strong evidence for believing that in the 'pre-industrial' era it was state policy to favour building more than most other economic activities as a means of creating new employment. Elizabeth I and her ministers were hardly original in this. Although Elizabethan and Jacobean governments were profoundly exercised by the problem of creating new employment for the vast increase in population that had occurred, they did not want to create any type of employment at any cost. Building, so long as it was sited well away from London, possessed specific advantages.

The first arose from the government's anxiety over the fluctuating and seasonal pattern of work created by the growth of London which has already been noted. Similar problems were associated with England's staple industry, woollen cloth, to which the astronomical growth of London was related. Because much cloth was exported clothworkers were exposed to the fluctuations of the trade cycle. Whenever trade fell off 'infinite numbers of Spynners, Carders, Pickers of woll are turned to begging with no smale store of pore children, who driven with necessitie (that hath no lawe) both come idelie about to begg to the oppression of the poore husbandmen, And robbe their hedges of Lynnen, stele pig, gose, and capon'. Just such a slump occurred in 1552 when exports of shortcloths dropped by a quarter and remained at a depressed level for quarter of a century before recovering.[89]

Those were the problems of failure, but there were also problems of success, which could be even greater in that they caused permanent distortions in the pre-existing economy and society. When the cloth trade was flourishing a large proportion of the exports went through the Port of London and the hands of the Merchant Adventurers. Thus the growth of London was heavily dependent upon the fortunes of the cloth trade. If the growth of London with all its attendant problems was to be contained then so too must cloth exports and manufacture. People at the time had a shrewd and practical grasp of what economists today call backward linkages.[90] They did not need statistics, they could *see* the results with their own eyes as in the case of Southampton and other decayed towns. Here is an example that illustrates both this vivid way of spelling out the implications of economic policies and which also serves as a further instance of the effects of a flourishing cloth trade: 'dere clothe doth engender dere wolle, and dere wolle doth engender many scheppe [sheep], and many scheppe doth ingendar myche pastor and dere, and myche pastor is the dekaye of tyllage [crop farming], and owte of the dekaye of tyllage spryngthe ii evylls, skarsyte of korne and the pepull unwroghte, and consequently the darthe of all thynges'.[91] These considerations led Burghley himself to observe that employment should be directed away from the manufacture of cloth in the interests of preventing social disorder, depopulation, vagabondage, as well as to maintain the food supply and prevent the country's dependence upon imported corn and hence upon a foreign power such as France. 'It is to be thought', wrote Cecil in his own hand in 1564, 'that the diminution of clothying in this realme were proffitable to the same for many causes: first, for that therby the tilladg of the realm is notoriously decayed, which is yerly manifest in that, contrary to former tymes, the realme is dryven to be furnished with forayn corne, and specially the Citee of London. Secondly for that the people depend uppon makyng of cloth ar worss condition to be quyetly governed than the husband men. Thyrdly by convertyng of so many people to clothyng the realme lacketh not only artificers, which were wont to inhabitt all corporat townes, but also laborers for all comon workes.'[92]

There was, therefore, a close connection between economic policies to encourage tillage and prevent enclosure and rural depopulation, and policies which prohibited new building in London and encouraged the gentry and nobility to reside on their estates. Building, particularly the building of mansions scattered fairly evenly across the country, was an ideal form of job-creating activity. Indeed by the early seventeenth century the building industry probably employed the largest number of industrial workers after cloth.[93]

What exactly were the specific social and economic advantages of country house building? First of all, as seasonal work, it could complement and support tillage. Thus it strengthened the rural economy and tied people more closely to the land, making work in the cities correspondingly less attractive. Building was also labour-intensive, and the aim of policy was to employ as many of the poor as possible rather than to increase the productivity or efficiency of labour through the use of machinery or other means: 'that being the best form of tillage which employeth most about it, to keep them from stealing and starving'.[94] This also accounted for the importance of the 'costlie gardaines, walks, and places of pleasure', for after the houses had been completed they provided permanent employment of gardeners, labourers and maintenance men. The upkeep of gardens is notoriously labour-intensive, particularly those of the period, with their well-trimmed topiary and knots so despised by Francis Bacon and later by Addison and Pope for being more to the taste of children than adults. The sixty-six or so labourers who were paid over £10 a year at Theobalds may well have been employed as gardeners.

Given the length of time over which the building programmes often stretched some craftsmen would be guaranteed long term if not a lifetime's employment. The Talbots and Cavendishes kept large numbers of craftsmen employed for over a century on building their many mansions. We know of at least sixteen craftsmen employed at Chatsworth who also worked at Hardwick.[95] And it seems highly probable that Burghley employed the same team of highly trained craftsmen on both Burghley House and Theobalds and simply moved them from Northamptonshire to Hertfordshire in 1567 and back again to Burghley. In effect, these great magnate families owned their own private firms of building contractors who were engaged in the aristocratic equivalent of a public works programme.

Once those mansions were completed their contribution to employment did not cease. As we have seen labourers might be employed about the house and gardens while many of the more highly skilled craftsmen, administrators and architects were itinerant and moved on, like the cathedral masons, to other projects. The most famous example of this was Robert Smythson who after twelve years at Longleat moved in 1580 to Wollaton Hall where he worked until 1588 taking with him several masons and carpenters.[96]

But the prodigy houses did more than simply provide employment for skilled men in the course of their construction; they were themselves a school for craftsmen where those skills could be nurtured, where apprenticeships could be provided and future generations of craftsmen could be trained.

We can be almost certain that this consideration, indirect as it may seem, would have been uppermost in the minds of the government, and it provides supporting evidence that the prodigy houses were an intentional and positive act of policy and not the products of 'a lust for power, a thirst for admiration, an ambition to outstrip all rivals'.[97] We find exactly the same indirect method of promoting an industry in other areas of economic policy. In 1548–9 there was the declaration of 'political Lent'. The long-suffering JPs had to enforce the compulsory eating of fish on Fridays and Saturdays. In 1563–4 Wednesday was added. The purpose was not religious, but economic and military: to encourage the fishing industry, shipping, shipbuilding and also to serve as a 'school for mariners'. It was to create the industry and the skills which could be turned to naval use in time of war – an aspect of economic stimulation that constantly recurs in the next four centuries.[98] Almost a century later Christopher Wren, visiting Paris in 1665, described the Louvre, then in the course of construction, with a thousand craftsmen working on site, as the greatest school of architecture in the world, indicating that the notion of great building works serving the purpose of training centres was still current in the seventeenth century.

Another example where the aims of a sumptuary law (a law that regulates consumption) were designed more to regulate economic than social behaviour was that of the acts to force everybody over the age of six to wear a cap of English woollen cloth on a Sunday. This was introduced in 1571 because the cappers had complained that people had ceased to wear caps, but was also intended to encourage English manufacturers of woollen cloth and to prevent imports of silk. There are many other examples, all of them framed by Lord Burghley and his fellow councillors in pursuit of their ambition to reduce unemployment.[99]

Evidence that the building of prodigy houses was a sumptuary regulation designed to foster employment in the building trades is provided by *The Statute of Artificers* of 1563. This statute was devised to prevent mobility of labour, to retard the expansion of output particularly in cloth manufacture, and correspondingly to bolster agrarianism.[100] In order to restrict clothmaking there were strict regulations upon those who could take up apprentice-ships. The building trades, in contrast, were favoured as much as agriculture itself. Article 23 specifically opened apprenticeship for the trades of 'carpenter, rough mason, plaisterer, swayer, lime burner, brickmaker, bricklayer, tiler, slater, healyer, tilemaker, thatcher or shingler' to people whose parents did not possess the financial qualifications required for more favourably regarded trades. Very few builders or carpenters were prosecuted for breaches of the apprenticeship laws.[101] Moreover an official memorandum on the Statute of Artificers of 1573 explains this greater licence towards such crafts on the grounds that 'theis seem to be such trades as are for divers respectes to be planted as well in countrey townes and villages as in cittyes and townes corporatte'.[102] Finally, as late as 1597, a memorandum linked the justification for the laws restricting building in London and those encouraging tillage in the following terms: 'The grate decay of people. The ingrossing wealth into few hands. Setting people to work in husbandry, whereby idleness, drunken-ness and vice are avoided. Swarms of poor loose and wandering people bred by those decays, miserable to themselves, dangerous to the state. Subjecting the realm to the discretion of foreign states either to help us with corn in time of dearth or to hinder us by embargos on our cloths, if we stand too much upon that commodity. Danger of famine.'[103]

Like the intended effects of political Lent the potential contribution of a workforce of skilled and experienced builders to the country's military capacity must also have been an important consideration. It is significant that the largest section of the two great volumes of architectural drawings assembled by Lord Burghley and his son the Earl of Salisbury consisted of forts and military engineering. When muster rolls were drawn up listing the able-bodied men of each county capable of bearing arms, each man's occupation was listed so as to make it possible to match his civil skills to his military contribution. Men with building skills had an obvious contribution to the construction of fortifications and machines of war.[104]

Such building programmes not only created employment on the building site itself. They also created a huge demand for building materials and hence stimulated those industries. Stone quarries were opened and quarriers employed, trees were felled and woods replanted, stimulus was given to the establishment of glassworks, ironworks and brickworks, quite apart from the subsequent demand for furnishings and plate when the house was completed – all those things that economists refer to as backward linkage and which the Elizabethans thoroughly appreciated.

Bricklaying is a perfect illustration of the long term influence of the building of the great houses upon the local economy and indeed upon the quality of the local environment as well. Many stone buildings, even the very grandest, were built of brick and faced in stone for reasons of cost, speed of construction and habitability. A stone building took time to dry out, until then it was 'green, moist, cold and unfit to dwell in'.[105] The prodigy houses used millions and millions of bricks. Between one and three million bricks were made annually over a period of four years for Robert Cecil's Hatfield House. Hatfield was built quickly, in almost one third of the time that it took to build Theobalds, but another major advantage of bricks was that they could be fired near the house, saving the costs and problems of transporting stone (Plate 25). The cost of setting up a brickworks was fully justified by the huge demand during the decade of construction. And once these estate brickworks had been established they often kept producing for years, even for centuries, afterwards. Holkham in Norfolk was one of several that continued until about 1900. Sir Robert

25 Fore Street, Hatfield, Herts. Brickworks set up to build Hatfield House 1607–12 remained in production to provide for the rebuilding of the town.

Walpole's brickyard at Houghton Hall was another.[106] These produced bricks both for the needs of the estate, for the repair and construction of farm buildings and estate cottages, and also for sale in the area. An ample illustration of the combination of business sense and philanthropy of the gentry is given by Roger North's observations while he was rebuilding Rougham Hall in 1693: 'I have contracted for 100,000 bricks to be made next summer, and of all one 10,000 will not come to my share, for I do but contrive, for the benefit of mankind, to convert rascally clay walls that the wind blows through and through, to bricks that will keep folks warm and alive.'[107]

In the century following the completion of the massive brick-built Hatfield House in 1612 the town of Hatfield had been transformed from one 'all of wood clay and plaster', the reason being that 'everyone now, from the richest to the poorest, will not build except with brick'. This must have been both because of the example set by Hatfield House itself, but also because of the availability of brick from the local brickworks that the great house had made possible. There is evidence that estate tenants came to expect their landlords to provide them with brick at cost price. Correspondingly the shift to brick had the added advantage of conserving timber – a point at issue in the London building proclamations – so long as coal was used to fire the brick kilns.[108]

Summing up, one can make the generalisation that the construction of the prodigy houses was intended to create employment and to provide training and apprenticeship for skilled craftsmen, which fulfilled one of the major objectives of Elizabethan employment policy. It also provided additional work for unskilled labourers in their own localities, both during the period of construction and thereafter. The huge capital costs justified the opening of estate and local brickworks, which provided additional employment but which also remained a source of building materials for the use of local people from the gentry downwards, in imitation of the example set by Burghley and his peers. Thus the building of prodigy houses not only set up a model for imitation but also helped to establish the manufacturing infrastructure that made it possible for the less well-off to follow suit. It was economic pump-priming on a grand scale.

We have seen that one of the government's greatest fears was that of vagrancy – of bands of unemployed beggars roaming the country. The whole system of local administration through the lords lieutenant, their deputies and the JPs was designed to stabilise the situation through local administration and jurisdiction, but it can also now be seen how superbly the building and rebuilding of the mansion houses of England contributed to this policy. The establishment of fitting residences for the gentry provided additional local employment for that most problematic group of the poor, the unskilled labourer. The seating of the gentry was an occasion for the stabilising of the entire working population.

To return to the starting point of this chapter – my rejection of the orthodox explanation of why country houses were built, as status symbols erected by the heads of private magnate families in a game of competitive consumption with their rivals. Of course these buildings were symbols of status amongst many other things, but in a very strict sense! They were what someone of a certain rank was expected to possess, just as a lawyer or a college fellow was expected to wear a gown of a certain kind. It is true that families competed to some degree in the size and splendour of their houses, but the heads of these families were not 'private' individuals in our sense. The competition between them was far less a matter of what we understand by the word and far more a matter of imitation – of their measuring up to what was expected of a particular rank. Moreover, even competitive display may have been the instrument of statecraft. The governors of England, educated in the humanist tradition as many of them were, would have been familiar with Tacitus's description of Agricola's policy as governor of Britannia: 'To induce a people, hitherto scattered, unciv-ilized and therefore prone to fight, to grow pleasurably inured to peace and ease, Agricola gave private encouragement and official assistance to the building of temples, public squares and mansions. He praised the keen and scolded the slack, and competition to gain honour from him was as effective as compulsion.'[109]

To return to Lord Burghley: the interest of the nation and his own private interest simply could not be separated, and this applied to his so-called prodigy houses. A parallel situation can be observed in Burghley's administration of affairs of state. There was no professional civil service. When Burghley took office the work that nowadays would be done by a ministry, its staff of civil servants, and the minister's private office was done by the senior members of his 'private' household. The same was true of the sovereign: 'the Queen's government was essentially personal, and service at least in part was domestic. Thus one spoke of the Queen's servants, or of Lord Burghley's servants, but not of civil servants.' And just as there was no civil service so there were no ministry buildings from which to work. Burghley's servants worked in his houses. His house was almost literally a microcosm of the state. But so too were the houses of lesser landlords.[110]

In like manner the financial affairs and the policy that governed Burghley's personal estate simply could not be separated from the affairs of the nation. *He was both ruler and ruled.* His steward, Thomas Bellott, was responsible both for administering Burghley's personal estate and for the conduct of Treasury business. The policies according to which he conducted the business of the nation and that of his own petty kingdom had to tally, and be seen to do so.

Returning to the argument about motivation at the beginning of this chapter, it seems incorrect to say that the difference between then and now is that the 'concept of a great nobleman serving the public for duty rather than gain' did not then exist. There is strong evidence of a sense of duty amongst leading statesmen and lesser gentry. But perhaps they did not possess our clear-cut distinction between the public interest and the private interest of a leading public figure who was a member of the government. This blurring of distinctions is clearly seen in Burghley's gardens, one of the rare arts in which he seems quite genuinely to have delighted, so much so that one of his few relaxations was to travel round his gardens on a donkey. Such gardens as these were ornamental, 'the purest of human pleasure . . . the greatest refreshment to the spirit of man' but they also had a scientific and commercial importance. Burghley cultivated exotic plants, he imported fifty kinds of seed from Florence, he imported lemon and myrtle trees and he was advised by the leading botanist and horticulturalist of the day, John Gerard, who dedicated his famous *Herbal* to his patron and was keeper of the physic garden of the Royal College of Physicians. John Tradescant, the naturalist, played the same role for his son, the Earl of Salisbury.[111] John Evelyn, who will be discussed in more detail, in his *Silva* of 1662 and his other writings on gardens also played a key role in developing the horticulture and arboriculture of the nation.

As a patron of botany and horticulture Burghley's pleasure in the beauty of plants could not be separated from their practical uses. Indeed it seems that man's relation to nature at this period was imbued with the idea that all creation was there for man's use and delight. Burghley's expenditure on his garden not only provided work for the labourers and gave him personal pleasure, it was also inconceivable without his desire to improve the economy through the domestication and improvement of species of medicinal and even industrial value.[112]

Further evidence of the way in which his supposedly 'private' concerns were an extension of his public policies is given by his ambition to re-establish the town of Stamford, of which he was lord of the town and market and which stands on the very borders of the park of Burghley House. But this aspect of policy is the subject of the following chapter.[113]

In conclusion, I have emphasised Burghley's utilitarian motives in building in order to redress the biassed, partisan and anachronistic explanation of his actions and those of others in terms of competitive consumption. How could so sober, prudent, calculating and indeed puritanical a statesman be seized by such a mania in this one single area of his life? But one must not go to the other extreme and deny him and his fellow peers any desire to create places of magnificence and beauty as well. It was not just a matter of putting the poor to work any old how, but putting them to such work as provided a 'school for craftsmen' whose skills would contribute to the creation of beautiful things: the culture that was created by these means sustained the economy rather than vice versa. Moreover, it would not have escaped the awareness of these members of the ruling class that the magnificence, splendour, richness and beauty of the country palaces of the chief nobility were a potent advertisement to foreign ambassadors and observers of the country's prosperity, the power of the sovereign manifested in the magnificence of the court, and of the nation's potential military might as well.

CHAPTER 3
The Control of Consumption

'NIFLES, TRIFLES' – THE ENCOURAGEMENT OF MANUFACTURES

So far we have seen two elements of a general policy to stabilise the economy and the social order: restrictions on the growth of London; seating the gentry and nobility. Besides these, however, there was a third: the manufacture of what we today call consumer goods, particularly those of high quality and 'Good Design'. For if the first two policies were devised to stimulate agriculture by correcting the imbalance of the economy towards sheep rearing, cloth production and London based trade and consumption, it was not the aim to have no manufacturing at all. On the contrary, the government's objective was as much to revive the regional towns whose trade and industry had decayed as to revive regional agriculture.

Its objective was also to establish in England such luxury industries as glassmaking, tapestry, carpets, fine porcelain and furniture whose products had previously to be imported, nowadays called import substitution. Even Adam Smith acknowledged that: 'From the beginning of the reign of Elizabeth too, the English legislature has been peculiarly attentive to the interests of commerce and manufactures, and in reality there is no country in Europe, Holland itself not excepted, of which the law is, upon the whole, more favourable to this sort of industry.' He recognised that as a result: 'commerce and manufactures have accordingly been continually advancing during all this period.'

As early as 1436, in the very first economic treatise ever to be written in English – manuscripts of which subsequently belonged both to Lord Burghley whose copy is annotated, as well as to Samuel Pepys – we find criticism of a policy which permitted the export of substantial English products '. . . our best chaffare, Clothe, woll and tynne' in exchange for imports of the unnecessary luxuries of Italy.

> The grete galees of Venees and Florence
> Be wel ladene wyth thynges of complacence,
> All spicerye and other grocers ware,
> Wyth swete wynes, all manere of chaffare,
> Apes and japes and marmusettes taylede,
> Nifles, trifles, that litell have availed,
> And thynges wyth whiche they fetely blere oure eye,
> Wyth thynges not endurynge that we bye.[1]

The spirit if not the high literary quality of this jeremiad against the folly and frivolity of imported luxuries considered from a moral, social as well as economic standpoint was to survive almost to the present day. We catch an echo of it in Shakespeare's dialogue between the ailing John of Gaunt and the Duke of York as they discuss their spendthrift nephew Richard II, whose ear is always open to

Report of fashions in proud Italy,
Whose manners still our tardy apish Nation
Limps after in base imitation[2]

Nonetheless it was during the Elizabethan and Jacobean periods that the general principles for handling the problem were developed. Those foreign products, particularly raw materials, that were essential to England's economy and military strength such as pitch, wood for ships' masts, hemp for canvas sails, iron and steel would have to be imported in exchange for our wool, cloth and tin. Indeed it was a tenet of the time that foreign trade was divinely sanctioned, a law of nature. It was believed that God had, by creating in different countries 'a lacke of necessarie commodities, dryven all the nations of the earth to seke one upon another, and therby to be knyt togither in amitye and love'. This argument even applied to arts and manufactures. 'He ordains that some nations excel in one art and others in another . . . He wished human friendships to be engendered by mutual needs and resources.'[3] On the other hand luxuries such as wines and spices that were inessential and that could not be produced easily in the English climate would be subject to high tariffs that the rich could well afford to pay and that contributed to the government's revenue. But those luxuries and frivolities that could as well be manufactured in England as abroad were to be actively encouraged – goods such as linens, silks, carpets, tapestries, paper, drinking glasses, windows and looking glasses, pins, knives, lace, perfumed gloves and playing cards. If people had to possess such vanities then, at least as a result of their manufacture 'twenty thousand persons might be set awork within this realm' instead of providing work in foreign countries through importation.[4]

The government (if one can speak confidently about such an entity at this period) believed that the market for luxuries was restricted to the rich, and that the goods themselves would therefore be of high quality both in manufacture and in design. It certainly did not intend to create a mass market in goods of lower quality, the production of which would draw more and more workers out of agriculture and into manufacturing, out of the country and into the towns where they might prosper alongside their masters and place fresh tension upon the existing social order. In theory at least, and to some considerable degree in practice, the objective was to achieve a balance of agriculture and manufacturing, and thereby to maintain social stability.

As with other aspects of policy so in this it was essential for Lord Burghley to be seen to put his principles into practice, in particular as lord of Stamford which had fallen on hard times since the fourteenth century (Plate 26). Then it had been the market centre of Europe's greatest wool-producing district, its port on the River Welland was the resort of European merchants and the town itself became for a while the seat of a university when some Oxford colleges took themselves off in one of their periodic exiles.[5]

Throughout the sixteenth century and most of the seventeenth, when the population of the country as a whole nearly doubled, that of Stamford was stagnant. In 1560 Lord Burghley, Sir William Cecil as he was then, supported a proposal to start a canvas-weaving business which would employ 300–400 people, but it was turned down by the town council. In 1567 some ten households of Dutch immigrant weavers of the 'New Draperies' such as bays, says, stammets, fustons, carpets, as well as ropemakers and workers in steel and copper, were invited to settle in Stamford and were provided with houses by Burghley.[6] Unfortunately they were not successful in establishing the New Draperies in Stamford. In 1571 Burghley assisted the settlement of a Dutch congregation led by a draper, Caspar Vosbergh, who brought woad, alum, copperas and teasels in his baggage. In the dire economic circumstances of these 'decayed towns' the economic effects of the renewed rebuilding of Burghley House in 1575 can easily be imagined. So too can the appeal of projectors like Robert Payne who wrote the following letter to Burghley in April 1580: 'I

26 St Mary's Hill, Stamford – one of the decayed towns of the sixteenth century; Lord Burghley introduced new industries to revive the town.

have heard by divers that your Honour would have Stamford a clothing town. If your Honour would but procure your own tenants to convert the most part of their wool into yarn and train up their poor people in spinning but two years at the most, there would not be so few as a thousand poor people presently set a-work; but also they would be so perfect in that space that clothiers would sue to your Honour to set up there.' Burghley's continuing concern for his town is obvious.[7]

It seems as if Stamford's fortunes were finally revived only through the opening up of a canal to remedy the silting up of the Welland. An Act to this effect was passed in 1570 and again in 1620, but it was not till after 1664 that the work was actually accomplished and the river 'made navigable, which affordeth no small advantage to the town and adjacent places'.[8] By 1705 the number of households had risen to over 470, and by 1688 it was as high as 856. Stamford's renewed prosperity was broadly based upon the malt trade, innkeeping, leather, weaving, metalwork and the building trades, and there were even two firms of cabinet-makers. Benjamin Tipping was paid for joinery and repairs by the eighth Earl of Exeter at Burghley House between 1722 and 1727. The other cabinet-maker, Robert Tymperon, was paid £9. 5s. 6d. in 1750 for a not inelegant sofa bed upholstered in green cut-velvet, a piece of furniture that survives to the present day (Plate 27).

27   Sofa bed, 1750, by Robert Tymperon, upholsterer of Stamford, made for Burghley House. Great houses supported local businesses.

Tymperon figures frequently in the account books over the century and he received a pension from the Exeters at the end of it. Most of the high quality furniture ordered in the second half of the century came from a single London firm, but the work received by Robert Tymperon for smaller jobs and maintenance illustrates the economic relations between an established prodigy house and the local market town in underwriting the economic survival of such a business.[9]

There was however a price to be paid for this secure prosperity. Throughout the eighteenth and much of the nineteenth century Stamford was a notorious pocket borough of the Earls of Exeter, whose control was described in a radical Stamford newspaper in 1839 as 'a state of barbarous intervention and blindness, which resembles more an African domination than an English ward and wholesome interference'.

The Exeters used every low trick of the hustings, not only bribing the voters but in 1831 at the time of the Reform Bill, when for the first time an opposition candidate was elected, hiring a gang of prize-fighters to intimidate them. They also resorted to gerrymandering in opposing the enclosure of open fields to prevent new housebuilding and to keep out of the town newcomers who might not vote in their interest. Since the park of Burghley House prevented expansion in the other direction the population grew very slowly. Thus a town that was half the size of Leicester at the beginning of the eighteenth century was a mere twentieth its size at the end of the nineteenth.[10]

Looked at objectively this was exactly the situation that the architects of the system, such as Lord Burghley, the direct ancestor of the anti-Reformist Exeter of the nineteenth century, intended: a stable, prosperous, unequal and deferential society without great economic growth or social change. Stamford exemplified the national plan in miniature.

Burghley's second son and his successor as Lord Treasurer, the Earl of Salisbury, continued his policy. Upon acquiring Hatfield House from the crown, Salisbury made an agreement with Walter Morrell of Enfield to teach 'the art of clothing, weaving, spinning, carding [to] . . . 50 persons' to be chosen by the earl, who gave Morrell a house rent free and paid him the large salary of £100 a year for ten years to underwrite the scheme: 'for the said parish of Hatfield . . . the said Walter Morrell shall find stuff and make enough to set all these 50 persons at work, so as to avoid idleness and also for the education and teaching of them in the skill and knowledge of the said trades for the better getting of their honest livings afterwards.'[11]

This project seems to have enjoyed some considerable success since Morrell attempted to extend the scheme to Hertfordshire as a whole and to the counties beyond, using a Corporation of gentry to underwrite it on similar lines. In 1615 Morrell successfully petitioned the Privy Council, Francis Bacon worked out the details, and later in 1616 some thirty of the leading gentlemen of Hertfordshire were incorporated as the Company of Drapers of the 'ars, trade and misterie of the new Draperie of Hatfield'.

However, such efforts were in conflict with the local agrarians who claimed that this county, devoted to tillage 'has better means to set the poor children on work without this new invention than some other counties, viz. by employing the female children in pulling of their wheat a great part of the year and the male children by straining before their ploughs in seedtime and other necessary occasions of husbandry.'

Despite a summons to the gentry by the lord lieutenant they refused to subscribe unless underwritten against their losses. So the project fell to the ground, only to be revived again during the trade depression of the 1620s when the Committee on the Decay of the Cloth Trade in 1622 recommended a corporation of 'the most able and sufficient men' in every county to investigate the possibility of cloth manufacture.

In 1625 charters for each company in Hertfordshire, Essex, Middlesex, Buckinghamshire, Devon, Dorset and Shropshire were drafted by Morrell and approved by the king and Privy Council shortly before the death of James I. The scheme was resurrected by Charles I on an even grander scale involving thirty-two counties. Although it never saw the light of day, it does provide the context within which to understand the widespread efforts of the nobility and gentry to set the poor at work by capitalising new businesses not only in the towns over which they presided but also on their own estates. For in spite of the conflict between manufacture and tillage the policy of restricting the former to towns was not pursued with doctrinaire intensity since the major problem was as much seasonal underemployment in the country as outright unemployment. Hence we find many examples of businesses set up on country estates by the gentry and nobility as an extension of the obligation of housekeeping, using the machinery of the Poor Laws of 1596/7 enacted in the aftermath of the great dearth. This in turn provides the background to the whole spirit of 'Improvement' of the subsequent three centuries both in agriculture and manufactures as well as in the support of arts and sciences within which the relatively unregimented efforts of individual landowners were deployed.

At Wollaton, for example, the same Robert Payne who in 1580 had been offering his services to Burghley at Stamford made proposals to Sir Francis Willoughby, the builder of Wollaton Hall, to invest in woad cultivation for dye. In partnership with a Merchant Taylor in London, Ralph Worthington, he successfully petitioned the Privy Council for exemption from a proclamation against woad growing on the grounds that there were few opportunities for work in Nottingham itself and the surrounding areas. The cultivation of woad in summer could be combined with converting wool into jersey in the winter, thus as many as four hundred could be employed. Problems arose, however, in selling the woad, so in 1587–8 Payne opened a dyehouse at Wollaton and in 1589 he was negotiating with a dyer and clothier from Leeds, Randall Tenche, to set up an arras tapestry works there for a fee of £50 a year, which Willoughby refused to pay.[12]

This project collapsed and litigation followed between Willoughby and Payne, who fled to Ireland. In the next generation Sir Percival Willoughby's coal factor, or manager, looking for a vent for the produce of his master's mines, suggested that in the light of the 1615 proclamation against making glass in wood-fired furnaces they should consider settling some coal fired glassworks at Wollaton. Detailed costings and estimates of profits were made, Sir Robert Mansell agreed to finance the works and Willoughby to supply the coal. However, because of the high cost of transporting the glass along poor roads and navigable rivers to Hull before shipment to London the profits were too low, so the Wollaton glassworks were closed.[13]

The Vale of Tewkesbury, which suffered from extreme poverty on account of poor land and the dissolution of four monasteries which had formerly provided employment and relief through housekeeping and hospitality, was the scene of another venture combining philanthropy and business enterprise. John Stratford the younger son of a local gentry family, had prospered as a London merchant selling English cloth to the Baltic and importing flax and other commodities. The loss of the flax trade led him into tobacco growing at Winchester in 1617, employing as many as one member from each poor household for six months of the year. When English tobacco cultivation was banned to favour the Virginian growers he turned to flax and created employment for 200 people on forty acres, in the face of opposition by his former partners in the import business. It was his firm belief that it was better to give work to the English 'seeing an inconceivable distress and misery increasing amongst the multitude of poor people that live in cities and towns where no clothing or help of other work is.' He argued that, once manufactured into linen, the produce of forty acres would create employment for 800 people. It would actually create more tillage, since woad prepared the ground for growing corn afterwards. It would not only prevent crime amongst the poor and turn their labour to the profit of the commonwealth but it would also provide them with the conditions to 'live according to God's ordinance by the sweat of their face in a more religious order'.[14]

Perusal of county histories could produce any number of comparable examples of what was a far more widespread practice than most economic historians are prepared to admit. However two more will suffice to round off the picture.[15]

First, Sir Richard Weston (1591–1652) of Sutton House in Surrey close to Guildford, was one of the very first pioneers of scientific agriculture in England, and the first to cultivate clover as a means of enriching the most barren heathland for the cultivation of wheat and oats by rotation. He was also the first to grow turnips as a cattle crop, the importance of which cannot be overestimated, and he advocated the cultivation of flax on the grounds that it was worth four or five times the value of corn. In addition he was the successful projector of the first canal in England to use locks, which he had studied alongside agricultural improvements in the Low Countries. For a total investment of £10,000, employing 200 men he canalised fourteen miles of the River Wey from Guildford to Weybridge in 1651. The work was opened in 1653, a year after his death. The effect was to open navigation from London to Guildford and provide a better vent for the crops of the neighbourhood, establishing the practice which Joseph Addison's *Guardian* recommended sixty years later, as a means of bringing great profit to the farmers and landlords of the country.[16]

Finally there was the 'godly' Sir Anthony Cope of Hanwell in North Oxfordshire, a 'hot Puritan' whose activities in relief of the poor were comparable to those of Sir Richard Grosvenor and Sir John Newdigate. In 1597 Cope protested to Lord Burghley about the weakness of a bill before parliament to curb enclosures, on the grounds that enclosure drove the poor into the great cities where they died 'in the streets and highe wayes for wante of soccour'. He grew woad at Hanwell and kept great state there dying with debts of £20,000. His son William leased 2,000 acres of marsh in Lincolnshire in 1616, which he also improved, for growing and producing dyes. A later Cope, another Sir Anthony, created one of those elaborate watergardens with a 'House of Diversions' on an island in the middle of a fishpond, with balls supported on a column of water and a waterclock which told the time 'by the rise of a new gilded sun, moving on a hemisphere of wood'. But these were merely

the fantastic and pleasurable by-products of the same science which lay behind the establishment on his estate of water-mills for grinding corn, cutting stone and boring guns.[17]

DESIGN MANUFACTURE

Many of the improvements effected by the country gentry and nobility were in the
production of staples and raw materials, rather than what they called 'delicacies' and later
became known as luxuries. Nonetheless, this general picture provides the setting for
understanding the efforts to domesticate luxury manufactures.

As we have seen, it was no part of the government's plan for the poor themselves to
prosper and create a demand for a mass market in luxuries. We have observed James I's
disgust, in 1623, at finding the luxury jewellers and goldsmiths shops of Cheapside replaced
with 'poore pettie trades'. Moreover, until 1604, when they were repealed because they
gave James I general powers of enforcement by proclamation, which parliament wished to
prevent, there were in existence sumptuary laws designed to keep people's expenditure and
personal display within the bounds of their station in life. In a real sense the subsequent
efforts to 'improve' or 'reform' the design of manufactured goods were an attempt to
reinstate sumptuary law by other means. The connection between taste and snobbery is a
vestige of just this legislation.[18]

Sumptuary laws were common throughout Europe in the late Middle Ages and England
was no exception. Acts were passed in 1337, 1363, 1463, 1483, 1510, 1515, 1533 and 1554
but were mostly unenforced. Under Elizabeth I and particularly by Lord Burghley, however, they were enforced – from a royal proclamation in 1562 until Burghley's death in
1598. In 1566 four watchmen were appointed to be on duty at the gates of London,
morning and afternoon, to restrain those 'using or wearing any great and monstrous hose,
silk, velvet or weapons'. Of particular concern was the wearing of the elaborate slashed and
ornamented hose or stockings of the period (Plate 28), and punishment was by fine or
public ridicule. In 1570 Thomas Bradshaw was led through the streets of London to his
'missus house' in the offending doublet and hose, and in 1565 an offender was imprisoned
until he got some decent and lawful hose while his 'monsterous hose' were publicly
displayed to be seen by the people 'as an example of extreme folly' – a technique akin to
that employed by Henry Cole in his Chamber of Horrors of 1852, as we shall see.

As well as having a moral and social basis Sumptuary Law was very much a part of the
policy to restrain the growth of London, promote the residence of gentry on their estates,
encourage agriculture and make England as independent as possible of foreign imports.
Throughout the seventeenth century efforts were made to re-introduce sumptuary laws.
John Evelyn promoted the idea in the first year of the Restoration in his pamphlet *Tyrannus*
and Bishop Berkeley recommended them in 1721, favouring expenditure upon the public
and 'noble arts of architecture, Sculpture, and painting' as a means of employing the poor
without encouraging imports while at the same time inspiring the people 'to an emulation
of worthy actions' and discouraging private luxury – very much the Elizabethan policy of
favouring building. But this is to run ahead of our story.

Government policy was simply directed at encouraging the two ends of the spectrum of
consumption: food and cloth for the subsistence of the poor and high quality goods for the
rich, disregarding the consumption of those in between. In turning at last to consider design
or art manufactures, therefore, we note this peculiarity: during the long history of government efforts to encourage such productions, most initiatives have been directed against the
tastes and fashions of the mass market and have been preoccupied with high quality, a
feature now partly explained. And nowhere was this feature more pronounced than in the
growing phases of the policy to reduce England's dependence upon imports.[19]

28 Sumptuary laws strictly enforced by Lord Burghley between 1562 and his own death in 1598
prohibited 'great and monstrous hose' like these. For that reason no English paintings show such garments.
This is a detail from a French painting.

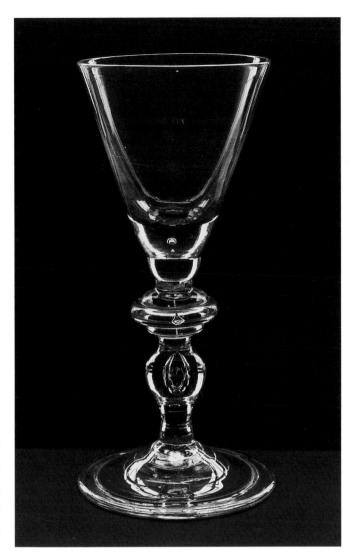

29 Baluster stem lead-crystal glass, English, early eighteenth century. Before 1567 most glass in England was imported and very expensive. To prevent imports Burghley encouraged the industry which flourished subsequently particularly with the invention of this highly refractive lead glass at the end of the seventeenth century which could also be used for lenses.

Two of the products introduced into this country in the Tudor and Jacobean period were glass and tapestry. Glass, both for industry and for drinking vessels, was the ultimate luxury: as recently as the early nineteenth century a poor Scottish labourer and his wife 'had a window (the house had none) consisting of one small pane of glass, and when they moved from one house to another in different parts of Berwickshire in different years, they carried this window with them, and had it fixed in each hovel into which they went as tenants'.[20]

Before 1567, when the total amount of window glass imported or manufactured in England was the equivalent of the output of only one glasshouse, windows were rare and were indeed counted as moveable goods like furniture, remaining so till glass became more plentiful around 1600. Window glass for churches and palaces was imported from Flanders. Before 1580 no craftsmen's houses recorded in Oxfordshire inventories had glass windows. And the stained glass of the English churches was not destroyed at the Reformation, alongside other religious icons, because in the 1550s it was too expensive to replace with clear glass whereas, by the time of the Civil War of 1642–8, the iconoclasts could destroy with impunity because white glass was readily available as a replacement.[21]

More prosaically, the cost of a large ordinary beer glass in 1621 was 6d., equal to a poor labourer's daily wage, or perhaps £25 in today's money. Before the 1570s it was very uncommon for even the gentry to own glasses (Plate 29); in 1613 Sir Robert Drury possessed only four wine and three beer glasses. Most preferred plate, pewter, treen and horn, which must therefore have been cheaper.[22]

The technique of glassmaking was complicated and a closely guarded secret. Glassmakers in France had the status of gentlemen and enjoyed a comparable income. Glass did not become plentiful in England until the immigration of glassmakers was officially encouraged in 1567 by licences granted by Burghley to Jean Carré from Antwerp to establish glassworks both in London and the Weald with a twenty-one year monopoly in the manufacture and sale of window glass on the grounds that none was being produced here. In Burghley's words it was 'her Majesties intention to have the Science of the making of that kinde of glass within her realme'. One condition, therefore, was that Carré's men should train Englishmen in the art so that at the end of their monopoly it would be in the hands of the natives. Imports of glass, however, were still permitted and Carré had to pay the equivalent of customs duty on his products so that, although his transport costs were lower than for imported glass, the price he could charge for his products was controlled by competition. For drinking glass no monopoly at all was granted.[23]

All manner of problems arose. The foreign glassmakers vehemently refused to train the English so as to 'kepe the science out of the Realme'. Some returned to France to set up near the port of Boulogne. And the queen's own glazier still bought most of his glass from France, since the cost of overland transport from Alfold in Surrey was greater than that of sea carriage from Normandy.

Carré died in 1572, his business bedeviled by financial problems, but, in the previous year, Jacob Verzelini, a Venetian, took over his fine glassmaking business in London and obtained a monopoly in 1574 with a prohibition on imports from Venice on the grounds that glasses were 'unnecessary' works.[24]

By 1590 there were some fifteen glasshouses disposed around the country, many of them, because of their voracious demand for timber as fuel, sited on country estates such as Knole, Bagot's Park and Petworth. Glassmaking became a highly itinerant manufacture contributing to the local economy only in providing a vent for its fuel. It was the need to develop coal-fired glasshouses as an alternative, after a proclamation of 1615 which forbad wood, as well as the need to be within easy reach of a port, that led to the failure of the Wollaton works near Nottingham and the success of those in Newcastle and, later, at Bristol and Kings Lynn. This change in fuel also gave England a huge technological lead not only in production but also in the type and quality of glass that could be produced. For the stronger and more stable heat produced in coal furnaces was one of the chief factors that enabled George Ravenscroft, between 1673 and 1676, to develop lead crystal glass with its high refractive index, ideal for optical and scientific instruments, and its far greater durability, which finally enabled England to reverse the situation and to win a commanding position in the export trade. It is a classic illustration of how to build up a new industry behind a protective wall.[25]

The domestication of glassmaking seems to have had an immediate effect upon architecture. An outstanding feature of all the prodigy houses begun in and about 1567 is the huge areas of glazing. We find this at Burghley's own Theobalds, Thynne's rebuilt Longleat, Hatton's Holdenby, Willoughby's Wollaton and Bess of Hardwick's Hardwick Hall: 'More glass than wall'. Almost 10,000 feet were proposed at Petworth in 1615. The cost of the glass for these houses, however, can easily be exaggerated to serve the conspicuous consumption theory. The cost of the new house at Petworth proposed by the ninth Earl of Northumberland in 1615, but not built, was estimated at £25,572 of which the cost of glazing was £243. 6s. 0d., – under 1 per cent of the total. Even in the 1560s the cost of

30 Raphael, *St Paul preaching at Athens*, cartoon for tapestry manufacture. One of seven purchased by the crown in 1623 for the state-funded Mortlake Tapestry Works, the cartoon epitomises state encouragement of luxury industries and classicism as the chosen style for Great Britain.

glazing the far smaller Losely House close to the Alford glasshouse was only 1.74 per cent of the total. We know however that glazing for Petworth was estimated at 6d. a foot and ashlar walls at 4d. a foot. Had the windows been only half the size the saving through using less glass would have amounted to only £40 – a negligible sum in £25,000.[26]

The truth seems to be that once they became readily available glass windows were introduced for pleasure. But it seems quite probable that a 'generous emulation' was initiated amongst the higher nobility building prodigy houses to provide a vent for the produce of the infant industry which even its monopoly could not have obtained for it.

Thus, in the manufacture of glass, we see on a national scale a reflection of Burghley's policy for the finances of his own estate and market town: on the one hand trying to stimulate new manufacturing by importing foreign craftsmen, on the other hand trying to sustain those industries by patronising their wares as a large scale consumer.

We also observe how in addition to patronising the new industry as customers the gentry and nobility formed a co-partnership with the manufacturers in the supply of fuel – first wood and then after 1615 coal – as well as in providing sites for glassworks and even, as in the case of Sir Francis Willoughby, making a direct investment. Particularly after 1615, when glassmaking in England came under the monopoly control of one man, Sir Robert

Mansell, the younger son of a Glamorganshire squire who had risen to be Vice Admiral of England and the Treasurer of the Navy in 1604, we find a perfect example of a gentleman courtier in business who successfully laid the foundations for an emerging industry of national importance. In the process of building his glassmaking empire – manufactured window glass, looking glass, hour glasses, wine bottles, medicine bottles and phials, spectacles, luxury glassware – he helped to develop the coalmining industry on the Tyne, in Scotland, south Wales, the Forest of Dean, Staffordshire and Nottinghamshire, and the clay extraction industry at Stourbridge and Newcastle for making the pots in which the glass was fired. The result was to develop new employment throughout the country.[27]

Mansell is a typical swashbuckling but intelligent gentleman-courtier, entrepreneur and administrator who in return for monopoly rights put the commercial and industrial policy of the Stuart and Tudor governments into effect. A similar character was Sir Francis Crane who, within a decade, put England in the very forefront of the manufacture of one of the most sumptuous luxuries of all, woven tapestry, and was producing it to designs by Rubens, Van Dyck and Raphael.

This story must be seen in the larger context of efforts to adapt the English weaving industry. First, as we have already noted, there was the introduction of the so-called 'New Draperies' – bays and says, serges and perpetuanoes, camlets and callinancoes – which were lighter and more colourful than the so-called 'Old Draperies' in which England had excelled and which were increasingly in demand at home and abroad. Second, there was the fact that much of the English 'Old Drapery' was in the form of undyed, unfinished, semi-manufactured goods which were then exported to the Low Countries for dyeing and finishing, before being re-imported.[28]

As early as 1550 William Cholmeley had brought a master dyer over from Antwerp and they set up a dyehouse at Southwark in partnership. Three years later, he addressed to the queen a pamphlet about his 'enterpreys', arguing that the 150,000 unfinished English broadcloths provided work for 200,000 people in the Low Countries worth £150,000 a year. This sounds pitifully little even for those days when a labourer's wage was between 6d. and 8d. a day, but in addition there were the profits from growing and refining dyestuffs such as woad, madder and alum, as well as the value of conducting the market in finished cloths. All this value added to the raw cloth by others was profit and employment lost to England as a result of the lack of up-market skills and inventions.[29]

Other gentry, as we have seen, made efforts to cultivate woad for dyeing, while Burghley himself tried to settle dyers at Stamford in 1571. These efforts resurfaced in the second decade of the seventeenth century, following an economic boom that had lasted almost a decade from 1606, with a record 127,000 shortcloths being exported in 1614, a figure not attained since the 133,000 recorded in 1550. That earlier boom had been succeeded by the great depression which led to Burghley's policy of stabilisation and diversification. Now English governments turned once again to arguments like those of Cholmeley. This was not unreasonable in view of the fact that the Dutch estimated dyeing alone added 160 per cent to the value of the unfinished cloth, while fully finished the cloth sold for over three times the unfinished value. Sir William Cockayne, former Lord Mayor of London, succeeded in persuading the government to forbid altogether the export of unfinished cloth, which he promised could be dyed in England and exported by his company.[30]

The effect of this was disastrous. England simply did not possess sufficient industrial capacity or know-how to finish cloths; the Low Countries and Germany in retaliation refused to buy finished English cloth and were in any case awash with large stocks of unfinished cloth as a result of the boom. Cockayne's new company had insufficient ready money to pay the clothiers who, in turn, had to pay the weavers; foreign weavers set up to supply the unfinished cloths instead so that by 1616 the total export of shortcloths from London fell to 88,000. Customs revenue for cloth had fallen by 25 per cent, half the looms

31 Map of London, detail from a Sheldon tapestry, seventeenth century. Sheldon was one of the first English tapestry works established in the countryside in the sixteenth century to create employment and prevent imports.

in the West Country were unused, and unemployment was heavy. In theory there was nothing against the scheme. It is one followed successfully by companies in developing countries today. In Kenya the leather industry instead of exporting all its leather hides raw, whose value, like that of unfinished cloth in the seventeenth century, only amounts to one-third of the finished value, is opening a high quality tannery which will export a quarter of its production to Italy for shoemaking. Unlike the Kenyan scheme however, Cockayne's scheme was put into effect without adequate preparation.[31]

But it is an indication of the continuing ambitions of the government to increase the value-added of English produce; to create a more self-reliant and more vertically integrated industry; and to introduce higher skills in textile manufacturing. The Mortlake Tapestry Works, instituted soon afterwards in 1619, in the wake of a further deep depression in trade, was a signal example of this policy.

Mortlake was not the very first tapestry works in England. We have already seen Robert Payne negotiating with Randall Tenche in 1589 to set up an Arras tapestry works at Wollaton and, even before that, William Sheldon, a Warwickshire squire set up a tapestry works in the manor of Barcheston (Plate 31). He had obtained this through his marriage to the heiress of William Willington, a wealthy clothier who, when he bought the manor in 1509, had promptly turned 530 acres of arable land to pasture putting twenty-four people out of work; Sheldon's manufactory may have been an act of reparation for his father-in-law's actions. He established Richard Hicks, a native of the parish whom he sent to the Low Countries to be trained as a weaver, in a disused mansion house. There Hicks turned out not only tapestry but also other 'New Draperies'.[32]

The number of employees was large and Sheldon, in his will of 1569, enjoined his heir to carry on the works as a trade 'greatly beneficial to this commonwealth to trane youthe in and a meane to secure great sums of money within this Realme'. The works continued until as late perhaps as 1684.

Sheldon was a dutiful adherent of Burghleyan policy. His funeral in 1569 was conducted with great pomp with the Clarenceaux King of Arms and other heralds in attendance and his grand monument mentions his bringing the art of tapestry to England as an act of public spirit: 'viro ad publicum bonum nato.'

Although the Mortlake works were by far the most ambitious in scale, aiming to supply tapestry not only to the English royal family and nobility but also to Europe and as far afield as Persia and India, their economic objectives were similar to those of their precursors: namely that their 'example may likewise prove of very great advantage to the commonwealth by *showing men* [my italics] a better way of charity than of hospitals, which only provides for the poor.' In other words Mortlake was explicitly devised not merely as a commercial enterprise but as a model to all rich men in curing poverty by setting the poor to work.[33]

Its story is simply told. Sir Francis Crane was secretary to the future Charles I when he became Prince of Wales on the death of his brother Henry in 1612. He was also closely associated with the Earl of Arundel. In 1619 James I took the advice of the then Marquis of Buckingham and the prince in following the example of Henry IV of France by setting up a tapestry manufacture, and Crane was appointed to direct it. He had a guaranteed vent for his products in royal patronage, a twenty-year monopoly in addition to about £4,000 in grants. The promise or expectation of patronage or customers was an important means of underwriting a new business venture.

Crane secretly brought over fifty weavers and their families from the Low Countries in 1620 and settled them in Mortlake. Production began immediately on a suite of nine scenes of Vulcan and Venus, presumably to cartoons that had been brought by the weavers themselves, and finished two years later.

Francis Cleyn, a Flemish painter, was appointed limner or designer in 1623 at a lifetime pension of £100. Also in 1623 Charles I, then Prince of Wales, purchased the Raphael Cartoons of the Acts of the Apostles for £700 on the advice of Rubens and the Earl of Arundel (see Plate 30). Cleyn made copies of the originals to serve as cartoons for the factory and the first Raphael tapestries were completed in 1629.[34]

Apart from near bankruptcy in 1623 due to under-capitalisation, the works prospered greatly as did their owner Sir Francis Crane, particularly after Charles became king. Crane was also involved in other royal speculations including the draining of the Fens, and he had a house in Covent Garden. In addition to the Raphaels, whose borders were designed by Van Dyck, there were cartoons produced by Rubens for a set of Achilles tapestries, while Mantegna's *Triumphs of Caesar* were also reproduced. Francis Cleyn himself was a highly accomplished artist who painted some of the rooms in Somerset House and other houses of the nobility in addition to his work designing tapestry. Within an extremely short space of time Mortlake had become the producer of probably the best designed tapestries in Europe, acknowledged to be of exquisite quality even by the French in the early eighteenth century on account of the soft and even texture of the English wools.[35]

32   Stoke Bruerne, Northamptonshire, *c.*1628. Built by Sir Francis Crane, Director of the Mortlake Tapestry Works, the house was a showcase for state policy.

In 1628, in settlement of crown debts to the Mortlake Works, Crane was granted the Manor of Grafton Regis in Northamptonshire and a year later the adjacent Stoke Park. At Stoke Bruerne, Crane built what has been described as 'the first Palladian style country house in England' supposedly with the assistance of Inigo Jones on the basis of plans brought back from Italy. There is, as usual, no documentary evidence of Inigo Jones's involvement and the house has nothing distinctively Palladian about it. Be that as it may, it is certainly very grand and Italianate (Plate 32).

Its building is almost contemporaneous with the development of Covent Garden in the Italianate manner. A branch of the tapestry works was intended at nearby Grafton Manor house to train apprentices and provide employment. Although nothing came of this it is an indication of the broader economic policy of which it was a part. Cleyn moreover painted decorations for Stoke Bruerne and it seems inconceivable that Crane would not have hung examples of his own tapestry there. A tapestry portrait of Crane after Van Dyck exists, probably dating from the period after Van Dyck's return to England in 1632, intended presumably for the new house, which would have been a showpiece for the artistic, architectural, social and economic policies of Charles I's period of personal rule. In short, Stoke Bruerne was the very epitome of everything discussed in the last three chapters: a physical demonstration of the complex state policies governing the relationship between luxury manufactures, country houses and the planning of towns.[36]

But far and away the grandest example of the country house performing the function of a lesser court, similar to one of the smaller European kingdoms, was Wilton House in Wiltshire. Here manufacturing, architecture, poetry and natural sciences were patronised by the Herbert family, Lords Lieutenant on many occasions not only of Wiltshire but of much of the West Country as well.[37]

One need only mention the glittering literary court gathered there by the second Countess of Pembroke, Mary Sidney, sister of the poet Philip Sidney, who himself lived nearby between 1580–3 while he was writing the *Arcadia*. This led Aubrey to describe Wilton as 'an Academie, as well as Palace, and (as it were) the Apiarie, to which Many that were excellent in Arms, and Artes, did resort, and were carress't; and many of them received honourable Pensions.' 'In her time,' he continued, 'Wilton House was like a College there were so many learned and ingeniose persons.' These included Ben Jonson, Donne, Samuel Daniel, who was also tutor to the third earl and author of one of the first treatises on English poetics, probably Spencer as well as the Earl of Pembroke's players who produced and acted in the first performance of Shakespeare's *As You Like It* at Wilton in 1599. The play was dedicated to the countess's two sons in 1623. But she was not only a patron of literature. Dr Thomas Moffett, the distinguished physician was persuaded to settle at Wilton with a pension, became MP and published a treatise in verse upon the silkworm. Dr Adrian Gilbert, Raleigh's half brother, was a 'chymist' maintained by the family, no doubt with practical ends in view.[38]

The family tradition of patronage was maintained by the third earl described by Aubrey as 'the greatest Maecenas to learned Men of any Peer of his time: or since', as well as by his brother the fourth earl whom Charles I was supposed to have persuaded to rebuild the garden front 'all al Italiano' to designs which we now know to have been made not by Inigo Jones, whom the earl hated and nicknamed 'Iniquity' Jones, but by Isaac de Caus, who may also have been responsible for Covent Garden.[39]

It would be tedious to rehearse all the subsequent artistic splendours of Wilton, but little attention has been drawn to the commercial and industrial aspects. Wilton had been the capital of Wessex in the ninth century and a flourishing cloth town in the thirteenth and fourteenth centuries, but had subsequently lost ground to Salisbury. This and the large proportion of surrounding downland given over to pasture and the increasing monopoly in sheepraising by a single family, the Twogoods, led to acute poverty and unemployment. Wiltshire as a whole had been a major manufacturing centre of 'Old Draperies' and in the peak year of 1614, before the Cockayne scheme, 41,758 cloths, 60 per cent of the total number exported by the Merchant Adventurers Company, were made there. It suffered correspondingly as a result of the slump with 3,000 unemployed in 1616. Efforts to develop new lines of cloth ensued, and even Dr Moffett's researches on silk growing, though earlier, were probably associated with the search for a solution to the long-term decline of the Old Draperies. In the late seventeenth century it seems as if flat Kidderminster carpets and tapestry were made at Wilton. But these were of inferior quality. This may have led the ninth Earl of Pembroke, 'the architect earl', in about 1740 to smuggle into England, in breach of French prohibitions on the emigration of skilled men, two French carpet weavers, Anthony Duffossee and Peter Jemaule, in empty wine barrels, so it is said. Their skills were the basis for the revival of Wilton's fortunes as a cloth town and, by all accounts, for the establishment of carpet manufacture in this country.[40]

The nobility and gentry, then, were closely associated with this large-scale and long-term enterprise to stabilise the British economy and its social order by encouraging the manufacture of high quality, artistic consumer goods – elegant drinking glasses, fine tapestries, beautifully designed carpets, amongst other things. They were involved in two ways; first as actual entrepreneurs and financiers, and second, probably more important, as the customers whose patronage of luxury manufactured goods on a grand scale not only kept hundreds of firms of upholsterers and every kind of craftsman in existence but whose palaces in the country as in the town acted as showcases for British manufactures. By sporting English silks, for instance upon their backs, they acted as an example to everyone else to buy English.

From its outset, therefore, Good Design was associated with policies intended to restrict the consumption of the lower classes, particularly of the poor. Because of this, it was set against the diversity of quality, price and styles that cannot be avoided in a mass consumer market – a market inevitably brought into being by the increase, however small, in the income of the poor that was the direct result of the increase in employment.

Part Three

THE LUXURY DEBATE

PREFACE
History and Ideas

IN PREVIOUS SECTIONS we have been immersed in the physical world of brickmaking, tapestry-weaving, speculating, dye-works, woad plantations, urban unemployment, and the growth of London with its furniture shops and many factories; however we have also seen that certain ideas about social and economic life were implicit in these activities. Not only were the events directed by certain ideas and policies, but the events were also perceived, accurately and inaccurately, through the filter of certain theories. To ignore these often shadowy ideas and to seek the 'historical truth' purely through archival research can have the result of further consolidating a one-sided picture of the past. We have already examined an instance of this in the persistence of competitive consumption as an explanation for the motives of people who built and furnished country houses, an explanation which was current in the past as much as it is today but which is not, on that account or any other, necessarily 'true'.

And this leads on to a weightier reason for treating ideas in history with more seriousness and delicacy: namely, that even false constructions of events, false perceptions and misleading interpretations of people's motivation such as the legendary 'bad press' suffered by 'bad kings' like Richard III or bad classes like the 'extravagant' British aristocracy, frequently prove to have been ideas which, in their own period, were bandied about in the hustle and bustle of social and political life by the enemies of kings, political parties or social classes. The historian who fails to recognise the sources of these ideas may end up, partly unawares, merely rehearsing one or other partisan position of the period. This is the opposite vice to anachronism: not the unwitting imposition of the assumptions of the present upon the past, but the unwitting adoption of a partisan point of view belonging to the past itself. In some cases it can result in the lack of any historical perspective altogether.

In a famous paragraph John Maynard Keynes, who in his own career combined action with theory, expressed a similar view about the importance of even misguided ideas:

> the ideas of economists and political philosophers, both when they are right and when they are wrong, are more powerful than is commonly understood. Indeed the world is ruled by little else. Practical men, who believe themselves to be quite exempt from any intellectual influences, are usually the slaves of some defunct economist. Madmen in authority, who hear voices in the air, are distilling their frenzy from some academic scribbler of a few years back. I am sure that the power of vested interests is vastly exaggerated compared with the gradual encroachment of ideas.[1]

This point of view has hitherto been tacit. So too has been the idea that the writing of history begins its life as the continuation of a contemporary debate or struggle for power, though it is not intended to suggest that good history should remain partisan. More to the point is that the 'History of Ideas' cannot be consigned to a category separate from the 'History of Events', first because ideas influence events, and vice versa, as Keynes described, second because ideas become modified in the light of ensuing events, and third, still more important, because historical enquiry is itself guided by ideas of which it is best to be aware.

To avoid the problems of the more naive forms of empirical history more is required than that historians acknowledge their assumptions; it is necessary to disinter the historical origin and form of those ideas and see how they were propagated and criticised at the time. In this way one might portray a history in which events and ideas are intrinsic to one another. One might even achieve something more: a portrayal of ideas always struggling into existence in the form of events or social conditions, and of the lessons of events being distilled into an idea and that idea being embodied in a programme or policy – so that the passage of time and of history comes to be seen as both a physical and an intellectual process in which ideas are like the fruit of the past and the seeds of the future.

Through the beginnings of such an approach we have already seen how the 'country house' was both a concrete reality and an ideological construct of the established authorities of the sixteenth, seventeenth and eighteenth centuries. We have also seen how the bustling, flourishing marketplace of London at the time was in part a fact and in part an idea of the traders and property developers coming to power – notably Nicholas Barbon, who promoted the concept as part of his economic theories.

In the eighteenth century Barbon's theories influenced Adam Smith and subsequently the later classical economists, who criticised and disparaged the stable aristocratic world of country houses, 'extravagant' expenditure, fine clothes, equipage and state to such a degree that, until very recently, this anti-aristocratic viewpoint has dominated and distorted the writing of history itself. This will be examined in the chapter on Adam Smith. It is time to look at these theories, these sixteenth, seventeenth and eighteenth-century ideas about the political economy of personal consumption, especially as they were deployed in the Luxury Debate. This was a continuing debate about whether spending one's income on luxury goods and services was good or bad for the individual, for the public and for the state. In unravelling the arguments, we shall witness how a battle of ideas between two great political systems took place not on some lofty plane far from the heat of battle, not in some ivory tower, but in the very midst of affairs.[2]

Adam Smith, although himself one of the first *academic* economists, was totally aware that tracts and pamphlets on economic matters 'were addressed by merchants to parliaments and to the councils of princes, to nobles and to country gentlemen, by those who were supposed to understand trade to those who were conscious to themselves that they knew nothing about the matter'.[3] He himself, in spite of his extended attack upon the aristocracy, was of course conscious of addressing the same largely aristocratic legislature, while most of the leading writers of the books and pamphlets – Thomas Mun, Sir Joshua Child, Nicholas Barbon – were leading actors in the drama which they were also describing and analysing. As early as 1691, Sir Dudley North composed his *Discourse upon Trade* while steering a tariff bill through a House of Commons Committee, and whilst reading the eighteenth-century tracts we overhear parliamentary debates and conversations in the coffee houses. The merchants committed their ideas to print to petition the ministry of the day and thus to further their interests: calling for prohibitions on imports of French finery, reductions in import duties on commodities brought to London for re-export, or the removal of duties and prohibitions altogether. (Nowadays only the means of persuasion have changed: newspaper articles and television interviews instead of pamphlets.)

This had been true since the earliest recorded beginnings of English economic thought in *The Libelle of Englyshe Polycye* composed in vivid verse in 1436 or 1437 shortly before printing was invented by Adam Moleyns, Clerk of the Privy Council, to which the *Libelle* must have been addressed as a policy document.[4] As we have already noted, Lord Burghley himself owned a manuscript copy a century and a half later. Projectors like Robert Payne petitioned the Privy Council in favour of their schemes, deploying economic theories in their support. Similarly, Nicholas Barbon's *Apology for the Builder*, a printed pamphlet of 1685, was directly involved not only with the continuing post-Restoration political argument about whether or not to restrict the growth of London but also with a threatened Privy Council suit against him on the charge of incitement to riot in the wake of the battle, mentioned in an earlier chapter, between his workmen and the conservationists of the day at Red Lion Square in the previous year.

Early British economic writing was never pure theory, if such a thing exists, it was often representative of some interest or another, the product of the tavern and the coffee house, the forum and the market place. This gave it an earthy quality that continued to pervade its prose even after David Hume and Adam Smith had begun to withdraw the subject into the world of universities – though their idea of the university was strongly practical. Indeed right at the start of Adam Smith's career in a lecture on the 'Division of Labour' delivered in 1749 he felt obliged to answer the implied question of what use an academic like himself might be to a working class porter:

> The philosopher is of use to the porter; not only by being sometimes an occasional customer, like any other man who is not a porter, but in many other respects. If the speculations of the philosopher have been turned towards the improvement of the mechanic arts, the benefit of them may evidently descend to the meanest of the people. . . . Whoever eats bread receives a much greater advantage . . . from the inventors and improvers of wind and water-mills. Even the speculations of those who neither invent or improve anything are not altogether useless. They serve, at least, to keep alive and deliver down to posterity the inventions and improvements which have been made before them. They explain the grounds and reasons upon which these discoveries were founded and do not suffer the quality of useful science to diminish.[5]

And Adam Smith would surely have justified his own lifetime's work on political economy to the porter on the grounds that in preparing substantial arguments for the removal of the obstacles and restraints upon manufacturing and commerce he was providing for the improvement of laws and institutions to benefit the labouring classes above all.

In the following section an attempt will be made to place some of these economic theories in the context of the Britain we have been looking at and hence to indicate how ideas and events interacted with one another, as well as to suggest ways in which those ideas continue to influence historical interpretation.

CHAPTER 1
The Luxury Debate
1559–1660

IN THE LIGHT of the importance to historical writing of misguided ideas, it is essential to see how Adam Smith suffered from some himself. For one thing, he thought that the legislation dating from the start of Elizabeth's reign was *intended* to result in the economic growth which actually took place in the seventeenth and eighteenth centuries, whereas, as we have demonstrated, its aims were precisely the opposite: containment; social stability; a modest national self-sufficiency.

This latter aim, self-sufficiency, was especially misunderstood by Smith. Whereas Burghley and others had attempted to inhibit foreign trade in the interests of stability, to minimise social instability in a world of great political and dynastic unpredictability, Smith assumed that they had believed that their own country's manufactures would prosper if international competition were prevented: that 'mercantilist' prohibitions would produce faster growth. The evidence, of course, points the other way; they were well aware that prohibitions would restrict growth, and that was what they wanted. But Smith and other later economists took it for granted that Burghley and his successors had wanted growth, and that the theoretical basis of their economic policies was simply incorrect.

Not only was the theory behind the Tudor and Stuart policies not 'incorrect', it was also far more sophisticated than subsequent theorists acknowledged, for much of it was a subtle interweaving of ideology with pragmatism, of theory with practical knowledge. A case in point is the work which is widely regarded as the first major economic treatise in English worthy of the name. This is Thomas Mun's *England's Treasure by Forraign Trade or the Ballance of our Forraign Trade is the Rule of our Treasure*, published posthumously in 1664 but written in 1623 as a memorandum for the Privy Council inquiry into the causes of the trade depression of 1622, to which Mun as a director of the East India Company, Gerard de Malynes, a currency expert, and Edward Misselden were appointed. It was what we would now call a royal commission, and in Mun's book we find a thorough treatment of the policy of import substitution and national self-sufficiency in luxury goods. In addition Mun's book has been credited as establishing the 'first paradigm' in economics as an independent discipline.[1]

If finery were desired, wrote Mun, let it be produced at home so that 'the excess of the rich may be the employment of the poor'. Almost directly contemporary with the establishment of the Mortlake Tapestry Works, this is as good an explanation as any for the official encouragement given to a luxury artistic enterprise of this kind.

England's Treasure by Forraign Trade is often represented as the classic exposition of the supposedly mercantilist doctrine of 'beggar my neighbour', Mr Micawber's adage applied to the affairs of the nation. If we were to sell our surpluses of cloth, lead, tin, iron and fish to foreign countries for £2,200,000 and use our gains to buy abroad wares to the total of £2,000,000, we would enrich the kingdom by £200,000 annually. This could only be achieved if 'we were not too much affected to Pride, monstrous fashion, and Riot, above all other Nations'. Then 'one million and a half of pounds might plentifully supply our unnecessary wants'. We would have a surplus of £700,000 instead of £200,000, half a million more to invest in circulating capital for foreign trade. Frugality in the consumption of foreign luxuries was the precondition of prosperity. Mun scourged his countrymen for 'the general leprosie of our Piping, Potting, Feasting, Fashions, and mis-spending of our time in Idleness and Pleasure (contrary to the Law of God, and the use of other Nations) [which] hath made us effeminate in our bodies, weak in our knowledge, poor in our Treasure, declined in our Valour, unfortunate in our Enterprises, and contemned by our Enemies'.[2]

The analogy upon which Mun was drawing, like all other economic writers of this period, was that between the affairs of the estate of the realm and the housekeeping of a private man's estate: 'For in this case it cometh to pass in the stock of a Kingdom, as in the estate of a private man; who is supposed to have one thousand pounds yearly revenue and two thousand pounds of ready money in his Chest: If such a man through excess shall spend one thousand five hundred pounds *per annum*, all his ready mony will be gone in four years; and in the like time his said money will be doubled if he take a Frugal course to spend but five hundred pounds *per annum*.'[3] But although Mun was director of the East India Company, and it was therefore in his interest to call for bullion to be spent buying goods from distant countries like India, to be imported to England and re-exported at high profit in Europe, his economic theories were much more sophisticated than the conventional account suggests. Here we will concentrate more upon his view of consumption than of foreign trade.

Mun had very precise observations to make on the proper balance between spending and saving on the part of the king, nobility and gentry. Central to his concern about that issue and the balance of foreign trade was the crucial importance of the circulation of money, of circulating capital, to the economies of the period. As Professor Supple has demonstrated, fixed capital investment in machinery played a very small role in the industry and commerce of the period compared to recurrent investment in raw materials, wages and transport. This was part of the reason why a slump in foreign trade, despite its very small percentage contribution to total national production, could have so sudden and serious an effect upon the economy. If the merchants could not sell English wares abroad, they did not bring returns of bullion and could not pay the clothiers, who in turn could not pay the weavers and artisans in the cloth works, who in turn lacked coin to circulate within the local economy. And in spite of the fact that most workers were involved in agriculture, in satisfying the needs of their local communities, nonetheless, as Tawney estimated, as many as 20–25 per cent of the population of an agricultural area like Gloucestershire were employed in cloth manufacture in 1608. Thus the effects of a sudden slump abroad were likely to have been immediate and catastrophic for local areas that were already industrialised to some considerable degree and where up to half the population was already employed in occupations other than agricultural. 'Plenty of money is the life of trade, scarcity the maim of trade.' Professor Supple has done much to explain Mun's advocacy of a healthy balance on foreign trade in terms of the contemporary situation and the need for circulating coin.[4]

Mun's observations on domestic consumption were also based on concern for the same principles. For, in spite of the ferocious rhetoric of his attack on luxury, Mun nonetheless advocated that 'all kind of Bounty and Pomp is not to be avoided' even when it did involve 'forraign wares'; without pomp there could be no vent for English commodities abroad and what then, he asked, 'will become of our ships, Mariners, Munitions, our poor Artificers, and many others?' Thus the interpretation of so-called mercantilist theory as 'beggar-my-neighbour' is a caricature of Mun's position at least, for Mun recognised reciprocity in trade. He also defended some luxury expenditure on the grounds of providing employment and distributing wealth. 'Again, the pomp of buildings, Apparel, and the like, in the Nobility,

Gentry, and other able persons, cannot impoverish the Kingdome; if it be done with curious and costly works upon our Materials, and by our own people, it will maintain the poor with the purse of the rich, which is the best distribution of the Commonwealth.' But he did consider that employment in the fishing trade would be more profitable still, and his reasons were interesting.[5]

Even though he was a great foreign trader and a doughty defender of trade, Mun nonetheless believed that the foundation of a country's prosperity lay in primary production: agriculture and food production. The Dutch fishing ships were 'unto them as our Ploughs to us, the which except they stir, the people starve' giving 'Foundation, Trade and Subsistence to those multitude of Ships, Arts and People'.[6] These sustained public revenues which would collapse without fishing. For parallel reasons he stood by Burghley's policy of maintaining a proper balance between agriculture and cloth-making, 'for in times of War . . . if some forraign Prince should prohibit the use thereof in their domains, it might suddenly cause much poverty and dangerous uproars especially by our poor people, when they should be deprived of their ordinary maintenance'.[7] Instead Mun advocated as an insurance policy a diversity of employments balanced between primary production and manufacturing. In large measure, therefore, he was expounding how policy must operate in the real world with all the tact and practical intelligence of a thoroughly experienced foreign trader.

On the other hand, and this is a point we will enlarge upon in due course, Adam Smith was knowingly constructing a *theoretical* model of how an economy might work in *ideal* and unrealisable conditions.

Mun's analysis of the effect of what we would call spending on public works, but which he referred to as 'Pomp and Bounty' or 'Liberality amongst Princes, Nobility and Gentry', also depended upon his perception of the importance of circulating money. He advocated a policy of 'spending moderately', but the form of his argument is also interesting. First he dismissed the 'weak arguments' in favour of unlimited spending which used the 'examples of Caesar, Alexander, and others, who hating covetousness, achieved many acts and victories by lavish gifts and liberal expenses'. These examples, in his opinion, did not answer the arguments in favour of wise thrift and restraint. He accepted the need for liberal expenditures but attacked what he described as 'Excessive Bounty' which depended upon inequit-able and oppressive taxation which, as it had in Solomon's case, could cause a rebellion. But on the other hand a miserly king who had say £9m in reserve and who spent only £4m would not merely 'Fleece, but Flea his Subjects' because 'all the money in such a State would suddenly be drawn into the Prince's treasure, whereby the life of lands and arts must fail and fall to the ruin both of publick and private wealth' through the withdrawal of circulating capital. So while being in favour of a degree of thrift he also warned against the dangers of hoarding, what we call today a 'sudden tightening of monetary policy'.[8]

Although a state should build up a reserve fund for its defence against 'Forraign Invasions', yet even this money must not be 'massed up in treasure' but should be spent fruitfully in building a navy, arsenals of weapons and ammunition and granaries in which to store corn as an insurance against dearth. In the process this would provide employment for the subjects from whose labour the revenue was taken in the first place: 'for a Prince is like the stomach in the body, which if it cease to digest and distribute to the other members, it doth no sooner corrupt them, but it destroys itself'. Moreover these granaries and arsenals, like 'that famous Arsenal of the Venetians are to be admired', and doubtless feared, 'for the magnificence of the buildings, the quality of the Munitions and Stores, both for Sea and Land, the multitude of the workmen, the diversity and excellency of the Arts, with the order of the government.' This argument is as good a demonstration as any of a major contention of this book: that, in a period of imperfect or non-existent statistics, buildings were visible statistics, or what the author of an economic tract of 1677 called 'Signs of Wealth'.[9]

In spite therefore of Mun's oft-quoted attack upon luxury his real position was very similar to that of Burghley. By no means did he deny the importance of luxury or beauty, only he advocated a temperate bounty in the public spending of the king as well as that of his nobility and gentry. Although Mun did not enter into the issue, the implication is that like most senior London merchants he would surely have favoured the restrictions upon the growth of London. He would also have supported the policy of the residence of the nobility and gentry upon their estates for the purpose of maintaining the circulation of money in those highly localised economies as well as to encourage husbandry, which he regarded as the foundation of a wealthy, stable and secure society.

Many subsequent writers echoed Mun's prescriptions, advising parliament to do everything possible to make foreign trading advantageous by reducing duties on goods imported for the purpose of re-export, by lowering interest rates while increasing duties on goods bought abroad for home consumption. The most common adduced single constraint upon our increasing trade was the 'leprosie', as Mun had put it, of our taste for foreign luxuries. Samuel Fortrey, writing in 1673, produced figures to show that we were losing £1,600,000 a year in our trade with France. He provided a long list showing the value of goods bought from France, presumably compiled from customs records: velvets, satins, cloth of gold and silver, Lyons silks, taffeta, ribbons, felt hats, perfumed gloves, beds, mattresses and other household stuff, feathers, belts, girdles, fans, hoods, masks, gilt looking glasses, cabinets, watches, pictures, medals, bracelets and, of course, wines and Aqua Vita. He called upon the king, Charles II, as the man who set the fashion for the court and thus for his people, to refrain from following the 'humours and fancies of other nations', and to set an example by wearing clothes manufactured in England.[10]

Fortrey was echoing and endorsing the ideas of John Evelyn who, in December 1661, published and presented to Charles II his 'little trifle of Sumptuary Laws intitled *Tyrannus*' or '*The Mode in a Discourse of Sumptuary Laws*'. This attacked the Restoration courtiers for being slaves to French fashions and dressing up in so many silk ribbons that they could be likened to 'a May Pole or a Tom a Bedlam's cap'.[11]

Evelyn had proposed the revival of sumptuary laws, regulating the costumes for each and every rank in society both as a means of maintaining the social hierarchy and prohibiting imports while encouraging domestic manufactures. When within a month of the Fire of London in September 1666 the king and court renounced 'the French mode' for the Persian as part of a national atonement for the 'burning lusts, dissolute Court, profane and abominable lives', for which the Fire was God's punishment, Evelyn felt great satisfaction.[12]

Finally, in 1680, the anonymous author of *Britannia Languens*, using Fortrey's figures, argued that the restrictions in trade with France which had been imposed would have little effect, for we would simply buy our luxuries elsewhere, further afield, and that they would as a consequence impoverish us even more because of the extra cost of transport. He demanded more than a general prohibition on importations of gauderies, but a total moral reformation as well. 'Shall we continue rolling in Forreign Silks and Linnens? or be still sotting in Forreign Wines, whilst they pick our pockets? Shall we be curious in Trifles, seeking after our private interests? or like blind Sodomites groping after our filthy pleasures, whilst the Wrathful Angels of God stand at our elbows?' He called for a 'general Humiliation of ourselves towards God, accompanied with an abhorrence of our past intemperances, Corrupt Passions, Pride, Avarice, Lusts, Prophaneness, mutual Oppressions, Perfidies, and other Impieties'.[13]

CHAPTER 2

Barbon:
The Infinite Wants of the Mind

THERE COULD HAVE been no greater contrast to this long tradition of arguing for economic stability than the theories put forward in the late seventeenth century by Dr Nicholas Barbon.

Barbon's two pamphlets *An Apology for the Builder* of 1685 and *A Discourse of Trade* of 1690, which was an expansion of the earlier argument, called into question the closely interlinked policies of restraining the growth of London and encouraging the domestic manufacture of foreign luxuries through tariffs, prohibitions and new manufactures. They explicitly attacked the Elizabethan building prohibitions as obstacles to economic growth, and blamed them for what Barbon thought had been the stagnation of London's population in the early seventeenth century and for emigration to North America. They also attacked Thomas Mun, unfairly as we have seen, for commending 'Parsimony, Frugality and Sumptuary Laws' and for making a simple-minded analogy between the frugal household economy of an individual family and that of a nation.[1]

Barbon further attacked the puritans for their belief in the efficacy of sumptuary laws to discourage fashion, which he regarded as essential for prosperity, and criticised import prohibitions and other restraints upon foreign trade on the grounds that they were both ineffective and counter-productive.[2] In short he believed that continuous economic growth, both in total output and output per head was not only possible and desirable but *natural*: that artificial legislative restraints, in effect, hindered God's purposes for mankind.

He had two grounds for this belief. First there was what he called the 'natural increase of mankind' since the day of creation. As mankind grew more populous so the superfluous population of the country moved into the towns and, as the towns grew, bigger markets were created. This natural increase would obviously lead to a greater total wealth, though not necessarily greater wealth per head. But in addition a totally new situation prevailed because, in cities, trade increased even more rapidly than population. Simply because they lived in close proximity different tradesmen and business people created a market for one another's wares which would not otherwise have existed.[3]

The increasing size and concentration of towns increased the easy vent, supply and hence demand for goods. Two additional factors increased demand still further. One was the development of greater inequality, of social distinctions between rich and poor as society grew more complex. The other was the resulting appearance of competitive consumption. Both multiplied the wants of mankind far beyond mere necessity and created more internal and more international trade, more employment for the poor and more revenue for the state. This was a good thing and should not be hampered by ill-considered legislation.[4]

Barbon's explanation of these processes was very ingenious and interesting. It also marked another sharp break with the past. While he used traditional language to describe the causes of economic demand, 'Liberality in the Rich', which he distinguished as a mean between the vices of Prodigality and Covetousness, his underlying social psychology was fundamentally new. Barbon's 'liberality' was not the self-conscious premeditated bounty described by Thomas Mun or by Lord Burghley's obituarist, but an almost demonic urge to consume goods for one's personal benefit alone. As people became richer so the more they desired 'things that promote the ease, pleasures and pomp of life' over and above 'the first natural necessities from hunger, cold, and a house only to shelter their young'. Moreover not only did the rich already possess 'Variety of Dishes, several suits of Clothes, and larger Houses' but 'as their riches increase, so do their wants'. Barbon believed that the reason for this was that whereas the 'Necessitys of the Body', for basic food and shelter, were finite, once they had been satisfied 'those wants, most of them proceeding from imagination' which he described as 'the Wants of the Mind' were infinite. Moreover the raw materials and live produce required to satisfy them, the riches of the kingdoms of the earth, were inexhaustible, so he believed. Thus no *natural* obstacle stood in the way of this Faustian dream of unlimited growth in wealth. Only ill-conceived man-made laws could prevent it happening.[5]

Barbon's description of desire is worth quoting in full:

> Wares that have their Value from supplying the Wants of the Mind, are all such things that can satisfie Desire: Desire implys Want; It is the Appetite of the Soul, and is as natural to the Soul as Hunger to the Body. The Wants of the Mind are infinite, Man naturally Aspires, and as his Mind is elevated, his Senses grew more refined, and more capable of Delight; his Desires are inlarged and his Wants increase with his Wishes, which is for everything that is rare, can gratifie his Senses, adorn his Body, and promote the Ease, Pleasure and Pomp of Life.[6]

This development in human wants and economic demand from the necessities of the body, such as basic food and shelter, to the Wants of the Mind in civilised nations is fundamental to subsequent theories of political economy, including William Jevons's theory of the diminishing marginal utility of goods.

Equally important to subsequent theory is the reductive and materialist idea that the desire for these higher wants is prompted by people's competition for the ownership of marks of social distinction, rather than by any sensual or intellectual desire for perfumes, printing, music or books to 'gratifie the Sense or delight the Minde'.

Barbon enumerated the 'Wants of the Mind'. There was the adornment of the body as a consequence of the Fall of Man, not for pleasure but primarily as a sign of social distinction. Precious stones and animal skins, 'things rare and difficult to be obtained, are General Badges of Honour'. Amongst the trades that 'express the Pomp of Life' were the manufacture of clothes, including all the luxuries such as gloves and shoes, 'Equipage for Servants, Trappings for Horses; and those that Build, Furnish and Adorn Houses'. He considered building to be 'the most proper and visible Distinction of Riches and Greatness' because the cost was so great as to deter emulation. In addition a 'Magnificent Structure doth best represent the Majesty of the Person that lives in it, and is the most lasting truest History of the Greatness of his Person'. And fashion, in Barbon's opinion, was 'the spring of trade . . . the Spirit and Life of Trade; It makes a Circulation and gives a Value by Turns, to all sorts of Commodities, keeps the Great Body of Trade in Motion; it is an Invention to Dress a Man, as if he lived in a perpetual Spring; he never sees the Autumn of his Cloaths.'[7]

The effect of the multiplication of these three factors − social distinction, emulation and fashion − upon the efficient marketplace provided by large towns was to increase production of man-made goods astronomically. An additional effect was to create a demand for foreign luxuries which instead of competing with domestic goods, as commonly believed, were yet further additions to 'the wants of the Mind, Fashion, and desire of Novelties'. Someone would readily eat Westphalian bacon where he would not have eaten English at all.[8]

The value of things, then, arose from their use: 'Things of no Use, have no Value, as the

English phrase is, They are good for nothing.' Use, however was not limited in any way to what was purely practical or physical such as basic food, clothing or shelter; use was defined by the 'wants of the mind', wherever fashion, social emulation or novelty might lead. Since those wants were continually fluctuating the only sure judge of value was the marketplace where prices were determined by demand and supply.[9]

This was a fundamental challenge to earlier ideas, even although there are certain continuities. Certainly there was the common aim of maintaining 'a circulation', as Barbon called circulating capital, through the liberality of the rich. This set the poor to work. And in both systems this consumption and circulation centred around the building and furnishing of houses, as well as clothing. The builder 'provideth the place of birth for all the other arts'. But whereas the liberality spoken of by previous writers aspired to a calculated, temperate balance between prodigality and covetousness, Barbon's 'liberality' was a potentially uncontrollable appetite, a hunger for *things*. Nor did it arise from a noble generosity, but from selfish greed.[10]

The prodigality of the individual, moreover, was by no means prejudicial to the economy as a whole, only to that person's fortunes. Covetousness on the contrary was a 'Vice prejudicial both to Man and Trade; it starves the Man, and breaks the Trade'. By not consuming, by having no use for the products of the tradesmen, the miser helped to reduce their value and ultimately to destroy all the Nation's wealth: 'a Conspiracy of the Rich men to be Covetous, and not Spend would be as dangerous to a Trading state as a Forreign War'. If, for the Tudors and early Stuarts, hoarding and avarice had been a threat to static prosperity, to Barbon it was an obstacle to the natural growth of wealth.[11]

Previous writers and statesmen had wished to control the process of social emulation. It had been the duty of the king to set an example to his courtiers and for them to do likewise to the gentry and so on down the chain in order to prevent covetousness and hoarding. That was called 'setting up an honourable emulation'. But Barbon's emulation was something uncontrolled, a ruthless 'outvying', a clawing at any sign of distinction that could not be easily imitated, such as a very large mansion. Whereas such building was of great economic importance to both systems, earlier it has been subject to much planning and forethought regarding its location, layout and design. But none of these considerations mattered a jot to Barbon. If all building were concentrated in London it would still benefit England as a whole, in his view, by increasing the demand for building materials, stone, brick, lime, iron, lead and timber coming from the rest of the country. Moreover the inhabitants of the houses of Bloomsbury, Leicester Fields, St James's, Spitalfields, which Barbon compared to 'so many new towns', through their consumption of food, clothing and furniture, created a further demand for the natural produce of the country which led to such improvements as the draining of the Fens, and an increase in arable land, resulting in oversupplied markets, falling prices and reduced rents.[12]

Consumer goods which had previously been regulated by sumptuary law, or by the taste established by Charles I or Arundel through ventures such as the Mortlake Tapestry, were in Barbon's world to be governed by the caprices of fashion in freely traded goods. Prudence, taste, prohibitions and moralising all interfered with the potentially infinite growth in prosperity – as, indeed, we know that they were intended to.

Barbon was not alone in defending free trade, internally and externally, and in justifying unrestrained consumption. Sir Dudley North's anonymous *Discourses upon Trade* of 1691 virtually paraphrased Barbon's arguments stressing the importance of domestic consumption and foreign trade. North affirmed that the main spur to trade, industry and ingenuity was 'the exorbitant Appetites of Men' which they will work for to satisfy: 'For did Men content themselves with bare Necessaries, we should have a poor World'.[13]

The occasion for both these pamphlets was the beginning of an enormous increase in customs duties from 1690 onwards to pay for the French War, but we are less concerned with the *immediate* circumstances in which the pamphlet literature was written, more with the broad drift of the argument, between the advocates of growth through trade and the supporters of a stable economy, as it developed over the coming decades. We therefore need to turn next to the classic work that gave currency to the luxury debate, Bernard de Mandeville's *Fable of the Bees*.[14]

CHAPTER 3
Bernard de Mandeville

BERNARD DE MANDEVILLE was born in Holland in 1670 and, before coming to England, was trained like Barbon as a physician at the University of Leyden, where he specialised in the 'hypochondriack and hysteric passions', what we would call psychiatry, which he practised professionally in London without great success. In 1699 he married an English woman and continued to live in London until his death in 1733. His *The Grumbling Hive: or Knaves Turned Honest* was published as a doggerel poem in 1705, fifteen years after Barbon's *Discourse of Trade*, and enlarged in subsequent editions by prose commentaries on the poem which reappeared with its full title of *The Fable of the Bees: or Private Vices, Publick Benefits* in 1714 which was reprinted in six editions before his death (Plate 33).

Mandeville added little to Barbon's assessment of the growth of wealth: free trade based on competitive consumption was a more effective engine to turn the wheel of trade than noblesse oblige or aristocratic liberality. But Mandeville is significant, at least for this study, because he was the first to relate economic activity on a theoretical level to civil society as a whole, to social and moral issues, to the psychology of the individual and to the nature of government. It is surely significant that both he and Barbon shared a physiological training encouraging them to regard all members of society as having the same bodily and psychological appetites which merit equal satisfaction, in distinction to earlier writers who regarded the nobility as governed by motives different to the rest.[1] He laid the foundations of what came to be known as *political* economy developed as a system by David Hume and Adam Smith. He was not an adjunct to that world of petitioning merchants but an ideologist who, alone amongst the early free traders, held the view that the nature of a society's consumption of even the most trivial toys determined the political constitution of that society. Hence, if wealth were to grow, the whole structure of aristocratic bounty and the polity that it supported must be questioned and demolished.

Mandeville also insisted that compromise was not possible. A society could not enjoy great riches at the same time as a moderate, frugal and virtuous consumption. He saw the latter polity, moreover, for what it was: not as a collection of miscellaneous obstructions and petty constraints upon trade which were the product of ignorance or puritanism, but as part of a system.

This may make Bernard de Mandeville sound very dry, whereas of all economic authors he is the most entertaining. A coffee-house philosopher, forerunner of the modern café intellectual, enormously free-ranging in the scope of his knowledge and the thrust of his arguments, he not only foreshadowed quasi-psychoanalytic notions of individual repression as an instrument of civilisation, but he was also an early analyst of the subtle use of sexuality in commerce and salesmanship. Like Freud two centuries later, he outraged respectable opinion by uncovering unconscious motivation. He was also one of the forerunners of an anthropological approach to human society, one whose relativism about morality and customs gave him the manoeuvrability to perceive the rationale of different social systems.

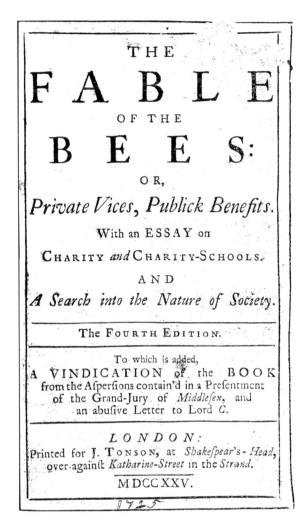

33 Title page of *The Fable of the Bees* (first edition 1714). Mandeville denied the good intentions of high-spending aristocrats and invented the idea of competitive consumption – a private vice with public benefits.

Finally, and oddly for a relativist, he was a passionate vegetarian and defender of animal rights. Mandeville was above all a lover of paradox.

Mandeville's importance to the present argument, then, lies not in his discovery of economic mechanisms but, first, in supplying the market economy with a philosophy by laying bare the psychological logic of competitive consumption. And he further used his psychological theory of consumption to satirise and dissect the then still dominant ideology of the 'temperate bounty' of the aristocracy – where Barbon had merely questioned its economic efficacy – doing this so successfully that, to this day, virtually no one credits the nobility and gentry of England for building grand country houses and living high out of a sense of duty.

Mandeville's theory that their motive was simple swank came to be central to the ideas of Adam Smith, Herbert Spencer, and Thorstein Veblen in his *Theory of the Leisure Class*, the account most familiar to us today. Through Veblen and through Adam Smith the theory has been a major influence upon historians such as Tawney and Lawrence Stone whose objective history appears to confirm the theory, whereas it is in fact the other way round. And recent cultural critics of modern society such as Bourdieu and Baudrillard are also heavily indebted to Mandeville through Veblen.[2] Moreover, because of the intermeshing we have seen of economics with design, Mandeville's ideas had an indirect effect on the history of design itself, since many of the movements to *reform* design have been driven by the desire to contrive objects of consumption that could avoid censure as vulgar ornaments in purely competitive display.

Mandeville, then, welcomed economic growth and its effects in creating large cities, the 'seething hive', and he was the first to reveal the workings of its culture and how it was regulated through the dextrous management of its individual members by the conscious play of shame and honour upon their self esteem. His role as a writer he saw, quite self-consciously, as the anatomist of human society who looked beneath the skin, bones and nerves at the 'small trifling Films and little Pipes' overlooked by the vulgar, but which were the true mechanisms making people and societies work. In particular he claimed to look beneath men's hypocritical self-images as public-spirited creatures at their true selfish motivation. We ought not to be moralists, he believed, teaching man what he should be but scientists examining what he really was. Man's passions made him tick.[3]

Here we shall focus upon five parts of Mandeville's anatomy: the psychology of the individual as it might exist outside society; the way individual passions are regulated to make man a social animal; the social psychology of the competitive consumption of luxury goods; a critique of aristocratic bounty; and finally the 'publick benefits' to society which arose from the exercise of these so-called vices. In addition, good relativist that he was, he gave some account of the positive virtues of the social system based upon aristocratic bounty, the object of his critique.

Primitive Psychology

The human individual, in the 'state of nature', possessed no moral virtues but was a 'compound of various passions' and appetites for selfish pleasure. Foremost were Hunger, Lust and Fear, each directed towards the self-preservation of the individual and the species. When someone's hunger or sexual lust was obstructed they were roused to anger and ferocity. However Mandeville's view of human nature was not so Hobbesian as this may sound, since human-beings were neither so salacious nor so ravenous as other animals. Since they possessed great cunning they could usually satisfy both hunger and lust without violence. Human beings were naturally prone to love peace, quiet, ease and pleasure. They were, in short, naturally lazy.[4]

Social Psychology

Left to his or her own devices in the savage state the human creature would have lived a peaceful, solitary and selfish existence. Those therefore who wanted to establish human societies (and it is a weakness of Mandeville that he gave no explanation of why any human being should want to do so) had to invent some way of encouraging people to act in the public interest. The means they discovered was to play upon people's selfishness and self-love by praise and flattery on the one hand and contempt on the other, appealing to the emotions of Honour, or esteem, and its opposite, Shame. Once these psychological mechanisms for the control of the passions had been discovered there was virtually nothing that people could not be made to do.[5]

Naturally slothful and peaceable man, for example, became as ferocious as the wildest bear when his honour was at stake or his courage shamed. Virtues and vices, therefore, were no more than the names given by the dextrous managers of society, be they politicians or parents, to those actions rewarded with honour or punished by shame. The virtues and the vices, moreover, were not fixed or universal; they differed according to the customs of different societies. All of them however – pride and vanity, envy, ambition, emulation and avarice – were variants or transformations of the three fundamental passions of hunger, lust and fear. Through honour and shame, moreover, all good manners, modesty, piety, self-denial and public-spiritedness were inculcated into people at a very early age for the benefit of society. Thus a fundamentally selfish passion lay at the root of every virtue and all so-called virtues were really hypocrisy.[6]

A refutation would begin by questioning Mandeville's premise that all motivation could be reduced to variants on hunger, lust and fear, but the aim here is to expound his theory and to show how his contemporaries and successors responded to it.

Mandeville illustrated the hypocritical nature of the social virtues and the education of the passions in a short fable which exposed sexual modesty, chastity and polite marriage as the means by which we were taught to satisfy our raging sexual desires without coming into conflict with others. Both men and women were naturally lustful, not modest. They would, if they could, satisfy their sexual desires whenever they arose with dire consequences for social harmony. Thus from childhood we were taught by the use of shame to stifle our appetites. The lessons of modesty 'like those of *Grammar*, are taught us long before we have occasion for, or understand the Usefulness of them . . . A girl who is modestly educated, may, before she is two Years old, begin to observe how careful the Women she converses with, are of covering themselves before Men; . . . it is very probable that at Six she'll be ashamed of showing her Leg, without knowing why such an Act is blameable, or what the Tendency of it is.[7] But if the enforcement of modesty were too extreme 'Propagation must have stood still among all Fashionable People'. So the male sex, naturally more lustful, was permitted more sexual liberty than the female so as to take the initiative in courtship.[8]

A civilised man, therefore, instead of telling a woman that he 'found a violent Desire that Moment to go about' propagating the species upon her person, was trained to achieve his objective by hiding his appetite, neither revealing his desires openly, for fear of offence, nor stifling them completely. Instead he had to flatter the girl with gifts and attentions, pay court to her father, and show himself to be prosperous and respectable. The result of a successful courtship would be that on their wedding night they go to bed together where 'the most reserv'd virgin very tamely suffers him to do what he pleases, and the upshot is that he obtains what he wanted without having ever ask'd for it' with the approval of 'the most sober matrons'. This fable of the quest for sexual satisfaction was used by Mandeville to illustrate how the rules of polite society operated by means of 'a dextrous Management of ourselves, a stifling of our Appetites, and hiding the real Sentiments of our Hearts before others'. By analogy everything desired was obtained by subterfuge, nothing should be judged by appearances, which are always deceptive. This in turn opens the way to a social analysis that takes nothing at its face value and always searches for damaging motives.[9]

Social Psychology of Competitive Consumption

Mandeville's explanation of the social psychology of competitive consumption was an elaborated version of Barbon's. We were motivated to acquire possessions, clothes, furniture and houses to outvy our neighbours with signs of our distinction and to satisfy our lusts, hunger, pride and vanity; but without competing so blatantly as to cause civil conflict.

The worldly-minded, voluptuous and ambitious Man, notwithstanding he is void of Merit, covets Precedence everywhere, and desires to be dignify'd above his Betters: He aims at spacious Palaces, and delicious Gardens; his chief Delight is in excelling others in stately Horses, magnificent Coaches, a numerous Attendance, and dear-bought Furniture. To gratify his Lust, he wishes for genteel, young, beautiful Women of different Charms and Complexions that shall adore his Greatness, and be really in love with his Person: His

Cellars he would have stored with the Flower of every Country that produces excellent Wines: His Table he desires may be serv'd with many Courses, and each of them contain a choice Variety of Dainties not easily purchas'd, and ample Evidences of elaborate and judicious Cookery; whilst harmonious Musick and well-couch'd Flattery entertain his Hearing by Turns.[10]

The novelty in Mandeville's account lay in his attempt to puncture the self-justifications of aristocratic bounty. He dismissed all such arguments as mere window-dressing: 'whilst thus wallowing in a Sea of Lust and Vanity . . . provoking and indulging his Appetites' the aristocrat like the gallant lover and the modest maid wished to be honoured and admired for his virtues, not condemned for his vices. So he claimed to spend all his money only 'to promote the publick Welfare'.[11]

Mandeville hinted that taste could be used as a justification for unbridled extravagance, in just the same way as the satisfying of lust in marriage was disguised as a moral virtue. Taking the example of clothing, he elaborated Barbon's simple description of competitive consumption. Clothing was made originally to protect us and keep us warm. But in civilised society ornament and hence fashion were added as emblems of honour: Hottentots adorned themselves with the guts of their enemies. Handsome apparel, then, was worn, according to Mandeville, to display our wealth and our taste; but particularly in large cities, where individuals were relatively anonymous, people tried to display themselves as having a higher rank than they really possessed. He illustrated this with a tale showing the reluctance of lower-class women dressed in their Easter finery to answer his questions about their homes or occupations: 'they hug themselves in their disguise' being unwilling to reveal anything lest their 'Golden Dream' of being thought better than they really were should be destroyed.[12]

Everyone, he argued, was engaged in the same masquerade. To appear genteel the labourer's wife half starved her family; the shopkeeper's wife imitated the wholesaler's wife who imitated the merchant's wife, who went to live in the West End and imitated the ladies of the court who contrived new fashions to escape the imitation of 'those saucy Cits'. Finally, to escape the affordable imitation of clothing altogether, the greatest people in the state were 'forced to lay out vast Estates in pompous Equipages, magnificent Furniture, sumptuous Gardens and princely Palaces'.

The human trait of imitating others more richly favoured than oneself was, moreover, spurred on by envy, the desire to possess the good fortune of others. Thus honour and shame, pride and ambition, emulation, envy and fashion cooperated with the basic appetites of lust and hunger to keep this great treadmill of competitive consumption turning, setting the poor to work.

But something vastly more important was achieved than employment and wealth, for it was by stimulating and channelling humankind's desires for vanities like furniture, clothing and great buildings that the selfish passions were educated and man was socialised: this is the true importance of luxury in Mandeville's system. Thus transformed, selfish urges could be satisfied not merely in a relatively harmless but in a positively beneficial way.

Critique of Aristocratic Bounty

Mandeville took three of the arguments which were commonly used by the very rich and great to justify huge extravagance and scornfully dissected each to reveal their true motives. First there was the argument that to such noble minds as theirs the possession of more suits of clothes or other pomps or luxuries was a burdensome duty assumed only in order to encourage particular branches of trade and to promote public welfare. It was, in effect, a kind of tax. Mandeville disposed of that argument with the rejoinder that, if it were a tax, one would surely pay no more than was required instead of outreaching oneself and endangering one's estate, as actually happened.[13]

The second apology, that rulers had to engage in pomp and pageantry to awe the populace and keep them in order by a show of magnificence as a sign of power, he dismissed on the grounds that those functions were performed by the army, the police and the courts and not by scarlet gowns and gold chains. Furthermore this pretext, argued Mandeville, did not explain purely private extravagance, 'the pomp and Luxury of the Dining Room and the Bed Chamber, and the Curiosities of the Closet'. Larks at half a guinea and paintings costing thousands of pounds were not acquired for political show but to gratify the appetites of princes and ministers.★[14]

Finally he explained away even charitable expenditure on the grounds of personal pride and desire for an honourable memorial to leave to posterity: 'Pride and Vanity have built more Hospitals than all the Virtues together'.[15]

The argument that even the great must exercise a 'temperate bounty' in their public-spirited consumption, recommended by Lord Burghley and Thomas Mun and which Mandeville attributed in his own time to the Earl of Shaftesbury, was dismissed both on the grounds that the greater their frugality the smaller the circulation of money and hence the less employment. Finally, with a great display of scorn, Mandeville accused them all of dishonesty, in a passage which summarises his own views of human motivation.[16]

> These are the Apologies, the Excuses and common Pleas, not only of those who are notoriously vicious, but the generality of Mankind, when you touch the Copy-hold of their Inclinations; and trying the real Value they have for Spirituals, would actually strip them of what their Minds are wholly bent upon. Ashamed of the many Frailties they feel within, all Men endeavour to hide themselves, their Ugly Nakedness, from each other, and wrapping up the true Motives of their Hearts in the Specious Cloak of Sociableness, and their Concern for the publick Good, they are in hopes of concealing their filthy Appetites and the Deformity of their Desires; whilst they are conscious within of the Fondness for their darling Lusts, and their Incapacity, barefac'd, to tread the arduous, rugged Path of Virtue.

His attack upon the whole political ethos of the aristocratic leadership went a stage further in the introductory essay on the 'Origin of Moral Virtue'. In this fable of the history of social morality, he mocked the pretensions of the upper classes to have mastered their sensual appetites in the interests of the public good and to have set themselves up as models to guide the lower classes into the paths of virtue. This, he claimed, was a conspiracy on the part of the rich to press morality and religion into the service of dominating the poor. He also claimed that virtue and vice, thus defined, were no more than what the ruling class, people like the Earl of Shaftesbury, chose to call them.[17]

It was this onslaught upon every facet of aristocratic bounty and his injunction to dissect motives, to probe the *real* motives, the *real* chain of causes, that made his alternative explanations of competitive consumption so convincing. If surface appearances are always deceptive then every attempt to justify them must be dismissed. Nonetheless, and this is a point which tends to be neglected, Mandeville was not denying the feasibility of societies other than the one he was describing. In the poem, *The Grumbling Hive*, Jove finally gives in to the prayers of the moral reformers, and 'At last in Anger swore, He'd rid The brawling Hive of Fraud: and did.' And in spite of the fact that luxuries and fashions disappear '. . . Still Peace and Plenty reign, And every Thing is cheap, tho' plain.' Hospitality for the poor returns, the clergyman

> chas'd no Starveling from his Door,
> Nor pinch'd the Wages of the Poor;

★ This, of course, undermines the logic of Mandeville's own argument that such purchases were made to compete with others, not for personal pleasure or greed.

But at his House the Hungry's fed,
The Hireling finds unmeasur'd Bread,
The needy Trav'ller Board and Bed.[18]

Mandeville argued that a society based upon temperate aristocratic bounty, the stable state envisaged by Burghley, was certainly possible, but that it would inevitably involve a return to the middle ages. Far from deriding it he claimed to prefer it, but he denied that one could enjoy the best of both worlds. A deferential, hierarchical society composed of 'harmless, innocent and well-meaning people, that would never dispute the Doctrine of Passive Obedience, nor any other Orthodox Principles but be submissive to Superiors and . . . in Religious Worship', was incompatible with a growth economy.

> Would you banish Fraud and Luxury, prevent Profaneness and Irreligion, and make the generality of the People Charitable, Good and Virtuous, break down the Printing-Presses, melt the Founds, and burn all the Books in the Island, except those at the Universities, where they remain unmolested, and suffer no Volume in private Hands but a Bible: knock down Foreign Trade, prohibit all Commerce with Strangers, and permit no Ships to go to Sea, that ever will return, beyond Fisher-Boats. Restore to the Clergy, the King and the Barons their Ancient Privileges, Prerogatives and Possessions: Build New Churches, and convert all the Coin you can come at into Sacred Utensils: Erect Monasteries and Alms-houses in abundance, and let no Parish be without a Charity-School. Enact Sumptuary Laws, and let your youth be inured to Hardship: Inspire them with all the nice and most refined Notions of Honour and Shame, of Friendship and of Heroism, and introduce among them a great variety of imaginary Rewards: Then let the Clergy preach Abstinence and Self-denial to others, and take what Liberty they please for themselves; let them bear the greatest Sway in the Management of State Affairs, and no Man be made Lord-Treasurer but a Bishop.
>
> By such pious Endeavours, and wholesome Regulations, the Scene would soon be alter'd; the greatest part of the Covetous, the Discontented, the Restless and Ambitious Villains would leave the Land, vast Swarms of Cheating Knaves would abandon the City, and be dispers'd throughout the Country: Artificers would learn to hold the Plough, Merchants turn Farmers, and the sinful over-grown Jerusalem, without Famine, War, Pestilence, or Compulsion, be emptied in the most easy manner, and ever after cease to be dreadful to her Sovereigns.[19]

Ironic as this is, it is also a fairly accurate characterisation of Lord Burghley's political objectives and of Thomas More's *Utopia*. Mandeville's recognition that the principles of an alternative society and source of earnings could make sense on their own terms, as they had in the past, distinguishes him from his long stream of followers. He did not assume that economic inefficiencies were necessarily the result of ignorance.

Public Benefit

Finally, Mandeville described the public benefit brought about by a social economy based upon the covert practice of vices. Through the consumption of luxury goods, mankind's selfishness was kept in social check and turned to good. Not only did luxury transform the evils inherent in human nature into social benefits it had the same influence upon the evils of external nature.

If mankind had been as well adapted to living in the open air as other animals there would have been no need to invent the arts and skills of making clothes, shelters, ships and tools. The combination of natural adversity and human vice were the origins of both society and civilisation. On the other hand 'the Amiable Virtues and Loving Qualities of Man', which he did not deny, practised in Paradise in the Golden Age would have produced neither.[20]

In his defence of what Adam Smith was to call the 'progressive state' of society he argued that one should not term luxuries merely the gaudy ornaments of the very rich but *anything* that was not absolutely necessary for subsistence. Strictly speaking nothing was a luxury because everything was. The very beginnings of luxury had to be sought in the simplest crafts and skills of savage peoples. 'Emulation and continual striving to out-do one another' were the spurs to progress and improvement, even the linen gown of the parish pauper was a luxury and the product of centuries of social and industrial evolution. It depended upon an enormous chain in the division of labour involving farmers, labourers, weavers, spinners, dyers, packers, millwrights and chemists.[21]

In conclusion – and in criticism of the then current theory that the protestant ethic was responsible for the growth of capitalist manufacture – Mandeville declared that it was not the success of the Reformation in making people more virtuous in countries like Holland and England that had made them 'flourishing beyond other Nations' but 'the silly and capricious Invention of Hoop'd and Quilted Petticoats'.[22]

34 Joseph Addison by Michael Dahl, 1719. Addison, a Whig politician and intellectual was co-editor with Richard Steele of *The Spectator* which shaped the opinions of the nation on every topic from food and gardening to high politics and economics. *The Spectator* believed that the moral standards of puritanism should control personal consumption.

CHAPTER 4

The Spectator

MANDEVILLE'S TALK OF petticoats was almost certainly aimed at his greatest adversaries, the journalists Richard Steele and Joseph Addison (Plate 34), who in essays censoring the more extreme fashions of the age had singled out for ridicule the hooped petticoat. Steele and Addison published and wrote in *The Tatler* and *The Spectator*, periodicals which, along with *The Guardian, Englishman, Freethinker and Lover*, exerted enormous influence on the thinking of eighteenth and nineteenth-century England. Specifically this is the place where the old patronising attitudes and the new economic point of view were first reconciled and consequently it is here that the ancestry of modern design ideology begins.

The Spectator, probably the most important of these, was founded in 1711, thirty-three years after England's first daily newspaper, *The Observer*, and three years before *The Fable of the Bees* was first published in full. It provided a mixture of news, advice and 'observations on life and manners' for a readership indistinguishable from the clientele of the coffee houses: merchants, barristers, politicians, a newly emerging bourgeoisie in the process of shaping its ethics and aesthetics. *The Spectator*'s success was rapid; Addison, albeit optimistically, calculated the number of its readers at approximately half a million (assuming that there were twenty readers per copy), or slightly less than 10 per cent of the population of the country. Certainly, a collection of its essays, of which the first edition consisted of 9,000 copies, went into eleven editions over twenty years, while the readership of the magazine continued to expand to include such people as shopkeepers, craftsmen and clerks, and women whose husbands' status and wealth debarred them from either domestic or public work.[1]

Like Mandeville, Addison and Steele were Whig in their outlook and politics: all three shared the view that the bounty of the landed rich was no longer the best nor the only means to create employment. But, on the central issue of the relationship between economic and other social objectives, they adopted very different positions. Mandeville argued that there was only one way for a state to be rich, but many ways to be poor. The authors of the Whig periodicals, to whom I shall refer collectively as *The Spectator* for convenience, believed that there were distinct kinds of wealth, of which only some were morally and aesthetically desirable.

They presented two alternatives, simply personified, as fictional members of Mr Spectator's club: the London merchant, Sir Andrew Freeport, and the old country squire, Sir Roger de Coverley – the first representing the monied and the second the landed interest. 'The Coverley Papers' is an important section of *The Spectator*: a dialogue between these two representative tendencies, it amounts to a parliamentary debate. But it is also a political allegory and a programme: Sir Roger dies without issue and shortly afterwards Freeport retires from trade investing his wealth in a country estate which he intends to improve through the application to agriculture of the economic principles acquired in the City. Thus, in a manner of speaking, *The Spectator* envisaged the monied interest as the 'heir' to the landed interest, both as Britain's ruling class and as the source of her wealth. Unlike Mandeville *The Spectator* believed that the two systems could be reconciled.

The fictional Mr Spectator's denial that he ever 'espoused any party with violence' and his promise to 'observe an exact neutrality between the Whigs and Tories' has a hollow ring,[2] seeing that Joseph Addison had been a leading office holder in the Whig administration under the Earl of Wharton. *The Spectator*'s cry of 'No Party' was a clever political ploy to win over, ideologically, protestant, loyalist, pro-Hanoverian Tories with the promise that the landed interest would be safeguarded and, more important, that the commercial interests would not be given full sway. Indeed, Mr Spectator is a canny diplomat and negotiator, well practised in dividing the opposition. For example, the author of *Spectator* 200 checks his argument in favour of opening the country to immigration, getting rid of the laws of parish settlement and removing all legislated obstructions to a free commerce when he recalls the force of English xenophobia. As we shall see, this political shrewdness was shared by Adam Smith, while Mandeville, by contrast, seems not just an extremist but severely limited in his awareness of the political obstacles to economic progress.

The Spectator, then, wished at all costs to avoid the real danger of another Civil War and to carry a majority of the country along with it in its campaign for essentially Whig objectives:[3] promotion of the monied interest, foreign trade and the improvement of the nation's resources. But *The Spectator* did not regard prudence as merely a negative virtue. As well as being committed to commercial values, *The Spectator* adhered to certain religious, moral and aesthetic values so fundamental to its vision of social life that nothing, not even the pursuit of wealth, could be permitted to override them. It was this pervasive willingness to judge, and, in the process, to instruct its readers in the minutiae of how they should live, that both distinguished it from Mandeville and led, for the first time ever, to a fusion of the new, expansionist economic theory with the old paternalism.[4]

Sir Roger de Coverley was a paradigm, almost a caricature of all those familiar squirearchical virtues. He was the benevolent ruler of his province and his parish, a great paternalist, father to his people, affable and a liberal host who maintained housekeeping for his neighbours and hospitality for the poor, particularly at Christmas when he held open house and his chimneys smoked with the roasting of eight fat hogs to feed the whole village which crowded into his hall. He even extended his charity to a London waterman who had lost a leg in the Queen's Service.[5] In religion he was High Church but not papist, horrified by the absence of steeples in the West End – 'A most heathenish sight!' – so much so that in his will he bequeathed money for a steeple to be built on his own church at Coverley, which inexplicably lacked one. As landlord to the whole congregation he saw religion essentially as a means of civilising the villagers. He lorded it in church, where he suffered 'nobody to sleep besides himself'. As he departed, the whole village had to bow to him. He was a dutiful JP, who died from a chill caught justicing for a poor widow. All his actions and principles were based upon his stated resolution to 'follow the steps of the most worthy of my ancestors who have inhabited this spot of earth before me, in all the methods of hospitality and good neighbourhood, for the sake of my fame; and in country sports and recreations, for the sake of my health'. He also avoided the pitfalls of extravagance.[6]

While *The Spectator* honoured the man, the death of Sir Roger, without direct issue, was nonetheless represented as the death of the policy of old-fashioned bounty and the passing of the torch to Sir Andrew Freeport, to whom Coverley significantly bequeathed his JP's *Collection of Acts of Parliament*. For while *The Spectator* admired Sir Roger's personal piety and dutifulness, and his lack of fashion and modishness in both dress or behaviour, the old gentry and nobility were criticised on three grounds: their extravagance and lack of thrift, the economic limitations of their bounty and charity as a means of creating employment; and their patronage and paternalism on a social and personal level. The attack upon patronage seems to be written from bitter personal experience: patrons were accused of failing to honour their obligations to their clients and of callous pride towards them. Most offensive was the personal servility, the passive obedience they demanded, in evidence in the deference demanded by Sir Roger from the congregation in church.[7]

For all these reasons *The Spectator* welcomed the new dispensation personified by Sir Andrew Freeport. No one worked for him as a servant, so no one was personally obliged to him in the old servile way. He was thrifty and hard-working; his self-interest worked to the public good by exporting all that was superfluous to Britain's needs and importing what was needed, thereby creating mutual intercourse between nations which promoted the international division of labour and a ready supply of raw materials. The result of Sir Andrew's labours was that British ships were 'laden with the harvest of every climate: our tables . . . stored with spices and oils and winces; our rooms . . . filled with pyramids of China, and adorned with the workmanship of Japan . . . we repair our bodies by the drugs of America and repose under Indian canopies'.[8]

Like Barbon, *The Spectator* also supported the growth of London, since the greater wealth of London's citizens meant that their consumption was far in excess of their population, creating a demand for the produce of the rest of the country which paid a large part of the nation's rents and its taxes. In Sir Andrew's view, paid employment and the division of labour, rather than charity or bounty, were to be the principles by which the poor were relieved. They would even work to the benefit of the country interest, of the Sir Rogers of England. As a result of the division of labour the prices of everything would fall and everyone's real wages and wealth would rise. Old-fashioned charity, on the other hand, had subsidised idleness. Freeport argued that this most sacred of Christian obligations should be dispensed through the 'new bounty' of trade and commerce.[9]

In a letter to *The Spectator* he explained that his new estate would give him the 'great opportunity of being charitable in my way, that is in setting my poor neighbours to work – My garden, my fish pond, my arable and pasture grounds shall be my several hospitals, or rather workhouses, on which I propose to maintain a great many indigent persons, who are now starving in my neighbourhood'. This he would achieve by investing in all kinds of improvements, planting woods and draining marshes, in the process also making his landscape as beautiful as could be. Nor did his new 'modes of charity' exclude the erection of almshouses for his retired husbandmen. Sir Andrew's plan for the economy was extended in *The Guardian* in the character of Sir Harry Lizard of Northamptonshire, who inherited his estate and applied to it the new methods of accounting *as well as* maintaining the old hospitality, a fine stable and most of the other appurtenances of his forefathers.[10]

Three issues later a Mr Charwell, a former City merchant purchased a 10,000 acre estate nearby. Because the local river was not navigable and canalising it had been opposed by the whole county for fear of opening their markets to external competition – rather like the actual case of Stamford – the whole economy of the area was stagnant in the absence of any effective external demand for its produce of corn, timber, coal. So the population was small and there was little building.[11]

Charwell's methods of dealing with this were to reduce his park from 2,000 to 200 acres and use it for livestock breeding, to reduce his household and move into a new, smaller house. Then in order to provide alternative employment and a vent for his tenant farmers' produce he built a town for 5,000 people over a period of twenty years on the site of his old house. The need that his housekeeping had fulfilled within the old economy thus disappeared, and its disappearance was no longer resented by the tenant farmers; his rents had risen and the farmers of the district were now ready to make the river navigable to provide a larger market for their produce.

The Spectator sought to prove that the landed and the moneyed interests could be reconciled and that all would benefit as a result. The only thing which prevented this happening was the ignorance of the country squires.[12]

Likewise *The Spectator* insisted that in its manners, morals and the nature of its consumption the new world dominated by trade must not be a free-for-all with everyone bent upon satisfying their over-stimulated appetites, in the way that Barbon or Mandeville had described. The reasons they gave for this were different, in emphasis at least, from those of Burghley or Mun a century earlier, when the chief concern in moderating consumption had been to prevent the growth of an urban proletariat and the decline of tillage with all the resulting social disruption. Now the concern was for the ethical character of individual and of private family life, particularly that of the middling classes.

The manner of life through which this was to be achieved will be the subject of a later chapter. But the gist of it was that, while all unnecessary consumption was vain and idolatrous, some kinds of consumption were less bad than others and some were even positively improving. But most important of all was not the outward material objects which people acquired so much as their attitude of mind in acquiring them.

This position could lead to surprising judgements. We might believe a housewife who spends her time making cushions and curtains, jams and preserves to be a paragon of domestic virtue compared to one who goes shopping for these small luxuries. But *The Spectator* did not agree. If she spent so much time on her needlework that the education of her children was neglected then she was as much at fault as if she had wasted her money. To read improving literature was obviously good for trade as well as for the soul, but the mere possession of a library as an object of display was a vice. Virtually the only activity, in itself, which escaped censure from these self-appointed censors was gardening and the laying out of woods, in the belief that communing with nature was inherently innocent and improving.[13]

Thus we find not only in the productive side of the economy but also in consumption that *The Spectator* represented a fusion of the older polity and the new. We have to wait for Adam Smith, who provided an economic rather than a moral justification of personal thrift as the fundamental means by which wealth could be increased through investment, before the circle of personal middle class morality was squared with economic efficiency, but the ethic of those manufacturers of the late eighteenth and early nineteenth centuries whose favourite reading was Adam Smith *and* William Cowper, the poet of retirement, was in large part adumbrated by *The Spectator*. What one could call the self-limiting ideology of British capitalist enterprise was formed long before the public school ethos of the later nineteenth century and manufacturers' retreat into gentility.[14]

In outline at least it should now be apparent that the seeds of a design reform, an attempt to make the appearance of domestic consumer goods, clothes and even food adhere to certain moral and aesthetic norms, can be found in the Whig response to the challenge presented by the growth of the consumer economy. And this will be discussed in greater detail when we return to *The Spectator* in Part IV. In contrast to Barbon and Mandeville, who advocated the unchaining of the forces of greed, fashion and free commerce, and to the Sir Roger de Coverleys who still believed in what we have called the Burghleyan dispensation of paternalism, sumptuary law, deference and a stable agrarian economy, Mr Spectator and his highly influential friends – who included Henry Martyn, Addison, Steele, Pope, as well as magnates like Thomas Wharton and the young Robert Walpole – laid the foundations of a new polity incorporating features of the old and the new. Country house building and landscape gardening were favoured alongside the improvement of agricultural practices. London and other cities would be permitted to expand without any restrictions other than the counterweight of a flourishing agriculture, and they would continue to be built to the standards of taste set by Covent Garden as well as by the regulations of the Act of 1667. In the area of personal consumption, although there were no more sumptuary laws, the moralist, the Censor, was there to restrain the excessive idolatry of worldly things though the influence of lay sermons, attempting to reform both the appearance of and people's attitudes to material things through the exercise of a form of taste which was both moral and aesthetic.

The Spectator believed in governing the free market by means of tariff and tax controls and governing consumption through the rules of taste. But, although the most common, theirs was not the only solution to the dilemma propounded by Mandeville. Far more ingenious and possibly unique, was that of the Scottish philosopher and historian David Hume, who set out to show that all *The Spectator* stood for could be achieved by the totally unconstrained consumption of luxury goods. Far from being the source of all kinds of debauchery and absurd fluctuations in fashion, it would produce a society at once more humane and more cultivated.

35 David Hume in 1754 by Allan Ramsay. An optimist about economic progress, Hume believed that free trade would stimulate morality and the arts as well as national prosperity.

CHAPTER 5
David Hume – Commerce and Refinement

Born in 1711, David Hume was the second son of a landed Scottish lawyer (Plate 35). His inheritance of £100 a year was modest enough to oblige him to supplement his income and although, after leaving Edinburgh University in 1726, he devoted himself single-mindedly to writing *A Treatise of Human Nature*, he was also apprenticed in 1734 to a Bristol sugar merchant and slave-trader. This post, however, did not last long, Hume leaving in disfavour for criticising his master's grammar and style. (His master retorted that his style had earned him a fortune of £20,000.) On its publication in 1739, *A Treatise of Human Nature* was less than successful, and Hume turned to writing something more saleable, *Essays: Moral and Political*, in open imitation of Addison and Steele's *Tatler* and *Spectator* essays.[1] Hume's essays, published in 1741, are not light reading however. In them, he attempted to apply to social and political questions the principles of the *Treatise*: in particular his ingenious theory of cause and effect. The gist of this was that there was no necessary relation between a cause and its effect; there was only a statistical probability founded upon the experience of the observer that when A happened B invariably followed. When, for example, a moving billiard ball struck a stationary one, the stationary ball would be set in motion on impact. Since the probability of this occurring was very high, we formed a 'belief' that the one event was the cause of the other. But it remained a 'belief', one that could be disproved by subsequent events.[2]

Applied to more complex social events and situations Hume believed that one could treat historical events as a series of experiments from which to infer the connections between a variety of causes and their probable effects. 'There is nothing which requires greater nicety, in our inquiries concerning human affairs, than to distinguish exactly what is owing to chance, and what proceeds from causes, nor is there any subject, in which an author is more liable to deceive himself by false subtleties and refinements.' Even more than in the case of physical events, there could be little certainty that one had discovered the true causes since the total number of experiments was very small. 'If I were to assign any general rule . . . it would be the following, *what depends upon a few persons is, in a great measure, to be ascribed to chance, or secret and unknown causes: What arises from a great number, may often be accounted for by determinate and known causes.*'[3] Thus all Hume's reasonings upon political or economic issues were provisional and hedged around with scepticism.

In common with Addison, Steele and Mandeville, Hume's contributions to economic theory were not occasioned by specific economic crises requiring solution, though Hume, like other Scottish writers, may have been prompted to consider the general effects of the Act of Union of 1707 upon Scotland's economy, particularly in the years around the 1745 Rebellion. They were part of his system of political philosophy, based upon a far more considered account of human psychology than that of Mandeville. Despite his failure to obtain a university chair, Hume wrote as an academic political economist.

Indeed, both *Essays: Moral and Political* and *Political Discourses* (1752) were published while Hume still nursed ambitions for a chair. He even presented a copy of the earlier volume to the Duke of Argyll, who was the source of all government patronage in Scotland. The works mark a major change both in the nature of economic literature and in the very conception of what university studies ought to be. In Scotland, at least, the university was being transformed into the modern state-funded institution for the encouragement of the Arts and Sciences, whose functions were intended to be of direct utility to their paymasters, the state or the City Corporation headed by city bosses like George Drummond. In the *Political Discourses* Hume stated that his own observations on economics served 'to employ the thoughts of our speculative politicians. For to these only I all along address myself.' It has been argued that Hume's reason for adopting *The Spectator* essay as his form in preference to the philosophical treatise was on account of his commitment to instructing the citizens of a modern commercial society in practical morality.[4]

Hume's scheme of economics was not only intricate but, at first sight, highly Utopian. Not only did it have no place for the philistine Bristol slave-trader, but everyone in it seemed to be happy, cultivated, law-abiding and free. It was almost a prophetic parody of Mr Podsnap's view of the world when Hume wrote: 'Can we expect that a government will be well-modelled by a people, who know not how to make a spinning-wheel, or to employ a loom to advantage?'[5] But although Hume was certainly an optimist, and did not share that view of human nature as fundamentally self-interested and self-seeking expounded by Mandeville, Thomas Hobbes and Puffendorf, his model was not altogether as simple-minded as it seems upon first reading. Far from being Utopian, it demonstrated how such a remarkable society could come about only if a whole series of subtly inter-related conditions obtained. For central to Hume's philosophical approach to cause and effect applied to human societies was his doctrine of united causes and his rejection of those philosophers of human nature, like Mandeville, who sought a simple underlying principle of motivation, such as self love, from which all other more generous and social passions were derived. Hume humorously invented a new 'philosophic' passion, the love of simplicity, to explain their false reasoning.[6]

His own argument was that humanity, benevolence to others, was not merely enlightened self-interest but a distinct innate passion – one, however, which might be *strengthened* by self-interest. Man has almost constant occasion for the help of his brethren and it is vain for him to expect it from their benevolence only; he will be more likely to prevail if he can interest their self love, their enjoyment of doing good and of being seen to do good, in his favour.[7] Accordingly Hume argued that, although a flourishing society might be motivated by its citizens' passion for the public good or their patriotism, such principles were 'too disinterested' and 'too difficult to support'. Men should be animated 'with a spirit of avarice and industry, art and luxury'.[8] He was not of course denying the existence or the effectiveness of public-spiritedness as a motivation, simply stating that, unless it was united with self-interest, it would be unlikely to have effect.

This reasoning was supported by another principle: that objects immediate in time or space had a greater effect on the imagination, and therefore upon the passions, than more remote ones. This explains Hume's view that governments would be well-modelled by those who knew how to make a spinning wheel and could employ a loom to advantage, for the flourishing of the mechanic arts led people to flock to cities and to towns not only for markets for one another's produce, as Barbon had argued, but to socialise as well, and hence they felt more humanity for their fellows because their sufferings were closer to hand. Thus benevolence, paired with self-interest, animated by immediate observation, would result in milder laws and better justice.[9]

But what makes Hume's model thoroughly non-Utopian is the way that it demonstrates by implication the would-be effects, in the real world, when such causes were *not* united.

This was especially apparent in two key chains of cause and effect: one concerning the motivation to work, the other concerning the growth of knowledge.

In his essay on the *Rise and Progress of the Arts and Sciences* of 1741 Hume argued that the arts and sciences could only arise in a free government – a republic – because only there was the rule of law to be found. He proceeded to argue that 'from law arises security: from security curiosity: and from curiosity knowledge'. Thus, 'Law must precede Science'.[10] This is so condensed a statement as to be thoroughly opaque, particularly in the causal connection that he made between security and curiosity, but the explanation is to be found in Hume's account of curiosity and love of truth in the *Treatise* of two years earlier. There, he deployed an analogy between the pursuit of truth and hunting, one of several ideas later adopted by Hogarth, as we shall see.

The pursuit of truth, Hume argued, was agreeable only insofar as the mind was exercised by the overcoming of difficulties. But that in itself was not a sufficient stimulus: the researcher also had to be convinced of the importance and utility of the truth he was seeking even if, like a hunter, his sense of its importance evaporated once the hunt was over. In a typical case of united causes, the dependence of curiosity upon security now becomes apparent: only if the law secures to the individual the fruits of his labours, his intellectual property and his self-interest, can curiosity be of any utility to him. Only under such conditions will he be motivated to pursue it.[11]

Thus, according to David Hume, only in a free republic governed by sound laws of intellectual and physical property, would the conditions obtain for the pursuit of knowledge, either for its own sake or for the benefit of manufacturing and commerce. This principle was also to be at the core of Adam Smith's theory.[12]

The motivation to work in general depended upon similar principles. And here Hume raised yet another issue, both moral and political, which was to preoccupy succeeding generations as the Industrial Revolution progressed: the necessity for the labourer to obtain some personal satisfaction, in addition to wages, from his work. Here was the problem of alienation and the motivation to work that so much concerned Marx and Ruskin, amongst others, in the nineteenth century. Human happiness, claimed Hume, had three ingredients: Action, Pleasure and Indolence. And, again, the effect of these depended on all three causes being united. Action in one's work gave pleasure but it was exhausting, so indolence, if it followed hard work, gave additional pleasure. Finally there was the pleasure of enjoying the fruits of one's labours: namely the conveniences and luxuries one could buy with one's wages, as well as indolence and recreation. If we now put these two chains or equations together we find that, if the causes are not united in the correct proportions, or if any are missing altogether, the whole system will collapse. So: if work itself were excessively monotonous, either the fruits of the worker's labour would have to be increased to compensate, or else he must have more leisure. If his work were excessively extended in time, as well as being monotonous, so that the worker had little leisure and little time to enjoy the fruits of his labour, then motivation would collapse for a different reason. If wages were very low, then only the threat of starvation and destitution would keep people working. In each case of imbalance, the members of the state would be unhappy and would only work from necessity. The fundamental cause of this must be some injustice in the *system of law*: namely a disregard for the property acquired directly through work.[13]

Hume examined the nature of this injustice, this inadequate framing of law, in another remarkable equation to be found in the previous essay, 'Of Commerce', where he observed that, in effect, an excessively unequal distribution of wealth weakened the state because it gave rise to social disharmony: 'Every person ought, if possible, to enjoy the fruits of his labour, in a full possession of all the necessaries, and many of the conveniencies of life.' When the rich engrossed the fruits of people's labour, when the poor were exploited, then the rich became still more powerful, could engross the power of the state and thereby shift the burden of taxation onto the poor and create laws to prevent the poor combining against the rich to raise their own wages.[14]

To sum up so far: if the state did not frame just laws concerning the right to private property and its distribution, curiosity, hence knowledge, hence the progress of the mechanic arts, would either not flourish at all or would flourish less.

This demonstrates the way in which the different parts of Hume's model concerned with individual motivation, happiness and national prosperity were inter-related. We are now in a better position to examine Hume's demonstration that a prosperous state whose individual members were indeed thoroughly motivated and happy as a result of their plentiful production of luxury goods would also, as a direct result, be highly cultivated, refined and artistic as well. In advancing this proposition Hume differed from both Mandeville and *The Spectator* writers, since the former argued that rapidly changing fashions, as distinct from static 'good taste', must prevail in a successful commercial society in order to stimulate demand, while the latter believed that taste must be *imposed* to moderate the excesses of luxury, for moral and religious reasons, even if the result were a lower consumption and hence less circulation of wealth. (Adam Smith took a more non-committal but probably equally pessimistic view of the tastefulness of the productions of a commercial society.) But Hume, an agnostic, did not share Addison's religious scruples, even though he may have shared Addison's account of human appetite. The problem, then, as Nicholas Phillipson has argued, was how to control appetite without resorting to abnegation and stoic virtue. Hume's solution was that luxury was far from vicious, it was beneficial, innocent even, and that tastefulness did not have to be imposed but would grow naturally in a commercial society. It was the productions of non-commercial societies that lacked all refinement. He stated this theme in the opening sentences of his 1752 essay 'Of Refinement in the Arts'. 'Luxury', he wrote, 'is a word of very uncertain signification, and may be taken in a good as well as in a bad sense. In general, it means great refinement in the gratification of the senses . . .'[15]

As so often Hume appears to set out as a premise or definition the very subject of dispute. Elsewhere he seems blithely to have assumed that whereas a wise framework of property laws was necessary to safeguard the conditions upon which the growth of political, economic and personal benefits depended, artistic achievements would develop of their own accord under the same conditions. (He did, however, have his doubts about this.) But to understand his reasoning we must look at another aspect of his model as a whole. It presupposed a group of small nation states like the City States of ancient Greece or late mediaeval Europe trading freely with one another and each enjoying an internal trade unrestricted by local tolls and customs. An empire would have been oppressive, while tariff barriers would inhibit the operation of the principles of natural law as expounded by the founder of modern international law, Hugo Grotius, in his *Mare Liberum*, (*Freedom of the Seas*) of 1608: 'it is not [God's] will to have Nature supply every place with all the necessaries of Life, He ordains that some nations excel in one art and others in another . . . [because] He wished human friendships to be engendered by mutual needs and resources.' Free international (or internal) trade was the means of righting the imbalance in the geographical distribution of commodities.[16]

In his essay 'The Balance of Trade' Hume echoed Grotius's formulation almost word for word. But a free trade between states did not merely correct the imbalance in the distribution of necessary commodities – wine from France to England, wool and cloth from England to France – it also brought into contact the peoples themselves, their manufactures and their culture, arousing first assimilation and then imitation and competition. Thus one country would import those manufactures of another which were more advanced than its own and, after a time, it would not only learn to make them itself but improve upon them, raising the standard of manufacturing and the mechanic arts everywhere.[17] And the same process, according to Hume, occurred in the liberal arts, the fine arts particularly. Adhering to the same experimental principle of cause and effect that he applied to the natural sciences and to the social sciences, he denied that there were any settled principles of taste, but equally denied that beauty was in the mind of the beholder, or that 'About taste there is no disputing'. On the contrary, repeated experiments conducted on the same works of art over many generations or between several countries would isolate those works which appealed not to the caprice of a particular time or a particular place but to 'the uniformity of sentiment among men'. So, likewise, the more critics from different cultures who had judged an artist to be great, the nearer that judgement would approach to a truth or a certainty. The corollary held also for the critic. The larger the sample of works of art from different periods and places that he had 'tasted' the nearer would his standard of taste approach to the truth.

The smaller a critic's sample, however, the more likely he was to be led astray: 'the coarsest daubing of a sign-post contains a certain lustre of colours and exactness of imitation, which are so far beauties, and would affect the mind of a peasant or Indian with the highest admiration.'[18] Thus it was that non-commercial societies, primitive societies whose members had not enjoyed commerce with other cultures, would not, according to Hume's reasoning, possess good taste or good artistic judgement, and this would apply both to the producer and the consumer. Hence the second proposition of the essay the 'Rise and Progress of the Arts and Sciences': 'That nothing is more favourable to the rise of politeness and learning than a number of neighbouring and independent states connected together by commerce and policy.'

The problem with such a theory is obvious: it equates excellence in the arts with cosmopolitan values, and rudeness with provincialism, but in Hume's own time this was a widely held point of view. More controversial to his peers was his contention that free trade, far from setting loose an insatiable greed and demand for exotic luxuries, polished the tastes of the nations involved and created a demand for, and hence a supply of articles of 'great refinement'. This was the justification of Hume's definition of luxury as *great refinement in the gratification of the senses*.

Besides, when importing nations learnt to manufacture the goods for themselves, this would further encourage the primary division of labour between agriculture and manufacture.[19] Agricultural productivity would thus improve and the state would be better able to meet the emergency of a war, since it would be self-sufficient in food, whilst the production of luxuries could be diverted to defence when the need arose. New social classes would emerge as a result of the division of labour and hence the stark divide between landowners and peasants would be remedied by the refined middle classes who would hold the balance and ensure the development of civil liberties.[20]

Such nations would be happy ones, because the desire to buy objects capable of gratifying the senses in a refined manner motivated everyone to work hard and live more elegantly. As a result of the growth of knowledge and the development of manufactures men and women 'flocked to cities' where their social intercourse promoted more refinement, criticism, taste, knowledge and humanity amongst cultivated consumers.[21]

All that was required to preserve this self-sustaining cycle of happy civilisation were good laws: good international law founded upon the natural principles of Grotius, that nations trade freely with one another and do not seek to conquer one another, good internal laws to guarantee the right to private property, the fruits of one's labours, and a just distribution of wealth and power.

36 Adam Smith by unknown painter. By emphasising saving and investment Smith solved the dilemma for puritans that their moralistic habits of consumption would reduce economic growth.

CHAPTER 6

Adam Smith

BEAUTY AND ECONOMIC GROWTH

David Hume represented the high point of Enlightenment optimism, offering a vision of society in which luxury, humanity and good taste; increasing wealth, morality and beauty; economics, ethics and aesthetics could be perfectly reconciled so long as certain conditions were met. In his view, aesthetic taste, far from putting a brake on growth, was a major force in economic advance as well as one of its fruits.

In the mature economic theory of Adam Smith (Plate 36), although he warmly acknowledged Hume as his mentor, neither the taste for beauty nor personal consumption itself are presented as being so important to the growth of wealth. This of course does not mean that Adam Smith dismissed art or the pursuit of beauty out of hand. *The Wealth of Nations*, his most influential book, published in 1776, does not, I believe, represent the exclusively 'economicist' view of the world for which it has often been condemned. Smith was not insisting that every course of action must be decided purely on the basis of its economic benefits. On the contrary, as Hont and Ignatieff have argued so persuasively, Smith was not preoccupied with riches to the exclusion of social justice but it was a central aim of his project to show that although 'modern commercial society was unequal . . . it was not unjust. It did not purchase civic virtue at the price of misery for its poorest members.' However *The Wealth of Nations* did establish, as far as was possible, what the purely economic criteria were and distinguished them clearly from other social aims and objectives.

Smith was realistic about the fact that these other aims and objectives were sometimes, though not invariably, in conflict with economic advantage. The most famous case of such a conflict (or externality, as modern economists would call it) described by Smith was the soul-destroying work resulting from the division of labour – which was at odds with Hume's criterion that the pleasure of work must be a major motivating factor in human industry. These conflicts between competing benefits and motivations give rise to apparent contradictions within Smith's work – the 'Adam Smith problem' as it has come to be known.

By distinguishing such conflicts logically, and honestly admitting their existence, Smith gave policy makers a basis upon which to alleviate, avoid, resolve or otherwise compensate for them.

Nonetheless a highly simplistic version of Adam Smith's attitudes to beauty and the fine arts (which were certainly complex if not ambivalent, as we shall see) has come to prevail. Both by later economists and those politicians who have sat at their feet, the arts are now customarily perceived as a drain upon the wealth of nations: 'toys and baubles', frivolous things, barely tolerated as objects of either private indulgence or public expenditure. Adam Smith himself was not directly to blame for this.

It should be said that it was only gradually that Smith moved away from the accepted view that consumption and hence taste were central to economic growth. In his earlier writings, which we shall examine first, he shared this assumption.

121

Born in 1723, Smith, like Hume, was a Scot, but unlike Hume he became Professor of Moral Philosophy at Glasgow in 1752. In his first major publication, *The Theory of Moral Sentiments* of 1759, the importance of 'taste' was emphasised by his devoting the whole of Part IV to the subject. The desire for aesthetic pleasure, Smith proposed, actually initiated the passion for acquiring riches and, as a consequence, set in motion the process of economic growth. He set special store by his own elaborate variant of this idea both for its originality and because it formed a link between ethics, which was the subject of that book, and political economy that was to the subject of his next.[1]

His theory was in three parts: first of all he gave a description of the psychological satisfactions arising from beauty; then an account of how the desire for beautiful things motivated individuals to acquire wealth; finally an analysis of the wider effects of the individual pursuit of riches on society.

Some would say that Smith defined beauty narrowly, as virtually identical with fitness for use, or utility. Certainly, he acknowledged his debt to David Hume's idea that the pleasure of looking at a beautiful object, something fit and trim like the symmetrical facade of a building, arose from one's being reminded of the pleasure to be had from using it: 'every time he looks at it, he is put in mind of this pleasure; and the object in this manner becomes a source of perpetual satisfaction and enjoyment'.[2] Someone who does not own the object can nonetheless enjoy its beauty by sympathy with the feelings which its owner enjoys. If, however, the pleasure of beauty arises from the satisfaction of contemplating an object's *potential* practical benefits, Adam Smith's refinement upon Hume's theory was to deny that this pleasure depended upon any *real* practical usefulness, or even any promise of it. It was often the case, he argued, that the fitness of an object in and for itself came to be valued more than its practical usefulness. He cited the example of people who made a fetish about the accuracy of a watch. 'A watch . . . that falls behind above two minutes in a day, is despised by one curious in watches. He sells it perhaps for a couple of guineas, and purchases another at fifty, which will not lose above a minute in a fortnight.' Yet the only real use of watches, Smith wryly observed, was to ensure our punctuality, and this connoisseur of accurate watches 'will not always be found either more scrupulously punctual than other men or more anxiously concerned upon any other account, to know precisely what time of day it is. What interests him is not so much the attainment of this piece of knowledge, as the perfection of his machine which serves to attain it.'

There follows a wonderfully wry and scornful account of the contemporary collector of mechanical automata, which merits quoting in full. It applies to the lovers of gadgets and articles of 'frivolous utility' of all ages. It is also a kind of allegory of modern consumption once the need for the necessities of life has been satisfied.

> How many people ruin themselves by laying out money on trinkets of frivolous utility? What pleases these lovers of toys is not so much the utility, as the aptness of the machines which are fitted to promote it. All their pockets are stuffed with little conveniencies. They contrive new pockets, unknown in the clothes of other people, in order to carry a greater number. They walk about loaded with a multitude of baubles, in weight and sometimes in value not inferior to an ordinary Jew's-box, some of which may sometimes be of some little use, but all of which might at all times be very well spared, and of which the whole utility is certainly not worth the fatigue of bearing the burden.[3]

This wonderful vignette completes Adam Smith's account of the ways in which beautiful things – by his definition, objects of apparent utility – satisfied the mind. His next step was to generalise from this to an explanation of the ambition for acquiring riches: that favourite topic of the period, 'The Pursuit of Riches'. Smith told a parable of the poor man's son whom heaven in its anger had 'visited with ambition'.[4] This unfortunate soul was fired with the desire to possess not mere clockwork machines, but 'the palaces, the gardens, the equipage, the retinue of the great'. As operating social systems, these possessed the same mechanical perfection, desirable in and for itself, as mechanical toys and, in the final reckoning, were also mere trinkets of frivolous utility, only bigger. Enchanted by his idea of the ease and happiness that the ownership of such property would bestow upon him, the young man devoted himself to the pursuit of wealth to pay for them. As a result he submitted 'in his first year, nay in the first month of his application, to more fatigue of body and more uneasiness of mind than he could have suffered through the whole of his life from the want of them.' Throughout his life the mirage of 'artificial and elegant repose' keeps him going till, rich at long last, though 'wasted with toil and diseases', he finds out that 'power and riches appear to be, what they are, enormous and operose machines contrived to produce a few trifling conveniences to the body . . . immense fabrics which it requires the labour of a life to raise, which threaten every moment to overwhelm the person that dwells in them'. Like the toys they were 'not worth the fatigue of bearing the burden', the only difference being that palaces were bigger and thus better adapted than mechanical toys to serve as status symbols. In short, Adam Smith argued that the real pleasures arising from the possessions of the super-rich, looked at in isolation from their beauty, were always 'contemptible and trifling', but that their beauty deceived people into rating them as 'grand and beautiful and noble', and hence a fit object for ambition.

Beauty then was a snare and a delusion, but as the motivation for great ambitions it possessed considerable social utility, since as Smith explained, 'It is this deception which raises and keeps in continual motion the industry of mankind' and effects all the increase in the wealth of mankind and the improvements in the means of creating that wealth. It was as well that man was not a natural stoic who could see through the superficial glitter of trinkets and baubles, for this lure was the source of much good.

This formed the last section of Adam Smith's explanation of the utility of beauty. The rich man's expenditure, his consumption of luxuries great and small, his troops of servants, helped to redistribute his wealth and the produce of his improvements to thousands of unpropertied poor people employed by him directly or indirectly. This, of course, was by now a commonplace theory, but it occasioned Smith's invention of the term the 'invisible hand', by means of which 'the proud and unfeeling landlord' was led to make 'nearly the same distribution of the necessaries of life, which would have been made, had the earth been divided into equal portions among all its inhabitants'. Or, as Alexander Pope had expressed it: 'what his hard heart denies his charitable vanity supplies'.

Three or four years after the publication of the *Theory of Moral Sentiments*, in some lectures on economics of 1762/3 for which a student's notes survive, Smith still appeared to be experimenting with the importance of beauty in economic and social life. By that time however he had revised his reductivist and utilitarian definition of beauty. He now defined the 'taste of beauty' as consisting of three qualities − 'proper variety, easy connection, and simple order' − as well as the pleasures of imitation, rarity and novelty to be found in gems and other exotic objects.[5] Possibly, in the intervening time, Smith had read Hogarth's *Analysis of Beauty* (1753), since variety, simplicity and composition were, as we shall later see, central to Hogarth's conception of beauty. But even if Smith had not read Hogarth he must have read Alexander Gerard's *Essay on Taste* and Gerard was heavily influenced by Hogarth.[6] Smith was a member of the Select Society of Edinburgh, founded in the 1750s for the same purpose as the Society of Arts of London, later the Royal Society of Arts: to encourage the arts and sciences by the award of premiums for the best manufactured goods and pattern designs. And, in line with the contemporary interest in the economic signifi-cance of beauty, the Select Society offered a gold medal for the best essay on taste, which was awarded in 1756 to Alexander Gerard, Professor of Philosophy at Aberdeen. Gerard's theory depended very heavily upon Hogarth, particularly in distinguishing the beauty of fitness (upon which Adam Smith's ideas in the *Theory of Moral Sentiments* had exclusively depended) from the beauty of form, which Gerard defined in terms of 'uniformity, variety and proportion' – terms which correspond closely to Adam Smith's 'proper variety, easy connection, and simple order'. It was this non-utilitarian taste for beauty which Adam Smith adduced in 1762/3 in the section entitled 'Of the Natural Wants of Mankind', dealing with the causes of economic growth.

Here he proposed that the 'taste for beauty' served two immensely important purposes:[7] first, as a major characteristic of human nature by which man was distinguished from other animals; second, as the distinctive feature of the human mind which gave rise to economic growth. Human beings differed from other animals in their natural wants. All animals including humans wanted food, covering and shelter, but whereas other animals were satisfied with what nature provided, man was not. 'Such is the delicacy of man alone, that no object is produced to his liking.' Everything was in 'need of improvement'. It was therefore a distinctively human necessity to cook, make clothes and (though Smith did not mention it specifically on this occasion) build and furnish houses. This dissatisfaction with raw nature, this implanted desire to *improve* raw materials before they are thought to be useful even as necessities, can be seen to correspond with that obsessive concern for utility as an end in itself discussed in *The Theory of Moral Sentiments*. It also corresponded in certain ways with 'the uniform, constant and uninterrupted effort of every man *to better his condition* . . . powerful enough to maintain the natural progress of things towards improvement' which was to be the motive force of the economy in *The Wealth of Nations*.[8]

But over and above the utilitarian need of human beings to satisfy the wants occasioned by the physical delicacy of their bodies, Adam Smith argued that the 'much greater delicacy' of the human mind, compared to other animals, was the cause of even greater wants. The essence of this delicacy of the human mind was a dissatisfaction with or distaste for ugliness, and a corresponding 'taste for beauty', associated with the desire to improve the form of things. This taste did not operate independently from the functional and materialistic desire for what we might call 'improved necessities' but in conjunction with it. People's wants, therefore, were for the natural commodities of food, clothing and shelter improved in practical ways to satisfy their physical requirements and fashioned to appeal to their taste. In Smith's own words: 'The whole industry of human life is employed not in procuring the supply of our three humble necessities, food, clothes and lodging, but in procuring *the conveniences of it according to the nicety and delicacy of our taste*. To improve and multiply the materials, which are the principal objects of our necessities, gives occasion to all the variety of the arts.'[9]

At this point in the development of his ideas, Smith was following Hume in arguing that the taste for luxury was not something vicious and debased but was identical to a taste for beauty and refinement. He took the argument one step further, however, in suggesting not only that luxury was identical to the taste for refinements in form, to the taste for beauty, but that this was inherent in human nature, whereas Hume gave emphasis to increasing refinement arising more from the social process of increased intercourse and competition between different cultures.

In two respects, this account was unlike the analysis of mankind's desire for goods advanced in the earlier *Theory of Moral Sentiments*.[10] First, as we have already observed, Adam Smith did not on this occasion reduce the beauty of things to 'one of its principle sources', utility or fitness, but distinguished between the desire for things that were functionally fit and the desire for things that were beautiful in form even when they were to be found in the same object. Second, he did not argue this time that the addition of beauty, however defined, to the objects of human desire was merely a cosmetic deception concealing the real value of consumer goods, whose real satisfactions were 'contemptible or trifling', in order to make us all work harder. In the 1762/3 Lectures, physical beauty and practicality were presented as 'real' rather than imaginary or apparent qualities, and the object of equally real satisfactions, giving rise to consumer demands which, in turn, gave rise to the practical arts and sciences, good government and law. The optimistic tone of the following passage describing this chain of consequences is very similar to David Hume's, apart from the characteristic reference to inequality of fortune. Adam Smith's usual love of paradox is almost entirely absent:

> Agriculture, of which the principal object is the supply of food, introduces not only the tilling of the ground, but also the planting of trees, the producing of flax, hemp, and innumerable other things of s similar kind. By these again are introduced different manufactures, which are so very capable of improvement. The metals dug from the bowels of the earth furnish materials for tools, by which many of these arts are practised. Commerce and navigation are also subservient to the same purposes by collecting the produce of these several arts. By these again other subsidiary [arts] are occasioned. Writing, to record the multitude of transactions, and geometry, which serves many useful purposes. Law and government, too, seem to propose no other object but this; they secure the individual who has enlarged his property, that he may peaceably enjoy the fruits of it. By law and government all the different arts flourish, and that inequality of fortune to which they give occasion is sufficiently preserved. By law and government domestic peace is enjoyed and security from the foreign invader. Wisdom and virtue too derive their lustre from supplying these necessities. For as the establishment of law and government is the highest effort of human prudence and wisdom, the causes cannot have a different influence from what the effects have.[11]

The lecture subsequently gives an account of how the division of labour and other improvements in manufacturing were the mechanisms by which the wealth of nations increased; an account which reappeared changed only in wording in the famous three opening chapters of *The Wealth of Nations*. But the section on the 'Natural Wants of Mankind' and the crucial role of the taste for beauty in creating and enlarging those wants – a section which in 1762–3 actually preceded those on the division of labour – was altogether omitted in 1776. In those thirteen years, during which Adam Smith perfected the construction of his economic model, the specific character of mankind's wants almost ceased to matter to him from an economic point of view. And because *The Wealth of Nations* had so overwhelming an influence in determining the major issues in political economy as it subsequently developed, the 'taste for beauty' never again figured as a subject in mainstream economic analysis. Beauty came to be seen 'hors de commerce', outside economic theory and policy-making, often indeed antagonistic to them, an 'externality'.

It is true that in *The Wealth of Nations* immediate consumption remained 'the sole end and purpose' of Adam Smith's economic system, 'To maintain and augment the stock which may be reserved for immediate consumption is the sole end and purpose both of the fixed and circulating capitals. It is this stock which feeds, clothes and lodges the people.'[12] Thus, in the history of mankind, once agricultural improvements had progressed so far that the work of one family could provide food for two, because 'the desire of food is limited in every man by the narrow capacity of the human stomach', the work of the other families would be employed in 'satisfying the other wants and fancies of mankind', principle amongst which were '*the conveniences and ornaments of* building, dress, equipage and household furniture'.[13]

The desire for these things, not being circumscribed by the size of the stomach, 'seems to have no limit or certain boundary . . . to be altogether endless'. It could therefore be the *basis* of an unlimited growth in human needs, hence in economic demand, and hence in the wealth of mankind.

But while Adam Smith, and certain of his successors, argued that demand for such goods would go on growing, they certainly did not assume that the demand must be for *beautiful* things, nor for any particular quality or description of things, but simply for convenient and ornamental things. More important, consumption itself – whether of the beautiful, the ugly, the useful or the frivolous, whether caused by a belief in hospitality, the desire for beauty or competitive consumption – did not have the same importance within Adam Smith's mature economic system as it had had within every system of theory and of policy since the Elizabethan period. Consumption for Smith may have been the basis of unlimited growth, but it was not its cause. Indeed, Adam Smith's most revolutionary break with the pre-existing economic tradition, and perhaps his greatest discovery – greater by far than laissez-faire – was that personal consumption, or expense as he called it, which put circulating capital into motion, did *not* cause a growth economy; it would only, perhaps, keep an economy ticking over in the unfavourable conditions of considerable unemployment and low real wages for labourers. If immediate consumption was, quite obviously, a necessary it was not a sufficient condition for a prospering economy.

To define the nature of those sufficient conditions was the aim of Smith's investigations: consumption and circulating capital were moved from their traditional position centre stage and replaced by the factors which Smith believed to be responsible for creating continuously growing wealth: saving, and the investment of savings in improvements to the manufac-turing process. Smith was not indifferent to consumers; he did not favour producers above them, nor the process of production; nevertheless his attention was turned from consumption and circulating capital to saving and fixed capital.

Adam Smith's account, or model, of the wealth-producing and wealth-augmenting machinery of society has been examined many times before, but the expert in the history of economic thought must forgive my doing so again. It is necessary in order to bring to the fore the place occupied within it by taste, beauty, design and the arts, in addition to associated matters, such as the alienation of labour within the structure of classical economics. These aspects of Adam Smith's work are almost entirely neglected in the scholarly literature, and this makes it difficult to discuss Ruskin's objections to the legacy of Smith's ideas in the nineteenth century. But, before embarking upon this examination, the character of Adam Smith's model, as distinct from its content, needs to be defined, for at first sight it appears to be highly systematic, with the chain of causes and effects established more in accordance with the laws of physics or astronomy than human affairs; it seems to lack those provisional and empirical qualities Hume's system so notably possessed.

THE LIMITATIONS OF ECONOMIC SYSTEMS

There is no doubting that one of the most original features of *The Wealth of Nations* was the enormous scope of the system, within which more aspects of economic life were incorporated than had ever been accomplished before. This, rather than the complete originality of his ideas on division of labour, or freedom of trade, for instance, was the mark of Adam Smith's astounding genius. 'The Wealth of Nations* put all earlier treatises of political economy in the shade because it was so comprehensively systematic, not because it blew the trumpet of free trade. It became the standard model to be studied, tested, revised and improved.' One of the editors of the bicentennial edition of Adam Smith's works has described it as 'a comprehensive system of the whole economic process, all parts of which interact with each other so as to maintain a self-adjusting balance and steady growth.' It is this character that makes *The Wealth of Nations* such a pleasure to read, even for those who are not professional economists.[14]

However, it is still more remarkable in such a systematic thinker that he should have been so aware of the pitfalls and limitations of systems themselves. In *The Theory of Moral Sentiments* written shortly before embarking upon the construction of his own great economic system he made the following observation on the vanity of the inventor or the reformer of systems of government: 'The man . . . of system is apt to be very wise in his own conceit; and is often so enamoured with the supposed beauty of his own ideal plan of government that he cannot suffer the smallest deviation from any part of it . . . He seems to imagine that he can arrange the different members of a great society with as much ease as the hand arranges the different pieces upon a chess board.'[15] He contrasted such a mentality, which he saw as containing the poison of absolute tyranny, when it was put into practice, with 'the man whose public spirit is prompted altogether by humanity and benevolence . . . [who] like Solon, when he cannot establish the best system of laws, he will endeavour to establish the best that the people can bear'. Although Adam Smith was clear in his own mind about the value of systematic thought in explaining society, he still understood that a system was 'necessarily simplified' and was not, therefore, an infallible guide to action. 'Some general, and even systematical, idea of the perfection of policy and law, may no doubt be necessary for directing the views of the statesman. But to insist upon establishing all at once, and in spite of opposition, every thing which that idea may seem to require, must often be the highest degree of arrogance.'

He took account of his own warnings. For example, in the case so close to his own heart, that of re-establishing free trade in foreign goods after a period of protective import controls or prohibitions, Adam Smith warned that in order to prevent widespread unemployment in those domestic industries which had grown up under protection 'Humanity may in this case require that the freedom of trade should be restored only by slow gradations, and with a good deal of reserve and circumspection.'[16] This is a general point which free-market advisers to the Russian government in the 1990s would have done well to have borne in mind!

But Smith had in mind more than a warning against the precipitate implementation of policies, he was also enjoining us to regard his own systematic model of a *perfect* system for nations to acquire wealth as something which could never be put into practice unmodified, as something not even attainable in the best of all possible worlds. Like Plato's *Republic* his great model was an ideal towards which to aspire and primarily a tool of analysis; it enabled governments to pinpoint some of the obstacles to economic growth in their society and, in attempting to make their economy more productive, to remove those obstacles which were the most obstructive. He was well aware of the rash rationality of the inveterate reformer or innovator.

In addition he was perfectly aware that some so-called 'obstacles' to increasing wealth had real value in human, moral, or even aesthetic terms: that there could be a real conflict between trying to increase wealth and achieving other benefits. Unlike Hume, therefore, he did not assume that a richer society was *necessarily* a better and more civilised one. The poor man's son of his fable, for example, was alienated from the fruits of his labours, his palaces of 'frivolous utility', quite as much as a labourer could be alienated from work itself by its extreme monotony. Also, in Adam Smith's opinion, the great and generous landlord who spent his fortune on bounty and hospitality did not contribute to economic growth at all, whereas he who spent it on luxury goods 'of frivolous utility' did – although Smith fully recognised that the bountiful landlord possessed the virtue of a generous spirit whereas the other often displayed 'not only a trifling, but a base and selfish disposition'.[17]

These harmful side effects or externalities of growth are often seen as extreme limitations of Adam Smith's vision. A recent writer accuses him of 'profound pessimism' because his system appears to terminate not in universal wealth and happiness but in economic stagnation, poverty and unemployment for the labouring classes and in the most degrading conditions of work resulting from the division of labour.[18] But seen in the light of Smith's warnings about the dangers of an excessively systematic approach, his drawing attention to these undesirable side effects was not a sign of his pessimism but of his realism: there was no perfect system that produced benefits in every aspect of life and consequently really difficult political choices were unavoidable. Public expenditure on education, for instance, which he advocated as a remedy for the corrupting effects of division of labour in the common people, must increase taxation and reduce the revenue which contributed to economic growth through the employment of productive labourers and investment.[19]

The immediate occasion for these paradoxes in Smith's model was probably an attempt to explore the problems and conflicts implicit in the political calculus of Hume's model. What would happen to the sum of human happiness if labourers did not derive pleasure from the performance of their work? Would the pleasure deriving from the enlarged fruits of their labour, the increased quantity of goods they could buy, be enough to compensate? But Smith and Hume, like the *Spectator* writers, were also responding to the challenge of Bernard de Mandeville's simplistic idea that wealth could only be attained at the cost of moral virtue: 'Private Vices, Publick Benefits'. Addison, the most morally committed, tried to identify certain morally innocent luxuries like gardening and the reading of improving literature upon which people could spend money; Hume argued that all luxury was almost inevitably civilised, civilising, refined and largely innocent. Both tended to accept, however, the premise common to every writer on economics back to the Tudor period: that high spending and circulating capital were essential to prosperity. Adam Smith, as we shall see, by questioning this premise opened the way to showing, even if he did not pursue the argument himself, that increasing prosperity could be reconciled with a concern for beauty and morality, even though it by no means gave rise to them.

With these reservations in mind we must turn at last to the system itself. There are three components to Adam Smith's explanation of continuous economic growth. The first dealt with the system of production and showed how improvements in manufacturing led to real improvements in the qualitative standard of living of all members of society, measured by the increased quantity and diversity of the household possessions they could acquire. In this section Smith demonstrated the beneficial effect of division of labour. The second section dealt with saving and consumption and showed how improvements in manufacturing could be paid for only if part of people's total income, instead of being spent on immediate consumption, were saved, and spent upon improved transport, machinery, or the organisation of labour – what we call capital investment. From the point of view of the fine arts and design this is the most important section, since it was here that Adam Smith introduced the crucial distinction between productive and unproductive labour and discussed the contribution of expenditure on the arts to economic growth. Finally these systematic and rather abstract models or explanations of production, consumption and saving were combined and applied in an historical account showing how a dynamic commercial society of free and independent labourers, based upon frugality and high investment, had emerged from the static agricultural society ruled by the aristocrats and great landlords who showered profuse bounty and hospitality upon teams of subservient serfs and unproductive flunkies. It is this section, violently attacking the landed aristocracy, which has been the primary source for the highly prejudiced historical account of aristocratic extravagance – a major obstacle, as we have seen, to our own historical understanding of the policy initiated by Lord Burghley.

IMPROVEMENTS IN PRODUCTION

Division of Labour etc.

According to Adam Smith the wealth of a nation did not consist simply of its total annual production. The true measure of a nation's wealth was the average share enjoyed by each member. In modern jargon, national wealth was to be measured by real income per head, not by gross national product. He also included a nation's accumulated stock of buildings, plant and goods.

The magnitude of a nation's real wealth therefore was determined both by the productivity and efficiency of the work-force and by the size of the population. If the population grew too fast fewer goods would be available to each and real wealth must drop – the Malthusian effect. The problems which arise when population growth exceeds the growth of production are not germane to the present discussion; however, I do not take the view that Adam Smith shared the theory of Thomas Malthus and David Ricardo that, according to the iron law of wages, the worker must always remain poor because the population increase always keeps pace with the increase in production. Smith stated that the potential for economic growth, on his own definition, was unlimited. And Malthus had no doubt that his own theory was quite original and had not been adumbrated by Smith; indeed Malthus was refuting Smith's optimism about growth. The only serious obstacles to unlimited growth identified by Adam Smith himself were institutional - bad laws and constitutions, which *The Wealth of Nations* was written to reform.[20]

Putting that to one side, the factor with which we shall be most concerned in Adam Smith's theory of how wealth can be increased, is the improvement in the productiveness or productivity of labour, the amount of goods that each worker can produce, his or her efficiency. In the first book of *The Wealth of Nations* Smith investigated the 'Causes of Improvement in the Productive Powers of Labour'. These are not difficult to grasp. If a worker takes less time to finish a job more work can be done and more goods produced. Adam Smith believed that the key to such improvements in efficiency was the division of labour: the specialisation of a worker upon a single, often very small step in the total process. The smaller and simpler each step, the more rapidly it could be performed and the more goods that could be turned out.

But a prior condition for even the simplest division of labour was the size of the local market. Only a large market could support specialist workers. An example was the porter, whose work was too specialised even for a market town, which could not provide him with sufficient work to keep him permanently employed. Likewise, in a country town a carpenter would also have to be a joiner, cabinet-maker, woodcarver, wheelwright, ploughwright, cart and waggon maker. The size of the market, however, was not determined simply by the local population but by the speed and ease of communications. Thus proximity to the sea, a navigable river or a canal would create a large market out of a number of settlements. Stamford, as we have seen, was a town whose economic problems had been solved within Adam Smith's lifetime by the building of a navigable canal and this problem was also discussed by *The Spectator* writers.[21]

Improvements in transport, however, were expensive, so the size of markets could only be extended through the investment of capital, which only became available when the commercial process had begun.

Adam Smith's famous example of division of labour was pin making. An individual pin maker, who personally performed each of the eighteen operations into which pin making was divided, could make perhaps a maximum of twenty pins a day. But in a manufactory where each operation was exercised by a skilled specialist he or she could turn out the equivalent of 4,800 pins a day. The simpler the operation the greater the dexterity, and the less time wasted in passing from one operation to the next. Labour-saving machines, which could be invented only when their minute operations had been identified through the division of manual labour, increased productiveness still further.[22]

As a result things cost less and could be produced in greater quantity. If the population remained the same, wealth per head must grow. Thus each individual could afford to buy more goods with the same wages and a wider range of goods became accessible to the poor. A watch that had cost £20 a century earlier now cost 20 shillings. But within a flourishing economy, or the 'progressive state' as Adam Smith called it, the wages of the poor did not remain the same, they actually rose in money terms in response to the greater demand for labour.[23]

In an extended and justly famous passage already quoted Adam Smith described the benefits not to the rich but to the 'most common artificer or day-labourer in a civilised and thriving country'. Smith made no bones about his belief that the possession of an increased quantity and variety of material possessions must add to the total happiness of a society.

Is this improvement in the circumstances of the lower ranks of the people to be regarded as an advantage or as an inconveniency to the society? The answer seems at first sight abundantly plain. Servants, labourers, and workmen of different kinds, make up the far greater part of every great political society. But what improves the circumstances of the greater part can never be regarded as an inconveniency to the whole. No society can surely be flourishing and happy, of which the far greater part of the members are poor and miserable. It is but equity, besides, that they who feed, clothe, and lodge the whole body of the people, should have such a share of the produce of their own labour as to be themselves tolerably well fed, clothed, and lodged.[24]

To sum up: a society could become increasingly wealthy through improvements in manufacturing brought about by the division of labour and the replacement of workers by machines. And not only would the lower ranks become richer, they would also be made happier by being 'tolerably well fed, clothed and lodged'.

Saving

Such improvements, however, cost money over and above the circulating capital for wages, raw materials and profit. Where was this money to come from? The answer to this question was given in the second book, 'Of the Nature, Accumulation and Employment of Stock', often regarded as his most original contribution to economic thought and the feature which most clearly differentiated him from his free-trade predecessors such as Barbon.

Once again the idea was very simple. The money to pay for improvements must be saved from manufacturers' profits, or from anyone's savings, if these were lent to manufacturers.

Simple as it seems in retrospect, it marks a major reversal of perhaps the most fundamental principle of earlier economic theory, which stressed the importance of liberality, even extravagance in expenditure, whether via country house hospitality or rip-roaring, free-for-all acquisitiveness. Contradicting this long held principle, Adam Smith, in an extended paeon of praise to the virtues of frugality (and probably overstating the case to make his point) proclaimed that 'every prodigal appears to be a public enemy, and every frugal man a public benefactor'.[25] The increasing wealth of nations depended upon the division of labour which depended upon the increase in capital. 'Parsimony, and not industry, is the immediate cause of the increase of capital.' Parsimony, and not great personal expenditure, was the key to ever-increasing wealth.

That is the whole idea in a nutshell, except for the crucially important rider that parsimony must never be an end in itself, the money saved must not be hoarded, because hoarding would cause unemployment. Savings should either be invested personally or lent to a manufacturer to invest. Moreover they had to be wisely invested since 'the effects of misconduct', of an injudicious and unsuccessful project were 'often the same as those of prodigality' in that the capital would be diminished by failure or bankruptcy. So 'parsimony' was really a bit of a misnomer, since, as Adam Smith was at pains to explain, 'what is annually saved is as regularly consumed as what is annually spent . . . but it is consumed by a different set of people': in other words, not by 'idle guests and menial servants' but by productive industrial workers.[26]

The frugal man, Smith continued, was not a miser nor a miserable man; the effect of his actions was more generous than 'the founder of a public workhouse, he establishes as it were a *perpetual* fund for the maintenance of an equal number in all times to come'. Moreover this employment fund, unlike the old kind of charitable endowment, needed no 'trust right or deed of mortmain' to ensure its perpetuation; that would be guarded by the interest of its owner in maintaining his income.

Saving and Human Nature

So much, then, for the simple principle which deals with the crude distinction between spending and saving, between prodigality and frugality. We shall shortly examine Adam Smith's refinements upon that hackneyed pair of opposites but, before doing so, we must look at the way that he extracted the fundamental premise of this system, which rooted it in the principles of nature – both external and human. In contrast to the frugal man whose parsimony endowed him, albeit unwittingly, with the virtues of a public benefactor, Adam Smith likened the prodigal to the embezzler of a charity. A prodigal beggared not only himself but the whole nation by diminishing its capital. Smith argued that 'the principle which prompts to expense is the passion for present enjoyment', momentary, violent and unrestrainable. This corresponded to the appetites and passions which Mandeville regarded as fundamental to economic activity, and it also corresponded to David Hume's character-isation of the Epicurean 'idea of human life and happiness':[27] one in which youthful voluptuaries, satiated by the soft seductions of love and every assorted pleasure, find justification in the melancholy awareness of the transitory nature of human life alleviated only by the certainty of sensuous pleasure.

Frugality on the other hand, Smith argued, was prompted by a *fundamental* principle of human nature: the desire to better our condition, a desire which, 'though generally calm and dispassionate, comes with us from the womb, and never leaves us till we go into the grave. In the whole interval which separates those two moments, there is scarce perhaps a single instant in which any man is so perfectly and completely satisfied with his situation as to be without any wish of alteration or improvement of any kind. An augmentation of fortune is the means by which the greater part of men propose and wish to better their condition. It is the means the most vulgar and the most obvious; and the most likely way of augmenting their fortune is to save and accumulate some part of what they acquire, either regularly and annually, or upon some extraordinary occasions.'[28]

This clearly corresponds to the Stoic's outlook: 'the primary influence upon Adam Smith's ethical thought' according to the editors of the Glasgow edition of his works. But here too Smith seems to have been building upon Hume's ideas.[29] For Hume's essay on 'The Stoic', paired as it was with his essay on 'The Epicurean', presented the Stoic approach to life as industry, in contrast to Epicurean pleasure-seeking idleness, as life steered by skill, reflection and intelligence rather than 'by the blind guidance of appetite and instinct'. Where Hume, however, had emphasised the *pleasures* of a laborious existence, by his analogy with hunting, as opposed to the insipid and transitory joys of epicurean luxury, Smith gave far more emphasis to the desire for bettering one's condition. He believed this principle to be so very powerful that not even the errors of government and law, which he held primarily responsible for the failure of nations to grow more opulent, could halt it in its path.

The uniform, constant, and uninterrupted effort of every man to better his condition, the principle from which public and national, as well as private opulence is originally derived, is frequently powerful enough to maintain the natural progress of things toward improvement, in spite both of the extravagance of government and of the greatest errors of administration. Like the unknown principle of animal life, it frequently restores health and vigour to the constitution, in spite, not only of the disease, but of the absurd prescriptions of the doctor.[30]

And he returned again in Book IV to this train of thought in his observations on the contemporary French economist Quesnai who, Smith claimed,

> seems not to have considered that, in the political body, the natural effort which every man is continually making to better his own condition is a principle of preservation capable of preventing and correcting in many respects the bad effects of a political economy, in some degree, both partial and oppressive. Such a political economy, though it no doubt retards more or less, is not always capable of stopping altogether the natural progress of a nation towards wealth and prosperity, and still less of making it go backwards. If a nation could not prosper without the enjoyment of perfect liberty and perfect justice, there is not in the world a nation which could ever have prospered.[31]

Elsewhere, in talking about agriculture, Adam Smith identified the principle of economic growth in external nature as well as in human nature:

> No equal capital puts into motion a greater quantity of productive labour than that of the farmer. Not only his labouring servants but his labouring cattle, are productive labourers. In agriculture too, nature labours along with man . . . The most important operations of agriculture seem intended not so much to increase . . . as to direct the fertility of nature towards the production of the plants most profitable to man.[32]

Nonetheless man was not exclusively a stoic for if he were he would be immune to the lure of trinkets and baubles, to the pursuit of riches and hence the whole wealth-creating system would be inoperative. Man was also epicurean. However Smith seems to have been claiming that the stoical desire for self-improvement predominated over the epicurean passion for present enjoyment.

Here we are looking at the very heart of Adam Smith's system of economics: the fundamental motivation which caused man to save some of his revenue, and to put those savings towards improving the means of production, was a kind of life force, the same as that which made nature so fertile; it was an unremitting, virtually involuntary desire to improve things, arising from a perpetual dissatisfaction with things as they were. Looking back, now, at his position in *The Theory of Moral Sentiments* and in the 1762/3 Lectures we see how he had succeeded, by the completion of *The Wealth of Nations*, in generalising upon the motive forces which he had formerly identified as responsible for economic growth: in *The Theory of Moral Sentiments* it was the poor man's son's dissatisfaction with his lot when he contemplated the frivolous utility or beauty of the possessions of the very rich; in the 1762/3 Lectures it was the human being's dissatisfaction with nature unimproved both from a utilitarian point of view and his aesthetic distaste for ugliness and his taste for beauty. Now these early ideas were subsumed in a far more general and by no means specifically aesthetic or economic desire to better oneself *in every possible way*. The reason why this desire was so influential in the economy was simply that 'the most vulgar and the most obvious' means, as Smith put it somewhat contemptuously, by which the majority of people envisaged bettering their lot was by becoming richer and the best means they knew was to save.[33]

But it was not the *only* way of improving oneself – one could try to become wiser, or more elegant, or better behaved. 'To deserve, to acquire, and to enjoy the respect and admiration of mankind, are the great objects of ambition and emulation. Two different roads are presented to us, equally leading to the attainment of this so much desired object; the one, by the study of wisdom and the practice of virtue; the other, by the acquisition of wealth and greatness.' Adam Smith, academic to the last, was in no doubt about which form of self-improvement he most admired: 'They are the wise and the virtuous chiefly, a select, though, I am afraid, but a small party, who are the real and steady admirers of wisdom and virtue. The great mob of mankind are the admirers and worshippers, and, what may seem more extraordinary, most frequently the disinterested admirers and worshippers, of wealth and greatness.'[34]

Adam Smith's view that the human desire for beauty was an inadequate explanation of the causes of economic growth was to have huge consequences, in that beauty and all other associated so-called 'externalities' came to be seen not merely as irrelevant to wealth creation but even as obstacles to it. Smith himself certainly did not intend to outlaw from society the pursuit of beauty let alone wisdom. He was arguing two things: first that man's efforts to improve his condition manifested itself in a number of different forms such as the pursuit of riches, the pursuit of beauty, the acquisition of knowledge or trying to be good, all of which were laudable; second, that the pursuit of riches could only be successful under certain conditions and other pursuits could be in partial conflict with it. This leads us on to his distinction between productive and unproductive labour.

Consumption: Productive and Unproductive Labour

Even amongst those people who practised thrift, not all kinds of personal expenditure were equally beneficial for the economy, in Smith's opinion. Some spending, that resulting in the employment of what he called productive labour, helped an economy to grow. Other kinds, that resulted in unproductive labour, made no contribution to growth at all, even hindered it. His definition of productive labour was labour to which improvements in efficiency could be applied – like making pins. So although all forms of prodigality, in the sense of spending one's income without saving, were economically harmful, some forms of prodigality were less harmful than others. This theory had major implications for architecture and the fine and decorative arts and the economic effects of expenditure upon them.

First we must examine Smith's definition of productive and unproductive labour, which is quite difficult to grasp and gave rise to much controversy.

> There is one sort of labour which adds to the value of the subject upon which it is bestowed: there is another which has no such effect. The former, as it produces a value, may be called productive; the latter, unproductive labour. Thus the labour of a manufacturer [i.e. a labourer] adds, generally, to the value of the materials which he works upon, that of his own maintenance, and of his master's profit. The labour of a menial servant, on the contrary, adds to the value of nothing. Though the manufacturer has his wages advanced to him by his master, he, in reality, costs him no expense, the value of those wages being generally restored, together with a profit, in the improved value of the subject upon which his labour is bestowed. But the maintenance of a menial servant never is restored. A man grows rich by employing a multitude of manufacturers: he grows poor by maintaining a multitude of menial servants.[35]

Adam Smith did not mean that the labour of a menial servant had no value and deserved no reward. Unproductive labour could be useful, honourable, and highly desirable.

> The sovereign, for example, with all the officers both of justice and war who served under him, the whole army and navy, are unproductive labourers . . . In the same class must be ranked, some both of the gravest and most important, and some of the most frivolous professions: churchmen, lawyers, physicians, men of letters of all kinds; players, buffoons, musicians, opera-singers, opera-dancers, etc.

What he did mean, however, was that productive labour was the kind of work, like pin making, which could be made more efficient and thereby increased the wealth of the nation.

He seems to have had two major factors in mind in assessing whether labour was productive. First, the labour must have contributed to making some physical object that could be sold so as to recover the costs of manufacture, and second the price must have yielded a profit. To be productive the labour must 'fix or realise itself in any permanent subject or vendible commodity, which endures after that labour is past, and for which an equal quantity of labour could afterwards be procured.'

From the standpoint of the arts, the problem with this definition is Adam Smith's insistence that productive labour was only that which resulted in some permanent object 'which lasts for some time at least after that labour is past'. This distinguishes in a quite arbitrary way between different arts. Moreover his apparent prejudice against the economic benefit of the arts was emphasised by his list of 'gravest and most frivolous professions' and his observation that 'like the declamation of the actor, the harangue of the orator, or the tune of the musician, the work of all of them perishes in the very instant of its production'.

By this token a painter's work was productive labour because like that of an upholsterer it was fixed in a permanent and vendible commodity but a singer's labour was unproductive. This is plainly ridiculous. A singer who appears in a concert for which tickets are sold at a price which yields a profit either to herself or the concert promoter enjoys both revenue, which she can spend, and the savings from the profit which can be invested in the promotion of more concerts. From an economic point of view the chief difference between her activity and that of the pin manufacturer is that there is a very low limit to the improvement in efficiency through the division of labour that is possible in her profession, unless we take into account her recordings (which Adam Smith could not have envisaged, but which fall into the general category of productive improvements) or the possibility of hiring a larger hall for her to sing in, which would reduce her unit costs to the promoter or increase their total takings. Nonetheless part of her savings could be invested by others upon 'productive labour' in industry or commerce, just as it would be by a parsimonious landowner or by a manufacturer himself, and almost certainly would be, were she highly successful, in order to provide herself with a pension. That itself would fulfil one condition of productive labour even if her notes did indeed perish at the very instant of their production. Of course the painter's labour was more obviously productive: it was fixed in a permanent and vendible object and was a form of manufacture upon which a profit could be earned. Moreover painting even during Smith's own lifetime satisfied the condition of contributing to the increase of wealth through improvements in productiveness. Portraits were often produced in multiple editions quite apart from the direct manufacturing process of print making. Joshua Reynolds's studio was very much a portrait manufactory operating on a strict division of labour in which Reynolds struck the pose of the sitter and painted the face before sending the canvas down to the drapery painter, the copyist and the mezzotinter in turn before it was framed, packed up and dispatched to the client.

Adam Smith cannot be blamed for failing to work through all the implications of this broad distinction between productive and unproductive labour, which continues to mislead economic policy-makers, prejudicing them in favour of manufacturing and technology and against the arts, entertainment and services in general. His chief point was that it would be pointless to invest profits in improving manufacturing efficiency if there were no demand for manufactured goods and consumers continued to spend their incomes on great banquets, hunting, teams of liveried servants, everything in short summed up in housekeeping and hospitality. Hence a precondition for growth in the wealth of nations was a change in their culture – an issue he explored in Book III.

The Implications of Expenditure on Productive and Unproductive Labour for the Arts and for Morals

Adam Smith was also arguing, implicitly, that the policy of old-fashioned bounty, hospitality and household economics could only keep an economy ticking over. It could not make either the nation or its citizens any the richer. The man of fortune who spent 'his revenue in a profuse and sumptuous table, and in maintaining a great number of menial servants, and a multitude of dogs and horses' might indeed provide employment, but neither he nor the nation would be any richer next year or the year after as a result. But if the same man laid out his future 'in adorning his house or his country villa, in useful or ornamental buildings, in useful or ornamental furniture, in collecting books, statues, pictures; or in things more frivolous, jewels, baubles, ingenious trinkets of different kinds; or, what is most trifling of all, in amassing a great wardrobe of fine clothes' then his expense would have 'employed masons, carpenters, upholsterers, mechanics, etc.', productive rather than unproductive hands with the effect of increasing 'the exchangeable value of the annual produce of the land and labour of the country'.[36]

The flaw in Adam Smith's definition in fact shows up here very clearly. Unless the work of these labourers could be made more productive through the division of labour and the employment of machines, then the only differences to the wealth of the nation between expenditure on the products of their labour and upon servants, hunting and hospitality would be to employ a different set of people, i.e. those who live in towns, and to add to the permanent stock of goods. The crafts which Adam Smith listed were those where improvements in productivity had long since advanced as far as they ever would before the invention of power tools. But Smith's broad position is clear: he favoured expenditure upon manufactured goods which could store up labour value for a long period of time and remain exchangeable, and which were moreover the type of manufactures to which the division of labour could in principle be applied.

As well as the benefit of such spending to the nation's economy, there were a number of benefits to the consumer himself and to the nation. First the 'magnificence of the person whose expense had been chiefly in durable commodities would be continually increasing', in that he who spent his money on building and furniture would own a stock which, should he want to, he could sell, even if not for all that it cost.[37] Then, too, it was obviously much easier to retrench upon expenditure on durable things without any loss of face than to reduce the lavishness of one's entertaining. Finally, even when the man of fortune had tired of his household furniture, it still remained part of the general stock of the nation since it could be purchased secondhand by the 'inferior and middling rank of people'. 'What was formerly a seat of the family of Seymour is now an inn upon the Bath road. The marriage-bed of James the First of Great Britain, which his queen brought with her from Denmark as a present fit for a sovereign to make to a sovereign, was, a few years ago, the ornament of an alehouse at Dunfermline.' Smith was no advocate of planned obsolescence or of a disposable society.

In addition, Smith admitted that the nation benefited in less tangibly economic ways from the creation of magnificent artefacts.

> Noble palaces, magnificent villas, great collections of books, statues, pictures, and other curiosities, are frequently both an ornament and an honour, not only to the neighbourhood, but to the whole country to which they belong. Versailles is an ornament and an honour to France, Stowe and Wilton to England. Italy still continues to command some sort of veneration by the number of monuments of this kind which it possesses, though the wealth which produced them has decayed, and though the genius which planned them seems to be extinguished, perhaps from not having the same employment.

Here survives more than a trace of the sixteenth-century household-based economics associated with the practice of making a survey either of the individual estate or of the realm, the practice of stocktaking, which in Thomas Fuller's list included medicinal waters and herbs, musicians and worthies, buildings and bridges, alongside the raw materials, arts and manufactures. In the work of the 'founder of modern economics', art and architecture can still be a form of visible statistics.[38]

However Adam Smith admitted that the balance of economic virtue did not necessarily coincide with the balance of moral virtue. As we have seen the rich man who spent his money on hospitality and entertaining was certainly more generous and liberal than the person who spent it on durable commodities: 'the little ornaments of dress and furniture, jewels, trinkets, gewgaws, frequently indicates, not only a trifling but a base and selfish disposition'.

To sum up the moral and aesthetic implications of Adam Smith's distinction between expenditure on productive and unproductive labour: the opulence of the nation would increase if people spent their income upon durable things such as clothes, furniture, houses, pictures and luxuries which were made by productive labourers. There were other economic benefits of such spending, both to the individual and to the nation, but there were also non-economic effects which were important enough to be pointed out. From an aesthetic point of view, a monument like Stowe or Versailles was 'an ornament and an honour' to a nation. Implicit in this was the belief that ornaments and buildings of lasting beauty would inevitably serve such a purpose, whereas those of an ephemeral and fashionable style or of frivolous utility would not. From a moral point of view, such spending was probably more selfish than spending upon ephemeral things like entertaining, but that had to be balanced against the 'new bounty' of commerce: 'What his hard heart denies his charitable vanity supplies.'

There begins to emerge a complex calculus of benefits very different in character to that of Mandeville's 'Private Vices, Publick Benefits' or of Hume's belief, for all his subtle provisos, that economic progress led infallibly to moral and cultural improvements. For Adam Smith, economic progress was not totally in conflict with morality or beauty, but neither was it necessarily in total harmony with them. The balance of advantage had to be carefully weighed.

Most people, besides, were not habitual prodigals: 'Though the principle of expense, therefore, prevails in almost all men upon some occasions, and in some men upon almost all occasions, yet in the greater part of men, taking the whole course of their life at an average, the principle of frugality seems not only to predominate, but to predominate very greatly.'[39] By virtue of Smith's belief in the human propensity to save – one aspect of the drive for self-improvement – he implicitly provided a solution to the profound moral dilemma raised by Mandeville and to which, as we have said, Addison and the other writers of *The Spectator* had no real answer: if prosperity depended upon massive personal spending, how could this spending be reconciled with virtue, with the avoidance of greed, vanity and the idolatry of personal consumption? Addison had suggested that the solution lay in expenditure on improving literature and gardening. But by changing the chain of causes, Adam Smith solved the problem. Whereas before it was believed that more spending created a greater demand for goods and services and hence more employment, and that anything such as moral or religious scruples, aesthetic standards, or political considerations that reduced the amount that people spent tended to diminish employment and prosperity, Smith showed that only if people saved, and only if those savings were invested, could the greater demand for goods be satisfied and result in fuller employment:

Savings $\rightarrow$ Capital investment $\rightarrow$ Greater productiveness $\rightarrow$ More and cheaper goods $\rightarrow$ More employment

If morality restrained personal expenditure and resulted in savings then it contributed to economic growth. Through the invisible hand, moreover, the poor became less wretched. Implicit, therefore, in Adam Smith's theory was an absence of inevitable conflict between moral values, or aesthetic standards, and the growth of the economy. According to this theory, prosperity could increase even though *The Spectator's* virtuous married couple did devote themselves dutifully to the upbringing of their children. The cause of prosperity did not require them to spend all their time and trouble on the frivolous luxuries of cushions and curtains and furniture and jams and other domestic delights, spending up to the hilt of their incomes; nor did they have to change their fashions every six months. Far from it. Their regular savings would make a greater contribution to sustainable employment than extravagance. But their good taste and virtue did not in themselves make a positive contribution to growth.[40]

In conclusion: although increasing wealth was not caused by the desire for beauty, and did not inevitably lead to an increase in the demand for beautiful things, it was by no means *incompatible* with a love of beauty, nor with restraints in personal consumption on religious or moral grounds. Aesthetic objectives only came into conflict with economic benefits insofar as the activity in question was one which resulted in the production of an immediately perishable performance, by a musician or actor, rather than contributing to a substantial product like a sofa, a table, a fine building or a painting. But even this did not represent any prejudice against artistic activity as such. It merely warned of the directly economic effects of employment in certain kinds of artistic activity on account of the features they shared with other services that could be classed as 'unproductive labour' not all of which were unworthy.

Perhaps this helps us to understand the type of early Victorian businessman, an ardent Evangelical whose favourite reading included Cowper, the poet of nature and retirement, as well as Adam Smith![41]

THE PROGRESS OF OPULENCE

Thus far Adam Smith's analysis was largely technical. He was describing his system or, as today's economists call it, his model of the economy. But in the third book of *The Wealth of Nations* Smith left this realm of pure theory behind to describe events in the real world, to write the economic and political history of Western Europe. Indeed he must be acknowledged as the founder of the economic interpretation of history.

And here a problem arose: for, in their interaction with the real world, the forces which led naturally to continuously increasing wealth met the social and political impediments which prevented mankind from enjoying its productive potential.

Without these impediments, what would occur was what Smith called 'The Natural Progress of Opulence'. First there would be a division of labour between the cultivators and the artificers – blacksmiths, wheelwrights, carpenters and so on – and then the tools that the latter made would help the cultivators to increase the fertility of the soil and thereby to support even more people in occupations other than farming. The practitioners of these trades would gather in towns where a larger market would facilitate further subdivisions in occupation, so that as well as an ever-increasing production of farm produce, and raw materials for manufacture connected with farming, there would also be an increase in production of finer and finer manufactures for convenience or luxury. 'According to the natural course of things, therefore, the greater part of the capital of every growing society is, first, directed to agriculture, afterwards to manufactures, and last of all to foreign commerce.'[42]

In the British colonies of North America and in the Roman Empire, Smith hinted, some approximation to this natural course of events had taken place. But in modern Europe after the fall of the Roman Empire this natural order of things had been 'entirely inverted'. The first step in the revival of prosperity had occurred when foreign commerce had introduced finer manufactures and these in turn had prompted improvements in manufacture, and in farming – the very reverse of the natural progress of opulence where improvements in farming led to luxury manufactures. How had this unnatural situation arisen?

Smith identified certain social and political impediments. Foremost amongst these were attempts by one group of people or another, whether landlords, farmers, merchants or artisans, to create a monopoly in whatever they supplied – be it land, a commodity, a skill or a service – in order to force up its price or the price of their labour, reduce the supply and prevent the process of increasing division of labour and improvement. This was summed up in the pithy and memorable epigram that 'People of the same trade seldom meet together, even for merriment and diversion, but the conversation ends in a conspiracy against the public, or in some contrivance to raise prices'. In Book I Smith expressed the view that this was the major obstacle to the continuously increasing wealth of a nation, rather than a nation attaining economic saturation. Perhaps no country, he observed, had 'ever yet arrived at this degree of opulence'. China's wealth, for example, had long since ceased to grow but this was the result of 'the nature of its laws and institutions'. China's wealth was far smaller than what 'with other laws and institutions, the nature of its soil, climate and situation might admit of'.[43]

Turning to Europe since the fall of the Roman Empire Smith traced the history of a particular set of obstacles and identified the monopoly in the ownership of land by great landlords as the fundamental source of all other forms of monopoly.

We also find that, in his role of historian, Adam Smith adopted a new personality: in place of the patient and scholarly analyst illuminating his argument with colourful examples, well-turned phrases and witty paradoxes, there emerged Smith the polemicist. Much of the third book consists of a violent diatribe against landlords and the hereditary aristocracy which presented a complete caricature of British history and economic policy.

Smith made no distinction between those landed aristocrats who improved their estates and even encouraged manufactures and the prodigals who consumed 'unproductive labour'. Likewise, all merchants and manufacturers were portrayed as parsimonious consumers of the products of productive labour. As we have seen, this historical caricature proved immensely influential, the major source of the belief in an extravagant and irresponsible aristocracy. At the same time, to a degree unmatched even by earlier Whiggish polemicists such as Barbon, Mandeville or *The Spectator* writers, Adam Smith totally misrepresented the aims of what I have called the Burghleyan policy of maintaining a balanced economy. Finally, as a corollary to this, Smith's view of the future of agriculture and the countryside was exclusively commercial to a degree not exceeded even by Sir Andrew Freeport. Thus, in general, the balanced, intelligent and subtle calculus of economic, moral, aesthetic, social and political benefits sketched in our earlier discussion of Books I and II is belied by Book III.

Smith's Economic History of Europe

The natural progress of opulence under the Roman Empire had been interrupted by the barbarian invasions which put an end to the commerce between town and country upon which naturally increasing wealth depended. The barbarian leaders usurped the land which was left uncultivated and the cities were largely deserted, impoverished and servile. The barbarians set aside the Roman laws of inheritance by which land was divided equally between the proprietor's children in favour of primogeniture which permitted only the eldest son to inherit the whole property. They regarded land not primarily as a means of subsistence but as a bastion of power. Hence they prevented the subdivision of their great landholdings. This was the original form of monopoly and engrossment.[44]

It had two pernicious results – one political and the other economic – which affected the economy both of the countryside and the towns. The political result was that each landlord by virtue of his monopoly over the very fount of prosperity, the land, became 'a sort of petty prince. His tenants were his subjects. He was their judge, and in some respects their legislator in peace, and their leader in war.'

But why, long after the turmoil had subsided, had these laws of primogeniture survived and, with them, the political power of the landlords and the economic order? Smith's answer was given in the spirit of Montesquieu, whom he greatly admired: 'Laws frequently continue in force long after the circumstances which first gave occasion to them, and which could also render them reasonable, are no more'. As a result, in the absence of commerce, the proprietor consumed the whole of his produce 'in rustic hospitality at home' maintaining through his bounty 'a multitude of retinues and dependents', feeding them in great halls such as Westminster Hall. This state of affairs had survived to recent times in the highlands of Scotland where a vassal of the Duke of Argyll, Mr Cameron of Lochiel, only thirty years earlier 'without being so much as a justice of peace used, notwithstanding, to exercise the highest criminal jurisdiction over his own people'.[45]

So much for the broadly political effects. The economic effects upon the countryside were twofold: first in the conduct of the landlords themselves as potential agricultural improvers, second in their influence upon their tenants.

In Book III Smith completely identified the landlord with his portrait of the prodigal 'man of fortune' of Book II. In the earlier section however he had been at least prepared to concede that rich merchants were just as likely to spend their incomes in the employment of unproductive labourers as great lords.[46] Now he made no exceptions. 'It seldom happens, moreover, that a great proprietor is a great improver', Smith wrote. If the expense of his house and person

> either equalled or exceeded his revenue, as it did very frequently, he had no stock to employ in this manner. If he was an economist, he generally found it more profitable to employ his annual savings in new purchases than in the improvement of his old estate. To improve land with profit, like all other commercial projects, requires an exact attention to small savings and small gains, of which a man born to a great fortune, even though naturally frugal, is very seldom capable. The situation of such a person naturally disposes him to attend rather to ornament which pleases his fancy than to profit for which he has so little occasion. The elegance of his dress, of his equipage, of his house, and household furniture, are objects which from his infancy he has been accustomed to have some anxiety about. The turn of mind which this habit naturally forms follows him when he comes to think of the improvement of land. He embellishes perhaps four or five hundred acres in the neighbourhood of his house, at ten times the expense which the land is worth after all his improvements; and finds that if he was to improve his whole estate in the same manner, and he has little taste for any other, he would be a bankrupt before he had finished the tenth part of it. There still remain in both parts of the united kingdom some great estates which have continued without interruption in the hands of the same family since the times of feudal anarchy. Compare the present condition of those estates with the possessions of the small proprietors in their neighbourhood, and you will require no other argument to convince you how unfavourable such extensive property is to improvement.[47]

In this passage, unlike those we have just been examining, landlords were not even given credit for the beneficial economic effects of that part of their expense that went on the products of productive labour such as clothes, equipage, architecture and household furniture. They stood totally condemned as improvident spendthrifts totally out of tune with the spirit of improvement.

As bad if not worse was their effect upon their own tenants who had been at first virtual slaves with no property, no security of tenure, and no opportunities to enjoy the fruits of their own labours. As a result they had 'no interest but to eat as much, and to labour as little as possible'. They had no interest whatsoever in bettering their conditions through their own efforts.

This attack on inequality based upon class – founded, in turn, upon entailed land holdings – was written with great passion. Entails, Smith wrote, 'are founded upon the most absurd of all suppositions, the supposition that every successive generation of men have not an equal right to the earth, and to all that it possesses'. The great merit of the colonies of North America lay in the abundance of land, the absence of rent and hence the fact that the cultivator had 'every motive to render as great as possible a produce, which is thus to be almost entirely his own'. Nor was Smith blind to the evils of slavery in some of those colonies which he condemned on moral as well as economic grounds.[48]

So how had this 'unnatural' situation been reversed? How in the fact of primogeniture had Europe recovered its prosperity? How had it been possible to break the economic monopoly and political stranglehold of the great proprietors who, Smith reminded his readers, 'were anciently the legislators of every part of Europe', with the result that 'the laws relating to land, therefore, were all calculated for what they supposed the interest of the proprietors'?

The explanation was clearer about the sequence of events than about their causes. Serfs gradually gave way to *metayers*, with whom the landlord shared the produce equally thus providing the latter with some interest in increasing the produce. Metayers gradually evolved into tenant farmers paying rent for their farms. Security of tenure increased, particularly in England, and long leases encouraged them to build upon the land that they did not own. This was the result of the self-interest of the landlord, who wanted a greater yield from his land, of the efforts of monarchs to undermine the power of their barons by supporting the serfs against their masters, as well as of papal bulls from the twelfth century onwards emancipating the serfs.[49]

The second means by which European prosperity was restored was that the towns and cities wrested control from the domination of the nobility. This they achieved by tax privileges granted to them by the king. This created cities with a degree of legal independence and self-government, and these grew into the city states of Italy and other parts of Europe. Assisted by the monarch, these cities formed mutual defence leagues against the nobility on the principle of the enemy of my enemy is my friend.

In these free towns, secure against the power of the nobility and also 'secure of enjoying the fruits of their industry', the citizens naturally exerted their labour 'to better their condition, and to acquire not only the necessaries, but the conveniencies and elegancies of life'.[50]

But the progress of these cities was still held back by the low level of agricultural efficiency within their adjacent territories caused by the economically backward nobility. It had to be a particular type of town, therefore, which set progress in train. Ports, for example, derived their natural produce not from the immediately surrounding countryside but from 'the most remote corners of the world'. Ports moreover could exchange not only their own manufactures for food and raw materials but also perform 'the office of carriers between distant countries . . . exchanging the produce of one for that of another. A city might in this manner grow up to great wealth and splendour, while not only the inland country in its neighbourhood, but the country of all those cities to which it traded, were in poverty and wretchedness. In Europe it was the cities of Italy, their shipping favoured by the crusades, which first developed in this way through foreign commerce.' The next step was an extraordinary one. The power of the greater nobility, which even the feudal system had failed to diminish, was now undermined not by force but by the imported luxuries of these great trading cities. The glitter of these luxuries attracted the vanity of the nobles and tempted them to send their 'rude produce' to market in exchange for such toys and baubles instead of sharing their produce with their servants and dependants through bounty and hospitality.

As a result of a cultural revolution involving this shift in expenditure from the direct employment of unproductive labour to the indirect employment of productive labour, the

37 Shoe buckles, late eighteenth century, Lady Mante Collection; Iveagh Bequest, Kenwood House, Hampstead. According to Smith aristocratic extravagance on such luxuries had destroyed their power and paved the way for a commercial society.

economic decline of Europe was reversed. To pay for his extravagance upon manufactured luxuries the great proprietor dismissed his household, and got rid of his less profitable tenants. Both classes left the country to seek their livelihoods in the towns where the demand for labour to import and manufacture luxuries grew steadily. As a result of the depopulation of the countryside and the enlargement of the size of the farms held by the more efficient tenants agriculture itself improved. The landlord could raise his rent and increase his consumption of luxuries still further. But when he tried to increase his rents above what his tenants could afford they were able to exact the condition of extending the terms of their leases to enable them 'to recover with profit whatever they should lay out in the further improvement of the land'. Long leases and increasing security of tenure reached a point where the farmers became virtually independent. In one of his great rhetorical passages Adam Smith summed up the effect of this noble extravagance:

For a pair of diamond buckles perhaps [Plate 37], or for something as frivolous and useless, they exchanged the maintenance, or what is the same thing, the price of the maintenance of a thousand men for a year, and with it the whole weight and authority which it could give them. The buckles, however, were to be all their own, and no other human creature was to have any share of them; whereas in the more ancient method of expense they must have shared with at least a thousand people. With the judges that were to determine the preference this difference was perfectly decisive; and thus, for the gratification of the most childish, the meanest, and the most sordid of all vanities, they gradually bartered their whole power and authority.

141

Specifically, when the nobility lost their political power, they were:

> no longer capable of interrupting the regular execution of justice or of disturbing the peace of the country. Having sold their birthright, not like Esau for a mess of potage in time of hunger and necessity, but in the wantonness of plenty, for trinkets and baubles, fitter to be the playthings of children than the serious pursuits of men, they became as insignificant as any substantial burger or tradesman in a city. A regular government was established in the country as well as in the city, nobody having sufficient power to disturb its operations in the one any more than in the other.[51]

However there is a problem with this explanation, and it lies in its one-sided rhetorical exaggeration. In Book II when he discussed the difference between the 'prodigal' who spent his fortune upon housekeeping and hospitality and the one who spent it upon a country house, furniture, collections of pictures and books, Adam Smith indicated that the latter objects of expenditure were admirable from an economic and aesthetic viewpoint even if not from that of personal morality. He made no generalisations about the motivation for such acquisitions. But here, in Book III, he reverted to the facile paradoxes that he had employed in the fable of the poor man's son in *The Theory of Moral Sentiments*.

Were it not for the enormous influence of *The Wealth of Nations* as the first systematic treatise on economics, this exaggeration would not matter, for Smith's systematisation of economics was a far greater achievement than his polemical effort to systematise the economic and social history of Europe since the Renaissance. But it is essential to the present argument to show that the stereotype of aristocratic extravagance and competitive consumption which, until recently, has so obsessed modern historians bears a very strong family resemblance to the historical section of *The Wealth of Nations*. Tawney in his seminal essay 'The Rise of the Gentry, 1558–1640' argued that the cause of the crisis of the landed aristocracy was that in addition to the traditional 'conspicuous waste' in which they were bound to engage as befitted their position, they also had to compete with 'the demands of a new world of luxury and fashions'. 'London, rapidly advancing in financial and commercial importance, with a Court that under James is a lottery of unearned fortunes, exercises a stronger pull. Town houses increase in number; visits to the capital are spun out; residential quarters are developed; to the delight of dressmakers, something like a season begins to emerge. Culture has demands to which homage must be paid.'[52]

But the aristocrats' estates, administered according to Tawney in the most conservative way, could not cope with the expense. So, 'As the tension tightened, something had to go. What went first was an aspect of life once of the first importance, but to which justice today is not easily done. The words "hospitality" or "house-keeping", its ordinary designation, were the description, not of a personal trait or a private habit, but of a semi-public institution . . .' And, as hospitality and housekeeping disappeared, the solution was for the aristocracy to 'go into business and prosper'. Tawney specially mentioned aristocrats who got rid of 'the unprofitable copyholders when lives ran out', who bought out small freeholders and who threw 'the land so secured into larger farms to be let on lease'. Other means of raising the landowners' incomes were investment in home farms, draining marshes and clearing waste, and 'other types of enterprise' such as the timber trade, mining and urban property development.

Is it not curious, but perhaps not so surprising, that Tawney, the Christian Socialist, seems to have been oblivious to the fact that his account of the final passing of the middle ages he so much admired and the birth of the heartless impersonal world of 'economic man' was in all its essentials derived from the philosophical history written by the very man who had codified the principles of that new economy 165 years earlier? It is perhaps more surprising that in the ensuing historical debate on 'The Rise of the Gentry' none of the participants seem to have appreciated that they were fighting an ideological battle whose roots lay so deep!

It is important to pinpoint the source of these ideas because this interpretation of history has largely obscured the full significance of those regional policies, centred around the country houses and their estates, which we examined in the previous section. Adam Smith's interpretation of aristocratic behaviour and of the policies of largely aristocratic legislators and governments was that by virtue of the traditions of their class they were helplessly committed to expense instead of frugality. Insofar as their expense had more recently fuelled the growth economy of manufacturing through their taste for 'toys and baubles' it was only because they had swapped one kind of unthinking, compulsive and showy behaviour for another. Thus Smith credited the social order that had already ruled England for two centuries and was to do so for at least a further century, with virtually no prudence, no foresight, no intelligence, no business sense.

And yet in the conclusion of this historical account Smith could observe that 'From the beginning of the reign of Elizabeth too, the English legislature has been peculiarly attentive to the interests of commerce and manufactures, and in reality there is no country in Europe, Holland itself not excepted, of which the law is, upon the whole, more favourable to this sort of industry. Commerce and manufactures have accordingly been continually advancing during all this period.'[53] But he seemed entirely oblivious of the fact this far-sighted legislature was largely composed of the very people whom he had just classified as vainglorious prodigals! It is far more serious, however, that he did not understand that the kinds of encouragement given to commerce and manufactures in the reign of Elizabeth were of a kind very carefully calculated to create not a fast-growing manufacturing economy but a stable and flourishing one balanced with the interests of husbandry and social harmony. He therefore failed to understand that the apprenticeship laws, for instance, were not an aberration, nor merely the result of the desire on the part of a particular profession to monopolise their trade, but a conscious effort to *restrict* certain kinds of commercial activity in the interests of social stability. In general Adam Smith, unlike even Mandeville for example, or Addison with his caricatured merchant and squire, Coverley and Freeport, failed to recognise that the policy of restraint of trade and manufacturing which had been initiated in the reign of Elizabeth was a fully conscious and calculated one, and that it was not the unintended result of benighted ignorance rooted in the lingering barbarism of the Dark Ages.

————Part Four————

STYLE AND ECONOMICS

PREFACE

It is clear that considerations of art, design and fashion, architecture and town planning, aesthetics and, in particular, taste were essential components of social and economic theory – indeed of policy and action – from at least the latter half of the sixteenth century. Moreover, these issues were inextricably linked to that of morality, to consideration of the vices and virtues of different kinds of consumption. But the actual *appearance*, character or style of buildings and possessions has not, so far, figured prominently in the controversies we have examined. The policy that the gentry should reside on their country estates was not accompanied by a recommendation that their country houses should be gothic in style or neo-palladian; nor could it be directly inferred from Hume's economic theories that the form of refinement produced by commercial society would be classical.

Alongside the events and the arguments which have been described, however, there was taking place a closely related debate, one which *was* specifically concerned with the character and the style, or manner, of manufactured objects and buildings. This will be the subject of Parts IV, V and VI – both the debate about style itself, and the nature of its relationship to the issues of theory and policy.

My approach to this large and complicated question is not based on any particular theoretical foundation, whether Hegelian, Marxist, Veblenite or some more recent fashionable structure for theorising about the relationship between the arts and other social institutions. This is not, it should be said, on account of any antagonism to such theories. Perhaps one problem with the 'grand narratives' of Hegel and Marx and their successors is that they best apply to the kinds of unified and well-disciplined states with which such writers were most familiar or which they hoped to see emerge. In other words, such theories are themselves the product of particular times and circumstances, even more highly determined perhaps than the situations and events they seek to explain – as already observed in the case of Mandeville's and Veblen's theory of competitive consumption. Such theories are also strongly contested.

Nonetheless, on the face of it, the following chapters might be said to offer some considerable evidence in support of a materialist explanation of economic cause and cultural effect. Almost all the key figures and institutions to be discussed were associated with the ruling elite which had an over-riding concern to preserve the social order. The elite was very small and socially coherent. Yet, in practice, this did not prevent considerable disagreement amongst its members over the preferred style for British architecture and design – classical, gothic, vernacular, naturalistic, eclectic and even Islamic. Meanwhile a country which traded with the world was open to all manner of imported exotic styles in the applied arts which no amount of persuasion from on top could control short of closing her borders to international trade, as Japan actually did. Moreover the situation was very different in different fields. Town planning and urban architecture are relatively permanent and public manifestations involving high capital outlay. For reasons already touched upon they were controlled fairly tightly and successfully by government and landowners. Personal possessions are more ephemeral, more private and far less amenable to control even when that is felt to be desirable. Of course it could be argued that Britain's stylistic heterogeneity was precisely the predictable product of a country in the process of a major revolution from agrarian aristocracy to commercial and industrial democracy. Maybe.

To address such issues adequately would require another book, but it is hoped that the following chapters will make some contribution to this important and interesting subject particularly insofar as they deal with a succession of major writers, architects and designers over a very extended period deliberating upon the issue of what *should be* the nation's predominant artistic style in full awareness of the social, moral, political and religious factors which for much of that time placed their society under great strain. In short, here is an opportunity to observe the inner workings of such a debate as well as to see its outcome, an opportunity denied one for the gothic middle ages or the early Italian Renaissance when, before printing, fewer records of such debates have come down to us.

However, the present work deals only with the applied arts of design, where the relationship between the ruling elite and the practitioners of these arts is extremely close, even to the point of members of the aristocracy acting on occasion as their own architects. It deals barely at all with painting and sculpture where such relationships are often more tenuous and difficult to establish, due in part to the fact that the professionalisation of these arts occurred far earlier than in architecture, planning or design.[1].

There is one final problem with the historical and sociological approaches developed in the nineteenth century to explain the relationship between art and society, namely that sometime they confuse what *ought to be* with what is or has been. The following pages deal with people who made no pretence that they were explicitly talking about what ought to be, people who often possessed the power and influence to put their ideas into practice.

CHAPTER 1

The Early Stuarts

THIS CHAPTER, WHICH is divided into three sections, will look at the debates about the nature of the relationship between social and economic policies and the appropriate styles, both in architecture and design, to be adopted in pursuit of them. It is often taken for granted that the classicists like Inigo Jones, the Earl of Arundel, Christopher Wren and his friend the diarist John Evelyn were antagonistic to the rudeness of the gothic and the vernacular, but it will become apparent that the lines of the seventeenth-century 'Battle of Styles' were not so sharply drawn. The choice of style being an issue of appropriateness or decorum was subject to some subtlety depending on circumstances. The grand (classical) style might be considered appropriate to buildings of national importance, while the gothic or vernacular could be used in more homely or local situations. But even that was not an invariable rule. Moreover the court, beyond its own specific projects, might encourage the classical through example or, in the case of London, through building regulations and bye-laws, but local patrons were free to go their own ways. Even in the case of national edifices, as demonstrated by the controversy over the style of St Paul's Cathedral, the gothic retained a strong appeal. At the very least, as John Summerson has remarked, gothic survived as a 'second language' for classical architects in Britain. Moreover the classicists did not have a monopoly of the best arguments. A good case could be made both for gothic and vernacular. It is also often supposed that the Goths veered towards more traditional patriarchal values of country living and that the classicists were associated with metropolitan life and the court. That also is far from being the case.

PENSHURST AND THE OLD FASHION OF ENGLAND

If the proclamations of the Stuart kings were negative, mandatory instruments for returning the gentry and aristocracy to their country estates, there was also in operation a positive, subtler means of coercion. The arts, especially poetry, were pressed into service as an ingenious form of 'state propaganda'.

What is termed 'The Country House Poem' of the seventeenth century has been widely discussed in terms of the way that it 'reflected' such changes as the decline in housekeeping and the increase in time spent in London. In reading these poems as symptoms of the decline of the rural community and hospitality, taking their ideas at face value, their real purpose and beauty has been lost. Raymond Williams's alternative approach, of regarding them as reflections of a Golden Age which turns out always to have belonged to the past, however far back one goes, also seems to miss the point. Court propaganda, I would suggest, is precisely how we should regard them. In Howard Erskine-Hill's apt words, the poems should be seen as panegyrics, exercises in the art of praise, referring neither to the norm nor the exceptions, but to an ideal. Virginia Kenny has observed that 'the country house panegyric was a public poem about public and private virtue'.[1]

38   Penshurst Place, Kent, *c.* 1341, hall and porch. Penshurst was eulogised by the Poet Laureate, Ben Jonson, in 1616, as a symbol of housekeeping and hospitality.

We have to remember that Ben Jonson, who wrote 'To Penshurst', perhaps the very first of these poems and certainly the one which gave dignity to the whole genre, was the Poet Laureate and an official of the court of James I, who himself wrote a poem on gentry residence in 1622. 'To Penshurst' dates from between 1608 and the death of Henry Prince of Wales in 1616, a period that marks the very height of James's campaign. It was originally published, moreover, very prominently, as the first long poem of Jonson's collection *The Forrest* in 1616, just a few months after the Star Chamber speech of James I, whose personal injunction to the aristocracy to 'leave these idle forreigne toyes, and keepe the old fashion of England' it so richly echoes and illustrates. Moreover, the poem immediately following it in the collection, 'To Sir Robert Wroth', has a similar theme, praising the country life of the son-in-law of Penshurst's owner, Sir Robert Sidney. These poems were 'public utterances' within which life in the English country house becomes a metaphor for the state.[2]

Wroth's own father also happens to have been one of the 'most persuaded proponents' of the great Elizabethan Poor Law legislation which passed through the 1597/98 session of parliament. He had been one of the chief parliamentary leaders and allies of Burghley alongside Sir Francis Bacon, Sir Nicholas Bacon and Sir Thomas Cecil, who nursed the bill in its passage through the House.[3] Both Penshurst, the building and seat of the Sidney family, and Sir Robert Wroth, the man and his way of life, were epitomised by Ben Jonson in glowing terms as the very embodiment of the 'old fashion of England' and the antithesis to the snares of metropolitan and courtly luxury (Plate 38).

Jonson portrayed Wroth, for example, as a man who disdained the thrilling and artificial pleasures of 'the better cloth of state; the richer hangings, or crowne-plate . . . the jewels, stuffes, the paines, the wit/There wasted', a man who preferred to enjoy the peaceful and natural beauties of life in the security of his own estate, living off his own 'unbought provision'.

> 'Mongst loughing heards, and solide hoofes
> Along'st the curled woods, and painted meades
> Through which a serpent river leades
> To some coole, courteous shade, which he calls his,
> And makes sleepe softer than it is![4]

The pleasurable occupations of hunting, shooting and fishing, the ever-changing spectacle of the fertile landscape throughout the seasons in place of the everchanging fashions of the town,★ the heartiness of housekeeping filling the 'open hall with mirth and cheere' at Christmas, are all vividly contrasted in the poem with the scars and braggadoccio of war, the wrangling of the bar, the rapine and injustice of trade and the flattery of life at court. Jonson specifically compared this country life with the Golden Age, but he did not believe that it was something that already existed in full perfection. It was an ideal to strive for and to cherish.

The preceding poem, 'To Penshurst', deals less with the ethical conduct of an individual squire and more with the practice of housekeeping.[5] Its subjects include the moral and social virtues of the country house to which it is addressed: the seat of a stable, deferential, rural community and a mansion whose virtue glows through its very stones, 'rear'd with no man's ruine, no man's grone'. Its woods, its meadows, its streams and even 'the blushing apricot and woolly peach' ripening on the walls of the kitchen garden: all these *things*, these products jointly of nature and man's art, are enumerated by Jonson in a very thingy and matter-of-fact way, in just the same way, indeed, as moralists used to list luxury goods. And that very similarity points to the difference: that every detail of the glowing portrait of Penshurst is the antithesis and the antidote to luxury.

The poem concludes with the neat conceit of the mansion's preparedness – despite the absence of its lady, Barbara Gamage, Lady Sidney – to receive a totally unexpected visit by the king and the Prince of Wales when they were 'hunting late this way'.

> and what high praise was heap'd
> On thy good lady, then! who, therein, reap'd
> The just reward of her high huswifery;
> To have her linnen, plate and all things nigh,
> When she was farre: and not a roome, but drest,
> As if it had expected such a guest!

This episode draws together the important themes of hunting and the ideal of well-ordered housekeeping and generous openhandedness at which such people were expected to aim – and none more than wives who, to paraphrase the king's own admonition, should neither risk their own reputations nor rob their husband's purses on shopping expeditions to the capital but ought instead to preside over their protestant 'abbeys' with an almost religious devotion.[6]

It is hard to avoid the comparison between such poems and that tradition of thought, to which we have already referred, represented by the whole enterprise of Fuller's *Worthies of England*, begun less than thirty years after *The Forrest* was published. Just as Fuller's work describes the minutiae of idealised lives, in order to provide an example, so 'To Penshurst', for example 'takes stock' of an idealised house and estate in the long inventories which make up the very form of the poem: Penshurst's woods and ponds and rivers, its livestock, sheep, cattle, horses, game and fish, its orchard, fruit and other produce, Penshurst's own 'worthies', 'thy lord and lady', its tenants and guests, its hospitality and piety, take stock of Penshurst's housekeeping, Penshurst's private economy glowing in the golden light of Jonson's poetry: statistics made palpable to sight and touch by means of the art of poetry.

But there is more to the poem than this. If we recall Sir Henry Wotton's characterisation

---

★ Barbon in *A Discourse of Trade*, London, 1690, compared fashion to a Ver Perpetuum:– 'it is an Invention to Dress a Man, as if he lived in perpetual Spring; he never sees the Autumn of his Cloaths.'

of 'every man's proper Mansion house and Home' as 'a kinde of private Princedom; Nay to the Possessors thereof, an Epitome of the whole Worlde', there seems every justification for believing that Jonson meant his portrait of Penshurst to be seen as an epitome of the old fashion of England itself. For Ben Jonson not only was Penshurst England; England was the sum of many Penshursts.

But country house poems like 'To Penshurst' did more than echo the general objective and voice of the Stuart proclamations. They were also, by their nature, *specific*. Penshurst, for instance, was built in a particular style, fourteenth century gothic, whose revival was favoured by the Stuart court – the 'Gothic of Good King James'.

> Thou art not, Penshurst, built to envious show,
>   Of touch, or marble, nor canst boast a row
> Of polished pillars, or a roof of gold:
>   Thou hast no lanterne, whereof tales are told;
> Or stayre, or courts; but stand'st an ancient pile,
>   And these grudg'd at, art reverenc'd the while.

And this look, this physical appearance became part and parcel of the virtues ascribed to the Sidneys – as, by the self-same process, did the nature and design of their household goods. In contrast to the evils of 'idle foreign toyes' and vanities, here, simply, were food and buildings: essential goods as distinct from the inessentials of jewellery, plate and lace-bedecked finery. Their very appearance was homely, old, natural and above all English. It is the same spirit as John of Gaunt's dying evocation in Shakespeare's *Richard II*:

> This happy breed of men, this little world,
> This precious stone, set in a silver sea,
> . . . This blessed spot, this Realm, this England

which Gaunt contrasted with the foreign luxuries devouring the kingdom as a result of the example set by the King.

The country house poems of royalists and parliamentarians alike rehearsed these themes, counterpointing town and country, old and new, English and foreign, throughout the succeeding decades of the seventeenth century. For example, in an anonymous poem probably dating from the Restoration, 'The Old and Young Courtier', the ancient manor house

> With an old study fill'd full of learned old books
> With an old reverend chaplain, you might know him by his looks;
> With an old buttery hatch worn quite off the hooks,
> And an old kitchen, that maintain'd half a dozen old cooks;

is contrasted with the 'new fashion'd hall'

> With a new study, stuft full of pamphlets and plays,
> And a new chaplain that swears faster than he prays,
> With a new buttery hatch that opens once in four or five days
> And a new *French* cook to devise fine kickshaws and toys;
>   Like a young courtier of the King's
>   And the King's young courtier.[7]

Here fashionable and frivolous foreign extravagance, epitomised by French food, becomes the cause of the demise of old-fashioned English hospitality to the poor, hospitality equated with another architectural feature of Tudor and Jacobean manor houses:

> ...the towered chimneys, which should be
> The windpipes of good hospitality,
> Through which it breatheth to the open air
> Betokening of life, and liberal welfare;[8]

The symbolism of the high smoking chimneys (Plate 40) was a common theme in poetry and prose: 'The niggardness of the lord or master is the cause no more chimneys do smoke: for would they use ancient hospitality as their forefathers did . . . then you would see every chimney in the house smoke.'[9] Each house, and each portion of each house, was regarded as an emblem which should be hallowed by piety.

> To the worn Threshold, Porch, Hall, Parlour, Kitchin,
>   The fat-fed smoking temple, which in
> The wholesome savour of thy mighty Chines
>   Invites to supper him who dines,
> Where laden spits warp't with large Ribbs of Beefe,
>   Not represent, but give reliefe
> To the lanke Stranger, and the sowre swain;
>   Where both many feed, and come againe:
> For no black-bearded Vigil from thy doore
>   Beats with a button'd-staffe the poore:[10]

This charitable piety should also be accompanied by architectural humility as Marvell recommended in 'Appleton House'

> Within this sober Frame expect
> Work of no Forrain Architect

Rather, the very architecture was to be constructed from social and religious virtues, and the idolatrous worship of material possessions stood condemned.

> A Stately Frontispiece of Poor
> Adorns without the open Door;
> Nor less the Rooms within commends
> Daily new Furniture of Friends.
> The House was built upon the Place
> Only as for a Mark of Grace;
> And for an Inn to entertain
> Its Lord a while, but not remain[11]

Marvell also drew an explicit moral in telling the history of Appleton Nunnery, which had preceded the house on the same site. He argued that the original pious intentions of the Founder had been better fulfilled since the Reformation and Dissolution than before.

> Though many a *Nun* there made her Vow,
> Twas no *Religious House* till now

When we turn to the buildings themselves their very form embodies the themes of the country house poems. Chantmarle in the village of Cattistock in Dorset can stand for the many hundreds of Jacobean manor houses (Plate 39). Its builder, Sir John Strode, younger son of the family seated at Parnham, was a successful London lawyer who bought estates to refound his family's fortunes. He was a godly man who as MP for Bridport drew up an Act against profane cursing and swearing. He was clearly a man who also exemplified the words John Dryden applied to his own kinsman, who steered a course betwixt the county and the court.

39 Chantmarle, Dorset, rebuilt in 1612 by Sir John Strode, a pious London merchant, in traditional style in tune with government policy.

40 Theobalds, Herts., the second of Lord Burghley's mansions 1564–74, demolished in the 1650s. The drawing shows 'high smoking chimneys', a symbol of generous housekeeping in country house poems.

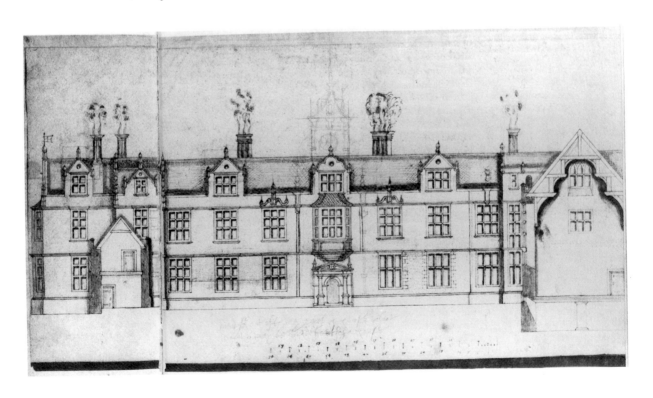

Sir John Strode has left us his own manuscript account of the rebuilding of Chantmarle, in which he placed overwhelming emphasis upon his pious motives.[12] The old manor house, he explained, had an oratory which was 'low-rooft, little and dark' and therefore the building of a new chapel – splendidly 'fretted over on its inside' with decoration derived from the symbolism of Solomon's Temple 'sun, moone, starrs, *cherubims*, doves, grapes and pomegranates, all supported by 4 angells in the 4 corners of the roofe' – took precedence over the building of the mansion house itself and was sited, appropriately, in a former herb-garden. The psalms and lessons that were sung at the service of dedication by the Bishop of Bristol in September 1619 make it clear that Sir John Strode saw himself following the example of King David.

> Lorde, remember David with all his affliction Who sware unto the Lorde, and vowed unto the mightie God of Jacob, saying, I will not enter into the Tabernacle of mine house, nor come upon my pallet or bed, nor suffer mine eyes to sleepe nor mine eyelids to slumber, until I finde out a place for the Lorde, an habitation for the mightie God of Jacob.

The blessing from Psalm LXXII shows him drawing a parallel between his mansion house and the heavenly city: 'Pray for the peace of Jerusalem: let them prosper that love thee. Peace be within thy walls, and prosperity within thy palaces.' One must infer that, as ruler of his own estate, Strode saw himself aspiring to imitate the conduct of King Solomon.

Also in tune with the poems was the traditional style of the new house in local stone, a hint of gothic in the window mullions with triangular gables of the same form as the surviving wing of the fifteenth-century house, which Strode seems to have preserved out of reverence, perhaps because it contained the original chapel.[13]

After the service of dedication attended by his family, the county gentry and 400–500 people, a ceremonial observance of housekeeping and hospitality was performed in feasting all those of good quality in the new house while 'the poor had bread and meate at the doores'. This completed the hallowing of the house which was shaped in the form of an E to represent Emmanuel, also carved over the door with the date of the laying of the foundation stone, 1612. Strode later endowed almshouses for six poor people in 1630, which were inscribed:

God's House
Sit honos Trino Deo
Anno Dom.
1630

THE 'MEANING' OF CLASSICISM

An almost inescapable impression is given by this evidence that the traditional, vernacular gothic style of the English mansion house, cherished in the country house poems and actually constructed during the early decades of the seventeenth century, was directly associated with the maintenance of the traditional social values. Penshurst according to Jonson was explicitly not

> . . . built to envious show,
> Of touch, or marble; nor canst boast a row
> Of polish'd pillars

Marvell used Italianate or foreign architecture as an emblem of pride, and Appleton as an emblem of humility. Thus

> Within this sober frame expect
> Work of no Forrain Architect;
> That unto Caves the Quarries drew,
> And Forrests did to Pastures hew;
> Who of his great Design in pain
> Did for a Model vault his Brain,
> Whose Columns should so high be rais'd
> To arch the Brows that on them gaz'd.

He poked fun at architects inspired by Vitruvius and sacred geometry.

> *Humility* alone designs
> These short but admirable Lines
> By which, ungirt and unconstrain'd,
> Things greater are in less contain'd.
> Let others vainly strive t'immure
> The *Circle* in the *Quadrature*!
> These *holy Mathematics* can
> In ev'ry Figure equal Man.

As we have seen, he argued that pious Appleton was constructed and adorned not with the classical orders and enrichments, but with the social and religious virtues, foreswearing the idolatry of material possessions.

> A stately Frontispiece of Poor
> Adorns without the open door:

Reading these country house poems it seems almost impossible to escape the conclusion that the paternalistic policy of bounty, hospitality and regionalism, the protection of English husbandry and manufactures, and the concomitant love of Englishness must have been intrinsic to the vernacular gothic of the Elizabethan and Jacobean period. On the other hand the association of classicism with absenteeism at court and a denial of bounty, hospitality and paternalistic regionalism is equally inescapable. After all, the style of classical buildings was *foreign* in origin. Such buildings were rather grand and haughty. Poets and moralists found it irresistible to use this fashionable style as a moral emblem.

But the truth, of course, is that style can play different roles in different games – the architectural, the political, the literary, the moral – and, as we shall see in a moment, there were other debates where classicism was held to be the most truly traditional, moral style of them all, embodying much the same virtues as those ascribed to vernacular gothic. The constant factor was the attribution to one kind of form, design and style of intrinsic political, social and ethical goodness.

But while all is fair, perhaps, in the polemics of any period, what is surprising is that sober social and architectural historians today reiterate one set of these associations, the rhetoric of the country house poets, as though it were a logical argument. Maurice Howard, in the most recent addition to this genre of interpretation, argues of classical Longleat, built by Sir John Thynne (who was, like Burghley, one of Lord Protector Somerset's protegés, all of them committed to the ideal of the patriarchal Common Weal discussed in Part II):

> Like many (though by no means all) former monastic sites, it lies remote from other settlements. Whilst the majority of country houses were still close to, or on the edge of villages in the sixteenth century, as time progressed more and more country houses were built in the way with which we are most familiar, at the centre of a great walled park and at the end of a long drive. This development has much to say about the place of the great

156

landowner in society and about how the relationship between the powerful and their immediate local communities had changed over the centuries since the Middle Ages. This visual evidence for a change in what was represented by the outward aspect of the great house was mirrored in much polemical literature of the mid-sixteenth century, which portrayed the landowner as no longer in a patriarchal and therefore protective relationship with his servants and tenants, but rather as a distant, managerial and self-seeking figure.[14]

In support of his argument Howard quotes a writer of 1563 who compared the new type of remote country house with the villas of the ancient Roman nobility, used as places of private retreat from the life of the city rather than as places of duty and hospitality:

> For flyeng cities . . . to build outleyes [outlying] farre from townes, to dwell scatteringe as the people Nomades [like Nomadic people], what it availeth . . . I can not yet reache by conjecture. For safe, it is not as already proved. And living solitary, they purchase envy . . .[15]

Howard, in my view, all too readily takes the sixteenth century critics of aristocratic remoteness at face value.

Even Felicity Heal, in her very careful article on the idea of hospitality, has argued that hospitality declined with the rise of Italian Renaissance and humanist ideals of gentility and social refinement disseminated through the English translations of Castiglione's *The Courtier* and other manuals of courtesy. It was to get away from 'your rude Country Gentleman, or rustical neighbours' that one writer of this period recommended the gentry to live in the city where they would learn the virtues of civility. Once again we find Italianate and classical ideals held responsible for the decline of the English traditions of charity and community.[16]

It may not be altogether surprising to discover this association of the classical style with the disintegration of the old organic English community of the middle ages among writers of the Ruskinian and Tawneyite tendency. But even amongst those historians who personally cherish the classical tradition, we find the same identification. Sir John Summerson, for example, has observed that

> Taste in architecture reached London about 1615; taste that is, in the exclusive, snobbish sense of the recognition of certain fixed values by certain people. Taste was a luxury import from abroad, received and cherished by a small group of nobleman and artists whose setting was the not very polished Court of James I. Architecture was a late comer to this little circle of intelligence in a still half-medieval England.[17]

According to Summerson, the harbinger of this taste was Inigo Jones, appointed Surveyor to the King in 1615. Summerson painted a vivid portrait of the half-gothic, 'barbarian' and traditional London (and England, by extension) upon which the Italian style of Inigo Jones burst:

> The freshness, the stark novelty, of Jones's work in Jacobean London cannot be overstressed. Here was a city built by a generation of closely organised carpenters and masons, a city of gables, mullioned windows, carved barge-boards, corner-posts and brackets, a city in which architectural novelty consisted in exceptional feats of carpentry, or in the extravagant use of stone . . . To put up a pure Italianate building in such a setting was sensational.

Both classicist and anti-classicist architectural historians have shared a picture of a pre-classical England which was homely, bountiful and good, half-gothic and not a little barbarian, and of an emerging classical England which was extravagant, cosmopolitan, proud and uncaring, absentee and money-mad though tasteful and civilised. Both groups regard the supposed 'arrival' of classicism in about 1615 as a watershed in English culture and society. The difference between the two camps lies in the fact that one lot regards the change as having been to the good aesthetically, and the other lot believes that it was to the bad socially.

Yet nothing, in fact, could be further from the truth. Indeed, some of the very people who were strongest in promoting traditional social values favoured the Italianate or classical style. Burghley House itself is an obvious example of a mansion quite rigorously classical in style – even if curiously hybridised with many vernacular features such as the bustling skyline of high chimneys above the cornice – which, as we have seen, was also a symbol of hospitality. Burghley was also surrounded by a park and detached from the town of Stamford, as its predecessor had been, yet Lord Burghley's paternal concern for the town could not have been greater. And no one could have been stronger, after all, in his advocacy of the traditional duties of the aristocrat than James I, yet it was he who commissioned the Banqueting House in Whitehall designed by Inigo Jones in 1619.

Throughout James's reign, moreover, in his own highly personalised London Proclamations after 1607, regulations increasingly favoured a classical style of house, explicitly espousing, in July 1615, the ambition to do for London what the Emperor Augustus had done for Rome:

> Onely, as to private houses, We could design and wish, according to Our former Proclamation and Ordinances touching Brick buildings, that as it was said by the first Emperour of Rome, that he had found the City of Rome of Bricke, and left it of marble, So that Wee whom GOD hath honoured to be the first King of Great Britaine, might bee able to say in some proportion, That Wee had found Our Citie and Suburbs of London of stickes, and left them of Bricke, being a Materiall farre more durable, safe from fire, beautifull and magnificent.[18]

As we have seen the proclamation of July 1618, which stipulated that window lights should of 'of more height than bredth', effectively specified the design of the classical London terrace house for the next 250 years.[19] Charles I's proclamation of 1632, returning the gentry to their estates, coincided with the laying out of Leicester Square and Covent Garden. Indeed, far from the adoption of classical architecture and urbanism being regarded by its supporters as a contradiction of their social and economic principles, the orderliness and uniformity which the 'classical' system encouraged in urban building was totally in accord with the ambition to prevent an uncontrolled clutter of new buildings in lanes and back gardens with overhanging jutties built of wood.★[20]

Sir Henry Wotton, himself the younger son of a Kentish squire and as ambassador in Venice one of the leading italianisers and classicists of the day, began the second part of his *Elements of Architecture* of 1624, the section dealing with ornamentation, with the most succinct and beautifully expressed summary of all the major social ideals we have been looking at. He certainly did not regard them as incompatible with classical forms, even if Marvell did.

> Every Mans proper Mansion House and Home, being the Theater of his Hospitality, the Seate of Selfe-fruition, the Comfortablest part of his owne Life, the Noblest of his Sonnes Inheritance, a kinde of private Princedome; Nay, to the Possessors thereof, an Epitomie of the whole World: may well deserve by these Attributes, according to the degree of the Master, to be decently and delightfully adorned.[21]

★ See, for example, the proclamation of May 1611: 'also observing how much it would grace and beautifie the said Cities, being the principall places of this Kingdome, for the resort and intertainment of forreine Princes, which from time to time doe come into this Realme, if an Uniformitie were kept in the sayd Buildings, and the foreparts or forefronts of the houses, standing and looking towards the Streets, were all builded with Bricke and Stone.'

41 King James I gold laurel, 1619–20. James I, as the first ruler of Great Britain since Roman times, adopted a classical imperial style with laurel wreath for his coinage.

Style, in other words, was an issue of decorum or appropriateness. Wotton did not deny, however, that the Italian style needed to be adapted to the different social customs prevailing in Britain. Whereas in Italy the kitchens, buttery and other domestic offices were placed underground in order to raise the main front of the house upon a basement 'to adde Majestie to the whole Aspect', he considered that 'by the naturall Hospitalitie of England, the Buttrie must be more visible; and wee neede perchance for our Raunges, a more spacious and luminous Kitchin, then the foresaid Compartition will beare'.[22]

It seems inconceivable that Charles I should have seen any contradiction between the classical style and his social policies.

What arguments, then, were employed to show that the aesthetic virtues of classical architecture were indeed compatible with the social virtues of traditional patriarchal government? Nothing, of course, could be more Roman in spirit than the power of the paterfamilias which James I, Charles I and others such as Sir Robert Filmer, the author of *Patriarcha, or the Natural Power of Kings Asserted*, wished to sustain and even extend.[23] But the fuller explanation, though it may encompass patriarchy, is infinitely more curious and complex than this.

This explanation relates to the larger political and constitutional issue of Britain's national identity once the accession of James VI of Scotland as James I of England had unified the countries and nations of the island of Britain under one rule.[24] James I was the first sovereign to style himself King of Great Britain, France and Ireland on his coinage: 'Magnae Britanniae Rex'. He was, moreover, the first sovereign since Alfred to be represented on British or English coins with a wreath, imperial style, rather than with a crown (Plate 41). However, the nature and origin of this revived political entity was not a simple one, as is apparent when we read William Camden's *Britannia* published in successive editions after 1586.

Camden was one of the founding fathers of modern British history, an exact historian with a critical and humanist approach to his sources, whose declared aim was to 'restore antiquity to Britaine, and Britain to his antiquity'. Following earlier humanists like Polydore Virgil and John Major in the first half of the sixteenth century, Camden therefore rejected the myth – still current as a popular legend in the early seventeenth century – that Britain had been founded by the Trojan Brutus. Moreover, his enterprise seems to have been to show that there was no such person as a 'True-born Briton'. Britain was an island into

159

which many nations had migrated and which had been conquered many times. It did not possess any clear-cut racial or cultural identity. The only unity and civilisation which the whole island had ever possessed in the past was that conferred upon it by the Roman conquest. By analogy Camden led his readers to suppose that only Roman culture could be an appropriate common culture or lingua franca for such a mongrel nation.[25]

The original inhabitants of Britain, according to Camden's history, were descendants of Noah's son Japheth who had colonised Britain from Gaul. These were subsequently subjugated and civilised by the Romans, with whom they largely intermarried, but the disappearance of the Roman legions in the early fifth century AD drove some of these romanised Britons to Brittany, others to Wales, others to Cornwall, as they fled such barbarian invaders as the Picts, the Jutes and the Saxons.[26]

Once they had established their conquest, the Anglo-Saxons initiated the re-unification of Britain: 'all the conquered', according to Camden, 'became one nation, used the same lawes, tooke their name, and spake one and the selfesame language, with the conquerors'. Their territory moreover included the greater part of Scotland which was inhabited by the Anglo-Saxons, so that Anglo-Saxon had been the common language of much of England and Scotland for the previous 1150 years.[27]

The next step in reunification came when Egbert, King of Wessex replaced the Saxon Heptarchy, the seven kingdoms, with one King of the English nation. Although fragmented by the Danish conquest of Northumberland in the ninth and tenth centuries, the unity of England was once again restored by the Danish kings of England and in turn by their Anglo-Saxon successors. Indeed, Camden reported, King Eadred had even used the name and title of King of Great Britain on documents in AD 948. Finally, all of England was conquered by the Normans, a mixed nation of ferocious Norwegians, Swedes and Danes who had settled in Neustria, or Normandy.[28]

With the Welsh House of Tudor and the Scottish House of Stuart, the whole of 'England and Scotland, long time divided' was 'most happily now in the most mightie Prince King James, under one imperiall Diademe conjoined and united'.[29]

But such was the confusion of nations over which James I reigned that Camden was moved to quote Seneca to characterise the flux of historical change: 'nothing hath continued in the same place, wherein it had the first beginning. There is daily stirring and moving to and fro of mankind: some change or other there is every day in so great a revolution of this world. New foundations of Cities are laid: New names of nations spring up, whereas the old are either growne out of use, or altered by the comming in of a mightier.'

This chaos alone would explain the value of a universal, unifying classical culture to the official historians of the late sixteenth and early seventeenth centuries. But Camden presented a stronger case for affinity between Britain and Rome. First, it was as a result of the Roman conquest that Christianity had come to Britain, initially under the Emperor Commodus and then, when Christianity became the state religion, under Constantine the Great. Second, Constantine the Great was himself half British, since his mother, the Empress Helena, was the daughter of the British prince Coelus – or so it was believed by Camden and his contemporary. Constantine also had assumed the imperial purple on British soil at York, to which he had travelled by post horse from Rome to be by his father's death bed. 'O fortunate Britaine and more happy now than all other lands, that hast the first sight of Constantine Caesar.' But as we have already seen, Camden believed that the Roman soldiers and colonists had so abundantly intermarried with the original Britons that they had 'by a blessed and joyfull mutuall ingrassing, as it were, ... growen into one stocke and nation'. So Constantine the Great was the epitome both of the union of the Roman and British nations and of the blessings of Roman-Christian civilisation, founded, or so Camden believed, by the product of this happy union of two great nations.

160

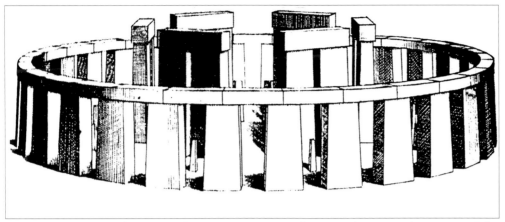

42 Stonehenge, engr. after drawing by Inigo Jones *c.* 1620, from *Stone-heng Restored*. Jones argued that Stonehenge was a Roman temple in the plainest Tuscan order built to set the ancient Britons on the path to civilisation. The buildings of the Kings should do likewise.

Third, despite the severity of the yoke that they placed on the Britons, by their conquest the Romans 'chased away all savage barbarism from the Britons minds'. They governed the country with good laws, reduced diverse nations into a unity and taught the Britons 'good maners and behaviour so, as in the diet and apparell they were not inferior to any other provinces'.

Among the instruments and benefits of Roman civilisation, Camden singled out building, architecture, the construction of roads and bridges as well as the draining of marshes and fen. 'They furnished them also with goodly houses and stately buildings in such sort, that the reliques and rubbish of their ruines doe cause the beholders now, exceedingly to admire the same . . . Certes, they are works of exceeding great admiration, and sumptuous magnificence.' Camden drew attention to the fact that the Romans set in progress public works like road building both to improve communications but also 'to exercise their souldiers, and the common multitude, lest being idle, they should grow fractious, and affect alteration in the State'. Moreover, as we have seen, Tacitus, from whom Camden derived his account of Roman architecture in Britain, refers to the way that Agricola set up competition amongst the Britons as being a more effective means of gaining honour from him than compulsion.[30]

Camden, in fact, was far more interested in language than in architecture but his history of Britannia implicitly addressed the whole question of the nature of cultural identity, which was determined not only by language but by law, religion, manners, building and the liberal arts.

The question which arose for the architecture of the new *Great* Britain of the Stuart dynasty was 'in what style should we build?' The obvious answer was 'in the British style'. But what was the British style? Was it the same as the English style, epitomised by Penshurst or Chantmarle? Or was it necessarily different? And, if it was different, were there buildings surviving from the pre-Roman era upon which to base such a style?

Here the argument was taken up by the King's Surveyor-General, Inigo Jones, who had been commanded by James I 'to produce, out of mine own Practice in Architecture, and Experience in Antiquities Abroad, What possibly I could discover concerning this of Stone Heng'. This command arose from James I's visit to Stonehenge on his Progress of 1620, and Jones's book was apparently written in 1620, although not published till after his death by his pupil John Webb in 1655, in a revised and polished form.[31]

Inigo Jones based his historical account closely upon Camden's *Britannia*, his argument

161

being this: there were no buildings worthy of the name by either the pre-Roman inhabitants of Britain or the Anglo-Saxon barbarians who had invaded the island when the Romans departed. The reason was that the Britons, the Druids, their priests and the Anglo-Saxons were all barbarians and hence deficient in knowledge of the liberal arts essential to architecture.

The Druids lived in 'Caves of desert and darksom Woods' and had no public works either sacred or secular let alone buildings of stone. Their *only* temples were 'Groves of Oak'. The Britons themselves were ignorant of all the arts except for the art of war. They didn't even know how to clothe themselves, let alone how 'to erect Stately Structures'. They were as primitive as the people Vitruvius had described in the first Age of the World. They were the British Nomads; their notion of a town or city was a thick wood enclosed by a ditch. It was only Agricola who had encouraged in them the arts of peace. Why, asked Jones, should Tacitus have told us that they had had to be compelled to build magnificent Temples if they had already been able to do so.[32]

As for the period of the Saxons, 'the Arts of Design, of which Architecture is chief, were utterly lost even in Rome itself, much more in Britain, being then but a Tempest-beaten Province and utterly abandoned by the Romans.'[33]

Only the Romans, therefore, during the period between Agricola and Constantine the Great, could have been responsible for Stonehenge (Plate 42).

Inigo Jones's subsequent explanation of the history, significance and the meaning of Stonehenge is highly instructive from the viewpoint of the history of British architecture and the arts of design, even if it is almost totally fabulous. Stonehenge, according to Jones, was a Roman Temple dedicated to the father of all the Gods, Coelus or Uranus. This he deduced from its situation on a plain remote from any town or village and from its being unvaulted and open to the skies, which, according to Vitruvius, was customary in Temples to celestial gods such as Coelus, Jove, the Sun and Moon. He deduced it also from the circular plan which was considered by the Egyptians to be 'an Hieroglyphick of Coelus' because the circle was suggestive of the sphere of the heavens. Finally, he deduced it from the severity of the order, which Jones considered to be Tuscan, appropriate to the most ancient of the Roman deities. Moreover, the fact that four equilateral triangles, representing the harmony of the twelve astrological signs, could be inscribed within Stonehenge was additional evidence for its dedication to the God of the Heavens.[34]

The reason why the Romans chose to dedicate a temple in Britain to this god was that Coelus was the bringer of civilization to mankind: 'he invited Men, living dispersedly before throughout the Fields, to convene, and dwell in Companies together, exhorting them to build towns, and reducing them from wild and savage to the Conversation of civil Life: Taught them also to sow corn and feeds, and divers other things belonging to the common Use of Mankind.' Such a Temple would both symbolise civilisation and encourage the Britons to become civilised.

In addition Jones implied that the date of the building of Stonehenge concurred with the period when the Romans had 'reduced the natural Inhabitants of this Island into the Society of Civil Life, by training them up in the Liberal Sciences'. He also referred to the passage in Camden's *Britannia* which told of the Roman practice of building great public works in order to keep their soldiers and the common people employed as deliberate policy to prevent them from growing rebellious. In other words, the building of Stonehenge epitomised the dissemination of the liberal arts and the employment of both skilled and unskilled artisans. Its building was an instrument of the civilising of Britannia. It was both a great school of architecture and of culture.[35]

Finally, Inigo Jones attached great importance to the Order which the Romans had chose for Stonehenge – the Tuscan Order, in his opinion. To understand his emphasis it is necessary to appreciate the significance which Inigo Jones attached to style, or manner as he called it. The manner of any work was profoundly characteristic of its maker. Thus any good judge of architecture could distinguish the structures of one nation from another, the Egyptian from the Greek and Roman, the Italian from the French or Dutch. Even a nation's shipping could be identified by its appearance: 'Is not our shipping, by the Mould thereof, known throughout the World English built?' This corresponds to Camden's notions about the manners, religion and language of a nation, but also extends the idea specifically to encompass the style and visual appearance of a structure or manufacture.

So why did the Romans choose the Tuscan Order for Stonehenge? First, the Tuscan Order was the only *Italian* order, invented by the Etruscans and adopted by the Romans. As the aboriginal Italian or Roman order its use in Stonehenge, designed to instruct the Britons in the art of architecture, was also a celebration of the virtue of the Roman 'Ancestors for so noble an Invention' as well as a means of making 'themselves the more renowned to Posterity, for erecting thereof, so well ordered a Building'. Moreover, reflecting the virtues of these first Italian buildings, the Tuscan Order was 'a plain, grave, and humble manner of Building, very solid and strong' of which 'Stone-Heng principally consists'.

Thus Stonehenge was a morally didactic work, teaching the Britons about the fundamentally spartan virtues of simplicity, sobriety and strength possessed by the Romans.

Inigo Jones provided his own summing up to what is, I would suggest, his manifesto of the architecture most appropriate for the newly united kingdom of Magna Britannia:

> I suppose, I have now proved from authentick Authors, and the Rules of Art, Stone-Heng anciently a Temple, dedicated to Coelus, built by the Romans; either in, or not long after those Times (by all likelihood) when the Roman Eagles spreading their commanding Wings over this Island; the more to civilize the Natives, introduc'd the Art of Building amongst them, discovering their ambitious Desire, by stupendious and prodigious Works, to eternize the Memory of their high Minds to succeeding Ages. For, the Magnificence of that stately Empire, is at this Day clearly visible in nothing more than in the Ruins of their Temples, Palaces, Arches Triumphals, Aquaeducts, Thermae, Theaters, Amphitheaters, Cirques, and other secular, and sacred Structures.[36]

Here it should be said that Inigo Jones was not the first architect in England or Britain to design in the classical or Roman style – despite the chorus of architectural historians who, over four centuries, have reiterated that he was. The style had been well-established in Britain for more than a century. Quite apart from buildings like Burghley House, Kirby Hall and the work of Robert Smythson in the reign of Elizabeth, there was the work of Nicholas Gerbier, Nicholas Stone, Isaac and Salomon de Caus, as well as that of the Florentine Constantino de' Servi (1554–1622) who was appointed architect to Henry Prince of Wales in 1611 at £200 a year, four times Inigo Jones's salary as the prince's surveyor.[37]

It is impossible that Inigo Jones himself was unaware of this. So of what, precisely, was *Stone-Heng Restored* a manifesto? The answer is to be found in Jones's only other extended statement about architectural style, inscribed in his Italian sketchbook and dated 20 January 1615.

> And to saie trew all thes composed ornaments the wch Proceed out of ye aboundance of dessigners and wear brought in by Michill Angell and his followers in my oppignion do not well in sollid Architecture and ye fasciati of houses, but in gardens loggis stucco or ornaments of chimnies peeces or in the inner parts of houses thos compositions are of necessety to be yoused. For as outwarly every wyse man carrieth a graviti in Publicke Places, whear ther is nothing els looked for, yet inwardly hath his immaginacy set on fire, and sumtimes licenciously flying out, as nature hir sealf doeth often tymes stravagantly, to dellight, amase us sumtimes mouve us to laughter, sumtimes to contemplation and

horror, so in architecture ye outward ornaments oft [ought] to be sollid, proporsionable according to the rulles, masculine and unaffected.[38]

In other words, Jones disapproved of the use of fantastic 'composed ornaments' introduced by Michelangelo, what we would call the Mannerist style, especially for the public facades of buildings – and this opinion tallies completely with the argument of *Stone-Heng Restored*. There, Jones praised not Michelangelo but Donato Bramante who 'attaining admirable perfection in Architecture, restored to the World again the true Rules of Building, according to those Orders, by the ancient Romans in the most flourishing Times observed'.[39] From statements such as these we can see that Jones perceived himself not as the man who merely restored to Britain a classical architecture, but as the man who restored it in its truest and purest Roman form, purged of all the licentious ornament of Michelangelo and his mannerist followers. Moreover, he saw himself as holding not only the British but the European stage: he would be the scourge of license everywhere, the guardian of the true manner and spirit of classicism as exemplified in the works of the Emperor Augustus, Vitruvius's treatise and the modern work of Bramante and Palladio. When John Webb called Inigo Jones 'the Vitruvius of his Age' he meant the Vitruvius of Europe, not just of Great Britain.

Thus, from about 1615, as we have already observed, a relatively pure form of classicism was adopted, both in buildings and in schemes like the Queen's House at Greenwich, the Banqueting Hall at Whitehall, Covent Garden piazza, the portico of St Paul's Cathedral, Stoke Bruerne in Northamptonshire and Wilton House, as well as in the purchase of the Raphael Cartoons for the Tapestry Works at Mortlake and the depiction of James I in Augustan fashion on his coinage. This kind of classicism was distinctively different to that of the previous half-century or so, exemplified by Longleat, Burghley or Wollaton, which, although it may seem to us the essence of Tudor vernacular architecture, was certainly regarded by contemporaries as being Italianate. Worksop Manor Lodge, for instance, a tall, thin and modest brick house with Tudor windows, was used as a reference by Thomas Coke when describing the Medici villa of Pratolino: 'The house is in show much what about the show of R. Portlington's Lodge in Worksop Park, and the chambers in it very like to those.' It is possible that the great staircases and terraces of the house of Lord Burghley's eldest son, Thomas Cecil, were likewise inspired by the Villa Farnese at Caprarola, designed by Vignola.[40]

Such an interpretation of classicism can make sense in the context of late sixteenth-century humanist conceptions about translation summarised in John Donne's Latin verses to Ben Jonson:

O Poet, if our lawyers and theologians, students of human and divine law, had the courage you showed in your art in *Volpone*, in your method of both following and yet rivalling the classical writers you drew on, we should all of us be in possession of the wisdom we need to save our souls. But for them the classics are dead and covered with cobwebs. None of them knows how to make use of the classics as you do, who treat the authors you translate in a creative, revolutionary way, making new art of old.[41]

Ben Jonson's poem 'To Penshurst' was also a creative translation: a translation of Martial, Horace and Pliny into English verse and English life. So, by the same token, were those Elizabethan prodigy houses I have mentioned. But Inigo Jones set himself against this 'creative' assimilation of the classical; he desired the letter as well as the spirit. The reason for this lay in a belief that the spirit and the letter were inseparable, that the outward appearance of a building as well as its underlying principles, its manner, should be appropriate to its purpose. The purpose of monumental or public architecture was to civilise a country, to teach its citizens the civic virtues of sobriety and a well-ordered life and, by so doing, to assist the constitutional ambition of unifying the two kingdoms and all the different races of Magna Britannia. The logic behind this becomes clearer when we examine the career of Thomas Howard, Earl of Arundel whose patronage of the visual arts marks him out as the first of a long line of arbiters of taste in Britain.

ARBITERS OF TASTE

The Earl of Arundel was no passive patron; not an original scholar nor a practitioner of the arts, he was part of that circle of great antiquarians and historians that included Sir Henry Wotton and William Camden and he had, it appears, formed a powerful ambition to foster the revival of learning and the arts in Britain. Rubens described him as one of the 'four evangelists of our art'.[42]

Something of the intensity of Arundel's application is suggested by the true story of how he and his countess, an equal partner in their enterprise, immured themselves for six weeks within the Monastery delle Grazie in Siena learning Italian, resolutely refusing an invitation from the Duke of Tuscany to join him at court. Their Grand Tour, or perhaps we should call it their great Study Tour of Italy between 1612 and 1614, on which they were accompanied by Inigo Jones, was not only the prototype for those of future generations of British aristocracy, it was, it seems, undertaken very much in the spirit of a mission to educate their countrymen, the ruling class in particular. And so it was understood back at home. One courtier wrote to the Arundels in Italy to tell them that 'the exercise you are in is much applauded of all men'.[43]

The details of what they did on the tour are amply described by David Howarth in his admirable book on Arundel's career as a patron. For my purposes, the repercussions of that tour upon their return home are most important. First there was the influence of the collections they made, particularly the famous Arundel Marbles. The purpose of forming great comprehensive collections of marbles or drawings at that period, long before cheap processes of reproduction and cheap travel, was primarily educative and to some degree, certainly in the eighteenth and nineteenth centuries, commercial. With access to the Arundel Marbles and the subsequent collection of drawings including two hundred volumes of Michelangelos, Leonardos, Raphaels and other old masters, British artists possessed an essential study collection and the basis of an academy of art.[44]

Second was the impact of the tour upon the career of Inigo Jones. In September 1615, shortly after the Arundels and Jones returned from Italy, Jones succeeded Simon Basil as Surveyor of the King's Works. In that office, first at the Banqueting House built between 1619 and 1622, then in the Queen's House at Greenwich begun in 1616 but not finished until 1638, and finally in the casing of St Paul's during the 1630s, Jones set the model for a correct style of architecture grounded in Palladio, Bramante and the remains of antiquity (Plate 43).

Third, as Surveyor of the King's Works, Inigo Jones had overall responsibility for enforcing the proclamations on building in London – and the first proclamation to be issued during his tenure of the office, that of July 1618, certainly bears his stamp. Its detailed regulations concerning construction and the design of facades were prescriptive enough to act as specifications for the London terrace house of the subsequent 250 years.

And further, That all and every person and persons, which at any time hereafter shall erect, build, or set up within any of the Limits, Places or Precincts aforesaid, any manner of Houses, or other buildings whatsoever, shall make and build the same of such height, & in such manner and forme as heerein is expressed [That is to say] every whole Story of and in such Houses & Buildings; and all & every the Roomes of such whole Story

43 New facade of old St Paul's by Inigo Jones, 1634–42. The Corinthian portico, reminiscent of Hadrian's Temple in Rome, must have been a striking vision of ancient Rome when approached from the timber houses of Ludgate Hill.

shalbe of the height of ten foote of Assise at the least; And every halfe story of and in such Houses and Buildings, shalbe of the height of seven foote & a halfe of assise at the least; And that the Forefront & outer Walles & windows thereof shalbe of Bricke, or of Bricke and Stone: And if the said building do not exceede two Stories in height, then the walles therof shalbe of the thicknes of one Brickes and halfe a Bricks length from the ground unto the uppermost part of the said wals . . . And that in building of the said Houses, there shalbe no Jutties, or jutting Windowes; either upon Timber joysts, or otherwise, but the walles to goe direct & straight upwards, and at the setting off, a water table to bee made. Also the Lights in the Windowes of every whole Story to be of more height then bredth, to the end there may bee a sufficient peere of Bricke betweene the Windowes for strength: And likewise the Windowes of every halfe Story to be made square every way, or neere thereabouts. And lastly, that all Shops in every principal Street of Trade be made with Pillasters of hard Stone or Bricke cut in Wedges Archwise, Upon paine that all persons directly or indirectly neglecting or disobeying this our Proclamation, or doeing any thing contrary to the tenor thereof, or any part thereof, shall endure & abide such Censure in Our high Court of Starre-Chamber . . .[45]

It was as members of the Building Commission that Inigo Jones and Arundel contributed to the successive efforts to introduce the Moorfields solution to urban development. At Lincoln's Inn in 1618, Jones was mentioned specifically as surveying the Fields to lay them out in 'the manner of Moorfields'. At Leicester Square in 1630, Arundel was one of

166

the three commissioners who reported to the Privy Council in favour of turning half the Lammas lands into a public open space laid out in walks and planted with trees. And Jones was involved at Covent Garden between 1632 and 1638 – though not, it seems, as architect.[46]

Besides all this, there exists sufficient circumstantial evidence to suggest that Arundel may have been the prime mover in the purchase of the Raphael Cartoons and the founding of the Mortlake Tapestry Works by Sir Francis Crane. As early as 1613, when Arundel was in Venice, he had attempted to buy the Grimani tapestries, the second of two sets woven from the Raphael cartoons in the early sixteenth century. Although he failed in this attempt, he was a close personal friend of Crane and he would certainly have favoured the Mortlake project. For Arundel was far from an unworldly connoisseur. He had had to work hard to re-establish his own estates, buying them back from relatives, and he employed Francesco, son of Giacomo Verzellini the glassmaker, as his Italian secretary. He would not therefore have been unaware or uninterested in the commercial and industrial aspects of the fine arts. Indeed, so much is indicated by his own much later investment in opening up marble quarries at Drean in County Donegal in Ireland and importing the material to England on a commercial basis to offset some of his costs in using the marble. To obtain permission he wrote the Earl of Strafford, Lord Deputy of Ireland, whose own interest in encouraging the building industry we have already noted, a letter to accompany two members of his household – one of them a Roman sculptor Clemente Coltreci who had worked for him since 1619: 'to the end, that if they [the quarries] prove so well, as is enformed me, I may not only make use of them myself for a whole room that I am about, but set up a trade of them hither, and increase shipping with the good of both kingdoms and benefit to the undertakers'. Strafford heartily approved, as one might expect, and ventured to hope that he himself might 'get a barque laden to send about to Hull and so into Yorkshire, to make a Chimney peece or two at Woodhouse'.[47]

We have already discussed the creation of employment through aristocratic expenditure on houses and their furnishing. Here, the issue is more specific: the *aesthetic character* of the edifices and objects created by that expenditure. Arundel exemplifies a dual concern with beauty and profit.

The true fruits of his enterprise were to be seen in the initial stages of the great neo-Palladian building and rebuilding of the English country house. The first example of this, to which reference has already been made was Sir Francis Crane's great house at Stoke Bruerne in Northamptonshire, built with the profits of the Mortlake Tapestry Works and which would, had Crane not died prematurely in 1636, have been a model of policy: a grand house in a pure Italianate manner, furnished with tapestries manufactured at Mortlake, maybe including the Raphaels themselves, as well as a tapestry works providing employment on the estate itself. Likewise, on a still grander scale, there was Wilton House, the truly viceregal country palace which Charles I commanded the Earl of Pembroke to rebuild in 1636 and which, in the next century, not only housed another notable collection of marbles but also became the centre of a major 'art manufactory': the Wilton Carpet company.

Integral to this building and rebuilding was the idea that the visual arts not only *reflected* the character of a nation and of an era, as Camden had believed, but would actually incite those exposed to them to behave in a corresponding manner. The theory was propounded by Arundel's librarian, Francis Junius, in his book *De Pictura Veterum* of 1637, where he argued that the presence of noble statues in a house could inspire the inhabitants with the desire to commit noble deeds. He was not, however, alone in his views. As we saw in relation to the belief that the monarch and the aristocracy should set a good example to the people, Junius' basically magical concept of cause and effect was widely accepted.[48]

This process was often termed 'fascination' because, as if they were under a spell, individuals involved in it had no choice but to imitate the behaviour and images surround-

Ἡ δὲ μετάνοια ἐστὶ φιλο-
σοφίας ἀρχὴ γίνεται

44 John
Evelyn by
Robert Walker.
Evelyn, though
a royalist, was
severely
puritanical in
his views on
clothing and
design.

ing them. Moreover, the actions and productions of a person must inevitably bear the stamp of his or her character – their *virtu*. Thus, for Giorgio Vasari, writing in sixteenth-century Florence, Fra Angelico's paintings were naturally pious because he was a pious man, and Botticelli's paintings were full of caprice and conceit because he was something of a practical joker. Cervantes, in the Prologue to *Don Quixote* offered an ironical command on this belief:

> Idle reader, you can believe without any oath of mine that I would wish this book, as the child of my brain, to be the most beautiful, the liveliest and the cleverest imaginable. But I have been unable to transgress the order of nature, by which like gives birth to like. And so, what could my sterile and ill-cultivated genius beget but the story of a lean, shrivelled, whimsical child, full of varied fancies that no one else has ever imagined – much like one

engendered in prison, where every discomfort has its seat and every dismal sound its habitation?

The idea was of great antiquity. It lay at the root of Plato's concern, in both the *Laws* and the *Republic*, to banish or at least to control the arts by law, in order to prevent corrupt and effeminate forms and styles such as the Ionic from corrupting the citizens. The Doric mode was to be preferred for its greater simplicity and self-control. In architecture, Leon Battista Alberti, whose treatise *De Re Aedificatoria* of 1452 was the first European work on the subject since antiquity, also subscribed to the notion. 'In that Apartment which is peculiar to the Master of the Family and his Wife, we should take care that nothing be painted but the most comely and beautiful Faces; which we are told may be of no small Consequence to the Conception of the Lady, and the Beauty of the Children. Such as are tormented with a Fever are not a little refreshed by the Sight of Pictures of Springs, Cascades and Streams of Water.' Alberti also argued that the physical beauty of the buildings in a city could be a form of defence in itself, since 'Beauty will have such an Effect even upon an enraged Enemy, that it will disarm his Anger, and prevent him from offering it any Injury.' By extension, the divine harmonies of a well-planned and proportioned city would calm and compose the passions and regulate the minds of all the citizens and contribute to the good government of the state.[49]

There still survived more than a trace of this belief in the magical power of imitation and of images among the rational protestants who founded the Royal Society: men such as John Evelyn, who seems to have regarded himself as the Earl of Arundel's successor as arbiter of taste under the restored government of Charles II. It is to Evelyn's career and publications that we now turn.

In the decade following the Restoration, John Evelyn (Plate 44), as a familiar at court, played an important role in re-establishing the aesthetic and architectural programme initiated by Arundel and Jones. He was a regular attender at meetings of the new Royal Society, was appointed to various building commissions, gave informed advice to the king and inspected and commented on the new country houses of the nobility. Above all he published a series of pamphlets and treatises all aiming at the improvement of taste, the control of luxury and of environmental pollution and the orderly augmentation of the wealth of the kingdom. His career overlapped with that of his close friend Sir Christopher Wren though once the latter was launched upon his own career as architect and surveyor, from 1665 onwards, Evelyn's contribution to public affairs in this field faded out.

The first of Evelyn's post-Restoration publications provides evidence of a continuing superstition about the quasi-magical effects of style or manner. *Tyrannus or the Mode*, which Evelyn presented to the king on its appearance in January 1661, was a 'Discourse of Sumptuary Lawes', whose reinstatement Evelyn favoured. The first sentence declared that 'Garments in Animals, are infallible signs of their Nature; in Men of their Understanding.' So far so good, but on the next page Evelyn observed that clothes not only *signified* the character of the wearer but that the style of clothing itself could affect the wearers. Thus 'when a Nation is able to impose, and give laws to the habits of another, (as the late Tartars in China) it has (like that of Language) prov'd a Fore-runer of the spreading of their Conquests there, as it has something of Magisterial; so it gives them a boldnesse, and an Assurance which early introduces them, without being taken notice of for Strangers where they come; so as by degrees, they insinuate themselves into all those Places where they Model is taken up.' He also argued that 'the People of Rome, left off the Toga, an Antient and Noble Garment, with their power'. Evelyn's specific complaint was against effeminate and ever-changing French fashions (Plate 45):

> It was a fine silken thing which I spied walking th' other day through Westminster-Hall, that has as much Ribbon about him as would have plundered six shops, and set up

twenty Country Pedlers: All his Body was dres't like a May-Pole, or a Tom'a Bedlam's Cap. A Fregat newly rigg'd kept not half such a clatter in a storme, as this Puppets Streamers did when the Wind was in his Shroud's; the Motion was Wonderfull to behold, and the Colours were Red, Orange, and Blew, of well gum'd Sattin . . .

His proposed solution was to regulate attire partly through Sumptuary Laws and partly through the king setting a good example. (Wasn't Charles II, just returned from France, wearing French ribbons himself at this time?) He recommended a virile and more constant style which made a clear distinction between the sexes: 'whatever is comely, and of use, and to that I would be constant, choosing nothing that should be capricious, nothing that were singular' – a modern equivalent to the Roman toga. The only form of variety and change he approved of was one based upon natural decorum; in words echoing those of Bacon's essay on gardens he proclaimed, 'Let men change their Habits as oft as they please, so the change be for the better: I would have a Summer Habit, and a Winter; for the Spring, and for the Autumne: Something I would indulge to Youth, something to Age, and Humour.' In addition he admitted a degree of variety based upon people's trade and status. Finally English costume should be English in cut and cloth so as to prevent the waste of bullion through the import of French materials as well as to encourage English manufactures and promote a national style.[50]

In fact, as Evelyn noted in his diary, during hostilities with France in 1666 Charles II ordered the adoption of Persian vests for the court in order, as Lord Halifax noted, that 'we might look more like a distinct People, and not be under the Servility of Imitation' (Plate 46). Louis XIV's response was to snub Charles II by dressing his footmen in the Persian vests, an interesting illustration of the way imitation and the avoidance of imitation were understood to operate.[51]

Evelyn himself, as far as can be seen from portraits, adopted the severe, puritanical style he recommended. As Addison and Steele were later to do, he was setting himself up explicitly as the aesthetic and moral censor of the fashions of his age. With tedious regularity his private diary commented upon the luxurious manners of the court and the French-style furnishings of the king's mistresses:

Following his Majestie this morning through the Gallerie, [I] went (with the few who attended him) into the Dutchesse of Portsmouths dressing roome, within her bed-chamber, where she was in her morning loose garment, her maides Combing her, newly out of her bed: his Majestie & the Gallants standing about her: but that which ingag'd my curiositie, was the rich & splendid furniture of this woman's Appartment, now twice or thrice, puld downe, & rebuilt, to satisfie her prodigal & expensive pleasures, whilst her Majestie dos not exceede, some gentlemens Ladies furniture & accommodation: Here I saw the new fabrique of *French Tapissry*, for designe, tendernesse of worke, & incomparable imitation of the best paintings; beyond any thing, I had ever beheld: some pieces had *Versailles*, St *Germans* & other Palaces of the French King with Huntings, figures, & Landscips, Exotique fowle & all to the life rarely don: Then for *Japon Cabinets, Skreenes, Pendule Clocks*, huge *Vasas* of wrought plate, *Tables, Stands, Chimny furniture, Sconces, branches, Braseras* &c they were all of massive silver, & without number, besides of his Majesties best paintings: Surfeiting of this, I din'd yet at *Sir Steph: Foxes*, & went contentedly home to my poore, but quiet *Villa*. Lord what contentment can there be in the riches & splendor of this world, purchas'd with vice & dishonor . . .

And he much approved a sermon given by his local curate which condemned the age as 'Wanton, madd, and surfeiting with prosperity, every moment unsettling the old foundations, and never constant to any thing'.[52]

In contrast his preface to a poem written by his daughter, which satirised young women's

45 The waxwork funeral effigy of Charles II in Westminster Abbey. Evelyn did not approve of the beribboned French fashions of the court.

fashions, pulled out all the familiar stops about the virtues of the preceding age, much as the Jacobean writers had done before him.

They had cupboards of ancient useful plate, whole chests of damask for the table, and store of fine Holland sheets (white as the driven snow), and fragrant of rose and lavender, for the bed; and the sturdy oaken bedstead, and furniture of the house, lasted one whole century; the shovel-board, and other long tables, both in hall and parlour, were as fixed as the freehold; nothing was moveable save joynt-stools, the black jacks, silver tankards, and bowls . . . Twas then ancient hospitality was kept up in town and country, by which the tenants were enabled to pay their landlords at punctual day; the poor were relieved bountifully, and charity was as warm as the kitchen, where the fire was perpetual.

In those happy days, Sure-foot, the grave and steady mare, carried the good knight, and his courteous lady behind him, to church and to visit the neighbourhood, without so many hell-carts, ratling coaches, and a crue of *lacqueys*, which a grave livery servant or two supply'd, who rid before and made way for his worship.

Things of use were natural, plain, and wholesome; nothing was superfluous, nothing necessary wanting; and men of estate studied the publick good, and gave examples of true piety, loyalty, justice, sobriety, charity, and the good neighbourhood compos'd most differences.[53]

172

46 *The Viner Family* by J.M. Wright, 1673. During war with France in 1666 Charles II ordered the adoption of Persian vests (worn here by Sir Robert Viner) to Evelyn's great satisfaction.

47 Late seventeenth-century panelling, Buckingham Street, Adelphi. The masculine severity of panelled rooms of this period reflects Evelyn and Wren's preference for things of use to be 'natural, plain and wholesome'.

The chief difference between this and earlier writings on the same theme is Evelyn's greater emphasis upon the iniquity of domestic luxury in furniture and household goods and the contrasting virtues of things of use that were 'natural, plain and wholesome' – a comparison which lies at the very root of design reform as it developed over the succeeding two centuries (Plate 47). Evelyn did not object to magnificence in the external architecture of great palaces and country houses: public magnificence was welcome, private luxury and indulgence was not.

Not every kind of public display or splendour, however, was equally acceptable. Evelyn's colleague and friend Christopher Wren, on his famous visit to Paris in 1665 to study Renaissance architecture at first hand at the outset of his architectural career, condemned the exterior of Versailles because its style was both effeminate and indecorous. It resembled the furnishing of the interiors and there was no proper distinction between inside and out. 'The Palace, or if you please, the Cabinet of *Versailles* call'd me twice to view it; the Mixtures of Brick, Stone, blue Tile and Gold make it look like a rich Livery: Not an Inch within but is crouded with little Curiosities of Ornaments: the Women, as they make here the Language and Fashions, and meddle with Politicks and Philosophy, so they sway also in Architecture; Works of Filgrand, and little Knacks are in great Vogue; but Building certainly ought to have the Attribute of eternal, and therefore the only Thing uncapable of new Fashions.' Clearly Wren did not care for the style of the interior of Versailles either.

173

In contrast 'The masculine Furniture of *Palais Mazarine* pleas'd me much better, where is a great and noble Collection of antique Statues and Bustos, (many of Porphyry) good Basso-relievos.'[54]

Wren was making a very similar observation about the decorum appropriate to the public as opposed to the private side of a building as Inigo Jones had made in 1615: 'as outwardly every wyse man carrieth a graviti in Publicke Places . . . so in architecture ye outward ornaments oft [ought] to be solid, proporsionable according to the rules, masculine and unaffected.' But whereas Inigo allowed that the inner man (and hence the interior of his home) could have his 'immaginacy set on fire, and sometimes licenciously flying out', both Evelyn and Wren seem to have insisted upon a 'masculine' unaffectedness in the private as well as in the public side of life. In so doing, the distinction on which Alberti had insisted − between public life, where a strict code of manners and decorum obtained, and private life, where far greater freedom was permitted − was in danger of being eroded, in theory if not in practice.

Public architecture, according to Wren should aim at 'Eternity; and therefore the only thing uncapable of Modes and Fashions in its Principals, the orders'. The orders of architecture were a kind of bulwark against the mutability and the fashions of the age of luxury, and therefore a direct means of regulating its temper while not actually restricting economic growth. Similarly, as Evelyn envisaged them, sumptuary laws would regulate dress, keeping it decorous and in accordance with the wearer's rank, age, metier and temperament.[55]

Returning, in conclusion, to *why* the observance of decorum should be a necessity, not only in clothes but in architecture, Evelyn adduced the 'magical' explanation: 'It is from the Asymmetry of our Buildings, want of Decorum and Proportion in our Houses, that the Irregularity of our Humours and Affections may be shrewdly discerned.'[56]

This also explains the intensity of his famous polemic upon 'a certain Fantastical and Licentious manner of Building, which we have since call'd Modern (or Gothic rather)'. His grounds for this attack were that the 'sharp Angles, Jetties, Narrow Lights, lame Statues, Lace and other Cut-work and Crinkle Crankle . . . Turrets and Pinacles thick set with Monkies and Chymaeras (and abundance of buisy Work and other Incongruities) dissipate and break the Angles of the Sight, and so confound it that one cannot consider it with any Steadiness'. Consequently the mind of the 'Judicious Spectator is . . . Distracted and quite Confounded'. Evelyn's choice of words here makes it clear without a shadow of a doubt that he believed gothic architecture to have a debauching effect upon the mental state of the onlooker and, hence, upon the condition of the nation. In contrast, the sight of well proportioned and majestic architecture in the ancient manner − such as Inigo's Banqueting House, Wren's St Paul's or Greenwich Palace − composed and civilised the mind and hence contributed to social and political stability, a major concern in the Restoration.[57]

Both Evelyn and Wren were actively involved in the regulation of towns and cities, London in particular, but Evelyn also had broader interests in environmental planning. Evelyn's earliest opinions on town planning are to be found in two pamphlets of the 1650s. The first was on *The State of France* published in 1652 and the second *A Character of England* published in 1659 and written in the guise of a visiting French nobleman. These contain a comparison of Paris and London and are based upon Evelyn's extensive continental travels during the 1640s. Paris he considered infinitely to excel all the major cities of Italy − Naples, Rome, Florence, Genoa and Venice − in its palaces, gentlemen's houses, public buildings, streets, suburbs and common buildings. Only in ecclesiastical architecture did it fall short of Renaissance Italy. (Maybe it was on his recommendation that Wren only visited Paris and never toured Italy.) In contrast to those of Paris, the streets of London were wooden, northern, narrow and congested. As a whole the city was deformed and asymmetrical, and it possessed only two good classical buildings: the Banqueting House and

Inigo Jones's portico for St Paul's. The behaviour of the London populace towards the nobility in their coaches, 'cursing and reviling' them, was such that 'you would imagine yourself amongst a legion of devils, and in the suburbs of hell' – presumably as a result of the influence of gothic and barbaric architecture. Indeed, Evelyn described London's buildings as being 'as deformed as the minds and confusion of the people'.[58]

Another example of this deformity of mind was the inadequacy of the building laws and regulations, so that when there was a fire 'the magistrate has either no power, or no care to make them build with any uniformity'. The result of this lack of legal regulation was an ugly, ill-mannered and heavily polluted town

> pestred with hackney-coaches and insolent carre-men, shops and taverns, noyse, and such a cloud of sea-coal, as if there be a resemblance of hell upon earth, it is in this vulcano in a foggy day: this pestilent smoak, which corrodes the very yron, and spoils all the moveables, leaving a soot on all things that it lights: and so fatally seizing on the lungs of the inhabitants, that the cough and the consumption spares no man. I have been in a spacious church where I could not discern the minister for the smoak; nor hear him for the people's barking.[59]

In *Fumifugium: Or the Inconvenience of the Aer and Smoake of London Dissipated*, which appeared in the same year as *Tyrannus or the Mode*, Evelyn addressed some of these problems more fully, apparently with the intent of securing an act of parliament with the king's support. The control of atmospheric pollution had been a favoured cause of the early Stuart court, particularly promoted by Charles I's Archbishop of Canterbury, William Laud. Evelyn considered the problem of atmospheric pollution to belong essentially to the medicinal, or what we would call the public health aspect of architecture, as discussed by Vitruvius in his section on the siting of cities. Evelyn discussed in great detail both the physical and psychological harm caused by smoke. It was the cause of all manner of respiratory illnesses but, since the smoke was borne upon the air, and the air was also the vehicle of the human spirit, he also believed that the corrupt air of London 'prohibits necessary transpiration for the resolution and dissipation of ill Vapours, even to disturbance of the very Rational faculties, which the purer Aer does so far illuminate'. He suggested that 'grosse and heavy' air was a 'potent and great disposer to Rebellion'. Thus many of England's political as well as social ills were caused by the smoke of London. In addition he cited the effect of the soot upon buildings and their contents and upon plants, insects and animals, 'suffering nothing in our Gardens to bud, display themselves or ripen'.[60]

His solution was three-fold. First to remove by Statute all industries using coal from London to a spot beyond the hill at Greenwich in order to prevent the prevailing winds blowing the smoke back again: what we would call industrial zoning. As a precedent to such legislation Evelyn cited an Act of 1610 to prevent the burning of gorse to clear heaths. He also recommended the removal of smelly and offensive trades such as abattoirs, fishmongers and tallow makers. Their removal would free land within the city for domestic occupation and the citizens of London would enjoy a clean and well-aired city. His second remedy, dependent upon the first, was to lay out plantations in square fields of between twenty and forty acres each to the east and the south-west of the city as market gardens for all kind of 'most fragrant and odoriferous Flowers', such as musk roses and woodbines, lavender and above all rosemary whose scent would sweeten the air of London, as well as providing marketable produce and vegetables. His third remedy was to use smokeless fuel charcoal, though not coke.[61]

In addition Evelyn desired the enforcement of the early Stuart proclamations against London's expansion, which had already been reintroduced in August 1661, maybe on his advice, a month before he presented *Fumifugium* to Charles II. This was a point he reiterated in the Epistle Dedicatory to his translation of Fréart's *Parallel*, adding his opinion that the

175

king should use powers of compulsory purchase to demolish buildings in the suburbs in order to 'bring this monstrous Body into Shape'.[62]

Although most of these ideas came to nothing and it was not in fact until 1956 that the Clean Air Act finally tackled London's problem effectively, the principle of establishing laws for regulating the uniformity of buildings was established.

Another essential component of the policy of reforming the architecture of England was education: the education of those who commissioned buildings, the Architectus Sumptuarius, and of those, the Architect and the Architectus Manuarius (to use Evelyn's terms) who made and executed the designs. How was this to be accomplished?

In the case of the Architectus Sumptuarius the first necessity was that the king should set an example in encouraging fine building for the nobility and others to follow, as Augustus and other great rulers had done. But example was not enough. Evelyn also believed that each type of architect required a degree of formal education in architecture, part of it provided by the fourth type of architect, the Architectus Verborum, the theoretician like himself.[63]

He therefore recommended that the gentry and nobility on their Grand Tours ought to make a special study of architecture as the Romans had done and the Italians still did. In addition he favoured the establishment of Professors of Architecture at the universities amongst the Humanities and not, as such studies were at the time, 'thrust out as purely Mechanical'. Indeed he implicitly compared architecture to the experimental sciences in which both he and Wren, Savilian Professor of Astronomy at Oxford, were so much involved at the Royal Society. He also promoted the idea that the king should fund an Academy of Design in the rooms of the new Royal Palace at Whitehall when it was finished, 'for the Ease and Encouragement of the ablest Workmen in this, as in all other useful, Princely and Sumptuous Arts: I mean for Printers, Painters, Sculptors, Architects'. In his *Scultura* of 1662 he insisted upon the necessity of academies of drawing for the encouragement of the arts of design, in obvious imitation of the French Académie Royale de Peinture et de Sculpture founded in 1648.[64]

But a still more fascinating reflection upon the academic ideal appears in Wren's letter concerning his Paris visit of 1665, on which he also served, as was the case with most such travellers, as a kind of industrial spy: 'my Business now is to pry into Trades and Arts, I put myself into all Shapes to humour them'. Wren briefly described the Académie Royale in the Louvre but his most interesting observations were devoted to the rebuilding of the Louvre – for it was these building works themselves which he regarded as the true academy in which all three forms of architect might be educated:

> the Louvre for a while was my daily Object, where no less than a thousand hands are constantly employ'd in the Works; some in laying mighty Foundations, some in raising the Stories, Columns, Entablements, &c. with vast Stones, by great and useful Engines; other in Carving, Inlaying of Marbles, Plaistering, Painting, Gilding, &c. Which altogether make a School of Architecture, the best probably, at this Day in Europe.

Do we see here the germ of the idea upon which Wren was to base his own administration of the Royal Works, which he treated as a school where designers as well as executive architects and craftsmen could learn together in a thoroughly practical way? The observation is also interesting in that it tends to confirm the theory expressed in a previous section that the prodigy houses of the Elizabethan period were also intended as 'schools of architecture', just as subsequently so too was the rebuilding of the Palace of Westminster under Barry and Pugin. Certainly Wren's unfinished treatise on architecture opens with the following resounding sentence, which summarises one of the dominant themes of this present book: 'Architecture has its political Use; publick Buildings being the Ornament of a Country; it

The Oak Tree.

Publish'd Jan.y 1.st 1776 by J. Hinton, N.16 as the Act directs.

J. Miller del.t & Sculp.t

48   *The Oak Tree* by J. Miller from the 1776 edition of Evelyn's *Silva*. 1664, which encouraged landlords to replant their estates with timber for building warships.

establishes a Nation, draws People and Commerce; makes the People love their native Country, which Passion is the Original of all great Actions in a Common-wealth.'[65] In their great undertakings Evelyn and Wren firmly re-established the work begun by Arundel and Jones in matters of style or manner, in the control of new building in London and in promoting an educational system through which the Arts of Design might be taught.

Economic considerations were also in the forefront of their minds, as Wren's words indicate, and perhaps in a more systematic form than earlier in the century. Both of them were founder fellows of London's Royal Society – indeed it was Evelyn who named it – and the Royal Society's objectives were economic and practical as much as they were purely scientific. In the first year of the society many of the meetings of 'our society', as Evelyn called it, were devoted to Boyle's experiments with air pressure, vacuums, air pumps, barometers, clocks, pendulums, hydraulics and Saturn's rings. But Evelyn was encouraged by the Fellows to publish his treatise on engraving which appears as *Scultura* in 1662, and included his account of Prince Rupert's method of mezzotint which subsequently 'set so many artists on Worke'.[66]

There were also experiments in the refining of metals. Evelyn went to see the Revd Wm. Lee's stocking machine, invented in 1596 but not put to practical use at the time for fear of putting handcraftsmen out of work. He also inspected a diving bell at Deptford and heard Sir William Petty deliver an 'excellent discourse of the Manufacture of Wollen-Cloth, & propos'd divers things concerning the improving of Shipping'.[67]

Perhaps Evelyn's greatest contribution to the aesthetic and economic well-being of the nation was his *Silva or a Discourse of Forest-Trees and the Propagation of Timber in his Majesty's Dominions* written after the Commissioners of the Navy consulted the Royal Society about the timber shortage (Plate 48). It was presented to the Royal Society in 1664. The problem he sought to redress was the enormous consumption of timber for glassworks, iron furnaces as well as for shipping and housebuilding. His solution was a careful programme of arboriculture on the part of the great landlords, for the beauty of their estates as well as for use and profit. His tribute is given in the words of Isaac d'Israeli: 'Inquire at the Admiralty how the fleets of Nelson have been constructed, and they can tell you that it was with the oaks which the genius of Evelyn planted.'[68]

To sum up: from the outset of the seventeenth century certain important scholars, artists and patrons, including Camden, Wotton, Jones, Wren, Arundel and Evelyn, conceived the idea that the ancient or classical style of architecture and design would serve as an instrument of state policy within a racially and politically divided Magna Britannia, Great Britain, facing the ever-increasing pressures of urbanisation and industrialisation. Among the reasons why they felt that the ancient manner would serve this purpose better than the gothic or the vernacular seems to have been that its regularity, simplicity and harmony of proportion were not only symbols of good order and good government but also induced harmony within the souls of the members of society by the operation of natural magic.

These classicists, however, shared many social ideals with those such as Ben Jonson, or Andrew Marvell, who supported more traditional architecture. The notion that gothic or vernacular was associated with traditional, homely, squirearchical virtues, and classical with the values of those who lived it up at court, could not be further from the truth. No one was a more committed classicist than Evelyn and yet there was no one more devoted to what he saw as the traditional pieties of the local gentry (even though his own family's fortunes were based not upon land but gunpowder manufacturing.)

In any case, the conflict between gothic and classical was less extreme than a reading of Evelyn might lead one to believe, and even Evelyn in his diary was warmly appreciative of the great English cathedrals. Arundel as Earl Marshall was one of the pioneers of the scholarly study of mediaeval art, as was Sir William Dugdale, a member of his circle. This is not so much of an inconsistency as it may seem.[69] A better way of thinking about the two major styles, perhaps, is as alternative manners appropriate for different uses according to the rules of decorum as the passage quoted from Wotton suggests. The classical, therefore, was the style appropriate to national monuments, to the planning of cities and to country palaces of the greater nobility. It was the style of Magna Britannia, epitomised by the Banqueting House, Wilton and the new St Paul's, Gothic or vernacular, in contrast, was more a regional manner, an English manner, the manner of Penshurst. Both styles were needed.

CHAPTER 2

Luxury, Virtue and the Imagination:
The Spectator and Pope

THE RENAISSANCE, THAT revival of classical antiquity that spread throughout Europe from Italy in the fifteenth and sixteenth centuries, is commonly described as a flourishing of scientific discovery and the start of the modern world. In fact, as we have glimpsed, it was a major retrenchment: a cultural and economic movement to stabilise an immensely turbulent and uncontrollable state of affairs caused at least in part by the growth in private ownership of furniture, household goods, jewellery and clothes. The manufacture of these personal possessions, or the foreign trade to import them, led to increased numbers of workers living in manufacturing towns who might be thrown out of work at any time because of a foreign war, or slump, or be left starving because of a bad harvest. The dangers of civil unrest were enormous.

Contrary to popular belief, the great inventors of the Italian Renaissance, like Leonardo da Vinci, were the exception rather than the rule. Not only were they ill-understood but when, as in the case of Galileo, they challenged the harmonious cosmology of the period, they were repressed. Leon Battista Alberti is a far more typical figure of the movement we call the Italian Renaissance. In *De Re Aedificatoria*, his great treatise on the town planning and architecture of the well-governed society, Alberti strongly advised against the siting of cities by the sea, because trading ports and their population of foreign merchants and sailors led to the mixing of alien elements and hence to the corruption of the national way of life. He barely mentioned manufacturing in this book, in spite of the importance of the cloth industry in towns like his native Florence, yet he devoted pages of painstaking analysis to the requirements for farm buildings. In short, for Renaissance humanists like Alberti, good government was based on a stable, self-sufficient agrarian economy, with minimal foreign trade and few inessential manufactures. The culture and religion of this state should be based on eternal truths and absolute beauty and harmony: finely turned Ciceronian prose; beautiful and well composed narrative paintings; ordered, harmonious, beautiful and awe-inspiring buildings. Much of this policy was adopted by the Common Weal men of the reign of Elizabeth such as Thomas More, Thomas Cromwell and their followers.

In its extreme form such a policy for building and personal possessions amounted to an absolute prohibition upon all new building on green-field sites near towns and strict sumptuary laws: a process attempted in England, as we have seen, by Burghley and others. Later, as evolved by such planners as Evelyn and Wren, it involved a complete subordination of the private life to public concerns, so that even the *interiors* of houses were considered to be suitable for regulation. Alberti at least recognised that behind the walls of their palazzi the household had far greater freedom in the appearance of their rooms and furnishings than on the facade itself or the more public areas of the house. Perhaps those dark-panelled, severely architectural rooms of Evelyn's period exemplify the subordination of private to public values. (See Plate 47)

But, as a control upon the dangerously volatile nature of personal desire, Evelyn's austere

Weake as you say we are, yett wee command
all flesh to fall, that doth against us stand.
The light within us, of such force is found,
showld satan come, twill lay him on the grund.

The Light they talke of keepes a heavy rout,
ile search all corners, but ile find it out.
By yea and nay, she is a dareing Girle.
ile try a fall or els I am a Churle.

With face of brass, this woman that you see
most Impudently doth afirm, that shee.
The mind of God, in all poynts, more doth know,
then from the Sacred Scriptures, ere could flaw.
Presumptious wretch, it were more fitt that shee,
at home showld keepe, and mind hir howsewifery.
And if noe meanes to live on, worke for bread,
then idlye gossop with hir maget head.
Their light within doth so prevayle,
it makes them hot about the Layle.
Exsept afreind that poynt doth cleare,
they could them selves in pecces teare.

49 *A Quaker, c.* 1700, engr. after E. van Heemskirk. Because of the Quaker rejection of vanity there are no portraits showing Quaker dress. This is a caricature.

sumptuary code was crude and inflexible. Moreover, as Mandeville pointed out, it simply could not be reconciled with the tremendous growth in personal consumption, foreign trade and the importation of exotic novelties that actually took place in the period between the Restoration and the Hanoverian Succession: that period in which there emerged the London of street upon street of glittering shops, of seemingly ever-changing fashions and exotica portrayed in Part I of this book.

The moral dangers of that society were wonderfully portrayed in Daniel Defoe's great novel about the courtesan *Roxana*, published in 1724, in which her very identity appears to be continuously shifting and changing as she changes her lovers, her clothes and her houses, operating by counterfeit and dissimulation until finally, in her desperate attempt to escape from her identity as a whore, she leaves the West End of London to take lodgings with a Quaker lady who lives in a courtyard in the City. There she adopts Quaker dress (see Plate 49), the very essence of the dourest of sumptuary codes, devised to control worldly vanity and desire: not to reform her behaviour, however, but as a more perfect disguise. There could have been no greater irony, nor a more complete refutation of the idea that the mind might be reformed by the censorship and control of worldly goods. It was also a perfect example of Mandevillian hypocrisy.

> By accustoming myself to converse with her, I had not only learn'd to dress like a QUAKER, but so us'd myself to THEE and THOU, that I talk'd like a QUAKER too . . . When we came to talk of Equipages; she extoll'd the having all things plain; I said so too; so I left it to her Direction, and a Coach-Maker was sent for, and he provided me a plain Coach, no gilding or painting, lin'd with a light-grey Cloath, and my Coachman had a Coat of the same, and no Lace on his Hat.
>
> When all was ready, I dress'd myself in the Dress I bought of her, and said, Come, I'll be a QUAKER to-Day, and you and I'll go Abroad; which we did, and there was not a QUAKER in the Town look's less like a Counterfeit than I did: But all this was my particular Plot to be the more compleatly conceal'd, and that I might depend upon being not known, and yet need not be confin'd like a Prisoner, and be always in Fear; so that all the rest was Grimace.[1]

Here, there is no asumption that a sober style could instil sober conduct. If, as Defoe was suggesting, no degree of sumptuary restraint was much use against a false attitude of mind, then a far more sophisticated, intellectual and reasoned approach was needed to the problems of personal consumption and social morality. And this is where we must return to *The Spectator*, that extremely influential periodical, to examine in detail how it tried achieve to just that.

We have already seen how *The Spectator*, especially in the contributions of Joseph Addison, evolved a calculus of consumption and a 'Political Economy of Design'. But in addition, *The Spectator* also offered reflections on how the design of man-made things could be made to serve moral and social ends more satisfactorily than the crude abnegations of sumptuary laws, whether those of the state or of particular religious groups such as Quakers. How could you make things that, in their very nature, so delighted the mind as to lead it towards innocence – particularly at a time when, following Locke's *Essay on the Human Understanding*, no intellectual believed any longer in inherent and magical causes? People could no longer believe, as even Evelyn had, that the soul might be put under a spell, for good or ill, simply through the appearance of things. But Addison argued that a solution might be found in the exercise of taste and an interest in the arts, in what he called the 'pleasures of fancy and the imagination'. The contribution of *The Spectator* to the notion that luxury consumption could be rendered less morally offensive by taste has been neglected in favour of later writers such as Jonathan Richardson and David Hume. Here an attempt will be made to stress the centrality and primacy of *The Spectator* to the developing argument.[2]

The Spectator and its predecessor *The Tatler* took upon themselves 'The Title and Dignity of Censor of Great Britain . . . to look into the Manners of the People, and to check any growing luxury, whether in Diet, Dress or Building!'[3] For example, in the course of a mere two months in 1711, *The Spectator* discussed jealousy, hen-pecked husbands, the population of France under Louis XIV, cruelty to children, seduction, jilting, religious enthusiasm, prostitution, gambling, inherited characteristics, the Levée, the art of good conversation, relations between the sexes, economics, medicine, diet and longevity, devotion, exercise and the comforts of life. Its collected essays more frequently reprinted than any other secular book in the eighteenth century, *The Spectator* in particular became the vade-mecum of orthodox moderate Whiggery in every department of social life, and perhaps did more than any other influence to shape the ideology and behaviour of the English for the next one hundred and fifty years. It was the first English *arbiter elegantiarum*, or 'judge of propriety', published, according to Dr Johnson, in order 'to teach the minuter decencies and inferior duties, to regulate the practice of daily conversation, to correct those depravities which are rather ridiculous than criminal' – an English equivalent of Castiglione's *Courtier*.

Amongst the Censor's particular targets were women's fashions, their consumption of domestic ornaments and furniture, their grand extravagance and behaviour. In the absence of sumptuary laws, in a situation where everyone could dress and buy as they pleased, and in preference to such laws the Censor saw his duties as 'reprehending those vices which are too trivial for the chastisement of the law, and too fantastical for the cognisance of the pulpit'. For reasons to which we shall return, the Censor was altogether opposed to the reimposition of law to regulate such behaviour and in favour of 'the Chastisement of Wit . . . Ridicule' and good sense as the instruments with which to effect a Reformation of Manners. Nonetheless much of the spirit of sumptuary law was to survive in the Good Design Movement.[4]

We have already referred to the mock trial of the hooped petticoat in *Tatler* 116. Hung like an umbrella in the Censor's court, where it formed a 'splendid Canopy over our Heads', the petticoat itself formed a comic setting for the case. Counsel for the petticoat pleaded in Mandevillian fashion on behalf of the woollen manufacturers, since the petticoat required twenty-four yards of cloth, on behalf of the manufacturers of cords and on behalf of the Greenland Company, which imported the whalebones. Finally counsel pleaded the cause of chastity, since the unwieldiness of the garment kept suitors at bay. The Censor's judgement against the petticoat, however, was partly on the grounds of its extravagance, but much more on the moral grounds that women's dress should enhance rather than disguise their natural beauty. The Goddess of Vanity, in a subsequent paper, wore a petticoat which, like all the rest of her clothes, was designed 'to show herself more beautiful and majestick' than she really was.[5]

Similarly the Censor attacked the high coiffures of the period, comparing them to gothic architecture and steeples (Plate 50) (which were essentially High Church and Tory) but censuring them above all as adornments of the outside of the head rather than of the inside, the mind, of which the head, in its natural state, already was the true ornament. For nature 'seems to have designed the head as the cupola to the most glorious of her works; and when we load it with such a pile of supernumerary ornament, we destroy the symmetry of the human figure, and foolishly contrive to call off the eye from great and real beauties to childish gewgaws, ribbands, and bone-lace'.[6]

At its very worst, female luxury in household furnishings, which extended to the taste for buying perishable, ephemeral and useless things like china ornaments, was associated with the snares of prostitution so dangerous to young men:

> The unguarded youth, in silken fetters ty'd,
> Resign'd his realm, and with ease comply'd.[7]

50 London steeples. Whigs like Addison regarded steeples as Tory and papist, comparing them to women's high coiffeurs as symbols of vanity and pride.

At best, women's extravagance, even where her own needlework and labour was employed, was a vanity and a diversion of the labour that should have been properly employed upon the upbringing and moral education of the children. A correspondent complained to *The Spectator* about his wife who, though exceedingly well-bred, well-educated, accomplished and skilled in domestic sciences, 'keeps four French protestants continually employed in making divers pieces of superfluous furniture, as quilts, toilets, hangings for doors, beds, window-curtains, easy chairs and tabourets' all of which she 'obstinately persists in thinking . . . a notable piece of good housewifery because they are made at home and she has had some share in the performance'. It was not the financial extravagance of the housewife that *The Spectator* condemned, but the misdirection of her labour; for, as the husband ironically observed, the only department of domestic life where she displayed frugality was in the nursery. All her children were confined under the tuition of an ignorant old nurse 'to one large room in the remoter part of the house, with bolts on the doors and bars on the windows'. The husband concludes with the moral that his wife's failings were, first, to fix her affections upon the 'trappings and decorations' of her sex rather than upon its true merits; second, to take the qualities which should be the blessings of a family to such an extreme that they were likely to become 'the bane and destruction of it'.[8]

At issue was not the *financial* extravagance of fashion, but the way that it diverted labour from life's true spiritual and moral ends. The worship of luxuries and vanities, even the worship of external human beauty, was a form of idolatry seducing people from true worship to that of false gods.[9]

The Spectator complained of a young woman, extremely beautiful and elegant though by no means extravagantly dressed, the very picture of modesty and innocence, who came to church and, while going through all the motions of a zealous participation in divine service, literally 'suspended the devotion of everyone around her'. This scene is almost a parable of what the paper was trying to teach: that the worship of external beauties and pleasures, whether natural or artificial, fashionable or homely, was a form of idolatry leading the soul astray. It was for this reason that a true Reformation of Manners could not be achieved by a re-enactment of sumptuary law, since the vice lay not in the object but in the mind and the emotions.[10]

The importance of *The Spectator*'s attack upon luxury for the later development of notions of Good Design cannot be exaggerated. Associated with luxury was the titillation of the appetites and animal passions, which was condemned not because these were bad in themselves but because, by giving rise to 'irregular Thoughts and Desires', they seduced people from the true paths of virtue. The Censor's attack upon the over-refinements of the modern diet pulled together many of these themes. On one level it was a patriotic counter-blast against the fashion for French fricassés and ragouts and a call for a return 'to the Food of (our) Forefathers', when Queen Elizabeth's Maids of Honour 'were allowed three Rumps of Beef for their Breakfast'. It was the roast beef of England and the good sense of the common people in keeping up 'the Taste of their Ancestors', that had produced the florid complexions, strong limbs and hale constitutions with which victory had been won at the battles of Blenheim and Ramillies. French ragouts and the consumption of lamb, veal, chicken and other 'immature' meats were the cause of 'a pale, sickly, spindle-legged Generation'. But deeper criticisms concerned the way in which such food-stuff was disguised and dressed up to deceive the eyes, and, still more seriously, the way that this highly spiced and seasoned kind of diet inflamed desire and heated the body without nourishing it. The imagery was directly sexual but the fundamental point was that such food symbolised a state of mind in which *all* the appetites, not just hunger and sex, were maintained in a dangerous state of perpetual arousal and desire.[11]

Greed, appetite and hunger, the very same human passions which were advocated by Barbon and Mandeville as fuel for the economy, were considered by *The Spectator* to be the very sources of the worship of false gods, despite the fact that the paper wholly favoured a commercial society. Taken to extremes, it indeed seems hard to see how they could reconcile such moral and religious ideals with their spirited support for an economy which loaded English tables with foreign spices, oils and wines, and English rooms with pyramids of China and the workmanship of Japan. This, of course, was the basis for Mandeville's disagreement with them.[12]

Nonetheless, these were the conflicting values and objectives which the Addisonian Whigs did wish to reconcile by guiding consumption into a course which Hume later called 'Innocent Luxury'. In setting up such an ideal, *The Spectator* set the course for much of the subsequent history of Good Design. For that magazine both contributed substantially and gave the widest currency to a domestic ideal founded upon a true love between men and women based not upon admiration for physical beauty but upon moral worth. Good women would 'distinguish themselves as tender mothers, and faithful wives' for 'the family is their proper province for private women to shine in'. Appearances were not what mattered. In a modern moral version of the Judgement of Hercules, men were advised to choose the plain sister, agreeably endowed with good sense, rather than the beautiful one whose head had been turned by flattery. The true marriage was painted in sober but glowing colours:

Aurelia, though a woman of great quality, delights in the privacy of a country life, and passes away a great part of her time in her own walks and gardens. Her husband, who is her bosom friend and companion in her solitudes, has been in love with her ever since he knew her. They both abound with good sense, consummate virtue, and a mutual esteem; and are a perpetual entertainment to one another. Their family is under so regular an oeconomy, in its hours of devotion and repast, employment and diversion, that it looks like a little commonwealth within itself. They often go into company, that they may return with the greater delight to one another; and sometimes live in town, not to enjoy it so properly as to grow weary of it, that they may renew in themselves the relish of a country life. By this means they are happy in each other, beloved by their children, adored by their servants, and are become the envy, or rather the delight, of all that know them.[13]

In contrast, the fashionable couple 'consider only the drapery of the species, and never cast away a thought on those ornaments of the mind that make persons illustrious in themselves and useful to others'. Aurelia is the abbess of the protestant monastery, itself the foundation of national virtue.

All the material aspects of the life recommended by *The Spectator* circulated around the sober domestic ideal, which was morally and naturally tasteful. Here was an ideal of innocent pleasures and recreations of the mind and body, based upon simplicity, nature and the imaginative pleasures of art: neither frugality nor parsimony, but a moral and aesthetic temperance, to be exercised not for economic but ethical reasons. Here is the basis for the ideology of design reform.

Of course, in a world where circulating capital was of prime importance, Barbon's and Mandeville's arguments that such restrictions in consumption would reduce the circulation of money and hence employment and the growth of wealth were recognised. But, by objecting not so much to the quantity of consumption as to its quality, and demanding not merely an absence of ornamental glitter but the right attitude in the minds of the consumers, *The Spectator* could to some degree answer these objections. Nonetheless it was a circle difficult to square, and it is perhaps for that reason that *The Spectator* did not altogether reject the contribution of conscious bounty and liberality albeit in the new form practised by Sir Andrew Freeport and Mr Charwell. Moreover, amongst the legitimate objects of expenditure, books and papers of an improving kind were included. In a not altogether facetious spirit, *The Spectator* 367 applied the arguments of Barbon and Mandeville to *The Spectator* itself, arguing that its success had stimulated British paper manufacture and provided employment for printers and post-boys: 'While I am writing a Spectator, I fancy myself providing bread for a multitude.'[14]

Other legitimate objects of expenditure for the rich were the gardens and landscapes. Here *The Spectator* was directly recommending the programme laid down by John Evelyn less than half a century before. Such activities were praiseworthy both because the contemplation of nature's beauty brought one closer to God and because the activity of planting 'has something in it like creation' and might not only transform the whole of England into 'one great garden' but also improve agriculture. It could also be a patriotic duty, since planting forests would supply the fleets of the future as well as raw materials for the economy in general.[15]

From one point of view, gardening was even better than another traditional activity of the great sanctioned by *The Spectator*, namely building, since as soon as a building is finished it begins to decay, whereas gardens grow of their own accord more and more perfect. Certainly, in a digression upon the economic virtue of building in biblical times, the essayist shows that he is fully conversant with those arguments in favour of building as a means of furnishing seasonal employment in an agrarian economy which we earlier argued would have been paramount in the minds of Queen Elizabeth and Lord Burghley.[16]

But *The Spectator's* commitment to gardens as morally impeccable objects for expenditure was by no means as simple-minded as it sounds. In eleven closely-reasoned essays, Addison presented the broad defence for the role of arts in society, and the exercise of what we might call the aesthetic faculties, as not only innocent but positively improving recreations and antidotes to luxury. These famous essays on the 'pleasures of the imagination or fancy' carry us far beyond the applied arts, with which we are primarily concerned, and into the domain of the fine and liberal arts: literature, music, history, the sciences. But the essays are nonetheless important to us because Addison's notion of imagination was transposed by his eighteenth and nineteenth-century successors to applied art, in the belief that manufactured objects could be ennobled by artistic elaboration and, moreover, that if they were decorated with appropriate pictures, cups and saucers, chairs and tables, carpets and curtains would help to transport fancy and imagination into the homes of city dwellers who could not afford expensive paintings or get out into the countryside. In other words, instead of using sumptuary laws to police personal possessions, the solution was to make household goods more like works of art, works which would give rise to the virtuous pleasures attendant upon the exercise of the fancy and the imagination. Here was a notion – the transformation of household goods into household gods – that would still reverberate in the works of Ruskin, Dickens and William Morris.

What, then, did Addison mean by imagination? How did it work, and why was it so valuable? By imagination, Addison meant the human capacity to receive images of the world. It was therefore a faculty of the mind and the soul quite different from intellectual activity on the one hand and from sensual experience on the other. At its simplest it amounted to the activity of gazing with pleasure at something beautiful like a sunset or a fern frond. But the imagination need not only be activated by looking directly at nature, what Addison called primary imagination; it could also be exercised by representations of nature in the medium of words, pictures, statues and music. This he called secondary imagination – we might call it simply the experience of works of art. And, in the case of the secondary imagination, both the operations of the mind and the objects of attention were more complicated in certain respects than those of the primary imagination.

As for the *pleasures* of imaginative activities, these arose from the size, the novelty or the beauty of things. One example of greatness, for example, was an unbounded landscape. This gave people a wonderful feeling of liberty and a sense both of the infinite and of the eternal.[17] Novelty and variety, whether in the changing seasons or new inventions or fantasies, gave pleasure because they were out of the ordinary and alleviated boredom. Finally beauty, whether in perfection of form, or in the arrangement of colours, proportion or composition, gave satisfaction through a sense of inner joy. Each kind of beauty, moreover, served a special purpose, or final cause: the pleasure in greatness was implanted in human nature so as to enable us to experience the awe of God; novelty encouraged curiosity and the search for knowledge; delight in the physical beauty of one's own species encouraged sexual reproduction. In general physical beauty served as an ornament to God's universe so that all His creation should seem glorious to the imagination.

The arts, or what Addison termed the secondary imagination, gave rise to all the same pleasures as those which arose from the nature which they represented. Hence in literature or painting the pleasures of greatness, novelty and beauty were to be found. But the arts also opened the way to sources of pleasure supplementary to those of nature. Not only did one get pleasure from the natural scene or event brought to one's mind by the description in words, or in paint, but one also got pleasure from the words or the brush-strokes themselves, from the artist's skill in the use of the medium, from the action of the mind 'which compares the ideas that arise from words, with the ideas that arise from the objects themselves'.[18] As a result objects which in nature were disgusting could give pleasure in art – an idea taken from Aristotle's *Poetics*. Milton's description of Hell pleased, not because Hell itself was pleasing but because of 'the aptness of the description to excite the image'. This example points the way to yet a further source of imaginative pleasure. Scenes and events which in real life excited the most unpleasant emotions like terror and grief could please one in art because, in addition to feeling frightened or depressed, we were 'not a little pleased to think that we are in no danger'. But not only was there this sense of security, the kind of pleasure that we enjoy reading horror stories and ghost stories; the mind was also stimulated to reflect upon the source of danger when it was met with in a representation, an experience which was clearly impossible in reality 'when the object presses too close upon our senses, and bears so hard upon us that it does not give us the time or freedom to reflect upon ourselves'. In a similar way to the pleasure arising directly from greatness – the sense of being at liberty and unconfined – so *representations* of horror provided the mind with another kind of liberty, the freedom to reflect upon the source of the emotion itself.

Those were the psychological benefits of those arts which were imitative of nature. But the powers of artistic or secondary imagination also extended the very resources of nature itself, so that art constituted a *new kind* of nature – both by adding greater beauties, strangeness and grandeur to that which existed in nature, by creating a new world of fanciful creation, as Shakespeare had done – and by concentrating the beauties which were dispersed and scattered in real life into the space of a single canvas or poem. This last idea, the concentration and intensification of the great wide world into the small space of a work of art, was summarised by Addison in his last essay devoted to the imaginative pleasures of reading history and science. A treatise on astronomy, for example, provided one, on a minute scale, with a model of the universe, bringing something so vast within the scope of the imagination, which was thereby enlarged as well as the understanding: 'when we survey the whole earth at once, and the several planets that lie within its neighbourhood, we are filled with a pleasing astonishment, to see so many worlds hanging one above another, and sliding with their axles in such an amazing pomp and solemnity'. But when we went beyond what was visible through a telescope and considered 'the fixed stars as so many vast oceans of flame that are each of them attended with a different set of planets' then 'we are lost in such a labyrinth of suns and worlds, and confounded with the immensity and magnificence of nature'.[19]

This may seem to carry us far beyond the humble concerns of teacups and gardens. But it is necessary to grasp the full grandeur of Addison's theory of the arts in order to see why he thought so highly of gardening. The reason can be given in a single sentence. Gardens were the creation of both nature and art, and they therefore exercised both the primary and the secondary imagination as nothing else could.

The essay on gardens opens with the observation that, in comparison to nature, works of art have a limited appeal.[20] This is because they commonly lack the magnitude of nature and hence the pleasures arising from immensity, eternity and so on. Addison particularly castigated the architectonic gardens fashionable in seventeenth century England in which 'we see the marks of the scissors upon every plant and bush', clipped as they were into 'cones, globes and pyramids' (Plate 51). Wild nature was more pleasing:

> Cool grots, and living lakes, the flow'ry pride
> Of meads, and streams that through the valley glide

But most pleasing of all were landscapes which resembled those of art – what later came to be called the picturesque. Such scenes appealed both directly to the primary imagination and to the reflective and meditative pleasures of secondary imagination as well. Correspondingly man-made gardens ought, in Addison's opinion, to have something 'grand and august' about them, rather than the 'neatness and elegancy' of a parterre, and he recommended a type of gardened landscape which combined both virtues with economic considerations as well: 'It might, indeed, be of ill consequence to the public, as well as unprofitable to

51 Parterre garden with clipped hedges from J. Bradley's *New Improvements of Planting and Gardening*, 1726. Pope and Addison abhorred the artificiality of clipped hedges and symmetry, associating them with French absolutism.

52　*Mr and Mrs Andrews*, by Thomas Gainsborough. This exemplifies Addison's virtuous couple seated in their estate 'thrown into a kind of garden', natural rather than formal, to their profit and pleasure.

private persons, to alienate so much ground from pasturage, and the plough, in many parts of a country that is so well peopled, and cultivated to a far greater advantage. But why may not a whole estate be thrown into a kind of garden, by frequent plantations, that may turn as much to the profit as to the pleasure of the owner (Plate 52).' He then painted a word picture of such an estate with its fields of corn, country lanes, 'the natural embroidery of the meadows' as well as some cultivated flowers, hedgerows planted with trees so that 'a man might make a pretty landskip of his own possessions'. In that productive landscape garden lay the epitome of the attempt by Addison and his colleagues on *The Spectator* to reconcile economic growth with the landed interest and with personal and social virtues without sacrificing the economic benefits of high consumption. Nor was it in any way impractical. Nurserymen in the vicinity of London and other large towns ran businesses that flourished upon this kind of virtuous consumption and great landscape gardens such as Stowe were justified, in part, for their economic side effects which included tourism.

Implicit in Addison's writing was the notion that the pleasures of the imagination were an antidote to luxury. This argument was made more explicit in an essay attributed to Bishop Berkeley that was published in *The Spectator*'s successor, *The Guardian*, in 1713.[21] There, in what is yet another rejoinder to Barbon and Mandeville, a distinction was drawn between *Natural Pleasures*, which corresponded largely with Addison's 'pleasures of the imagination' and *Fantastical Pleasures*, which included the pursuit of fashion. 'It is evident, that a Desire terminated in Money is fantastical; so is the Desire of outward Distinctions, which bring no Delight of Sense, nor recommend us as useful to Mankind; and the Desire of things merely because they are new or Foreign. Men, who are indisposed to a due Exertion of their higher Parts, are driven to such Pursuits as these from the Restlessness of the Mind, and the sensitive Appetites being easily satisfied.' One of the chief virtues of the exercise of primary imagination in gazing upon the beauties of the countryside lay in the fact that one could enjoy all these natural beauties without having to own them; they were free and, more than that, they freed one from the treadmill of the *fantastical pleasures* of avarice and ambition to obtain the money needed to buy the fields for oneself.

Alexander Pope, who also contributed to *The Guardian*, there presented, in his translation of the Garden of Alcinous from Homer's *Odyssey*, his ideal small garden of four acres whose beauty arose entirely from the fruits of the useful Part of Horticulture'.[22] It both exemplifies the idea of a ver perpetuum as a virtuous substitute for the novelties of luxury and illustrates Addison's conception of the secondary imagination as a delightful concentration of the scattered beauties of real life, a kind of Penshurst, but in classical costume:

> Close to the Gates a spacious Garden lies,
> From Storms defended and inclement Skies:
> Four Acres was th' allotted Space of Ground,
> Fenc'd with a green Enclosure all around.
> Tall thriving Trees confest the fruitful Mold;
> The red'ning Apple ripens here to Gold,
> Here the blue Figg with luscious Juice o'erflows,
> With deeper Red the full Pomegranate glows,
> The Branch here bends beneath the weighty Pear,
> And verdant Olives flourish round the Year.
> The balmy Spirit of the Western Gale
> Eternal breathes on Fruits untaught to fail:
> Each dropping pear a following Pear supplies,
> On Apple Apples, Figs on Figs arise:
> The same mild Season gives blooms to blow,
> The Buds to harden, and the Fruits to grow.

In contrast, Pope poked rumbustious fun at the fashion for topiary in his imaginary catalogue of a Town Gardener, including 'Divers eminent Modern poets in Bays, somewhat blighted, to be disposed of a Pennyworth'. It was not, however, until twenty years or so later that Pope returned to the fray in a poem which more completely and concisely summarised the Spectatorial rejoinder to the Mandevillians. This has come to be known as the Fourth Moral Essay, 'Of the Use of Riches', dedicated to the Earl of Burlington. It was first published in December 1731 with the title 'Of Taste' as well as an epistle to Burlington 'occasioned by his Publishing Palladio's Designs of the Baths, Arches, Theatres etc of Ancient Rome'.[23]

> At Timon's Villa let us pass a day,
> Where all cry out, 'What sums are thrown away!'

Pope presented the epitome of all the tasteless and unnatural extravagances represented by competitive consumption and vanity: the travesty of old-fashioned hospitality.

> Is this a dinner? This a genial room?
> No, 'tis a Temple, and a hecatomb.
> A solemn sacrifice performed in state,
> You drink by measure, and to minutes eat.

The counterfeit patronage of scholarship and learning:

> His study! with what authors is it stored?
> In books, not authors, curious is my Lord

190

and of course the regimentation of nature in the gardens:

> No pleasing intricacies intervene,
> No artful wildness to perplex the scene:
> Grove nods at grove, each alley has a brother,
> And half the platform just reflects the other.

as well as the infernal topiary:

> The suffering eye inverted nature sees,
> Trees cut to statues, statues thick as trees

Pope admitted, all the same, that Mandeville was in one sense correct about extravagance:

> Yet hence the poor are clothed, the hungry fed
> Health to himself, and to his infants bread,
> The labourer bears: what his hard heart denies,
> His charitable vanity supplies.

However, Pope concluded the poem with an affirmation of his belief that there was an alternative to turning the wheels of trade by Timon's tasteless extravagances. That was the 'well judg'd Bounties'* of noblemen like the Earl of Bathurst, who laid out Cirencester Park, and the Earl of Burlington. The final section of the poem requires quoting in full, familiar as it may be, since all the themes upon which the preceding account has touched are represented here: on the one hand, the concept of a self-conscious, aristocratic bounty that will assist the nation, the tenantry and the labourers by improving the land, planting useful forests and providing rural employment and, in so doing, create a beautiful landscape; on the other, an architectural revival of Palladio, to pioneer the patronage of public architecture until the state takes over the function.

> His father's acres who enjoys in peace,
> Or makes his neighbours glad, if he increase:
> Whose cheerful tenants bless their yearly toil,
> Yet to their lord owe more than to the soil;
> Whose ample lawns are not ashamed to feed
> The milky heifer and deserving steed;
> Whose rising forests, not for pride or show,
> But future buildings, future navies grow:
> Let his plantations stretch from down to down,
> First shade a country, and then raise a town.
> You too proceed! make falling arts your care,
> Erect new wonders, and the old repair;
> Jones and Palladio to themselves restore,
> And be whate'er Vitruvius was before:
> 'Till kings call forth the ideas of your mind
> (Proud to accomplish what such hands design'd),
> Bid harbours open public ways extend,
> Bid temples, worthier of the god, ascend;
> Bid the broad arch the dangerous flood contain,
> The mole projected break the roaring main;
> Back to his bounds their subject sea command,
> And roll obedient rivers through the land;
> These honours Peace to happy Britain brings,
> These are imperial works, and worthy kings.

---

* As is well known, Pope was criticised for appearing to attack the Duke of Chandos in the character of Timon. In 'A Master Key to Popery', anonymous but certainly written by Pope, he defended himself on the grounds, *inter alia*, that 'Timon was famous for Extravagances, the Duke for well-judg'd Bounties'.

53   Hogarth's Shakespeare Chair made for Garrick's Shakespeare Club. One of the only surviving objects
designed by Hogarth, it takes his key principle of intricacy as the basis of beauty to fanciful extremes.

CHAPTER 3
Hogarth's Analysis of Beauty

In ADDISON AND Pope we find a convergence of almost all the issues whose inter-relationship it has been the task of this book to trace and reconstruct: economic and social policy, the problem of regionalism and the growth of cities, the ethical and religious implications of consumption and the relation of these to the style or manner of buildings, landscapes and objects. There is, however, one subject that both men neglected: neither Pope nor Addison devoted the same attention as they gave to gardens to the style of household goods. It was not so much that the subject was beneath their dignity. Addison indeed had many strictures to make on private excess. But his recommendations about personal possessions were little more than simple prohibitions: man-made things should be kept functional, simple, natural and plain.

Among his contemporaries, however, there were those with more complex ideas. In that *Guardian* essay attributed to Berkeley, for instance, Addison's notion of imaginative pleasure was certainly extended to household possessions.[1] Berkeley, it will be remembered, was in favour of sumptuary laws. If Berkeley claimed to have chosen the furnishings of his own house so as to avoid luxury, status symbols and foreign imports, he had nonetheless not denied himself the pleasure of owning beautiful things.

> As I cannot go to the price of History-painting, I have purchased at easie Rates several beautifully designed Pieces of Landscape and Perspective, which are much more pleasing to a natural Taste than unknown Faces or *Dutch* Gambols, tho' done by the best Masters. My Couches, Beds, and Window-Curtains are of *Irish* Stuff, which those of that Nation work very fine and with a delightful mixture of Colours. There is not a Piece of China in my House, but I have Glasses of all sorts, and some tinged with the finest Colours, which are not the less pleasing because they are Domestick and cheaper than Foreign Toys. Everything is neat, intire, and clean, and fitted to the Taste of one who had rather be *happy* than *be thought rich*.

The most interesting observations here, from the point of view of imaginative and natural pleasure, concern the glass 'tinged with the finest colours' and the Irish fabrics in 'a delightful mixture of colours'. In them, Berkeley was associating imaginative pleasure in the composition of colour – one of Addison's characteristics of natural beauty – directly with private furnishings and utensils.[2] This idea was developed far more fully by William Hogarth, the painter and engraver, whose *Analysis of Beauty* of 1753 was the first work to analyse Good Design in any detail. Indeed, the importance of Hogarth within the history of Good Design rests precisely upon his effort to demonstrate in detail, rather than in general, how the design and appearance of objects could be shaped to obey the moral and social dictates that we have been examining.

In contrast to Addison or Evelyn, Hogarth did not advocate puritanical simplicity, which, as Defoe was only too aware, could easily be the greatest deceit. Hogarth like Mandeville recognised the subtleties of moral dissimulation and hypocrisy. What he tried to show was that there was a great range of pleasures to be had from furnishings and clothes that was compatible with the avoidance of vanity and luxury. To be more particular, he was the first theorist to integrate the moral, visual and practical components of designing a chair or a candlestick.

If Hogarth did not directly refer to wider social and economic matters or to the luxury debate, these are as implicit in his argument as they are central to his paintings and engravings: from the *Harlot's Progress* series of 1731 to *The Four Stages of Cruelty* of 1751. Moreover, as we have already observed, Hogarth was keenly read by Adam Smith and Alexander Gerard. In short, he lay the foundation for a tradition of theories of Good Design which would flourish in the following century, and within which each formal characteristic of style could be justified on the basis of 'principles' − part moral, part aesthetic − that amounted to a kind of moral calculus of design.

To suggest, however, as some have done, that Hogarth himself created the narrowly functional theory of design that we shall subsequently examine could not be more misleading. Nor was Hogarth responsible for what Geoffrey Scott called the 'ethical fallacy' − seeking to justify a style through its ethical associations. On the contrary, Hogarth's fundamental aim was to escape from those rigid identifications of moral and social virtue with fitness for use and simplicity that were current in his own time, and also from the corresponding association of luxury and vice with things that were intricate and finely wrought. Roxana's assumed plainness could clearly be the greatest hypocrisy of all.

I shall also show that Hogarth was trying to establish a distinction between the public and private aspects of life, between business and the pleasures of recreation, and that he believed the private life was an appropriate space for imaginative, ornamental and even aesthetically licentious pleasures. Finally I shall examine how Hogarth sought to indicate the true relationship between beauty and moral worth. His book, however, is so often interpreted as an early defence of functionalism that some considerable attention must be devoted to demonstrating how this totally misrepresents Hogarth's intention. Hogarth was a very sophisticated thinker and his writings on beauty make considerable intellectual demands upon the reader.

The confusion just referred to arises in part from Hogarth's own words and the arrangement of the book. The opening chapter of *The Analysis of Beauty* is entitled 'Of Fitness' and in it Hogarth stated that fitness for use was 'of the greatest consequence to the beauty of the whole'.[3] Yet that does not amount to his saying that 'fitness for use *is* the cause of beauty' or that 'fitness is *identical* to beauty'. On the contrary, Hogarth wished to demonstrate that fitness played a less important part in beauty than previous authors had contended. In his view people tended to conflate the two ideas, and he wished both to distinguish between them and to define their true relationship. A brief note which he wrote for his own benefit early on in the drafting of his manuscript states his intentions:

> Such power former Authors of the first rank have attributed to Fitness alone that they have condensed [?] the whole beauty of the creation into that one . . . have [?] given their preferences [?] to uniformity . . . Simplicity has been also alow'd as a great beauty, but for Intricacy they show most lowly of all . . .[4]

Confirmation that it was his intention to redress the balance between fitness and intricacy is also to be found in a manuscript preface to an unpublished second edition:

> The first attempts that were made to fix true ideas of taste upon a surer basis, were by *natural philosophers*, who, in their amplified contemplations on the universal beauty displayed in the harmony and order of nature, very soon lost themselves; an event that, from the way in which they set out, was inevitable; for, if I may be permitted to adopt

an allegorical figure, it necessarily led them into the wide road of *order* and *regularity*, which they unexpectedly found crossed and intersected by many other paths, that led into the *labyrinths* of *variety*; where, not having passed through the *province of painting*, they became confused, and could never find their way. To explaining the order and usefulness of nature they might be equal; but of her sportiveness and fancy, they were totally ignorant.[5]

But Hogarth does not want to suggest that the correct relationship between fitness and beauty is a simple one. This is reinforced by the very first paragraph of the chapter 'Of Fitness' where the reader faces considerable difficulty in working out exactly what Hogarth is trying to say. My belief, arrived at after discussing the passage with many puzzled students over many years is that Hogarth wrote it deliberately as a mind-bending riddle in order to convey his notion that the relationship between fitness and beauty was an extremely intricate one, a prime example, therefore of intricacy which he considered the crucial component of beauty.

In the same draft preface Hogarth also attacked Addison, Shaftesbury and, perhaps, Plato for over-emphasising the moral aspect of beauty. 'To extricate themselves from these difficulties, they ascended *the mound of moral beauty*, contiguous to the open field of *divinity*, where rambling and ranging at large, they lost all remembrance of their former pursuit.' In another manuscript note that he made for his first draft of the *Analysis* Hogarth expanded upon this distinction between the two sets of principles, which he tabulated as follows:

Fitness	Uniformity and Regularity	Fitness excites a pleasure equall or similar to that of truth and Justice, uniformity and regularity, pleasure and contentment
Variety	Simplicity Intricacy quantity and distinctness	Variety excites the lively feeling of of wantoness and play, Intricacy in the joy of persute, quantity excites the pleasure admiration and wonder[6]

Advised by his friend and neighbour, the classical scholar Revd Thomas Morell, Hogarth had studied the chapter of Xenophon's *Memorabilia* in which Socrates defines beauty in terms of fitness for use. The philosopher reasons that there is no single type of beauty: if an athlete were the epitome of beauty, then every other thing in art or nature that is not an athlete must fall short of the highest beauty. To avoid that problem Socrates argues that there is a beauty proper to each kind of thing: a beautiful building, a beautiful man, a beautiful girl. But even this is not fine enough: if among athletes a runner is considered beautiful then what about a wrestler? The solution, as Socrates sees it, is to define beauty in terms of perfect fitness or usefulness. A beautiful runner is one who is best made for running, a beautiful house is one best suited to its owner's needs, to the climate and to its situation. Beauty and perfect fitness are thus synonymous.

Hogarth did not agree. Socrates argued that a builder's hod might be beautiful, a golden shield vile, since the former is perfectly adapted to its use and the latter functionally useless. Hogarth wanted to know how one assessed an object, such as a builder's hod, whose form was perfectly fit for its function but whose 'real appearance exclusive of any other consideration were ugly in itself'. He did not deny that fitness for use was extremely important from a practical point of view, but neither the perfect blunderbuss nor the perfect builder's hod need be pleasing to the eye.[7]

But Hogarth also attempted to explain why people had been misled into believing the fallacy that beauty and fitness were identical. He fully appreciated the great satisfaction to be obtained from using a utensil which answered efficiently to its purpose: levers that were easy to pull, chairs that were comfortable and so on. He also appreciated that people often spoke of a well-running machine or utensil as 'working beautifully'. But the word 'beauty' in such cases was used as a metaphor. We ought not, in Hogarth's opinion, to confuse the true meaning of beauty with its metaphorical application. What he perceived was that the 'beauty' of fitness, which fundamentally appealed to the mind, so biased the sight that we might attribute beauty to an object which, though useful, was ugly. This sort of confusion was one which we ought not to make, and which he sought to disentangle.[8]

Hogarth's famous example of the well-wrought ship was chosen to demonstrate the way in which the two applications of the word beauty had become confused: 'in ship-building the dimensions of every part are confin'd and regulated by fitness for sailing. When a vessel sails well, the sailors always call her a beauty; the two ideas have such a connexion!' Hogarth did not deny that a good ship might also be beautiful to the eye. But, if it were so, it would be because the form which was perfectly fit for the purpose of sailing happened, by chance, to *coincide* with a form which pleased the eye. Edmund Burke later expressed the same idea when he suggested that

> The cause of this confusion, I imagine, proceeds from our frequently perceiving the parts of the human and other animal bodies to be at once very beautiful, and very well adapted to their purposes; and we are deceived by a sophism, which makes us take that for a cause which is only a concomitant: this is the sophism of the fly, who imagined he raised a great dust because he stood upon the chariot that really raised it.[9]

Perhaps Hogarth was also taking issue, to a lesser extent, with David Hume, who in his *Inquiry concerning the Principle of Morals*, published in 1751, two years before the *Analysis of Beauty*, had written:

> . . . how satisfactory an apology for any disproportion or seeming deformity, if we can show the necessity of that particular construction for the use intended! A ship appears more beautiful to an artist, or one moderately skilled in navigation, where its prow is wide and swelling beyond its poop, than if it were framed with a precise geometrical regularity, in contradiction to all the laws of mechanics. A building, whose doors and windows were exact squares, would hurt the eye by that very proportion; as ill adapted to the figure of a human creature, for whose service the fabric was intended.[10]

Although Hume is making a distinction in this passage between fitness for purpose and elegance of form, he is nonetheless arguing that the *fittest* shape for the ship's prow must appear more beautiful, to artist as well as to sailor, than a shape of perfect beauty which conflicted with fitness. Hogarth disagreed. To summarise Hogarth's 'dialogue' with Socrates and Hume: he concurred that it was use which had given rise to the characteristic shape of an object; he agreed that it was common linguistic usage to call useful objects beautiful; but he would not concede that all functional objects were appealing or beautiful to the eye, however fit they were for their purposes.[11]

Hogarth introduced an additional consideration, that of *apparent* fitness and unfitness. There might be instances of a fundamentally useful object, perfectly adapted to its purpose, whose form was also most elegant, but which disgusted the eye because it *appeared* to be unfit. He may well have had in mind Bernini's Baldacchino in St Peter's when he remarked that twisted columns were 'undoubtedly ornamental; but as they convey an idea of weakness, they always displease, when they are improperly made use of as supports to any thing that is bulky, or appears heavy'. Here the mere *suggestion* of impracticality detracted from the total pleasure. Hence, to be totally satisfactory on all scores, an object had to satisfy three criteria: it had to be fit for use; it had to please the eye, and it must not *displease* the mind by giving the *appearance* of being unfit for its intended use. And, because of this triple requirement, 'beauty' in man-made objects was something that frequently had to be added to, or developed from, the fit shape.[12]

To functionalists of all centuries this might appear a retrogressive step. But to anyone with practical experience of designing, even an amateur putting in new bathroom fittings, it is evident that a good solution to a functional problem – where to run the pipes, say – does not inevitably produce a beautiful appearance. Moreover there is often no single perfect formal solution to the demands of mechanical efficiency. Even the so-called functionalist, who would leave pipes exposed and paint them bright colours, must choose from the alternatives that arrangement which is the neatest or most attractive.

What were the practical repercussions of Hogarth's *Analysis of Beauty* for the actual design or judgement of a real object? We have already encountered his tabulation of beauty into fitness and variety; but, although this appears to give equal weight to both ingredients, there seems little doubt that he regarded fitness as a necessary but minimum requirement, also as a bit of a bore. Fitness, in Hogarth's opinion, was that which has to be 'strictly and mechanically complied with'.[13] 'In short, whatever appears to be fit, and proper to answer great purposes, ever satisfies the mind and pleases on that account. Uniformity is of this kind. We find it necessary, in some degree, to give the idea of rest and motion, without the possibility of falling.'

Hogarth in fact preferred objects that teetered on the very brink of stability, both real and apparent. 'But when any such purposes can be as well effected by more irregular parts, the eye is always better pleased on the account of variety.' His ideal shape had the minimum uniformity consistent with fitness, and the maximum variety. For example, a cube of wood is the most stable form for a table, both from the practical point of view and in its appearance of fitness. A table with four solid legs satisfies both conditions with less bulk and enables people to sit closer to the surface. But, for Hogarth, a three-legged table or stand was best because it just sufficed. 'How pleasingly is the idea of firmness in standing convey'd to the eye by the three elegant claws of a table, the three feet of a tea-lamp, or the celebrated tripod of the ancients?'[14]

When we examine Hogarth's only surviving design, the Shakespeare Chair which he designed for Garrick's Shakespeare Club, the real bias of his own tastes becomes clear. The chair is certainly stable and soundly constructed, but every opportunity to excite the eye through a wild fantasy of ornament and symbolism has been taken. For Hogarth fitness and its associated visual qualities were worthy but dull preconditions for the existence of an object. They gave the user of an article some pleasure, but satisfied the mind too quickly (see Plate 53).[15]

As manifested in the visual qualities of uniformity and regularity, fitness was similar to truth and justice in its psychological effects. It bore an *analogy* to moral virtues, though it was not identical to them. Beauty, however, had no such function nor was it directly related to moral qualities. Though, as we shall see, that it is not to say that beauty is either amoral or immoral. Hogarth's account of the true sources of beauty, found in variety and intricacy, depended upon a psychological account of the difference between boredom and excitation. The senses, he argued, were 'averse to sameness. The ear is as much offended with one even continued note, as the eye is with being fix'd to a point, or even to the view of a dead wall.' He anticipated the modern theory of the saturation of attention when he described an experiment demonstrating how constant movement of the eye is necessary for perception to take place at all. Thus, for interest to be aroused and attention to be maintained, an object must possess some degree of both variety and intricacy.[16]

The degree to which it had to possess these qualities, in Hogarth's theory if not in his practice, was also important. *Excessive* variety amounted in effect to sameness and repetition, so that the eye would once again become satiated. For sustained visual pleasure the greatest intricacy and variety consistent with clarity of composition was necessary, and it was from this principle that he derived his paradigm of beauty in the serpentine line, or the line of

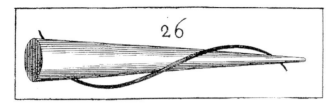

54 The serpentine Line of Beauty from Plate 1 of Hogarth's *Analysis of Beauty*, 1753.

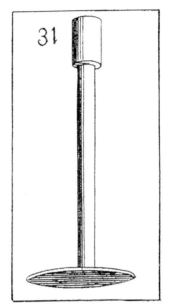

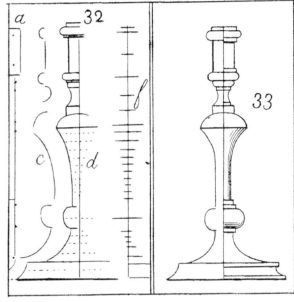

55 How to design a candlestick from Plate 1 of the *Analysis of Beauty*.

56 Dolphin candlestick engraved from a drawing in the manuscript of the *Analysis of Beauty*. This did not appear in the published book, but like the Shakespeare Chair it indicates Hogarth's personal taste in design and its fanciful naturalism was highly influential in the following century.

beauty (Plate 54). A rectangular box was unvaried and dull. Seen obliquely, in perspective, the gradual diminution of its width made it more interesting. Thus a pyramid was quite beautiful. Similarly, a straight line was less varied than a curved one. A cone because curved was more beautiful than a pyramid, and a curved line wrapped around a cone became the paradigm of beauty – a simple line continually varying in curvature and in its dimensions.[17]

But although the line of beauty was the paradigm, Hogarth did not suggest that only those objects which literally incorporated it would be beautiful. The art of designing a beautiful object lay in varying its elements, whether they were straight, curved, square or rounded.

In illustration of his theory, Hogarth took the case of women's dress. All women, he argued, applied the foregoing principles, often without even being aware that they were using principles at all. First of all they considered usefulness both from a physical and social point of view. But once that had been taken account of and a necessary uniformity, arising from the symmetry of the human body had been complied with, they applied themselves to the constant study of variety. No woman would place two feathers symmetrically on either side of her head, nor create any other symmetry, unless she was deliberately seeking to be 'formal'. She would attempt a certain fullness, even to excess as in the great ruff collars of the Elizabethan period or the hooped skirts of Hogarth's own day. She would find delight not only in variety and asymmetry but also in intricacy, which also implied the avoidance of immodesty: '. . . modesty in dress, to keep up our expectations, and not suffer them to be too soon gratified. Therefore the body and limbs should all be cover'd, and little more than certain hints be given of them thro' the cloathing.'[18]

Hogarth's belief in the supreme importance of intricacy and variety, his hatred of sameness, committed him to a belief in the importance of novelty and innovation, of creativeness, and an extraordinary unorthodoxy on the issue of style. Applied to a simple utensil like a candlestick, his practical method of design worked as follows: first one fixed a convenient height, then one made the socket of the necessary size, but 'after *fitness* hath been strictly and mechanically complied with, any additional ornamental members, or parts, may, by the foregoing rules, be varied with great elegance'. Thus in dividing the stem of the candlestick into balusters and knobs, all the distances between them should divide the stem into unequal parts, just as the width of each knob should differ from that of every other. The only necessity was to avoid such an excess of variety, such a jumble that the variations of size and proportions could not be perceived at all (Plate 55 and 56).[19] Using his method, Hogarth considered that all objects and buildings might be so designed as to give delight to the eye. He dismissed the claims of orthodoxy, tradition and particularly of classical architecture, and called for 'a completely new and harmonious order of architecture' founded upon the eternal principles of natural beauty.

> . . . nor can I help thinking but that churches, palaces, hospitals, prisons, common houses and summer houses, might be built more in distinct characters than they are, by contriving orders suitable to each; whereas were a modern architect to build a palace in Lapland, or the West-Indies, Paladio must be his guide, nor would he dare to stir a step without his book.[20]

And he recommended that these new ornaments might be based upon hints from nature, in shells and flowers.

This last point is an important one to emphasise. In the manuscript of the *Analysis* Hogarth instanced the flower of the cyclamen as the perfect example of the line of beauty: 'nature describes it more distinctly to the eye in a little flower call'd the Autumn Siclomon the outer edges of its five leafs gives a most clear conception of the precision of this line attach'd to the most simple form which neither twisted too much nor too little . . .'[21] There is a strong thread of natural theology running through Hogarth's thinking on the subject of design and ornament which points to the underlying affinity between his ideas on the design of domestic utensils and *The Spectator's* ideas on natural scenery and gardens. A letter from Hogarth, written to his friend and colleague the naturalist John Ellis four years after the publication of the *Analysis*, makes his worship of the beauty of nature quite apparent:

> It must be allowed your print is accurately executed, and very satisfactory too. As for your pretty little seed cups, or vases, they are a sweet confirmation of the pleasure Nature seems to take in superadding an elegance of form to most of her works, wherever you find them. How poor and bungling are all the imitations of art! When I have the pleasure of seeing you next we will sit down – *nay kneel down* if you will – and admire these things. (author's italics)[22]

Hogarth was justifying and giving currency to objects either shaped like plants or adorned with them as a means of bringing the imaginative pleasures of nature into the home. This type of naturalist ornament was extremely popular in the eighteenth and, particularly, the nineteenth century, when it became the target of criticism by the design reformers of the day. It remains very popular to this day.

Hogarth's arguments are often regarded as a defence of the rococo, and it is true that many of the artists and designers with whom he was associated in the art school known as the St Martin's Lane Academy were rococo.[23] But in fact Hogarth was not committed to any particular style or manner. He admired Windsor Castle for its grandeur and picturesque massing, St Paul's Cathedral for its richness, variety, quantity and simplicity, Wren's city churches and their steeples, Westminster Abbey and other gothic buildings for their 'consistent beauty' and even chinoiserie for its novelty. An object was to be judged not upon its adherence to a style, but upon its capacity to please the eye and the mind. Function must be fulfilled, but not necessarily expressed.

Addison and *The Spectator* writers, it will be recalled, had found it very hard to reconcile personal acquisitiveness with moral virtue, in spite of their recognition that the only real idolatry was of the mind. There was therefore a missing link in the chain of their economic theory and policy. Their moral principles would limit consumption and impede trade. This they attempted to surmount by approving of gardening and the pleasures associated with the gentle exercise of the imagination in art and nature: occupations upon which time could be spent in communion with God while money was being spent innocently. The flaw is obvious. If idolatry is of the mind then a person can as easily neglect their duties in tending their own garden as in making jam or buying fashionable furniture and flounces. From an economic point of view, a mass consumption based upon gardening would have had the curious, though by no means economically insane, effect of creating a growth-economy based upon market-gardening. This had actually happened in Holland to some degree and had led to the extraordinary speculation in tulip bulbs – tulipomania.[24]

Hogarth, arguing his case as always in full awareness that hypocrisy was an ever-present danger however plain one's tastes, showed that man-made things might possess some of the merits of nature herself in providing the opportunity for the mind to be virtuously exercised and entertained. But the practice of virtue did not depend upon the appearance or style of things consumed, just as beauty did not depend upon fitness.

Let us return to Hogarth's two aspects of beauty. Whereas fitness corresponded to truth and justice, variety excited 'the lively feeling of wantonness and play' and intricacy the joy of pursuit. Broadly speaking Hogarth believed that fitness corresponded to the business of our lives, beauty to its recreations. Thus he equated the pleasure of symmetry with the pleasure which a child finds in imitating the people around him as a means of learning the skills and customs of the world. This explained why we tire of symmetry. Imitation was a lesser and simpler faculty, whereas the faculties associated with variety and intricacy were higher, more complex and creative.[25]

Why this should be, he attempted to explain in the chapter on intricacy: 'The active

57 *The Rake's Progress*, Plate 2. Having inherited a fortune the Rake sets up house in the new, fashionable, neo-palladian West End. Palladian simplicity, for Hogarth, was no guarantee of virtuous behaviour.

mind is ever bent to be employ'd. Pursuing is the business of our lives; and even abstracted from any other view, gives pleasure.' At first sight it might appear that he believed the pleasures of pursuit to have been as functional as those of imitation, and as much a part of the business of our lives. Indeed he says so: 'This love of pursuit, merely as pursuit, is implanted in our natures, and design'd, no doubt, for necessary and useful purposes.' But what was curious about this faculty was that man and other animals seemed to possess it to a degree vastly in excess of any practical needs. In fact so heartily did we thrive upon difficulties that the more problems which arose in the course of our work the more enjoyable and stimulating work became, and 'what would else be toil and labour [becomes] sport and recreation'. Insofar then as a love of intricacy was part of the instinct of self-preservation, and associated with the business of our lives, it had to be considered a higher faculty to that of imitation. Associated with creativity and fertility of invention it enabled us to face up to new obstacles for which rote learning and knowledge from the past could be no guide: the more intricate and unfamiliar the problem the readier we were to solve it. But Hogarth did not rest his case concerning intricacy and variety on functional grounds alone. And in declining to do so he was taking issue both with Addison and with Hume.[26]

It will be remembered that Addison had argued that the final cause or purpose why

201

pleasure in variety was implanted in our nature was to stimulate curiosity and the search for knowledge: it was basically functional. We have already seen how David Hume in his *Treatise of Human Nature* of 1736 had developed this idea to explain the nature of curiosity and the search for truth, using indeed the same simile as Hogarth was himself to employ. Curiosity was like hunting. It was agreeable only insofar as the mind was activated and exercised by overcoming obstacles. But Hume denied that this 'love of pursuit' alone was an adequate stimulus to effort. The scholar like the hunter also had to be convinced of the practical importance of any enquiry, and of its utility to society, *even if* such a conviction were in fact a delusion.[27]

Hogarth disputed this – implicitly at least. The instinct for pursuit, in all its many manifestations, was so strong and super-abundant that it needed no functional justification. Its presence in mankind's make-up was vastly in excess of any functional needs. It constituted a great part of our leisure and recreation, in sports like hunting, in games and riddles, in art, literature and the contemplation of nature:

> with what delight does [the mind] follow the well-connected thread of a play, or novel, which ever-increases as the plot thickens, and ends most pleas'd when that is most distinctly unravelled. The eye hath this sort of enjoyment in winding walks, and serpentine views, and all sort of objects, whose forms . . . are composed principally of . . . the waving and serpentine lines.[28]

Furthermore the individual was not merely a passive recipient of such pleasures, for the mind must be actively employed to some degree in the overcoming of perceptual difficulties and riddles. Hence, even for the owner or beholder of intricately devised objects such as Hogarth's candlestick, a degree of visual skill and work was involved which further removed such experiences from the charge of idolatry. Such pleasures were the result of a kind of work. When the mind was occupied in these ways, the most creative, inventive and intellectual faculties of man were being exercised purely as an end in themselves. This was certainly innocent and perhaps even improving. Insofar as a God-given characteristic was being employed it could not be altogether bad.

Within the terms of the debate about luxury it was sufficient for Hogarth to show that the pleasures of contemplating beauty were morally innocuous, that beauty was not necessarily a Jezebel or painted whore. Hume in his economic essays had reached a similar conclusion on the issue of luxury in general. But Hume was very much a utilitarian, and he urged the argument that luxury was also useful to society. Was there a parallel case to be made for beauty in relation to morality? Did beauty have a *positive* moral contribution to make to life, or was it merely a means of titillating the mind, a harmless form of playful recreation?

We have seen earlier in his treatment of the relationship between beauty and fitness how sceptical Hogarth was of conflating or confusing discreet things; likewise in his discussion of beauty and behaviour in the final chapters of the book devoted to bodily and facial expression. His line of argument was very complex and, in the final analysis, perhaps not altogether clear – which is excusable in such a subject – but he was at pains to separate himself from the arguments of the physiognomists who believed that face and body were visual signs to be read for their underlying meaning. Up to a point Hogarth accepted that 'we have daily many instances which confirm the common received opinion, that the face is the index of the mind'. But nonetheless he argued that 'the old adage, "fronti nulla fides" – there is no trusting to appearances – was correct because there were 'so many different causes which produce the same kinds of movements and appearances in the features'. This was especially the case with beautiful people: 'Very handsome faces of almost any age, will hide a foolish or a wicked mind till they betray themselves by their actions or their words.' This presented particular problems to a painter like Hogarth who had to represent people's

58 Detail of *The Dance*, Plate 2 of Hogarth's *Analysis*. The graceful dance of the virtuous couple embodied the proper relationship between the independent qualities of beauty and goodness.

actions and thoughts through visual representations since 'the bad man, if he be an hypocrite, may' so manage his muscles, by teaching them to contradict his heart that little of his mind can be gathered from his countenance'. Of course it was true that the ill-natured man who habitually frowns or pouts might acquire an ill-natured appearance, and in general the habits and emotions of a person permanently mark the face through the habitual use of certain muscles. The relationship, however, was not inevitable. But more to the point was the fact, as Hogarth observed, that bad human characteristics were better marked than good ones, for 'beyond the appearance of common sense and placidity' there were no shapes to indicate human perfection. These must be indicated by other means: 'Deportment, words, and actions, must speak the good, the wise, the witty, the humane, the generous, the merciful, and the brave.' Visual forms constituted a restricted vocabulary and one which was therefore easily misinterpreted. Hence the acrobat's expression as he tried 'to preserve his balance, may look as wise at that time as the greatest philosopher in the depth of his studies'. The physiognomists therefore were wrong in believing there to be a *direct* relationship between the signs of human expression and character. However in his subsequent discussion of the movements of the body Hogarth provided some suggestions of what the relationship between beauty and morality might be.[29]

In our ordinary everyday occupations we did not make a conscious effort to make all our movements graceful: 'all useful habitual motions, such as are readiest to serve the necessary purposes of life, are those made up of plain lines'. Mere efficiency demanded so. And, as the satirist must observe, to perform every action with serpentine grace would be ridiculous and affected. Graceful movements 'are used but occasionally, and rather at times of leisure . . . they being properly speaking, only the ornamental part of gesture.' Even in our behaviour, then, there was an ornamental part and a business part. When we walked our body undulated in a waving line but, when we danced, this natural movement was augmented to a degree that would be preposterous were we merely pacing about our study.[30]

It was in his discussion of dance that Hogarth drew together the threads of his argument concerning the relationship between the ornamental and the business part of life and morality (Plate 58). Even in nature's finest machine, mankind, where beauty and fitness went closest in hand, truth and honesty did not in themselves create beauty – just as fitness alone could not make a chair or a clock beautiful. Conversely, just as an object's added elegance must not contradict its fitness, so the deportment of a good man or woman should correspond to their inner character and not give a contradictory impression. However graceful, deportment was not an *expression* of the individual's moral conduct, rather it was an added glory that crowned virtue. And perhaps in illustration of this, Hogarth quoted the lines from Shakespeare's *Winter's Tale* in which Florizel lavishes praise upon Perdita's gracefulness in all her doings, and especially in dancing:[31]

> What you do,
> Still betters what is done. When you speak, sweet
> I'd have you do it ever: when you sing,
> I'd have you buy, and sell so: so give alms,
> Pray so: and for the ord'ring your affairs,
> To sing them too. When you do dance, I wish you
> A wave o' th' sea, that you might ever do
> Nothing but that: move still, still so:
> And own no other function.

Perdita's dancing was a superfluous beauty, an end in itself, but as such both it and the grace of all her actions was the fitting ornament of moral worth.

> Each your doing,
> (So singular, in each particular)
> Crowns what you are doing, in the present deeds,
> That all your acts, are Queens.

To sum up: for Hogarth the good might fail to have a beautiful external appearance, and beautiful appearances might well disguise evil intent; but that did not mean that goodness had to be necessarily ugly or plain, or that beauty was *always* a snare and deception. On the contrary, plainness could also be deceptive. There was therefore no moral reason why beauty of an intricate kind and goodness should not go hand in hand within the same individual, or fitness and beauty be conjoined in objects of use. When this happened, both virtue and beauty were mutually enriched. Indeed people of the highest moral worth or artefacts associated with worthy purposes ought to be adorned with the greatest beauty, and when this occurred the most noble beauty was created. Such beauty, however, did not just happen. It was a moral imperative to create it, one arising from a profound sense of decorum. The highest form of beauty, illustrated by Perdita's dance, in which 'beautiful' behaviour, using the word metaphorically, was performed with an exquisite grace was, in practice, a living metaphor for virtue.

Part Five

GOOD DESIGN

PREFACE

LET US TAKE stock. In the previous section it has been seen how the momentous issues in social and economic policy engendered a parallel debate concerning the style and appearance of towns, of buildings, of furnishings and other personal possessions and of clothes. Writers struggled to resolve the moral and religious dilemmas of increasing personal consumption and they discovered in 'style' and an 'improved taste' solutions to the problem of reconciling high consumption, which before Adam Smith's emphasis on saving and investment was considered to be the major precondition for growth, with the moral sanctions against materialism. No longer was there need for puritanical self-denial if you spent your money on *innocent* luxuries such as gardening or household utensils with naturalistic ornament. Likewise towns and cities could be safely permitted to expand so long as they were classical in style and orderly in layout and design. These aesthetic issues were all part of a continuing public debate about attaining a balance between the different aspects of social and economic life.

Architecture and town planning, the public face of the Arts of Design, were subject to laws and proclamations, increasingly enforced, which subordinated individualism to the public good. But the private side – furniture and dress – was free from statutory controls such as sumptuary laws. The views of the Censor in *The Spectator* were intended to influence behaviour and curb the excesses of vanity and fashion; theories of design of great intellectual sophistication, such as Hogarth's, were propounded; but it was left to people's individual consciences, to the forces of social conformity and to the market to determine what people actually did. Calls for the reintroduction of sumptuary laws by Evelyn and later by Berkeley were unheeded.

However, a century later a government department was established 'to diffuse taste throughout the population'. If that fell short of sumptuary law, it certainly attempted to use the growing apparatus of the modern state, particularly education, to control the character of personal consumption in order to counteract some of the vicious consequences of the Industrial Revolution. The Spectatorial tone of detachment vanished and was replaced by the prophetic and prescriptive utterances of Pugin, Henry Cole, Ruskin, William Morris and a host of others. The tyrannical possibilities of taste censorship did not pass unnoticed. In Ruskin's work the whole equation between the arts of design and political economy was radically reconsidered. Another century passed and under the guise of Good Design and the stringencies of the war-time economy sumptuary laws actually *were* reintroduced in Britain, if only for a decade during and after the Second World War in what was called the Utility Scheme.

In the next two sections the key events of the mid-nineteenth century centring around the Great Exhibition and of the mid-twentieth century centring upon the rise of the Modern Movement will be examined in the light of the increased urgency to control the moral consequences of economic progress through design and taste. This story is much concerned with the institutions founded to implement the policies of control; hence for a full understanding of the issues some survey, however brief, needs to be provided of the development during the eighteenth century of the institutional framework for the encouragement of arts and manufactures, loosely described as mercantilism. In addition it is necessary to be briefly reminded of the shift in attitude from the optimism of the Enlightenment view of British progress to the anxieties of the period of Chartism and Reform which provide the background for much of what follows.

CHAPTER 1

The Encouragement of the Arts of Design in the Eighteenth Century

MERCANTILISM

Since the early seventeenth century there had been an evolution rather than any radical change in state policy concerning political economy. Stability was the continuing aim: to preserve a balance between existing interests – land, trade and manufacturing – by means of an ever-shifting complex of tariffs, prohibitions, claw-backs and bounties. The Corn Laws protected the landed interest, the Navigation Acts protected trade, other measures protected the woollen industry against foreign competition and the competition from other domestically produced textiles such as cotton. New industries, however, were not discouraged so long as they did not jeopardise existing interests or threaten the balance. That, at least was the theory.

There has been much recent argument as to whether this really did add up to a systematic policy, known as Mercantilism, or whether it was simply an ad hoc and pragmatic method of raising government revenue, a rag-bag of measures. For Adam Smith, who coined the term Mercantilism, it was a coherent system. Even his recent critics agree that tariffs were 'infinitely tempting for they could bring revenue, protect industry, satisfy interests, and . . . import substitution seemed a path not only to economic wealth but also to social stability'.[1] These critics acknowledge that governments may have used tariffs to encourage manufacturing 'to employ the poor and create national wealth'. But this was exactly Smith's point – that muddled as it was, a policy existed which was coherent enough to amount to a system.

> By restraining, either by high duties or by absolute prohibitions, the importation of such goods from foreign countries as can be produced at home, the monopoly of the home market is more or less secured to the domestic industry employed in producing them . . . So the prohibition of the importation of foreign woollens is . . . favourable to the woollen manufacturers. The silk manufacturer . . . has lately obtained the same advantage.[2]

Smith described the results of these efforts by the producers, achieved through unrelenting lobbying of government 'to extort advantages from the legislature' as 'a monopoly against their own countrymen' – the poor consumers. Contradictory though the hotch-potch of regulations was, as *The Wealth of Nations* amply demonstrates, it had a coherent purpose. And historians today acknowledge that several industries flourished under the Mercantile System that might never have existed without it: silk, linen and paper for example. By their own admission, cotton manufacturing might never have been established in Britain but for the prohibition on the import of East Indian printed cottons in 1700.[3]

But in the nature of a system driven by lobbying, there was no overall pattern of protection and encouragement of industry – depending upon circumstances some new industries were protected by outright prohibitions against imports and by tariffs as well as receiving encouragement through investment by government and the nobility; others were encouraged but not protected by tariffs; others were neither much encouraged nor protected but flourished through entrepreneurship; and others were actually discouraged and prohibited. In the following section silk, carpets, pottery and cotton will be examined as examples of each category. It will also become apparent that even if one cannot call it a 'system' there was a climate within which manufactures were encouraged, an informal system perhaps, which could be put to good use by an entrepreneur like Josiah Wedgwood.

NEW INDUSTRIES AND THE MERCANTILE SYSTEM

Silk

Since Dr Thomas Moffat's efforts at the 'academy' at Wilton presided over by the Countess of Pembroke and James I's attempts to encourage the planting of mulberry trees, England had ambitions to become a major silk producer. All efforts were unsuccessful until Louis XIV's Revocation of the Edict of Nantes in 1685, which removed toleration for French protestants and resulted in the massive immigration of Huguenot weavers to settle in Spitalfields. Within seven years the Royal Lustring Company was incorporated by royal charter and foreign silks were totally prohibited.[4] Italy supplied the English silk industry with thread, but to escape this dependence as well, John Lombe, in 1716, in a classic exploit of industrial espionage, penetrated the spinning mills at Leghorn, made drawings of the machinery, and with the Tuscan navy in hot pursuit, escaped capture and returned to England. He and his brother Thomas were granted a fourteen-year patent in 1718 and built a water-driven mill on an island in the Derwent at Derby. Five hundred feet long, six stories high producing 300 million yards of thread a day: the first great machine-driven factory of the Industrial Revolution, it also produced the first personal account of the horrors of child labour. The Lombes may well have been supported with government subsidy as well as by patent; certainly, when the patent expired in 1732, they received a subsidy of £14,000 in lieu of an extension.[5]

Silk weaving was based in Spitalfields, the largest industry in the capital, and time and again parliament faced the threat of 20,000 distressed weavers marching through the streets of London with 'drums beating and banners flying', breaking the windows of mercers' shops which sold French silks, and demanding total prohibition. This was finally granted in 1766 and remained in force until 1826, when a free-trading Chancellor of the Exchequer repealed it and replaced it with a tariff of 30 per cent on imports.[6]

The unemployment caused by free competition both from abroad and from unregulated silk towns such as Coventry, Paisley and Macclesfield was partly the reason why the Commons Committee on Arts and Manufactures was set up in 1835. Their report set up the School of Design and led directly to the Great Exhibition and the great flourishing of British design manufactures in the later nineteenth century. The disproportionate attention paid to high quality artistic design, necessary for fine silks but not for cheap cottons, and the corresponding depreciation of the qualities of cheaper chintzes and calicoes will be examined subsequently.

Carpets

The British carpet industry owes its very foundation to public-spirited aristocratic patronage and investment, but unlike silk it did not receive any special protection. First imported in any quantity from Turkey by Venetian merchants, few carpets were woven in England during the sixteenth and early part of the seventeenth century. It was under the patronage of the

Earls of Pembroke at Wilton that the industry got under way. Tapestry carpets similar to those manufactured by William Sheldon at Barcheston had been produced at Wilton since the mid-seventeenth century for covering tables and upholstering chairs. As we saw earlier the eighth earl began the transformation of the industry when, probably in the 1720s, he smuggled two carpet-weavers out of France in empty wine barrels! The Wilton cut pile carpet was the result. It found a ready sale, created a large employment at high wages, and has continued to be manufactured there ever since.[7]

Other places followed suit and were supported by aristocratic or royal patronage. Two workmen from the Savonnerie who escaped to London in 1750 were told that 'to form an Undertaking of this kind, it would be necessary to procure the Protection of some Person of Fortune, who actuated by the motive of Public-spiritedness, might be both able and willing to sacrifice a Sum of Money, to procure to the Nation the Advantage of such an Establishment'. The king's son, the Duke of Cumberland, put up some money, and a factory was set up at Fulham with a hundred English employees. A school for designers and craftsmen was projected. But the enterprise was sold in 1755. Nevertheless it contributed to the establishment of the other great British manufacture at Axminster. Thomas Whitty, a weaver already interested in carpets, visited the Fulham works and based upon what he saw of the machinery, set up his own loom, on which he wove his first carpet on Midsummer Day 1755. The local gentry immediately patronised him with their custom, his carpet was shown to the steward of the Earl of Shaftesbury, the son of the author of the *Letter on Design*, which will shortly be examined in more detail, who agreed to 'encourage' the new manufactory. The newly-founded Society of Arts awarded him premiums in 1757 and in two subsequent years. His factory was a great success with aristocracy and royalty. The Prince of Wales, the future George IV, furnished his palaces at Carlton House and the Royal Pavilion at Brighton as far as possible with articles of British manufacture, including Axminster carpets.

Pottery and Porcelain

The potteries, in contrast to the carpet industry, were highly entrepreneurial (as they remain) and thus differed from their counterparts in Europe. In England they flourished without either protection or much in the way of aristocratic patronage. There was an industry producing high-priced luxury goods in great demand in the European courts. The Royal Saxon Porcelain Factory at Meissen, the leading European factory, had been founded by Augustus the Strong in 1710 to exploit Bottger's discovery of the secret of making hard-paste Chinese-type porcelain. French and other German courts followed suit in founding and subsidising factories producing soft-paste imitations. But in England, when the taste for the rococo wares of the Meissen factory began to establish itself in the 1740s, it was the heirs to the projectors of the period of the South Sea Bubble, the Bubble Age, who exploited the rage for collecting china and sought what financial backing they could obtain.[8]

Chelsea, the earliest of these factories, was founded in 1745 by Nicholas Sprimont, a silversmith from Liege who had been working in London. It seems that he received almost £1,500 from Sir Everard Fawkener, secretary to H.R.H. the Duke of Cumberland, and maybe from the duke himself. Fawkener certainly assisted him in 1751 by requesting the British Minister in Dresden to send examples of Meissen 'in order to furnish the undertakers with good designs'. The minister complied by making available a table set of Meissen given him by the King of Poland and valued at £1,500. But the Chelsea factory enjoyed no protection, as Sprimont complained in a petition, claiming that prohibitions had been 'the rule in every country upon the establishment of new manufactures'. Nonetheless, so long as it was the fashion to follow the German taste, and turn the dinner table into a semblance of the stage at the Italian opera with 'harlequins, gondoliers, Turks, Chinese and shepherdesses' rollicking about, the English factories were highly successful.[9]

Such an industry was heavily dependent both upon technical innovation and upon the arts of design. Chelsea seems to have maintained its own design school of some kind where 'thirty lads, taken from the parishes and charity schools [were] bred to designing and painting'. One of the factory's most popular lines was for figurines based on a variety of sources: engravings after Watteau, Boucher, Francis Hayman, Meissen originals, and terra-cotta or wax originals modelled by their chief modeller, Joseph Willems, a Flemish sculptor. For the manufacture of such wares, a training of the kind provided by the St Martin's Lane Academy was essential.[10] And although there was no direct connection between the academy and the factories, both belonged to the same milieu. Willems and Sprimont came from the same Huguenot background as several of Hogarth's colleagues, and shared the same style – graceful, rococo and naturalistic – which Hogarth had espoused in opposition to the Palladians. One of their wares, for example, was decorated with high naturalistic botanical specimens taken from plates of the plants in the Society of Apothecaries' Physic Garden at Chelsea. Another ware, soup tureens modelled in the forms of fruit, fishes and animals such as plaice, ducks and pineapples, was based upon Meissen but vastly extended the repertoire.[11]

Cotton

Far from receiving encouragement or tariff protection, cotton manufacturing, which was to grow into Britain's largest manufacturing industry, the centrepiece of the Industrial Revolution and champion of foreign trade, was actively prohibited throughout much of the eighteenth century. This was largely due to the combined opposition of England's staple industry, wool, and of the Spitalfields silk weavers to the threat presented by fine printed cottons imported by the East India Company, particularly under Sir Josiah Child. These had proved an extraordinary success, growing from 50,000 pieces a year in 1620 to 1,760,000 pieces in 1684 – the 'craze for calico'. Britain did not have its own native cotton industry – only coarse fustians for tickings, linings and for the garments of the poor were produced here. The lobby of wool and silk manufacturers succeeded in prohibiting the import of cotton fabrics in 1700 through an Act 'for the more effectual employment of the poor and for encouraging the manufacturers of England'. The importation of printed and dyed calicoes was absolutely prohibited and so was their use either for dress or furniture. The import of plain calicoes, however, was still permitted and despite the continued opposition of the silk and wool lobbies this actually stimulated the development of the English cotton printing industry which was producing 1,000,000 yards by 1711. Finally in 1721 a new Act prohibited the use or wear of all printed or dyed calicoes, even if they had been printed in England. But even this Act exempted fabrics actually manufactured in England. This in turn stimulated even more the printing of mixed cotton fustians and linen and the development of cotton manufacturing, with incalculable and uncalculated results. Another Act in 1735 expressly permitted the printing of British linens and fustians. In 1738 Messrs Wyatt and Paul set up their factory in Northampton to spin cotton thread mechanically by the use of rollers, a process that was only perfected by Richard Arkwright who obtained a patent in 1769 and in partnership with Jedediah Strutt, the stocking manufacturer, established his factory at Cromford in the Derbyshire hills in great secrecy and in buildings designed, quite literally, to withstand a siege – from machine-breaking mobs. In 1774 Arkwright succeeded in securing the repeal of the Calico Acts thus permitting the spinning and weaving of British cottons, for the employment of the British poor; and the growth in production of British cotton cloth began apace.[12]

Thus all this tariff legislation, culminating in Walpole's reforms of the 1720s, was carefully adapted to circumstances and the strength of lobbyists. The equivalent French policies begun by Louis XIV's chief minister, Colbert, had also established royal factories, producing every luxury associated with the furnishing and decoration of palaces, as well as the Royal Academies of Painting and Sculpture and of Architecture to raise standards of taste and to furnish designs. But nothing similar was attempted in England after the experiments in the monopolies of glass and tapestry under the early Stuarts. They smacked too much of absolutism. Even in architecture Christopher Wren preferred to train architects and other building trades practically on the job in the Royal Works rather than within a Royal Academy of Architecture.[13]

Hence in addition to fiscal protection, it was left to a hodge-podge of aristocratic patronage, private academies and encouragement societies, and to the initiative of individual manufacturers to encourage the arts, sciences and manufactures. Even voluntary societies made no headway in the 1720s after the South Sea Bubble. In 1722 proposals for a Chamber of the Arts 'to enquire into the Manner of performing any Thing Curious or Rare in all Arts, Trades, and Manufactures' were turned down on the grounds that it was not 'a proper time to introduce anything new, when Projects in general are under so much Disreputation, and so many people reduced to Misfortunes by playing with them'. For such reasons even the august Royal Society turned down a similar scheme in 1738 — for this was the age of 'bubbles', when stupendous sums of £1 million were solicited for such projects as 'raising the growth of raw silk' or manufacturing china and delftware. Not until the 1750s, when the odium had sufficiently lifted, was the Society (later the Royal Society) of Arts established; and not until 1768 was a Royal Academy of Arts founded, one which set itself apart from considerations of trade.[14]

The hostility to central government patronage is made explicit in Shaftesbury's *Letter concerning the Art, or Science of Design*. 'The long reign of luxury and pleasure under King Charles II' had done nothing to raise standards in English music. And it was 'one single court-architect', namely Christopher Wren, whom he blamed for spoilt palaces, ruined cathedrals and a London skyline infested with gothic spires, that very symbol of High Toryism. Anticipating David Hume he argued that only when public opinion, freely exercised by right of 'our Liberty and happy constitution', was permitted freely to judge on such matters would the arts and sciences improve. Freedom and security in the possession of the fruits of one's labours and industry had led to the growth of a vast metropolis like London, which was in turn 'a cause that workmanship and arts of so many kinds arise to such perfection'.[15]

Shaftesbury poured scorn upon the royal academies and the artistic achievements of 'our so highly assisted neighbours'. What was concentrated in the person of the king in an absolute monarchy should be diffused throughout the people in a legal monarchy. Consequently he considered that it was not only public monuments which were a public concern, but also those private houses which 'are of such a grandeur and magnificence as to become national ornaments'.

Aristocratic Patronage

Shaftesbury's *Letter* indicates the continuing rationale of country house building as a way of stimulating the arts and manufactures — just the kind of thing which Mandeville contemptuously dismissed as special pleading. Nonetheless it was a plea often heard not only from the nobility but also from manufacturers themselves such as Wedgwood, later in the

59 Houghton Hall and stables, built for Sir Robert Walpole, 1720–35, by Colen Campbell, Thomas Ripley and James Gibbs. The corner domes echo the turrets of Burghley with whose builder Walpole was often compared by friends and enemies.

61 (*facing page*) The fireplace in the Stone Hall, Houghton, by Michael Rysbrack. The bust displays Walpole as a Roman consul in front of a relief showing a sacrifice to Diana the Huntress. Houghton was used for only two months in the year when Walpole entertained the local gentry to an orgy of hunting and feasting.

60 *Moses striking the Rock* by N. Poussin. Part of Walpole's great collection, now the nucleus of the Hermitage Museum, St Petersburg, this picture was the basis of a eulogy of Walpole as Britain's saviour written by his son Horace.

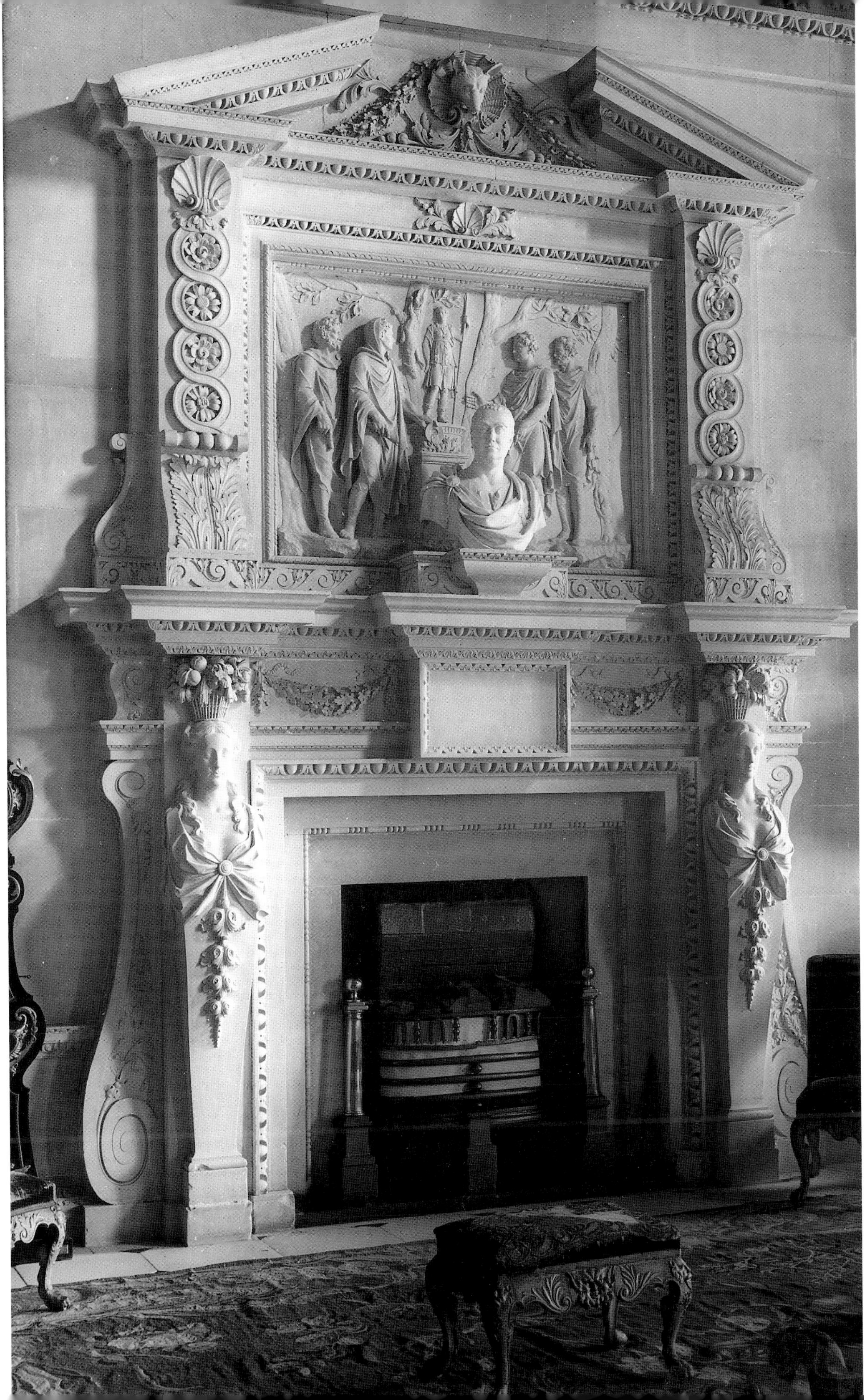

century. A somewhat fawning poem to Canons, the house of the Duke of Chandos, Pope's *Timon*, refers to it as an Eden, a Temple of the Arts and a 'grand Versailles'.[16] But probably the most significant of the new houses of the modern Maecenases was Houghton Hall in Norfolk rebuilt by Sir Robert Walpole between 1720 and 1735 during his period as prime minister within which time he gave special consideration to the management of the economy and the encouragement of British manufacturers (Plate 59). The Walpoles had been lords of the manor of Houghton since the eleventh century. Sir Robert Walpole's father though conventionally famed for his jovial disposition, housekeeping and hospitality was also a great improver, a pioneer of crop rotation who had trebled the rental income of the estate. His son, even during his years in office, continued the tradition of housekeeping with his biannual Norfolk Congresses for the local gentry which lasted a whole month and took place in the new neo-Palladian palace built at a cost of £200,000. His supporters 'applauded a mode of living so analogous to the spirit of ancient hospitality', his enemies accused him of corruption on an oriental scale.[17]

The outward form of the house, with four cupolas at the corners, like Burghley House in more correct classical dress, proclaims Walpole as the modern Burghley, bringing England the prosperity, security and stability of Elizabethan times. The staircase leading up to 'the floor of taste, expense, state and parade' is decorated with a mural of Meleager killing the boar which Artemis had sent as a punishment to lay waste the fields of Calydon, a subject which would have been understood as an allusion to Walpole's saving the nation from financial disaster after the South Sea Bubble. The stone hall, a severe almost sepulchral room, has a classical bust of Walpole placed amongst the Caesars over the fireplace and is an apotheosis of the great modern leader (Plate 61). The ceiling of the saloon is painted with the Gods on Mount Olympus who bless and protect the house; the dining room, ornamented with bacchanalian motifs overflows with the fruits of the earth. The walls of the major rooms used to hang with masterpieces by Andrea del Sarto, Titian, Rubens and Van Dyck, later sold to Catherine the Great of Russia, and with a set of Mortlake Tapestries of the House of Stuart, and the furniture was designed by William Kent – all indicating Walpole's stature as a great patron of the arts.[18]

That he himself conceived of the house in this way is strongly suggested by two contributions to *Aedes Walpolianae* of 1742, compiled and probably written by his son Horace in defence of his father at the time of his fall from power in that year.[19] The 'Journey to Houghton, a Poem' and the 'Sermon on Painting preached before the Earl of Orford at Houghton, 1742' make great play of Poussin's painting *Moses Striking the Rock*, which formed part of the collection (Plate 60). The parallel is drawn between Walpole's improvement of his own estate and his management of the affairs of the kingdom and Moses leading the Israelites out of the desert into the land flowing with milk and honey. This was entirely appropriate to a man whose economic policies were specifically praised by Mandeville as the epitome of 'the dextrous Management of the clever Politician', who used tariffs upon imported goods to turn private vices to public benefit.[20] The first speech from the throne of Walpole's administration had announced the policy of 'extending our commerce upon which the riches and grandeur of this nation chiefly depend'. Throughout the 1720s he implemented it by reducing or removing duties upon commodities needed by English manufacturers, facilitating trade in re-exported goods, actively encouraging silk manufacture with large subsidies, and introducing the Calico Act of 1720 to protect wool and silk. These were his policies as a statesman. It is hard to believe that the personal expenditure of this 'Minister of Industry' was not also conceived as a means of stimulating British manufacturers. Josiah Wedgwood certainly regarded the sale of the Houghton paintings to Russia in 1779 as a grievous loss of the nation's artistic capital.[21]

The academy at Wilton in the seventeenth century has been referred to earlier as has the eighth earl's patronage of carpet manufacture after 1700. The greatest 'privately' patronised academy in the early Hanoverian period was that of the third Earl of Burlington, Richard Boyle, said to have achieved for the arts what the 'bounty to learned men' dispensed by his great-uncle, the scientist Robert Boyle, had done for the sciences. Not only architecture and the fine arts benefited. On the earl's return from Italy in 1719, he brought with him two Italian musicians. Handel also lived in Burlington House.

The story of Burlington's espousal of the Palladian cause and his advancement of that style in the King's Works and amongst his fellow magnates is familiar.[22] He furthered the careers of Kent, Flitcroft, Isaac Ware and Vardy. Through them he monopolised the Royal Works and his fellow nobility followed his advice and example both in their country houses and in their urban estates. Such was his influence in the public domain of architecture that royal patronage could scarcely have accomplished more. However, as a result of English liberty in opinion and the relative freedom of the market, dissent arose both on aesthetic and on political grounds.

One focus for this was amongst the members of the St Martin's Lane Academy, led by William Hogarth. This had been founded as a drawing school in 1711 by Sir James Thornhill and Sir Godfrey Kneller. After various vicissitudes it was refounded by Hogarth around 1735 as a drawing school for painters and sculptors and for ornamental designers as well.

Hogarth himself had been apprenticed as an engraver of silver plate. He was intimate with the luxury trades. In 1720 he enrolled in Vanderbank's Academy, the St Martin's Lane Academy in one of its many pre-incarnations, and set up as an engraver. His early print *The Taste of the Town*, of 1723/4, was a satire upon Lord Burlington. Over the gate of Burlington House, inscribed 'Academy of Arts', stands Kent between Raphael and Michelangelo. To the left a motley crew of pimps, whores and prelates are being roped into a performance of one of Handel's Italian operas. On the other side a crowd is *freely* queuing up for a performance of Marlowe's *Dr Faustus*. The plays of Shakespeare, Jonson, Congreve, England's native dramatists, are being carted away from Lord Burlington's theatre in a wheel-barrow – echoing the early seventeenth-century arguments between Italian classicism and English culture.[23]

Hogarth also engraved plate, including a magnificent salver for Sir Robert Walpole in 1727, and made a design for a tapestry for the upholsterer Joshua Morris in the same year. (When Morris refused to pay, Hogarth sued him and won.)

When later in 1732 the print-sellers cheated Hogarth over his first great satirical series *The Harlot's Progress*, he petitioned parliament in 1734 to change the law and institute a fourteen-year copyright for the design of engravings. His grounds were conventionally patriotic and commercial: designing was the foundation of the useful arts, as well as of painting, sculpture and architecture. Copyright would give pattern designers the necessary security to enable British manufactures to compete with the French, and to assist the balance of trade. He also appealed to the principles of protecting what we now call intellectual property. For artists to be protected against the 'tyranny of the rich' print-sellers and to enjoy the just fruits of their labours they needed statutory protection against monopolies and combinations – an argument also to be found in Shaftesbury, Hume and Adam Smith.

The Act, known as Hogarth's Act, became law in 1735, and on the crest of his success the St Martin's Lane Academy was once again refounded.[24] This was not simply a training ground for painters and sculptors alone but Britain's first School of Design. The list of teachers at the school in 1745 gives an idea of the curriculum. Francis Hayman taught history painting, Roubiliac taught statuary, Yeo taught seal engraving and Hubert Gravelot taught design. The key figure was Gravelot. He had come to England from Paris is 1732 and appears at one time, perhaps before the establishment of the academy, to have run his own drawing school at the sign of the Pestle and Mortar in Covent Garden. He was a painter, book illustrator and engraver but he also, according to George Vertue, made 'drawings for . . . all other kinds of Gold and Silver works . . . he is endowed with a great and fruitful genius for designs, inventions of history and ornaments'. He made designs for cabinet-makers and joiners. Members of the Academy were largely responsible for the buildings and decorations of Vauxhall Gardens between 1732 and 1750, and students included the cabinet-maker and designer John Linnell and the architect James Paine.

Two treatises indirectly sponsored by the academy were based on its teaching and of use to practitioners of the applied as well as the fine arts. Joshua Kirby's *Perspective* of 1754 was based upon lectures given at the academy in the same year;[25] while Hogarth's own *Analysis of Beauty* of the following year summarises his teaching of twenty years. As we saw, he devoted as much space to the problems of the practical arts as to painting. It was vigorously anti-Burlington, anti-Palladian and anti-geometrical as indicated by Hogarth's mocking reference to the neo-Palladian architect not daring 'to stir a step without his book'.

Though conducted on private and informal lines the St Martin's Lane Academy, situated in the major cabinet-making district of London, was therefore a kind of English Gobelins and Academy rolled into one. Hogarth considered that presidents and professors were 'a ridiculous imitation of the foolish parade of the French Academy' and insisted upon a fully democratic constitution to which everyone contributed an equal share and had an equal right to vote. Deep was his disillusion, therefore, when in the 1750s his colleagues exercised that right and, leaving Hogarth in a minority of one, petitioned 'the three great estates of the Empire, about twenty or thirty students drawing after a man or a horse' – for the establishment of a hierarchical Royal Academy on French lines, which came to fruition in 1768, without any provision however for the applied arts other than architecture – and not much of that.

Such was the opposition between the Academy of Burlington House and that of St Martin's Lane. In the one case an aristocratic architect and patron headed a group of artist protégés; in the other case a group of distinguished artists and designers formed their own democratic association. In one case the admired style was Italian, neo-classical, based upon historical precedent and geometric principles; in the other case England's own national heritage was held up for admiration – Shakespeare, Westminster Abbey and Tudor together with a naturalism based upon the baroque and the rococo. Though the rococo was already fashionable and of French origin, it was reinterpreted as a natural style celebrating God's creation.

The 1750s, when Hogarth's own book was published, was a decade when public interest in design rose to fever-pitch. The presses groaned under the burden of proposals for academies and associations, treatises on taste, pattern books and new manufactories. In 1748 Stuart and Revett produced their *Proposals for Publishing an Accurate Description of the Antiquities of Athens*, set out on their travels supported by the Society of Dilettante in 1751 and published in 1762. Lock and Copland, who worked for Chippendale, published their *New Book of Ornaments* in 1752. Chippendale's own *Gentleman and Cabinet Makers' Director* followed in 1754, Thomas Johnson's *Twelve Girandoles* in 1755, and Ince and Mayhew's *Universal System of Household Furniture* between 1759 and 1762. On a theoretical level Burke's *On the Sublime and the Beautiful* of 1756 built upon Hogarth's foundations, as did Alexander Gerard's *Essay on Taste* of 1759, which won the Select Society of Edinburgh's prize in 1756. This was the period when Hume argued that luxury was nothing other than a general refinement in the senses and Adam Smith entertained the idea that the desire for beauty was the basis of economic growth.

62 Frontispiece to Thomas Johnson's *One Hundred and Fifty Designs*, 1758, dedicated like Pl. 3 to the Antigallican Society. A cherub is setting fire to French papier mâché, a threat to woodcarvers like Johnson.

Encouragement Societies

The 1750s also saw the establishment of several encouragement societies, including the Society of Arts, from which the Great Exhibition was launched a century later. The earliest of these was the Dublin Society, started by the Rev. 'Premium' Madden in 1739. In 1746 the lord lieutenant, the Earl of Chesterfield, obtained an annual grant of £500. Lady Chesterfield, in the spirit of Evelyn's advice to Charles II, set an example by appearing clothed in Irish materials.[26]

Prejudice against these societies was not unjustified. The Antigallican Association, the most bizarre example, was going strong in 1751 offering prizes for woven brocades and English bone lace. With the Seven Years War, its antigallican endeavours turned from commerce to piracy. Through the Stock Exchange, it financed its own privateer, The Antigallican, which attacked a French East Indiaman off the coast of neutral Spain creating a diplomatic incident. The backers resorted to fraud to maintain the values of the shares. However, the association remained in existence in 1758 when the woodcarver, Thomas Johnson, dedicated his *One Hundred and Fifty New Designs* to the president, the national hero Admiral Lord Blakeney. His frontispiece illustrates the national hostility, for it shows

St George piercing the arms of France and a cherub setting fire to a scroll bearing the words 'French Papier Mache' – a product which threatened the livelihood of woodcarvers such as Johnson (Plate 62).[27]

One of these societies survives to this day – the Society of Arts. Its founder, William Shipley, a London painter and drawing master, lived in Northampton between 1747 and 1753. A member of the flourishing local Philosophical Society, he met several of the pioneers of the Industrial Revolution. For it was there that, in 1739, Lewis Paul had built the first mill to spin cotton thread with rollers, the process which Richard Arkwright brought successfully into commercial operation thirty years later.[28]

Shipley issued his proposals to distribute premiums for improvements in the 'Liberal Arts and Sciences and Manufactures etc.' in June 1753, on the grounds that 'the introduction of such manufactures . . . may employ great numbers of the poor'. He also shared Hume's belief that these improvements would lead to a new golden age of universal refinement: 'The Augustan Age amongst the Romans and some preceding ages amongst the Greeks, were remarkable for the delicacy of their taste and the nobleness of the productions.'

The first premiums were offered for the discovery of cobalt mines and the growing of madder, favourite projecting eldorados. A cobalt mine *was* discovered in England, as Shipley happily reported in the *Gentleman's Magazine* in 1756. He stressed the utilitarianism of the society's awards and its concentration upon the applied arts, 'the society will not be misunderstood to aim at raising numbers of what are usually called painters; but it is earnestly solicitous to produce amongst boys ingenious mechanics, such as carvers, joiners, upholsterers, cabinet-makers'. Prize-winners included students of the St Martin's Lane Academy and John Flaxman the sculptor who made designs for Josiah Wedgwood.[29]

The two Scottish societies founded at the same time were associated with scientific advances and with the theories of Adam Smith. At Glasgow College, the theory of latent heat had been developed by Dr Black, and James Watt, mathematical instrument-maker to the college, invented the condenser for the steam engine there in 1764. Adam Smith was appointed Professor of Logic in 1751 and of Moral Philosophy a year later, and was already corresponding with David Hume on economic issues. He took an active interest in the Academy of Design founded in 1753. He chose pictures for students to copy, drew up a memorandum to enlist government support, and lectured upon the relationship between monetary value and aesthetic merit. He was also a member of the Select Society of Edinburgh, founded at the same time and for the same purposes of the Society of Arts in London, to give prizes and premiums for manufactures and designs, including the prize for the *Essay on Taste* awarded to Gerard in 1756.

JOSIAH WEDGWOOD

The view that a philosophical Treatise on Taste by Gerard or by Hogarth could make a serious contribution to the fortunes of the nation's traders and manufacturers did not arise from the vanity of artists and ivory tower academics, as the career of Josiah Wedgwood amply demonstrates. Wedgwood was keenly interested in the contribution of taste to business. I make no apologies for concluding this chapter with a brief account of his achievements, much discussed though he is, because to a remarkable degree he draws together and exemplifies almost all the threads of the argument of this book as well as demonstrating how the 'climate' of British industrial encouragement, described in this chapter, so curiously lacking in any centralised bureaucracy on account of British hostility to absolutism, actually worked.

The greater part of this book has attempted to unravel and explain the forces which brought into being 'London – the first modern city' portrayed in the very first chapter through the eyes of fascinated foreign visitors. Far from being the product of pure free-market conditions as writers like Nicholas Barbon and some recent historians have suggested, the economic system as well as the visual character of both London and Britain was the result of public policy grappling with and trying to control the market place. And just as the appearance of Georgian terraces typified the urban form of this society so the simple neo-classical wares of Josiah Wedgwood, whose showroom was one of the sights of London, have come to typify the domestic style of the interiors of those homes.

During the nineteenth and twentieth centuries Wedgwood has been variously interpreted as the epitome of a manufacturer with well-developed aesthetic principles, the forerunner of the late Victorian Art Manufacturer and of the Modern Movement. Eliza Meteyard, his chief nineteenth-century biographer, represented him as a philanthropist who pursued his aesthetic ideal almost regardless of commercial considerations. Others have argued that his success depended upon the application of division of labour both to reduce costs and to increase sales and profits, and upon his technical innovations as well. However a recent revaluation of the evidence by Neil McKendrick paints a very different picture, that of an active entrepreneur who regarded taste and quality merely as aspects of fashion to be exploited by clever marketing in order to increase sales.[30]

In more detail, McKendrick has argued that Wedgwood never tried to compete on price with other manufacturers – he always maintained prices substantially higher than those of his competitors because he was aiming for an exclusive market amongst the gentry and aristocracy. Second, Wedgwood derived little competitive advantage from his technical and artistic innovations since these were readily copied by other manufacturers who undercut him. And third, the real basis for his success was his brilliance as a salesman. He actively sought the patronage of the nobility and royalty in order to create a fashion for his wares amongst the rich and the great. To the same ends he sought the advice, support and patronage both of architects like Athenian Stuart and of arbiters of taste such as Sir William Hamilton. McKendrick has claimed that far from being committed to neo-classicism Wedgwood exploited commercially the new taste which had already been established by others. Moreover until he was absolutely sure which way the wind was blowing he kept a foot in both camps by continuing to make rococo and naturalistic wares. He was also exceptionally canny in matching his wares to the distinct tastes of particular national markets and to the moral foibles of the British public insisting, for example, that human figures derived from classical sculpture should not be naked. But over and above everything else his genius as a showman was exemplified by the way that he ran his shop in London, constantly changing the displays or putting on special exhibitions in order to draw the crowds, obtain press coverage and sell his goods.

This is an immensely stimulating and invaluable corrective to the earlier picture of Wedgwood seen through rose-tinted spectacles. Each major point is substantially correct. But the overall burden of the argument – that Wedgwood triumphed by exploiting the Veblen effect, or what one ought less anachronistically to call the Mandeville effect, playing upon the whimsicality of fashion, upon greed, appetite and people's desire to imitate their social superiors – is not borne out, and can only be supported by means of a partial and one-sided reading of the evidence. It goes without saying that both Wedgwood and his partner Thomas Bentley were extremely astute and calculating businessmen, but the evidence of their written correspondence points in a different direction – to two men of high principles intent upon steering a middle, and quite un-Mandevillean course between private profit and public benefits.[31]

For example, in the early years of the correspondence between Wedgwood and Bentley there was a protracted debate as to whether the intrinsic merit of an object or whether fashion was the way to sell most goods.[32] This was not an idle academic discussion but a vital contribution to their business plan, the foundations of which were being established

63 Wedgwood Creamware or Queensware. Wedgwood's career illustrates the informal, non-governmental institutions by which manufacturing was encouraged in eighteenth-century Britain.

in the years between 1767 when Bentley joined the partnership and about 1770. The issue of merit and fashion was first broached in September 1767 when Wedgwood was asking how much the success of his Creamware or Queensware depended upon 'its real utility and beauty' and how much upon 'the mode of its introduction' – Queen Charlotte had ordered a Creamware tea and coffee service two years earlier, a fact which Wedgwood had publicised heartily, and he had been appointed 'Potter to Her Majesty' in the summer of 1767 (Plate 63).[33] 'The government of our future conduct' would depend upon the answer to that question, for 'if a Royal or Noble introduction be as necessary to the sale of an Article of *Luxury*, as real Elegance and beauty, then the Manufacturer, if he consults his own interest will bestow as much pains, and expence too if necessary, in gaining the former of these advantages, as he would in bestowing the latter.'[34] Two years later he reported a discussion on this topic that he had had with Athenian Stuart in which they divided potential customers into three groups – those with a taste for 'show and glitter', who would not buy Wedgwood's neo-classical wares under any circumstances, those with a taste for 'a fine outline' who would, and third, those whose personal taste would be for 'show and glitter' but who would accept the advice of arbiters of taste, whether their architects or anyone else such as social superiors, upon whom they depended in these matters. Hence, if Wedgwood could gain the allegiance of the arbiters of taste and of royalty and nobility whose taste was imitated by others, he would acquire a greater share of the market. A decade later in June 1779 blaming poor initial sales of jasperware upon their failure to persuade the architects to promote the new product Wedgwood somewhat sourly observed that '*Fashion* is infinitely superior to *merit* in many respects.' But none of these discussions suggests that Wedgwood doubted the importance of 'merit' or, indeed, the actual merit of his own productions. His commercial analysis was based upon what he saw as a human reality, that while only a minority of potential customers had the ability to recognise real merit many others could be persuaded to follow the example of the recognised arbiters of taste.[35]

Far from displaying any cynicism about the quality of his own productions it is clear from these letters that he believed in the 'real Elegance and beauty' of Queensware, in the 'fine outline' of his neo-classical vases and was severely disappointed that the newly invented jasperware, 'a favourite child' of his, was not proving successful. Everything supports the view that like David Hume, Adam Smith in his 1762/63 lectures, William Shipley and many others, Wedgwood shared the optimistic belief of the 1750s and 60s that a taste for beauty operating in a relatively free market was the wheel that turned the trade and indeed the foundation of a new civilisation to rival those of antiquity. Writing to Bentley in November 1767 to overcome any residual doubts about his qualifications for joining the partnership Wedgwood stated, 'You have taste, the best foundation for our intended concern, and which must be our Primum Mobile, for without that all will stand still, *or better it did so*' (author's italics). He lured Bentley with the prospect of becoming a creator of beauty rather than a mere wholesaler.[36]

Wedgwood also had certainly read Hogarth's *Analysis of Beauty* whose principles of variety he tried to apply both to design and indeed to the changing displays in his showrooms; he was familiar with Slaughter's Coffee House in St Martin's Lane, the haunt of the members of the St Martin's Lane Academy; and he seems to have founded his own Society of Artists. In matters of taste he was proud to see himself rivalling and even surpassing antiquity, buying the great folios of the excavations at Pompeii and Herculaneum, Stuart and Revett's *Antiquities of Athens*, and of Sir William Hamilton's vases, and after the vases themselves had been purchased by the British Museum in 1772 he copied directly from the originals. He named his new factory on the Trent and Mersey Canal, Etruria. Wedgwood both benefited from the long tradition of classicism as the style appropriate for Magna Britannia and contributed to its further development, particularly in his imitation of the Portland Vase in the later years of his career between 1786 and 1790, his 'great work', conducted not in a spirit of absolute servility to the original but introducing his own variations. At the same period he financed John Flaxman who had been making designs for him since the 1770s to visit Rome, there to be 'still further improved, and enriched with antique love for the fountainhead of taste and the fine arts'.[37]

Indeed on the more general question of whether Wedgwood and Bentley were motivated primarily by high ideals, whether aesthetic or social, or by personal profit, everything in the correspondence points to the partners being strongly influenced by the Whig, puritan and improving ethos of *The Spectator* and of that attempt to strike a balance between personal profit and the public good in order to create the best of all possible worlds, as aspiration ridiculed in *The Fable of the Bees*. In many respects the two partners were the embodiment of Sir Andrew Freeport; projecting canals to create larger and more efficient national markets, encouraging division of labour, creating employment through the 'new bounty' of manufacturing and commerce, ardent believers in foreign and subsequently in free trade, while submitting themselves in addition to the rule of fancy and the imagination governed by taste.[38]

Two early letters in particular were concerned with the ethics of their business partnership which clearly mattered greatly to both of the partners who were devout nonconformists. In one of these written before the formation of the partnership Bentley, whose letter has not survived, seems to have praised the public spiritedness of most projectors who put the public good before personal profit. He argued however that the public good was not incompatible with private profit, instancing Brindley, the canal-builder, and Wedgwood

64 An engraving of figures from one of the Etruscan vases from Sir William Hamilton's Collection purchased by the British Museum in 1772 on commercial as well as antiquarian grounds and used by Wedgwood.

himself. Wedgwood replied with a certain coy modesty denying that he had either made a great fortune or that his trade was as noble or public-spirited as that of real public benefactors: 'Do you think my friend that the outline of a Jug, even a Bolingbroke, or the fine turn of a Teapot are synonims to creating a River, or building a City. No, No, my friend, let us speak softly, or rather be silent on such fribling performances.' Later in his career, however, he referred to Britain's manufacturers as her lifebelts. Two years after this first letter the partners were grappling with the problem of other manufacturers copying their wares and undercutting them. Should they fight their imitators by releasing very few new designs at any one time so as to maximise sales before their imitators caught up with them or should they throw caution to the winds and release all their new designs at once and let every manufacturer in England and Europe imitate them for the benefit of industry everywhere? In some disgust Wedgwood wrote that there was 'nothing relating to business I so much wish for as being released from these degrading slavish chains, these mean selfish fears of other people copying my works'. In reply Bentley, as before, argued that by attempting to inhibit imitations through reducing the release of new products it was actually possible to combine profit and personal fortune with fame and the public good.[39]

Turning to the issue of patronage, it is clear that Wedgwood actively sought out and encouraged influential patrons and did all he could to publicise their custom in order to encourage others to follow their lead. He certainly did not wait for them to come to him. And it is fascinating that in this unprotected and largely unpatronised industry Wedgwood sought to turn the tradition of the royal and aristocratic patronage of luxury manufacturing to his own ends by transforming his customers into his patrons, not, however, by encouraging them to invest in his business. While he sometimes bridled at the appalling arrogance and superiority of some members of the aristocracy he nonetheless expressed considerable appreciation for the tradition of public-spirited country house building and collecting upon which his own trade and art depended – he was ever alert to the opportunities offered for jasperware medallions and bas-reliefs for fireplaces, furniture and interior decoration when houses were being rebuilt. But his attitude was far from purely commercial. He had a strong sense of pride in his own contribution to the richness of such showplaces:

> Sir William's room is hung round with Corregios, Raphaels, Guerchinos, Bassans and many more great masters . . . it is *one* of the first rooms in the Kingdom. Among other great works of art Sir William particularly pointed out the chimney piece, assuring me at the

224

same time that he esteemed it the best piece in his room, and shews it as such to all his company. You know the pieces – Homer and Hesiod for the tablet, and the Muses for the frise. The statuary has done them justice and they look charmingly, and do more than merely support themselves in the very fine company into which he has introduced them.[40]

Consequently he was much saddened by the sale of Sir Robert Walpole's collection of paintings from Houghton to Catherine of Russia in 1779 and by a collection of marbles which followed them, both as a loss to the national stock, cultural and economic, and as a symptom of national decline at the time of the American War of Independence – whose colonists he nonetheless supported: 'Russia is sacking our palaces and museums, France and Spain are conquering our outposts.'[41] At the same time this reinforces the view that Wedgwood's primary concern, certainly in his ornamental wares, such as jasper bas-reliefs, was with the small luxury market and he set the process of social emulation to work not between social classes but within a single social class – the gentry and aristocracy. He wanted his wares to remain exclusive, *not* to trickle down.

On a more general level Wedgwood's career bears out the contention that the teacup and the candlestick were beginning to replace the palace as yardsticks of a nation's civilisation. Much as he denied any grander pretensions than 'pleasing the ladies' the export of his wares to such very grand ladies as Marie Antoinette and Catherine the Great ensured that the progress of British civilisation was being advertised throughout the courts and palaces of the world constituting tangible evidence of the British achievement in much the same way as the ceramic remains of classical antiquity, such as the Etruscan vases of Sir William Hamilton's collection – pottery being remarkably indestructible compared to buildings, paintings and textiles, or even silver and gold plate. As David Bindman has observed, 'Wedgwood saw his pottery not only as a commercial enterprise but as the new Etruria, where the crafts of antiquity were revived.'[42]

Related to the cultural importance of his pottery was his concern with its moral qualities as well. Early in the partnership he remarked that 'the Quakers have for sometime past been trying my ware, and verily they find it to answer their wishes in every respect.' He was indeed concerned that naked figures in bas-reliefs derived from classical sources would meet with strong moral and religious objections, but these concerns were shared by himself and his family, as is shown in a letter to Joseph Wright of Derby about his painting of 'The Corinthian Maid' which Wedgwood had commissioned: 'The objections were the division of the posteriors appearing too plain through the drapery and its sticking so close.'[43]

Finally the ample documentation of the Wedgwood-Bentley correspondence demonstrates how the 'climate' of encouragement actually operated in eighteenth-century Britain. While there were no centralised state academies or royal factories unlike those of 'our much assisted neighbours', there did exist a whole network through which an intelligent and enterprising manufacturer might serve his ends: lobbying government to obtain import tariffs or free trade; the use of country houses and their collections as a vent for their products and indeed as a showroom, as well as a source of models for imitation. The collection of Etruscan vases formed by Sir William Hamilton and sold to the British Museum in 1772 as well as the Portland Vase served as his models (Plate 64), as Sophie von La Roche recognised, and the inclusion of Wedgwood's showrooms on the itinerary of the essential sights of London alongside the British Museum is not so surprising. He was also indebted to the drawing schools like St Martin's Lane and to the Society of Arts for his artists as well as to the Society of Dilettantes for sponsoring Stuart and Revett's visit to Athens. Indeed the Secretary of the Society of Arts visited Etruria in 1774 and suggested that Wedgwood himself should form a collection of his own products for posterity. Wedgwood resolved to do so and this now forms the basis of the Wedgwood Museum – in effect, his own contribution to the system from which he had benefited.[44]

CHAPTER 2
The Condition of England

'CAN WE EXPECT that a government will be well-modelled by a people who know not how to make a spinning wheel or employ a loom to advantage?'[1] Posed by David Hume in 1752, the question was then largely rhetorical. The optimism of the period was such that even the more circumspect Adam Smith believed that the whole justification for a flourishing economy was the greater material well-being of the greater number. Nonetheless we have seen that both Smith and Hume were alert to the ways in which the new economic order might turn sour if a balance between wages, satisfaction in the work and pleasure in recreation were not maintained – as would be the case should combinations of employers drive down wages. Their opponents, meanwhile, those who represented the landed and agrarian interest and view of society, had long been aware of the social disadvantages of too much commerce and manufacture.

But none of them (except perhaps John Evelyn) foresaw a Britain whose foul rivers, dimly seen through fog and sleet, ran black with the effluent from dye-works, tanneries and sewers, whose landscapes had become an impenetrable darkness lurid only with flames, in which weird gloom there towered prison-like factories worked by armies of half-naked savages who lived in dank cellars and spent their leisure in drunkenness and dissolution. Less than thirty years after Sophie von La Roche's visit to London everything seemed to have gone wrong. The country was plagued with social and political unrest. Visitors no longer portrayed London as a paradise but as an inferno or a Babylon. That was the image of early nineteenth-century Britain which replaced the vision of Elysian splendour brought back by eighteenth-century visitors. By the early decades of the nineteenth century, as the imbalances and drawbacks so dimly glimpsed both by Hume and Smith became painfully apparent, Hume's question was no longer rhetorical. 'The Condition of England Question', as Thomas Carlyle called it, was the appropriate response to that polluted landscape and violently disturbed society.

The moral, social and economic repercussions of the Industrial Revolution were endlessly debated. The Old Polity had broken down, it had failed to stop the very thing for which it had been designed, namely the expansion of manufacturing industry and the growth of towns. By this account the Industrial Revolution was a mistake, a ghastly failure of policy, who knows maybe even an accident. And indeed there were plenty of people of that persuasion who struggled with all their might against parliamentary reform, against the repeal of the Corn Laws and who tried to reinstate what they perceived to be the merits of the pre-Industrial Age, which stood, after all, in the immediate past and was still surviving almost to the present day in many rural areas.

In the same period, between the 1830s and the 1860s, the design of manufactured goods – as well as of buildings and towns – became a major issue and focus within that debate, on account of the long tradition of policy and theory linking design to economic and social affairs. But, before examining those debates about design reform in detail, the familiar outlines of the 'Condition of England Question' need to be briefly recalled.

First of all, the facts. The population of England and Wales in 1700 has been estimated at between 5 and 6 million. Fifty years later it had grown little if at all, maybe to about 6 million. Fifty years later, at the first census in 1801, it was 50 per cent higher: about 9 million. Fifty years later, in 1851, it was 100 per cent higher and reached 18 million. In the century from 1750 to 1850, the population had trebled.[2]

The effect of this upon the great new manufacturing towns was dramatic. London had grown almost three-fold between 1550 and 1600; but the speed at which the new industrial metropolises – Manchester, Liverpool and even Huddersfield – grew was even faster. Between 1801 and 1851 Manchester grew four-fold, from 75,000 to 300,000; Liverpool by four and a half times, from 82,000 to 376,000; and even Huddersfield from 7,000 to 31,000. Brighton grew fastest of all: in 1851 it was almost ten times larger, at 66,000, than it had been in 1801. All the major towns grew at the same pace, and even those cities like Oxford, Cambridge, Bath and York, not ordinarily associated with the Industrial Revolution, doubled in tune with the overall increase in population during the same period. The whole balance between town and country had changed.[3]

As a result the amount of building was enormous. By 1852 there were almost $3\frac{1}{2}$ million houses, double the number in 1800. Annual brick production trebled from 700 million in 1801 to 2,200 million in 1852. Meanwhile, by 1815, cotton amounted to 40 per cent of total British exports, more than double that of wool, the traditional staple, and by 1830 cotton made up over half of total exports. Other industries grew as fast or faster. The production of coal was 50 million tons in 1850 compared to 11 million tons in 1800; iron was third only to wool and cotton in 1805; in 1851 there were 6,700 miles of railway track compared to 1,000 miles in 1840. And so on. There is no point in continuing the familiar statistical litany which represents the fulfilment of that enlightened and optimistic dream of the British economic miracle portrayed at the beginning of this book.[4]

But nineteenth-century foreign visitors, while they perceived as many signs of increasing production, splendour and wealth as their eighteenth century predecessors, were no longer able to ignore the living conditions in the industrial regions where much of the wealth was produced. Echoing Sophie von La Roche's description of Oxford Street fifty years earlier, the French writer Flora Tristan observed that it was at night that London should be seen at its best: 'Then, in the magic light of millions of gas-lamps, London is superb! Its broad streets stretch to infinity; its shops are resplendent with every masterpiece that human ingenuity can devise.' But she accused the fashionable visitors who stayed in the West End of ignoring the considerable proportion of the population – very nearly half – employed in the workshops, observing that 'in the metropolis itself there are many neighbourhoods which harbour all the misery, vice and evil known to mankind'.[5]

Tristan's censure is actually more applicable to eighteenth-century travellers, who showed not the slightest interest in the workshops of the East End or of Southwark and still less in the conditions of the new industrial cities such as Derby where the Lombes' silk mill stood, a miracle in the eyes of Defoe, who went into raptures over the fact that only one operative was needed to watch sixty bobbins, but the factory was perceived very differently by one of the very first of those operatives, whose personal experience was so much at odds with that of curious tourists who, he observed,

> have earnestly wished to see this singular piece of mechanism, but I have sincerely wished I never had . . . To this curious, but wretched place, I was bound apprentice for seven years, which I always considered the most unhappy of my life . . . My parents, through mere necessity, put me to labour before nature had made me able. Low as the engines were, I was too short to reach them. To remedy this defect, a pair of high pattens were fabricated and lashed to my feet, which I dragged after me till time lengthened my stature. The confinement and the labour were no burden, but the severity was intolerable, the marks of which I yet carry, and shall carry to the grave.[6]

But the nineteenth-century commentators made a special point of lifting the veil upon the apparent prosperity of the West End of London and the country estates. It became a literary convention: one that is well exemplified in Engels' famous analysis of the way in which the display of luxury in the shopping streets served as a false facade concealing the working-class misery which produced it.

> To such an extent has the convenience of the rich been considered in the planning of Manchester that these plutocrats can travel from their houses to their places of business in the centre of the town by the shortest routes, which run entirely through working-class districts, without even realising how close they are to the misery and filth which lie on both sides of the road. This is because the main streets which run from the Exchange in all directions out of the town are occupied almost uninterruptedly on both sides by shops, which are kept by members of the lower middle classes . . . hiding from the eyes of wealthy ladies and gentlemen with strong stomachs and weak nerves the misery and squalor which are part and parcel of their own riches and luxury.[7]

The only language these commentators could find to do justice to what they saw behind those facades was that of Dante's Inferno. Even Karl Marx in *Das Kapital*, that most theoretical and abstract of books which focuses upon the process whereby capitalism alienates all human relationships, echoed Dante's lines describing his descent into Hell, when he spoke of leading his reader from the market-place, where everything seemed open and above-board, in order to follow the owners of money and of labour power 'into the hidden foci of production, crossing the threshold of the portal above which is written: "No admittance except on business" to discover the secrets of creating capital.'[8]

What did they experience as they peered through the pall of ocean vapours created by 'the fuel of Hell, snatched from the very bowels of the earth' to feed the furnaces, the railways and the shops?[9] Initially they felt overpowered as by a colossus. When Ralph Waldo Emerson arrived in Liverpool in 1848 he observed that 'Everything in England bespeaks an immense population. The buildings are on a scale of size and wealth out of all proportion to ours, the colossal masonry of the docks.' To the French historian Hippolyte Taine, 'the warehouses of finished cotton goods and other fabrics are Babylonian monuments'. When Taine visited the Platt works in Manchester where the cotton-spinning machinery itself was made and entered the workshops, he stood dazed 'by a gigantic and orderly jumble of activity, a labyrinth of wheels, cogs, moving leather belts, a whole edifice of motion and action which, from floor to ceiling and storey to storey, is toiling and turning at a dizzy velocity like some obstinate and indefatigable automaton'. In relation to this man was like an insect. Among the highly regimented workers in English factories he complained that one never heard snatches of song, conversation or laughter, as one did in French factories. 'The master does not like his workers to be distracted from their toil for one moment by any reminder that they are living human beings; he insists on silence, and a deathly silence reigns, so much does the worker's hunger reinforce the employer's command!' Common humanity was absent in the relations between masters and men. 'In an English factory you would never hear the master say to a worker, "Good day, Baptiste, how is your wife and the little one?"'

These workers seemed the living proof of Adam Smith's grim prophecy concerning the division of labour, crushed as they were by a sense of their utter insignificance and their intelligences dulled through constant repetition of the same actions. After a day's work, at about six o'clock the factory gates opened to discharge 'an excited noisy crowd into the streets, men, women and children swarming in the turgid air. Their clothes are soiled; many of the children are barefooted; the faces are drawn and dismal.' Taine followed them home to their lairs in the dreary, uniform, smoke-stained streets paved with ironstone slag: 'You draw near a house, look in, and, in the half-light of a passage, see mother and grown daughter crouching, wearing little more than a chemise. What rooms! A threadbare slip of oilcloth on the floor, sometimes a big sea-shell or one or two plaster ornaments . . . The smell is that of an old-clothes shop full of rotting rags.'[10]

From our point of view it does not matter whether the condition of the working class was in fact as bad as these accounts suggest, or whether their standard of living, measured statistically, actually rose rather than fell during this period. What does matter are perceptions, correct or incorrect, of working-class conditions; what matters is working-class agitation and political activity, and their political and cultural results in the troubled first half of the nineteenth century.[11]

Britain was not in a state of continuous unrest, of course; nor did its rioting take the form of mindless violence. It was usually part of organised protest against specific industrial or political grievances at times of economic distress or crisis. The first major outbreak, the Luddite machine-breaking among the framework-knitters of Nottinghamshire, is particularly apposite to the theme of this book, since the original stocking frame or machine, invented by Revd William Lee in 1589, was, as we have seen, one of those inventions actively discouraged by Elizabeth I and James I in pursuit of Burghley's agrarian policy, on the grounds that increased productivity was undesirable because it put people out of work. Nonetheless, the machine was eventually introduced and in 1657 Cromwell and subsequently Charles II chartered a Framework-Knitters Company. The machine was the most sophisticated textile machine of its period with two thousand parts. It was improved by Jedediah Strutt, who subsequently invested the profits in the development of Arkwright's roller spinning machines. Its importance for the mechanisation of industry is immense.[12]

Framework-knitting was a domestic industry in which masters like Strutt rented out machines to the workers. The Luddites' great grievance was not, according to E. P. Thompson, over the use of machines as such (whose invention had been the basis of their livelihood) but partly over reductions in wages and increases in the rent of frames extracted by the hosiers during a period of recession. Still more serious apparently was the attempt to introduce a new kind of machine among the unemployed knitters, one which – unlike the older machine, which made the whole stocking in one piece – made large pieces of knitted fabric to be 'cut up' and sewn into the shape of stockings. Clearly the produce of the wide-framed machines could be used to undercut the others in price. The framework-knitters only resorted to violence after their efforts to obtain legal redress under the charter of the old Framework-Knitters' Company had failed. And they broke only the new machines.[13]

Most illuminating, in view of the discussion of design reform which follows, was the fact, declared by the radical *Nottingham Review*, that the machines were broken only 'in consequence of goods being wrought upon them which are of little worth, *are deceptive to the eye*, are disreputable to the trade, and therefore pregnant with the seeds of its destruction'. Here is perhaps one source of the strong attacks made by design reformers against designs which were deceptive or which concealed their mode of construction.[14]

After 1815 the agitations which took place at the end of the Napoleonic War, culminating in the Peterloo Massacre of 1819 in which eleven unarmed protesters were killed and 400 wounded, were of different origin. In part it was the new Corn Law of 1815 designed to maintain the price of bread, in part the post-war unemployment which led to the 'March of the Blanketeers' by Manchester factory workers. But the great difference between the way Burghley had handled economic distress just two centuries earlier and the approach of Lord Liverpool's administration is indicated by the latter's observation that there was no connection between social distress and political unrest, that government could do little about economic difficulties and that 'most miseries of mankind were beyond the reach of legislation, and government intervention into economic matters nearly always did more harm that good'.[15]

The sheer brutality of encounters between government troops and demonstrators is indicated by an incident in May 1832, when the passing of the Third Reform Act hung in the balance and 200,000 supporters of the Birmingham Political Union resolved to march on London. The Scots Greys, in barracks at Birmingham, were given orders to rough-sharpen their swords. 'The purpose of so roughening their edges, was to make them inflict a ragged wound. Not since before the battle of Waterloo had the swords of the Greys undergone the same process.'[16]

When Reform finally came, the working-class movements were rapidly disillusioned by the results. The New Poor Law of 1834 dismantled the relatively philanthropic Elizabethan Poor Law, designed to supplement housekeeping and hospitality and administered by the local JPs. No longer would the unemployed receive relief in their own homes; now they had to enter the dreaded workhouses whose strict discipline and bad food discouraged anyone from seeking benefits rather than working. Christian charity was to be supplanted by a free-market in labour. 'The poor-laws, as at present administered', wrote one reformer, James Kay, 'retail all the evils of the gross and indiscriminate bounty of ancient monasteries. They also fail in exciting the gratitude of the people, and they extinguish the charity of the rich.' Indeed, the Poor Law Commission declared that 'Every penny bestowed that tends to render the condition of the pauper more eligible than that of the independent labourer is a *bounty on indolence and vice.*' With the demise of bounty, the almshouse was replaced by the workhouse – a point graphically made by Pugin in his *Contrasts* of 1836.[17]

The Earl of Shaftesbury's Factory Bill, mangled by the House of Commons in 1833, had provided that no child under nine years old was to be employed at all, and that no one under eighteen should be employed for more than ten hours a day. Employers convicted three times would have been imprisoned. As amended the Act restricted the ten-hour day to children below thirteen years old, although it did introduce Factory Inspectors and the principle of two hours education a day. The watering down of the Factory Bill lent fire to the factory workers' campaign, led by Robert Owen, for a national eight-hour day. The cotton workers planned to strike for this cause in 1834.[18]

The Act's provision for two hours daily education was a dead letter because in many places there were no schools or teachers. A Bill, introduced by J.A. Roebuck in 1833, to make schooling compulsory between the ages of six and twelve, and administered by a Secretary of State for Education, was rejected. Instead a paltry £20,000 a year was dispensed after 1834 to provide for 'the Erection of School Houses, for the Education of the Children of the Poorer Classes'. Not until 1839 was that figure raised to £30,000, and Dr James Kay, later Kay-Shuttleworth, whose support of the New Poor Law we have noted, was appointed as Secretary to an Education Committee of the Privy Council. He was responsible for the appointment of School Inspectors. But his personal concern for the education of the working classes was to forestall the effects of division of labour anticipated by Adam Smith: 'The dull routine of a ceaseless drudgery, in which the same mechanical process is incessantly repeated, resembles the torment of Sisyphus – the toil, like the rock, recoils perpetually on the wearied operative.' And what really worried him were not the diseases of extreme poverty so much as the thriftless vices and luxuries of operatives on high wages who, in his opinion, possessed the habits of animals. The purpose of education was to instruct the poor 'in habits of forethought and economy'. And this, in turn, was essential because 'The preservation of *internal peace*, not less than the improvement of our national institutions, depends on the education of the working classes.'[19]

Deep dissatisfaction with the drear and self-interested utilitarianism of the reform parliament provides some explanation for Chartism, the last great demonstration of working-class unrest, supported by frustrated radical MPs like Roebuck. The Charter's six points included universal manhood suffrage and voting by secret ballot to ensure that neither landlords nor capitalists monopolised the law-making process. The National Petition for the Charter, with its 1,280,000 signatures wrapped round a huge roller was presented to the House of Commons in June 1839. In July the House of Commons rejected it. Disraeli declared that much as he disapproved of the Charter he sympathised with the Chartists. He traced the troubles to the new Poor Law, to an attitude of utilitarian parsimony towards the duties of government and to the Reform Act itself. The Commons vote was followed by looting and rioting in Birmingham, and the Newport Massacre in which ten Chartists were killed and fifty wounded.[20]

In that same year, 1839, when the press was already claiming the demise of Chartism, came the publication of the 'Essay on Chartism' by Thomas Carlyle.[21] It is not always easy for us today to grasp the contemporary appeal and importance of this rambling, long-winded, prophetic figure whom both Dickens and Ruskin looked upon as their mentor. But in 'Chartism' we can see how Carlyle commanded admiration for the manner in which he told against the laissez-faire and utilitarian currents of his age. 'A feeling very generally exists that the condition and disposition of the Working Classes is a rather ominous matter at present; that something ought to be said, something ought to be done, in regard to it.' So the essay begins, and the burden of Carlyle's message is that 'the matter of Chartism is weighty, deep-rooted, far-extending' – that it would not just go away, either by burning itself out or by the ferocity of the law. It was the expression of the condition of the working classes which could not be measured by wages alone but by what he called 'the quality of wages'; which included the labourer's prospects of self-improvement, his security of em-ployment, his human relationship with his employer, his sense of injustice, the way he spent his leisure. In Carlyle's opinion, laissez-faire amounted to an abdication by the ruling class of its responsibilities towards the governed; laissez-faire was 'do-nothing' government. Carlyle interpreted the 'thought which at heart torments these wild inarticulate souls, struggling there, with inarticulate uproar, like hurt creatures in pain' not as a cry for democracy but for real government: 'Guide me, govern me! I am mad and miserable and cannot guide myself.' And while he warned his readers against confusing the feudal ideal of aristocratic bounty with the 'poor imperfectual Actual' nonetheless he argued that the old aristocracy had indeed fulfilled their obligations as the rulers of society, and had not surrendered their relations with the lower orders to the cash nexus.

From the standpoint of Burghleyan policy (the 'old constitution' as Disraeli called it), the Industrial Revolution was a terrible failure because it was the very phenomenon that the policy had been designed to prevent. That policy had been under strain from the very beginning, but even in the eighteenth century a compromise between landed and commer-cial interests had permitted it to be maintained. Burghley, and his successors, had devised conditions for a stable, prosperous and predominantly agrarian economy. They failed to reckon with the effects of compound interest, investment and import substitution.

The object here is not to analyse the causes nor to trace the progress of the Industrial Revolution but to examine the ways in which the arts of design entered into the great debate on the breakdown of the old policy. As we have seen, the arts of design had always been an important component of that policy through the control of urban growth, the residence of the ruling aristocracy in their mansions on their estates, as well as the moralised consumption of goods. But, as the Burghleyan system fragmented in the 1830s, the old issues were re-opened with more urgency than at any time since the Elizabethan and Jacobean periods. On a political level, this was manifested in Disraeli and the 'Young England' movement trying to heal the wounds through the restoration of paternalism. But, in the arts of design, there appeared a new factor in the specificity of the solutions that were prescribed, particularly in the design of household goods. The sweeping relationship between British national identity and the classical style, or between innocent luxury and the worship of nature, no longer sufficed. The kinds of issue raised by *The Spectator* were now submitted to a peculiarly intense scrutiny: one which included not only the *appearance* of articles of consumption, or their psychological and moral effects, but their very construction, down to the types of nails and hinges that should be used in furniture, and the quality of the work that should go into making them. In the chapters that follow, we will look in detail at the most important of the solutions that were proposed between the 1830s and the 1860s: Pugin's attempt to build a theocratic Christian state around architecture and design; the efforts of the Design School movement to combine utilitarianism with art; and Ruskin's far-reaching analysis of the connection between the economic system and the physical environment which it was responsible for constructing.

CHAPTER 3

Pugin:
Preaching Design

AUGUSTUS WELBY NORTHMORE Pugin was born in 1812, the son of a refugee from the French Revolution. Pugin senior worked as a draughtsman for the architect John Nash and, with his son's occasional assistance, published books on mediaeval furniture and buildings.

Pugin himself achieved public notice when, in 1836, shortly after his conversion to Catholicism, he published a controversial book: *Contrasts, or A Parallel Between the Noble Edifices of the Fourteenth and Fifteenth Centuries, and Similar Buildings of the Present Day, Shewing the Present Decay of Taste.* As an architect, he proceeded to design a number of cathedrals and churches, but his most outstanding architectural achievement, in collaboration with Sir Charles Barry, was to design the Houses of Parliament in London.

In the twentieth century critics and historians have neglected Pugin in favour of Ruskin and Morris and members of the Arts and Crafts Movement, who owed so much to his pioneering career. Perhaps his insistent Catholicism is felt to be intellectually indigestible. Here the balance will be redressed by giving Pugin pride of place as the initiator of the arts and crafts. When his theories have been considered at all, it has largely been from the standpoint of our own architectural controversies. Because his 'two great rules of design' were that ornaments should never be constructed or tacked on, but 'should consist of enrichment of the essential construction of a building', he has been espoused as a pioneer of the Modern Movement; a slightly embarrassing one, maybe, in view of his backward-looking mediaevalism. On the other hand, for the critics of the Modern Movement Pugin was the first false prophet of the heresy that architecture could be good only if it were the product of a good society – the 'ethical fallacy' of Geoffrey Scott.

But both interpretations are based upon a degree of misunderstanding of Pugin's position. Pugin certainly believed that there was a moral aspect to architecture and design, building and manufacture but, as we have seen, he was hardly the first to believe this. He was also less guilty of the ethical fallacy than his critics affirm and in any case, as Louise Durning has shown, it is a misunderstanding of Geoffrey Scott to think that he proscribed *any* ethical content in architecture. Pugin was also far from being a functionalist.[1]

He was guided by three theories: a theory of what constituted a good society and of its relationship with good architecture; a theory of architectural appropriateness or decorum; and a theory about honesty of construction. There is nothing unusual about the first two. But the idea that buildings or furniture or other manufactured things ought to display their mode of construction, that one should be able to see the nailheads and hinges, was unusual and original. It is not to be found in the writings of the French rationalists such as Laugier. Here it will be argued that it was very much a response to the 'Condition of England Question' and to the new phase in the long-running debate about the politics of design. We shall take each of these aspects in turn.

65   The Christian Architect, frontispiece to Pugin's *True Principles of Pointed Architecture*, 1841.

Scarisbrick Hall in Lancashire is one of only two major country houses for which Pugin was responsible. Charles Scarisbrick, the owner and rebuilder, was head of an old Catholic family but, unlike Pugin's other Catholic clients and patrons such as Lord Shrewsbury (for whose Alton Towers Pugin designed some additions) or Ambrose Phillips de Lisle, he was not pious, certainly not a proselytiser and, through a common-law marriage in Germany, he was father of several illegitimate children. His family's development of Southport as a holiday resort in the 1820s made Charles Scarisbrick very rich, yet he lived in seclusion in Lancashire, dispensing little or no hospitality, even though he employed Pugin to continue rebuilding the Elizabethan house in the style of those mediaeval manor houses with which hospitality and housekeeping were almost synonymous.[2]

It must have been an odd relationship between this man and the passionate, idealistic young Pugin, who had only just published *Contrasts*, his architectural and social manifesto. I think that Scarisbrick Hall must be understood as a counterpart to that book, a manifesto in wood and stone for which Pugin was lucky to find a patron who gave him a relatively free rein. But the building is something more specific; it is itself a sermon, a homily upon the way that a squire ought to live, addressed to Scarisbrick himself and his heirs. That *does* mark a revolution in the role of an architect or designer. Pugin assumed the role of a priest and prophet, indeed portrayed himself as such in the frontispiece of his *True Principles* (1841) (Plate 65). In general, Pugin's architecture and the designs of his furniture and household utensils not only strove to obey the true principles in which he believed, but also to instruct others. Even a humble plate became a sermon shaped in pottery.

By 1836 there was nothing especially original in building a mansion in the mediaeval style. Strawberry Hill, Fonthill Abbey, Eaton Hall, Abbotsbury, Windsor Castle, to name only the most famous, had already been completed. Ten years earlier, when Pugin was only fifteen, he had himself been producing gothic furniture for Windsor Castle. His father's practice as an architectural draughtsman had flourished on this trade and his two volumes of beautifully detailed measured drawings of *Specimens of Gothic Architecture*, published between 1821 and 1823, was essentially a pattern book to meet this demand.[3]

What makes Scarisbrick special is the fact that it broke away from the tradition of gothick toys. It was built in an archaeologically coherent style, English perpendicular of the late fifteenth or early sixteenth century, the period just preceding what Pugin regarded as the catastrophe of the Reformation, and it looks much like Hengrave Hall in Suffolk or even Penshurst itself (Plate 66). Pugin's conception was for the main front to centre around the entrance porch, with the Great Hall to the left, the chapel to the right and the kitchens, modelled upon those at Glastonbury, beyond. The chapel though essential to Pugin's idea was never built, but enough was built to enable us to see the sort of statement about the social order that Pugin was making. This is reinforced by the carved and painted inscriptions. The porch, unlike a classical portico, is raised on only three steps and both welcomes and protects the visitor, while its inscription proclaims 'This hall was built by me Charles Scarisbrick, 1842. Laus Deo.' The two double-height oriel windows of the Great Hall, with its high crested roof crowned by the fanciful lantern, signify the household assembled at meals and is the most richly decorated section of the exterior (Plate 67). 'I have raised up the ruins and I have built it as in the days of old', reads the inscription of the frieze over one of the windows. The other reads 'Every house is builded by some man, but he that buildeth all is God.'[4]

Here then was a church-shaped society in which the secular hall was intended to be subordinate to the unbuilt chapel. Yet there is no pretence of the house having been built in the middle ages. It is emphatically a house of 1842, but one which aims to reinstate the architectural standards of the past, if not to reconstruct the whole way of life (Plate 68). The

66 Scarisbrick Hall, Great Hall and Porch, by A.N.W. Pugin from 1836. 'This hall was built by me Charles Scarisbrick' is inscribed over the Porch.

67 (*facing page*) Great Hall photographed in the late nineteenth century.

68 Hall fireplace, Scarisbrick, with the inscription 'Make the Pile for Fire Great'.

interior of the hall itself, with its splendid timber roof, carved screen and encaustic tiled floor, is a restatement of the generosity of baronial housekeeping signified by the inscription on the fireplace: 'Make the Pile for Fire Great.'

In a letter to the Earl of Shrewsbury concerning a proposed hall at Alton Towers, Pugin wrote, 'I have nailed my colours to the mast, – a bay window, high open roof, lantern, two good fireplaces, a great sideboard, screen, minstrel gallery – *all or none*. I will not sell myself to do a wretched thing.' His generous vision applies equally to Scarisbrick.[5] The inscription in the Great Hall reads: 'Except the Lord build the house they labour in vain that build it; except the Lord keep the City, the watchman watcheth but in vain.' The form of the house and the sentiments expressed clearly put us in mind of the 'old fashion of England' at Chantmarle or Penshurst. God endows the landlord with his bounty and he, as God's Steward, bestows it in turn upon the members of his own household. The chief rooms were the places where such a way of life was to be celebrated – and, even if that did not occur in reality in this case, the house was certainly intended to mould the lives of its future occupants through text, symbol and design.

Whether or not Pugin believed in natural magic (one suspects he did not) he did believe that physical surroundings could influence people's conduct. 'Do not these arches, these mullioned windows, these cloistered alleys, tend to cherish and preserve within their breasts that gravity and religious composure so essential to the high state to which they belong?' he wrote of the palaces of bishops, and the same applied to the mansions of the nobility. Although his *True Principles of Pointed or Christian Architecture* was published in 1841, it was based upon lectures given in 1838 which were themselves the expansion of ideas in the last chapter of *Contrasts*. There he portrayed the English manor house in familiar terms (Plate 69).

> The old English Catholic mansions were the very reverse of those I have been describing; they were substantial appropriate edifices, suited by their scale and arrangement for the purposes of habitation. Each part of these buildings indicated its particular destination: the turreted gate-house and porter's lodging, the entrance porch, the high-crested roof and Louvred hall, with its capacious chimney, the guest chambers, the vast kitchens and offices, all formed distinct and beautiful features, not *masked or concealed under one monotonous front*, but by their variety in form and outline increasing the effect of the building, and presenting a standing illustration of good old English hospitality . . . under the oaken rafters of their capacious halls the lords of the manor used to assemble all their friends and tenants at those successive periods when the church bids all her children rejoice, while humbler guests partook of their share of bounty dealt to them by the hand of the almoner beneath the groined entrance of the gate-house. Catholic England was merry England, at least for the humbler classes; and the architecture was in keeping with the faith and manners of the times, – at once strong and hospitable.[6]

Pugin's objective was nothing less than the re-establishment of a Catholic theocracy in which state was subordinated to church and the ruled to the rulers. One hundred and fifty years later, it is easy to regard Pugin's ambitions as the ultimate in lost causes, a self-deluding attempt to turn back the clock. But throughout the early years of reform, in spite of rapid industrialisation and urbanisation, the Corn Laws remained in force and the power of agrarian interests was still considerable. The Oxford Movement flourished and Tories such as the Earl of Shaftesbury were leading the campaign for Factory Acts and the ten-hour day against industrialists and free-traders. So it was by no means unreasonable to cherish the hope that the inexorable movement towards a fully-industrialised society could be slowed down and perhaps halted and even reversed. After all, a future prime minister, Disraeli, expressed his support in the House of Commons for the underlying causes of Chartism and, shortly afterwards, joined in the movement known as Young England which sought a

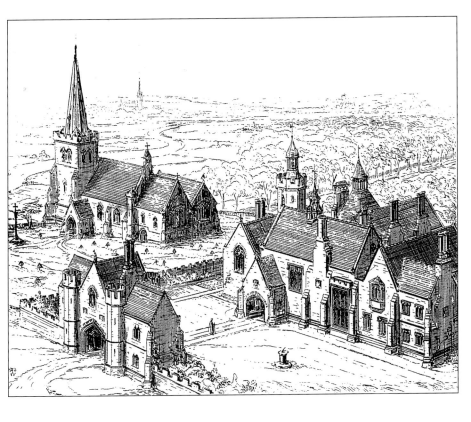

69 Old English Manor House from *True Principles*. Pugin's evocation of the bounty, hospitality and architectural form of the old English mansion derives from houses like Penshurst and Chantmarle (Pls. 38 and 40).

return to the principle that great duties were an obligation of great wealth – Carlyle's tenet. Young England supported the campaign of Pugin's patron Ambrose Phillips de Lisle for union with Rome.[7]

Eustace Lyle, the master of St Genevieve, the house which figures in Disraeli's novel *Coningsby*, 1844, was modelled on de Lisle. Disraeli's description of his house is obviously derived from Pugin's writings and buildings:

> In a valley, not far from the margin of a beautiful river, raised on a lofty and artificial terrace at the base of a range of wooded heights, was a pile of modern building in the finest style of Christian architecture . . . The first glance at the building, its striking situation, its beautiful form, its great extent, a gathering as it seemed of galleries, halls, and chapels, mullioned windows, portals of clustered columns, and groups of airy pinnacles and fretwork spires, called forth a general cry of wonder and of praise.

And the description of Christmas at St Genevieve is the very epitome of Pugin's social values – and of those of English hospitality.

> It was merry Christmas at St Genevieve. There was a yule log blazing on every hearth in that wide domain, from the hall of the squire to the peasant's roof. The Buttery Hatch was open for the whole week from noon to sunset; all comers might take their fill, and each carry away as much bold beef, white bread, and jolly ale as a strong man could bear in a basket with one hand . . . Within his hall, too, he holds his revel, and his beauteous bride welcomes their guests, from her noble parents to the faithful tenants of the house. All classes are mingled in the joyous equality that becomes the season, at once sacred and merry. There are carols for the eventful eve, and mummers for the festive day.[8]

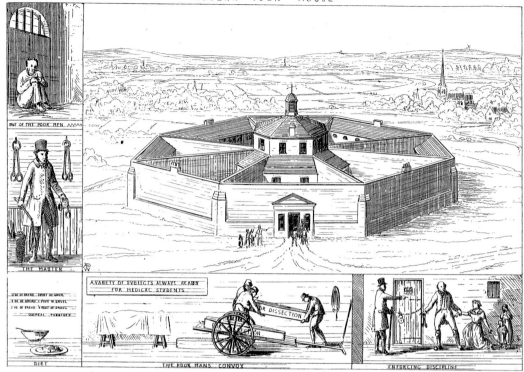

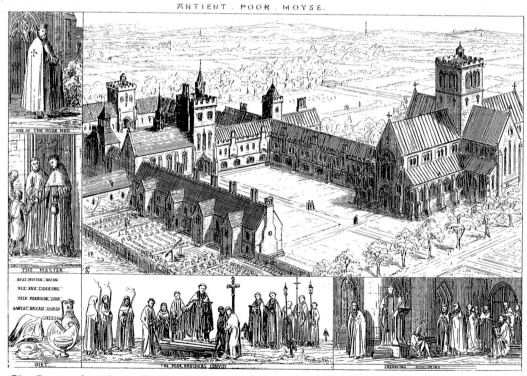

70 Contrasted residences for the poor from *Contrasts*, 1836. The Benthamite New Poor Law of 1834 dismantled the relatively generous Elizabethan legislation.

The plates of *Contrasts*, and the additions made in 1841 particularly, extend our sense of Pugin's social vision. In front of the Palladian arch of King's College in the Strand (a pioneer of Benthamite vocational education) stands a man with a placard reading:

CHEAP
KNOWLEDGE
LECTURE
MECHANICS
INSTITUTE
Mr. GAB
ON
THE POWER
OF THE
PEOPLE

In contrast to this is the grand perpendicular arch of Christ's College, Oxford, through which a solemn academical procession passes bearing a crucifix. Similarly, the Poor House of the New Poor Law, on the outskirts of town, is in the form of Bentham's windowless octagonal panopticon, the diet is bread and gruel, the paupers are whipped and kept in solitary confinement. The 'antient Poor House', meanwhile, is a splendid almshouse built around a courtyard attached to a grand church, where the poor consume beef, mutton, bacon, ale and cider, milk and porridge, wheaten brad and cheese – redolent of the 'gross and indiscriminate bounty of ancient monasteries' so loathed by the utilitarian reformers (Plate 70). Finally the town of 1840, in contrast to the fair-walled town of spires and towers of 1440, is the polluted mill town described by nineteenth-century foreign travellers and English novelists.

All Pugin's values and ideals were opposed to the utilitarian reforms of the 1830s and 1840s and, even though he had no truck with either socialism or democracy, he did, as we shall see, share certain remedies with the working-class movements.

PUGIN'S THEORY OF PROPRIETY

Pugin's first great rule for design was the 'there should be no features about a building which are not necessary for convenience, construction, or propriety' and he glossed this with the rider that 'the smallest detail should have a meaning or serve a purpose'. He was not therefore what we call a functionalist, since the purposes that he considered a building might serve included spiritual ones, and the details that might be appropriate included decoration and symbolism. Although he insisted upon a rigorous logic to ensure that meanings and architectural imagery were strictly appropriate, his was far from the reductive utilitarianism or mechanistic approach sometimes mistakenly associated with twentieth-century functionalism.

First of all Pugin considered ecclesiastical architecture to be the crowning glory and central focus of the ancient city, in which the mother church stood 'vast in height, rising above all the towers of the parochial churches which surrounded her'.[9] It would therefore be an impropriety for any civic or private buildings to dwarf the cathedral. Moreover, Pugin's objection to modern churches, particularly to the Commissioners' Churches, financed by the State through the Church Building Act of 1818, was that they employed decorative facades as screens to disguise the penny-pinching halls behind. This did not mean that he would condemn the thatched barn used as a church by a poor congregation, only that the House of God ought to be the finest building in the town, finer than any private dwelling, and 'should be as good, as spacious, as rich and beautiful, as the means and numbers of those who are erecting them will permit'. As a society grew richer so it should rebuild its churches on a more glorious scale, just as happened in the middle ages. This

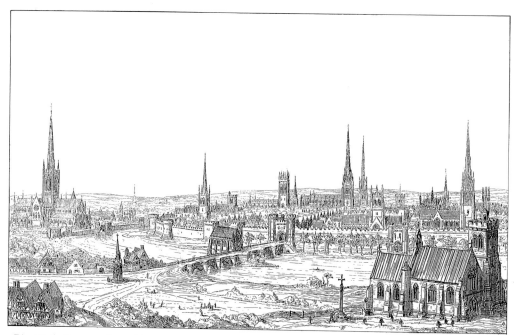

71 Catholic town from *Contrasts*. Pugin believed that the skyline should reflect the pre-eminence of the town's major church.

principle had a bearing upon Pugin's ideas about honesty. The showy facade to the parsimonious Commissioners' Church was contemptible because it was a dishonest and vain attempt to 'escape the all-searching eye of God'. Nothing in a church should be shoddy, even if out of human sight. Moreover no cheap materials should be painted to resemble more expensive ones like wood or stone. Were the real thing too expensive, a deceptive imitation was, in a church, inappropriate.

Since Pugin's theory was strictly hierarchical, everything fell into place around the building and decoration of the church (Plate 71). In collegiate architecture, exemplified by Winchester and Oxford, the students' lodgings ought to be 'severe, elegant, and scholastic' as Henry VI had specified for King's College Cambridge – 'without too great superfluity of detail or busie moulding'. The few ornaments ought to include sacred images. Therefore he condemned modern colleges in a 'bastard Greek' style which 'might be taken for a barrack hospital or asylum'.[10]

Domestic and civil architecture next fell into place. We have already considered Pugin's views about mansion houses, and most of his observations consist of an attack upon the rootless cosmopolitan eclecticism of the modern day which failed above all in propriety, both to climate and to the nation's history and characteristics. 'We have Swiss cottages in a flat country; Italian villas in the coldest situations; a Turkish kremlin for a royal residence; Greek temples in crowded lanes; Egyptian auction rooms; and all kinds of absurdities and incongruities.' Although he didn't say so, this diversity of inappropriate foreign styles was the inevitable result of Britain's position as an international trading nation. In contrast, a self-sufficient agrarian society would not have deserted the architecture appropriate to its climate, national materials, religion and settled way of life.[11]

Pugin's belief that gothic, or what he called Christian or Pointed architecture, was the right architecture for England derived from this insistence upon the rules of propriety. The climate dictated steeply-pitched roofs to throw off snow and rain, substantial walls

242

and large windows.[12] Next, taking materials into account, the pointed arch was a masonry form of construction based upon the availability of small stones. This is more questionable, since the pointed arch also arises in the wooden cruck arch and, conversely, the availability of small stones might be a determinant of *any* arched architecture: round, pointed or Islamic, as Christopher Wren had observed. Nonetheless, such was Pugin's theory; and its bedrock was religious and symbolical. The pointed arch, allowing a far greater ratio of height to width than the round headed arch, was an emblem of the resurrection. There is an obvious flaw in this argument but, when presented in one of Pugin's most inspired passages of writing, it is easy to be swept along by his conviction.

> What a burst of glory meets the eye, on entering a long majestic line of pillars rising into lofty and fretted vaulting! The eye is lost in the intricacies of the aisles and lateral chapels; each window beams with sacred instructions, and sparkles with glowing and sacred tints; the pavement is a rich enamel, interspersed with brass memorials of departed souls. Every capital and base are fashioned to represent some holy mystery; the great rood loft, with its lights and images, through the centre arch of which, in distant perspective, may be seen the high altar blazing with gold and jewels, surmounted by a golden dove, the earthly tabernacle of the Highest; before which, burn three unextinguished lamps. It is, indeed, a sacred place; the modulated light, the gleaming tapers, the tombs of the faithful, the various altars, the venerable images of the just, – all conspire to fill the mind with veneration, and to impress it with the sublimity of Christian worship. And when the deep intonations of the bells from the lofty campaniles, which summon the people to the house of prayer, have ceased, and the solemn chant of the choir swells through the vast edifice, – cold, indeed, must be the heart of that man who does not cry out with the Psalmist, *Domine dilexi decorem domus tuae, et locum habitationis gloriae tuae.*[13]

HONESTY

Pugin's attempt to forge a necessary and sufficient connection between gothic architecture and English culture is almost certainly the weakest link in his discussion of architectural propriety, since it is perfectly possible to have an architecture adapted to the English climate and local building materials, with churches of a cruciform plan, of tall and lofty proportions, without the pointed style being employed. In his insistence upon constructional honesty, however, Pugin was on stronger ground. In the first place, as we have already observed, honesty could be a species of propriety, as in the case of churches. No deceit or attempt to pass off an inferior material under an imitative disguise was to be tolerated if the congregation could afford better.

But Pugin took his insistence upon honesty much further than this, further than any writer on architecture or design had taken it before. He argued that 'hinges, locks, bolts, nails, etc., which are always *concealed in modern designs*, were rendered in pointed architecture *rich and beautiful decorations*', both in buildings and in furniture.[14] Not even the humblest nail should be disguised: 'Bolts, nails, rivets, so far from being unsightly, are beautiful studs and busy enrichments, if properly treated.' The more important parts of an object such as the lock, especially those in churches, should be 'adorned with sacred subjects chased on them, with the most ingenious mechanical contrivances for concealing the key-hole' (concealment here apparently being appropriate on the grounds of security) (Plate 72).

For similar reasons Pugin objected to illusionistic wallpapers of a gothick pattern, in which a shaded perspective of a gothic arch was repeated at odds with the spectator's viewpoint and the natural lighting of a room. He did not object to the adornment of walls or floors, but only if the patterns were flat, unshaded and non-illusionistic, like those of Turkey carpets, mediaeval tiles and brocades. These contrasted with contemporary practices

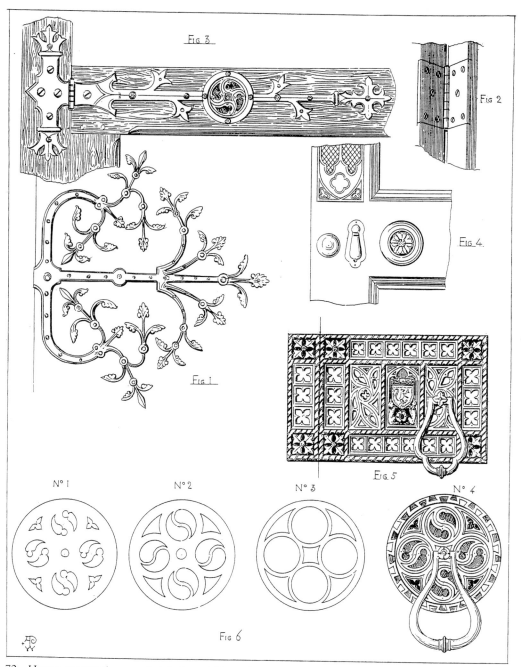

72 Honest construction revealed: locks and hinges from *True Principles* contrasted with modern concealed door furniture. Pugin's object was to prevent the concealment of shoddy workmanship.

in which a form for a utensil was chosen and a decoration then added to it: in which the fit form, as Hogarth would have called it, was disguised instead of beautified. Hogarth, of course, believing that fitness of form was not necessarily beautiful, supported the addition of elegance. Pugin, however, objected strongly.[15]

Part of his reason was that such adornments frequently breached propriety in an utterly silly fashion, such as a firegrate made to look like a miniature castle complete with portcullis and battlements. But, in the equipment of the rooms of a private house, one might have thought that such harmless frivolities could be allowed. One reason that Pugin

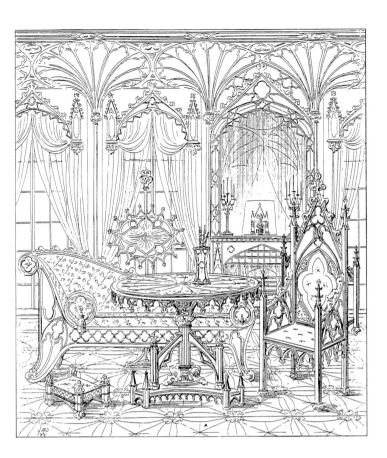

73 Pugin condemned this Gothick furniture in *True Principles*. The table can be compared with his own design for the House of Lords below.

74 Octagonal oak table from the Prince's Chamber, Palace of Westminster. Decoration should never be constructed, but construction might be decorated. Here, however, Pugin has gone for construction overkill.

would not allow it was his belief that 'cheap deceptions of magnificence encourage persons to assume a semblance of decoration far beyond either their means or their station' – a return to the rigours of sumptuary law as a means of maintaining the social hierarchy. Pugin attacked 'that mockery of splendour which pervades even the dwellings of the lower classes of society',[16] but his insistence upon the thorough-going display of the very construction of a building or object was so unusual at this period as to require a further explanation. It is not, let us remind ourselves, that he merely required things to be soundly constructed; they had to be *seen* to be soundly constructed, and nothing, not even appropriate and meaningful decoration, should conceal the construction – all must be open to inspection.

We have observed that the opponents of utilitarianism had much in common with the radical working-class movement in their opposition to the parsimony of the New Poor Law, the conditions in the factories, the conditions in industrial towns, even if they did not share a belief in unionism, socialism or manhood suffrage. There is also a striking parallel between the grievances of the Luddites in 1811, relating to the use of machinery to make stockings whose manufacture was 'deceptive to the eye', and Pugin's ideas about honesty of construction. Pugin had no *a priori* objection to modern inventions and mechanical improvements – 'In matters purely mechanical the Christian architect should gladly avail himself of those improvements and increased facilities that are suggested from time to time' – but he did object to their use for degrading design. Here as an architect he stood shoulder to shoulder with the proud artisans who foresaw the redundancy of their skills and livelihoods through the use of machines to reduce quality and cut corners.[17]

> All the mechanical contrivances and inventions of the day, such as plastering, composition, papier mâché, and a host of other deceptions only serve to degrade design, by abolishing the variety of ornament and ideas, as well as the boldness of execution, so admirable and beautiful in ancient carved works. What can be so ludicrous as to see one of those putty-stamping manufacturers, with a whole host of pieces, cutting, paving, brading on, and contriving an ornament? Then covering the whole with priming to hide the joins: and when done, it is a heavy, disjointed, ugly, composition. Yet it is cheap – that is, it is cheaper than what an artist can design and produce.[18]

Pugin's attack upon deceits was as far-reaching in the implications it held for the future of industrial society as anything the later Arts and Crafts Movement was to advocate. His objection to the cosmopolitan eclecticism of style, the 'carnival of architecture' and the post-modernism of its day, in which 'every architect has a theory of his own . . . One creates nothing but the Alhambra . . . a third is full of lotus cups and pyramids', was that it was destroying the art and skill of the carver, metalworker and plasterer. He believed that people of wealth, instead of filling their houses with mass-produced ornaments and the contents of antique shops, should follow the example of 'the fostering care of the Catholic church, and its noble encouragement' in restoring the skill and art which produced the antiquities in the first place.[19]

What was the source of his ideas? At the back of his mind he must have recalled the censure by the preachers of the middle ages of craftsmen and merchants who practised 'falsities and tricks to deceive people'. The preachers advised craftsmen to refuse to do a job if the client insisted upon inferior materials being used. If a carpenter were asked to lay floors for a house with planks that were too short, he should say, 'I will not take the wage or have anything to do with it, because that timber is no use'.[20]

This was why Pugin, in the new conditions of the 1830s, demanded that all goods, all artefacts be completely open to inspection, not only as a display of honest practice but also as a sermon fixed in the very material and form of the thing, an icon of itself, and a moral lesson of the dangers of deceit, bad craftsmanship and un-Christian work (Plates 73–4).

His insistence upon honesty brings us back, therefore, to Pugin's social ideas, his conception of a Christian society. There were inescapable political implications to Pugin's ideas about the kind of social and industrial organisation that would guarantee the revival of high quality craftsmanship. He believed this could only be achieved within a hierarchical Christian society in which the craftsman knew his own subordinate place but would also insist upon the standards of his craft against the efforts of his employers to reduce the costs of the work. It is absolutely inconceivable that Pugin was unaware of the great efforts by Robert Owen, in association with Joseph Hansom, to set up a Grand National Guild of Builders in 1833. For one of Pugin's very earliest jobs in 1833 was detailing the Birmingham Free Grammar School whose contractors, Walthen's, dismissed all its union members, provoking an uproar in which the Owenites played a large part. Pugin's criticisms of the new capitalist system of general contracting in the building industry must have been close to those of the union and of Hansom, though his remedies were different.[21]

Another figure of the period with whom Pugin shared ideas about craftsmanship was Alfred Bartholomew, who followed Hansom as the second editor of *The Builder* for a short period between 1843 and 1844. Bartholomew was the son of a Clerkenwell watchmaker and therefore brought up in a community of proud craftsmen implacably opposed to capitalist methods. He had been apprenticed to a pupil of Sir John Soane and, in a book of 1840 called *Specifications for Practical Architecture*, fulminated like Pugin against modern eclecticism and the neglect of sound structure. In 1842 Bartholomew set up an elaborate organisation called 'The Freemasons of the Church' whose vice-presidents included two of the three leaders of Young England – Disraeli and Lord John Manners. Associated with the Freemasons was a plan for a National Architectural College to reform training. It would have taken twenty years for the architect to become fully qualified. The college itself was envisaged as an estate of the realm controlling all appointments to public surveyorships, which were to be limited to Master Masons. In short, Bartholomew dreamed of an architectural profession tied to the state with the monopolistic powers it was to achieve only a century or so later – and then only for a short period.[22]

In purely practical and political terms, both Bartholomew's and Joseph Hansom's ideals have come closer to realisation than Pugin's. But neither of them had the same influence upon the ideals that inspired generations of architects and designers down to and including the present. For Pugin was the seminal figure in the Good Design Movement, awkward though his religious beliefs make it for us to accept him. All the subsequent individuals and institutions, however unlike him in philosophy, either developed or modified his ideas: the teachers and administrators of the Schools of Design including Redgrave, Owen Jones and Henry Cole, Ruskin himself and his Arts and Crafts disciples including William Morris. Above all, it was Pugin who, under the pressures of the intense social and political turmoil of the 1830s, perceived that any artefact, be it a building, a chair or a dinner plate, could be made an object lesson in how we should conduct our lives, both spelling out the lessons concerning the work that went into its construction and teaching us how we should behave when we use it. Whereas Lord Burghley had enacted sumptuary laws which told people what they could and could not wear, and *The Spectator*'s authors had developed a non-statutory moral code of taste governing the ways people should spend their leisure and their money, and Hogarth had shown how innocent luxuries might be contrived through design, Pugin discovered a means by which the very objects themselves, including their mode of construction, would preach to their users. Perhaps we should leave him with the last word:

A witty writer in a recent periodical advised me to stick to my trowel; but I reply that I am a builder up of man's minds and ideas as well as of material edifices, and there is an immense work and a moral foundation yet required before they are prepared to receive, understand, and practically realize the glories of Christian Art. Building without teaching or explaining is useless.[23]

CHAPTER 4

Design Reform and the Great Exhibition

THE SCHOOLS OF DESIGN

We now reach the strangest episode so far in this history. Since the ending of sumptuary laws in 1604, the state's intervention in the Arts of Design had been limited to their public aspects, to efforts to control both the size of towns and the relationship between private building and public areas within them. The decoration of a person's teacup, for example, had been a matter of moral and aesthetic dispute, at most persuasion, but beneath the notice of the state or legislation. Yet, after 1835, the state took an increasing interest in such apparently private matters. It established and financed public schools to train designers. It promoted the first and grandest international trade fair, the Great Exhibition of 1851. It founded one of the finest museums of applied art in the world. All this to regulate the appearance of the humble teacup. Why?

Had the motives been purely commercial, to improve the competitiveness of British goods in world markets, this would not have been surprising. But, although that was the ostensible purpose of the enterprise and the pretext for enlisting the power of the state, the real motif of those involved was to reshape personal morality by implementing the kind of control over individual consumption about which *The Spectator* contributors, or Pugin, had merely written – and which *The Spectator*, in any case, had insisted should *not* be imposed.

The outline of events is easily told. In the aftermath of the Reform Act, the reformers' utilitarian attentions turned among other things to art education and, in particular, to the monopoly enjoyed by the Royal Academy, which was seen as a redoubt of the ancien regime.[1] In 1835 a Select Committee of the House of Commons was appointed and heard a succession of witnesses carefully picked by the reformers to support their contention that it was essential to establish schools of design in order to supply British manufacturers with the skills to compete with foreign producers, in particular the French. The Committee's Report in 1836 led to the Board of Trade opening a Government School of Design the following year. In 1838 the Scottish painter William Dyce became director, on the strength of his report upon the continental schools, and ran the school successfully with the help of J.R. Herbert, a friend of Pugin who taught figure-drawing, until he resigned in 1843 to return to his own painting. Towards the end of his term of office he began the publication of the school's first textbook on ornamental design, *The Drawing Book of the Government School of Design*, which attempted to define a grammar of ornament. Also during this period the first regional branch schools were founded with government grants.

The departure of Dyce and his replacement by C.H. Wilson led, in 1845, to a rebellion first of the students and, within months, of the staff. Herbert, with whom Wilson had clashed, was dismissed. New staff, including the painters Richard Redgrave, Harrison Townsend and John Horsley and the sculptor Alfred Stevens, were appointed. In 1847, the council of the School of Design presented a report on these troubles to parliament. As a

75 Caricature of Sir Henry Cole (1808–82) by James Tissot from *Vanity Fair*, 1871. An unsung Eminent Victorian, it was Cole who set up the Great Exhibition, not Prince Albert, as well as the Victoria and Albert Museum and the British art school system.

result, in 1848, Wilson was sacked and both Dyce and Pugin's friend Herbert returned as teachers of ornament.

Meanwhile, design had begun to attract the attentions of a hyperactive Benthamite civil servant in his early forties, Henry Cole (Plate 75), who had won his spurs as the reformer of the Public Record Office and as Rowland Hill's chief aide in the Penny Post campaign.[2] Cole was looking for new fields to conquer. In 1845 he joined the Royal Society of Arts which Prince Albert was trying to revive, won a prize in 1846 for a design of a teacup and teapot; in 1847 he employed several of the teachers of the School of Design to design articles for a concern called 'Felix Summerly's Art Manufactures' and, in 1848, sowed the seed of what was to grow into the 1851 Exhibition; this he largely masterminded though Prince Albert still gets all the credit especially in the absence of a modern biography of Cole. Cole also launched the *Journal of Design* and, between 1848 and 1852, edited it as a platform for his views and those of his fellow reformers. In 1848 he was brought in by the Board of Trade to help put the School of Design on a sound footing. He wrote three reports and, in 1849, set up yet another Select Committee of the House of Commons, whose report, however, he failed on that occasion to fix. Nonetheless, in the aftermath of the Great Exhibition, Cole finally had his way and established a Department of Practical Art of the Board of Trade to administer the London school and the Museum of Ornamental Art, as well as to supervise the provincial schools according to the principles which he and his fellow reformers had developed.

That, then, is the outline. The details are more confusing – if only because the aims of the whole enterprise were confused. And this is hardly surprising, since its starting point was a one-man campaign whose aim was not to improve industrial design at all, but Fine Art. In 1808, the painter Benjamin Robert Haydon saw the Parthenon (Elgin) Marbles newly arrived in London and became convinced that he possessed the entire secret of artistic beauty. Britain, he hoped, might lead a cultural renaissance. His plan was that patrons would be instructed at the universities in the principles of taste – in the way that Evelyn had proposed – and that, throughout the country, there would be art schools for painters and sculptors where teaching would be based upon anatomy and the antique. Haydon made no headway until, in an audience with the Prime Minister Lord Melbourne in October 1834, he deployed the commercial argument: 'High Art does not end with itself. It presupposes great knowledge, which influences manufactures, as in France. Why is she superior in manufactures at Lyons? Because by State support she educated youth to design.'[3]

What had been merely a pretext for Haydon became the chief objective of such utilitarian MPs as William Ewart, who furthered the cause on the Select Committee. They were faced, however, with a problem. British manufactured goods, unlike those of France, did not compete in the luxury markets of the world, had never really done so, and did not depend upon the highest standards of artistic design. Cheap cotton goods, produced by the most advanced industrial machinery in the world, were in fact the staple of British trade and – attractive though these were, to judge from surviving examples – they did not sell on the basis of luxurious designs but because of their hardiness and their price. To make out a case for design schools to assist British manufacturers, it was necessary to identify some other threat to Britain's commercial interests. The key lay in silk manufactures.

As we have seen the British silk industry had been fully protected by prohibitions on imports until, in 1826, it became the first industry to be exposed to foreign competition as a result of Huskisson's Free Trade legislation. The removal of these prohibitions – even though imports remained subject to a high 30 per cent tariff – happened to coincide with the trade depression of 1826 to 1830. And there were 25,000 silk looms in Spitalfields in 1824, making silk-weaving the major single industry in the capital. Tens of thousands of unemployed operatives rioting in the streets of London was an uncomfortable prospect in a period of working class agitation as it had been a century earlier when the Spitalfields anti-calico riots of 1719 had rattled a nation recovering from the 1715 Jacobite uprising and had led to the 1721 Calico Act.

One answer was a Buy British Campaign of the kind traditional since the seventeenth century.[4] On the accession of William IV in 1830, Queen Adelaide ordained that all the ladies attending her first drawing room in February 1831 must wear dresses of British materials, made by British dressmakers. The queen herself appeared in a brocaded dress of Spitalfields silk. Presented by Spitalfields operatives with six pieces of silk, she declared, 'As far as I can judge . . . English silks are very superior to the foreign.' Queen Victoria's wedding dress was Spitalfields silk and was bought by Madame Tussauds for £1,000 and put on show.

But another answer lay to hand in Haydon's existing campaign for art education. John Gwynn, the eighteenth-century campaigner for town planning and good design, as early as 1749 in an appeal for French-style design education had specifically referred to Spitalfields silk and although it was not openly referred to in 1835 it is surely no coincidence that over a quarter of the hand-picked witnesses to the 1835 Committee, eight of the thirty, were either silk manufacturers or traders, or were questioned on the subject of the silk trade: a representation out of all proportion to the national importance of the industry. Almost all of these specialists, in answering the leading questions put to them, agreed that French silks were better than English in point of design, though not so good in manufacture. All of them agreed with the gentlemen of the Committee that the reason for French pre-eminence was the existence in France of schools for training designers and of public museums and exhibitions to diffuse taste amongst the whole population. They also agreed that, as a result of this superior artistic education, the French workman in any material was better able to use his intelligence in transferring the design to the manufactured product. (Subsequently, when the Government School of Design was founded, silk manufacture continued to receive a disproportionate degree of attention. And it was in Spitalfields, in 1842, that the first branch school was established.)[5]

But amongst the witnesses to the Committee there were a few dissenting voices who refused to accept that France had all the answers. The manufacturer of that characteristic example of so-called Victoriana, japanned papier-mâché, agreed that public taste would be improved and that their operatives would benefit by learning to draw, but also divulged that his best wares sold very well in France and that English designs were superior. The French 'do not seem to raise the japan trade to an art; they appear merely to daub it over and call it japan; there is neither design nor beauty of execution'. Moreover, the workmen in the English factory were responsible for designing their own patterns and had acquired knowledge of decoration as part of their training. They were also, by the standards of the time, extremely well paid.[6]

The chief hostile witness, however, was J.C. Robertson, editor of the *Mechanics Magazine*, who amazed the MPs by refusing to accept their basic assumption that the British were behind the French in any but a very few branches of manufacture. Indeed, he gave the lie to the superiority of French designs with the following anecdote:[7]

> You commonly hear it said that the patterns of French prints are much superior to ours. Now it is notorious (abroad at least, if not at home,) that most of the engraved cylinders used in France are supplied from this country. A friend of mine went into a Mercer's shop in Paris and was shown there some very beautiful printed cloths; chintzes, I believe; he dropped an expression of surprise that our English manufacturers could not produce such elegant patterns as those he saw before him. The shopman smiled and replied, 'To tell you the truth, sir, the cylinders from which these cloths were printed, came from Manchester.'

Recent evidence seems to support his arguments. His major point, however, was that the British competed in a different sector of the market to the French. While the French might excel in 'fancy goods' or the luxury market, the British were unequalled in producing long runs, of a high quality, for a mass market, in which there was a steady demand, no sudden fluctuations in taste and, although the unit profit was lower, overall profits were far higher.

When Robertson was asked whether the taste of the mass market might not be improved, so that demand might be increased, he dismissed the argument on the grounds that the taste of the West End would probably be undesired in Wapping, and he even hinted that the taste of Wapping was ahead of that of the West End. He attacked the snobbery and vulgarity of customers who were attracted by a French 'label' even when the origin of the design was English. Above all, he warned of the danger of putting British commerce in jeopardy. The demand for fancy silks, ormolu and fine porcelain was very small, even though the percentage profits on such a trade might be great. British manufacturers and artisans could, if they so desired, produce goods to satisfy that demand, but they didn't desire to because 'Kings can never be numerous as customers'. If Britain decided to satisfy one market she could not so easily satisfy the other. The worst thing to do would be to confuse the different natures of the different markets. 'You might produce patterns so elegant that they would not sell' to the negro markets of America, for instance, who preferred lots of 'red and yellow in barbarous combination'. And that, he asserted, with a nice dig at the uncommercial fastidiousness of the 'quality', was not an extreme example: 'People of taste are fond of complaining of the many ugly patterns which our manufacturers are constantly sending forth, when with the same trouble, and at the same expense, so much finer patterns may be produced; but they would not do so, if they only considered how many ugly tastes our manufacturers have to cater for.' To this assertion of the marketing principle that different groups of consumers have different tastes and that manufacturers were only following their commercial common sense in catering to such taste, the Committee had no reply. In vain did it adduce the example of Wedgwood to prove that classical elegance could be responsible for creating a large demand. Robertson, more aware than they that Wedgwood's classical designs were of appeal to a small market, pointed out that the most popular Wedgwood ware in universal use, the Willow Pattern, had nothing classical about it at all.

Robertson, however, did not prevail and from its inception the School of Design aimed to train designers for industries and markets in which Britain did not much excel – a project entirely at odds with the concurrent pursuit of free trade. Another anomaly arose in the school's first year, when it was directed by the architect J.B. Papworth, and the Council actually *prohibited* students from learning to draw the human figure on the bizarre grounds that its aim was to train industrial designers and pattern makers, not people who might become artists or history painters, as poor Haydon had wished. When Dyce was appointed at the end of the first year, the Council resolved, on his suggestion, that 'the human figure, for the purposes of ornament, be taught in the School'.

NATURALISTIC ORNAMENT

Such switches of principle became the norm, the two main contending forces consisting of the naturalists, who thought that ornament should be based on a realistic representation of natural forms, and the conventionalists, who believed that ornament had its own rules, quite different to those of fine art, requiring the ornamentist to abstract features from natural form and thus conventionalise nature rather than imitate it. The naturalists included several of the artists appointed by C.H. Wilson, such as Richard Redgrave, John Horsley, H.J. Townsend, all of whom produced distinctively naturalistic designs for Henry Cole's 'Summerly's Art Manufactures' in 1847. The conventionalists included Dyce, whose *Drawing Book* was the first to state the principles of conventionalism, and the architect Owen Jones; also, from around 1850, Richard Redgrave and Henry Cole suddenly changed sides.

Behind the conventionalists, though they barely referred to him openly, stood the overtowering figure of Pugin, and it was the conventionalists who finally won the day in devising the principles upon which design would be taught in the art schools of Britain – not to mention its primary and secondary schools where, until as late as the 1950s, exercises in designing repeating wallpaper patterns and abstracted natural ornament were inflicted upon children in art classes. First, however, we will consider the naturalists' ideas, looking at conventionalism only later, in relation to the period following the 1851 Exhibition.

Richard Redgrave, both in his evidence to the 1847 Committee of Inquiry into the Schools of Design and in his designs for Felix Summerly's Art Manufactures, is probably the most lucid protagonist for the naturalists. Although he was also influenced by Pugin's strict sense of propriety, his conception of design and ideology derived from Addison, Hogarth and William Paley's *Natural Theology*. The study of nature was fundamental because, as Redgrave stated in his evidence, 'the perfect beauty and works of the Great Ornamentist, ought to be deeply studied by those who, in humble imitation of His goodness, attempt to add beauty to utility'.[8] Moreover, a study of nature, botany in particular, was a means of guarding against ornamental design plagiarising from the past, while simultaneously satisfying the human love of variety.

The variety of nature was a virtuous and improving substitute for that of fashion – an idea which goes back to Ben Jonson and Francis Bacon. Drawing upon the researches of the great classifying botanists, from Linnaeus to Lindley, Redgrave pointed to the enormous numbers of species of plants of even a single order, and of the even greater number of varieties of a single species, in which, in a single plant, not one leaf is identical to another. 'With such an inexhaustible fund of ideas as is here offered, is not the plagiarism that we see around us most lamentable?' The ornamentist must therefore study nature for his innovations, observing how the foliage and flowers of a particular variety were adapted to their purposes of respiration and growth in a particular habitat, creating a wonderful union of 'elegance with strength and utility'. To these ends he considered it essential for students to study 'the wild luxuriance of the plant in its natural habit' in order to see its 'true growth' and 'the natural prehension of the climbers', instead of the 'stunted abortive growth in pots' provided by the School of Design.[9]

Like Hogarth, Redgrave believed that nature provided the designer with ideas both ornamental and functional; he gave the examples of the Greek use of the ammonite as a source for the Ionic capital, Wren's study of the structure of shells as the basis for spires (a specific echo of Hogarth), and Smeaton's use of the oak tree as a basis for the lighthouse. He also strongly favoured life drawing for two reasons: first, because it was a 'means by which we acquire the greatest command of hand and education of eye, as it were a grammar use, to lead us to a mastery over all forms'; second, more straightforward, because it provided designers with the skill to incorporate human and animal motifs in their designs. At this period of his life Redgrave had little time for geometry or diaper patterns. Cross-examined during the 1847 Inquiry by the architect C.R. Cockerell on whether anatomy had any connection with practical matters – 'with chintzes, with the printing of cottons, with brass works, with stove and iron castings', Redgrave replied, 'It might be asked also, what has geometry to do with chintzes and cottons?'[10]

Redgrave also considered that an ornamental art based upon nature would be genuinely popular.[11] The ornamentist, he wrote, 'to make his art widely popular, must address it as much as possible to the knowledge and sympathies of those whom it is intended to please.' The advantage of employing botanical ornament was that:

> The written and unwritten poetry of our land is constantly conversant with them; their very names endear them to use, those simple names which so often express their sensible qualities; such as 'the traveller's joy', whose exquisite scent from the cottage porch or the hedge-row side refreshes the weary; the 'meadow sweet', the 'hart's tongue' fern, which seems to pant for the water-springs, lining with nature's own living tapestry our cottage wells.

Through the local associations of this language of flowers, therefore, it might be possible to develop a national English style, appropriate to the age as well, instead of rehashing old motifs in a meaningless jumble of symbols, such as he had found in Dorney Church, Berkshire, where lictor's rods were 'coupled with the thyrsus of Bacchus, in a Christian temple'.

Redgrave even had hopes that nature might provide some solution to the deskilling effects of the extreme division of labour and mechanical production: 'the continual machine repetition of small portions to form a whole . . . whereby the labour of the skilled hand is superseded and replaced by the dull uniformity of the machine. How opposite is this to the unending variety of nature's works! While nature and art are both engaged in producing parts having a constant uniformity, nature graces them even in their likeness with an endless change.'[12]

But over and above all these considerations was the idea deriving originally from Addison: that is that our love for nature and the gratification of the senses that we derive from it was protected against the charge of sensual indulgence, for these were pleasures expressly provided for Man by the Great Creator and Ornamentist. In having nature on our ornament, we were not indulging in vicious and self-regarding luxury but engaging in a hymn of praise to the Creator and Provider of all things.

Redgrave's own designs for Felix Summerly's Art Manufactures are an admirable illustration of his principles of ornament. They also show that he made a careful study of the fitness for use of each article to achieve that union of fitness and beauty which Hogarth had advocated. His water-jug can be grasped with a firm hand around its neck, while the rushes, which appear to grow out of the water within, form an attractive conceit. His papier-mâché wine tray is admirably shaped to fit the body of the person carrying it; it has two lugs at each end to enable it to be held firmly and two hollows on either side in which to place the decanters or bottles to prevent their sliding around.

Felix Summerly's Art Manufactures – launched in 1847, at the same time as the Inquiry into the Schools of Design – seems to have arisen partly from the fact that Cole edited a series of children's books called *Summerly's Home Treasury* (Felix Summerly was his nom de plume) for which artists such as Mulready, R. Cope, J.C. Horsley, Redgrave, Webster, Linnell and H.J. Townsend drew the illustrations. Through Townsend and Horsley, Cole got to hear about the row in the School of Design and the problems of good design for industry. And when, in 1845, the Society of Arts offered prizes for the design of a tea service and a beer jug for common use, Cole persuaded Herbert Minton to manufacture the tea service and the beer jug designed by himself and Townsend respectively.[13]

Cole had never before had occasion to design an object in his life, but he had great self-confidence and so, according to his own account, he went to the British Museum, to the Hamilton Collection, and 'consulted Greek earthenware for authority for handles'. Looking at the tea service he did produce, it is very clear that he had consulted Greek earthenware for more than handles. The creamer and the teacups are patently derived from Greek sources, though the teapot itself is reminiscent of Lambeth teapots loosely based on Chinese ginger jars. What is surprising, though, is that he had any need whatsoever to consult original sources, since all his shapes, the Greek ones in particular, were extremely popular at the time, and derived directly from Wedgwood's neo-classical designs in the late eighteenth century. To these he added some singularly inappropriate but not unattractive embossed ornament in the shape of rams heads on the teapot lid. The one feature possessing any originality was the unpainted white body of the ware. This, however, was not a revolt against ornament, as twentieth century commentators have interpreted it. It was simply that Cole was designing the body of the ware leaving it for the factory to decorate – a standard practice. And there are in existence examples of the Summerly teacups decorated in different styles of ornament.

Cole's tea service and Townsend's beer jug won the silver medal in April 1846 and, from that point, things moved fast. First Cole enlisted the patronage of Prince Albert, who approved his designs. Then he joined the Society of Arts and started to put some zest behind their schemes for exhibitions of the products of industry, two of which had been held at the end of 1844 and the beginning of 1845. Next he organised his artist friends into Summerly's Art Manufactures. Their manifesto stated principles similar to Redgrave's and may well have been drafted by him.

> Franceso Francia was a goldsmith as well as a Painter. Designs for pottery are attributed to Raffaelle. Leonardo da Vinci invented necklaces . . . and, in fact, there was scarcely a great mediaeval artist . . . who did not essay to decorate the objects of everyday life. Poetry of form, and color, and poetic invention were associated with everything. So it ought still to be, and, we will say, shall be again.
>
> Manufacturing still is pre-eminent and abounds; but artistic skill has to be wedded with it. . . . It is the purpose of this Collection . . . to revive the good old practice of connec-

76 Fish server by the sculptor John Bell for Felix Summerly's Art Manufactures, established by Cole as models of good design and ornament which while as naturalistic as any other of the period was more rigorously appropriate to use – as here.

ting the best art with familiar objects in daily use. In doing this, Art Manufacturers will aim to produce in each article superior utility, which is not to be sacrificed to ornament; to select pure forms; to decorate each article with appropriate details relating to its use, and to obtain those details as directly as possible from nature. These principles . . . may possibly contain the germs of a style which England of the nineteenth century may call its own.

It is significant that the productions of Summerly's Art Manufactures were extensively advertised and sold around Christmas; for, far from being objects of daily use, they were delightful, whimsical, poetic and ingenious fancy goods. Townsend's beer jug, for instance, is conventional in shape, and it is 'an art-manufacture' only in that art, in the form of relief figures gathering hops, forms a decoration around the body of the pot. A snoozing cherub sprawling between two sheaves of barley forms the knob of the lid and a rather inebriated adolescent cherub, emptying a jug of beer down the side, hangs on to the handle of the jug which is formed of twined hop stems. Richard Redgrave's water jug is in the form of a Greek pitcher and has received painted decoration in the form of rushes. John Bell's fish servers are in the form of a trident and a slice whose blade is in the shape of a fish (Plate 76). All kinds of marine creatures are engraved or embossed on the handles and the blade. Bell's bread-board has a handle in the shape of an ear of maize and other cereals around the rim of the board. In other words, all the designs consist of basic conventional shapes to which *pictures* appropriate to the function have been added. And in fact there was nothing profoundly unusual about designs of this kind at this period. It was not uncommon to have fish servers in the shape of fins or fish bones, or ewers shaped like eighteenth-century wine bottles and embellished with a silver gilt handle and a rim in the form of a vine. What distinguished Summerly's Art Manufactures were that they were very carefully designed and

255

that – unlike objects created by the general run of manufactures, where fancy often ran riot – their allegories and poems are always appropriate.

Meanwhile, ever active, Cole founded the *Journal of Design and Manufactures*, edited by himself and Richard Redgrave. It appeared from March 1849 until February 1852 and was used to provide running commentaries upon the preparations for the 1851 Exhibition, the enquiries into the Schools of Design and the issue of design copyright, as well as being a monthly review of manufacturers' products. These included textiles and wallpapers, hundreds of actual samples of which were pasted into the magazine, giving us the most vivid impression of the original colours, totally belying the popular image of Victorian drabness, since they have almost never been exposed to light and remain unfaded. But the main interest of the *Journal of Design* lies in the way that it reflects the development of the views of Henry Cole and his associates during the critical three years covering the period of the Great Exhibition, concluding with the establishment of the Museum for Ornamental Art and the School of Practical Art in South Kensington.

Although by the end of the period these people had formulated a clear and consistent set of principles, later to be consolidated as doctrine by Owen Jones in *The Grammar of Ornament* – the principles upon which the School of Design and the Museum of Ornamental Art were based – much confusion reigned in the editorial office about which principles they ought to adopt. The editors indeed were rather disarming in their admission that they lacked a consistent theory. Cole himself was quoted in the Commons Committee on the Schools of Design as saying that in a project so experimental complete agreement could not be expected. In the penultimate issue of January 1852 it was argued that the controversies of the preceding fifteen years had been the necessary result of ignorance. By then the editors did not believe there could be genuine differences of principle, any differences arose simply from ignorance.[14]

The confused editorial policy was particularly striking in the earliest numbers. All kinds of designs, later to be the targets of scorn and anathematisation, were approved. Floral illusionistic carpets shaded to suggest three dimensionality, chandeliers with panthers and dancing satyrs, a gilt centre-piece designed by Prince Albert and featuring the royal family's favourite dogs: all these were admired unreservedly.[15] Even as late as November 1851 the journal printed a favourable review of some examples of fabrics *printed* to imitate lace and muslin, and suggested that such patterns be used in the schools of design. This is extraordinary in a magazine which had for some time been crusading against 'shams and imitations' in woven fabrics, on the grounds that the imitation must be inferior to the object imitated and that, worse still, falsehood would lead to moral degeneration: 'We think we could prove, without great difficulty, that there is some damage even to good morals in the long run to the housemaid, who, parading in a Glasgow printed shawl, affects to pass for her mistress in a cachmere one.'[16] But this was a common complaint at the time: mill girls wearing to church silk dresses which they had helped to manufacture had been ushered mistakenly into pews reserved for the gentry!

The early admiration for naturalistic floral patterns with a strong element of fancy is somewhat less surprising, in view of the positive admiration expressed by the design pundits for the productions of France. In 1849 Henry Cole and Matthew Digby Wyatt visited the ninth French Exposition to have been held since 1797 and the *Journal's* report, probably written by Wyatt, is couched in tones of almost uncritical admiration. Most peculiar was Wyatt's admiration for a pendant lamp embellished with pineapples: 'Among the various objects contributed by M. Susse, the one more directly utilitarian is the pendant lamp we engrave. It is a happy adaptation of the plant, and if it were possible to substitute a lighter form for that of the *ananas* (pine-apple), it would be full of elegance.'[17] There was no

77   Pugin's Mediaeval Court at the 1851 Exhibition, lithograph by L. Haghe from Dickinson's *Views of the Great Exhibition*. One of the most popular exhibits. Pugin's designs, despite their Catholicism, were admired by Cole and his utilitarian colleagues.

78   Moresque Ornament from Owen Jones, *Grammar of Ornament*, 1856. Jones was one of Cole's colleagues all of whom rejected naturalism in the 1850s for geometric designs derived partly from Pugin, partly from the Moresque.

FALSE PRINCIPLES. 10

ECT IMITATIC OF NATUR

80 and 81 on following page: surviving examples of False Principles of Design with their original labels exhibited in the Chamber of Horrors, in the first exhibition of the Museum of Ornamental Art, 1852, later the Victoria and Albert Museum.

79 (*facing page*) Sample of contemporary wallpaper from the *Journal of Design*, vol. 2, September 1849–February 1850.

reference to the fact that pineapples are totally unconnected with the idea of lighting, nor that these ones happened to be growing from vine stalks. One suspects that Cole and his chums shared the prejudices of fashionable society that French was always best.

This point becomes clearer when it becomes apparent that, as the pundits saw more and more French goods and as their principles developed, they did begin to appreciate that French stood for all that was incorrect and unprincipled. The first signs of disenchantment with France came during the Exposition of French manufactures at George Street, Hanover Square – a selection from the Paris Exposition of 1849. The reviewer made the usual noises in praise of French manufactures and the excellence of the French system of design education, but then launched into a diatribe against the ostentation, the shams in the imitation of materials, the lack of flatness in ornament, the lack of simplicity and the use of the rococo. The carpets were condemned for all these reasons – 'even fruits are there to crush beneath the feet that tread them' – and, worse still, for exhibiting a trellis pattern which might be found upon a wall but never on the floor. By September 1850 the Louis Quatorze scroll had become the symbol of 'the debaucheries of courts, the corruption of the people, Voltaire and infidelity' – everything, in other words, associated with the ancien regime, including those who opposed it most strongly![18]

A year later, when the products of the industry of all nations had been on show at the Great Exhibition for three months, disillusionment was complete. The absence of principles was not restricted to England, it was universal. France, previously considered the paradigm of taste, was by now 'only the leader in what should rather be avoided than imitated in manufactures'. *The Times* and *The Morning Chronicle* were quoted in support of the view that fitness and propriety had been ignored in Europe, that fireplaces were ornamented with human figures inappropriately placed next to 'an element which must inevitably destroy them'![19]

So where, now that France was no longer the model of taste, should guidance be sought? Here, for the first time, the primitive enters the scene. Since European art was exhausted, the reformers turned to the Indian section of the Great Exhibition, and there discovered the true canons of taste and the laws of beauty. The adage that 'tastes vary' was dismissed. The right question was: '*Should* tastes be *allowed* to vary?' What was needed was the foundation of a set of rules for a new national style appropriate to the age. The article concluded with the clarion call: 'Truly "art has its dogmas and orthodoxy", which our Schools of Design have yet to learn and teach.' A month later, with the conclusion of the Great Exhibition, the editorial tune had totally changed. Now the British manufacturers, for so long the villains of the piece, were the heroes; the foreigners had been routed, and the only obstacle to universal progress was the taste of the British people. The whims and fancies of novelty and fashion must give way to truth based upon inalienable principles, those of the conventionalists, who were by now set to win the day within the *Journal of Design* and the team that Henry Cole had assembled around him. It is now time to look at them more closely and to trace their evolution.[20]

CONVENTIONALISED ORNAMENT

As early as Dyce's regime at the School of Design, conventionalist ideas had been current. For Dyce's *Drawing Book* made a sharp distinction between the skills of a designer or orna-mentist and those of an artist. For an artist, beauty was an individual quality, 'the beauty of a horse, of a man, of a flower; and hence the expression of his ideas is necessarily made by a fictitious resemblance of the object in which the beauty naturally resides.' For the ornamental designer, on the other hand, beauty was 'a quality separate from natural objects', and Dyce made the separation in order to impress what he called the cosmetic of nature on the production of human industry. Works of industry should not be imitations of nature covered with pictured or sculptured resemblances of natural objects, instead they

82 Illusionistic floral floor carpet *c.* 1850. These were the chief butt of the Design Reformers – floors were flat so carpets must appear to be flat.

should be 'adorned on the same principles as the works of nature themselves'. The designer, therefore, rather than giving the impression of three-dimensional form, needed to possess 'the power of representing objects in the form of diagrams'.[21]

Thus the major object of a designer's education was to learn to draw outlines rather than drawing from nature, and the *Drawing Book* was devoted to this end, with a series of exercises starting from outlines and modelled forms. Dyce was certainly one of the first to talk about abstract diagrammatic, or conventionalised, ornament and to criticise designs that were imitative of nature. He was, therefore, much at odds with Richard Redgrave and the Summerly people in the mid-1840s. Nature's inexhaustible variety, the variations in individual leaves or of species did not interest him. What impressed him were the principles of repetition and uniformity in nature's processes of self-reproduction. He considered that pattern-making should be based upon the model of the honey bee, in the regular hexagons of the honeycomb.[22]

Dyce was forever contemplating the idea of 'stumbling and impediments'. Since a floor was flat, its decoration should be flat, and not such as would suggest 'inequality of surface and insecurity of footing' (Plate 82). The geometrical patterns which we ought to use for such a purpose were the most natural since they embodied the principle of repetition in nature. His only concession concerned mural paintings properly framed and related to the wall surface. Although walls, insofar as they were flat, ought to be decorated like floors with flat geometrical patterns, they might also be pierced with windows, real or even imaginary – so long as they did not suggest instability. And through such apertures we might expect to see 'Landscapes, historical subjects, pictures of flowers, ornamental trellis-work, these are all appropriate.': an opinion not altogether surprising from a painter of mural pictures and grand historical subjects.

262

In spite of this concession to his own profession, Dyce had no truck with the idea of giving the public or the manufacturers what they wanted, or with fashion: 'Our business here is not with fashions, but with good taste in design.' Whereas Redgrave had hopes that picturesque poetic ornament would have a profound appeal to the traditional culture of the nation, Dyce was altogether more dispassionate. For him, the correct application of ornament was not determined by the appropriateness of the poetic idea or the symbolism to the *function* of the utensil, but the appropriateness of the character of decoration to the *form* of the object. Finally, Dyce was one of the first to suggest that ornament was, like spoken language, a system of conventional signs that had evolved over time, and which therefore possessed a history as well as principles akin to grammar. There was a language and a historical literature of ornament that the student needed to learn before starting to design.[23]

Dyce's ideas about flat patterns were not entirely original. We have already met them in Pugin's *True Principles* of 1841 and they are plainly manifested in Greek Revival stencil patterns. Indeed, the more one thinks about it, the clearer it becomes that Pugin had a major formative influence upon Design Reform, one which was little acknowledged both at the time and today. The single major difference between Pugin's designs and those of the reformers is the Christian, or ecclesiastical, appearance of the former compared to the secular, or at least 'Protestant', appearance of the latter – though Dyce himself was also Catholic.[24] And Pugin, after all, had been involved in design education from his early years, as one of his father's numerous articled pupils: the stern regime, starting at six o'clock in the morning and not ending till eight at night, is vividly portrayed in Benjamin Ferrey's biography. From 1837 he had been Professor of Ecclesiastical Architecture at St Mary's College, Oscott, outside Birmingham, where the lectures reprinted as *True Principles* were first delivered. By 1840 he had assembled his team of craftsman-manufacturers including John Hardman, the Birmingham button maker whom Pugin persuaded to produce mediaeval ironwork, and Herbert Minton, the Stoke pottery manufacturer, as well as his builder George Myers.[25] It was by working with these firms that he could restore something of the quality of relationship that had existed between designer and craftsman before the introduction of the system of general contracting in the building industry. Pugin, moreover, had strong views about the education of architects, which he expressed in the 1836 edition of *Contrasts*, in the 1843 *Apology for the Revival of Christian Architecture*, as well as in a letter to his friend J.R. Herbert who taught life drawing at the School of Design. This letter is virtually a blueprint for a reformed school of design, and most of its principles were adopted either by the government schools or by members of the Arts and Crafts Movement. It was published in *The Builder* of 2 August 1845.

Pugin's ideal was to combine the old principles with modern improvements in science and mechanical skill to create a school of national artists which would be 'a true expression of our period'. He insisted upon the importance of designers respecting the materials for which their designs were made, for 'wood, stone, glass, silk and metal require totally different treatment in their enrichment'. He also was concerned to train operatives as well as designing artists: 'We want artist smiths in silver and ivory, artist chasers in metals etc. . . . well grounded in the fundamental principle of adapting the style and the working of its ornament to . . . the material.'

The design reformers, then, were certainly not unaware of Pugin's ideas nor his work, though they were highly critical of his Roman Catholic allegiances and mediaevalism, which the *Journal of Design* described as being like a crab crawling backwards.[26] The same reviewer disliked his 'Gothicky principles applied to articles of modern invention, for which, indeed, they appear quite unsuitable'. He objected particularly to Pugin's magnificent bread plate, 'Waste not want not', on the grounds that it was made on 'the encaustic tile principle: very dark and massive in colouring, and disagreeably associating with the bread. The design might do very well for a pavement.' But even though the reviewer disputed that the world would revert to mediaeval Catholicism, he argued that 'the art of the Middle Ages was a genuine thing to be respected and studied, because it was based upon *principles*, which principles are equally applicable, with modifications, to altered circumstances'.

With this objective of modifying Pugin's principles to the altered circumstances of a protestant and reformed Britain, Henry Cole's team took Pugin on board. He was invited to design the Mediaeval Court at the Great Exhibition, with his own team of Minton, Hardman, Myers and Crace, and this proved to be one of the greatest popular successes of the event (Plate 77). Following the exhibition, Pugin was one of the four people, together with Cole, Redgrave and Owen Jones, appointed to spend the £5,000 voted by the government to buy exhibits from the exhibition for the Department of Practical Art, to be selected 'without reference to styles, but entirely for the excellence of their art or workmanship'.[27] No one seems to have an explanation for how Pugin was invited to do the Mediaeval Court. One suspects that it was one of Henry Cole's publicity stunts, and that Cole may have encountered Pugin in connection with the Royal Society of Arts 'Exhibition of Works of Ancient and Mediaeval Art', to which Pugin lent nine objects early in 1850. It was about this time, in March 1850, that Pugin began work on the Mediaeval Court, and the *Journal of Design* began to comment favourably on his work.

Even before the exhibition was opened on May Day, Pugin's contribution had begun to stir up the hornets' nest of 'No Popery', on account of his suspending a crucifix high above the court, which was not by any means exclusively devoted to ecclesiastical objects. One clergyman wrote to *The Times* complaining of this insult to his country's religion and, although Pugin was persuaded to lower it and place it in a corner, the story neatly illustrates the attitude to Pugin's designs, and explains why the reformers considered it so essential to de-Catholicise them.[28]

Nonetheless, there is evidence that even on a popular level Pugin's severe principles stole the show. Cassell's *Illustrated Exhibitor*, in its article upon the Mediaeval Court, which it considered one of the most attractive courts, made the extraordinary observation that the steam engine itself was a manifestation of Pugin's principles of honesty, and marked the reaction against the deceits, shams and decadence of recent ornamental art. The steam engine was 'the most sternly real and truthful exhibition of constructive art ever realised. One may wander from engine to engine in the machinery department without seeing one superfluous detail, or pretty disguise, or adventitious ornament . . . Every particular of form and colour tells its unvarnished story, and if these characteristics be, as we believe, common to it with the arts of the ante-Renaissance period, there is no reason, in respect of principle, for excluding a steam-engine from Mr Pugin's Mediaeval Court.'[29]

Henry Mayhew in *1851: or the Adventures of Mr. and Mrs. Sandboys* believed that the exhibition would 'decrease the large amount of sloppy or inferior productions' which were palmed off on the public as a result of honourable masters reducing the wages of 'the more dexterous hands' in order to remain competitive against those who undercut them by reducing quality. Greater knowledge, through the exhibition, was the best antidote for these deceits. By encouraging a higher artistic standard of labour, assisted by machinery, the Great Exhibition of the Industry of all Countries was nothing less than 'a huge academy for teaching the nobility of labour'.[30]

Richard Redgrave, in his 'Supplementary Report on Design' published in the *Report by the Juries*, leaned over backwards to praise Pugin: 'It is impossible to refrain from speaking in high terms of the works contained in the Mediaeval Court . . . for just principles of decoration, for beautiful details, for correct use of materials, and for excellent workmanship, the general collection is unique.' However, the lesson that 'the true ornamentist' would learn would be to seek out 'the *principles* on which the by-gone artists worked, and the rules by which they arrived at excellence, and discarding mere imitation and reproduction of details', he would endeavour 'by the application of new ideas and new matter on principles which he believes to be sound, on which time and the assent of other minds has approved to be fundamental, to attain originality through fitness and truth'.[31]

Likewise Owen Jones, in an article in the *Journal of Design* published a month after the exhibition opened, began to expound the principles which were to be fully worked out in his *Grammar of Ornament* of 1856.[32] All or most of them were derived from Pugin, in particular the idea that 'The construction is decorated; decoration is never purposely constructed.' In the *Grammar of Ornament* there were no fewer than thirty-seven principles, but these can be summarised in just seven categories:

1   The decorative arts arise from, and are attendant upon, architecture; architecture is the material expression of the age in which it was created.
2   The principle of constructive ornament, as opposed to constructed ornament. By this Jones meant that ornament should be integral to the construction of a building or object, a carved or surface decoration upon a necessary part of the construction, not upon a feature specially constructed to serve as a ground for ornament.
3   Ornamentation should possess meaning to the society which uses a building or object. Egyptian ornament is praised for being based upon plant forms which possessed symbolic meaning, Greek ornament on the other hand is condemned for its absence of symbolism.
4   The lines of, particularly, natural ornament should curve gradually and continuously; all the lines should be traceable back through its branches to the root or centre; the junction of all curved lines with either curved or straight lines must be tangential.
5   All ornament must be based upon a geometrical construction. Within this geometrical reticulation the branches of ornamentation should subdivide and further subdivide the spaces, thereby creating different levels of decoration, perceptible at different distances. The result should be an overall decoration of great variety and complexity.
6   All natural objects used for ornamental purposes should be represented in a simplified or conventionalised form, in which their ideal nature is exhibited, not their appearance.
7   Colour should be used to separate the parts of the decorative motif from one another. They should be combined according to the rules of harmony for primary, secondary and tertiary colours and their complimentaries. Shading should never be used.

Jones's final proposition asserted that: 'No improvement can take place in the Art of the present generation until all classes, Artists, Manufacturers, and the Public, are better educated in Art, and the existence of general principles is more fully recognised.'

In the opinion of Owen Jones, the 1851 Exhibition had revealed the total decline, the utter disorder of European decorative art, corrupted as it was by the ceaseless search for novelty. And while Jones was able to sympathise to some degree with the public's boredom with the endless repetition of the conventional ornament of the past, by which he meant the classical, he rejected the 'return to nature' as a source of new vitality, if it were to mean the mere imitation of natural appearances. The Europeans had to learn from those surviving primitive civilisations, such as the Indians and the Tunisians, which had exhibited to such good effect in 1851. These were remarkable not only for their adherence to design principles, but for the evidence they provided of a civilisation which still retained a common faith and purpose. In other words, principled ornament indicated a principled civilisation.

This was made quite clear in Jones's account of ancient civilisations. The Romans in their temples, for example, were only concerned with arousing admiration by dazzling the spectator with the quantity of unprincipled ornament which they lavished on such buildings. Greek ornament, on the other hand, was symptomatic of a society in which 'we must believe the presence of refined taste was almost universal'. It only lacked the mark of the most perfect style, and the most perfect civilisation – meaningful symbolism. This was to be found in the Egyptian and the Moresque (Plate 78).[33]

Owen Jones's admiration of the Egyptian depended upon three qualities: first, since it was the earliest style known, it must be the 'original' style of the earliest civilisation and, hence, the Egyptians must have gone directly to nature for it; second, the forms of the lotus, papyrus, birds' wings and palm suggested the ideas of food for mind and body, and kingship – simple and highly moral ideas on which their civilisation was based; third, the ornament remained unchanged and immune from fashion throughout almost the whole period of Egyptian civilisation, and had done so, presumably, because based upon true principles, there had been no need for change.[34]

Moresque ornament, while not being the original style, nor unvarying, and even though it lacked symbolism because of the Islamic prohibition upon representation, still possessed moral purity and avoided the vanity of modern or of Roman ornament.[35]

The search for true ornament in the present day, therefore, was not a purely aesthetic matter, nor was the aim to provide additional sources of pleasure. Since true ornament was the sign of a God-fearing and nature-loving society, free from vanity and pride, the desire for a new ornament of the nineteenth century arose from the desire to construct such a society in the present.

Owen Jones's primary preoccupation, even though he was an architect by training, was with patterns and with the decoration of structure. His disciple and pupil Christopher Dresser was to take his principles a stage further and to show how they could be applied to the structure of utensils and articles of use as well as to surface decoration.

One of Dresser's earliest writings was a series of articles in the *Art Journal* in 1857 on the subject of *Botany as Adapted to the Arts and Art-Manufacture*. Dresser was only twenty-three but he had absorbed the teaching of Redgrave, Dyce and Owen Jones and was a committed adherent to the principles of conventionalised ornament. Indeed, he was so taken with the principle of the study of botany as a basis for ornamental art that he was at one time undecided on whether to become a botanist or to continue as a designer.

Dresser stood at the opposite extreme to Redgrave's love of picturesque variety, a variety warranted by the researches of the classifying botanists. While he shared Redgrave's and Owen Jones's opinion that flowers and plants were provided for man by the Great Ornamentist himself as sources of pleasure and utility, his grounds for approving only of a conventionalised method of treatment were different. Where Jones believed that conventionalisation represented an *understanding* of the underlying structure of the plant, Dresser believed that it most truly *represented* the plant. Writing just two years before Darwin's *Origin of Species*, he was a committed creationist – he believed that God had created the universe in seven days and that no further changes had occurred through evolution. 'It is a world to which nothing shall hereafter be added', he observed, and the only change was the continuous circle of birth, life and death. The perfect adaptation of plants to the uses of man and other creatures was explained entirely in terms of God's foreknowledge of the requirements of the animals he would create. Likewise the adaptation of all the different plants to their different habitats and conditions was the result of God's design. How then did Dresser seek to explain the variations between one plant and another, between one leaf and the next, and all the irregularities of nature which are observable? Quite simply through the time-honoured aesthetic argument that external influences cause deformities in the normal or unmodified *natural state* of the plant. Putting aside any inconsistency between this explanation of variation and his theory that each plant had been perfectly adapted to its habitat by God in Creation, it is clear that for Dresser convention was a means of representing the *natural state* of a plant. It was far more than a diagram of the structure, it was the essence of the plant as God had designed it. Dresser therefore had a licence to identify the true laws of growth and form in natural organisms. He deduced for each plant

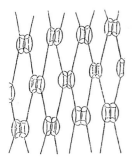

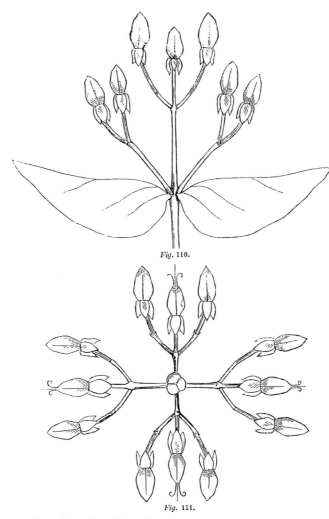

Fig. 110.

Fig. 111.

83   Microscopic cellular structures and Hypericum by Christopher Dresser, *Art Journal*, 1857. Dresser believed that ornament should be based upon an idealised diagram of the plant's true structure, not upon its appearance, and that repeating patterns could be justified by cellular structures.

a law governing the radiation of the leaves and stems around the central axis, a distinct one for each class of plant. In these, all discrepancies from the rule were dismissed as distortions. Likewise the leaves of a single specimen were reproduced as conforming to a single type, and as exhibiting a perfect symmetry between one side and the other. These perfect structures were to be observed at every level of order in the plant, from the veins and fibres seen in microscopic cross-section to the overall shape (Plate 83).[36]

Nature, therefore, in its *natural state*, served not merely as a source from which ornamental patterns and designs could be abstracted but it actually *was* ornamental when represented so as to show the true form. Botany, as Dresser understood it, provided him with the source of the true principles of decorative ornament and of the design of utensils. The arrangement of the parts of a plant, or the parts of its members – twigs, veins, leaves, petals, stamens – were the basic decorative groupings and arrangements of ornament. At the same time, since all the parts of a plant were necessary to it and essential to its structure and function, the plant was a perfect exemplification of the principle that ornament should not be specially constructed but intrinsic to the structure. Finally, natural colours were also, in Dresser's view, the justification for Owen Jones's classification of colour into primaries, secondaries and tertiaries. But whereas Jones had based his principles upon the practice of his favoured periods of civilisation, and had argued that the primaries should be used predominantly so that the overall appearance of the *Grammar of Ornament* is of bright, almost fairground combinations of colour and pattern, Dresser argued that, since the primaries in nature were restricted to flowers and blossoms, which represented only one small stage in the development of the plant, ornament should follow suit and primaries be used only sparingly compared to the secondaries, and even more the tertiaries – citrine, russet and olive. Hence the source of what Darwin called the 'dingy high-art colours' (the true origin of the misconceived Victorian dinginess) which he compared unfavourably with the bright tints of nature, his favourite orchids for example.[37]

Whether one believes Dresser to have been misguided or not, he was nothing but consistent in his principles, if not always in his practice. For Dresser there was no tension between the demands of decoration and beauty in an artefact and the basic rule of truth to nature. An object would be beautiful when proper attention was paid to its utility and its construction. A chair, he argued, was simply a stool with a backrest. The designer of a chair had to ensure that the material for construction – wood – was used so that its strength was fully exploited. All vertical supports must use the wood in the direction of the grain, so that the grain would lie in the direction of compression. Curved supports, in which the stress was at an angle to the grain, would weaken the chair and arouse fear in the user that the chair might collapse. Likewise there was always a danger that the back of the chair, being subject to the weight of the sitter, might snap or might give the suggestion of being liable to snap. Consequently the back ought to be supported by triangular brackets attached to the seat. In addition the physical means used to construct the chair ought not to be disguised – 'an obvious and true structure is always pleasant'. The pins of mortice and tenon joints ought therefore always to be exhibited (Plate 84).[38]

Dresser's principles were similar to Pugin's. But he was critical of Pugin's actual productions insofar as the furniture was excessively enriched with carving, even though the carving was not extraneous to the construction of the piece of furniture.[39] The designs which he favoured, his own and those of Bruce Talbert, were very much of the belt-and-braces type of construction. Backs of chairs were of a piece with the back legs, and were further strengthened by brackets connecting them with the stretchers of the seat. Alternatively the back was a separate bracket supported by the elongation of the rear legs. Brackets were used to strengthen the joins between the legs and the stretchers. Indeed, Dresser's designs for chairs are more like wooden scaffolding than anything else and, apart from the fact that his theories allowed for some degree of decoration in the form of turning and relief carving, we have in his designs many of the principles of the Modern Movement. Such was his concern for the visible expression of construction as a means of allaying his obsessional fears of instability that he suggested, in the case of a reclining chair where the stress upon the backrest would be considerable, an extension of the seat behind the backrest in order to provide space for an additional buttress supporting the back from behind. The extension would not, of course, be cantilevered, which might have provided a more fascinating solution to the problem Dresser set himself, but had to be supported by a fifth leg. His own furniture designs, such as that for his solicitor at Bushloe House in Leicester, applied his theories quite consistently. The junction between the seat and the legs is strengthened by arched brackets. The backrest is formed of a series of bars which also form a bracket between the seat and the back. The only problem is that, while the chair could doubtless survive any amount of punishment, even be thrown around a room without damage, it is itself grotesquely uncomfortable: what was later nicknamed 'a punishment chair'. The back, being innocent of any suspicion of a curve, bites into the spine without mercy. Compared

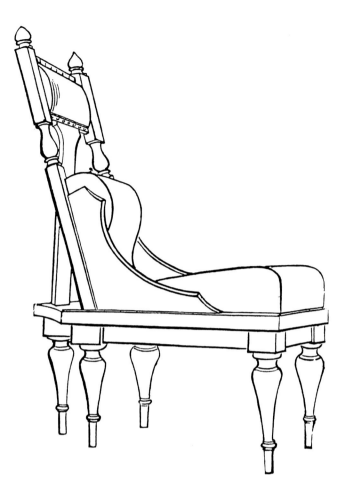

84 Five-legged chair from Dresser's *Principles of Decorative Design*, 1873. In the pursuit of stability nothing must be left to chance – five legs were better than four!

to the graceful bucket curves of early Victorian furniture, it totally failed to serve the utility for which it was presumably intended.

Another interesting example of Dresser's approach is to be found in his metalware, particularly his teapots. He rejected conventionally-shaped teapots on the grounds that the distance of the centre of gravity from the handle was so great as to require 'a much greater expenditure of force in order that the teapot be put to its use than is necessary were it properly formed'.[40]

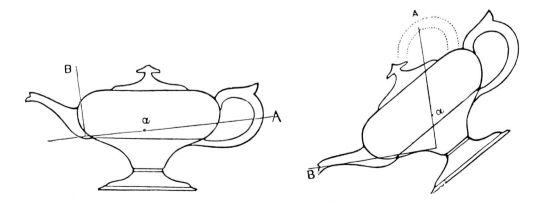

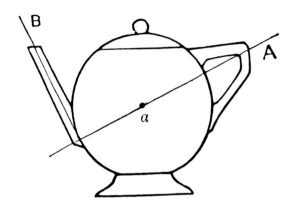

The correct law for the design of a teapot, or any other pouring vessel, was that the spout should be at right angles to the line passing through the handle and the centre of gravity of the pot. Of course, this ignores that the human arm possesses any strength at all.

Every article one could imagine to furnish the house was subjected to this kind of minute functional and constructional calculus, which was also a moral calculus. Dresser believed that ornamentation 'if properly understood, would at once be seen to be a high art in the truest sense of the word, as it can teach, elevate, refine, induce lofty aspirations and allay sorrows'. It could also be 'a fine art, administering to man in his various moods, rather than the handmaid to religion or morals'.[41]

Dresser was the epitome of the state's protestant alternative to Pugin. He had devised a set of principles for designs to fulfil every need of the average household in such a way as to fulfil the most stringent moral requirements and though purged of Pugin's papist imagery, to be didactic as well. By this means, all the members of the household, the children in particular, would be surrounded by active influences which would silently mould their morals and behaviour by virtue of being practically involved in every minute province of life. Thus the concerns about materialism voiced by *The Spectator* amongst others might be answered.

From the point of view of production, goods so designed would raise the dignity of labour because of the relatively high levels of craft involved and the ordinance against shoddy trade practices, deceits and shams. While, from an economic point of view, well-constructed items of household equipment, which would last for generations and never go out of fashion, would become part of the owner's stock or capital, and hence, as Adam Smith had argued, form a permanent addition to the nation's stock as well. Moreover, because design in general added considerable value to raw materials, it was wise policy for the state to encourage what Dresser called 'art knowledge'.[42]

In the two decades after 1835, the state had thus acquired new and costly national institutions to implement a policy governing the appearance of everyday things. The Great Exhibition itself – and the Crystal Palace, which has become the most striking symbol of the whole Victorian Age – were devised by Henry Cole and Prince Albert as a publicity stunt, no more nor less, as an object-lesson directed to British manufacturers in the poor design of their goods compared to that of other countries. But of course it became something grander, this 'Beehive of the World', as George Cruikshank called it; it became a huge model of something huger still, of the political economy of the whole world, comprising raw materials, machines and the finished manufactures themselves. It was, in a way, the transformation of Smith's *Wealth of Nations* into a tableau. And, in drawing attention to the great engine of the nineteenth-century economy, it focused and publicised the questions which the Luddites and the Chartists, Carlyle and Pugin had already voiced. In the following chapter we will examine how this argument developed amongst those who called into question the objectives of Henry Cole and the design reformers.

CHAPTER 5

The Opponents of Design Reform

TRUE PRINCIPLES OF Design had been established! And, over the same period, the institutions for disseminating those principles had been reformed and consolidated by Henry Cole, Richard Redgrave and Owen Jones: the Triumvirate of Taste, as they became known. In 1849 Cole had tried and failed to persuade the Commons Select Committee on the Schools of Design to adopt his proposals for a Benthamite institution efficiently and centrally managed, whose objective would be the vocational training of pattern designers for industry, not the aesthetic education of artists. Two years later, however, in January 1852, Cole was appointed to undertake the management of the School of Design and created a Department of Practical Art with himself as the fulltime permanent superintendent directly responsible to the Board of Trade with Redgrave as his deputy.[1]

Meanwhile Prince Albert, with a surplus of £186,000 from the exhibition of 1851 and in connection with the purchase of a large site in South Kensington, was planning to set up some sort of institute through which science and art might be applied to industry. He wanted Cole to bring the Department of Practical Art and the School of Design into his scheme and, as a first step, offered to lend Marlborough House for the use of the school and its museum. On 19 May 1852, the Museum of Ornamental Manufactures (it soon changed its name to the Museum of Ornamental Art) opened to the public in Marlborough House, and the School of Design followed from Somerset House in 1853.[2]

Cole clearly wanted his new museum to become one of the shows of London and with his flair for public relations, the museum opened with an exhibition of students' work and a course of four lectures on general principles of design given by Owen Jones to advertise the new regime and to educate manufacturers and the general public. But, although a large proportion of the exhibits consisted of the historical collections which were to grow into the Victoria and Albert Museum, it was a tiny little ante-room nicknamed the Chamber of Horrors, after the original in Madame Tussauds, in which eighty-seven examples of 'decorations on false principles' were displayed, that has subsequently attracted most attention, and which may have been the inspiration for the 'bad taste' house, Gremlin Grange, on the LCC's model Lansbury Estate in 1951.[3]

Oddly enough, the Chamber of Horrors passed unnoticed in the press at the time and existed for only a few months at the most. All our knowledge of it comes from the catalogue to the museum, a satirical article 'A House Full of Horrors' which appeared in Charles Dickens's *Household Words* for 4 December 1852, and a pseudonymous pamphlet entitled *A Mild Remonstrance against the Taste Censorship at Marlborough House*, which was published early in 1853. Dispersed throughout the collections of the Victoria and Albert Museum, there also survive a number of the exhibits from which it is possible to reconstruct the appearance and contents of the room.

The catalogue declared that, in addition to the vast majority of exhibits illustrating correct principles, 'it has been deemed advisable to collect and exhibit to the student

85 Mr Crumpet of Clump Lodge, Brixton, the subject of a satirical sketch in Charles Dickens's *Household Words*, a suburbanite who visited the Chamber of Horrors to discover that he had been living amidst hideous horrors. Drawing by M.S. Walker, 1979.

examples of what, according to the views held in this Department, are considered to illustrate wrong or false principles'. It warned of the appearance of an aesthetic plague spreading across Europe: 'There has arisen a new species of ornament of the most objectionable kind, which it is desirable at once to deprecate on account of its complete departure from just taste and true principles. It may be called the *natural* or merely imitative style.' The surviving exhibits, some of which still retain their original paper labels (which were stuck directly onto the materials), expand upon the story (Plates 80 and 81). The simplest case of the 'disease' was demonstrated by a glazed floral chintz labelled 'FALSE PRINCIPLES 10. DIRECT IMITATION OF NATURE'. But there were 'complications', such as No. 17 'IMITATION OF ONE FABRIC UPON ANOTHER: FESTOONS OF RIBBON UPON CHINTZ; DIRECT IMITATIONS OF NATURE'. We are thoroughly familiar with the false principles in paper hanging. Here, the examples included, 'PERSPECTIVE REPRESENTATIONS OF BATTLES, FREQUENTLY REPEATED' and 'PERSPECTIVE REPRESENTATIONS OF A RAILWAY STATION, FREQUENTLY REPEATED AND FALSIFYING THE PERSPECTIVE' (see endpapers). Even a pair of check trousers was displayed – an echo of Lord Burghley's technique of using public ridicule to punish offenders against the sumptuary laws.[4]

These provided Dickens's journalist Henry Morley with a golden opportunity for burlesque.[5] A City gent and the archetypal 'man on the Clapham omnibus', Mr Crumpet of Clump Lodge, Brixton, has visited the Chamber of Horrors and been converted to correct principles of taste (Plate 85). He is now haunted with hideous horrors all around him: in his home, on the bodies of his beloved wife and daughter, on the Clapham omnibus itself and in the Stockwell home of his fellow suburbanite, Mr Frippy, where he finds the very objects he has seen in Marlborough House and which he decries in the very words of the catalogue. Mr Frippy, for instance, is wearing a waistcoat 'buttoned with half a dozen studs of horses, and a large pin stuck through the face of an opera girl who danced upon the bosom of his shirt. On the head of the pin there was a jockey riding at full speed.' He is also wearing a shirt made from one of the calicoes, No. 50, 51, 52, 'DIRECT IMITATIONS OF FIGURES AND ANIMALS; BALLET GIRLS, POLKA DANCERS, AND RACE HORSES'. Mr Crumpet solemnly explains to Mr Frippy that these patterns are ugly because ornament must be appropriate 'and vex the eye with nothing that suggests consciousness of incongruity or contradiction . . . there is no fitness in stamping racehorses over a shirt, and tucking them away under your outer garments.' The tableau reaches its climax when the Crumpet and Frippy families sit down to have dinner in Chimborazo Villa. Mr Crumpet tries to dine and talk of other matters, 'but I saw that I had boiled fish and oyster sauce put on my plate over a delicate bouquet of pink and yellow flowers, and I knew what I had learnt at Marlborough House of the impropriety of putting elaborate patterns – to say nothing of direct imitations of Nature – on that part of a plate or tray which is intended to be covered'. Jugs and glasses, equally offensive, continue to pass before the poor man's eyes until finally, just as he is finishing his cup of tea, he drops his cup and saucer with a cry of agony:

'Papa, papa, what is the matter?' cried my child; and my wife ran to me, and Mrs. Frippy, for I had fallen back in my chair almost deprived of reason.
'A but –' I gasped.
'But what, my dear?' asked my wife.
'Butter-fly – inside my cup! Horr-horr-horr-horr-ri-ble!'
I was taken home in a cab.

This essay is especially interesting since, in the very form of the moral fable, there is a direct link with *The Spectator* and the Censor. And Clump Lodge and Chimborazo Villa are archetypes of the moralised, suburban home which Addison and Steele recommended. Here the Cheapside merchant could retire from the world of business and, as he drew the curtains on the twilight and lit the camphine lamp, shut out care as well. In his large easy chair he 'seemed to have put on inside as well as outside comfort and ease'. He was a man who lived his business life according to the principles of Adam Smith and his domestic life according to those of William Cowper or Addison, in a protestant monastery presided over by his comforting wife. Moreover, the furniture of his home, so many potential vanities and idols, had been purged of luxury and vice by the incorporation of God's Nature. Yet Cole's government Department of Practical Art, representing that sterner moral calculus of design whose development we have been tracing, had taken over as the state-subsidised Censor of this innocent world of fancy and imagination. Admittedly, the Department possessed no legal powers to impose its laws of taste upon manufacturers or consumers. It fell short, therefore, of sumptuary law. But unlike *The Spectator* it was a public body with the backing of the state and was certainly in a position to impose its rules upon students in the Design Schools as well as children in the National Schools.

One F.J. Prouting expanded on this, at length and with great gusto, under the pseudonym 'Argus' in a pamphlet entitled *A Mild Remonstrance against the Taste Censorship at Marlborough House* published in the first months of 1853. It is not known who Prouting was, except that he lived in Manchester and represented the free trade principles of the Manchester School in all their purity. He regarded Cole's Taste Censorship as 'an encroachment on our liberties' and argued that it was no small matter because, 'If you can establish a Censorship over a Pattern, where is our security against the Censorship over the Press?' This, he argued, was the first step towards the state's intrusion into the citizen's private domesticity and the next step would be interference in the cause of commercial freedom, which had only just been won with the repeal of the Corn Laws in 1846 and Gladstone's renewal of Huskisson's tariff reforms.[6]

Prouting dismissed the idea that there could be any absolute dogmatic standard of taste and, somewhat like Mandeville, argued that fashion was the best and safest arbiter, both in providing the people with what they wanted and from a commercial point of view. In his opinion there had been a change for the worse between the two Commons reports on the Schools of Design, from the attitude of 1836 that 'the best is that which sells the best' to 'what sells the best is that which embodies the best rules'. He may have been factually wrong in believing that the 1836 committee was so libertarian, but his scorn was directed at the inadequacy of the rules proposed by the Triumvirate. 'Think of Mr Hume turning his attention to the subject! or Mr Drummond! or Mr Osborne! or Mr Locke! Nothing . . . can be more impertinent . . . than the employment of this draper-shop verbosity and market salesman slang by which your Catalogue is characterised.' The tone of the catalogue, he said, was that of the auctioneer's clerk, and he invented a scene with an auctioneer knocking a spice-box down to the nation. 'Well, gentleman! what shall we say for it? £200? £150? £50? £30? £10? gentlemen! gentlemen! £5, thank you, Sir. £5 only bid for this exquisite "Enamelled Spice-Box" . . .' The Nation was 'buying in' all the things that nobody wanted under the guise of forming the Museum of Ornamental Art.[7]

Prouting's strongest scorn was reserved for the silliness of the principles and for the inconsistency with which they were applied to the objects in the Chamber of Horrors and in the museum as a whole. He pointed out that although geometry was claimed as the basis of all ornament by the Triumvirate, not one twentieth of the objects in the museum conformed to the principle. Although it may have been true that ornament should not be stuck on to objects, that was a principle that only the very rich, or those who, like the Triumvirate, were paid out of the public purse, could afford to practice. Most people, if they were to have ornament at all, had to have it 'stuck on'. As for the principle of utility, he condemned as excessive the belief that the harmless fancy of making a pair of scissors in the form of a stork was corrupt and morally degrading. As for flatness in the ornamentation of walls and floors, if this principle were to be applied literally there should be no decoration allowed at all. And as for the 'too direct imitation of nature', what of Summerly's art-manufactures themselves? How could one talk of the dangers of over-ornamentation when the much-admired Indian designs were just that? Prouting got particularly worked up over the belief of the Triumvirate, especially Jones, in conventionalised ornament, and their corresponding admiration for Indian designs. Jones he described at one point as 'that patron and admirer of Flats; that Mohammedan in Taste; that disciple of Buddha Vishnu, Fo; that honey-tongued sorcerer, Jones'. Prouting disliked geometric and conventionalised ornament partly because he saw it as 'barbaric glitter', partly because he regarded it as symptomatic of everything stereotyped and predetermined in oriental and pre-industrial society: 'We do not acknowledge "Castes" in our social economy. We could not submit to hereditary occupations; nor tie ourselves down to the fixity of forms and fashions which Conventionalism imposes on the nations where it reigns.' Fixed taste and conventional ornament, therefore, were the causes of a non-progressive and tyrannical civilisation. Moreover, since Owen Jones had claimed in the catalogue that the reason for the correctness of Indian designs was that they were 'the works of a people who are still as faithful to their Art as to the Religion, habits, and modes of thought which inspired it', then logically he must have desired Europe to convert to Mohammedanism or Buddhism. But, Prouting went on, Europe and Britain possessed their own civilisation, which was Christian, and their own art, which was naturalistic, and which he justified with a quote from Paley's *Natural Theology*: 'If one train of thinking be more desirable than another, it is that which regards the phenomenon of nature with a constant reference to a supreme, intelligent Author . . . The world henceforth becomes a temple, and life itself one continued act of adoration.' In the absence of a proper

86   Convulvulus Gas Lamp – another false design.

education system, Prouting argued that 'the majority of people *never see Nature*; and that millions never would have seen it, had they not been taught to see it through the works of the Poet and the Artist'. The mission of commerce which multiplied the production of utensils upon which direct imitations of nature were impressed was to recall to the minds of millions those childhood instincts that had been crushed by the force of circumstances, or blunted by neglect, and 'to bring them closer to God'. This was the chief use of Art if it were to be anything more than pampering luxury. This, moreover, had been the principle to which Redgrave, as one of the Felix Summerly designers, had himself subscribed only three years earlier, before 'that "honey-tongued" sorcerer, Jones' had inveigled him into conventionalism.[8]

These aesthetic and theological justifications for naturalistic ornament were finally linked together with the civilising mission of free commerce in Prouting's Christianised version of David Hume's vision of progress.

> . . . for many centuries natural ornament has been applied to everything. How far our liberty in this respect has had to do with our progress in Civilization cannot be estimated with much certainty; but this we know, that for many centuries Turkey and Arabia has in everything been standing still, if not retrograding, whilst England for as many centuries has been rapidly advancing. It is true all Christendom has not kept pace with England. But why? Because ever since England began to make any appreciable advance in refinement and intelligence, she has been commercial. It is easy to perceive that Commerce, though its immediate end is Gain, is, and must be, the great civilizer of the world; inasmuch as it is the originator, the encourager, the protector, and the disseminator of the Arts, – the proper and legitimate end of which, whether practical and useful, or refining and luxurious, is mentality, morality, religion. If Commerce trades in natural ornament it disseminates a natural luxury, a mental luxury, and, therefore, the means of mentality and enlightenment.

In splendid manifesto style, Prouting concluded with a statement of his own principles:

> ULTIMATE PRINCIPLE – HUMAN PROGRESS AND ENLIGHTENMENT.
> This demands ART, and deprecates Conventionalism.
> IMMEDIATE PRINCIPLE – COMMERCE.
> This demands the COMPLEX in Ornamentation in preference to the
> Simple.
> These, Sir, are Principles, whether you approve of them
> or not; and we hope they are intelligible.
> The first aims to advance the Mental interests of
> humanity.
> The second aims to supply the Physical means through
> which all aids to Mentality are best secured.
> We advocate the Complex in Ornamentation, first,
> because it supplies most labour; secondly, because in this Complex
> Ornamentation there is the largest demand for ART.

Finally, still addressing 'Redgrave the Renegade', he reminded him of Raphael's tapestry cartoons, which were designed for the loom, for making mechanical copies 'wrought in the tints and lines of Nature' to be hung on walls for decoration. What a touching irony this was, in view of the importance of Raphael's Cartoons within the history of British design and the fact that only a decade or so later, in 1865, the Cartoons came to rest on the walls of the Museum of Ornamental Art, subsequently the Victoria and Albert Museum, where they remain to this day.[9]

Whoever Prouting was, his pamphlet represents more clearly than any other piece of writing the complex intertwining of economic, political, aesthetic, theological, national and moral ideas which it has been the function of this book to reconstitute. Although it is not a great piece of writing, it succeeds better than any of the productions of more original minds in laying open the widely-held assumptions of the period. It is probably the very best document of the popular phenomenon of high Victorian taste in furnishings and design. This was not just 'bad taste', as we have tended to regard it for the past century or more, but one possessing its own rationale, which derived, in the final analysis, from *The Spectator* and Hogarth's *Analysis of Beauty*.

Dickens himself returned to the attack eighteen months later. While he was working out the plot for his new novel *Hard Times*, he became aware of a darker side to the dotty didacticism of the Triumvirate. He had never been very impressed by the Great Exhibition; it was not that there was 'nothing in it – there's too much'. Writing in November 1854 of the 'terrific duffery' of the Crystal Palace, by then re-erected in Sydenham with large-scale models of buildings in the recommended styles and a permanent bazaar of British manufactures, he strongly objected to having 'so very large a building continually crammed down one's throat, and to find it a new page in *The Whole Duty of Man* to go there'. Contem-plating the miseries of the workers of the northern industrial towns, he concluded that amusement and entertainment for its own sake, in whatever taste, were inalienable rights. 'The English are, so far as I know, the hardest-worked people on whom the sun shines. Be content if, in their wretched intervals of pleasure, they read for amusement and do no worse. They were born at the oar, and they live and die at it. Good God, what would we have of them!'[10]

Henry Cole, moreover, who represented the new class of Benthamite civil servant, was doubly tarred, perhaps somewhat unfairly, in Dickens's eyes: not only as a kill-joy, but also as a representative of an administration whose 'addled heads would take the average of cold in the Crimea during the twelve months as a reason for clothing a soldier in nankeens on a night when he would be frozen to death in fur . . . Bah! What have you to do with these?' And Cole was cruelly caricatured in the first scene of *Hard Times* as the government officer who, hand-in-glove with the industrialist Mr Gradgrind, is determined to implant facts, facts and more facts, for practical purposes, in the heads of the working-class children of England. He became the personification of utilitarian education, put in motion by Sir James Kay-Shuttleworth.[11]

In the novel, Cole examines the class of Mr Gradgrind's school on their knowledge of true principles of design. When Sissy Jupe, the circus girl, proves to be the only child to stick to her principles – those of fancy and the imagination – the Inspector makes an example of her:

'Girl number twenty,' said the gentleman, smiling in the calm strength of knowledge.
    Sissy blushed, and stood up.
'So you would carpet your room – or your husband's room, if you were a grown woman, and had a husband – with representations of flowers, would you?' said the gentleman. 'Why would you?'
'If you please, Sir, I am very fond of flowers,' returned the girl.
'And that is why you would put tables and chairs upon them, and have people walking over them in heavy boots?'
'It wouldn't hurt them, Sir. They wouldn't crush and wither, if you please, Sir. They would be pictures of what was very pleasant, and I would fancy –'
'Ay, ay, ay! But you mustn't fancy,' cried the gentlemen, quite elated by coming so happily to his point. 'That's it! You are never to fancy.'
'You are not, Cecilia Jupe,' Thomas Gradgrind solemnly repeated, 'to do anything of that kind.'

'Fact, fact, fact!' said the gentleman. And 'Fact, fact, fact!' repeated Thomas Gradgrind. 'You are to be in all things regulated and governed,' said the gentleman, 'by fact. We hope to have, before long, a board of fact, composed of commissioners of fact, which will force the people to be a people of fact, and of nothing but fact. You must discard the word Fancy altogether. You must have nothing to do with it.'

The point needs no underlining. Dickens, standing in the tradition of Addison and Hogarth, was affirming the positive value of fancy and imagination in contrast to the world of utilitarianism, where only work and business mattered.[12]

CHAPTER 6

John Ruskin:
The Political Economy of Design

ONE MAN WHO wholeheartedly shared the analysis of industrial society presented in *Hard Times* was the influential critic John Ruskin (Plate 87). A rigorous yet hugely popular writer on art and its place in society, Ruskin had published his first essays before he was twenty years old and, by 1854, the year in which *Hard Times* appeared, was the widely read author of *Modern Painters*, *Seven Lamps of Architecture* and *The Stones of Venice*. Despite his regret that Dickens chose 'to speak in a circle of stage fire', and lost the support of many people by his caricature and exaggeration, Ruskin considered *Hard Times* to be quite right in its main drift and recommended that it should 'be studied with close and earnest care by persons interested in social questions'.[1]

It might seem odd for Ruskin to have found the True Principles of the Triumvirate so inimical. The second volume of the *Journal of Design* had quoted with approval a passage from his 'Lamp of Truth' condemning painted shams like the marbling of shop fronts as 'utterly base and inadmissible'. Owen Jones, in a prospectus for his lectures at Marlborough House, had quoted Ruskin's definition of architecture as the art 'which so disposes and adorns the edifices raised by man, for whatever uses, that the sight of them contribute to this mental health, power and pleasure', and this very passage asserted that architecture was concerned only with those characteristics of an edifice which are over and above its common uses.[2]

Restricting ourselves to Ruskin's views on painted shams, it is worth stressing how misleading it can be to quote Ruskin selectively, perhaps because of the dialectical nature of his arguments. It is true that Ruskin was saddened by the wasteful extravagance of such vanities as marbled shop fronts but, like Pugin, he made a clear distinction between the abuse of the principle of truth in such a trivial case and its abuse in an important building like the British Museum or a church. Ruskin had an acute sense of appropriateness and decorum, the lack of which amongst the reformers makes their statements so comical.[3]

But more than decorum and common sense marked Ruskin off from Henry Cole and his chums; his basic premises about architecture and design, particularly concerning the relationship between structure and ornament, were at odds with theirs. Ruskin was in many respects the heir of Hogarth and Addison; his views on 'shams and deceits', that great issue of the day, was merely a small component in his broad position. He has been described by Asa Briggs as uniting 'in one synthesis a theory of economics, an approach to art criticism, and a new prescription for national policy'.[4] Indeed, his was an extraordinary achievement, equalled in scope by none of the other writers whom we have examined so far, with the possible exception of the contributors to *The Spectator* as a group. Although Ruskin is regarded as a critic of industrialisation, of classical economics and of modernity, his own theories nonetheless essentially belong to the great tradition of political economy – the policy of national housekeeping – which has been traced in this book. From his starting point as a critic and theorist of art and architecture, he developed a profound critique of the more recent contributions to that tradition.

87 John Ruskin, self-portrait, 1864–5. Ruskin, the great critic of art and society, was contemptuous of the principles of the Design Reformers because their utilitarianism denied the role of the imagination. Ruskin sided with Dickens and was heir to the ideas of Addison and Hogarth.

In this chapter we will start by exploring Ruskin's criticism of the True Principles of design reform. Then we will look at his more general theory of the relationship between beauty and the fitness of an object, which will lead on to his view of beauty itself and its relation to nature. Finally, we will examine his reflections on the Political Economy of Art and its relation to society.

RUSKIN AND THE TRUE PRINCIPLES

As the orthodoxy of the reformers concerning flatness and conventionalisation of ornament hardened and was consolidated in Owen Jones's *Grammar of Ornament* in 1856, so Ruskin's irritability increased. At a meeting of the Royal Society of Arts in March 1856 he replied to a paper by the headmaster of one of the provincial schools of design. The headmaster's complaint was that, in spite of all that had been done by the schools of design, in spite of all the efforts of the Department of Practical Art, in spite of the availability of 'the best geometric designs' for carpets and fabrics, ladies still preferred to buy 'roses done in wool'. His implication was not, of course, that the True Principles might be wrong, but that an even greater effort at the diffusion of taste was necessary. Ruskin called the attack 'ungallant' and refused to join in condemning the ladies, 'chiefly because he knew a most respectable and long-established firm, engaged in carpet manufacture on an extensive scale, which conducted its business on the principle Mr. Wallis opposed. He referred to the firm whose head partners, the months of April and May, supplied a large part of the world with green carpets, in which floral design was largely introduced, and he believed generally to the satisfaction of the public.'⁵

This gibe had much in common with those of Dickens and Prouting. Ruskin, however, defended naturalism further, pointing out the parallel between the representations of flowers upon carpets and their scattering in festival processions: another instance of his sophisticated historical understanding of the function of ornament.

This seems to have been the earliest public occasion upon which Ruskin attacked the True Principles. Moreover, his attack upon South Kensington was not purely theoretical. He wrote to his father in July 1858 to say that he wanted to change Cole's system. Like Redgrave in 1846 and Prouting, he believed you could not teach design, only drawing.⁶

The new buildings for the Museum of Ornamental Art and the Department of Science and Art in South Kensington were completed by the early summer of 1857 and the Architectural Museum Society moved into its headquarters there shortly after. In January 1858 Ruskin gave the inaugural lecture. Although there is no record that the Triumvirate were among Ruskin's audience, it would have been very odd had they not been, and they must have been a little taken aback even if not altogether surprised by what they heard in the lecture entitled 'The Deteriorative Power of Conventional Art over Nations'. For Ruskin chose to apply his main attack to the most vulnerable point in the reformers' argument: that conventional ornament was symptomatic of the high moral stature of a nation. He conjured in the minds of his audience a picture of the solitary wilds of northern Scotland, where the crofters' cottages completely lacked the refinements of ornamental embellishment, and contrasted this to the refinement of the exquisite examples of Indian art collected together in the South Kensington Museum. The latter had been praised by Owen Jones as the product of a 'common faith' and a unified civilisation, yet, while Ruskin had been holidaying in the Highlands, the Indian Mutiny had given rise to acts more bestial than anything in the history of mankind, while, in the Crimea, the Scots soldiers had been fighting with courage and self-sacrifice. In the spirit of Rousseau, Ruskin reminded his audience that periods when great art has flourished seem to portend the ruin of a nation: 'races who live by depredation and slaughter nearly always bestow exquisite ornaments on the quiver, the helmet and the spear'. Although he exonerated Henry Cole and Richard Redgrave personally from desiring the moral and economic corruption of their nation, he asked his audience whether they were assembled 'to any good purpose'. 'Are we met here as honest people? or are we not rather so many Catilines assembled to devise the hasty degradation of our country, or, like a conclave of midnight witches, to summon and send forth, on new and unsuspected missions, the demons of luxury, cruelty and superstition?'⁷

The chief error of Indian and exotic ornament, in Ruskin's view, arose from its conventionalisation and its avoidance of the use of the human figure and nature: 'it will not draw a man, but an eight-armed monster; it will not draw a flower, but only a spiral or a zig-zag.'⁸

281

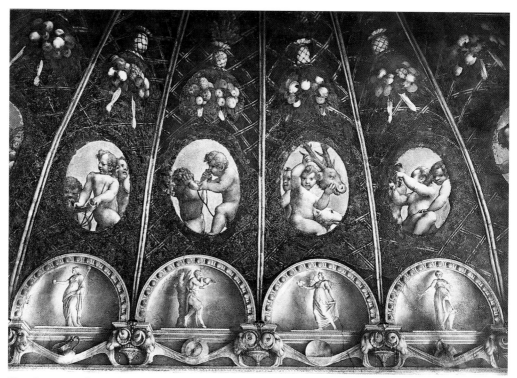

88　Correggio, frescoed cupola, Convento di San Paolo, Palma, 1518–19. Ruskin approved of illusionism, adducing the great fresco painters of the Italian Renaissance in its defence.

In the art of ancient Greece, Florence and Venice, on the other hand, the human figure was central to architecture and decoration. Even if the surrounding ornament was conventionalised to some degree, as in the portals of the west front of Chartres, its purpose was to set off the figure, to integrate it into the architecture, and it should not be an end in itself. Ruskin condemned the wilfulness of forcing natural facts into a geometrical form. However, he neither condemned all conventionalisation out of hand, nor did he recommend perfect imitation of nature. The real error lay in turning aside from nature or reducing her to 'heartless laws'.[9]

Ruskin returned to the theme a year later in the inaugural lecture given to the students of the newly formed Bradford School of Design. First, he disputed the division between ornamental and other forms of art. Raphael's School of Athens was merely the decoration of one of the suite of papal apartments in the Vatican; Michelangelo's Sistine ceiling, the decoration of the Pope's private chapel. Decorative art was simply art adapted to the decoration of a particular place, event or object, and a due sense of decorum should be flexibly applied. He attacked the dogmatism of the reformers:

You will every day hear it absurdly said that room decoration should be by flat patterns – by dead colours – by conventional monotonies, and I know not what. Now, just be assured of this – nobody ever yet used conventional art to decorate with, when he could do anything better, and knew that what he did would be safe . . . Correggio gets a commission to paint a room on the ground floor of a palace at Parma: Any of our people – bred on our fine modern principles – would have covered it with a diaper, or with stripes and flourishes, or mosaic patterns. Not so Correggio: he paints a thick trellis of vine-leaves with oval openings, and lovely children leaping through them into the room; and lovely children, depend upon it, are rather more desirable decorations than diaper, if you can do them – but they are not so easily done [Plate 88].[10]

Ruskin was far from dogmatic about the *avoidance* of convention. He knew that all art is based upon conventions. Hair, in a sculpture, can only be suggested; to represent each hair would be a servile degradation of the art. And sculpture will be seen from a particular place. High up on a cathedral, the carving has to be simplified and emboldened to make it visible from the ground. Similarly, in domestic implements, the finest carving should not be applied to the blade of a knife where it will wear away.[11] These were rules of convention-alisation by virtue of material, of place and of function. But Ruskin's main point, as before, was that to be any good conventionalisation and ornament must be based upon the study of nature and figure drawing. In his opinion, even the Greek fret or the honeysuckle patterns were dependent for their subtlety on the skill which the artist had acquired in the drawing of the outlines of the human figure – the same point as Redgrave had made before his conversion to conventionalism.

To illustrate the inadequacy of the principles of the reformers, Ruskin reprinted a correspondence with Ralph Wornum, whose essay on the 'Exhibition as a Lesson in Taste' had propounded principles similar to those of Owen Jones and Redgrave.[12]

My friend had been maintaining that the essence of ornament consisted in three things: contrast, series and symmetry. I replied (by letter) that 'none of them, nor all of them together, would produce ornament. Here' – (making a ragged blot with the back of my pen on the paper) – 'you have contrast; but it isn't ornament: here, – 1, 2, 3, 4, 5, 6,' – (writing the numerals) – 'you have series; but it isn't ornament: and here,' – (sketching this figure at the side) – 'you have symmetry; but it isn't ornament.'

My friend replied: Your materials were not ornament because you did not apply them. I send them to you back, made up into a choice sporting neckerchief:

Symmetrical figure . . . . . . Unit of diaper
Contrast . . . . Corner ornaments
Series . . . . Border ornaments

Each figure is converted into a harmony by being revolved on its two axes, the whole opposed, in a contrasting series.

would produce ornament. Here" — (making a ragged blot with the back of my pen on the paper)—" you have contrast; but it isn't ornament: here, — 1, 2, 3, 4, 5, 6,"— (writing the numerals) — " you have series; but it isn't ornament : and here,"— (sketching this figure at the side)—" you have symmetry; but it isn't ornament."

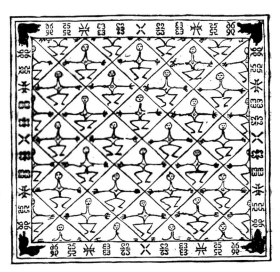

Ruskin replied that the design, based upon such rotten components, was admirable, but it was not so much an application of rules as a *sense* of design which led Wornum to determine a border of just such a breadth, to place each of the component motifs in such a place and in such numbers. The success of the design depended therefore not upon symmetry, contrast and series, but upon judgement and sense.

BEAUTY AND STRUCTURE

Ruskin's ideas about nature and convention, and his attacks upon dogma, were part of a broader conception of the way in which ornament should relate to the fitness of an article of use. His formulations on this subject, as we indicated earlier, have been widely misunderstood. On the one hand, many of his contemporaries, particularly his followers in America, regarded him, as an advocate of the theory that beauty arises from the fitness of the structural means to the end and as the scourge of all concealing ornament and decoration. On the other hand, more recently, modernists have seen Ruskin as the source, even the inspiration, of the wrong direction taken by the architecture and design of the period: the fancy-dress parade of styles. Thus Pevsner's *Pioneers of Modern Design* opens with a quotation: '"Ornamentation", says Ruskin, "is the principal part of architecture." It is that part, he says in another place, which impresses on a building "certain characters venerable or beautiful, but otherwise unnecessary." '[13]

Yet neither reading of Ruskin is accurate or true to the spirit of his writings. If we continue with the quotation chosen by Pevsner, taken from the *Lectures on Architecture and Painting* delivered at Edinburgh in 1853, we find that Ruskin was defending himself against just such simple-minded misinterpretations of his doctrine: 'my most heretical proposition' as he called it.[14] His defence is an admirable summary of his ideas on the relationship between fitness and ornament, between building and architecture.

Far from demanding that the convenience of a building should be sacrificed to its appearance, he insisted that the prior consideration in any building was that 'it shall answer its purposes completely, permanently, and at the smallest expense . . . If it be a public office, it should be so disposed as is most convenient for the clerks in their daily avocations . . . and all being done solidly, securely, and at the smallest necessary cost.' Planning and construction, utility, were essential, just as they had been for Hogarth; but, if utility was the first thing required of a building, it was not 'the highest thing'. It did not constitute architecture as a fine art.

Nonetheless, Ruskin did not dispute, just as Hogarth had not disputed, that a building constructed for function alone could be pleasing, 'just as a ship, constructed with simple reference to its service against powers of wind and wave, turns out to be one of the loveliest things that human hands produce'. And he took Edmund Burke to task for denying '*any* value or agreeableness in constructive proportion' as he had called it. Indeed, its absence would be highly disagreeable – yet it had nothing to do with beauty. The beauty, as distinct from the loveliness, of a building must derive from some other source than the frank exhibition of sound construction or convenient planning.[15]

That being the case, it might well appear that Ruskin believed that the beauty of the building derived from the ornaments stuck onto the structure. And such an interpretation of his thought might appear to be confirmed in the following quotation from *Lectures on Architecture and Painting*:

> And it is to be done by painting and sculpture, that is to say, by ornamentation. Ornamentation is therefore the principal part of architecture, considered as a fine art . . . This is a universal law. No person who is not a great sculptor or painter *can* be an architect. If he is not a sculptor or painter, he can only be a *builder*.[16]

What makes misinterpretation of Ruskin's thought so easy is that, as well as being a subtle theorist, he was a deliberately provocative polemicist.* In the *Lectures on Architecture and Painting* he was making coarse and effective public distinctions between his position and that of the functionalists, leaving his more refined arguments to his books. Nonetheless, we are faced here with a real problem, since Ruskin would appear to have rejected the three possible positions current at the time: the beauty of revealed construction; the beauty of applied, constructed and arbitrary ornament; and the beauty of ornamented construction. And this indeed appears to have been the case. For what Ruskin had in mind when he spoke of the architect as a painter or a sculptor was the notion of the beauty of architecture arising from the *imaginative elaboration* of the building, shaped and carved as by a sculptor.

That the essential quality of architecture as an art should reside in the transforming and enriching power of the imagination is hardly surprising in a fervent disciple of Wordsworth. Few would doubt, reading Wordsworth's theoretical writings, that he conceived of a hierarchy in which truth of description, while necessary to poetry, stood on a lower rung than fancy and imagination; Ruskin's ideas have not been perceived so clearly.

The essential document is the second chapter of *Seven Lamps of Architecture*, 'The Lamp of Truth'. This has frequently been read as a defence of honesty of construction and an attack upon shams. Ruskin stated unequivocally 'Do not let us lie at all.' And he meant it. The only question was what constituted a lie in art or architecture and, in this, Ruskin was aware that 'there arise, in the application of the strict rules of right, many exceptions and niceties of conscience'. The chapter is therefore more concerned with defining which falsehoods, in the eyes of a rigorist, were permissible. For imagination itself, which for Ruskin was essential to art, might be construed as falsehood or deception.[17]

The argument which Ruskin used to demolish this position was one borrowed from Letter 26 of Schiller's *On the Aesthetic Education of Man*, the English translation of which had appeared in 1844, and references to which had appeared in the second volume of *Modern Painters* in 1846. Schiller had distinguished between two species of untruth, what he called 'logical semblance' and 'aesthetic semblance'. In logical semblance, a falsehood with respect to matters of fact or knowledge was, for Schiller as for Ruskin, always a fraud and deceit. Aesthetic semblance, that imitation or illusion essential to art, 'could, however, never be prejudicial to truth, because one is never in danger of substituting it for truth'. Because we knew full well that it was a semblance and not the real thing, we were able to enjoy the pleasures of beauty without being in any moral danger of being fooled. Ruskin, like Schiller, was making more than a straight-forward epistemological point. 'It is necessary to our rank as spiritual creatures, that we should be able to invent and to behold what is not.' Architecture and the arts in general were luxuries, but necessary ones, most valuable in that they denoted man's spiritual freedom from basic needs.[18]

As Peter Fuller has explained in his magnificent account of Ruskin's theory of beauty, these ideas about the beauty of man-made things were derived from his conception of nature itself. To conflate the perception of the beauty of a plant or animal with its construction or its fitness was tantamount to excluding God from His own creation. For, if the experience of beauty were in fact a judgement of the utilitarian qualities of the object in question, then there could be no spiritual dimension to man's experience.[19]

In 'The Lamp of Truth' Ruskin indicated three classes of deceit or falsehood in architecture: structural deceits, in which the appearance of the building did not reflect its real construction; surface deceits, in which the facing materials disguised the real building materials; and operative deceits, wherein surfaces which appeared to be hand-made were in fact machine-made. On the face of it, each category except for the last would appear to correspond directly to those of Pugin or the South Kensington set. And yet, in each

* 'Perhaps some of my hearers this evening may occasionally have heard it stated of me that I am rather apt to contradict myself. I hope I am exceedingly apt to do so. I never met with a question yet, of any importance, which did not need, for the right solution of it, at least one positive and one negative answer . . . Mostly matters of any consequence are three-sided, or four-sided, or polygonal . . . For myself I am never satisfied that I have handled a subject properly till I have contradicted myself at least three times.' (*Library Edition*, XVI, p. 187.)

89   Detail of exterior of Baptistery, Florence by John Ruskin, 1872. Appealing to the principles of imagination he disputed that structure had to be exhibited. The external walls of the Baptistery had 'no more to do with the real make of the building than the diaper of a Harlequin's jacket has to do with his bones.'

instance, the exceptions to the rule were more important to Ruskin than the rule itself.

Thus the very first point that he made about the criterion of structural honesty was that it did not bind the architect 'to exhibit structure'. On the contrary, implicitly referring to Pugin and Owen Jones, he attacked 'the false theory that ornamentation should be merely decorated structure' giving as an example a major work of architecture

> in which the structure is wholly concealed . . . the Baptistery of Florence [Plate 89], which is, in reality, as much a buttressed chapel with a vaulted roof, as the Chapter House of York; – but round it, in order to conceal that buttressed structure, (not to decorate, observe, but to *conceal*,) a flat external wall is raised . . . on the surface of which the eye and intellect are to be interested by . . . pieces of encrusting marble of different colours, which have no more to do with the real make of the building than the diaper of a Harlequin's jacket has to do with his bones.

The architect, then, might conceal structure, as skin and clothing conceal skeleton and muscle, so that only a learned observer could penetrate his secrets. Even in gothic buildings where it seems as if decoration is applied only to the structure he might off-load the thrust of the roof of a church from the columns to concealed flying buttresses, so as to build columns which unassisted would be too slight for the weight, in order to create 'the arborescent look of lofty Gothic aisles', because that was a 'legitimate appeal to the imagination'.[20]

This appeal to the constructive imagination in architecture was no different from the pleasure we enjoy in contemplating clouds, which arises from our imagining them to have 'massive, luminous, warm, and mountain-like surfaces' when we know that they are really damp fog. Moreover, not only did Ruskin deny that fitness, or apparent fitness, was essential to beauty, but he also went one stage further than Hogarth, insisting that even *apparent* unfitness could be highly pleasurable 'as in the unnatural and seemingly impossible lightness of Gothic spires and roofs'.[21] Of course, it was no good if they came crashing down as mediaeval spires or the tower at Fonthill had done, but even their structural failure did not make them ugly. So long, therefore, as there was no real attempt to deceive, so long as an observer could, like an anatomist, search out the truth of the structure, so long was the affecting of the mind with a contradictory impression 'no dishonesty, but on the contrary, a legitimate appeal to the imagination'.

Turning next to surface deceits, Ruskin had no quarrel with illusionistic fresco-painting since no one was deceived by the Sistine Chapel ceiling or Correggio's *Assumption* in Parma. But marbling wood or painting plaster to look like rustication was reprehensible because it was an economy designed to deceive. Yet, even here, degrees of culpability might be discerned, so that it was less venial to simulate marble on a shop front than in a grand public or religious building. The latter kind of building might, however, have its surface veneered with precious marbles or with gold mosaics, because no-one would be under any illusion that the walls were built of solid marble or gold. Besides, in the case of a church, the gold leaf or mosaic was a symbol of heaven and made a legitimate appeal to the imagination.

Finally, in the case of operative deceits – the machine production of decoration which ought to be hand-made – Ruskin did not demand that everything be hand-made. On the contrary, bricks, tiles or moulded terra-cotta were customarily made in moulds, as were bronze and iron decorations. The use of a carving machine for stone, however, he considered deceitful.

The chief criterion of architectural dishonesty for Ruskin was intention, or 'mens rea'. Where the intention in juggling with the structure was to create a poetry of architecture, almost anything was acceptable. When one grasps that the central cohesive force in Ruskin's architectural theory was this conviction of the ennobling power of the human imagination when stimulated by the objects of nature, or by the production of men who were at one with nature, then many of the seeming inconsistencies in his writings disappear. Likewise, all the ramifications of his theory fall into place. If he seems contradictory it is because the subject requires great subtlety.

Since beauty in architecture did not arise from the honest exhibition of the structural skeleton, then it must arise from the elaboration of the building, its decoration, so long as this was appropriate to its purpose. But, by decoration, Ruskin did not mean only inlays, cornices, carved capitals; he meant everything from the composition of the mass of the building down to the carving of the most insignificant moulding. He conceived of a building as a subtly coordinated whole, in which each order played its part when seen from the appropriate distance. From afar it would be the great masses of a cathedral which inspired the imagination; at a closer distance, the arcades, traceries, shafts and pinnacles; still closer, the niches, statues, tracery and carved flowers. From no point should a building fail to engage, delight and stir the mind of the spectator. Everything had its appropriate viewing distance, and everything had a distinct species of beauty when seen from there. Drawing upon an analogy with nature itself, he compared these distinct effects with the view of a ridge of pine trees with the sun rising behind them, in which the 'whole form of the tree . . . becomes one frostwork of intensely brilliant silver'. He invited the reader to consider the amazement of someone who had never seen a pine-tree when he approached the ridge 'to find that the fiery spectres had been produced by trees with swarthy and grey trunks, and dark leaves! We . . . should have built up trees of chased silver, with trunks of glass.'

BEAUTY AND NATURE

We have seen that beauty, for Ruskin, served to reveal God's glory to mankind. But what *was* beauty in architecture, ornament and decoration?

On the most obvious level, beauty 'derived chiefly from the external appearances of organic nature'. Equally, 'all noble ornamentation was the expression of man's delight in God's work'. Ignoble ornament was an expression of man's delight in his own work, like the ornament on the base of the columns in the Place Vendome 'composed of Wellington boots and laced frock coats', or Ruskin's ironic suggestion of the ornament appropriate to the new Bradford Exchange: its frieze decorated with 'pendant purses . . . its pillars broad at the base, for the sticking of bills'. Against this, Ruskin provided a long list of God's ornament, including the forms of the four elements – earth and mineral crystals, water and the waves of the sea, flames of fire and rays of light, the clouds of the air – and the varieties of animal and vegetable creation.[22]

But, in a building, beauty did not arise simply as a result of ornament applied, or of nature directly imitated. It was more a matter of a certain resemblance to nature, as in the affinity between the Ionic capital and the spiral of shells. Likewise, the rounded arch was the type of the vault of heaven, and the pointed arch 'the termination of every leaf that shakes in summer wind'. He also believed that beauty was to be found in leaves and flowers, the most frequent things in nature, because God had 'stamped those characters of beauty which He made it man's nature to love'.[23]

So much for beauty suggested by, or imitative of, the outward shapes of Nature. But Ruskin did not deny the existence of a more abstract kind of beauty derived from nature, although this differed considerably from the conventionalised abstraction of the 'South Ken. Set'. The examples which he gave included the profile of the glacier at Chamounix, the spruce fir branch, the willow leaf, and it ought to be no surprise that these natural forms are almost identical to those recommended by Hogarth, nor that Ruskin's reasons for preferring them were similar. The variety to be found there was not reducible to rules, and the mind never tired of it. Ruskin too was opposed to beauty based upon geometric and

90 'Abstract Lines' from Ruskin's *Stones of Venice*, I, 1851. Ruskin did not dispute than some ornament could be abstract, but it should retain the serpentine forms found in nature.

mathematical principles, and thought natural serpentine forms superior because they kept the mind in action (Plate 90). But, while Hogarth certainly would have admitted that the beauty of natural variety was a reflection of God's handiwork, his focus was more purely psychological. Ruskin, on the other hand, emphasised, on lines similar to Addison, that such infinite variety reflected the infinite nature of god – 'the least material, the least finite . . . the most typical of the nature of God, the most suggestive of the glory of His dwelling place'.[24]

These abstract lines of exquisite subtlety could be incorporated in the profile of a stone or wooden moulding or the shape of a pointed arch, and their beauty was the result of the infinite variation of their curvature, which suggested the infinitude of God. But other kinds of visual quality could be beautiful by analogy. So the infinitely varying gradation of shadow or colour was a form of beauty, so too, of particular importance to architecture, was proportion.

Proportion in a composition existed whenever the parts were unequal, when one part was larger than another. Equality of the parts gave rise to symmetry and, while symmetry was essential to beauty, Ruskin believed, as Hogarth had done, that it was one of the least necessary and most easily accomplished features of beauty. Proportion, in contrast, was difficult to achieve and, consequently, it was a vain 'endeavour to reduce this proportion to finite rules'. But there were two general rules which offered some kind of guide. First, there should be one principle thing in a building or group of buildings bigger than all the rest, such as a spire, gateway or tower. Second, a proportion was only to be found between at least three components, and the more subtle the ratios the better. Indeed, even in the case of symmetry, such as in the arches on the West Front of Pisa Cathedral, beauty would be achieved only when the symmetrical elements were not exactly equal. These 'exquisite delicacies of change in the proportions and dimensions of the apparently symmetrical arcades' gave rise not only to beautiful architecture but also to what Ruskin called 'Living Architecture. There is sensation in every inch of it, and an accommodation to every architectural necessity . . . which is exactly like the related proportions and provisions of the structure of organic form.'[25]

However, not every kind of variety, not all change, was beautiful or good. People's craving for novelty in dress and other fashions was a decided imperfection. A beautiful variety, one which gave rise to healthy sensations, had to belong to some larger order or unity within which harmony was created. This could be the unity of origin, as Ruskin called it: the relationship between the branches and the tree, for instance. Or it could be the unity of sequence or of influence, as in the case of waves or clouds. In such man-made things as buildings, this balance between unity and variety had to be created, avoiding monotonous and repetitive order on the one hand, the order of a plodding, unvarying iambic metre in poetry, and on the other hand avoiding undisciplined and extravagant wildness. As in poetry, Ruskin argued, where it is the play of the irregularities of the verse against the sustaining rhythm of the metre which creates the true variety and beauty of which one never grows tired, so it should be in a building. The uncontrolled application of naturalistic representations in carving, or any other materials which sprawled over the structure and the geometry of the building, was inadmissible. At the other extreme he warned against a rigid subordination of ornament to the geometry of a spandrel or a capital. Worst of all was the equivalent to poetry where the words are cut around to fit the metre, as would be the case were one to cut out a branch of hawthorn as it grows and rule a triangle around it, putting it into a cage as it were. Instead, what Ruskin recommended was that the spirit of the triangle should be put into the hawthorn; it should be trained around the triangle, like a vine or a rose is trained about a trellis.[26]

It has to be remembered that for Ruskin the purpose of recreating this natural beauty of infinitude in buildings was fundamentally religious. What Ruskin called Typical Beauty was based upon the idea that nature itself was a book of divine revelation, and he suggested to his readers that the experience of 'the still small voice of the level twilight behind purple hills, or the scarlet arch of dawn over the dark, troublous-edged sea' was 'one of the principal and most earnest motives of beauty . . . the farthest withdrawn from the earthly prison house, the most typical of the nature of God, the most suggestive of the glory of his dwelling-place'. It was for Turner's power to reveal this vision that Ruskin described him in the first edition of *Modern Painters* as 'standing like the great angel of the Apocalypse, clothed with a cloud, and with a rainbow on his head, and with the sun and stars given into his hand'.[27]

Buildings could never have the effect of nature; on the contrary, buildings and towns buried nature beneath bricks and mortar, as London's citizens had complained in the early seventeenth century. Builders therefore had a duty to incorporate as much natural beauty as possible as a recompense for what they destroyed.[28]

THE POLITICAL ECONOMY OF ART

For Christmas 1850, Ruskin published a fairy-tale that he had written almost ten years before for the girl who had since become his wife. Called *The King of the Golden River*, it remains in print, and many who know Ruskin's name know it only from this.[29]

The fairy-tale tells of three brothers: Schwartz and Hans, the older, who are cruel and covetous, and Gluck, the youngest, who is kind and generous. They are farmers in Treasure Valley, an area of extremely fertile farmland watered by the Golden River. All the farmers in the area are efficient and very prosperous. But Schwartz and Hans are tight-fisted and mean. They work their servants to the bone without paying their wages, they exterminate all the wild animals and insects that threaten their profits, they keep their corn from market until there is a scarcity and the price is doubled.

91 The Golden Goblet comes to life, from Ruskin's *King of the Golden River*, drawn by Richard Doyle. A parable of the political economy of art.

One cold day, while these evil brothers are out, a goblin comes to visit. The goblin is cold and hungry, but young Gluck is frightened to provide any hospitality. However, the goblin persuades Gluck to let him in and give him something to eat. When the older brothers return they throw the goblin out, but he threatens to return at midnight. Night falls, the wind howls and the goblin returns, tears off the roof, leaving his visiting card and promising to return never again. The card is engraved with the words 'South West Wind Esquire'.

The flood that night sweeps all away. The farm is ruined and, subsequently, a terrible drought destroys the valley's fertility. Finally, in despair, the brothers give up trying to farm, pack up the remnants of their gold plate and set off to the city to make their living as goldsmiths, mixing the gold with copper to make more money at their customers' expense.

They do not prosper. They take to drink. And, finally, Gluck is left to melt down the last remaining gold mug, his own and his special favourite. It is 'a very odd mug to look at. The handle was formed of two wreaths of flowing golden hair, so finely spun that it looked more like silk than metal, and these wreaths descended into, and mixed with, a beard and whiskers of the same exquisite workmanship, which surrounded and decorated a very fierce little face.' The mug has the most intensely staring eyes and Gluck almost imagines that they wink. But he puts it into the furnace as he had been ordered.

Immediately the pot begins singing and demands to be poured out of the crucible. When this is done, there emerges a living figure eighteen inches tall who introduces himself as the King of the Golden River. He tells Gluck that whoever casts three drops of Holy Water into the Golden River will find the river turn to gold, but he who casts unholy water will turn into a black stone.

When the older brothers hear the story, they steal Holy Water from the church and set off greedily for the Golden River. On their journey, they meet a dying dog, a dying child and a dying old man. They refuse to give away any of their water and are turned into black stones. But, when Gluck passes the dog, he freely gives him the Holy Water. The dog is transformed into the King of the Golden River who tells Gluck to cast dew into the waters, at which a new river springs out of the rocks and Treasure Valley becomes fertile once again: 'the inheritance, which had been lost by cruelty, was regained by love.'

This wonderful parable, written when Ruskin was only twenty-two, in the same year as Pugin's *True Principles* and at the time of the Young England movement with which, as he have seen, Pugin was associated, contains the kernel of Ruskin's mature theories of Political Economy. Schwartz and Hans are miserable and covetous men. They embody the very vices condemned by the government of Elizabeth and the early Stuarts. They personify the worst aspects of contemporary political economy. They are selfish and uncharitable, they maltreat their workers, exploit nature and, as goldsmiths, trade in deceitful practices and destroy their own stock of beautiful art-workmanship. Gluck's beautiful little mug is the epitome of the kind of naturalistic beauty we have been discussing. It is to be valued for something over and above its monetary worth. It incorporates true wealth and civilisation, which must not be squandered but treasured and used – the true meaning of consumption. The political economy of Hans and Schwartz, which seeks to destroy such beautiful things only to replace them with adulterated rubbish, is destructive of true wealth, of real capital. Finally, fertility and true prosperity, which must be based upon nature, are restored by Gluck's charity or love – the chief of the Christian virtues. Ruskin's moral was that true political economy, or housekeeping, respected nature and worked with it. It was just and charitable, it produced goods of real art and beauty, and it conserved the best of the past – the nation's stock, to use Adam Smith's term.

Because of its influence upon people's souls, beauty, for Ruskin, was an absolutely necessary 'luxury'. But during the 1840s, while he was writing primarily about painting, he was most concerned with the effects of art and nature upon the observer. He could take for granted that a major artist such as Turner was not subjected to servile and soul-destroying labour. When he turned to think about architecture and the products of industry, however, he was compelled to think about the workers who had to execute the ideas of an architect or designer. And the more he thought, the more difficult it was for him to entertain the facile optimism of a writer like Prouting, with his theological version of Hume's idea that economic progress would lead to the diffusion of goods which, by their very nature, would spread increasingly civilised values throughout the population. Even naturalistic objects like Summerly's art-manufactures could not, in Ruskin's view, be evaluated solely in terms of their effect upon their owners if, as Adam Smith had predicted, their manufacture reduced the worker to a situation in which 'the torpor of his mind' rendered him 'as stupid and ignorant as it possible for a human creature to become'.[30]

Adam Smith's solution, followed subsequently by the utilitarian reformers, was an improved education system. But Dickens showed that the system of education which was being instituted, partly at the instigation of the Department of Practical Art was as destructive of human imagination as the factory system itself. Moreover, if people spent twelve hours a day for most of their working lives in such factories, then a few years of education, even the best, could not compensate. The whole system of production and political economy had to be re-examined if the kinds of benefit which Hume had predicted were to be realised, where pleasure in work, pleasure in recreation, and pleasure in the fruits of one's labours were to be equally balanced in a refined civilisation.

There is a tendency to regard Ruskin's work on political economy to be in diametric opposition to the works of the great classical economists, but he was in fact posing their own questions in the altered circumstances of almost a century of industrial and commercial development.

Between the publication of *Seven Lamps* in 1849 and the second volume of *Stones of Venice* in 1853, which included the famous chapter on the 'Nature of Gothic', a major shift can be observed in Ruskin's thinking. In *Seven Lamps* he looked at the issues from the standpoint of the consumer of goods and of the patrons and the users of buildings. In 1853 he tried to consider the entire process of production. The 'Lamp of Life' had briefly noted that 'living architecture' could not be produced either by machines or by workers whose labour was reduced to that of a machine. When work had been done by men whose hearts were in their work, it could always be detected: 'there has been a pause, and a care about them; and then there will come careless bits, and fast bits' and, in this, lay the poetry of true Architecture. But even in that famous passage Ruskin's emphasis was more upon the aesthetic effect and the quality of the finished work and less upon the value of the human process.[31] On his return to the issue in the 'Nature of Gothic', he evaluated the famous six 'characteristic or moral elements of Gothic', which correspond closely to the elements of Beauty – Savageness, Changefulness, Naturalism, Grotesqueness, Rigidity and Redundancy – far more from the point of view of the experience of the workmen, and as the epitome of the whole social economy in which things were manufactured. Thus Ruskin could invite his reader, the consumer, to

> look round this English room of yours, about which you have been proud so often, because the work of it was so good and strong, and the ornaments of it so finished. Examine again all those accurate mouldings, and perfect polishings, and unerring adjustments of the seasoned wood and tempered steel. Many a time you have exulted over them, and thought how great England was, because her slightest work was done so thoroughly.[32]

But in fact, 'read rightly', such perfect order was the product of servile and soul-destroying work resulting from the

> great civilized invention of the division of labour; only we give it a false name. It is not, truly speaking, the labour that is divided; but the men – Divided into mere segments of men – broken into small fragments and crumbs of life; so that all the little piece of intelligence that is left in a man is not enough to make a pin, or a nail, but exhausts itself in making the point of a pin, or the head of a nail.[33]

A truly Christian civilisation, Ruskin argued, would give each workman a degree of creative freedom; one capital, one moulding in a building would differ from another so that the workman himself would enjoy the experience of change and variety as opposed to soul-destroying repetition and monotony. And, although Ruskin found these qualities in gothic rather than in Greek or Renaissance architecture, his theory was not yoked to a particular style.[34]

There are many problems in Ruskin's conception of work. For one thing, he does not seem to have realised that the work of a stone-mason who carved the mouldings of a gothic cathedral using a template was always servile and repetitive to some degree, like that of a bricklayer. All the intricacy and variety of which he was talking were to be found in the work of the ornamental carvers who were a separate class of workman, closer to the sculptor. Second, there is indeed a paradox that increased production can only result from increased productivity, and hence from the division of labour with those drawbacks of which Adam Smith had been so aware. But oddly enough neither of those points, nor any other fallacies that can be detected, invalidate Ruskin's approach, which was to insist upon looking at society as a whole (though not to assume that it was a single unified entity) rather than to divide it up into unrelated parts such as economics, art, architecture, justice, work, leisure, consumption and production, religion, nature and so on. For there was, as we observed in Section III, a fatal reductivism in the thinking both of Hume and, particularly, Adam Smith. The latter, having initially conceived of beauty as synonymous with fitness – then having briefly toyed with a larger, more complex notion of beauty derived from Hogarth – finally dispensed with the desire for beauty as the motive force behind increasing opulence and replaced it with the will to self-improvement. And what this meant, in practice, was the materialistic craving for more and more *things*.

One way of characterising Ruskin's achievement in his economic writings of the late 1850s and early 1860s is to say that he fundamentally re-examined the underlying motivation and objectives of the economic system derived from Smith's *The Wealth of Nations*. In particular, he raised once again the question of the relation of economics to beauty, which had been so central to the work of David Hume and, indeed, of Adam Smith in his 1763 lectures, but which had been dislodged from Smith's mature system.

In *Unto this Last*, which appeared as four articles in the *Cornhill Magazine* in 1860, until they were discontinued as a result of a public outcry, Ruskin questioned the basic presuppositions of political economy. For example, he drew a distinction between the pursuit of riches and the desire for real wealth. Political economy as it stood was 'simply the science of getting rich'.[35] But no-one bothered to ask what true riches really were. Accepting Smith's labour theory of value, Ruskin argued that riches as property amounted basically to one man's power over the labour of others poorer than himself. If someone possessed lots of money but had nobody to work for him, either as servants or as operatives in a factory making goods for him to buy, then his property would be valueless. It mattered not, according to this definition of riches, how they were distributed or what conditions the operatives lived in, or whether they had been acquired dishonestly. But the real value of a nation's *wealth*, as distinct from its riches, depended upon 'the moral sign attached to it, just as sternly as that of a mathematical quantity' depended upon the algebraical sign.

So one line of Ruskin's argument was to reintroduce morality or justice into the affairs of commerce. The title of the third paper, 'Qui Judicatis Terram', was taken from an inscription on Ambrogio Lorenzetti's allegory of the well-governed and prosperous city in the council chamber of Siena: 'DILIGITE JUSTITIAM QUI JUDICATIS TERRAM' ('Love Justice, You who judge the earth').[36] The rich city was nothing if it were not also a just and well-governed city. In this, he in fact had much in common with both Hume and Smith, neither of whom equated free trade with a free-for-all. Both had insisted upon the necessity of just laws to prevent any social class or professional group from creating a monopoly of power and wealth. Ruskin declared himself 'an utterly fearless and unscrupulous free-trader' on the old Grotian grounds of exchanging the natural produce of one part of the world for that of another – Tuscan olive oil for Sheffield steel. Ruskin also shared with Smith the belief that, when protection was dismantled, it should be done little by little to avoid sudden and calamitous unemployment. Where he fundamentally disagreed with the classical economists was over the distinction, invented by Smith, between productive and unproductive labour.[37]

It will be remembered that the point of making this distinction was to refute both the Burghleyan and the Mandevillean arguments that all expenditure, all consumption, helped create prosperity because it gave people jobs. Smith's rejoinder had been that if economic growth were one's objective all forms of consumption were not equally effective. Wealth would only increase if people spent their money on things which could be made cheaper and more plentiful through the kinds of investment which improved the productiveness of labour. Productive labour was labour engaged in production where the profits could be invested to improve efficiency. Productive consumption was the purchase of things produced by such labour. We have already examined the inconsistencies in Smith's definition. Yet his reasons in 1776 for making the broad distinction were sensible enough, part of his refutation of the theory that prodigality was always beneficial to the nation, if not to the individual. In the hands of his successors, and in the minds of the Manchester School manufacturers, the elegant distinction between productive and useful labour was inevitably lost, so that only productive labour was deemed to be useful, just as only money riches were counted amongst the nation's wealth.

John Stuart Mill in his *Principles of Political Economy* of 1848, with which Ruskin took issue, went one stage further than Adam Smith. Mill argued that 'consumption on pleasures or luxuries . . . since production is neither its object nor is in any way advanced by it, must be reckoned unproductive'. Only the consumption of the essentials to life could be considered productive.[38] One would have thought that this obviated the whole point of economic growth, but that, of course, was not Ruskin's criticism. Ruskin challenged the whole distinction between useful and productive labour.

Mill had argued that if a hardware manufacturer spent his profits upon jewellery and plate, his consumption would be unproductive, but if he spent it on hiring more factory workers 'more food would be appropriated to the consumption of productive labourers'. But what about the jewellers or silversmiths? asked Ruskin. Why was a steel fork more productive than a silver one? And what if it were the case that the hardware manufacturer produced bayonets and other instruments of destruction rather than knives and forks? For what reason, on what basis, could Mill make such a judgement?[39]

The fundamental inconsistency which Ruskin laid at Mill's door was his claim that political economy had 'nothing to do with moral values – the comparative estimation of different uses in the judgement of a philosopher or a moralist'.[40] According to Mill political economy had only to do with the exchange value of a thing, which depended in part upon its use in satisfying people's desires. But, argued Ruskin, if the economic value of things was determined by people's desires, and since people's desires must be based upon their estimate of the agreeableness of the thing, which must in turn be determined by their moral dispositions, then economic value must be influenced by moral values – a point Barbon would have accepted. In a society which disapproved of alcohol, wines and spirits would be worthless. Therefore, in determining which forms of consumption were productive or unproductive, moral judgments could not be avoided. In general, our wealth as a nation must lie in our capacity to produce the things and services and activities that we valued most highly from a moral standpoint.

Ruskin was certainly no relativist in moral matters, even after 1858 when he had abandoned Christianity. He defined wealth as our stock of those things that 'avail towards life'. Wealth was independent of mere human opinion. Productive labour, therefore, was that which produced life, and unproductive labour that which produced death – in the biblical or spiritual sense. In Ruskin's terms, therefore, productive consumption would lead to the construction of what he described as 'living architecture', or to the performance of a harmonious piece of music which inspired one with the infinitude of God and Nature. It would also include well-made clothes, or carriages, or good food, so long as a person's desire for such things was not the product of greed or vanity.[41]

Nor did Ruskin deny the role of capital investment in increasing the production and hence the wealth of nations; but he insisted, logically enough, that capital accumulation could not be an end in itself. As he put it: the political economy of Europe had hitherto devoted itself wholly to the multiplication of tulip bulbs rather than flowers, to plough-shares begetting more ploughshares rather than corn. This was production as an end in itself. The true test of a nation's wealth must be the *quality* of what it *consumed* rather than the quantity of what it produced – and here too there was a certain affinity between Ruskin and Adam Smith, who had attacked the mercantile system because the 'interest of the consumer is almost constantly sacrificed to that of the producer'. But of course this did not rule out Ruskin's deep concern for the conditions of employment and the quality of working people's lives.

It can be argued that to adopt this as a working definition of capital would lead to a society with no economic growth or increase in wealth. But Ruskin would have argued that if, say, the material things produced by a society were of lasting quality, which aroused the appreciation of nature in all its richness and variety in their owners and hence quelled the human craving for mere novelty, then the nation's existing stock of wealth would only be slowly consumed, through wear and tear, and constantly increased by the productions of each succeeding generation, as opposed to being constantly destroyed as one fashion superseded the last. In a small parable which echoes the *King of the Golden River*, he wrote of a young couple setting up home who have to have new plate – for which the old, however beautiful, had to be melted down. The silversmiths, knowing that this will be the fate of their own work in another generation, do not bother to put their souls into the work.

> You ask of him nothing but a little quick handicraft – a clever twist of a handle here, and a fret there, a convolvulus from the newest School of design, a pheasant from Landseer's game cards; a couple of sentimental figures for supporters . . . then a clever touch with the burnisher, and there's your épergne, the admiration of all the footmen at the wedding breakfast, and the torment of some unfortunate youth who cannot see the pretty girl opposite to him, through its tyrannous branches.[42]

Instead, what Ruskin wished to see was a Political Economy in which skilful workers, satisfied in their labour, could produce workmanship of 'imperishable splendour' and 'wilful fancies . . . as their dreams require', the finest of such treasures accumulating over the ages.

Finally since the aim of all art had to be the worship of God through Nature, no economic system which destroyed or polluted Nature could be considered wealthy. The land could indeed support a very large population, all England could well become a factory with the complete loss of the countryside, but, since wild flowers, birds and even insects were also a source of human happiness, they too were essential to any definition of real wealth and true riches.

Part Six

GOOD MODERN DESIGN

PREFACE
A Tyranny of Taste

Every one of us should consider the problem of working-class housing. Perhaps the average owner or tenant of a privately-built house will ask what business it is of his. All design is everybody's business. I would almost go so far as to say that . . . behind all this business of taps and teapots and where to put electric light, there lies a very big idea – the idea of man planning and making a civilized life.[1]

What right indeed did the professional middle classes have to interfere with the design of teapots in working-class homes? The author of this 1938 Pelican Special on Design was clearly aware that he and his fellow design pundits could be accused of unwarrantable intrusion into the privacy of family life, even if they only restricted themselves to preaching their gospel, as in earlier centuries, which they were not in fact content to do. They believed it to be so important as fully to justify the state in assuming powers to stop people buying teapots, chairs and tables of 'bad design' by outlawing their manufacture. Under wartime conditions they actually achieved this ambition. For ten years (eight of them in peace-time) the Utility Scheme prohibited the sale of clothes, furniture and pottery unless they were made to state-approved designs. Sumptuary laws were back in force and with a vengeance for the first time in almost four hundred years. This was indeed a Tyranny of Taste. How did it come about?

In the other areas of design such as architecture and town planning where the state had for long been directly involved, it increasingly supported the aspirations of the design professions, architects in particular, to shape every aspect of the physical environment. For a period of almost half a century, from the 1940s till the early 1980s the architect-planner-designer became a figure of great power and influence, designing everything from teapots to new towns within a legal framework of planning law and aesthetic control which gave him almost dictatorial powers and immunity from interference either by the owners or residents of private property or by the general public who opposed the new projects. These were on a colossal scale involving the demolition of huge areas of existing towns and cities and their rebuilding in a totally new style and layout as well as building New Towns all over the country.

Like it or not (and at the time of writing public opinion is strongly disenchanted with much post-war so-called modern architecture) it was an extraordinary period in terms of the scale of the power of the design professions but even more of their scope.

This question of teapots was the starting point for this book and has led us back to the Elizabethan period and through the work of *The Spectator*, David Hume, Adam Smith, Hogarth and Ruskin, amongst others, all of whom participated in the debate concerning the 'Political Economy of Design' and were clearly aware of the interconnections between economics, social policy, morality and design.

In the twentieth century, to which we now turn, perhaps as a result of the rise of the professional expert in each of these fields, the sense of the interconnectedness of all the different issues seems somewhat obscured, even from the contributors to the debate themselves, and we must be at somewhat greater pains to reconstruct it.

Because the reappearance of sumptuary law is the most exceptional aspect of the period and also because concern for the proper conduct of people's private lives held great sway in the design of buildings and in turn upon the way cities were planned, we shall start there.

CHAPTER 1
Modern Leisure and Sumptuary Law

PART OF THE explanation for this concern with the minutiae of domestic design, consumption and style – that part specifically related to the design professions and to the issue of what style was appropriate to the modern age – can be traced directly to a continental debate about the importance of good modern design. We shall need to examine the ideas of the Austrian architect Adolf Loos and the Franco-Swiss architect Le Corbusier. The other part arises from specifically British debates relating both to design and also to practical social and economic policies such as rehousing and slum clearance. We shall deal with each in turn.

THE MODERN STYLE: LOOS AND LE CORBUSIER

The author of the 1938 tract on design, Anthony Bertram, claimed that good modern design and civilisation were one and the same, the essential features of which, sound function and good form, did not need to be tricked out with 'trappings and trinkets, make-up and tattooing'. Civilised design, he implied, was the antithesis of effeminacy, degeneracy and primitivism.[1]

The origin of this ideology is to be found in the writings of Adolf Loos and Le Corbusier; in particular Loos's famous essay of 1908, 'Ornament and Crime' ('Ornament und Verbrechen') which Le Corbusier republished in French in the first number of his propagandist journal *L'Esprit Nouveau*, from the pages of which he compiled his own highly influential books on the subjects of consumer design, architecture and town planning: *L'Art decoratif d'aujourdhui* (1925), *Vers une architecture* (1923), and *Urbanisme* (1924).

Both Adolf Loos, before the First World War, and Le Corbusier afterwards lived in countries which were significantly less industrialised and urbanised than Britain. Loos, who predicted Austria's military defeat in the First World War and attributed it to the country's backwardness in design, and Le Corbusier, who had experienced that of France, both believed that modernisation was the solution to their countries' problems. This had to be a modernisation not merely of factories and cities, but also of the homes and the very hearts and minds of the people, of their life-styles as a whole. Both writers, moreover, felt a degree of optimism in progress and laissez-faire that smacks of David Hume in his less guarded moments.

Loos, the earlier figure, was the more content to allow the change in style to occur of its own accord, as Austria's economy became increasingly liberalised. His writings, therefore, although polemical, seem to have been aimed more at forming public opinion by passing comment upon and analysing the personal styles and fashions of the day in fin-de-siècle Vienna.[2]

'Ornament and Crime' was written in the lively and provocative style which Loos adopted in his polemical writings to shock his readers and make them think. The essay

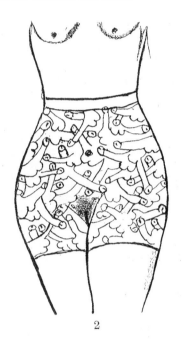

92 Adolf Loos (1870–1933), the Viennese architect and polemicist who gave rise to the modernist slogan 'Ornament is crime'. He considered the English gentleman's suit (worn here) to be the epitome of modernity.

93 Tattooed prostitute from Césare Lombroso's *L'Uomo delinquente*, 1897. Lombroso was a highly influential criminologist who considered criminality to be genetic and from whom Loos took the connection between ornament and crime.

2

draws upon wide reading and is very much the product of Viennese cafe culture. It opens with a paradox concerning moral relativity and social evolution. 'The child is amoral. So is the Papuan, to us. The Papuan kills his enemies and eats them. He is no criminal. But if a modern man kills someone and eats him, he is a criminal or a degenerate!'[3] Loos then applied this idea to decoration. Whereas the Papuan who 'tattoos his skin, his rudder, his oars' was no criminal, 'the modern man who tattoos himself is a criminal or a degenerate. There are prisons where eighty percent of the prisoners are tattooed.'

Observing that it was possible to estimate a country's culture by the amount of graffiti on lavatory walls, Loos enunciated the following law: 'Cultural evolution is equivalent to the removal of ornament from articles in daily use.' And elsewhere he claimed that 'The lower the culture the stronger the ornament. Ornament is something which must be conquered. The Papuan and the criminal ornament their skin (Plate 93). Indians decorate their boats and their oars with ornament. But the bicycle and the steam-engine are free of ornament. Advanced civilisation eliminates the ornament from objects.' Here were the seeds of the machine aesthetic and the simple unadorned modern style.[4]

Loos's justification for this rule drew upon three sources: the theories of the English sociologist and evolutionist Herbert Spencer whose ideas were virtually plagiarised by

302

Veblen in his *Theory of the Leisure Classes*; the notion of the English Dandy as the archetype of the heroic modern man advanced by Charles Baudelaire amongst others; and the thesis of the influential Italian criminologist, Cesare Lombroso, that criminals were a degenerate species of humanity and that their condition was an inherited one.

The function of ornament and its origin lay at the heart of the matter. For Herbert Spencer ornament originated as a trophy of conquest and of the hunt. This was also the case with jewellery and even of ordinary clothes, whose primary function was not therefore protective. Their original function was as signs of masculine prowess and they continued to serve a social function as status symbols. He did not even entertain the possibility that ornament could serve any other end. As society grew more complex and intricate mon-archical and aristocratic hierarchies developed so ornament and clothing developed into a system for expressing minute distinctions of rank. But when, with the development of a commercial society, contractual relationships replaced hierarchical status, these decorations, previously enforced by sumptuary laws, gradually disappeared under the influence of fashion and the imitation of the rich by the less well-off.[5]

Fashion, according to this view, was a modern phenomenon and a challenge to inherited status tending towards equalisation. Burghley or Evelyn would have agreed – if disapprov-ingly. Accordingly, Loos himself believed that in a modern society where 'dress code regulations' had been done away with, everyone enjoyed the right to dress as he pleased. But that did not mean they would use their freedom to dress in an individualist or showy style, but they would dress 'in such a way that stands out the least'. Since wearing a top hat on the ice rink made one stand out, it was unmodern to wear a top hat there. One might suppose that social freedom would have the reverse effect, but the logic of the theory as well as observation of sartorial conventions in the more industrialised countries such as Britain and America led Loos, and Spencer before him, to the opposite conclusion. There men of all ranks and classes wore suits, except on ceremonial occasions; whereas in Austria or Russia officials of the vast imperial bureaucracies still wore court dress at work festooned with medals and decorations. Decoration in the general sense was for Loos virtually identical with honorific or ceremonial decoration. An absence of decoration was therefore a repudiation of feudal society.[6]

Loos narrowed the scope of his axiom still further. The test of being well-dressed and modern was to be *inconspicuous* in the very centre of modern culture, which at that time was London. Loos's ideal of the well-dressed modern man was one who abided by the well-cut, well-tailored, monochrome and unadorned English style established at the beginning of the nineteenth century by Beau Brummell, the King of the Dandies, and developed subsequently into the gentleman's suit (Plate 92). There was an equivalent style in household furniture.[7]

Loos used the style of dress to exemplify his grand theory concerning the relationship between the economic modernity of a society and the manner or style of all its products. The English and the Americans, as the economically most advanced nations, not only dressed in a simple style for reasons of fashion, but also for efficiency. Because for modern man, in Benjamin Franklin's adage, 'time was money', it was, in Loos's view, 'necessary for us to walk more quickly every year'. Consequently, shoes with laces would predominate in the twentieth century because they made this possible.[8]

Turning to personal hygiene he claimed that modern people used water for washing themselves. But the French and the Austrians did not wash. They used water as a thing of beauty for ornamental fountains. Their railway waiting rooms stank. In contrast, 'Every English washbasin with its spigot and drain is a marvel of progress.' For this reason, the plumber was the pioneer of modernity, 'the State's chief craftsman, the quartermaster of . . . today's prevailing culture'.[9]

The equivalent of the English suit in furniture and therefore the most modern was English furniture of the late eighteenth century (Plate 95). Loos believed there was no need

94   Iced Cakes from *Icing made Easy* (n.d.) by Geo.F.Burton. According to Loos and his disciple Le Corbusier these, and fancy food in general, were unmodern. Like Addison they advocated plain English food.

95 Dining Room of the Schwarwald House by Adolf Loos, 1905. Loos attacked the architect-designed interior, his own were equipped with reproduction English eighteenth-century furniture which he thought as modern as the suit.

to design chairs afresh. They had already been perfected. One needed only to copy them or buy them from the famous London furniture store, Maples. Not only did artefacts obey this rule, so too did food. English, that is to say modern, food was roast beef, grilled steaks, boiled cabbage and raw tomatoes, in contrast to French stew, Wiener Schnitzel and other fancy recipes.[10]

This point of view reminds us of that of Addison and *The Spectator*, and it is fascinating to observe that many of the features Loos saw as epitomising the modern English style of life echo those emphasised by German travellers to England and London in the eighteenth century. Since there is no positive evidence that Loos ever visited London, though he did spend several years in America, one must assume that he was drawing upon this literary stereotype. Indeed, the very form, as well as the wit, of these essays which he contributed in 1898 to 'The Times of Austria', the *Neue Freie Presse*, seems modelled, indirectly perhaps, upon those of *The Tatler* and *The Spectator*, just as Austrian theories of an industrial economy were drawn from the classical English economists. The progressive classes of turn-of-the-century Vienna were thoroughly Anglophile. Several younger architects recalled that, when they asked Loos what they should see in London, he would recommend the eighteenth-century London squares and Maples in Tottenham Court Road.

If the Dandy epitomised all that Loos admired in the Modern Age, then the fop, the peacock and the aesthete stood for everything that he loathed. Writing only three years after the trial of Oscar Wilde, Loos accurately judged the eclipse of Aesthetic Movement and of 'camp'. He castigated the German aesthetes and Art-Architects, the leaders of movements like the Vienna Secession, whose chief ambition was, in his opinion, to stand out from the crowd. These idolaters made 'altars of their bodies, on which beauty in the shape of velvet collars, fancy trouser materials, and secession-style ties, shall be sacrificed'.[11] He called them criminals and degenerates because they were openly resisting the tendencies of the modern age. And they were aided and abetted by the Austrian state which had financed schools of design and museums of ornamental art (on the English model) in order to 'retard the cultural progress of the people'. All such people were active 'criminals' because they knowingly resisted modernity on account of its undermining the ancien régime upon which their status depended. Through positive encouragement of the use of ornament, in schools of design and elsewhere, as a means of sumptuary and hence of social control, they were engaged in a conspiracy to preserve the outward distinctions of rank and, thereby, to obstruct the economic, social and cultural development of the people.

This paradox, that the architects and designers supposedly the most 'advanced' of their day were akin to criminals and degenerates derives from the ideas of Cesare Lombroso who believed that criminality was caused by genetic inheritance and not by social conditions, that criminals were reversions to apes and the so-called lower races of mankind. He was the source of Loos's statement that 80 per cent of all prisoners were tattooed – only he had claimed only 8 per cent. He supported his argument both by references to the shape of criminal skulls and the similarity between the behaviour of criminals, savages and apes, all of whom supposedly engaged in 'tattooing, excessive idleness, love of orgies'. Loos, however, unlike Lombroso was not a eugenicist but a social evolutionist and environmentalist who was using Lombroso's ideas in a highly polemical and playful manner.[12]

Loos drew a clear distinction between, on the one hand, those who wilfully clung to decoration even though they were in a position to know better, 'degenerate aristocrats' and art-architects, and, on the other hand, the continuing traditions of ornament in the artefacts of culturally backward peoples both from other cultures and from within the Austro-Hungarian Empire. Thus his own shoemaker, who gained pleasure from covering brogues with unmodern scallops and perforations, was not open to criticism, but the advanced ornamentalists of Art Nouveau, like Van der Velde, were blameworthy because they were *knowingly* sustaining the craft-based, unmechanised and pre-industrial economy which kept artisans on the verge of poverty, and also sustained a socially degenerate state, backward and incapable of defending itself in war against advanced industrial nations like Britain and America.[13]

The undecorated modern style was, therefore, the result of modern industry and the social order associated with it. Loos was convinced of a causal set of relationships between the social hierarchy of the ancien régime, its commitment to ceremony and ornamental status symbols, and the economic arrangements by which the equipment for this way of life was produced. He was equally convinced of a causal relationship between the modern world of competitive businessmen, dressed in their egalitarian suits and setting about their business in the most efficient way possible, and the well-paid factory workers who were not employed to make useless handcrafted ornaments at starvation wages.[14]

It is a theory which stems directly from the intellectual tradition of the political economy of design, Loos siding with Adam Smith (who objected to ceremony as a non-productive form of consumption) and with Herbert Spencer, and, on this issue, against Ruskin, Morris and those who wished to revive the arts and crafts.

Despite what may seem like a flaw in his association of mass production with simplicity of style, such concerns as these obviously made the appearance of everyday domestic goods a matter of acute interest to Loos's audience and clients, the readers of *Neue Freie Presse*, who were in the forefront of efforts to modernise Austria's economy.

Loos was, therefore, a major influence on the idea of the unadorned modern style and upon the idea that time-consuming, hand-made, architect-designed 'ornament is a crime' against social and economic progress, against equality and against democracy.

But Loos himself did not adhere to the view expressed in some of the English pamphlets of the 1930s, that Good Design should be *imposed* by the state upon its citizens. He was also quote opposed to the notion that *architects* should be the pioneering experts of the modern age. First of all, he really did believe that the modern style would evolve naturally step by step with economic modernisation, as in England and America. But, second, he was profoundly sceptical of the ambitions of the architectural profession. He was committed to tradition, as we have seen in his attitude to English eighteenth-century furniture, and saw no need to reinvent the wheel.

Thus the interiors of many of the houses Loos designed were furnished not with pieces stamped with an exaggeratedly individualist personal style, instantly recognisable, as in the contemporary interiors of Frank Lloyd Wright, Voysey or Hoffmann, but very much in the classic English style, with reproduction Sheraton and Hepplewhite chairs, akin to what Norman Shaw and the English Neo-Georgians and Queen Anne style architects were doing at much the same time. So too the gentlemen's tailor shops, which constituted an important part of Loos's practice, were very much in the style of the English gentleman's outfitters.

One of the most moving of Loos's writings describes the furniture in his childhood home, and especially the table around which the whole family used to sit:

> I did not grow up, thank God, in a stylish home. At that time no one knew what it was yet. Now, unfortunately, everything is different in my family too. But in those days! Here was the table, a totally crazy and intricate piece of furniture, an extension table with a shocking bit of work as a lock. But it was *our* table, *ours*! Can you understand what that means? Do you know what wonderful times we had there? Evenings, when I was a young boy and the lamp was burning, I was never able to tear myself away from it! Father always imitated the night watchman's horn so that I would run – terrified – into my bedroom. And there was the writing table! There was an ink stain on it; my sister Hermione had knocked over the inkwell when she was a little baby. And there was the picture of my parents! What a hideous frame! But it was a wedding gift from the workers at my father's shop . . . Every piece of furniture, every thing, every object had a story to tell, a family history. The house was never finished; it grew along with us and we grew within it. Of course it did not have any style to it. That means there was no strangeness, no age. But there was one style that our home did have – the style of its occupants, the style of our family.[15]

Dickens would have approved. Loos believed that 'neither the archaeologist nor the interior decorator, nor the architect, nor the painter, nor the sculptor should design our homes'. Everyone should be their own decorator. He praised a room designed by Otto Wagner for its beauty 'not because, but in spite of the fact that it was designed by an architect'. And one of his most telling essays, which sums up all his feelings about the tyranny of good taste, is in the form of a parable: 'The Story of a Poor Rich Man' who, possessing everything that there was to possess except art, hired a famous art-architect to design for him an artistic home in which every single thing had its own special place. This was taken to such extremes that 'once you held an object in your hand there was no end to guessing and looking for its proper place' and sometimes the architect had to be called out to 'unroll his working drawings' in order 'to rediscover the place for a match-box'. When the millionaire remembered all the homely things from his childhood, like his father's big armchair and the old family clock, tears used to spring to his eyes. He appreciated that one had to make sacrifices for art, but this was taking things too far: all human sentiment was excluded, replacing the individuality of the client with the tyrannical artistic egotism of the architect. In contrast the interior of Loos's own flat, with its heavily corbelled fireplace, inglenook, roof beams and benign clutter, perfectly exemplified his expressed beliefs.[16]

For all his attacks upon decoration and his belief in the modernity of simple form, Loos was far from simplistic in making the traditional distinction between the well-groomed *public* face which decorum required in one's clothing or in the facade of a building and the *private* informality permissible within. Indeed, for all Loos's talk of modernity, it seems likely that in today's climate Loos would see himself as a classicist as much as a modernist. 'Our education,' he wrote, 'rests on the classical tradition. An architect is a builder who has learned Latin. But our modern architects appear rather to have learned Esperanto.'[17]

The importance of Adolf Loos as a pioneer of the Modern Movement needs to be stressed, since apart from the slogan 'Ornament is Crime', derived from the title of his essay, his contribution is less acknowledged, particularly in English-speaking countries, than that of Le Corbusier or Walter Gropius. This was partly a question of translation. 'Ornament and Crime', 'The Plumbers' and 'The Poor Little Rich Man' did not appear in English till 1966, and his seminal articles of 1897 and 1898 in *Neue Freie Press* not until 1982. The writings of Le Corbusier, which first appeared in *L'Esprit Nouveau* from 1920 onwards and which were published in book form almost immediately, were devoured by British and American architects and critics on their appearance and long before they were translated in 1927 and 1929.[18]

It is through Le Corbusier that Loos's ideas have been widely disseminated. Many of Le Corbusier's ideas as well as his polemical style come, as we shall see, from Loos, whose influence he generously acknowledged, claiming that 'Ornament and Crime' marked a decisive turning point for Modernism. As already noted *L'Esprit Nouveau* published a translation of 'Ornament and Crime' in its first issue.[19]

The similarities between the two writers are very strong. Le Corbusier adopted Loos's attack upon applied ornament and upon the schools of decorative art which taught the subject; he also believed that ornament belonged to the pre-industrial world of the great monarchies and aristocracies not to the modern world of democracy, equality and industrial society; he too attacked the attempts to revive craftsmanship, folk art and the vernacular while at the same time acknowledging the beauty of the original artefacts as products of their own time and place; he too praised the virtues of modern industrial society for its efficiency, its hygiene, its food and its self-effacing aesthetic; and he admired Maples, the London furniture store.

Le Corbusier's differences to Loos lie in the scope of his ideas and in his more extreme iconoclasm: his scope, in that he believed the subject of architecture to extend to 'everything man makes . . . from the dressmaker's hat box to the future town plans of Paris, London or Moscow'. His *Pavilion de L'Esprit Nouveau* at the Paris Exposition of 1925 was designed, he wrote later, indissolubly to link 'the equipment of the home (furniture) to architecture (the space inhabited, the dwelling), and to town planning (the conditions of life of a society).'[20] He was even more vitriolic than Loos in his attack upon the art-architects whose decorative and dictatorial whimsies were manifested in the 'Art Deco' of the 1925 exhibition as they had been in the 1898 Vienna Jubilee Exhibition which had provided Loos with his targets; but whereas Loos's alternative was that of an easy-going personal or family style, corresponding to 'English Comfort', Corbusier wanted to sweep all clutter aside in favour of an ascetic and efficient living space – the 'house as a machine for living in', although this was not so mechanistic a concept as it seems (see Plate 97).

Above all Le Corbusier was by far the greater figure – visionary town planner and designer as well as architect, painter, prolific and brilliant writer, organiser of international movements – whose sheer energy as well as his highly ambitious conception of the architect provided the younger generation of architects throughout the world between the 1920s and the 1970s with a wonderfully inspiring vision of their role in society. Even today, when we find Loos's modest conception of the scope of an architect's work far more to our liking, it is easy to put ourselves in the place of a student listening to Corbusier's lectures in those early years, swept along with a sure sense of purpose, wanting nothing more than to join Corbusier's crusade to change the world.[21]

So what was Le Corbusier's doctrine concerning furniture and personal possessions? He rejected Romanticism in almost all its forms. He abhorred trashy manufactured objects covered with historical ornament, he attacked the bric-à-brac mentality and the fashion for what we today would call ethnic products and their industrial imitations – 'Russian embroidery, Breton wardrobes, fancies from almost everywhere, Japonaiserie of all kinds . . . bathing us in P-o-e-t-r-y,' and he had no time for efforts to revive the traditions of handicraft in industrial countries. He attributed the blame for all these things in part upon the modern museums of decorative art, based upon the prototype at South Kensington, and in part upon the ethnographic museums.[22]

THE MUSEUM IS BAD
BECAUSE IT DOES NOT TELL THE WHOLE STORY.
IT MISLEADS, IT DISSIMULATES, IT DELUDES.
IT IS A LIAR.

The principles according to which museum objects were chosen were biased towards a special class of highly decorated and enriched objects from churches and palaces designed to dazzle, overawe and impress whereas none of the simple utensils of the everyday life of the past were included. The same problem arose with ethnographic museums, because 'a colonial . . . prefers to bring back . . . an object of display belonging to a negro chief or the local deity, rather than to encumber himself with numerous utensils that would give a picture of the cultural condition of the people.' These collections had come to serve as models for the decorative artist. But however impressive the provenance of the artefacts one should not be discouraged from using one's critical faculties and seeing it as the 'disgustingly drawn, cheap rubbish' it really was.[23]

Patterns, decorations, baubles which flooded 'the shelves of the Department Stores' and sold cheaply to shop-girls, stood condemned as meretricious rubbish. He even verged upon condemning the shop-girl's printed cotton dress, but relented – 'What would spring be without it?' The problem was that decoration nowadays covered everything so that the healthy gaiety of the shop-girl became rank corruption when surrounded by 'Renaissance stoves, Turkish smoking tables, Japanese umbrellas, chamber pots and bidets from Luneville or Rouen, Bichara perfumes, bordello lamp-shades, pumpkin cushions, divans spread with gold and silver lame, black velvets flecked like the Grand Turk, rugs with baskets of flowers and kissing doves, linoleum printed with Louis XVI ribbons' – all the products of the modern western bazaar, turning 'our houses into museums or temples filled with votive offerings'.[24]

This kind of criticism echoes those of the British design reformers of the 1830s and 1840s, but Le Corbusier also attacked their own remedies, the museums and schools of ornamental art, even more directly than Loos had done before him. And he also attacked their own detractors, Ruskin in particular, 'the romantic and Ruskinian baggage that formed our education', the whole naturalistic movement upon which generations of art students had been reared since the mid-nineteenth century guided by Ruskin, Owen Jones and others in the study of flowers, insects, trees, clouds and birds whose 'life-curve' they

96   Modern commercial glass and crockey from *The Decorative Art of Today* (1925) by Le Corbusier who loved the platonic perfection of machine-made goods.

had tried to understand, as well as the study of those cultures which had excelled in this type of decoration – the Gothic, the Savage, the Assyrian, the Chinese.[25] All of this and its modern consequences in the Arts and Crafts Movement and Art Nouveau was to be abominated and swept away:

> Such stuff founders in a narcotic haze. Let's have done with it.
> It is time to crusade for whitewash and Diogenes.

That sums up Le Corbusier's positive alternative. As he put it, the very idea behind the title of his book *The Decorative Art of Today* was a paradox because, as Loos had put it so neatly: 'the more cultivated a people becomes, the more decoration disappears.' With true Loosian style he summed up the change like this: 'When my aunt gave me twenty sous, I ran off to buy cakes covered with cream and icing sugar, masterpieces of craftsmanship, pagodas! I thought myself a prince [see Plate 94] . . . The whole oxen that were once roasted at ancestral banquets now fill no more than the centre of a dinner-plate: the beef steak.'[26] In short, the inside of the home should be equipped with furniture as functional as the Roneo metal equipment used in the modern American office, furniture which ought to be regarded as tools and as extensions of our human limbs and faculties. 'adapted to human functions that are type-functions. Type-needs, type-functions, therefore type-objects and type-furniture. The human-limb object is a docile servant. A good servant is discreet and self-effacing, in order to leave his master free.'[27] Home furniture then should be seen purely as mechanical equipment and stripped of all its romantic poetry. This was not to suggest that it did not possess its own beauty, but that would be the totally new geometrical beauty of the machine, never seen before and far removed from that of nature itself, since 'the machine brings shining before us disks, spheres, the cylinders of polished steel' in place of,

310

and even more perfect than the roundest and most polished pebble from the sea-shore. As Philip Johnson was later to point out, these were the forms of perfect Platonic beauty.[28]

The epitome of Le Corbusier's vision of the 'decorative arts of today' was the shop-girl in her flower-patterned cretonne dress surrounded not by the commercial trash of that modern bazaar, the department store, but 'in a pretty room, bright and clear, white walls, a good chair – wickerwork or Thonet; table . . . painted with ripolin. A good, well-polished lamp, some crockery of white porcelain; and on the table three tulips in a vase . . . It is healthy, clean, decent. [Plate 96]'[29] Personally assuming the mantle of a modern Solon (the seventh-century BC Athenian reformer who abolished serfdom, laid the foundations of Athenian democracy and introduced sumptuary laws to restrict luxury), Le Corbusier proposed his own sumptuary law:

THE LAW OF RIPOLIN
A COAT OF WHITEWASH

Every citizen is required to replace his hangings, his damask, his wall-papers, his stencils, with a plain coat of white ripolin. *His home* is made clean. There are no more dirty, dark corners. *Everything is shown as it is.* Then comes *inner* cleanness, for the course adopted leads to refusal to allow anything at all which is not correct, authorised, intended, desired, thought-out: no action before thought. When you are surrounded with shadows and dark corners you are at home only as far as the hazy edges of the darkness your eyes cannot penetrate. You are not master in your own house. Once you have put ripolin on your walls you will be *master of yourself.* And you will want to be precise, to be accurate, to think clearly.[30]

Here was a declaration of intent, maybe slightly tongue-in-cheek, by the leader of the modernists, to introduce sumptuary law.

To what end? What did Le Corbusier hope to achieve? What can explain intolerance for decoration taken to such extremes? His reasons, as we shall see, are even more interesting than his prescriptions.

First of all, decoration, as the etymology of the word suggests, was that which promotes decorum and both 'serve a certain caste of persons who practise decorum'. But as a result of the Industrial Revolution, democratisation and greater equality that 'hierarchical system of decoration has collapsed'. Whereas Louis XIV is pictured strutting around Versailles in a costume of ostrich feathers, ermine, silk, brocade and lace murmuring to himself 'By G– we're going to stun them!' Lenin, the modern ruler, is shown seated at the Rotonde before the war in the ideal Corbusian surroundings – 'on a cane chair; he has paid twenty centimes for his coffee, with a tip of one sou. He has drunk out of a small white porcelain cup. He is wearing a bowler hat and a smooth white collar. He has been writing for several hours on sheets of typing paper. His inkpot is smooth and round made from bottle glass.'[31]

Second, the post-war period was no longer the epoch of Ruskin. In the age of science and the machine people approached the mysteries of nature not through Ruskinian poetry but scientifically, without losing any sense of its profundity while gaining hugely in their power to cater for human needs. *This* was the culture of the modern age.[32]

Nothing however could be further from the truth than to suppose that Le Corbusier was a heartless, unspiritual worshipper at the altar of pure technology. He believed that in life there was a hierarchy of work and of leisure. Correspondingly there were functional equipment and furniture both in the workplace and the home to make work and household chores more efficient, while the fine arts of painting, sculpture and architecture, should serve the ends of spiritual recreation. The reason for advocating the uncluttered and efficient house as a 'machine for living in' was to free people from drudgery and chores so that they had the leisure to enjoy spiritual satisfactions.[33]

This was all the more necessary because of the mechanical nature of modern working conditions, in factory or office, which provided 'marching orders of Prussian vigour; blinkers so one can't see, shafts to keep order, and a whip behind and on the behind to maintain contact with guiding intelligence'.[34] Not that people found this unpleasant, only it left no room for their own thoughts, for personal reflection and meditation. All the more necessary, therefore, that leisure should provide the tranquillity for introspection. Le Corbusier's worry was that because modern working conditions were so hostile to it people had become terrified at the prospect of being alone and having the time to fill with their own thoughts. This was the root of his antipathy to newspapers, cinemas, dance halls, jazz, all the fashionable manifestations of modern leisure as well as the material furniture of modern life – ethnic artefacts, museums of decorative art, trashy decorated objects. All these activities and things were resorts 'to get away from oneself, never to be alone. If I were to come face to face with my soul (fearful thought)? What would I say to it?'

The targets of his animosity were condemned and proscribed, therefore, on profoundly spiritual and religious grounds. Factory and office denied the opportunity for spiritual reflection at work, and cluttered furniture denied it at home. House tools on the other hand would free the mind for contemplation.

But the situation of modern man thus furnished and entertained was even more serious, for old fashioned furniture and objects were not simply *distractions* from higher spiritual activities, they could become agents of the worst vices imaginable. Here is a strange passage objecting to the elegant wood and marble veneers of the Art Deco furniture at the 1925 Exposition:

> The final retreat for ostentation is in polished marbles with restless patterns of veining, in panelling of rare woods as exotic to us as humming birds, in glass pastes, in lacquers copied from *the excesses* of the Mandarins . . . At the same time, the Prefecture of Police has set about pursuing the pedlars of cocaine. This is all of a piece: feverish pulses and nerves shattered in the aftermath of war like to cool themselves by contact with these inhuman materials that keep us at a distance.[35]

It is not only the luxurious Art Deco of the Jazz Age which stands condemned in these terms but the naturalism of the Ruskinians, romantics and aesthetes of the fin de siecle which he regards as a 'malaise', an opium den, a narcotic haze where people 'lounge on ottomans and divans among orchids in the scented atmosphere of a seraglio'. Even bohemian cafe society on the Boul' Mich stood condemned.[36]

Here lies the nerve of Le Corbusier's ferocious attack upon decoration and the associated leisure time distractions of modern life. He feared the orientalisation of advanced Western civilisation and a loss of moral integrity in a narcotic haze induced by sensational music, cinema and decoration.

The origins of Le Corbusier's iconoclasm lie therefore in a Calvinist revulsion from everything that can distract a person from self-knowledge. His father worked in the Swiss watch-making industry and his mother came from a line of French Huguenots. His ideal home is nothing less than a secular monastery. 'We long to leave this den,' he wrote, 'to seat ourselves in a cell such as that in the convent at Fiesole.'[★37] He speaks of himself as one of the 'men of vigour in an age of heroic awakening from the powers of the spirit, in an epoch which rings out with a tragic thunder not far from doric'. Not for nothing, then, were his allusions to the perfect geometrical forms of machines as a near approximation to Plato's ideal forms, nor his invocation of the philosopher Diogenes who practised a life of austere simplicity and who was the disciple of one of Socrates's most ardent followers. Likewise Corbusier's identification with Solon. Technology was not an end in itself but a means to the end of a profound spiritual purification for all members of modern society.

★   The fifteenth-century Badia designed by Michelozzo and Cosimo de Medici.

Major design debates seem to hit Britain at intervals of every century or half-century – the 1600s, 1700s, 1750s, 1850s, 1930s and 1980s. In the 1930s there was the familiar flurry of interest manifested in books, articles, broadcasts, exhibitions, but also in a far more concerted effort to enforce the principles of good design in each of the three domains identified by Le Corbusier as the province of the architect. What is strange is that it should have been pragmatic Britain rather than systematic France where Le Corbusier's ambitions were most fully implemented, a point which did not escape the French themselves.[38]

The chief issues that were aired in the 1930s are those familiar to us in the two theorists just considered: the dangers of kitsch, of frivolous and sensationalist forms of personal consumption and recreation, of domestic inefficiency, and the related issues of poverty, slum clearance and rehousing. But these were also related to pressing issues of a macroeconomic nature which we will examine in more detail in the chapter on planning: foreign competition and protection, the drift of new industries and with them of population to London, the Midlands and the south-east of England leaving the north in a state of deep depression, high unemployment, poverty and social unrest while London suffered the problems of urban sprawl and traffic congestion.

As a focus we shall concentrate upon the 1937 government report on *The Working Class Home: Its Furnishing and Equipment* written under the chairmanship of Frank Pick who as head of London Transport had been a leading patron of good design and architecture. He was chairman of the Board of Trade's Council for Art and Industry under whose auspices the report was produced, with much of the work done by the housing expert Elizabeth Denby. She advised the London County Council and collaborated with Maxwell Fry, the pioneering British modernist, on the Kensal House working-class housing scheme for the Gas, Light and Coke Company completed in 1937.[39]

The report picks up many of the issues aired by other crusaders of the time, in particular the failure of industry to supply good modern design to consumers, particularly to the poor and those of moderate means. It also incorporates tacit assumptions which help us to understand why it was felt that sumptuary law needed to be imposed, and third, its recommendations prefigure the Utility Scheme of five years later - unsurprising since Elizabeth Denby herself was one of the experts appointed by the Board of Trade to advise on the scheme in 1942.

The background to the report was twofold. On the one hand government had to some degree initiated the renewed interest in design with the publication of the 1932 Gorell Report into the 'Production and Exhibition of Articles of Good Design and Everyday Use' and in whose wake the Council for Art and Industry was established, with a brief to promote the education of designers, industrialists, middlemen, retailers and consumers as the best solution to the problem. On the other hand between 1933 and 1939 there was a major campaign of slum clearance and rehousing in which 245,000 slums were demolished and 279,000 homes built to replace them and as a solution to overcrowding, in addition to the reconditioning of a further 439,000 existing houses.[40]

A major concern was that if former slum-dwellers brought their old bug-ridden furniture and bedding with them to their new homes the problem of infestation would start all over again. Under Section 72(2) of the 1936 Housing Act, housing authorities and associations were authorised to provide new furniture for tenants on easy terms under some kind of hire purchase. In any case it was supposed that slum clearance would itself increase the demand for cheap furniture.[41]

The purpose of the report, then, was to show that a family of two adults and two children in a two-bedroom dwelling with one living room could refurnish in approved modern design on a budget of £50 – the rough equivalent of £2,500 in 1994. The working assumptions of the report were quite unrealistic even for better-off working class families, let alone for the poorest, namely that only new furniture would be purchased, that it would be bought all at once rather than being built up gradually, and that it would be paid for in cash rather than through some form of hire purchase.[42] The lack of realism of these assumptions was acknowledged, but on careful reading it becomes apparent that the report was not aimed at the education of the families in question, even though education in design was proposed as one remedy. The target group was in fact housing authorities, both public and voluntary, using their statutory powers to provide tenants with furniture at some small addition to the rent under a form of hire purchase, either by means of the authorities buying their own stock or by ear-marking goods in local retailers which tenants could acquire with vouchers. The related exhibition of sample rooms furnished by Miss Denby was held in the Building Centre in New Bond Street, the classiest shopping street in Britain. The idea underlying the report and exhibition seems therefore to have been to show housing authorities that they could operate furniture schemes as cheaply using articles of approved design as they could if they simply took the cheapest goods on current offer in local stores.

The obvious implication is that if such schemes were stocked exclusively with such designs then the very poor who were compelled to use these furniture schemes would thereby be compelled to acquire good design, circumventing their own 'popular taste' as well as the bad taste of the buyers for the local furniture stores themselves who were also given a commercial incentive to stock such designs by a captive market. These buyers were widely regarded by campaigners for good design as perhaps the major obstacle to its wider dissemination. Nikolaus Pevsner in his 1937 *Enquiry into Industrial Art in England* observed that the usual argument – that the public wanted 'poor quality', metalwork gates, for example, did not hold good 'for the public is hardly ever asked. Almost all his trade is done through builders' merchants. It is they who dictate the taste.' And John Gloag referred to the 'reactionary retail buyers who insist that they know what the public wants' as 'those arrogant obstructionists'. This was part and parcel of a widespread disillusion with free markets and laissez-faire during the 1930s.[43]

The policy implicit in the report, therefore, was to impose a limited form of sumptuary control, if not actual sumptuary law, upon the poorest section of the community, less able than any to call their homes their castles.[44]

Nonetheless at first sight the content of the Report seems quite sensible and far less extreme and doctrinaire than the opinions of other modernist campaigners of the time. It pays attention to the practical issues of wear and tear caused by children and by men engaged in dirty trades. On the level of taste it admits 'that there is a desire for pattern . . . There seems to be a general reluctance to look at anything bare and plain.' While clearly disapproving of this – 'in many houses there is an accumulation of patterns which is often conflicting and tiresome' – it nonetheless accepted, grudgingly maybe, that some compromise between the high principles of the Council for Art and Industry and popular taste was necessary. 'We felt, however, that it would be unreasonable to expect the average working-class home, or any other class of home, to be furnished with the uncompromising severity which some modern tastes dictate.' Even so tacit assumptions emerge: first of all in the report's criteria of good and bad design; second, and more interestingly, in their reasons for believing that it was necessary to promote good design.[45]

Bad design in furniture comprised things that were flimsy in construction because more money had been spent upon making them showy and decorative and less upon their basic durability. Highly decorated things were also less easy to keep clean and hence posed a potential threat to hygiene. The basic reason given for why people might have preferred decorative or showy pieces of furniture – upholstered three-piece suites were singled out for special condemnation – was that they wanted to impress their friends and neighbours or they were imitating the past fashions of the higher social classes, a reason also advanced against the practice of buying secondhand. It was however just permissible to have decoration on curtains and crockery.

Good design, on the other hand, comprised things that were durable above all, but also simple in form, of a 'reserved taste', well proportioned, highly practical, hygienic and easy to clean because of the absence of moulded decorations. In addition good design would be classless design – there should be no need for the trickle-down effect of secondhand status symbols from one social class to another, instead there should be a single tradition of good design for all.

The reasons for the necessity of good design are more complicated and peculiar. It seems to have had something to do with character training through the ownership of personal property, as a means of acquiring self-respect, tidiness and personal and social hygiene:

> It was thought that something should be done to give each member of the family a place for his own personal possessions . . . Only in such circumstances, it seems to us, can personal respect be properly developed and the elements of a tidy manner of life secured. Human character would seem to be enlarged by owning something, so long as it is something of daily use and service and not something held for the mere sake of ownership, and ownership is not complete without a place in which to maintain it.[46]

The 'mere sake of ownership' seems to suggest status symbols, but could also refer to any form of cupidity, acquisitiveness or desire to own articles of beauty or curiosity as opposed to objects of utility. This seems to be confirmed by the next observation: 'Personal hygiene again depends upon the separate ownership of the means to cleanliness. The Committee could hardly contemplate common use of toothbrushes, for example, and added to the toothbrush there might quite well be a coloured mug, in the new plastic materials, which was readily identifiable as mine or thine.' Finally, there comes an observation that Loos would have considered quintessentially Anglo-Saxon: 'One witness went so far as to say that the fitted wash basin was the most civilizing influence of which she could think.'

The report also paid a great deal of attention to the design and layout of working-class living rooms in the new flats, which were indeed small for a family, varying between 170 and 200 square feet, 13 or 14 feet square, and which had to serve most of the social needs of the family. Two important paragraphs are entitled 'The uses to which the home is put: congestion in the home' and 'The use of the living room – its multiple purposes'. If the word 'congestion' suggests the contemporary problem of traffic congestion in London on account of the unplanned shift in the location of industry, this is not coincidental. These paragraphs stress that with so many different activities – children's play, homework, family meals and social life – taking place in the living room, the most careful planning of layout and furniture was essential, hence another reason why the three-piece suite was unsuitable.[47]

This concentration upon planning and household efficiency is another more general theme in the design propaganda of the period prefigured by Loos's interest in plumbing and by Le Corbusier. His maisonette '*de l'esprit nouveau*' was designed to replace 'human labour by the machine and good organisation' (Plate 97). This stems directly from Taylorism, the American system of scientific management based in part upon what have come to be known as time-and-motion studies of a worker's movements. Frederick Taylor's work began in the 1880s, and his *Principles of Scientific Management* was published in 1911. Le Corbusier's 'Manual of the Dwelling' was intended as an antidote to houses whose occupants 'hardly dare to walk through the labyrinth of their furniture'. Elsewhere he described his modern block of maisonettes in which

> modern achievement, applied to so important an enterprise, replaces human labour by the machine and by good organisation; constant hot water, central heating, refrigerators, vacuum cleaners, pure water etc. Servants are no longer of necessity tied to the house;

97 *Pavillon de L'Esprit Nouveau* by Le Corbusier at the 1925 Paris Exposition des Arts decoratifs. A prototype home for the Ville Contemporaine – the tree shows that nature was integral to Corbusier's vision of 'Soleil, l'Espace, Verdure'.

they come here, as they would to a factory, and do their eight hours; in this way an active staff is available day and night. The provision of food, whether cooked or not, is arranged by a special purchasing service, which makes for quality and economy.

It is a wonderfully aseptic document, the kind of thing that inspired Aldous Huxley's *Brave New World*.[48]

On a more practical level, Elizabeth Denby herself reported the American finding that a cook took 281 steps to make a cake, which could be reduced to 45 simply by replanning the kitchen. The kitchen was 'a vital domestic workshop' from which much of the work of the rest of the house was directed: supplying food, hot water, management and cleaning to the other rooms as well as providing a dining and sitting room for the servants in a large house and the family in a small one. Consequently, Denby drew a parallel between the wasteful effects of a badly-planned kitchen and those of an unplanned town. If there were muddle and congestion in the kitchen, there would be dirt, disease and wasted work in the rest of the house, likewise in the town or city. Moreover, wasted work in the home must have social and economic repercussions for society as a whole (Plate 98).[49]

But far more than efficiency, domestic or even national, was at stake. The clue to the underlying issue is given by the following statements: 'Any scheme for assisting the furnishing of working class homes should start from the basic idea that the home is to be made as far as possible a retreat and a refuge from the rigour of daily life.'[50] The heart of this sanctuary was the living room: 'the place where warmth and comfort and some repose

98 Modern Kitchen by Maxwell Fry, 1930s. Modernists considered the kitchen to be the engine room of the house – if it were planned the efficiency of the family and hence of society as a whole would be improved.

have to be found, and where, with the minimum disturbance, the family must read, eat, talk, work and play, see their friends and generally employ their leisure *without spending money.*' The italics are mine, and upon their significance hangs the fundamental explanation we are searching for. To throw light upon this we need to turn aside from the working-class furnishing report to the influential and representative ideas of two men to whom much of the credit for the establishment of the Welfare State has been attributed – William Beveridge and Seebohm Rowntree.

Seebohm Rowntree (1871–1954) was the son of Joseph Rowntree, who founded the international cocoa and chocolate business based in York.[51] The family were Quakers, Liberals and devoted themselves to social work and philanthropy in the city where they became the largest employers. Seebohm himself was a director of the company but his reputation as the 'Einstein of the Welfare State' rests upon his 1901 book *Poverty: A Study of Town Life*, a meticulous analysis of 11,560 families, virtually the entire working-class population at the time. He was the first social scientist to make the crucial distinction between primary and secondary poverty, that is between those 'whose incomes were insufficient to provide the bare necessities of physical efficiency' however carefully they budgeted, which he estimated at 10 per cent of York's population (15 per cent of the working class population) and the further 18 per cent who suffered from secondary poverty, which meant that their income was adequate but was spent unwisely. His fundamental purpose was not, however, to argue that better management and morals could alleviate secondary poverty but that primary poverty was no fault of the poor themselves and could only be remedied by the state and other bodies in providing improved housing, slum clearance, pensions, unemployment benefit and a national minimum wage. Rowntree and his father were responsible for establishing the village of New Earswick, designed by Raymond Unwin who later designed Hampstead Garden Suburb and the first garden city at Letchworth; they instituted a form of minimum wage at their own works; and they introduced one of the first company pension schemes in Britain.[52]

In 1941 Rowntree published a 'second social survey of York' entitled *Poverty and Progress* based upon research done in 1935 and 1936, once again covering the entire working-class population of the city, 16,362 families. But on this occasion he extended his enquiries beyond family budgets on food and household expenses to include a new section on 'leisure time activities'. Part of the reason for this was that he discovered that the numbers living in primary poverty in 1936 had fallen from 15 per cent to 7 per cent of the working-class population and that the living standards of the working classes as a whole had improved by as much as 30 per cent in spite of the depression of the 1930s.[53] He was not complacent about this. Far from it, he considered that poverty must be eradicated completely and indeed that it could be 'without dislocating industry or our national finances. [It] can be removed just as the slums, once thought to be inevitable, are being removed today.' However, and this was the reason for his new emphasis upon leisure, he also considered that 'we must not rest content with raising to a higher level the physical standard of those who are living in poverty.' The case for eradicating poverty through state policies had been made, and poverty was in the process of being overcome, now his overwhelming concern was with the overall quality of life.[54]

While improving the material standard of living might be difficult, he believed that 'to raise the mental and spiritual life of the whole nation to a markedly higher level will be an infinitely harder task.' Hence his interest in leisure pursuits.[55] 'It is hardly an exaggeration to say that the way in which communities spend their leisure is a criterion of the national character. The kind of work people do . . . [is] largely determined by circumstances they cannot control, but they can do what they will with their leisure hours.'[56] He found that here too there had been a great improvement since 1900. Then, because there were few counter-attractions, working-class people spent their leisure either in pubs or, if they were young, lounging around their neighbourhoods or 'aimlessly' walking up and down the main street of York at night trying to 'get off with' the girls. But in 1936 people had far more comfortable homes with gardens, wireless sets, there were free libraries, cinemas, repertory theatres, music halls and dance halls to visit, they could bicycle out into the open country, play team games, take excursions and go rambling. While he welcomed this variety, particularly insofar as it led to a reduction in gambling and drinking, he wished to alert the nation to new dangers as well as to insist upon the inherent value or worthlessness of particular leisure-time activities.[57]

On the basis of the way they spent their leisure he divided the working class into 'the more and the less serious-minded members of the community'. The less serious were those who drank in pubs, gambled, went to the cinema, the dance hall, pursued the opposite sex and watched spectator sports. The more serious-minded were those who, if they drank did so in licensed clubs, those who went to the theatre, opera, concerts or engaged in choral singing, those who actively participated in team sports, went bicycling and rambling, and finally those who stayed at home tending their gardens, listening to the wireless, reading, doing their homework if they were at school, even perhaps having a quiet drink by their own fireside bought at the off-licence.[58]

This kind of attitude to leisure pursuits which Rowntree articulates so precisely in his survey was widespread during the 1930s and it explains the priority placed by the working-class furnishing report upon the living room uncongested by bulky and showy furniture where rehoused working-class families could 'employ their leisure *without spending money*'

SLUM HOUSES
(Before site was cleared)

COUNCIL HOUSES BUILT ON THE SAME SITE
(Occupied by tenants who previously lived in slum houses)

99   Slums and rebuilding from *Poverty and Progress*, 1941, by Seebohm Rowntree, with Beveridge one of the founders of the Welfare State. They believed that good homes with gardens would stop the working class squandering its money on drink and passive entertainments like watching football.

Magicoal Fires

BRITISH MADE

JACOBEAN. 3 kW.

Antique bright finish (rustless)

Supplied with 3 kW. heating and full heat control switch mounted on grate.

E.78916

Height 30 in.   Width 16 in.   Depth 16 in.

£12 0 0 each

E.78917

Height 30 in.   Width 20 in.   Depth 16 in.

£14 0 0 each

E.78918

Height 30 in.   Width 24 in.   Depth 16 in.

£16 0 0 each

Can be fitted with Magicoal-Plus without extra charge.

THE "STARBERRY" 2 kW.

A Magicoal-Plus model, with bright rustless bars. Supplied with full heat control switches and 6 ft. flex.

Height 21 in.   Width 16 in.   Depth 11 in.

E.78911   Oxidised Copper   ...   **72/6** each

E.78912   Oxidised Silver   ...   **72/6** each

If fitted with detachable Kettle Boiler 2/- extra

THE "LOUIS RAYBERRY" 3 kW.

Antique and bright rustless finish. Supplied with full heat control switches, 6 ft. flex and Magicoal-Plus.

Height 26 in.   Width 21 in.   Depth 11 in.

Height without back 20 in.

E.79399 With or without back   **£8 8s.** each

100   Artificial coal–glow electric fire from 1933 catalogue. Harmless as they appear, modernists anathematised them as escapist fantasies which could drug the populace into acceptance of fascism.

(Plate 99). These living rooms, if equipped with furniture of good design, would facilitate Rowntree's serious-minded pursuits within small families, headed by a non-drinking and non-gambling father and an efficient housekeeping mother who liked to read and listen to the wireless in her spare time, and children who had the space to do their homework, reminding us of the sixteenth-century ideal of the protestant monastery.

But why did Rowntree, along with others, consider certain pursuits to be unserious and others serious? The answer to this question provides a further explanation for why good design was thought, by some, to be so important. It is summed up in his definition of recreation: 'True recreation is constructive, and wholesome recreation implies *re-creating* physical, intellectual, or moral vitality.'[59] This kind of leisure pursuit would need to involve the active powers of the body and the mind. But other pursuits were likely to be escapist (cinema), undemanding (thrillers and sentimental lovestories), undiscriminating (Radio Luxembourg), or stimulating the craving for 'a bit of fun' and sexual adventure (cinema, music halls and dance halls). With the decline in the influence of parents and of the churches and the dangers of escapism, leisure carried the heavy burden of responsibility for the formation of the character of the nation's citizens, particularly of its youth.[60] Rowntree's concluding paragraph, published in 1941 when Britain stood alone, sums it up:

> Everywhere democracy is challenged. A totalitarian State does not demand high intellectual or spiritual standards from its people; on the contrary it can only function successfully when they cease to think for themselves and are willing to obey the command to worship false gods. But a democratic State can only flourish if the level of intelligence of the community is high and its spiritual life dynamic.[61]

We have met this concern with the quality of leisure and the dangers of escapism in the writings of Le Corbusier, and it was widely voiced in relation to the design of homes and their furnishings. For instance, the accusation that traditional styles of furnishings were escapist, was tied to the more general view that both suburbia and garden cities were a form of romantic escapism. This was considered a 'bad thing' because the tendency of artists, architects and designers to run away from the problems of life in the modern city in the early years of the Industrial Revolution was blamed for the failure of the nineteenth century to harness the power of the machine to the creation of beautiful cities and beautiful houses. As Pevsner put it in 1936, commenting upon the mid-nineteenth century,

> Demand was increasing from year to year, but demand from an uneducated and debased population, living a slave-life in filth and penury. The artist withdrew in disgust from such squalor. It was not for him to work for the needs of those classes, to condescend to the taste of the majority of his fellow men, to meddle with the 'Arts Not Fine'.[62]

A year later Pevsner took this argument a stage further, arguing that the imitative illusionism of popular furniture, such as those electric fires made to look like glowing embers (Plate 100), was a form of sensationalism invented to bring some pleasure into the joyless lives of working-class city-dwellers, and he associated it with Hollywood movies: 'A splendour which reality does not concede is brought into our humble surroundings by meretricious industrial products, which achieve in permanence some of the elating effect that for a few hours is bestowed upon us by the Hollywood heroes' fantastic mode of life in the pictures.' The contention here was that such furnishings were a narcotic, creating a permanent dream-world within the home. This was a widespread fear in the 1930s, not merely amongst design pundits but also literary critics. Dr F.R. Leavis employed the language of drug addiction to describe the effect of the popular novel in providing 'the very reverse of recreation, in that it tends, not to strengthen and refresh the addict for living, but to increase his unfitness by habituating him to weak evasions, to the refusal to face reality at all'. Kitsch was also associated with the dictatorships, who were accused of using it for the purposes of promoting 'the illusion that the masses rule', disguising the chains of the people with garlands of kitsch. This kind of attack echoes that of Rousseau upon the rococo of LouisXV and of Macchiavelli upon the pageant-laden tyranny of Medicean Florence, and perhaps explains how Pevsner could argue that the 'fight against the shoddy design of those goods by which most of our fellow-men are surrounded becomes a moral duty' – part of '*the* social question of our time'.[63]

To sum up. Good design in furniture and domestic equipment was of vital concern to the state because it contributed to personal and social hygiene. On another level it helped to promote good planning and hence efficiency in the home, both in the kitchen and in the family activities that took place in the living room. Efficient domestic 'production' necess-arily contributed to national production. But over and above, this good modern design in a comfortable well-designed modern home stimulated the intellectual and spiritual faculties while keeping at bay all the escapist, narcotic and sensationalist tendencies of modern life which discouraged a serious-minded approach to citizenship. Here, once again, applied at this period to working-class life, are the values of *The Spectator*.

While this explains why people should have felt that good design was a highly desirable civilising influence and very much 'everybody's business', it does not altogether explain why it should need to be made compulsory. To explain that we need to examine the workings of the Utility Scheme itself and to look at the highly influential ideas of William Beveridge in his report *Full Employment in a Free Society* published in November 1944 as a personal venture two years after his government report *Social Insurance and Allied Services*. This laid down the blueprint for the Welfare State with a comprehensive programme of social insurance, a national health service, old age pensions to tackle what he called the 'five giants on the road of reconstruction' – Want, Disease, Ignorance, Squalor and Idleness. Whereas the official Beveridge Report itself proposed remedies for Want and Disease, *Full Employment* was dedicated to the giant Idleness, but it also had another side, as we shall soon see.[64]

Although the picture of the 1930s in Britain as a 'Bleak Age' of unrelieved slump and mass unemployment has been challenged by recent historians who confirm Rowntree's observations that working-class living standards, even in a northern city like York, had risen considerably while the southern regions of the country enjoyed considerable growth, nonetheless at the time the problem of mass unemployment was regarded as the most important, requiring urgent action, by figures like Beveridge and Keynes, who had given Beveridge much advice on the 1942 report.[65] Beveridge was fully aware that the impact of mass unemployment was concentrated in the depressed regions but he insisted that it must be regarded as a national rather than a local problem. By virtue of the inequity of its impact – the country was divided into two nations, just as it had been in the nineteenth and in the sixteenth centuries. In the worst year, 1932, unemployment was double in Wales and the north than it was in London, 28.2 per cent against 13.5 per cent and in 1937 15 per cent against 6.3 per cent for London. Beveridge's concern, therefore, was not merely with achieving full employment but with ensuring that work should be available everywhere in Britain.

His definition of full employment was a state of affairs where anyone who had lost his job should be able to find a new one, without delay, at a fair wage and within his capacity. To find a new job he proposed that there should always be a small surplus of jobs over those seeking work in all parts of the country.[66]

Beveridge identified three causes of unemployment: the lack of an effective demand for the products of industry, sufficient demand in other words to require the full use of the entire labour force; misdirected demand, that is, demand for goods which the existing labour force were unable to make or for goods which were made in places where workmen could not easily go to; and third the practice of employers in maintaining a pool of unemployed workers to reduce wages and for other purposes.[67]

In the 1920s and 1930s, he argued, demand had been both inadequate and misdirected. War however had confirmed 'the possibility of securing full employment by socialization of demand'. The means to this end were two-fold – a new kind of annual budget designed to maintain effective demand to secure full employment in addition to the budget's traditional function of raising revenue to pay for government expenditure; second a system of national planning for land use to direct work to the existing areas where people were located rather than expecting people to move their homes to where businessmen wished to run their concerns. The issue of land-use planning is one which will be examined in Chapter 3. Here we shall look at the management of effective demand which also contributed to the location of employment.[68]

The annual budget would secure effective demand by influencing private spending and by determining public spending in five ways: through public spending by the government on defence, education, health etc.; through public investment both in state-owned businesses and in private businesses; through state purchases and subsidised resale of certain necessities of life; and finally through the control of private consumption by 're-distributing income, by measures of Social Security, and by progressive taxation.' Of these, the control of private consumption, through taxation, was the precondition for the other four, since taxation would provide much of the funds required, as well as being an end in itself. This Beveridge made clear in a short section of crucial importance where he explained his larger philosophy of Social Demand. There he vigorously rejected the alternative policy of creating effective demand by increasing private spending and consumption through reduced taxation and a minimum of state interference and planning. He gave three reasons for rejecting the policy of a free market economy.[69]

First, he argued, the employment so created 'might not be wisely directed', in other words popular consumption might create a demand for skills other than those which had lain unemployed, and in places where unemployment was low, as indeed had been the case during the 1930s. As he put it, 'Money spent on drink does not give employment to the miner but to the brewer; money spent on milk does not help to solve the problem of the unemployed engineer.' Since the problem was urgent, one could not wait for the miner to retrain as a brewer, nor was it acceptable to break up existing communities by expecting people to move to where work was to be found. In addition, privately directed consumption could well favour imported goods and provide employment for foreigners rather than the British. This marks a return to the mercantilist policies examined in the earlier sections of this book and would not have appeared unfamiliar to Lord Burghley.

Second, and more directly related to the issue of home furnishings, he argued that popular consumption might go on luxuries rather than necessaries like good housing and nutritious food, on things that were not socially the most desirable. Here his paternalism, and his affinity with Rowntree (whom he had consulted on his 1942 report) and the working class furnishing report, shows without disguise.

In a free market economy, consumers can buy only that which is offered to them, and *that which is offered is not necessarily that which is of most advantage to them*. It is that which appears to give the best prospect of profit to the producer. In a free market economy under pressure of salesmanship the negroes of the Southern States of America have, to a large extent, obtained automobiles and radios and have not obtained good housing, sanitation and medical service. In the free market economy of Britain under pressure of salesmanship the citizens have devoted appreciable parts of their increasing resources to funeral benefits of little social importance furnished at excessive cost or to the waste of football pools and other frivolous amusements.[70]

There can be no doubt that he had read *Poverty and Progress*, and he looked to State management of effective demand as a cure for regional unemployment but also as a way of killing two birds with one stone. It is equally clear from this that he had in mind high taxation not only of the middle but of the more prosperous working classes, to achieve the objective of improving the moral fibre of the nation. Money which they might spend unwisely should be taken from them for the state to spend wisely on their behalf.

But it was his third reason which was the decisive one against the policy of encouraging private consumption. This was the fact that many services considered to be essential for raising standards of health and happiness could only be obtained at reasonable cost through collective provision: state nursery schools, playgrounds, hospitals, libraries and good housing would achieve economies of scale. Not only, therefore, could people not be trusted to use their discretionary spending in their own, and the state's, best interests, but it was in addition more economical for the state to provide.[71]

Hence the need for compulsion in enforcing Social Demand. This was achieved through high rates of personal taxation for the less well-off as well as redistributive taxation of the better-off and was envisaged by Beveridge (who was representative of a very powerful body of opinion) as a means of redistributing the objects of consumption from the luxuries of what we have come to call the 'consumer society' to those things which Rowntree's more serious-minded members of the community would choose for themselves. In this emphasis upon public expenditure, upon public service architecture and upon the discouragement of private luxury consumption, we have the explanation for the fervent crusade for Good Design.

Obviously Beveridge writing in 1944 and Rowntree in 1941 could not directly have influenced the 1937 Furnishing Report nor the Utility Scheme of 1942, but their views are representative of the frame of mind which lay behind these manifestations of sumptuary control, echoing the Tudor Common Weal, and it only remains in this chapter to provide a short account of the Utility Scheme itself.[72]

When the Second World War started, the government controlled prices and restricted the supply of timber to the furniture and other industries. After the Blitz began in the autumn of 1940, however, some provision had to be made to supply household furnishings and equipment for bomb victims (bombees as they were called) as well as for newly-weds setting up home; otherwise, a black market would have led to high prices and profiteering in secondhand furniture. In the early stages of the scheme, in 1941, emergency furniture was manufactured to basic specifications and designs akin to those used for government offices. The idea was simply to make replacement furniture of a utilitarian kind available at the cheapest prices and with the least demand upon the supply of raw materials and labour. At this point aesthetics were not a primary concern.

So things might have continued, had not Hugh Dalton become President of the Board of Trade early in 1942. It seems that he – influenced presumably by the pre-war propaganda for Modern Design – grafted on to existing plans to control prices and the consumption of timber the idea of specifying 'furniture of good, sound construction in simple but agreeable designs for sale at reasonable prices'. And these few words were radically to alter the scheme's parameters. In July 1942 a committee of experts was appointed, several of whom, like John Gloag, Elizabeth Denby and Gordon Russell, had played leading roles in the campaign for Good Modern Design during the 1930s. By October prototypes had been designed, manufactured and put on public exhibition. By the beginning of 1943 the furniture was on sale in the shops. At the same time a similar scheme was introduced for pottery and, although there was no rationing, decorated and inessential wares were prohibited, and Dalton ordered that only undecorated natural clay colours were to be produced. It also, and most important of all for the wartime economy, applied to clothing (Plate 101).

Absolutely crucial to the Utility Scheme was its exemption from purchase tax, then as high as 33 per cent. This meant that any furniture manufactured to designs that were not Utility would have been priced out of the mass market. This is indeed exactly what

101　Wartime rationing provided the opportunity to impose sumptuary law in the form of the utility Scheme, in Britain for the first time since the death of Elizabeth I. Only furniture of approved designs could be manufactured and sold.

happened in the post-war period, for the Utility Scheme continued until the Conservative government repealed it in 1953 and removed the exemption from purchase tax, which by 1948 had risen to 66⅔ per cent. By 1949, because of increasing opposition from the furniture manufacturers, the scheme was changed from one that completely prescribed the appearance of all furniture to one which merely set limits on the size and quality of furniture, with the considerable inducement to the customers who enjoyed a tax discount of forty percent on what they would have had to pay for non-Utility goods. So, for the four years from 1949 to 1953, the scheme became a government-backed guarantee of good value and good design.

The essential point is that the design reformers of the 1930s used the exigencies of war to advance their objectives for the promotion, even enforcement, of Good Modern Design during peacetime. To achieve price control and the economy of raw materials alone, the Good Design aspect of Utility was clearly unnecessary. Indeed, in one respect, the scheme was quite extravagant, since only the more expensive hardwoods such as oak and mahogany were used.

Utility, then, was a wartime experiment in the imposition of Good Design, part of Planning for Reconstruction. Writing in 1946, Gordon Russell felt 'that to raise the whole standard of furniture for the mass of the people was not a bad war job', and he looked forward to the possibility of using 'the utility specification as the basis of a quality mark in the post-control period'. Moreover, the Council for Industrial Design, launched by Dalton in 1944 to 'promote by all practicable means the improvement of design in the products of British Industry', grew out of the Utility Scheme; its kitemark was just such a quality mark as Russell proposed in 1946, which is hardly surprising since he became its first director.

CHAPTER 2
Modern Architecture

THE INTERIOR

With the Utility Scheme, the sacred divide between public and private had been breached, justifying fully the widespread fear that an Englishman's home, particularly if he were poor, was no longer his castle. But this was far from being the only effect of the Modern Movement on the previously honoured distinction between people's private and public affairs. The movement's ideology also resulted in radical changes to the ways in which both architecture and town planning were controlled.

In its very early days, with figures such as Loos and even with Gropius and Mies van der Rohe, Modernism had much in common with earlier architectural styles in that it worked within the established framework of the city. The 'Looshaus' in Michelerplatz in Vienna, for example, represented a way of placing a building on one corner of a square that differed from more traditional approaches only in the amount and type of decoration that Loos used. The same is true of Modernist buildings in London from between the wars, constrained by the London Building Act regulations governing height and street lines: the Daily Express building in Fleet Street; Simpsons in Piccadilly; Peter Jones in Sloane Square. Mature Modernism on the other hand declared that it had no truck with 'style', that it was not a 'style' at all but a 'design method'.

The essential feature of this method was that the plan of a building must proceed 'from within to without', that the exterior was 'the result of an interior' and neither a buffer between public and private nor something superimposed upon a building by the laws and conventions of the city.[1] One crucial rationale of modern architecture, for reasons given by Le Corbusier and others, was that nothing should impede the achievement of the most desirable domestic or commercial interior; hence the unparalleled attention that was given by architects to the design of furniture and everyday things. Any obstacle that did impede the creation of the new interior, such as the existing pattern of streets or skyline, or the ownership of building plots, or regulations that insisted upon the adherence of new buildings to the pre-existing pattern: all had to be swept away. In the interests of creating a new kind of private interior, the Modernists declared war upon the traditional townscape.

For these reasons one cannot discuss modern architecture properly without discussing modern town planning. As the writers of the 1930s reiterated: the true modern architecture could only flourish and its benefits could only be fully enjoyed if the old regulations were to go. Thus F.R.S. Yorke began his often-reprinted anthology *The Modern House*, first published in 1934, with an apology for the fact that he dealt only with the 'individual villa type house'. He did not pretend that 'the building of villas was a good, or even a possible, solution to the problem of housing the people'. But he accepted that people would continue to want to live in detached or semi-detached houses until the time when 'land is so controlled that flats can be planned in proper relationship to neighbourhoods and to open

326

space'. The rules that were to govern the modern city, therefore, were to be determined to a considerable extent by the internal requirements of the modern home – or, rather, the interpretation of those needs by Modernist architects and their intellectual allies. In addition, the modern city needed to accommodate the motor car. There was to be no let or hindrance, in the form of public regulations, upon the freedom of architects to work out ways of satisfying these requirements and express and realise their ideas. We shall therefore proceed in a Modernist manner, from inside out, discussing here the architecture of individual buildings before turning to town planning in the following chapter.[2]

So what were the qualities of the new interior that determined the plan of the modern building? Several features have already been mentioned. There was the evolution to a greater simplicity of form and absence of decoration, the cult of hygiene and personal cleanliness, the contribution of time-and-motion methods to the design of the house and particularly to the kitchen, the machine aesthetic and the cult of mass production. We have also referred to Le Corbusier's idea of the home as a machine for living in, a 'House-Tool'. Over and above was the feeling, expressed in the most vivid terms by Le Corbusier in the following passage, that the style of living had totally changed and that the home had to adapt to these new conditions, in exactly the same way as the factory and the office had done.

THE MANUAL OF THE DWELLING

Demand a bathroom looking south, one of the largest rooms in the house or flat, the old drawing-room for instance. One wall to be entirely glazed, opening if possible on to a balcony for sun baths; the most up-to-date fittings with a shower-bath and gymnastic appliances.

An adjoining room to be a dressing-room in which you can dress and undress. Never undress in your bedroom. It is not a clean thing to do and makes the room horribly untidy. In this room demand fitments for your linen and clothing, not more than 5 feet in height, with drawers, hangers, etc.

Demand one really large living room instead of a number of small ones.

Demand bare walls in your bedroom, your living room and your dining-room. Built-in fittings to take the place of much of the furniture, which is expensive to buy, takes up too much room and needs looking after.

If you can, put the kitchen at the top of the house to avoid smells.

Demand concealed or diffused lighting.

Demand a vacuum cleaner.

Buy only practical furniture and never buy decorative 'pieces'. If you want to see bad taste, go into the houses of the rich. Put only a few pictures on your walls and none but good ones.

Keep your odds and ends in drawers or cabinets.

The gramophone or the pianola or wireless will give you exact interpretations of first-rate music, and you will avoid catching cold in the concert hall, and the frenzy of the virtuoso.[3]

This was taken up by the young British architects and writers of the 1930s who argued that the plan of a house had always been determined by its social functions. The mediaeval house centred around the hall while, in succeeding centuries, more and more private rooms were added for the purpose of display. But now, in the modern age of labour-saving devices, electricity, foreign travel, the disappearance of the dynastic family and the family home that went on for generations, out-of-door leisure pursuits, the cinema, dancing, motoring and motor-bikes, the old pretentious house plan had become obsolete (Plate 102). Boxy little rooms were unnecessary; modern people needed a large open-plan living apartment surrounded by smaller rationally planned service rooms such as the kitchen, bedrooms, bathroom.[4]

102 Modern Contrasts. One of a series much reproduced in the thirties allegedly showing a Victorian house transformed room by room, object by object, into a modern interior.

For the same reasons, the blazing Dickensian fire crackling in the hearth, standing for the very essence of English life and Cowper's ideal of 'the undisturbed retirement' of the family home, was out of tune with an age in which people went to the cinema, returning home to switch on an electric fire rather than facing the chore of relighting a heap of dead ashes. The living room no longer needed to be planned around the fireplace. With central heating and air-conditioning, the air could be heated, cooled, humidified, de-humidified and cleansed, and as a result the living room could be freely planned around different areas for different activities, removing internal congestion. Hence the importance of the flat roof which, unlike the pitched roof, did not dictate the shape of the house plan. With a flat roof the stairs could be top-lit and placed wherever it was convenient, instead of having to be next to an external wall for the purpose of lighting. Of course such an argument was absurd; for centuries in English terraced houses the stairs had indeed been tucked away in the centre of the house and, in grander examples, were top-lit as well.[5]

But over and above these functional arguments was the glamorous image, often reproduced, of the roof garden designed to echo the decks and sporting facilities of transatlantic liners: a new modern world of sunlight, hygiene and the breezy, unstuffy out-of-doors which Loos had celebrated, a little timidly perhaps, in his vignettes of the English sportsman riding his horse over heath and moor and madly peddling his bicycle.

THE STRUGGLE FOR LIGHT

There was widespread agreement that sunlight was a good thing both psychologically and for reasons of health. Indeed, one can go even further and say with Le Corbusier that the

Modern Movement was the culmination of 'the century-old struggle for light, the struggle for the window'. Light, daylight moreover, was a symbol with almost religious resonance for the Modernists. Sunlight breaking through the grimy windows of both the Victorian slum and middle-class home; sunlight sweeping away all the heavy drapes and encrusted wall-papers; sunlight cleansing the atmosphere of the heavily-polluted industrial city; sunlight warming and invigorating the bodies of a new generation. It became a moral duty in the minds of many architects to design buildings which permitted the maximum of daylighting.[6]

Black and white photographs of these modern buildings, as crisp and gleaming as a Cunard liner, could be found in any book on modern life or in the cinema, as well as in books on modern architecture itself. The twentieth-century attitude to sunlight was quoted as a key instance of the gulf that divided modern people from the past and from primitive peoples. 'In earlier times sunlight was regarded as harmful rather than beneficial', wrote Yorke. 'Through medical research we have learnt better . . . we take sun-baths and even artificial sun-ray treatments, we like large windows, and sometimes fill them with special glass to admit the ultra-violet rays.' (Today, of course, *we* have learnt better, and strive to protect ourselves against the carcinogenic ultra-violet rays and, in particular, to prevent any further deterioration of the ozone layer which protects us against them.)[7]

This propaganda culminated in one of the most sumptuous books of the Modern Movement in Britain, Raymond McGrath's *Glass in Architecture and Decoration* of 1937. McGrath saw two major virtues in large glass windows. The first was the view that they provided of external nature, the pure contemplation of which was, in his opinion, the mark of increasing intellectual enlightenment since the Renaissance in contrast to the more primitive attitude to nature in the middle ages when windows were small and filled with stained glass to encourage contemplation of the inner world and of the spirit. The second was, of course, the value of admitting daylight into rooms themselves. Together, these qualities gave rise to a third: the ideal of free internal planning. McGrath referred particularly to department stores and anticipated a new type, one in which there would be no facade, but the steel frame would be exposed, with glass forming the only screen between the street and the inside of the shop (Plate 103). He illustrated smaller shops where the use of huge plate-glass windows represented a step in the right direction, and contrasted this to shops like Selfridge's, designed, in his view, primarily to create an impressive building.[8]

McGrath's book is interesting in that both he and his co-authors understood the huge problems of having large areas of glass in a building. First there was the increased heat loss in the winter, putting the temperature of the building at the mercy of the weather. It was argued, however, that this could be prevented through a combination of double-glazing and air-conditioning. But double-glazing presented more problems. It was expensive, as was air-conditioning, and, by sealing the interior of the building from the outside, the *direct* contact between the occupant of a building and the open air was sacrificed, paradoxically, for the sake of the view. There was no mention of 'Sick Building Syndrome' and other problems associated with the hermetically sealed building – they were to be discovered fifty years later. But there was the problem of the greenhouse effect, namely that in summer an undesirable quantity of solar heat might be admitted but not allowed to escape owing to the operation of glass as a one-way heat valve. McGrath's suggested remedy for this was either forced ventilation, blinds, or, for the best results, two coats of whitewash. This last, of course, was recommended only for roof-lights; on any other type of window it would negate the visual advantages of having glass in the first place.[9]

Drawbacks on such a scale, openly admitted, would have deterred most people. But for the Modernists glass was the very symbol of liberation and enlightenment and it could not be sacrificed for reasons of pettifogging practicality. This commitment to daylighting could be taken to extraordinary lengths, as in the case of the 1950s slab-type office block whose form was developed to permit the maximum penetration of daylight into relatively shallow

103 Citroën showroom, Paris from McGrath's *Glass*, 1937. Plate glass admitting daylight was a symbol of modern enlightenment.

offices (their maximum depth from the window was about 20 to 25 feet). But, whereas half of this area would receive adequate daylighting, the inner half required supplementary, artificial light which had to be intense enough to harmonise with the daylight. This produced expensive electricity bills, on account not only of the lighting but of the air-conditioning required to remove the heat generated by the lights. Consequently, tinted glass and Venetian blinds were introduced in these buildings during the 1960s in order to lower the level of natural lighting on the periphery of the building, reduce the necessary level of artificial light at the core, cut energy bills and reduce glare. It might have been considered simpler to employ conventional sash or casement windows and have less daylight in the first place.[10]

This point becomes even more serious when it is realised that much of the thinking which led to both high-rise office building and to the comprehensive redevelopment of the cities after the war, was based almost exclusively upon the need to create the conditions in which such intensely sunlit buildings could be constructed. But this is a subject to which we will return in a subsequent chapter.

FREE LOVE AND FREE PLANNING

Modern architecture, therefore, was modern design writ large. Modern houses were the kind of buildings needed to accommodate all the new and legitimate desires of modern men and modern women and all the everyday furniture and equipment for those lives. Few people in England typified this new free modern life-style better than the businessman Jack Pritchard who, in the 1930s, set up the Isokon Furniture Company for which Marcel Breuer designed the famous reclining chair, and who also commissioned the Isokon Flats in Lawn Road, Hampstead (Plate 104). Pritchard had been brought up in Hampstead and Kensington before the First World War. His grandfather was a progressive Liberal and a republican, other members of his family had aesthetic tendencies. At Cambridge after the war, Pritchard studied engineering and economics and was deeply influenced by lectures on Taylorian time-and-motion study as well as by J.M. Keynes's ideas on post-war reconstruction. He married one woman by whom he had two sons; another woman to whom he was not married ran a nursery school for his children on the top floor of their house in Hampstead and bore him a daughter as well. His wife became a psychotherapist and the children were educated according to the progressive child-centred theories of A.S. Neill of Summerhill, and of Bertrand Russell to whose preparatory school at Beacon Hill they were sent before going to the progressive public school, Bryanston. The principle was not to impose discipline upon the children – classes at Beacon Hill were not compulsory – but to 'encourage the children to develop for themselves any need for discipline'.[11]

This notion of the child's right to creative freedom also extended to designers and architects. Describing the evolution of the design for the Isokon Flats in Lawn Road, Pritchard reveals an immense tolerance towards their architect, Wells Coates. At one stage there was an inevitable need to cut costs, towards which Wells Coates was very resistant. 'He had to be infallible', observed Pritchard in his memoirs, before going on to admit that, 'Of course, we had to go ahead after all. Wells's plans were so very good.' Over and over again in his memoirs Pritchard reveals his abdication of traditional authority and responsibility in favour of both children and creative professionals, though he was totally incapable of crediting furniture retailers and manufacturers with a knowledge of their own markets.[12]

The Isokon flats of course were the centre for a community of modern and progressive people. There was a dining club and a bar, called the Isobar, which was a meeting place for Hampstead artists like Henry Moore, Ben Nicholson, Barbara Hepworth and others, and Pritchard's daughter's mother's nursery school was incorporated in the plans. The building, with its long, white concrete access-corridors on the side facing the road, looked like one of Le Corbusier's favourite ocean liners, and the Pritchards had their own flat, complete with garden, on the roof.[13]

Here then was the epitome of the new forms of modern life and behaviour which were supposed to require a totally new plan of house and totally new buildings, made of new materials, because the old no longer fitted.

There were, however, two flaws in the argument. The first, was that buildings must be

104 Isokon flats, Lawn Road, Hampstead, 1934, designed by Wells Coates for Jack Pritchard, were a prototype for modern living, with a community centre for modern artists and a progressive nursery school.

tailor-made to house a particular social activity, rather than standard building types being adapted as they had, quite happily, been in the past.[14] Second, the Hampstead set, like the Beveridges and Rowntrees, never paused to consider whether the rest of society, especially the working-class families for whom such homes and such schools were to be built, were living, or even wanting to live, lives like Jack Pritchard and his friends.

In the early years of the war, *Mass Observation* carried out a detailed survey of people's attitudes to their existing homes and hopes for their dream home of the future. The following seems to sum up the desires of a large part of the sample. In spite of features in common, such as the desire for well-lit rooms and labour-saving equipment, they are very different in overall character from the Modernist ideal.

I should like a house with a kitchen-dining-room – you know, one room where you eat and cook and a scullery. And a sitting-room, not too big. Three bedrooms and a bathroom, and *two* lavatories, one upstairs in the bathroom and one downstairs. I'd like large windows, very light and airy, and of course, a garden. I like bow-windows really, the modern type that let in all the light. In the scullery I should like a sink and draining board all in one piece. Like those steel ones, I think they are. And I'd *like* – of course people in our circumstances can't have it, but I'd *like* a refrigerator. I would like a coal fire in the sitting-room, with a nice brick fireplace, and gas or electric in the kitchen. Gas, I think; electric really dries the air up worse than gas, I always think. Gas fires in the bedrooms. I'm not keen on central heating.[15]

CHAPTER 3
Town Planning

MODERNIST PLANNING

> Let us clear the ground first:
> *The 'corridor street' must be destroyed.*
>
> Le Corbusier, *Précisions*, 1929[1]

In order to construct the new kind of building, home or office, surrounded by open space, flooded with daylight, and served by rapid motor transport, a new type of city had to be created out of the old, on the very site of the old. A piecemeal approach, rebuilding the old masonry buildings with shining new concrete and glass constructions on the same site, would not work because both the shape of the site and existing bye-laws would reproduce the same shape of building, albeit in a different style and with freer internal planning, to fit into the existing pattern of dark and narrow streets. Down these more and more cars would continue to pour, creating more and more congestion, pollution and noise.

In the mid-1920s Le Corbusier had led the campaign against traditional urban regulations. 'If we set ourselves against the past, we are forced to the conclusion that the old architectural code, with its mass of rules and regulations evolved during four thousand years, is no longer of any interest . . .'[2]

He called for the repudiation of the existing layout of our towns.

> Instead of our towns being laid out in massive quadrangles, with the streets in narrow trenches walled in by seven-storeyed buildings set perpendicular on the pavement and enclosing unhealthy courtyards, airless and sunless wells, our new layout, employing the same area and housing the same number of people, would show great blocks of houses with successive set-backs, stretching along arterial avenues. No more courtyards, but flats opening on every side to air and light, and looking, not on the puny trees of our boulevards of today, but upon green sward, sports grounds and abundant plantations of trees.

He even condemned the much-loved Parisian cafe as 'that fungus which eats up he pavements of Paris' – another instance of his hatred for bohemianism, aestheticism and romanticism.[3]

The British contribution was not a slavish application of Le Corbusier's principles. British architectural writers of the 1930s expanded upon Le Corbusier's message and related it to British circumstances. The system of the 1947 *Town and Country Planning Act* was a sophisticated solution to the problem Corbusier had expounded. The prime objects of attack for these writers were both the older bye-laws and the more recent Town Planning Schemes. The former, it will be recalled, laid down the hard-and-fast rules which created the corridor street; the latter, which we shall examine later in this chapter, gave rise to a more villagey and picturesque garden city kind of townscape. For example, in 1937, F.R.S.

105 'A Typical London Suburb' from the first English edition of Le Corbusier's *Urbanisme* (1929). 'A charming picture which displays every vice of planning.'

Yorke complained that plans for private houses had to be approved not only by the landowners but also by the local authority, the town planning amenity council and the Restriction of Ribbon Development body. Thomas Sharp, who was to work in the research team of the Ministry of Works and Planning which helped prepare the 1947 legislation, berated the bye-law street introduced under the Public Health Act of 1875, for its 'all pervading dullness'. He accepted that the bye-laws had been a success in making the disease-ridden early industrial city more hygienic: 'Every family had an inalienable right to a certain minimum of light and air.' But the industrial town remained, in essentials, a barracks for its work force. 'Dreariness, drabness, dullness – the sanitary Victorian Town' (Plate 105). But Sharp also condemned the romantic escapism of the suburb, whose origin he found in Ruskin's outburst against Edinburgh New Town as well as in laissez-faire and economic individualism.[4]

The Modernists, therefore, opposed both the bye-law kind of planning and that of the garden cities, which they disparaged as the romantic reaction to it. The first was too restrictive and unimaginative, the latter too escapist and anarchic. In a small introductory book on the principles of planning, Sir Patrick Abercrombie, author of the 1943 County of London Plan and a major force behind the 1947 *Town and Country Planning Act*, made exactly this point in contrasting the architectural results of ancient Greek planning with those of Adam Smith's principle of the 'invisible hand': 'both are wrong', he argued.

> The plan should not be in the hands of the drill sergeant nor should the city be under the domination of the muddler who will talk about the Law of Supply & Demand and the Liberty of the Individual. Town and country planning seeks to proffer a guiding hand to the trend of natural evolution, as a result of careful study of the place itself and its external relationships. The result is to be more than a piece of skilful engineering, or satisfactory hygiene or successful economics: it should be a social organism and a work of art.[5]

But the question remained: What were the principles according to which the cities were to be reconstructed to achieve a modern harmony? Le Corbusier in the early 1920s had set his heart against the solutions proposed by the romantic school of town planning represented by Raymond Unwin in Britain and Camillo Sitte in Austria. He saw no future for cities that had enlarged themselves in a piecemeal fashion with their quaint winding streets – the 'pack-donkey' way – scatter-brained and distracted, zig-zagging to take the line of least resistance. He admired the city of the rational man who ruled 'brute creation by his intelligence'. He admired Roman town planning as well as that of Louis XIV whose image approving the plan for Les Invalides was the final plate in the book, captioned: 'Homage to a great town planner. This despot conceived immense projects and realised them. Over all the country his noble works still fill us with admiration. He was capable of saying, "We wish it," or "Such is our pleasure." '[6] Le Corbusier insisted that only ruthlessness could modernise the higgledy-piggledy city that had evolved in such a piecemeal fashion. If the house were a machine for the family to live in, the city was a machine for organising the whole of society, its government and business, and this machine was choking to death through cancerous congestion. Radical surgery was needed. The solution was to pull down the city centres and rebuild them as business and administrative centres and to transfer the 'urban troglodytes', as he called the inhabitants of the Marais, to garden cities farther out; not however garden cities of individual houses and gardens such as Hampstead, but of six-storey blocks of maisonettes with separate communal gardens and playground areas. In the *Parillion de l'Esprit Nouveau* shown at the 1925 Paris Exposition, Le Corbusier presented his scheme for a new Paris, which he named the Voisin Plan after the car manufacturer who appropriately had sponsored it. The centre of Paris, including areas like the Marais, would be demolished and only the churches and major monuments left standing. A great avenue 400 feet wide, parallel to the Champs Elysées would run through the city, with the administrative centre of 600-feet tower blocks arranged around it, but sufficiently remote to be quiet, and set in green parkland.[7]

If this was the ideal, it was not easy to see how it could be achieved in practice. Obviously changes to building regulations were essential, but one British writer acknowledged that, given the small number of clients committed to modern architecture and the slow pace with which taste changed, 'the coming generation of architects may not have their opportunity for twentieth-century design until London, Manchester, Birmingham, Liverpool, and a few other cities and residential areas have been levelled by the air raids of another war'. This was written five years before the Second World War, in 1934, and offers a horrifying reflection on the inhuman lengths to which Modernists were prepared to let their imaginations go.[8] But then, even John Betjeman, the future eulogist of Metroland, could write:

> Come, friendly bombs, and fall on Slough
> It isn't fit for humans now,
> There isn't grass to graze a cow
> Swarm over, Death!

Even while the Blitz was in progress, similar views were being expressed. One writer went so far as to argue that, because monuments in old cities were so hard to dislodge and therefore spoiled the accomplishment of the ideal town plan, this was 'where the Nazi bombers come in. As site-clearing agencies they have shown themselves to be incomparably effective.' Others such as Sir John Summerson and Sir James Richards expressed similar views, even in a volume of photographs commemorating the ruined buildings of Britain! Their disregard for the loss of life in the interests of modern architecture was a foretaste of what was to happen in the 1960s and 1970s.[9]

In itself, however, site-clearance, even on a massive scale, whether by bombers or bulldozers, was simply not sufficient to put the modern ideals into practice. A city might be almost completely flattened or swept away, as the City of London had been in the Fire of London, but would still be rebuilt to the same layout if the ownership of property, the lines of the streets and the building regulations or bye-laws remained unchanged. This is why the failure of Wren's plan for rebuilding London after the Great Fire was so often cited by Modernists as the greatest lost opportunity: a ruthless and noble idea obstructed by the claims of private property and of business to get started again as quickly as possible. It was considered essential to avoid losing the similar opportunity provided by the Blitz.

Le Corbusier proposed that the state should acquire the existing land and buildings in the inner city at their market price, fully compensating the owners of property; begin immediately upon the building of 600-feet office buildings upon 5 per cent of the area increasing the density of usable space twenty-fold; so that with the completion of the towers the value of the state's property would be worth correspondingly more. The next step was to move the businesses from their old offices to the new ones and to use the huge profits from the operation to finance the landscaping of the 95 per cent for open space, motorways and other communal facilities.[10]

Such a draconian scheme was not unrealistic, particularly with the example of Haussmann in the recent past. But it was not to become the way forward. The British contribution was to devise a piecemeal approach which aimed to achieve the same result. Even so, from where was the political will for such rebuilding to come in the post-war reconstruction period?[11]

In spite of the mass of propaganda about modern architecture in the 1930s, a post-war Labour government committed to a massive programme of legislation designed to transform society was not likely to find parliamentary time for legislation whose only purpose was to satisfy the ambitions of an architectural coterie. So the primary occasion for the new legislation was not architectural but social and economic, an attempt to remedy the problems of the 1930s – namely, the high levels of unemployment in the depressed regions – and of the Victorian industrial city through land-use planning or, in other words, through government control over the use to which any piece of land could be put. This was an issue which had greatly exercised the state during the Tudor and Stuart periods and which came to the fore again in the nineteenth century under the impact of the renewed expansion of British cities, London in particular, where industry and housing were crowded together in polluted and insanitary conditions in the very centre. Attempts to solve the problem by slum clearances and new wide roads only intensified the problem since the poor could not afford the cost of transport to enable them to live away from their work, and crowded into the surviving accommodation. Numerous remedies were proposed including those of Ebenezer Howard for satellite garden cities and of Raymond Unwin for low-density garden suburbs. Local authorities, the LCC in particular, built suburban housing estates. In 1938 the Green Belt Act encouraged the development of a *cordon sanitaire* to limit the size of London and its suburbs. Patrick Abercrombie's two plans for London, the *County of London Plan* of 1943 and the *Greater London Plan* of 1944, aimed to assist this process of thinning out the density of central London by dispersal of accommodation and industry.[12]

For these purposes, local planning authorities and the minister were given wide powers, to be employed at their discretion, and architect-planners were able to use these powers to achieve their own ambitions.

The wheel had, in a sense, turned full circle. Just as in the reign of James I it was the issue of controlling the growth of London, preserving open space and maintaining an economic balance between the capital city and the provinces that had provided the conditions within which the royal proclamations against building and, subsequently, the London Building Regulations were developed, so in the 1940s it was a similar complex of problems that gave rise to a new and radical form of development control: one which was very different from the old one, but which had no less a drastic effect upon the streets, squares and skyline of the 'bye-law' city as bye-laws had had upon the winding lanes of the mediaeval city.

DEPRESSED AREAS AND LAND-USE PLANNING

The Barlow Commission, or to give it its full title The Royal Commission on the Distribution of the Industrial Population, was appointed in July 1937 and reported in January 1940. Its appointment arose from concern at the very high levels of unemployment in the industrially depressed regions. This was coupled with an equal worry about the 'excessive growth of London' where many of the new light industries had been setting up, creating huge problems of congestion in addition to vulnerability from air attack. The Commission was charged to study the problem and consider whether 'further extension of industry in Greater London should be controlled, as a means of securing more even distribution of production'. It was specifically asked to suggest remedies.[13]

The report's findings confirmed that, whereas the old, heavy and extractive industries in the North of England and Wales were contracting and shedding labour through increases in productivity, the new light industries and services were mostly setting up in London, the home counties and the Midlands. A major reason for this was that electricity and motor transport had enabled industry to choose their locations for factories more flexibly. In the absence of any government regulation, the Commission believed that this trend would continue. This was thought undesirable for many different reasons, including health, smoke and noise, the excessive growth, overcrowding and congestion in London and its vulnerability to air attack. The suggested remedy was a National Industrial Board designed to encourage 'a reasonable balance of industrial development, so far as possible, throughout the various divisions or regions of Great Britain, coupled with appropriate diversification of industry in each division or region throughout the country'. The board would conduct research, advise ministers and also regulate the location of new industry in London and the home counties. This board would not necessarily be associated with town planning.[14]

The Commission, however, had also received evidence from various planning bodies which had found 'defects' in the existing system of town and country planning. Most important amongst these defects was that, although Town Planning Schemes under the 1932 Act would eventually cover the whole country, there was no provision for coordinating them into a national plan.

It may, therefore, be said that while present statutory town-planning tends towards producing a more pleasant, healthier and more convenient local environment, it is not adapted to check the spread of great towns or agglomerations, nor, so long as their growth continues, to arrest the tendency to increasing central density and traffic congestion. To say this is not in any way to diminish the importance of present town-planning, which is of essential value in the protection and creation of amenities. It is really to say that present town-planning does not concern itself with the larger question of the general and national grouping of the population which is the subject of this Commission's inquiry. Whatever policy of grouping is adopted, detailed planning on a local basis will remain necessary.[15]

The report tried to answer this point by suggesting that the National Industrial Board should inspect all planning schemes to provide a measure of national coordination. Evidence had also been given that the existing law did not regulate the use of land on a national scale. Finally, the cost to local authorities of compensating owners of property for restrictions upon the development and redevelopment of land was often too high. As a result, the decisions most desirable from a national point of view were not taken.[16]

But a minority report, headed by Patrick Abercrombie, made a far stronger recommendation, namely that there should be a new cabinet minister for the location of industry and national planning. This ministry would both conduct research and also produce an overall National Development Plan with the power to impose it upon local schemes. Abercrombie criticised the feebleness of the report's main findings on the defects in the existing planning system, arguing that this had simply not been devised for and therefore was not adequate for the regulation of the location of industry or population on a national scale. He believed that the new ministry should coordinate the planning of other departments.[17]

Abercrombie's minority report, articulating as it did the concerns of those in the Town Planning Movement who wanted a total reshaping of living and working conditions, marked the beginning of the process by which the requirements and objectives of national economic and land-use planning assumed greater legislative and political importance than planning to control appearance and layout. But it was on the back of land-use planning that the Modernists were able to achieve the means of 'clearing the ground' and destroying the corridor street.

TOWN PLANNING 1906–1947

The two existing types of planning which the Modernists needed to replace were the bye-law system and the more recent Town Planning schemes. The first of these had developed out of the London Building Acts from the seventeenth century onwards and has been discussed in Part II. It was applied to the rest of the country through the *Model Clauses* of the 1875 *Public Health Act* administered by the Local Government Board which prescribed minimum widths for streets depending upon their length and function. For example, any street longer than 100 feet had to be a carriage road and at least 36 feet wide. The model bye-laws were only advisory, and the actual bye-laws in operation could differ from place to place, but basically their virtue lay in being readily intelligible and easily enforceable through a corps of district surveyors. At the same time, like all simple regulations, they undoubtedly resulted in a somewhat regimented and unimaginative layout of buildings (Plate 106). But they did secure a minimum standard of light, density and space for new housing development and were a marked contribution to public health by preventing gross overcrowding.[18]

How, then, does so-called town planning differ from the bye-laws? A problem arises in answering that question because the term 'town planning' has been used in Britain to describe two very different systems. The first of these operated from the passing of the first *Town Planning Act* of 1909 until the *Town and Country Planning Act* of 1947; the second, an entirely different affair, has been in operation since then. To make matters more complicated still, certain provisions of the earlier system continued in the second. However, it is essential to clarify the distinction between the two, even at the risk of exaggeration.

The earlier inter-war system differed from bye-laws in two main respects. First, it limited the automatic right of some landowners to build upon his property however he chose.

338

106 Bye-Law Street, product of the 1875 Public Health Act to improve hygiene but attacked by Raymond Unwin, pioneer of garden cities and suburbs, for creating a dismal environment.

Second, the number of features governed by rules was considerably increased, and so, to some degree, was the discretion of the planning authority in deciding whether or not to apply those rules. In short, what was called town planning from 1909 to 1947 was a more extensive, more flexibly administered, system of bye-laws in all but name. But it only applied to areas 'ripe for development' designated by the local authority – and these were very few.

In the early part of this century, support for town planning and opposition to bye-laws came from those members of the architectural profession who wished architecture to be more of an independent, high-status profession like medicine or the law, free to develop and progress in ways which seemed best to expert opinion, and not bound by an inflexible local bureaucracy. They also wished the profession of architecture to acquire new and potentially lucrative lines of business in, for example, the huge and growing market for new houses to meet the 'house famine'. So long as those developments were controlled and to a large degree specified by bye-laws and standard house-plans, they could be built by ordinary builders and there was almost nothing for an architect to contribute and, therefore, very little opportunity for him to earn fees.

So one aim was to remove legal constraints upon an architect's creative freedom in designing a new estate. This was a determined bid by the architectural profession to wrest the control of building from the civil engineer and the surveyor, the two professions whose members filled the posts of Borough Surveyor or Engineer through which control of bye-laws was exercised. The Town Planning Committee of the RIBA argued that, 'For the design of the town plan, the architecturally trained mind is as essential as for the design of a single building; for the work consists in applying upon a wider field and with greater

339

scope the same principles which govern the designing of individual buildings.' The new breed of architect planner was essential if there was to be 'that spacious breadth of ordered elevation in the groups of buildings, which so largely constitute the beauty and grandeur of cities'.[19]

It would be altogether wrong, however, to imply that professional self-interest was the only, or indeed the leading, determinant of the Town Planning Movement, whose leaders were highly altruistic and very practical and indeed effective people. Dominant amongst them was Sir Raymond Unwin. Between 1914 and 1928 Unwin was Chief Technical Officer for Building and Town Planning at the Local Government Board and subsequently the Ministry of Health, which had responsibility for planning and for public housing, then fairly minor concerns of central government. Much earlier he and his partner, Barry Parker, had designed New Earswick for the Joseph Rowntree Village Trust in 1902, in which Seebohm Rowntree was involved; they had designed the master plan for the first garden city at Letchworth in Hertfordshire in 1903 which had been founded by Ebenezer Howard; and they had then been responsible for the layout of Hampstead Garden Suburb in 1906. In the words of the standard history, 'It was town planning of the kind advocated by Unwin which established itself as town planning in practice.' No-one had more influence upon the built environment in Britain in the first half of this century than Unwin.[20]

Unwin put the case for replacing bye-laws by town planning. In his definitive and epoch-making book *Town Planning in Practice* of 1909, he argued that, while the bye-laws and other measures of public health had done much to improve conditions in the rapidly-expanding towns of the nineteenth century, they were nonetheless productive of a dismal and ugly environment in which to live.[21] He wanted towns and cities to be enhanced by art and beauty in the true spirit of Ruskin and Morris whose ardent disciple he had been since his youth. In order to achieve this he believed that:

> *the range of building bye-laws must necessarily be extended*; it will not be practicable for a town plan to show everything that needs to be determined. The limitation of the number of houses to the acre; the reservation of sites for probable public buildings or other requirements; the proper distribution of works and factories; and many other similar matters, will need to be brought under some public control if towns are to be adequately managed, and developed along the best lines. Upon many of these points it will be peculiarly difficult to frame regulations, so difficult that it will hardly be practicable, *unless some means can be discovered of introducing an element of discretion* and affording some opportunity for the *individual case to be considered on its merits*. [my italics][22]

From an architectural and aesthetic point of view, Unwin's justification for this degree of administrative discretion was that

> the line laid down by the building bye-laws is a rigid and inflexible one. The builder is compelled to conform to it, and in seeking to secure the utmost which the bye-law will allow him, he pushes his building, as it were, against an unbending line or plane. His building becomes moulded by this, and from this moulding springs what I have called 'bye-law architecture'. It is the *hard-and-fast* form of these building regulations . . . resulting in mutual antagonism and suspicion between the builder and the man whose duty it is to enforce the restraint, which leads to so much harm. [my italics][23]

Unwin wanted individual cases to be negotiated between the architect and the local authority in a spirit of 'co-operation and sympathy'. At the same time he acknowledged the misgivings of the Local Government Board that such a broad measure of discretion would place the building inspectors in a position of undue influence and open the way for corruption. But the discretionary element in the legislation of 1909–44 was on a quite

107 Sketch of Hampstead Garden Suburb planned after 1906 by Raymond Unwin as a low-density suburb, separated from the existing town of Hampstead by a green belt and a model for how cities could expand without sprawl.

different scale to that brought in by the 1947 Act. In the earlier phase there were clear-cut rules to which all developments within a Town Planning Scheme had to conform, with the local authority possessing a limited and defined degree of discretion or latitude in their application, mainly to avoid the grid-iron rigidity of the Public Health Act bye-laws and to permit the kind of subtlety in the way that buildings defined the public spaces between them possessed by the historic towns of the middle ages and Renaissance which represented his ideal.[24]

Indeed, it is essential to appreciate that Unwin was by no means opposed to building being controlled through bye-laws. On the contrary, he argued that,

> So long as some definite standard of building is required, so long will bye-laws in one form or another be necessary. It is not a matter that can be *entirely left to the discretion of the building surveyor* [my italics]. It is as necessary to the builder in preparing his plans that he should know within fairly definite limits the standard required of him as it is for the building inspector to have some definite standard to keep his judgements regular and consistent and fair to all.

But it was essential, in Unwin's opinion, that, while rules could easily be framed to 'cover the majority of cases and work out satisfactorily', allowance had to be made for instances not allowed for in the regulations which had been devised with an urban context in mind. It was for these cases that a degree of administrative discretion was needed – to enable new developments to take advantage of the potentialities of sites outside the city-centre, to make the bye-laws workable and to prevent any outcry against them from architects or jerry-builders on account of patent unfairness. Unwin therefore was not advocating total discretion for planners; he was calling for the authorities 'to devote more care to framing and revising bye-laws, so that their action shall be as little arbitrary as possible'.[25]

This point becomes quite clear when we look at the first step taken to replace bye-laws with town planning controls. This was achieved not by national legislation but by private act of parliament: the 1906 *Hampstead Garden Suburb Act* (6 Edw 7, Ch. CXCII), moved by the Hampstead Garden Suburb Trust which had been formed to develop the new suburb. Unwin was its architect and chief planner. Assisted by John Burns, the former dock-workers' leader who was President of the Local Government Board, the Act suspended certain of the bye-laws of Hendon Borough Council and gave the Trust powers to make its own, so that the architects had far greater freedom of action. For example: 'Any road less than 500 feet long primarily to give access to houses, not designed for through-traffic may with the consent of the Urban District Council of Hendon be exempt from bye-laws relating to the width of new streets.' As well as rules governing the width of streets, a large set of special bye-laws was framed by the Hampstead Garden Suburb Trust covering matters from party walls to bay windows, from the height of rooms to the arrangement of houses on the corners of streets.[26]

Thus Unwin was able to provide cul-de-sacs and short narrow roads forbidden under existing bye-laws. The Trust's own regulations stipulated that the distance between buildings facing one another across the street or close had to be a minimum of 50 feet. The average density, including public open space, was, at eight houses to the acre, very low. In effect, the Act set aside the local regulations responsible for the kind of regimented terrace housing of the 1890s and early 1900s, which had simply continued the pattern of earlier decades and centuries and in its place created a pattern of broad, leafy, winding roads, of a wide variety of different kinds of streets, squares and open spaces, of picturesque bay-windowed houses set back from the road behind their own front gardens. This pattern is to be found in its richest and most picturesque form in Hampstead and other garden suburbs and cities (Plate 107). But it also became the model for the huge suburban developments that took place between the wars, permitted by changes in the bye-laws.[27]

There followed four public Town Planning Acts which applied to the country as a whole, in 1909, 1919, 1923 and 1932. The first of these, The Housing, Town Planning etc. Act of 1909 (9 Edw 7, Ch 44) simply provided local authorities with the power to prepare a Town Planning Scheme without having to obtain a private act of parliament, in exactly the same way that the Public Health Acts empowered them to make bye-laws. The only difference was that many hurdles had to be jumped before these powers could be obtained. Town Planning Schemes could only be drawn up for green-field sites 'ripe for development', and could not cover areas already built upon which might be 'ripe for *re*development'. Within major towns and cities the most serious problem was that of redevelopment rather than new development, and the Acts did nothing to help until 1932. Rural areas were also excluded. In other words, a scheme could only be introduced where the interests of the local authority and the property owners were in unison. It is hardly surprising that by 1913 only three schemes in the whole country, two in Birmingham and one in Ruislip, Middlesex, had been approved.[28]

By 1939, however, 1.1 million acres were covered by Town Planning Schemes, with a further 4 million acres awaiting approval. Moreover 26.5 million acres were covered by resolutions to prepare schemes and were therefore under the control of Interim Development Orders which gave local authorities both the power to refuse permission for developments likely to conflict with schemes not yet in force and the power to suspend existing bye-laws.

The matters that could be regulated by the scheme included the space surrounding buildings, the number of buildings that could be erected on an area: the density, as well as the height, size, design and external appearance of any building. To ensure that the interests of property owners and residents were fully taken into account, the local authority was required to compile and maintain a register of owners, owners' associations and business associations. These had to be informed of the contents of the scheme. So too did the occupier of every 'hereditament' in the area. Developers possessed the right to appeal and to be compensated financially if they lost potential profit as a result of the regulations, as did any resident or owner agrieved by the granting of permission. The Ministry of Health had to approve a scheme for it to become operational.

The specific regulations themselves differed from locality to locality but all were influenced by *Town Planning Model Clauses for Use in the Preparations of Schemes*. This were first issued by the Ministry of Health in 1923 to coincide with the operation of the 1919 Act and were regularly revised. An essential precondition to any Town Planning Scheme was the provision, first introduced in the Act of 1909, giving local authorities powers 'for suspending, so far as necessary for the proper carrying out of the scheme, any statutory enactments, by-laws, regulations, or other provisions . . . which are in operation in the area included in the scheme' to ensure that in a Town Planning Scheme there was no confusion between one set of rules or the other.[29]

Yet the Model Clauses were bye-laws in all but name. They set down quite stringent rules about what was permitted for particular kinds of buildings, for streets, and for the use to which buildings would be put in particular areas – 'zoning' as it is called. These zones, and the layout of major roads, were indicated in a map.

Under the Model Clauses of January 1935 there were three basic land use zones: residential, business and industrial. There were also mixed zones. In a residential zone no consent was required if someone wished to build houses, but industrial buildings for 'noxious' trades were absolutely forbidden. So permission was automatic for buildings whose use conformed to the basic character of the zone.

In all cases, however, whether consent was automatic or required, the building had to conform to the rules governing layout and appearance. Thus the width of streets was strictly related to their length. Then there were rules about density, limiting the number of houses in residential zones to between 6 and 12 to the acre. Then there were rules ensuring that there was a lot of open space around a building. Basically all buildings had to adhere to the building line in a street, and there was a maximum height of 70 feet.[30]

The character of these regulations was more flexible, certainly, than the Model Bye-Laws under the 1875 Public Health Act, but they were also far more comprehensive. It will readily be understood why the modern architects found the regulations of the Town Planning Schemes as irksome to the realisation of their kind of architecture as any pre-existing bye-laws or building regulations.

What was to have an influence upon inter-war Britain greater even than the new town planning legislation were the new bye-laws. The Local Government Board had the bit between its teeth and, in a circular of August 1912, it followed Unwin's advice about authorities taking more care in 'framing and revising bye-laws' and called upon local authorities 'to consider Byelaws made under Section 157 of the Public Health Act 1875' as to whether 'the ordinary clauses for the laying out of roads do not permit some of the classes of roadway which have been designed in some "garden cities"'. (The new layouts also permitted cheaper roadways.) By 1924, the Model Bye-Laws themselves had been adapted to permit layouts more in line with garden suburbs. It was this change, no doubt, that accounted for the garden suburb character of most of the so-called speculative housing of the inter-war period (Plate 108). This, rather than the Town Planning Acts themselves, which only took effect slowly, is Unwin's true legacy, which is hardly ever noted: he set the model and lay down the regulations for the 'suburban semi' and the shopping parade, for John Betjeman's Metroland normally characterised as unregulated speculative building or ribbon development, but in fact the product of government regulations.[31]

But, in addition to these regulations, one feature of the new system after 1935 threatened to make it impossible to design buildings that were modern in appearance even if they did

108 Inter-war suburbs. Unwin was highly practical and finding that planned garden surburbs were slow off the ground, he changed the old bye-laws to force so-called 'speculative builders' to create a watered-down version. Suburban sprawl was in fact the product of rigid planning like the old bye-law street.

obey all the rules. These were the rules governing the external appearance of a building – aesthetic control.[32]

Under Clause 44 of the 1935 Model Clauses, the local planning authority could call upon a developer to supply drawings which indicated the external appearance, including the materials which were to be used. This applied both to completely new buildings and to the redevelopment, extension or alteration of an existing building. If the council disapproved of the plans, the developer possessed the right of appeal to a three-man tribunal composed of an architect, a chartered surveyor and a JP. Their decision was final. Since the architect was in a minority of one on this tribunal – and since he had moreover to be a fellow of the RIBA appointed by the president and, therefore, a traditionalist in all likelihood, the chances of any buildings of a modern style being approved was very small indeed. The character of the controls over building development enacted between the wars, in addition to the survival of earlier bye-laws, explains why it was that, although both the Arts and Crafts and Garden City Movements led by Raymond Unwin and the Modernists believed in town planning, the two camps nonetheless parted company.

The philosophy and the provisions of the 1947 Town and Country Planning Act were totally different. The essence was to introduce national and regional planning for land-use along the lines advocated by the Barlow Commission, Beveridge and others. Gone were both bye-laws and Town Planning Schemes with their detailed maps and regulations governing layout and appearance. What replaced them was a Development Plan, which every local planning authority was obliged to produce within three years, showing 'the manner in which they propose that land in that area should be *used*'.[33] These were to be shown on maps designating roads, open spaces, and new buildings both public and private. No development could any longer be carried out without permission from the planning authority, and the authority had powers to give or to refuse consent 'as they think fit', so

344

long as they 'have regard to the provisions of the development plan'. The right of an owner to develop his land was nationalised (£300 million was paid out nationally) and the problem of property rights and compensation, which had proved a serious obstacle in former legislation, was removed.[34]

In addition, the local authority had powers to designate land for Comprehensive Development. The definition of a Comprehensive Development Area was one which 'should be developed or redeveloped as a whole' in order to deal with war damage, to remedy 'bad layout or obsolete development' or to provide for relocating population, industry or open space. These provisions – first introduced into an earlier Act of 1944, amending the 1932 Act – extended to powers to stop the existing uses of buildings and to alter or remove any building by order if 'expedient in the interests of the proper planning of the area'. In addition, the authority had the power to purchase land for these purposes not only by agreement with the owners but compulsorily. This supplied the kinds of powers which Le Corbusier had considered necessary 'to clear the site' of all impediments, legal and physical, to root-and-branch replanning.[35]

Subject to the right of appeal to the minister, the local authorities were given powers of almost complete discretion over development, a discretion totally different in kind from the administrative flexibility built into the pre-war statutes. The post-war planning authorities were not even bound to adhere to their own Development Plans as the basis for granting permission. They only had to 'have regard' to the plan, and could disregard its provisions if they thought it was better to do so.

Besides the enormous shift in power to the local authorities, the 1947 Town Planning Act marked another significant change. Unlike the earlier legislation, its emphasis was not upon the control of development in order to secure proper sanitation, amenity, convenience, or in order to preserve existing buildings and other objects of architectural, historic or artistic interest, but upon the far grander and more general purpose of setting up a rolling programme for the future use of all the land in an area. In effect this meant that amenity planning was incorporated within the wider purpose of land-use and general economic planning.

The Modernist architects now had much of what they had been calling for during the 1920s and 1930s. They were freed from the tightly-drawn rules of both the old bye-laws and the newer Model Clauses. But this was only a negative freedom. Because there were no longer any bye-laws or Model Clauses at all – not even Modernist ones – Modernist architects possessed the freedom to try out their proposals; but the exercise of their freedom depended entirely upon finding clients who wished to employ them and upon sympathetic local planning authorities who would use their almost unlimited powers of discretion favourably. We will see in the following chapter how those conditions were achieved, but first we shall examine more closely how this dramatic change to discretionary planning came about, and how it accorded with the aims of the Modern Movement.

FRAMING THE 1947 ACT

Barlow reported in January 1940. Dunkirk was evacuated on 30 May and the Battle of Britain began on 8 August. Within a fortnight a War Aims Committee of the Cabinet was set up, out of which, by the end of December 1940, at the very height of the Battle, emerged a small ministerial secretariat in charge of reconstruction. On the very next day, Lord Reith, the first Director-General of the BBC, who in October had been appointed Minister of Works with special responsibility to Cabinet for the machinery for reconstruction planning, presented his report (Plate 109). Reith, whose BBC Radio and its weekly journal *The Listener* had given a platform to the Modernists and planners throughout the 1930s, strongly advocated central planning along the lines of Abercrombie's minority report, for the 'execution of a national plan for the best use of land.' Although Reith's responsibilities had been limited to reporting, he nonetheless continued, throughout the following year and until his dismissal, to press for a central planning authority with a general authority for all social and economic development which would, inevitably, have preempted the authority of all the other ministries. But his somewhat megalomaniac schemes did not find favour with the bipartisan War Cabinet and he was dismissed in February 1942.[36]

He had, however, made several appointments who carried on the work and played key roles in the development of the 1947 Act. Foremost amongst them was W.G. Holford, later Lord Holford, who had succeeded Abercrombie as Professor of Town Planning at Liverpool at the age of only twenty-eight. Holford led the research team, which included a fellow ex-student from Liverpool, Gordon Stephenson, who had spent the years between 1934 and 1938 at the Massachusetts Institute of Technology studying the Tennessee Valley Authority. Also included was Thomas Sharp, a leading propagandist for planning between the wars, and Sir George Pepler who had succeeded Unwin at the Ministry of Health and was of like mind. In addition, Reith appointed Abercrombie to prepare the County of London Plan, as well as two special committees, the Scott and Uthwatt Committees, upon specific aspects of the proposed planning legislation.[37]

The chief idea to emerge from all this work in April 1943, and which was however accepted by the Cabinet, was that town planning should change from being essentially negative, regulative and local to playing a positive role in initiating plans throughout the country. The existing system of Town Planning Schemes, under which consent for development was automatic if the proposal conformed with the zoning regulations, was criticised for being static and inflexible because, once approved, the schemes were difficult to change. Instead an 'outline plan' was proposed, with an accompanying 'development programme', which would only lay down the broad outlines of the way a district should develop.[38]

Inevitably this would put an end to the system just beginning to get off the ground at the outbreak of war. Instead of permission being automatic for any proposal which conformed to the model clauses, all development of any kind was prohibited until consent was given. The notion of development included not only building but also changes in the use of existing buildings where the structure itself might be unchanged. (This was essential to the objectives of land-use planning and control over the location of industry.) Thus all the strings would be in the hands of the local planning authority and, ultimately, in the hands of the coordinating national minister, so that every individual new building or change of use could be fitted into the local plan for development, which would in turn fit in with national objectives. But in addition to these conditions for all forms of development, there would be special ones for what were initially called 'reconstruction areas' and were subsequently renamed Comprehensive Development Areas, CDAs. Here, as we have seen, the authorities would have the power not simply to refuse an owner permission, against which the owner could appeal, but the power to buy his land compulsorily if he would not do as he was told.

The essential feature was the broad outline plan to which, in the 1947 Act, the local authority merely had to 'have regard' in giving consent or refusing it. The planners in the Ministry of Works and Planning (the Ministry of Town and Country Planning after February 1943) deliberately wanted this to be vague, and not tied down to specific rules and roads. They wanted this because planning was, they argued, 'a continuous, not a static process', not an 'act of design'.

This simple formulation was a major break with the notion of civic design, which had been central to town planning in Britain since the Stuart proclamations. Second, it implied the total rejection of the participation of the public, for which reasonably good provision had been made in the 1932 Act with its registers of property owners and residents and forms of public inquiry. According to one internal memorandum, the paramount consideration

109 In 1940 Lord Reith, first Director-General of the BBC, became the government minister in charge of establishing the modernist system of town and country planning. The BBC, a public corporation which did not permit advertising, had promoted the Modern Movement and the assault upon consumerism.

'would be the planning merits or demerits of the outline plan in relation to local and national requirements'; and, in relation to this, 'the views of individual landowners and the effect of the plan on their particular interests in land would be largely irrelevant'.[39] Plato's Guardians were at work in this area as well.

Landowners were regarded as obstacles. It was proposed to nationalise their right to develop their own property and subject it to compulsory purchase. Neither did the residents of an area matter. Those drafting the legislation allowed that perhaps, if there were 'much adverse criticism or desire on the part of the public to suggest modifications in the specific proposals for the execution of the project', some kind of public inquiry might be necessary, but that should be left for the minister to decide. Even the wording is significant, because behind the bureaucratic language two things were implied. First, that the public should only have a say in a *specific* scheme for redevelopment, but not in the formulating of the larger outline scheme. Second, that the public's say would be limited to suggesting *modifications* of the proposal which would be worked out by the planners. Inevitably this idea of planning as a continuous process rather than an act of design must exclude the general public and property owners, because, if they could not see firm proposals, they would not have anything concrete to object to.

The 1947 Town and Country Planning Act is often presented as socialist in spirit, not altogether incorrectly, but like many of the other policies we have been examining it would be more correct to call it collectivist. It is very much a product of the ethos of Beveridge, Rowntree and Keynes. One specific source of the idea was the Tennessee Valley Authority, set up in the USA as one of the first acts of the Roosevelt New Deal administration in 1933 to regenerate the economy of the region which had suffered from terrible soil erosion and poverty. In the words of the TVA's chairman, the 'TVA idea of planning sees action and planning not as things separate and apart, but as one single and continuous process'. And he quoted Roosevelt's 1933 message to Congress: 'the TVA should be charged with the broadest duty of planning for the proper use, conservation, and development of the natural resources of the Tennessee River drainage basin and its adjoining territory *for the general social and economic welfare of the nation.*' The TVA was well-known in Britain as a shining model of total regional planning, social, economic and physical, within a democratic rather than a socialist or fascist state. Julian Huxley had written articles in *The Times* and *The Listener* in 1935, and, as we have already mentioned, one of Holford's team had written a thesis on the subject at MIT. Above all, the TVA covered an area about the same size as England which, for totally spurious reasons, recommended it as a model.[40]

In opposition to these dictatorial powers which Holford's team was formulating, Sir George Pepler, echoing Unwin's own words, defended the virtues of the existing system on the grounds that 'a considerable degree of precision and firmness was of great importance in planning both in guiding would-be developers with knowledge of what they could and could not do, and in controlling the local planning authorities, preventing them from being too loose and lazy.' He also believed that such precise plans must go to public inquiry, so as to get

> the best plan for the place in the interest of the people that live and work in it (subject to overriding national considerations) and those people are entitled to have a voice in the making of the plan and to have confidence that the local planning authority will keep to the plan, or that if important departures from it are proposed they will not be allowed without everybody being informed and given opportunity to express their views.★[41]

Although Pepler had his way over planning inquiries, Holford and the Modernists won their victory over the bye-law character of Town Planning Schemes. But Pepler's criticisms of the vague and over-flexible plans have been borne out both from the point of view of the developer and of the general public. The developer has every incentive to make a bid for planning permission for developments in conflict with the plan for the area because it is always open to the planning authority to disregard the plan. If he is refused permission, there is nothing to stop him making repeated applications or from appealing to the minister. Moreover, whereas he has the right of appeal, the general public or the residents have a capacity, not legally defined, only to make objections. They do not even have to be heard.

★ Minute of 15 September 1943: 'There is a danger that in our determination to throw off past shackles we under-estimate the importance of a considerable degree of precision and firmness in the processes of planning. Unless we have this, there will be a great temptation for local authorities to be lazy-minded and loose in their ideas; developers will be handicapped through lack of advance guidance; and none of us will really know where we stand.'

CHAPTER 4

Modernist Ideas in Action

As we have seen, the 1947 Act was essentially permissive legislation: it removed all statutory obstacles in the shape of bye-laws and Town Planning Schemes and imposed no new statutory regulations in their place. This was an article of faith. The Act had effectively nationalised the land by nationalising all its development rights; in theory, at least, planning authorities were placed in the position of the aristocratic landlords of the eighteenth century, with the same freedom to promote positive development on a large scale, instead of merely regulating the developments of other people and preventing abuses. There was therefore – again in theory – no need for bye-laws. Moreover, the memory of 'our endless miles of bye-law streets and the inchoate sprawl of the inter-war years' was a warning to many against the dangers of such controls.

'We cannot achieve fine design through controls,' wrote Gordon Stephenson in July 1949. 'From the great Public Health Act of 1875 to the First World War, we tried to improve new building through controls. We succeeded in driving speculating builders to produce the mechanical grids of bye-law housing.'[1]

But how without bye-laws or some kind of control were Modernist ideas to be carried out either in public-sector architecture and planning or in private, commercial developments? This problem, barely perceived by the Modernists in their euphoria over the 1947 Act, were admitted a decade later in an article of 1957 published in the *Architectural Review*, the flagship of the Modern Movement, entitled 'Europe Rebuilt 1946–56: What has happened to the Modern Movement?' This lamented the failure of Modernism to impose itself on post-war Europe. In Britain the overall impression was of architects or builders 'designing as they designed in the 1920s or even the 1900s'. The captions to the thirty-odd shock-horror photographs complain of 'pretentious mock-Georgian', 'tastelessly dolled-up factories', 'period-revival trappings', a 'mixture of styles' and 'poverty stricken design'.[2]

Looking back upon it from thirty years later, it is striking to discover that much of the architecture of reconstruction was indeed traditional in style. London offices of the period were predominantly neo-Georgian, followed the pre-existing building line and obeyed the 100 feet limit (Plate 110). Private housing built since the return of the Conservatives in 1951, was replete with bay windows, pitched roofs and half-timbered gables. What is more, most of the council housing erected under the post-war Labour government was in the form of red-brick houses or low flats with sash windows and pitched roofs. This was partly a matter of good sense. Even before the war ended, it had been found that a prefabricated house cost £100 more to build than a three-bedroomed house in brick, and the minister in charge of housing, Aneurin Bevan, had insisted upon high space standards and reliable, well-tried forms of construction. These houses have indeed proved a good investment, with the lowest level of maintenance problems of any post-war housing, whereas the high-rise Modernist flats whose erection began at about the time the article was being written were a disaster. This did not prevent the *Architectural Review* from attacking the traditional council houses as common-place 'borough engineers' housing'.[3]

110 Bank Buildings by Victor Heal, 1954, behind St Paul's. Despite the freedom from the 1890 100 ft height limit (Pl. 18) provided by the new planning system, almost all post-war building until the 1960s stuck to the old approach.

In 1957 hope, from the Modernists' point of view, was to be found only in the Royal Festival Hall, the slab flats at Churchill Gardens in Pimlico by the young firm of Powell and Moya, the pre-fabricated Hertfordshire schools, the LCC's Roehampton Estate and the replanning of Coventry 'where, as a result of the leadership of Donald Gibson, the city architect, a contemporary spirit now prevails in the rebuilt centre'.

The causes of this lack of progress, as the article's author and editor of the *Architectural Review*, J.M. Richards, saw it, were: first, the absence of a mechanised building industry, with the result that reconstruction had had to depend upon craft-based firms of builders who inevitably worked in largely traditional styles; second, that the bulk of commissions had gone to the older generation of architects who had kept up their pre-war commercial and official connections; finally he admitted that although Britain had ended 'the war with internationally admired planning legislation' whose 'planning controls were meant to stop such things' as 'badly designed speculative housing', the legislation had not been used. In short, the battle for modern architecture had not been won – yet.

Ten years later, the scene had changed. The major industrial cities were dotted with high-rise housing; the preeminence of St Paul's Cathedral to the east, and Big Ben to the west, upon the London skyline had been destroyed by the stumps of high-rise office slabs, which also broke up the old canyon-like streets of the City (Plate 111); much of Birmingham, Liverpool and Newcastle was being demolished and replanned. How had so unpromising a situation been transformed so rapidly?

The answer follows from the preceding analysis of the problem. Because the 1947 legislation was permissive rather than regulatory, everything depended upon key institutions and public bodies being under the control of the right chaps. And, in the rest of this chapter, I shall describe how borough engineers and surveyors were replaced by architect-trained planners, how public-sector architect departments, particularly dealing with education and housing, were taken over by Modernists and, finally, how the Modernists took power in the Council of the RIBA.

111 London skyline, 1994. The high offices of the 1960s were not the result of commercial pressures for more space, just the opposite – planning controls reduced office accommodation and imposed tall slabs upon developers to create open space.

There was, however, another crucial factor in the Modernists' bid for supremacy. Despite the prevailing permissiveness, one vital system of building control did get introduced – and, because its employment had enormous effect, we shall first look at that.

DAYLIGHTING AND DENSITY CONTROL

As J.M. Richard's article showed, there was nothing to stop a post-war authority continuing to enforce the old height controls, or even, because their discretion now was unlimited, imposing even lower limits. Moreover, there was nothing to prevent an architect or developer doing likewise. Anticipating this problem, some of the experts associated with Holford's wartime team in the Ministry of Town and Country Planning devised an ingenious regulatory mechanism which aimed to make it impossible to design the traditional type of city-centre office block: either the small building on a site fronting the street, or the larger stone-faced monsters created between the wars from the amalgamation of properties into a large block with internal light wells and courtyards. The mechanism – Plot Ratio and Daylighting Codes – was like a computer virus designed to destroy the 'programme' which had produced the traditional city.

This new regulatory mechanism depended upon the Modernist ideal of ensuring that rooms, whether in homes, factories or offices, were flooded with daylight. But the methods adopted ostensibly to increase the daylighting of the inside of buildings were also to determine the forms of much post-war building, to change out of all recognition large areas of the business centres of the great cities and, in the case of London, to destroy the existing skyline and replace it with another.

There is a long history of concern about the benefits of daylight in buildings, both for people's physical health and their psychological well-being. One reason why Florence Nightingale favoured long narrow hospital wards which projected from a central corridor

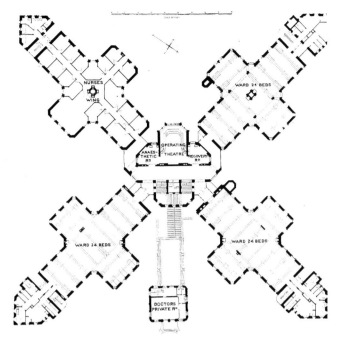

112 and 113   University College Hospital and plan, Gower Street by Alfred and Paul Waterhouse, 1894–1903. With its X plan set a 45° to the street this was a brilliant solution to improved daylighting in cities while respecting the line of the street.

so as to have windows on both sides – which became known as the Nightingale Ward – was her belief in the curative effect of daylight. She drew on statistics showing that patients in brightly-lit rooms in St Petersburg had four times the chance of recovering than patients in dingy rooms and concluded that it was 'essential to the recovery of the maimed and the sick' that the wards be 'flooded with sunlight'. Consequently St Thomas' Hospital, in whose design she was greatly involved, had a haircomb type of plan with the wards projecting onto the river so as to provide both light and a wonderful view of the Thames and the Houses of Parliament.[4]

The important thing to notice here is that solutions already existed to the problem of designing well-lit buildings in towns: solutions demanding neither a radical change of architectural style nor any drastic change to the relationship between building and street. Another good example of this is University College Hospital in Gower Street, built in 1903. Here, the wards radiate from the centre of the block in the shape of a cross set diagonally to the streets, but the building respects the line of the street both by being squared off at the corners and through its railings and ground floor entrance lobby (Plates 112 and 113).

In the late 1920s the architect Charles Holden applied this kind of building plan to the modern office building and drew also upon New York office types in his design for the headquarters of the London Passenger Transport Board on an awkward corner site behind Victoria Street. Unwin had been concerned for maximum daylight as early as 1902, and the deputy chief architect at the Housing Department of the Ministry of Health between 1920 and 1922, Manning Robertson, had proposals to extend the bye-laws in order to increase the lighting of terraced houses with back extensions.[5]

Concern for improvements in daylighting was not, therefore, the prerogative of architects in the modern camp. But what Modernists like Walter Gropius did when they latched on to Le Corbusier's urban ideas in the late 1920s was to demonstrate 'scientifically' that one could greatly increase the amount of daylight reaching each room by building a few ten-storey slabs on a site instead of many roads of two-storied terrace houses. And this could be achieved without reducing the density of population. The moral, in Gropius's view, was that the legislation restricting maximum heights should be abolished and new laws introduced to restrict only the maximum floor-space per acre, the density.[6]

Then, late in 1942, Bill Allen, a young Canadian architect who had been working on wartime factory design to save energy at the Building Research Station, drew Holford's attention to his own exciting refinement of Gropius's idea. Gropius had imagined high slab blocks as running parallel to one another, as in a street. But Allen showed that, if the blocks were turned alternately at right angles to one another, an intensity of illumination equal to 0.2 per cent of the light outside would reach as far as 15 feet into a room, farther than with parallel blocks where this level of lighting would only extend 10 feet into the room. The reason for this is given by the Waldram diagram illustrated below (Plate 114), which also shows the stepped form of skyline obtained as a result of this layout in comparison with the flat roofline of the buildings opposite, which is characteristic both of traditional street architecture as well as of that envisaged by Gropius.[7] The Waldram diagram shows that

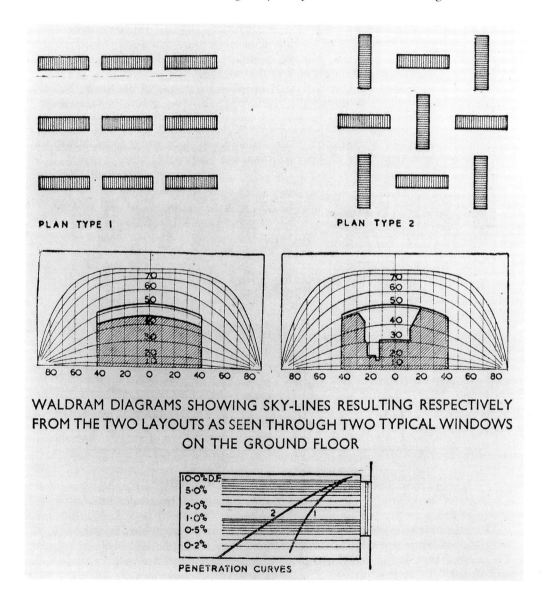

PLAN TYPE 1

PLAN TYPE 2

WALDRAM DIAGRAMS SHOWING SKY-LINES RESULTING RESPECTIVELY FROM THE TWO LAYOUTS AS SEEN THROUGH TWO TYPICAL WINDOWS ON THE GROUND FLOOR

PENETRATION CURVES

354

much more sky is visible with the alternating layout, and that is the reason for the increased daylight indoors.★8

There were, however, other good forms, including the 'Y' and the '+' plan. Indeed, according to the February 1943 paper, the '+' plan provided the highest level of illumination of all: 0.2 per cent as far as 14 feet from the window, compared to 12 feet 6 inches for the alternating arrangement of slab blocks.★★ In other words, from a purely quantitative point of view, the retention of the street coupled with cruciform buildings like Holden's London Transport offices, would have provided the very best lighting of all. Moreover, high windows reaching from table height to the ceiling gave better lighting levels than long low horizontal windows. And the deep reveals of Georgian windows reduced the glare caused by too abrupt a contrast between the sky and the dark wall. Holden's Neo-Georgian fenestration, therefore, was also best from this point of view (Plate 115).9

114 and 115 The Waldram diagrams indicate different amounts of light entering a building, while (left) the floor-ceiling Georgian windows allow good lighting levels.

★ Of course, this ignores the adaptability of the human eye to lower levels of lighting, as well as the compensating use of artificial light. Allen's work is intelligible in terms of the fact that he was working upon standard factory designs and investigating means of saving consumption of artificial light in wartime.
★★ In the 1944 *The Lighting of Buildings*, p. 24, the alternating scheme, however, had the advantage over the cruciform but only by a hair's breadth.

But those were not the conclusions which Holford and his team wanted to draw from the evidence. They wanted a technique which would help to specify a 'new type of street pattern'. And it was precisely because Allen realised that his elegant idea would assist this end that he mentioned it to Holford. Under the existing bye-laws, which restricted central city building heights to 100 feet, daylighting was relatively poor but there was, at the same time, only very weak control over the density of development. In Kingsway, where Allen carried out a survey, he found that buildings could contain office space up to twelve times the area of the ground site within the total height of about 100 feet. This ratio of floor area to ground site was named the Plot Ratio, and the building in Kingsway would have a Plot Ratio of 1:12.

The conclusion to be drawn was that, if London were to be reconstructed on pre-war lines with street-hugging, offices 100 feet tall illuminated by internal light-wells, then accommodation would increase, with increased urban congestion, while working conditions, as far as daylighting was concerned, would perhaps worsen. Indeed, the plan for reconstruction produced by the City of London Engineer, F.J. Forty, which envisaged the continuation of the height controls of the London Building Acts, foresaw an eventual increase in floor-space in the City to half as much again as had existed before the war when the old four-storey buildings were eventually redeveloped. Forty's plan was widely ridiculed by members of the Modernist town planning lobby such as John Summerson. However, Forty was more accurate than they in understanding that modern business methods would lead to a reduction of staff and an increase in the amount of space used by each, so that an increase in density of floor-space would not of itself necessarily result in an increase of the City's working population nor of traffic congestion. But this simple point was also one which Holford's team did not want to acknowledge. Allen's idea showed that height limits were neither effective as a means of controlling the overall density of floor-space nor as a means of ensuring good lighting.[10]

Holford then gave D.H. Crompton and another member of his team, G.T. Pound, an expert on planning controls, the task of translating Allen's idea into a workable set of regulations. They produced the idea of a Daylight Code in the form of compasses which enabled designers of buildings to assess whether adequate lighting was available to all rooms in a building from the irregular patches of sky visible as a result of the new shape of skyline. This made limitations of height obsolete as a means of ensuring good daylighting. The buildings could be any combination of height and breadth. Since height was also regarded as an inadequate control of density, and hence of congestion, there seemed no need to control height at all. Instead, a new control was invented for the purpose of controlling density and bulk: the Floor Space Index, a slightly different ratio to the Plot Ratio in that it included half the area of the surrounding streets in addition to the area of the ground site. It was a better measure of the overall density of the area of a town than Plot Ratio. One might, for instance, have a series of low Plot Ratios on very narrow streets and hence a relatively high density, whereas a high Plot Ratio on broad streets would give a lower overall density. Eventually, however, Plot Ratio was used, perhaps because it related more exactly to the specific development site. Low Plot Ratios, moreover, were intended to assist the dispersal of commercial activities from city centres and from London to other parts of the country, implementing the Barlow principle.[11]

One final problem remained. In 1943 Allen had pointed out that, where properties along existing city streets were redeveloped individually, his new system of arranging buildings would be impossible. 'Therefore it follows', he argued, 'that unless it becomes possible by some means to undertake comprehensive redevelopment in urban districts, no material improvement in daylighting can be obtained.' This opportunity was of course provided to some extent by the bombing, but above all by the powers of the local planning authority under the 1944 Town and Country Planning Act to declare Comprehensive Development

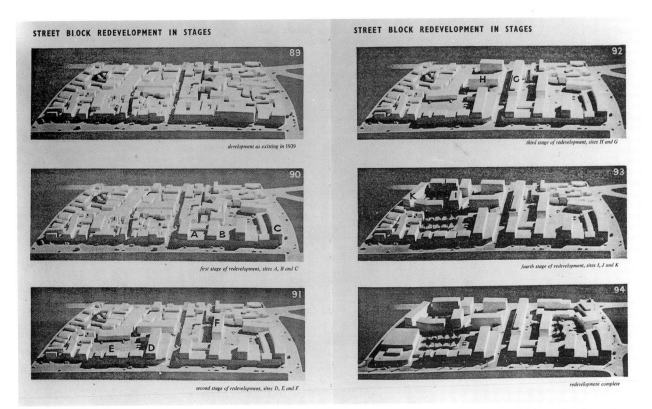

116   Diagrams from *The Redevelopment of City Centres*, 1947, show how the traditional street pattern could be replaced step-by-step with the new layout of slab blocks to create a Corbusian city.

Areas within which the piecemeal rebuilding or redevelopment of the larger site could be planned as part of the total pattern.[12]

In addition, as we have seen, the local authority acquired powers of compulsory purchase. The handbook, *The Redevelopment of Central Areas*, which appeared at the same time as the 1947 Act, showed how this might be done in a stage-by-stage process (Plate 116). It also illustrated the new appearance that cities would assume, though the height of the taller blocks was understated – presumably to avoid alarming the public (Plates 111 and 117).[13] Likewise in the *Report of the City of London* produced by Charles Holden and William Holford for the City Corporation in 1947 and published as a book in 1951, a maximum height of 120 feet was proposed as a general guideline within the new codes of control. The sketches showed a shape of building that was not so different as to frighten people. None of these building rises higher than eight storeys.[14] Armed with the powers of enforcing Plot Ratio controls and Daylighting Codes under a statutory development, any local planning authority who so desired now possessed the means for making it very difficult for an architect and developer to produce a building of the old type even if they wanted to. The tale is told that, in the case of one of the earliest of these buildings, Bucklersbury House in the City of London on Queen Victoria Street, the developer wanted to build a conventional, stone-fronted, street-aligned office block. It took long negotiations to persuade him to do as the architect-planners who controlled the City of London wanted. Holford was planning consultant to the City. Although Plot Ratio and the Daylighting Codes were purely advisory, the planning authority's discretionary power to withhold permission from any scheme which failed to comply was a formidable weapon in the hands of any authority committed to modern architecture. Here were bye-laws returning again through the back door.[15]

117   Slab office blocks on London Wall, Barbican, City of London, *c*. 1960. These were a model of modernist redevelopment. Sadly, since this photograph was taken in 1987 further redevelopment has destroyed a unique vista.

ARCHITECT PLANNERS

Even so, without the influence of planning officers who were also trained as architects, or at least sympathetic to the architect's point of view, there was of course little hope that Daylighting Codes would be employed, or modern architecture built. It was essential to ensure the appointment of Modernist architects to these jobs. Legislation, being permissive rather than prescriptive, was not enough.

We have observed that Modernist architects and their supporters had been vociferous during the 1930s in calling for an extension of the potential market for the architect's designs. An extreme advocate was John Gloag who declared in 1934 that:

> The architect is almost the only professional type of man in the community who is trained to think lucidly about design. He is trained to employ a perplexing diversity of materials for carrying out his work. His ability to plan may give him some exceptional

opportunities for affecting the life of the community in the future, not only in the obvious directions of building and town-planning, but by forming the character of industrial products, and by influencing the methods chosen for distributing such products to the general public.

He wished to see architects involved in the design of everything, including radio-sets and kettles, and indeed he believed that everything should be *compulsorily* designed: teacups; buildings; cities.[16]

Pevsner strongly supported Gloag in believing that the architect ought to become '*the* expert on design in the community', and he associated this with the Modern Movement in which he saw many symptoms of 'a legitimate widening of the architect's duties and rights'. Indeed most of the heroic pioneers of Pevsner's Modern Movement in Design were architects by training.[17]

But the case for the necessity of the architect as planner of cities was presented with all the scholarly authority of an historian by Sir John Summerson in his history of *Georgian London*, begun just before the war and published as it ended. His argument was based upon a fundamental assumption: there was a Good London and a Bad London. Bad London was mediaeval London as it stood before Inigo Jones's return from Italy, 'a city built by generations of closely organized carpenters and masons . . . a city in which architectural novelty consisted in exceptional feats of carpentry, in curious enrichment, or in extravagant use of stone.' Good London was the Georgian city whose design and planning was initiated by Inigo Jones under the aegis of the state and in which for some three centuries the great aristocratic landlords, and occasionally the crown estate, continued to employ architects as surveyors laying out their lands in the Spirit of Improvement. Taste during this period exercised some control over wealth. Bad London had returned with a vengeance after the Gothic Revival leading, in the twentieth century, to the 'out-thrust of estate development towards an incontinent suburbia created by . . . the overthrow of Georgian standards of taste under the assault of a new, combative attitude of mind better able to destroy than to create.'[18]

The moral to be drawn from this historical account was that the creation of some more publicly accountable equivalent to the aristocratic estates, namely the local planning authorities, through the nationalisation of development rights, was the necessary precondition for the employment of the right architects as planning officers. These architect-planners would provide the sufficient condition to ensure that the right modern buildings were built.[19]

In an article which Summerson wrote at about this time, for a book which formed a collective manifesto of modern thought in every area of life from science to theology, he drew attention to the first of such architect-planners to take over in the post of city engineer. This was Donald Gibson at Coventry, referred to with approval by J.M. Richards in his 1957 article.[20]

Gibson was appointed to head the newly created City Architects Department in 1938. After a battle between him and the City Engineer on whether reconstruction should be on the basis of the existing street plan or a new one Coventry Council backed Gibson, removing architecture and planning from the City Engineer and placing it in the hands of a trained architect. At the time, Coventry was the fastest growing city in Britain because of the expansion of its car assembly plants; its population jumped from 10,000 in 1901 to 305,000 in 1961. It exemplified all the problems which the Barlow Commission had been set up to examine. Gibson was soon joined by Percy Johnson-Marshall, with whose brother Stirrat he had worked as deputy county architect for the Isle of Ely. Even before the great bombing raid of 14 November 1940 which destroyed Coventry Cathedral, Gibson had started to devise a redevelopment plan, which was subsequently worked out, centring

118 Coventry city-centre shopping precinct planned by Sir Donald Gibson after 1940 and one of the earliest showcases for modernist ideas.

around the central shopping precinct in some areas of which traffic and pedestrians were separated (Plate 118). The 1969 guide to Coventry's New Architecture praised the precinct 'which allows for traffic-free shopping in over seventy shops and has multi-storey car parks behind'. One of these was proudly illustrated upon the cover, although even the authors had to admit that 'the individual buildings are not outstanding architecture'.[21]

The Modernists' next success was the 1946 appointment of Robert Matthew as architect to the LCC, also responsible for planning and housing, in succession to J.H. Forshaw who was Patrick Abercrombie's co-author on the 1943 *County of London Plan*. The LCC department became the largest architectural office in the world. Matthew's deputy was Leslie Martin. As well as ensuring that modern buildings were erected and modern planning methods adopted in their own localities, these two local authorities were a crucially important training ground and launch pad for city architects elsewhere.[22]

For example, Percy Johnson-Marshall left Coventry in 1949 to work for the LCC, first on the planning and design of the Lansbury Estate and then on the replanning of the South Bank and Elephant and Castle, all three of which had been declared Comprehensive Development Areas. Meanwhile in 1960 the new Labour leader of Newcastle, T. Dan Smith, later gaoled for corruption in connection with the architect John Poulson, appointed Wilfred Burns, who had worked at Coventry, as city planning officer on the retirement of the city engineer.[23]

A different example was the case of Liverpool which, as late as 1968, could be described as 'a Victorian city with much of its Victorian fabric still intact for redevelopment has come late'. Blitz damage had been replaced piecemeal under the regime of the city engineer. But under the control of a younger generation of Conservative councillors in the 1960s, Holford, supported by the permanent secretary at the Ministry of Housing and Local Government, exerted strong pressure on the city to appoint Modernist architect-planners. From the LCC's Comprehensive Development Areas at Lansbury, South Bank and Elephant and Castle came Graeme Shankland, appointed as planning consultant to Liverpool in 1960; and, in 1962, when the city engineer retired, Walter Bor, also from the LCC, was appointed as Liverpool's first city planning officer. Between them they produced the plan for the redevelopment of the centre of Liverpool.[24]

In securing control of the old city engineer's departments, the architect-planners also, inevitably, gained control of the local authority architects' departments, and were therefore in a position to design schools, colleges, housing, hospitals, council offices, police stations, multi-storey car parks, art galleries, municipal theatres, as well as to patronise private firms of modern architects. The best documented example of this is the case of Hertfordshire's architect's department formed in 1945 largely to cope with the school-building programme. Andrew Saint describes how between 1945 and 1948 Stirrat Johnson-Marshall, Percy's older brother and deputy county architect, created a team which developed a highly effective and flexible system of prefabricated building components which enabled Hertfordshire to meet its targets (at a time when traditional building materials and craftsmen were in short supply on account of the priority of the house-building programme, for which Aneurin Bevan had insisted upon traditional construction).[25]

Stirrat Johnson-Marshall moved to become chief architect to the Ministry of Education from 1948 to 1956, where he influenced the school-building programme of the nation as a whole through a development group which published design manuals, designed its own model schools and developed methods of cost analysis and yardsticks: all of which helped to cajole local authorities into using the kinds of approach which had proved so successful in Hertfordshire. Meanwhile Donald Gibson himself had left Coventry in 1955 to become chief architect of Nottinghamshire, and he moved in 1958 to hold that position in the War Office.[26]

What this amounted to was a State Architecture and Planning Service which, dispersed though it was through different local authority and government departments and lacking, therefore, *official* central control, was nonetheless coordinated both by strong personal links between the architects themselves who had trained together at the Architectural Association, the Liverpool University School of Architecture and elsewhere in the formative years of the 1930s, and through their professional body, the RIBA. The Modernists gained control of this in the early 1950s, partly through generational change, partly through stealth and tactics. This they reformed on quasi-Civil Service lines into a kind of Ministry of Archi-tecture which could negotiate with government and, through its Clients Advisory Service, recommend Modernist architects to private and public-sector clients.[27]

In addition, control of the RIBA gave control over architectural training in the schools of architecture which, under the Architectural Registration Acts of 1931 and 1938, had become a prerequisite to professional practice using the title of architect. And they used this

119   Flats at Alton West, part of the LCC Roehampton Estate, 1955–9, 'one of the masterpieces of post-war residential design' according to the *Architectural Review* but Pevsner detected 'more than a touch of the deliberate violence of the brutalists'.

power to ensure that all those schools which had continued to teach architecture on traditional lines were reformed on Modernist lines, many of them under the direction of the men who had headed the local authority architecture departments – thus Robert Matthew left the LCC to become head of the Edinburgh School in 1953 and his deputy, Leslie Martin, became Professor of Architecture at Cambridge in 1958.

It was in this way that the Modernists began to make their impact on British towns and cities in the years immediately following J.M. Richards's pessimistic article, as they pursued their long march through the institutions. Lionel Esher looked back upon 1960 as the *annus mirabilis* for the Modernists, with the unveiling of Stirling and Gowan's designs for Leicester University Engineering Building; the first major curtain-wall office block, Castrol House in London; the slab blocks at Roehampton (Plate 119); Park Hill housing at Sheffield; and Denys Lasdun's Royal College of Physicians in Regent's Park. J.M. Richards, in his 1961 forward to an exhibition 'Architecture Today', only four years after his gloom-ridden editorial, could take satisfaction in the fact that although the battle for modern architecture had not been 'won all along the line', and that 'freak returns to full-blooded nineteenth century historical revival' were still in evidence, nonetheless Modern architecture seemed to have established itself not just in schools and public housing but in every area of British life. Bill Allen, who had himself served as principal of the Architectural Association, wrote in 1966, with a crow of triumph, that the architecture 'profession in Britain is already in a relatively influential position, responsible for by far the largest sector of fixed capital investment in the country'.[28]

————Part Seven————

CONCLUSION
PLATO'S CONUNDRUM

CONCLUSION

WHEN PEOPLE TALKED about Britain entering a New Elizabethan Age on the accession of Elizabeth II in 1952, it was no empty rhetoric. The Welfare State, regional policy, social demand and the related policies of the Utility Scheme, dispersal from cities and town and country planning were an attempt to reinstate the benign paternalism and control both of personal consumption and urban growth that had characterised the efforts of Elizabeth I and Lord Burghley. Indeed, as we have seen, these policies were based in part upon historical interpretations of the Elizabethan and early Stuart reigns.

In the field of design, these policies enjoyed differing fortunes. The Utility Scheme was abolished in 1953 and free-market consumerism returned with the introduction of commercial TV and the rise of pop culture throughout the following decades. This reaction took place not only on a political, commercial and popular level. The Independent Group of artists, architects, designers and writers also espoused and promoted the values of commercial design against the stuffy good taste of an older generation of Modernists.

In architecture and planning, the new policies only fully made themselves fully felt in the 1960s and 1970s, so were out of phase with the design of furnishings and consumer goods, though the new public buildings gave rise to a demand for modern furniture if not for private domestic use. Then from the late 1960s onwards and particularly in the late 1970s and early 1980s, the Modernist policy suffered a series of assaults both at the level of public debate and public policy. Conservationists who deplored the wholesale destruction of older buildings and streets succeeded in setting up conservation areas under the Civic Amenities Act of 1967 which undermined comprehensive redevelopment; the famous collapse of the high-rise housing tower, Ronan Point, also in 1967, destroyed the case for the extra expense of housing people in tall buildings; in 1969 a group of influential authors published an article in *New Society* whose title speaks for its contents: 'Non-Plan: an experiment in Freedom' which challenged the most basic assumptions of 1947-type planning, namely the desire to control consumption, style, the use of the motor-car, urban sprawl and the freedom of industry and commerce to choose its location. More significant was the fact that in the correspondence columns of *New Society* a future adviser to Margaret Thatcher latched on to these ideas immediately and they formed the basis for free enterprise zones, the first of them in London's Docklands on the Isle of Dogs. Thatcher's government also responded to the public dissatisfaction with Modernist housing schemes with an election promise to introduce a right for tenants to buy the homes they had rented, a promise which was honoured, and also effectively ceased the building of new local authority housing. That in turn meant the end of the largest source of work for local authority architects departments and hence led to the dismembering of the 'State Architecture Service'. Community action also expressed itself in opposition to any further comprehensive redevelopment, particularly in Covent Garden, and succeeded not only in that specific case but also in changing public policy. Working-class community groups, particularly in Liverpool from the late-1970s onwards, obtained the power not only to manage their own public housing but also to act as clients for the design and building of their own small-scale, traditional housing schemes on a neighbourhood basis. Then in 1984 and especially after 1987, the Prince of Wales gave public expression in speeches, television and book to the widespread dissatisfaction with the surviving manifestations of Modernist architecture and planning, supported community architecture and called for a return to bye-law type amenity planning and a more humane architecture based upon traditional principles and craftsmanship. Local planning authorities responded by using their discretion under the planning laws, which had survived since 1947 effectively unaltered in principle, to favour schemes which respected the scale of the existing streetscape and townscape. At the same time, on a more purely architectural level, a fashion developed, dubbed Post-Modernism, for buildings which were more highly decorated in somewhat funky versions of traditional styles and in highly expressionist forms of Modernism. These 'signature buildings' acted in an opposite direction, using the freedoms permitted under the discretionary nature of the planning system to stand out against their surroundings both in height, scale and design. Furthermore, in the 1980s commercial property boom, which more than made up for the loss of work for architects in the public sector, a new breed of property developer took over greater control of the design process, displacing architects from their role as leaders of the building team. And finally, after the collapse of that boom in 1989, the construction industry entered its worst recession since the war, leaving the architectural profession without either bread or butter.

In 1995, at the time of publication, the whole Modernist system of design, architecture and planning in Britain lies in ruins and, even though the discretionary principles of the 1947 Planning Act remain in force, they have been used to implement quite different policies to those for which they were designed – as had indeed also happened during the first decade after 1947, as we have seen. Rather oddly, conservation has now caught up with the products of the 1960s and moves are afoot to preserve the best of the buildings and development schemes which are viewed with great admiration now there is no threat of comprehensive redevelopment (Plate 120), even by their former detractors, amongst whom this author is included.

The Modernist system has collapsed and a new orthodoxy seems to have replaced it, namely a return to the so-called traditional city of streets and squares. Despite its attractions I do not believe this to be an adequate approach to the complexity of life in what has aptly been called the '100 Mile City'. Indeed this new orthodoxy is almost as simplistic, and tyrannical perhaps, as modernism. But this conclusion is not the place in which to present arguments for alternatives.

The primary purpose of this book has been to present an historical reconstruction of a system of thought in which the design, manufacture and consumption of goods, architecture and town planning have been inextricably interlinked with issues of economic theory and policy, social policy and personal morality, from the Tudor period to that of the Welfare State, and to show how this 'Political Economy of Design' has shaped the physical environment of this country. At the same time it is hoped that this illustrates, for those who are interested in such matters, the kinds of ways in which art and society influence one another – though no claims are being made for a general theory, indeed it is doubtful whether any such theory can be formulated; the arts are all very different from one another and so are societies. In any case it must be acknowledged that the arts of design have, in general, a far more direct relationship to public policy than painting, literature and music.

The purpose of reconstructing this political economy of design was not, however, primarily for dry-as-dust historical explanation but to provide an holistic approach to thinking about the shaping of our surroundings in the present and future. The issues of the

120   Modernism with a comic face. Hayward Gallery, South Bank Arts Centre, 1965–8, GLC Architects Department, once threatened with demolition now saved, but in 1994 destined to be shrouded under a dome designed by Richard Rogers. It is one of the most charmingly quirky buildings of the 1960s with the most inventive use of concrete only requiring a periodic wash. It deserves to be seen.

next century are not going to be the same as those of the 1930s or of the 1830s or of the 1750s, but the kind of equation between consumption, taste, personal morality, the quality of work and of leisure and economic prosperity sketched out in so lucid a form by David Hume, amongst others, incomplete though it may be, provides a basis for thinking clearly about the repercussions of action and policy in any one sphere upon the others and for assessing the balance of advantage in an imperfect world. For example, one recent urban theorist who does possess a particular holistic vision of the future, Leon Krier, made the observation at a recent discussion that 'Suburban houses are not those little quiet things, which one imagines; they are really like mortars throwing cars at historic centres, creating every day about a dozen journeys.' To counteract this he believes, like Ebenezer Howard, that, instead of building new dormitory suburbs separated from places of work and from shops, we should build new towns where uses are mixed, not zoned, and small enough for everything to be within ten minutes walking distance. This in turn has vast implications for the way we might live.

Krier's position is not so far from that of Beveridge and his associates, that left to themselves and to the pressure of salesmanship, as he so quaintly called it, people will spend their money unwisely – on cars, funerals, drink, gambling and things offering sensual satisfaction – rather than wisely upon health, housing, education, a nutritious diet and provision for their old age. So they should be heavily taxed in order that the State can provide for them what they ought to have acquired of their own accord.

In both these cases, however, the decision rests with the wise minority in society, if they are able to acquire the power through democratic persuasion or other means. Implicit here is the notion of wise rulers or guardians of society which derives from Plato in Book II of his *Republic*. He was the first writer to analyse the implications of our style of life upon the economy and social structure and to examine the further implications for art and indeed ecology, No one's ideas have been more keenly studied and emulated by the ruling elite from Sir Thomas More to Keynes and Beveridge. Through the character of Socrates, Plato argues that human beings are not self-sufficient, and hence communities arise in which specialised workers, each expert in a particular craft or trade, can provide most efficiently for one another's needs by exchanging the products of their labours. As he sketches the simplest community needed to supply the fundamental requirements for food, shelter and clothing, so the number of specialists expands. A farmer, a builder, a weaver and a shoemaker need to be served by a smith to make tools, shepherds, foreign merchants for importing and exporting, sailors and shipbuilders, shopkeepers and labourers. He paints a picture of how they will live – their life-style:

> They will produce corn, wine, clothes, and shoes, and will build themselves houses. In the summer they will for the most part work unclothed and unshod, in the winter they will be clothed and shod suitably. For food they will prepare wheat-meal or barley-meal for baking or kneading. They will serve splendid cakes and loaves on rushes or fresh leaves, and will sit down to feast with their children on couches of myrtle and bryony; and they will have wine to drink too, and pray to the gods with garlands on their heads, and enjoy each other's company. And fear of poverty and war will make them keep the numbers of their families within their means . . . they will have a few luxuries, salt, of course, and olive oil and cheese, and different kinds of vegetables . . . And we must give them some dessert, figs and peas and beans, and myrtle-berries and acorns to roast at the fire as they sip their wine. So they will lead a peaceful and healthy life, and probably die at a ripe old age.

At this portrait of the simple, vegetarian life, one of Plato's own brothers, Glaucon, protests that this is a community of pigs not men; so Socrates offers to portray a society which enjoys the luxuries of civilisation, even though it will be like a man in a fever as opposed to a man in health.

> Such a society will not be satisfied with the standard of living we have described. It will want couches and tables and other furniture, and a variety of delicacies, scents, perfumes, call-girls and confectionary. And we must no longer confine ourselves to the bare necessities . . . but must add the fine arts of painting and embroidery, and introduce materials like gold and ivory.

As a result of this, many more kinds of occupation will be needed: hunters, fishermen and swineherds to provide the meat and fish; artists, sculptors, painters and musicians; poets, actors and reciters; cosmeticians, barbers, dressmakers, butchers and cooks. And, in order to treat the diseases of civilisation, doctors will be needed and armies of soldiers to defend the community and to conquer more land to provide for all these luxuries.

With great directness Plato shows how the provision of luxuries, including the arts, transforms not only the pattern of consumption and recreation but also the whole structure of the community, its industries, agriculture and ecology and its relation to neighbouring communities. And it becomes the task of the soldiers or guardians both to defend the society against its enemies and to maintain some kind of harmony within the body politic against its worst excesses. These austere guardians, educated in quasi-monastic surroundings in philosophy, mathematics and geometry in order that they should not be diverted from understanding the true nature of beauty and justice by the seductive charms of the fine arts and the sensuality of the world about them, have cast a spell upon the governors of Western societies, not least upon the protagonists who have figured in this book, upon Ruskin as much as Le Corbusier who was, as we saw, greatly inspired by both Plato and Diogenes and by the earlier reformer Solon.

I am far from advocating such remedies. Indeed there lurks the tyranny of taste. But Plato's conundrum, that when luxury enters human society innocence departs, is one to which there are no easy solutions. In Britain, as it entered the Industrial Revolution, from the sixteenth century onwards, politicians, philosophers (often the same people in those days), artists, designers and architects thought hard and deeply about the solution to Plato's conundrum. As we confront, on a global scale, the same set of problems, their system of thought, though not necessarily their conclusions, constitutes a tradition which can surely be of service to humankind.

NOTES

Introduction

1 Adam Smith, 'On the Nature of that Imitation which Takes Place in what are called The Imitative Arts', *Essays on Philosophical Subjects*, Basel, 1799, pp. 169–238.

Part One

1 *Discourses upon Trade*, London, 1691, in J.R. McCulloch (ed.), *Early English Tracts on Commerce* (1st ed. 1856), Cambridge, 1952, p. 528.
2 In general: P. Earle, *The Making of the English Middle Class, Business, Society and Family Life in London 1660–1730*, London, 1989 – especially chapters on 'The Metropolitan Economy' and 'Expenditure and Consumption'. For bibliographies of foreign visitors' accounts of England see C.T. Hagberg Wright, *Subject Index of the London Library*, 1909 and 1922 under England, Foreign Impressions and Travels; R. Bayne-Powell, *Travellers in Eighteenth Century England*, London, 1951; J.A. Kelly, *England and the Englishman in German Literature of the Eighteenth Century*, New York, 1921; A.D. Potts, 'British Romantic Art through German Eyes', in W. Sauerlander, *'Sind Briten hier?' Relations between British and Continental Art 1680–1880*, Munich, 1981, pp. 181–205.
3 *Joshua Johnson's Letter Book 1771–4. Letters from a Merchant in London to his Partners in Maryland*, ed. J.M. Price, London Record Society, 1979, p. 11 (7 August 1771); T.H. Breen, '"Baubles of Britain" the American and Consumer Revolutions of the 18th Century', *Past and Present*, 119, pp. 73–104.
4 W. Wordsworth, *The Prelude*, ed. Selincourt, 2nd ed., Oxford, 1959, Book VII, 97–104, 1805–6 version.
5 N.G. Brett-James, *The Growth of Stuart London*, London, 1935, pp. 495–513; R. Finlay and B. Shearer, 'Population Growth and Suburban Expansion', in A.L. Beier and R. Finlay, *London, 1500–1700*, London, 1986, pp. 37–59; Earle, op. cit., p. 17.

6 Daniel Defoe, *A Tour thro' the whole Island of Great Britain* . . . , London, 1725, Everyman Edition, London, 1962, I, p. 314.
7 Ibid., I, p. 355, 361–2.
8 Ibid., I, pp. 332–5.
9 Ibid., I, pp. 335–6.
10 Ibid., I, pp. 167–8; I. Macky, *A Journey through England*, London, 3rd ed., 1732, p. 4 (1st ed. 1722–3).
11 Defoe, op. cit., I, pp. 326–9; John Summerson, *Georgian London*, London, 1945 and later editions remains the most concise account of the growth of the West End; more detailed is Brett-James op. cit. See also relevant volumes of *The Survey of London*.
12 Brett-James, op. cit., pp. 73, 110–11, 152–60, 168–76, 178, 367–79, 452–6; John Stow, *A Survey of London*, ed. Henry Morley, London, n.d. (*c*. 1900) pp. 388–9; J. McMaster, *A Short History of the Royal Parish of St. Martin's-in-the-Fields*, London, 1916, pp. 254–9; see also below, Pt. II, Ch. 1.
13 Brett-James, op. cit., p. 154 for Privy Council, 20 March 1618.
14 R.H. Tawney and E. Power, *Tudor Economic Documents*, London, 1924, III, pp. 1, 7, 115–17; J.F. Larkin and P.H. Hughes (eds.), *Stuart Royal Proclamations, Volume I, Royal Proclamations of King James I, 1603–1625*, Oxford, 1973, pp. 267, 346, 429; Adam Smith, *The Wealth of Nations*, Everyman Edition, London, 1962, I, p. 311.
15 See note 2 above.
16 J.K. Hyde, 'Medieval Descriptions of Cities', *Bulletin of the John Rylands Library*, XLVIII, 1965–6, pp. 308–40.
17 G.F. Coyer, *Nouvelles Observations sur l'Angleterre*, Paris, 1779, pp. 34–36.
18 M. de Souligné, *A Comparison between Old Rome in It's Glory as to the Extent and Populousness of it And London as at Present*, 2nd ed., London, 1709 (1st ed. 1706), pp. 149–50.
19 Ibid., p. 154.
20 F. Braudel, *Civilization and Capitalism, 15th–18th Century*, II, London, 1982, pp. 60–75.
21 Smith, op. cit., I, p. 11.

22 I have in mind the highly graphic non-statistical model of economic flows that emerges both from the literary panegyric and from its pic-torial equivalent such as Ambrogio Lorenzetti's portrait of the well-governed City and its countryside in the Sala del Nove of the Palazzo Communale in Siena, dating from 1340. There we see the flow of trade back and forth between town and country: wool and food grown in the country, brought to market in town, manufactured there into cloth or shoes and returned to the country or exported. Political and re-ligious commentators of the time referred to Lorenzetti's frescoes as the basis for their own observations – see T. Burckhardt, *Siena*, Oxford, 1960, p. 40. The early literature of political economy retains this graphic quality, e.g. N. Barbon, *An Apology for the Builder*, London, 1685, and D. Defoe, *A Plan of English Commerce*, 3rd ed., London, 1749, pp. 20–7.

23 Count Frederick Kielmansegge, tr. Countess Kielmansegge, *Diary of a Journey to England 1761–2*, London, 1902, p. 18.

24 B. Faujas de Saint-Fond, *A Journey through England and Scotland to the Hebrides*, revised ed. of English tr. Sir A. Geikie, Glasgow, 1907. (1st ed. 1797. Faujas visited England in 1784.)

25 For Osterley and its owners see P. Ward-Jackson, *Osterley Park*, London, 1954.

26 M.S. von La Roche, tr. C. Williams, *Sophie in London, 1786*, London, 1933, pp. 224–8. For Horace Walpole's observations see Ward-Jackson, op. cit., pp. 8–9. 'The bed is . . . too theatric, and too like a modern head-dress . . . What would Vitruvius think of a dome decorated by a milliner?'

27 Tobias Smollett, *Travels through France and Italy*, London, 1778, II, pp. 103–4. His comparison between the French and Italian countryside and their peasantry and the English was a commonplace both amongst continental visitors to England and of English visitors to the continent.

28 J.W. von Archenholtz, *A Picture of England*, London, 1779, p. 132. (He visited London in the late 1770s.) Brett-James, op. cit., pp. 466 ff; P. Brimblecombe, *The Big Smoke*, London, 1987, pp. 40–2.

29 Il Conte G.L. Ferri de San Constante, *Londres et les Anglais*, 4 vols, Paris, 1802, I, p. 14.

30 Archenholtz, op. cit., p. 127.

31 Most of the travellers' accounts of England describe the inns; see too A.E. Richardson, *The Old Inns of England*, London, 1952 (6th ed.), pp. 20–1.

32 R. Edwards and M. Jourdain, *Georgian Cabinet Makers, 1700–1800*, London, 1955, pp. 39, 45, 50, 56, 61, 64, 85. For relative prices see Henry Phelps Brown and Sheila V. Hopkins, *A Perspective of Wages and Prices*, London, 1981. There are many difficulties in translating his-torical prices into contemporary values. I have used an index of prices in Douglas Jay, *Sterling*, Oxford, 1986, pp. 273–9, which brings Phelps Brown's series up to 1984.

33 Wendeborn estimated the average cost of building a house to be £300. For the number of houses a year built in London during the eighteenth century there are various estimates:

	Period	Total No.	Average/year
W. Petty	1682–1699	21,315	1,253
N. Barbon	1685		c. 1,000
Wendeborn	1746–1786	25,000	625
Grosley	1750–1765	20,000	1,333
Ferri	1750–1800	35,000	700
Archenholtz	1762–1779	42,000	2,470
M.D. George	1737–1801	37,739	590

Barbon, 1685, p. 18; G.F.A. Wendeborn, *A View of England towards the Close of the Eighteenth Century*, 2 vols, London, 1791, I, p. 254; M. Grosley, *A Tour of London*, London, 1772, I, p. 40; Ferri, op. cit., I, p. 10; Archenholtz, op. cit., p.118; M.D. George, *London Life in the XVIIIth Century*, London, 1930, Appendix 3. Earle, op. cit., p. 22 estimates that building was the second largest industry after clothing (25%) but gives no figures or references. There seems to be no accurate information here. For cost of construction (and much else) see Dan Cruickshank and Neil Burton, *Life in the Georgian City*, London, 1990, pp. 117–21.

34 Wendeborn, op. cit., I, pp. 190–2; Hoh-Cheung and Lorna H. Mui, *Shops and Shopkeeping in Eighteenth-Century England*, London, 1989, pp. 70–1; Earle, op. cit., pp. 44–5 (quoting Defoe) and Ch. 10; L. Weatherill, *The Growth of the Pottery Industry in England 1660–1815*, New York and London, 1986, p. 227 on London as an entrepot for England.

35 Braudel loc. cit. For the two shopping streets see J. Feltham, *The Picture of London for 1805*, London, 1805, pp. 44–5. Also Hoh-Cheung and Mui, op. cit., pp. 36–40.

36 Grosley, op. cit., I, p. 36; Hoh-Cheung and Mui, op. cit., pp. 17–18; Defoe, *The Complete English Tradesman*, London, 1745, II, pp. 332, 335, quoted in Braudel, op. cit., p. 69.

37 Ferri, op. cit., I, p. 26.

38 S. von La Roche, op. cit., pp. 141–2.

39 Von Archenholtz, op. cit., pp. 119–23.

40 Johnson, op. cit., p. 17, letter of 6 Nov. 1771 to partners in Maryland.

41 See Part II, Ch. 1 below for this debate. For the classic 'city' point of view see Thomas Mun, *England's Treasure by Forraign Trade*, London, 1664 in McCulloch, op. cit., p. 193.

42 For Barbon see Brett-James, op. cit., pp. 324–49 and J. Summerson, *Georgian London*, Harmondsworth, 1962, pp. 44–51.

43 Brett-James, op. cit., pp. 330–2.

44 Barbon, 1685, p. 6.

45 Ibid, p. 18.

46 Ibid, p. 28. Barbon was wrong. The increase in London's population was not natural, but the result of immigration. The population was falling, so high was the death rate. See below Part II, Ch. 1.

47 Ibid., p. 32.

48 Ibid., p. 30.

49 R. Campbell, *The London Tradesman*, London, 1747, pp. 155–77.

50 Barbon, 1685, p. 33.

51 Edwards and Jourdain, op. cit., p. 49.

52 For Seddon see R. Edwards, 'A Great Georgian Cabinet-Maker. New Light on the firm of Seddon', *Country Life*, 21 Oct. 1933, pp. 415–18.

53 Von La Roche, op. cit., pp. 173–5.

54 Campbell, op. cit., pp. 115–16.

55 Von Archenholtz, op. cit., pp. 221–2; Hoh-Cheung and Mui, op. cit., pp. 239–45; T.S. Willan, *Abraham Dent of Kirkby Stephen*, Manchester, 1970; Johnson, op. cit., p. 8; B. Lemire, *Fashion's Favourite*, Oxford, 1991, pp. 179–97 on ready-made clothes.

56 Von Archenholtz, op. cit., p. 223.

57 Wendeborn, op. cit., I, p. 195.

58 Campbell, op. cit., p. 192.

59 Barbon, 1685, p. 37.

Part Two

Preface

1 Bernard de Mandeville, 'A Search into the Nature of Society', *Fable of the Bees*, 4th ed., London, 1725, I, pp. 376–7.

Chapter 1

1 James F. Larkin and Paul L. Hughes (eds.), *Tudor Royal Proclamations, Vols 2 and 3, The Later Tudors*, London, 1969, Proclamation 649, II; 815, III; James F. Larkin and Paul L. Hughes (eds.), *Stuart Royal Proclamations, Vol. 1, Royal Proclamations of King James I, 1603–1625*, Oxford, 1973. See proclamations 25, 78, 87, 120, 121, 152, 175, 186, 204, 234, 255; James F. Larkin (ed.) *Stuart Royal Proclamations, Vol. II, Royal Proclamations of King Charles I, 1625–1646*, Oxford, 1983. See proclamations 9, 136; N.G. Brett-James, *The Growth of Stuart London*, London, 1935, Chs. 3 and 4, pp. 67–149; J. Summerson, 'The Surveyorship of Inigo Jones, 1615–43', Ch. 7 of H.M. Colvin (ed.), *The History of the King's Works*, III, Pt. I, 1485–1660, London, 1975.

2 'London in 1689–90', ed. D. Maclean and N.G. Brett-Jones, *London and Middlesex Archaeological Society Transactions*, n.s. VI, pp. 322–42; VII, pp. 133–57.

3 R. Finlay, *Population and Metropolis: the Demography of London, 1580–1650*, Cambridge, 1981, pp. 3–4 and 9–10; E.A. Wrigley, 'A Simple Model of London's Importance in Changing English Society and Economy, 1650–1750', *Past and Present*, 1967, XXXVII, pp. 46–8.

4 For the proclamations see Larkin and Hughes, loc. cit. and Brett-James, loc. cit. Also B.E. Supple, *Commercial Crisis and Change in England, 1600–1642*, Cambridge, 1959, p. 25.

5 M.J. Power, 'London and the Control of the "Crisis" of the 1590s', *History*, LXX, 1985, pp. 371–85; M.J. Power, 'A "Crisis" reconsidered: social and demographic dislocation in London in the 1590's', *London Journal*, XII, 1986, pp. 134–5; John Stow, *A Survey of London*, (ed. Henry Morley), London, n.d., p. 384 (7th paragraph of chapter on 'Suburbs without the walls'); J. Boulton, *Neighbourhood and Society: A London Suburb in the Seventeenth Century*, Cambridge, 1987, pp. 85–6; K.G.T. McDonnell, *Mediaeval London Suburbs*, Chichester, 1978, p. 121.

6 Proclamation of 2 May 1625 in Larkin, 1983, pp. 20–6; K. Sharpe, *The Personal Rule of Charles I*, New Haven and London, 1992, pp. 404 ff.

7 P. Clark and P. Slack, *English Towns in Transition, 1500–1700*, Oxford, 1976, p. 62; Proclamations of 7 July 1580 and 12 Oct. 1607, in Larkin and Hughes, 1969; II, procl. 649, and 1973, pp. 171–5; J.S. Davies, *A History of Southampton*, Southampton, 1883, pp. 256–62; Alwyn Ruddock, 'London's Capitalists and the Decline of Southampton in the Early Tudor Period', *Economic History Review*, 2nd series, II, pp. 137–51; Colin Platt, *Mediaeval Southampton*, London, 1973, pp. 215 ff.

8 'A Proclamation Commanding Noblemen, Knights, and Gentlemen of quality, to repayre to their Mansion houses in the Country . . .' 20 November 1622, Larkin and Hughes, 1973, pp. 561–2. See also proclamations 11, 23, 143, 158, 166, 241, 259. For similar orders in 1596 see Edward P. Cheyney, *A History of England from the Defeat of the Armada to the Death of Elizabeth*, 2 vols, London, 1926, II, pp. 13–14. Clark and Slack, op. cit., p. 68, mention that 30% of the Verney family's rental income during the 1680s and 77% of the Fitzwilliam family's in the late 1690s was being spent in London.

9 King James I, 'Speech in Star Chamber 1616', in *The Political Works of James I* (intro. by Charles H. McIlvain), Cambridge, Mass., 1918, p. 338; Hugh Ross Williamson, *Four Stuart Portraits*, London, 1949, p. 2. For the period following the Restoration see P. Earle, *The Making of the English Middle Class, 1670–1730*, London, 1989, partic. Ch. 2 'The Metropolitan Economy', and pp. 60–75 for

London as a centre for the pro-fessions. Earle estimates that around 1700 one fifth of the population of London, or 20–25,000 house-holds, belonged to the middle class in addition to 3–5,000 gentry and upper-middle class families. Even allowing for the growth in this professional section of the population between 1600 and 1700, the figures are indicative of the factors sustaining London's growth in population.

10 It is believed that during the seventeenth century between two-thirds and three-quarters of England's foreign trade passed annually through the Port of London. For the factors involved in London's expansion see four articles by F.J. Fisher: 'The Development of London as a Centre of Consumption in the 16th and 17th centuries, *Transactions of the Royal Historical Society*, 4th series, XXX, 1948, pp. 37–50, reprinted in E.M. Carus-Wilson, *Essays in Econ-omic History*, II, London, 1962, pp. 197–207; 'London's Export Trade in the Early 17th Century', *Economic History Review*, 2nd series, 1950, III, pp. 151–61; 'Commercial Trends and Policy in 16th century England', *Economic History Review*, 1st series, 1940, X, reprinted in E.M. Carus-Wilson, *Essays in Economic History*, London, 1954, pp. 152–72; 'London as an Engine of Economic Growth', in P. Clark (ed.) *The Early Modern Town: a Reader*, London 1976, pp. 205–15. All re-printed in F.J. Fisher, *London and the English Economy, 1500–1700*, London, 1990. See also the chapter on London in Clarke and Slack, op. cit., which estimates (p. 67) that by 1690 as much as 25% of London's population may have been employed in work related to the Port of London. For immigration to London from the rest of the country, especially the Midlands, see McDonnell, op. cit., p. 123.

11 McConnell, loc. cit.

12 *Remembrancia 1579–1664*, London, 1878, pp. 45–6, 48–9.

13 Larkin and Hughes, 1973, pp. 171–5.

14 Ibid, p. 268.

15 Ibid, pp. 345–7, and Brett-James, 1935, pp. 89–90.

16 Larkin and Hughes, 1973, pp. 398–400; Sharpe, op. cit., pp. 411–12.

17 But was not completely dead as an issue viz. 'The Debate of the Tax on New Buildings, 1677' in J. Thirsk and J.P. Cooper, *Seventeenth Century Economic Documents*, Oxford, 1972, pp. 687–91; and *A Discourse shewing the Great Advantages that New-Buildings, and the enlarging of Towns and Cities do bring to a Nation*, London, 1678 (ref. from Earle, 1989, p. 422). For the 1947 Act see Part VI, Ch. 3 below.

18 J. Summerson, *Georgian London*, London, 1945, pp. 13–17. For Summerson's espousal of 'planning' see 'New Groundwork of Architecture' in J.R.M. Brumwell (ed.) *This Changing World*, London, 1944, pp. 182–93, espec. p. 192; 'Ruins and the Future', *The Listener*, 17th April 1941, pp. 563–4; 'Rebuilding the City', *The Listener*, 24 August 1944, p. 6.

19 Stow, op. cit., p. 150 (Portsoken Ward – 17th paragraph); J. McMaster, *A Short History of the Royal Parish of St Martin's-in-the-Fields*, London, 1916, p. 259.

20 For Moorfields see: Brett-James, op. cit., pp. 451–60; Steen Eiler Rasmussen, *London, the Unique City*, 1948, pp. 79–84; *Fitzstephen's Description of the City of London*, London, 1772, pp. 50–2; Stow, op. cit. (Suburbs Without the Walls), pp. 387–9; Rev. W. Denton, *Moorfields. A Lecture to the Mutual Improvement Society*, London, 1863; Hall's *Chronical*, quoted in Denton, p. 12; Richard Johnson, *The Pleasant Walkes of Moore-Fields*, London, 1607 reprinted in J. Payne Collier, *Illustrations of Early English Popular Literature*, II, London, 1864.

21 Brett-James, 1935, pp. 152–60.

22 Ibid, pp. 110–11, 176–9; McMaster, op. cit., pp. 257–9; Duke of Manchester, *Court and Society from Elizabeth to Anne*, 2 vols, London, 1864, I, pp. 333–5; *Calendar of State Papers Domestic, Charles I, 1629–31*, CLXXXI, 1630? No. 27 (undated); *Acts of Privy Council of England*, June 1630–1, 22 June 1631, No. 1164, p. 50; *Cal. SPD, Ch. 1, 1631–3*, CXCVIII, 14 Aug. 1631, No. 36; J. Summerson, 'Prince Henry's Works, 1610–12', in ed. Colvin, op. cit., p. 144.

23 *Cal. State Papers Domestic, Ch. I*, CLXIII, No. 47, 25 March 1630; see also Sharpe, op. cit., p. 409.

24 Parishioners of St Martin's-in-the-Fields versus Earle of Bedford, 30 Nov. 1638, S.P. Dom, Ch. I, S.P. 16/402, No. 75. P.R.O.

25 For the 4th Earl of Bedford see *Dictionary of National Biography. Cal. S.P. Dom. Ch. I*, CLI, 1629, Nos. 24, 69, 70; Cal. S.P. in *Archives of Venice*, XXII, 1629–32, ed. Allen B. Hinds, London, 1919, Nos. 285 and 302; *Cal. S.P. Dom.*, CLXVII, Ch. 1, No. 44, 29 May 1630; S.P. 16/CLXXXII, No. 34, 10 Jan. 1631 P.R.O.; J. Summerson, 'Prince Henry's Works 1610–12', op. cit., p. 144; *Cal. S.P. Dom. Ch. I*, CLXXI, No. 30, 25 July 1630; CLXXII, No. 13, 3 Aug. 1630; CLXXV, No. 8, 2 Nov. 1630; CCIV, No. 39, 13 Dec. 1631; CCXXXI, No. 27, 13 Jan. 1633. See also Dorothy Summers, *The Great Level*, Newton Abbott, 1976; Keith Lindley, *Fenland Riots and the English Revolution*, London, 1982; Sharpe, op. cit., pp. 253–6.

26 E. Beresford Chancellor, *The History of the Squares of London*, London, 1907; Donald J. Olsen, *Town Planning in London, the 18th and 19th Centuries*, New Haven and London, 1964 and 1982; Brett-James, 1935; Andrew Byrne, *Bedford Square: An Architectural Study*, London,

1990, pp. 31–42, for a recent detailed analysis of the legal agreements which controlled building see D. Cruickshank and N. Burton, *Life in the Georgian City*, London, 1990, pp. 123–31.

27 T.F. Reddaway, *The Rebuilding of London after the Great Fire*, London, 1940; 18 and 19, Ch. 2, c. 8.

28 C.C. Knowles, *The History of Building Regulation in London, 1189–1972*, London, 1972, pp. 34, 49; J. Summerson, *Georgian London*, Harmonds-worth, 1962, pp. 123–9.

29 Knowles, op. cit., pp. 61 ff; Roger H. Harper, *Victorian Building Regulations*, London, 1985.

30 Ibid., pp. 88 ff; P. Metcalf, *James Knowles*, Oxford, 1980, pp. 299 ff; P. Metcalf, 'At Home in Westminster', *Architectural Review*, 155, Mar. 1974, pp. 135–8; *L.C.C. (General Powers) Act*, 1890, 53 and 54, Vict., Ch. ccxliii, sects. 28, 36; *London Building Act*, 1894, 57 and 58, Vict., cccxiii, sects. 47, 48, 49; *London Building Act*, 1930, 20 and 21 Geo 5, Ch. clviii, sects. 51–6. For 1947 see below, Part VI, Chs. 3 and 4.

31 Gilbert Elliott, *Proposals for carrying on certain Public Works in the City of Edinburgh*, Edinburgh, 1752; A.J. Youngson, *The Making of Classical Edinburgh, 1750–1840*, Edinburgh, 1960; James Wilson, *Miscellanies in Prose and Verse*, 4th ed., Edinburgh, 1771; W. Baird, *George Drummond*, Edinburgh, 1911; *The Present State of Scotland Consider'd*, Edinburgh, 1745, pp. 29–30.

Chapter 2

1 J.F. Larkin and P.L. Hughes, *Stuart Royal Proclamations, Vol. I, Royal Proclamations of King James I, 1603–1625*, Oxford, 1973, pp. 356–7. James I issued 8 proclamations on this issue compared to 3 by Charles I, 1 by Edward VI, 1 by Mary, and 2 by Elizabeth I (Larkin and Hughes, 1973, p. 22, n. 3).

2 M.M. Postan, 'The Rise of a Money Economy', (1944) in E.M. Carus-Wilson, *Essays in Economic History*, London, 1954, p. 1.

3 Mark Girouard, *Life in the English Country House*, New Haven and London, 1978, p. 3.

4 L. Stone, *The Crisis of the Aristocracy, 1558–1641*, Oxford, 1965, p. 551. See J.V. Beckett, *The Aristocracy in England 1660–1914*, Oxford, 1986 for a more positive view of the aristocracy, and John Cannon, *Aristocratic Century*, Cambridge, 1984 for a review of the chief issues relating to the aristocracy in the eighteenth century.

5 J. Summerson, *Architecture in Britain, 1530–1830*, Harmondsworth, 1955, p. 28.

6 R.H. Tawney, 'The Rise of the Gentry, 1558–1640' (1941) in Carus-Wilson, op. cit., pp. 173 ff.

7 The further history of this theory of consumption will be critically examined in Part III, particularly in relation to Barbon and Mandeville. Here it is enough to point out that the definitive modern statement of the theory appears in chapter 2 of Thorstein Veblen's *The Theory of the Leisure Class* (1899) 'Pecuniary Emulation' and was given wide currency by Vance Packard in *The Status Seekers* of 1960 (pp. 137 ff.), a study of upwardly mobile fam-ilies in the USA in the boom years following World War II, which Stone (op. cit., pp. 184–8, 547–55) used to explain the be-haviour of the Tudor nobility! Even the major critic of Stone and Tawney, H.R. Trevor-Roper, held contradictory views on this issue. He argued that 'it was the social duty of a gentleman not to "live like a hog",' not to live below one's income, but, like Sir George Holles, to 'maintain a port to the height of what his income would permit him'. Yet two pages later he seemed to identify with the disapproving puritan gentry of the period, who held no office and could not afford such port, when he wrote, 'The office-holders of the Crown might live up to the limit of their inflated incomes, vying with one another in "port" and "housekeeping", in ostentatious building and lavish feasts: recusants and puritans alike eschewed such waste.' H.R. Trevor-Roper, 'The Gentry 1540–1640', *Economic History Review Sup-plements*, No. 1, 1953, pp. 28–9. For a recent revaluation of the duties of the gentry and aristocracy see K. Sharpe, *The Personal Rule of Charles I*, New Haven and London, 1992, pp. 137, 235–6, 415 ff, 426, 431–2, 437, 447, 477; and for a balanced assessment of the com-plexity of an individual's motives in building see C. Saumarez-Smith, *The Building of Castle Howard*, London, 1990, Ch. 1.

8 *The Life of William Cecil, Lord Burghley*, (ed. Arthur Collins), London, 1732, pp. 42–3 (hereafter *Life of Cecil*).

9 (William Cecil, Lord Burghley) *Certaine Precepts, or Directions for the well ordering and carriage of a man's life . . . Left by a Father to his son at his death, who was sometimes of eminent Note and Place in this Kingdome*, London, 1617; Felicity Heal, 'The Idea of Hospitality in Early Modern England', *Past and Present*, No. 102, Feb. 1984, p. 77; Edward P. Cheyney, *A History of England from the Defeat of the Armada to the Death of Elizabeth*, London, 1926, II, pp. 3–15. *Life of Cecil*, p. 38.

10 E.g. *The Norfolk Congress*, London, 1728, pp. 3–5. This does not attack Walpole for building Houghton from the fruits of office but for encouraging luxury imports which threatened English goods: 'Who is there that doth not rejoice at the Plenty that is within his Palace? For he hath strewed Plenty over the Face of

the Land.' p. 4. See also *The Craftsman*, IV, No. 137, London, Sat. 15 Feb. 1728–9, pp. 134–7 and VII, No. 237, 16 Jan. 1730–1, pp. 211–12, both of which praise Elizabeth I's and Burghley's economic policy and implicitly attack that of Walpole.

11 R.C. (Ralph Courteville), *Memoirs of the Life and Administration of William Cecil Baron Burleigh . . . including a Parallel between the State of Government Then and Now*, London, 1738; W. Cox, *Sir Robert Walpole*, 4 vols, London, 1816, IV, pp. 318–21, 370–7.

12 Bernard de Mandeville, *The Fable of the Bees*, London, 1725, I, Remark M, pp. 127–30 ff.

13 J.T. Cliffe, *The Yorkshire Gentry from the Reformation to the Civil War*, London, 1969, p. 103, quoting from E. of Strafford's *Letters and Despatches*, 2 vols, 1739.

14 Cliffe, op. cit., p. 123. Thomas G. Barnes, *Somerset 1625–1640: A Country's Government during the 'Personal Rule'*, Oxford, 1961, pp. 23–4.

15 For Peter Walter see Howard Erskine-Hill, *The Social Milieu of Alexander Pope*, New Haven and London, 1975, pp. 103–31; *The Works of Alexander Pope* (ed. Rev. Wm. Bowles), London, 1806, 10 v, Moral Essays, Epistle III To Lord Bathurst, l. 123–6 and note by Pope and others in Vol. III, pp. 290–1. The description of his estate comes from Satire II of Dr John Donne versified l. 109–16, Vol. IV, p. 275. Walter is also Fielding's Peter Ponce in *Joseph Andrews*, Book III, chapter xiii. For elite withdrawal from the country 1660–1720 see J.M. Rosenheim, 'County governance and elite withdrawal in Norfolk, 1660–1720', in A.L. Beier et al. (eds.) *The First Modern Society*, Cambridge, 1989, pp. 95–125, and L. and J.C.F. Stone, *An Open Elite*, Oxford, 1984, pp. 269–75.

16 Larkin and Hughes, op. cit., 9 Dec. 1615, pp. 356–7; K. Sharpe, *The Personal Rule of Charles*, I, 1992, pp. 137, 195.

17 Larkin and Hughes, op. cit., p. 370, n. 2.

18 Ibid., p. 573.

19 Ibid., p. 608.

20 N.E. McClure (ed.), *The Letters of John Chamberlain*, Philadelphia, 1939, II, p. 328, 9 Nov. 1620 (hereafter *Chamberlain*).

21 *The Political Works of James I*, (intro. by Charles H. McIlvain) Cambridge, Mass., 1918, pp. 343–4. The Journal of Sir Roger Wilbraham, (1598), *Camden Miscellany*, X, 1902, p. 22.

22 McClure, op. cit., II, p. 502, 14 June 1623. For Charles I's action in closing non-goldsmiths in Lombard Street see Sharpe, op. cit., p. 247.

23 H.M. Colvin (ed.) *The History of the King's Works*, III, 1485–1660, Pt. I, London, 1975, p. 108.

24 Barnes, op. cit., p. 28 and n. 27. R. Cust and P.G. Lake, 'Sir Richard Grosvenor and the Rhetoric of Magistracy', *Bulletin of Institute of Historical Research*, LIV, 1981, pp. 40–1. V.M. Larminie, 'The Godly Magistrate: the private philosophy and public life of Sir John Newdigate 1571–1610', *Dugdale Society Occasional Papers*, No. 28, Oxford, 1982, pp. 15, 18. *Selections from Clarendon*, ed. G. Huehns, Oxford, 1955, p. 10 (hereafter *Clarendon*).

25 Cheyney, op. cit., p. 13.

26 Cliffe, op. cit., pp. 20–2.

27 Ibid, pp. 23, 24, 151, 153–4 referring to Sir Hugh Cholmeley, *The Memoirs of Sir H.C. . . .*, 1787.

28 T. Birch, *The Court and Times of James I*, London, 1848, 2 vols, 3 Jan. 1622–3, II, p. 354. *Chamberlain*, op. cit., suggested that the measures would 'beggar this towne quite' – II, p. 585; F. Heal, 'The Crown, the Gentry and London: the Enforcement of Proclamations, 1596–1640', in C. Cross et al. (eds.) *Law and Government under the Tudors*, Cambridge, 1988, pp. 211–26, partic. pp. 217–19. Charles I's campaign of 1632–6 was also enforced (p. 222). Heal (p. 214) also quotes a 1622 poem of James I on the subject, in *James I Poems*, (ed. J. Craigie), 2 vols, Edinburgh, 1955–8, II, p. 178. For the effect of the withdrawal of gentry from London and York upon their economies see Sharpe, op. cit., pp. 449–50.

29 Alfred Hassell Smith, *County and Court: Government and Politics in Norfolk, 1558–1603*, Oxford, 1974, p. 53 estimates the number of gentlemen in Norfolk in 1580 to have been at least 424; Cliffe, op. cit., p. 145, refers to 963 gentry families in the whole of Yorkshire between 1558 and 1642. In 1688 Gregory King estimated 16,586 lords, bishops, baronets and gentry. *Two Tracts by Gregory King*, ed. G.E. Barnett, Baltimore, 1936.

30 Cheyney, op. cit., II, p. 386–7; Gladys Scott Thomson, *Lords Lieutenant in the Sixteenth Century*, London, 1923, pp. 74–7; Barnes, op. cit., p. 85. The Webbs, in the first volume of their *English Local Government*, London, 1906, argue that although in law and theory JPs were a unit of obligation 'To execute policies and administer statutes for the State so strictly centralised as to leave no place for local autonomy,' in practice, by 1688, the rulers of the counties were self-governing to a considerable degree. The argument about the precise nature of the relationship between central government and the provinces continues. For a critique of the argument that there was a gulf between the traditional country gentry and an innovative cosmopolitan court, see K. Sharpe, *Criticism and Compliment: The Politics of Literature in the England of Charles I*, Cambridge, 1987, pp. 5–9.

31 Girouard, op. cit., p. 6, quoting from Stone, 1965, pp. 391–2, and J. Hurstfield, 'County Government: Wiltshire c. 1530–1660', *Freedom*

Corruption and Government, London, 1973, pp. 237–40. The lieutenancy of Wiltshire was held by a member of the Herbert family between 1551 and 1601, and from 1621 until the Civil War; Keith Thomas, *Man and the Natural World 1500–1800*, London, 1983, p. 252, quoting Dudley, Lord North, *Observations and Advices Oeconomical*, 1669, pp. 111–12.

32 Cust and Lake, op. cit., pp. 40–1, 45, 46, 48.

33 Larminie, op. cit., p. 17; W.K. Jordan, *Philanthropy in England, 1480–1660*, London, 1959, p. 93.

34 *The Diary of John Evelyn* (ed. E.S. de Beer), London, 1959, pp. 1–2.

35 *Clarendon*, p. 10.

36 Raymond Williams, *The Country and the City*, London, 1973. Henry Arthington in his *Provision for the poore* of 1597 attacked the present age for being 'iron and hard hearted' in which men had to be forced by law to exercise charity, compared to the generosity of the reign of Edward VI. In fact as W.K. Jordan, op. cit., p. 99, points out, the level of private charity had never been higher.

37 Izaak Walton, 'The Life of Sir Henry Wotton' in *The Lives . . .*, London, 1962, p. 97, and *Camden's Britannia: Kent* (ed. Gordon J. Copley), London, 1977, p. 16, re Penshurst.

38 Thomas Fuller, *The Worthies of England*, (ed. J. Freeman), London, 1952, pp. 1–2.

39 Heal, 1984, p. 82.

40 'The Treasure of Traffike' in J.R. McCulloch (ed.), *Early English Tracts on Commerce* (1st ed. 1856), Cambridge, 1952, pp. 87–8; Sharpe, 1992, pp. 188–9, 209–10.

41 Inscribed on his memorial in Sapperton Church.

42 For the Lords Lieutenant see Gladys Scott Thomson, op. cit., esp. pp. 16–29, 49–50, 77–8; S. and B. Webb, *English Local Government: The Parish and the County*, I, London, 1906, pp. 286–7; Hurstfield, op. cit., pp. 237–9; Barnes, op. cit., p. 101; Cliffe, op. cit., p. 233; John Chamberlayne, *Magnae Britanniae Notitia*, London, 1716, pp. 581–2. In Essex in the four centuries, 1545–1934, the post was held by a member of the nobility for all but 28 years, see Sir R.B. Colvin, *The Lieutenants and Keepers of the Rolls of the County of Essex*, London, 1934, pp. 11–13. See too Sharpe, 1992, pp. 267, 498.

43 For the JPs see Webb, op. cit., partic. pp. 281, 294, 535–43; Anthony Fletcher, *Reform in the Provinces, the Government of Stuart England*, Newhaven and London, 1986, pp. 159–62; P. Williams, *The Tudor Regime*, Oxford, 1979, pp. 147, 156, 178; Cust and Lake, op. cit., pp. 45–51; Larminie, op. cit., pp. 16–17.

44 Jordan, op. cit., pp. 68–74; *The Cambridge Economic History of Europe*, Cambridge, 1967 (repr. 1975), IV; Karl F. Helleiner, 'The Population of Europe from the Black Death to the Eve of the Vital Revolution', p. 32; F.P. Braudel and F. Spooner, 'Prices in Europe from 1450–1750', p. 428; Cheyney, op. cit., II, pp. 3–15, and Fletcher, op. cit., pp. 191, 200; A.L. Beier, *The Problem of the Poor in Tudor and Early Stuart England*, London, 1983.

45 Helleiner, op. cit., p. 31.

46 Jordan, op. cit., p. 67.

47 Mary Pawsey, in Gavin Weightman and Steve Humphries, *The Making of Modern London*, London, 1983, p. 63.

48 A. Hassell Smith, op. cit., p. 53 estimates the number of gentlemen in Norfolk in 1580 as at least 424, of whom there were 34 JPs in 1577 and 61 in 1602. However 84 new JPs were appointed between 1578 and 1603, and while in some few families a seat on the bench was almost hereditary in most cases sons did not succeed their fathers as JPs other than by their own deserts. Hence over several generations these offices would have been spread between a larger proportion of families.

49 For the great 'act for the relief of the poor' 39 and 40 Eliz. c. 3 and 43 and 43 Eliz. c. 2 see G.W. Prothero (ed.), *Select Statutes and other Constitutional Documents of Elizabeth and James I*, Oxford, 1894, 4th ed., 1913, pp. 96–100, 103–5; S. and B. Webb, *English Local Government: English Poor Law History: Part I*, VII, London, 1927, Ch. 2; Jordan, op. cit., pp. 91–101, and E.M. Leonard, *The Early History of English Poor Relief*, London, 1900.

50 Fletcher, op. cit., pp. 183–8 argues that although there was a decisive shift later in the century, particularly after the Restoration, from the traditional informal hospitality as a means of relief to the formal levying of parish poor rates, nonetheless the needy still looked to the gatehouse of the local squire who frequently relieved those who were refused by the over-seers. Also Jordan, op. cit., p. 171.

51 Heal, 1984, p. 75: True hospitality lay 'not in glutonous diversities, but rather in one kind of meat, in clothing the naked and giving alms unto the poor', William Vaughan, *The Golden Grove*, London, 1600, Bk 2, Ch. 25. 'Hospitalitie falsly so called is the keeping of a good table, at which seldome or never any other are entertained than kynsfolk, friends and other neighbours . . . This is no hospitalitie but it is good fellowship or some such like thing,' Caleb Dalechamp, *Christian Hospitalitie Handled Common – Place-Wise*, London, 1632, p. 6; McClure, *Chamberlain*, II, p. 475, suggested that the measures were actually counter-productive because the return of gentry to the country raised the price of food still higher. Even if landlords were absentees their stewards executed their political, business and social functions on their behalf, see D.R. Hainsworth, *Stewards, Lords and People*, Cambridge, 1992, pp. 3, 56 ff, 250 and Chs. 5, 8, 13; for a 19th-century example of the

dutiful aristocrat albeit imbued with the principles of political economy see E.A. Wasson, 'A progressive landlord: the third Earl Spencer, 1782–1845', in C.W. Chalklin and J.R. Wordie, *Town and Countryside: the English Landowner in the National Economy: 1660–1860*, London, 1989, pp. 83–101.

52 Jordan, op. cit., p. 171; Roger Backhouse, *Economists and the Economy, 1600 to the Present Day*, Oxford, 1988, p. 47: 'Underlying all this period's legislation was the notion of an ordered, controlled society' through measures to uphold the status quo, restrict industry and the development of a capitalist economy; J. Martin, *Francis Bacon, the State, and the Reform of Natural Philosophy*, Cambridge, 1992, pp. 7–22, quoting the first page of Marsiglio of Padua (1275–1342) *Defensor Pacis*. For the Cromwellian period see G.R. Elton, *Reform and Renewal: Thomas Cromwell and the Common Weal*, Cambridge, 1973; W.R.D. Jones, *The Tudor Commonwealth, 1529–59*, London, 1971.

53 W.G. Hoskins, 'The Rebuilding of Rural England, 1570–1640', *Past and Present*, No. 4, 1952–3, pp. 44–59; for a critique see R. Maclin, 'The Great Rebuilding, a Reassessment', *Past and Present*, No. 77, 1977, pp. 33–56. Maclin has done a very much more accurate count of 17 counties of all dated houses excluding the largest aristocratic houses but including barns etc. On this basis he points to a great rebuilding between 1650 and 1740.

54 Table of number of new country houses or manor houses built, substantially rebuilt or added to in each decade, 1500–1930. Figures derived from N. Pevsner, *Buildings of England*, Harmondsworth – Dorset, Kent, Wiltshire and Northamptonshire.

Decade	Total per decade	Large houses only
1500–10	11	
10–20	5	
20–30	12	1
30–40	10	
40–50	11	5
50–60	20	3
60–70	10	2
70–80	20	7
80–90	30	2
90–1600	26	3
1600–10	47	2
10–20	56	
20–30	24	1
30–40	31	
40–50	12	
50–60	42	1
60–70	24	
70–80	17	
80–90	22	
90–1700	43	
1700–10	56	
10–20	25	
20–30	31	1
30–40	28	
40–50	19	
50–60	33	1
60–70	19	
70–80	31	
80–90	17	
90–1800	28	
1800–10	28	
10–20	18	1
20–30	15	
30–40	15	
40–50	22	
50–60	22	
60–70	18	
70–80	19	
80–90	16	
90–1900	14	
1900–10	12	
10–20	9	
20–30	6	

55 Hoskins, op. cit., p. 50.

56 Ibid., p. 54.

57 E. Mercer, 'The Houses of the Gentry', *Past and Present*, May 1954, No. 5, pp. 11–31, 15, 18, 25–6.

58 Dr Christopher Clay (unpub. paper to Victoria and Albert Museum symposium, 1984) argued that very few could build such houses out of income except for people like the Willoughby family of Notts. who built Wollaton from their fortune. Otherwise brand new houses were built from the profits of office (e.g. Burley-on-the-Hill for the Earl of Nottingham as well as the couple already mentioned), the extended minority of an heir which allowed income to accumulate, or a fortunate marriage such as that of the 4th Earl of Pembroke with the daughter of the Duke of Buckingham which brought £25,000, which income directly went towards the rebuilding of Wilton. Unfortunately the young heir died on his Grand Tour and the Herberts had to repay the dowry. J. Cottis, 'A Country Gentleman on his Estates' in C.W. Chalklin and J.R. Wordie, *Town and Countryside: the English Landowner in the National Economy, 1660–1860*, London, 1989, pp. 25–6 for a lesser grandee.

59 'Considerations delivered to the Parliament, 1559', R.H. Tawney and E. Power (eds.), *Tudor Economic Documents*, London, 1924, I, p. 326 (hereafter *Tudor Economic Dowments*).

60 A. Oswald, *Country Houses of Dorset*, London, 1935, p. 66.

61 N. Pevsner, *The Buildings of England, Dorset*, Harmondsworth, 1972, p. 194. Mercer (op. cit.) argues that some people whose means enabled them to afford 'courtier houses' did not do so in reaction to the behaviour of the court from which they were politically

estranged, and believing Lulworth to have been erected in the 1580s attributed its scale and design to the fact that Henry Howard, Viscount Bindon was *persona non grata* at court. But Bindon's main seat was Bindon Abbey, in any case. Malcolm Airs in *The Building of England: Tudor and Jacobean*, London, 1982, p. 56 interprets the letter from Bindon to Salisbury as indicating that Salisbury was being 'consulted'.

62 Summerson, op. cit., p. 27.

63 Sir John Summerson, 'The Building of Theobalds, 1564–1585', *Archaeologia*, 2nd series, XCVII, London, 1959, p. 111.

64 Malcolm Airs, *The Making of the English Country House*, London, 1975, pp. 9 and 12. See too the whole of chapter 1 'Some Motives for Building'. He largely adopts the conventional approach and even explains the wit, emblematic informality and innovative styles of such houses on the competitive model. However Airs does allow that in at least one case, the buildings of Sir Thomas Tresham, who was converted to Catholicism in 1580, such as the Triangular Lodge at Rushton, Northants, 1594–7, were 'undoubtedly little more than public proclamations of his faith'. He also allows that the preoccupation with informality and fashion was not simply a matter of intense social rivalry . . . It was more a reflection of a contemporary concern with mortality, and of ways to outwit its effect . . .' In other words the country house, with its display of 'initials, dates, heraldic devices and mottoes' provided an acceptably Protestant alternative to 'the canopies and adornment of the parish church' as a means of ensuring immortality. In this kind of explanation there is some concession to explanations other than competitive consumption.

65 Airs, 1982 p. 50 and 1975, p. 12.

66 Hurstfield, op. cit., p. 229.

67 Scott Thompson, op. cit., pp. 46 ff.

68 J. Nichols, *The Progresses of Queen Elizabeth*, London, 1823, 3 vols. and *Progresses of James I*, London, 1828, 3 vols.

69 J. Hutchins, *History and Antiquities of the County of Dorset*, 3rd ed., IV, London, 1873, p. 5.

70 Airs, 1975, p. 12, quoting from H.G. Leach, 'Early Seventeenth-Century Houses in Ireland', *Studies in Building History* (ed. E.M. Jope), London, 1961, p. 244. Airs's interpretation of this is that although under Charles I 'the custom of royal progresses had declined in the face of the growing isolation of the Crown, there were still those who sought to ingratiate themselves with the monarchy by building on a grand scale.' See also *Gesta Grayorum AD 1594* (ed. D. Bland), Liverpool, 1968, pp. 48–9.

71 *The Complete Works of Sir Philip Sidney*, ed. E. Feuillerat, Cambridge, 1939, I, p. 15;

R. Strong, *Henry, Prince of Wales*, London, 1986, p. 8.

72 Summerson, 1959, pp. 110–11; Conyers Read, 'Lord Burghley's Household Accounts', *Econ. H.R.* 2nd series, 1956, IX, pp. 344 ff; B.W. Beckinsale, *Burghley*, London, 1967, p. 291; Sir William Petty, 'Observation No. 126', *Petty Papers*, ed. Marquess of Lansdowne, 2 vols, London, 1927, II, p. 236 – I owe this reference to Dr Christopher Clay. See also B. Murison, 'Getting and Spending: William Blathwayt and Dyrham Park', *History Today*, XII, 1990, pp. 22–8.

73 Read, op. cit., p. 345; Conyers Read, *Lord Burghley and Queen Elizabeth*, London, 1960, p. 437; A. Tinniswood, *A History of Country House Visiting*, Oxford, 1989, pp. 26–7.

74 Nichols, 1823 I, p. 205 and Read, 1960, pp. 315 ff and partic. p. 320.

75 L. Stone, 'The Fruits of Office: the Case of Robert Cecil, First Earl of Salisbury 1596–1612', in F.J. Fisher (ed.) *Essays in the Economic and Social History of Tudor and Stuart England*, Cambridge, 1961, pp. 89–116, partic. p. 108. Stone comments that the £40,000 cost of building Hatfield landed Cecil with 'a terrifying load of debt, nearly all of it at 10% interest' (p. 109). My reaction to this is to ask, 'terrifying to whom?' To Professor Lawrence Stone maybe, but clearly not to the first Earl of Salisbury whom Stone depicts borrowing a huge sum in 1603 to buy the lands of his treasonous brother-in-law, Lord Cobham, which he sold on a few years later for £74,000, making £37,300 profit, even if reduced by interest to a mere £20,185! His massive borrowings were contracted, it seems, in the spirit of a modern financier who saw an opening and took a chance. See also D. Thomas, 'The Elizabethan Crown Lands', in R.W. Hoyle (ed.) *The Estates of the English Crown, 1558–1640*, Cambridge, 1992, pp. 83–4 for the view that Cecil benefited more than James I in the exchange.

76 *The Life of Burghley*, 1732, p. 41.

77 Airs, 1975, Ch. 24, pp. 182–91 shows that the wage rates for different categories of worker differed widely. But over the period 1550–80 labourers seemed to get about 6d. a day and skilled craftsmen like masons and carpenters anything between 9d. and 14d. Assuming that approximately one third of the workmen were labourers, that makes an average wage of 9d. a day. According to Airs on pp. 157–8, 285 days/year were worked and there was little work in the four months from November to February, leaving about 190 working days a year for building projects. For Castle Howard, Maurice Barley, *Houses and History*, London, 1986, pp. 171–2 and Saumarez-Smith, op. cit.

78 Airs, 1975, p. 141, ref. Nottingham University Library, Mi A60/3. The table on p. 203 of *The*

History of the King's Works, III, Pt. 1, for the building of the Savoy Hospital 1512–17 is my basis for assuming that labourers were one third of the workforce at the height of building.

79 *Harrison's Description of England* (ed. F.J. Furnivall), pp. 241–2. For the standard work on hospitality see F. Heal, *Hospitality in Early Modern England*, Oxford, 1990. For a somewhat earlier period see K. Mertes, *The English Noble Household*, Oxford, 1988.

80 Cliffe, op. cit., p. 116.

81 Sarah Markham, *John Loveday of Caversham, 1711–1789*, Wilton, 1984, pp. 86–7.

82 Bernard de Mandeville, *The Fable of the Bees*, II, p. 29. Remark M.

83 Thomas Fuller, *The Worthies of England*, ed. J. Freeman, London, 1952 (Ref. supplied by Colin Ward).

84 Sir H. Wotton, *The Elements of Architecture*, London, 1624, p. 52.

85 *Tudor Economic Documents*, III, pp. 386–7.

86 McCulloch, op. cit.

87 *Life*, pp. 37–8, 43. The anonymous biographer estimated (p. 37) that Burghley's total household amounted to 80 in London, 26–30 as well as 67 labourers at Theobalds; assuming that he kept two-thirds of the total for Theobalds at Burghley this suggests that he employed a total of about 240 in London, Theobalds and Burghley in addition to a building organisation of 140.

88 *The Spectator*, No. 415; J. Appleby, *Economic Thought and Ideology in 17th Century England*, Princeton, 1978, p. 144.

89 Rawlinson Mss, D, 133 f. 46, quoted in F.J. Fisher, 'Commercial Trends and Policy in 16th Century England', 1940, in Carus-Wilson (ed.), 1954, p. 167.

90 Fisher, op. cit., p. 153 and B.E. Supple, *Commercial Crisis and Change in England, 1600–1642*, Cambridge, 1959, p. 4.

91 William Lane to Cecil on the coinage and other matters, 18 Jan. 1551, *Tudor Economic Documents*, II, p. 184, quoted in F. Fisher, op. cit., p. 157.

92 Memorandum by Cecil on the Export Trade in Cotton and Wool, 1564, *Tudor Economic Documents*, II, p. 45, also quoted in Fisher, op. cit., p. 166.

93 John U. Nef, *Industry and Government in France and England, 1540–1640*, Philadelphia, 1940, p. 44.

94 D.C. Coleman, 'Labour and the English Economy of the 17th Century', in E.M. Carus-Wilson, *Essays in Economic History*, II, London, 1962, p. 292.

95 Airs, 1975, pp. 136, 152.

96 Ibid., p. 140.

97 See note 4 above.

98 E. Lipson, *The Economic History of England*, III, 5th ed., London, 1948, pp. 117–9 and W.

Cunningham, *The Growth of English Industry and Commerce*, 2nd ed., London, 1890–2, I, pp. 443–4, II, p. 21.

99 Lipson, op. cit., III, p. 47; Cunningham, op. cit., II, p. 34.

100 Margaret Gay Davies, *The Enforcement of English Apprenticeship, 1563–1642*, Cambridge, Mass., 1956, p. 2.

101 G.W. Prothero, *Select Statutes of Elizabeth and James I*, Oxford, 4th ed., 1913, pp. 45 ff. and Davies, op. cit., p. 86.

102 *Tudor Economic Documents*, I, pp. 357–8.

103 Ibid., I, p. 89.

104 M. Girouard, *Robert Smythson and his Elizabethan Country House*, New Haven and London, 1983, p. 13; A.J. and R.H. Tawney, 'An Occupational Census of the 17th Century', *Econ. H.R.*, V, 1934, pp. 25–53.

105 Barley, op. cit., pp. 177–8.

106 Ibid, pp. 181, 183.

107 R. North, *Lives of the Norths*, London, 1890, III, p. 230, quoted in Barley, op. cit., p. 182.

108 'The Diary of Abraham de la Prynne', ed. C. Jackson, *Surtees Society*, LIV, 1870, p. 114, ref. Barley, op. cit., p. 184. R. Maclin's figures (see n. 53 above) lend some support to this hypothesis. The building of more modest houses lags behind that of major housebuilding from 1530 until the 1570s and 80s, and even in later decades middling houses peak in the 1610s, modest houses in the 1630s. Thereafter modest housebuilding continues to rise until the 1730s whereas larger houses never exceed the peak of the 1610s.

109 Tacitus, *On Britain and Germany*, Harmondsworth, 1951, p. 72.

110 Richard C. Barnett, *Place, Profit and Power: a study of the servants of William Cecil, Elizabethan Statesman*, University of North Carolina, 1969, pp. 5, 32–41; Virginia Kenny, *The Country House Ethos in English Literature, 1688–1750*, Brighton, 1984, p. 11.

111 Beckingsale, op. cit., p. 263; see too *Gesta Grayorum*, op. cit., p. 47 where Bacon recommends botanical and zoological gardens as part of the study of philosophy appropriate to a great prince.

112 Keith Thomas, *Man and the Natural World*, London, 1983, p. 17.

113 Beckingsale, op. cit., p. 275.

Chapter 3

1 *The Libelle of Englyshe Polycye*, ed. Sir George Warner, Oxford, 1926, p. 20, 1. 375–6 and p. 18, 1. 344–5.

2 Shakespeare, *Richard II*, Act 2, i.

3 Joan Thirsk, *Economic Policy and Projects: The Development of a Consumer Society in Early Modern England*, Oxford, 1978, p. 14; quoting *A Discourse of the Common Weal of this Realm of*

England, 1581, (ed. E. Lamond), Cambridge, 1893, p. 10 (attrib. to Sir Thomas Smith and probably written in 1545); *The Request and Suite of a True Hearted Englishman*, written by William Cholmeley, Londyner, in the year 1553, *Tudor Economic Documents*, III, p. 130; and Hugo Grotius, *The Freedom of the Seas*, (originally written 1608), tr. R.V.D. Magoffin and ed. J.B. Scott, New York and Oxford, 1916, p. 7.

4 F.J. Fisher 'Commercial Trends and Policy in 16th Century England', 1940 in E.M. Carus-Wilson, *Essays in Economic History*, London, 1954, p. 155; *A Discourse . . .*, pp. 126–7; Thirsk, op. cit., pp. 16, 49–50.

5 Alan Rogers, 'Mediaeval Stamford', in A. Rogers (ed.), *The Making of Stamford*, Leicester, 1965, pp. 43, 56; R.C.H.M., *The Town of Stamford*, London, 1977, pp. xii–xliii.

6 J. Thirsk, 'Stamford in the Sixteenth and Seventeenth Centuries', in Rogers (ed.), op. cit., pp. 38, 60, 65, 66. There were 242 households in Stamford in 1524 and 296 in 1603.

7 H.M.C., *Calendar of Mss. of the Marquis of Salisbury*, (ii), 1883, pp. 320, 837.

8 Thirsk, 'Stamford . . .', pp. 70–1, p. 63.

9 Eric Till, 'Georgian Cabinet Makers of Burghley', *Country Life*, 3 May and 7 June 1973, 29 Aug. 1974.

10 J.M. Lee, 'Modern Stamford', in Rogers (ed.), op. cit., pp. 92–103. For the reaction of a progressive aristocrat see E.A. Wasson, 'A Progressive Landlord: the 3rd Earl Spencer, 1782–1845', in C.W. Chalklin and J.R. Wordie, *Town and Countryside: The English Landowner in the National Economy, 1660–1860*, London, 1989, p. 91, see also p. 21 for landlords who facilitated urban expansion.

11 Victoria County History, *County of Hertford*, ed. W. Page, London, 1914, pp. 249–59; F.J. Fisher, 'Some Experiments in Company Organisation in the Early 17th Century', *Econ. H.R.*, 1st series, IV, 1933, pp. 191–3, reprinted in F.J. Fisher, *London and the English Economy*, London, 1990.

12 R.S. Smith, 'A Woad Growing Project at Wollaton in the 1580s', *Transactions of the Thoroton Society of Nottinghamshire*, LXV, 1961, pp. 27–46. For Sir Francis Willoughby and the interrelation between country house building and entrepreneurship see Alice T. Friedman, *House and Household in Elizabethan England: Wollaton Hall and the Willoughby Family*, Chicago, 1989.

13 R.S. Smith, 'Glassmaking at Wollaton in the Early Seventeenth Century', *Trans. of the Thoroton Society . . .*, LXVI, 1962, pp. 24–34.

14 Joan Thirsk, 'Projects for Gentlemen, Jobs for the Poor: Mutual Aid in the Vale of Tewkesbury 1600–1630', *The Rural Economy of England*, London, 1984, pp. 287–308.

15 'It is unlikely that these are the only examples of business enterprises mixed with philanthropy, of projects devised by gentlemen that created jobs for the poor.' Ibid., p. 307.

16 Frederic Harrison, *Annals of an old Manor-House, Sutton Place, Guildford*, London, 1899, pp. 120–33; S. Hartlib, *Sir Richard Weston's Legacy*, London, 1645, pp. 51–2; *Encyclopaedia Britannica*, 9th–11th eds., under Agriculture; County Histories of Surrey; see below Pt. III Ch. 4.

17 Thirsk, 1978, pp. 21–2; *Tudor Economic Documents*, I, p. 87; Victoria County History, *Oxon*, IX, pp. 114–16.

18 W. Hooper, 'Tudor Sumptuary Laws', *English Historical Review*, XXX, 1915, pp. 439 ff, partic. p. 441; N.B. Harte, 'State Control of Dress and Social Change in Pre-Industrial England' in D.C. Coleman and A.H. Johns (eds.) *Trade, Government and Economy in Pre-Industrial England*, London, 1976, pp. 131–64; J. Evelyn, *Tyrannus*, London, 1661, see below Part IV, Ch. 1, iii; Bishop Berkeley, 'An Essay Towards Preventing the Ruin of Great Britain' (1721) in *The Works of George Berkeley*, ed. T.E. Jessop, London, 1964, VI, pp. 65–85, partic. pp. 79–81.

19 Thirsk, 1978, pp. 115–17.

20 Anon. (Alexander Somerville), *The Autobiography of a Working Man*, London, 1848, p. 3.

21 Eleanor S. Godfrey, *The Develoment of English Glassmaking, 1560–1640*, Oxford, 1975, pp. 13, 208–9.

22 Ibid., p. 216.

23 Ibid., pp. 17–19, 24, 27.

24 Ibid., pp. 28, 47–8.

25 Ibid., pp. 69–88; Ada Polak, *Glass*, New York, 1975, pp. 115–17; W.A. Thorpe, *English Glass*, 3rd ed., London, 1961, pp. 154–8.

26 G. Batho, 'Notes and Documents on Petworth House', *Sussex Archive Collections*, XCVI, 1958, p. 128; Godfrey, op. cit., pp. 24, 205–6.

27 Thorpe, op. cit., pp. 115–28.

28 D.C. Coleman, *The Economy of England, 1450–1750*, Oxford, 1977, pp. 80–1.

29 Thirsk, 1978, p. 38; *Tudor Economic Documents*, III, p. 130.

30 Astrid Friis, *Alderman Cockayne's Project and the Cloth Trade*, Copenhagen and London, 1927; B.E. Supple, *Commercial Crisis and Change in England, 1600–1642*, Cambridge, 1959, pp. 27, 33–50; Fisher, 'Commercial Trends . . .', Carus-Wilson, op. cit., I, p. 153; C. Wilson, *England's Apprenticeship, 1603–1763*, London, 1965, p. 71. For Cockayne see D.N.B.

31 *The Economist*, 26 Dec. 1987, p. 86.

32 Aymer Vallance, *Art in England during the Elizabethan and Stuart Period*, London, 1908, pp. 99–100 (I owe this reference to Jenny Durkin); V.C.H., *Warwickshire*, II, pp. 263–5, V, pp. 5–9; T. Nash, *The History and Antiquities of Worcestershire*, 1781, I, pp. 64–6.

33 L. Martin, 'Sir Francis Crane', *Apollo*, Feb. 1981, p. 94; W.G. Thomson, *Tapestry Weaving in England*, London, 1914, p. 76; for Charles I's policies concerning projects and the commonwealth see Sharpe, 1992, pp. 257 ff.

34 J. Shearman, *Raphael's Cartoons*, London, 1972, pp. 145–7; Thompson, op. cit., p. 285.

35 V.C.H., *Surrey*, Vol. 2:2, P. 359.

36 Ibid., p. 356; L. Martin, op. cit., p. 94; on the authorship of Stoke Bruerne I am indebted to G. Roberts; R. Hoyle, 'Shearing the Hog' in R. Hoyle (ed.) *The Estates of the English Crown*, op. cit., p. 259.

37 Hurstfield, *Freedom, Corruption and Government*, London, 1973, p. 229; C. Hussey, 'Wilton House', *Country Life*, 9 and 16 May 1963, pp. 1044–8, 1109, 1113.

38 J. Aubrey, *Brief Lives*, London, 1960, pp. 138–9, 145–6; Hussey op. cit., p. 1048; for Moffett see D.N.B.

39 H.M. Colvin, 'The South Front of Wilton House', *Archaeological Journal*, CXI, 1955; A.A. Tait, 'Isaac de Caus and the South Front of Wilton House', *Burlington Magazine*, CVI, 1964.

40 Hussey, op. cit., pp. 1109–13; V.C.H., *Wiltshire*, IV, p. 151, 181–2, VI, pp. 1 ff, 25–6; C.E.C. Tattersall, *A History of British Carpets*, Rev'd by S. Reed, Leigh-on-Sea, 1966, pp. 42–50, 75, 128–30.

Part Three

Preface

1 J.M. Keynes, *The General Theory of Employment, Interest and Money*, London, 1973, pp. 383–4 (1st ed. 1935).

2 There is a growing and very interesting literature upon the luxury debate and upon consumption both from a historical and a theoretical standpoint much of which has unfortunately appeared since my own text was completed: Lorna Weatherill, 'The meaning of consumer behaviour in late 17th and early 18th century England,' in John Brewer and Roy Porter, *Consumption and the World of Goods*, London, 1993, pp. 206–27; L. Weatherill, *Consumer Behaviour and Material Culture in Britain, 1660–1760*, London, 1988; Colin Campbell, 'Understanding Traditional and Modern Patterns of Consumption in 18th century England: a Character-Action Approach', in Brewer and Porter, op. cit., pp. 40–57; C. Campbell, *The Romantic Ethic and the Spirit of Modern Consumerism*, Oxford, 1987; Amanda Vickery, 'Women and the world of goods: a Lancashire Consumer and her possessions, 1751–81', in Brewer and Porter, op. cit., pp. 274–301; John Styles, 'Manufacturing, consumption and design in 18th century England', in Brewer and Porter, op. cit., pp. 527–4; Terence Hutchison, *Before Adam Smith*, Oxford, 1988; for an ex-cellent introduction to the luxury debate, J. Sekora, *Luxury: the Concept in Western Thought, Eden to Smollett*, Baltimore, 1977.

3 Adam Smith, *The Wealth of Nations* (Everyman edition), London, 1964, I, p. 380; D.C. Coleman, 'Adam Smith, businessman and the mercantile system in England', *History of European Ideas*, IX, 1988, pp. 161–70.

4 *The Libelle of Englyshe Polycye*, ed. Sir George Warner, Oxford, 1926.

5 W.R. Scott, *Adam Smith as Student and Professor*, Glasgow, 1937, pp. 379–82.

Chapter 1

1 Thomas Mun, *England's Treasure by Forraign Trade*, London, 1664 in J.R. McCulloch, *Early English Tracts on Commerce*, Cambridge, 1952, pp. 115–209; Charles Wilson, *England's Apprenticeship*, London, 1965, pp. 58–60; B. Supple, *Commercial Crisis and Change in England*, Cambridge, 1959, pp. 66–8, 93, 211–9, 268–70; J. Appleby, *Economic Thought and Ideology in 17th Century England*, Princeton, 1978, p. 41.

2 Mun, op. cit., pp. 192–3.

3 Ibid., p. 126.

4 Supple, op. cit., pp. 1–14; A.J. and R.H. Tawney, 'An occupational census of the 17th Century', *Econ. H.R.*, 1st series, V, 1934, pp. 38–43.

5 Mun, op. cit., p. 180. Joyce Appleby while focussing upon Mun's frugality none-theless draws attention to the fact that he was not a simple-minded advocate of a positive balance of trade, see her *Economic Thought and Ideology*, pp. 38 ff, which gives an excellent account of the seventeenth-century debate.

6 Mun, op. cit., p. 199.

7 Ibid, p. 194.

8 Ibid, pp. 185–9.

9 *England's Great Happiness*, London, 1677, in McCulloch, op. cit., p. 271.

10 Samuel Fortrey, *England's Interest and Improvement*, London, 1673, McCulloch, op. cit., pp. 232–5.

11 *The Diary of John Evelyn*, ed. E.S. de Beer, Oxford, 1959, p. 432 (hereafter *Diary*); John Bowle, *John Evelyn and his World*, London, 1981, p. 110; John Evelyn, *Tyrranus*, London, 1661.

12 *Diary*, pp. 500–1.

13 *Britannia Languens*, London, 1680 in McCulloch, op. cit., pp. 503–4 and pp. 371–446.

Chapter 2

1 See notes of Part I for Barbon, n. 42; N. Barbon, *An Apology for The Builder*, London, 1685, pp. 28–9 (hereafter *Builder*); N. Barbon, *A Discourse of Trade*, London, 1690, p. 6 (hereafter *Trade*).
2 *Trade*, p. 66.
3 *Builder*, pp. 4 and 22.
4 *Builder*, pp. 5, 32–5; *Trade*, pp. 67–9.
5 *Trade*, pp. 5, 14–15, 19, 62; *Builder*, pp. 5–6.
6 *Trade*, pp. 14–15.
7 Ibid., pp. 16–17, 35, 67–9, 65.
8 Ibid., pp. 72–3.
9 Ibid., pp. 13 and 20; see John Law, *Money and Trade consider'd*, Edinburgh, 1705 for discussion of use-value, ref. in Appleby, *Economic Thought and Ideology*, Princeton, 1978, p. 180.
10 *Trade*, p. 65; *Builder*, p. 32; see also Marshall Sahlins, *Culture and Practical Reason*, Chicago, 1976 for a discussion of Homo Economicus.
11 *Trade*, p. 63.
12 *Builder*, pp. 22, 23, 25.
13 McCulloch, *Early English Tracts on Commerce*, Cambridge, 1952, pp. 505–40, partic p. 528.
14 Ralph Davis, 'The Rise of Protection in England, 1689–1786', *Econ. H.R.*, xix, 1966, pp. 306–17.

Chapter 3

1 Bernard Mandeville, *The Fable of the Bees*, ed. and intro. F. B. Kaye, 2 vols, Oxford, 1924; also ed. P. Harth, Harmondsworth, 1970; E.A.J. Johnson, *Predecessors of Adam Smith, the Growth of British Economic Thought*, London, 1937; B. Mandeville, *A Letter to Dion (1732)*, Augustan Reprint Society, 41, Intro. Jacob Viner, Los Angeles, 1953; J. Viner, *The Long View and the Short*, Glencoe Illinois, 1958; Nathan Rosenberg, 'Mandeville and Laissez-Faire', *Journey of the History of Ideas*, xxiv, 1963, pp. 183–96; Thomas A. Horne, *The Social Thought of Bernard Mandeville*, London, 1978; M.M. Goldsmith, *Private Vices, Public Benefits: Bernard Mandeville's Social and Political Thought*, Cambridge, 1985; on the democratisation of economics see Appleby, *Ecomonic Thought and Ideology*, Princeton, 1978, p. 115. For his life see D.N.B.
2 Pierre Bourdieu, *La Distinction: critique sociale du judgement*, Paris, 1979; J. Baudrillard, *For a Critique of the Political Economy of the Sign*, tr. C. Levin, St Louis, 1981.
3 Bernard de Mandeville, *The Fable of the Bees*, 4th ed., 2 vols, London, 1725, ɪ, A2, p. 25.
4 Ibid., ɪ, pp. 25, 28, 219–28, 212, 401.
5 Ibid., ɪ, pp. 28–9.
6 Ibid., ɪ, pp. 232, 34–5, 379, 71–4.
7 Ibid., ɪ, pp. 59–61.
8 Ibid., ɪ, p. 61.

9 Ibid., ɪ, pp. 61, 63, 65, 58.
10 Ibid., ɪ, pp. 157–8.
11 Ibid., ɪ, p. 159.
12 Ibid., ɪ, pp. 129–33.
13 Ibid., ɪ, pp. 127–9, 159–60; Appleby, op. cit., p. 116.
14 *Fable*, ɪ, pp. 175–7.
15 Ibid., ɪ, p. 294.
16 Ibid., ɪ, pp. 260–6, 197–8, 247–8.
17 Ibid., ɪ, pp. 20–5, 370.
18 Ibid., ɪ, pp. 3, 20, 16.
19 Ibid., ɪ, pp. 258–60.
20 Ibid., ɪ, pp. 398–9 and pp. 185–97.
21 Ibid., ɪ, pp. 108–10, 133.
22 Ibid., ɪ, p. 411.

Chapter 4

1 Per Gedin, *Literature in the Market Place*, (tr.), London, 1977; P. Smithers, *The Life of Joseph Addison*, 2nd ed., Oxford, 1968; L.D. Bloom, *Joseph Addison's Sociable Animal*, Providence R.I., 1971.
2 *Spectator* No. 1. (There are so many editions and each essay being so short only the number and journal will be given.)
3 Ibid., No. 126.
4 According to Joyce Appleby, in the 1690s the balance of trade theory offered a better defence of social stability than that of the old Tudor policy, see her *Economic Thought and Ideology*, Princeton, 1978, pp. 269 ff.
5 *Spectator*, Nos. 106, 424, 269, 383. The 1711 Act for Building Fifty New Churches insisted on church steeples. (Reference from Andrew Saint.)
6 *Spectator*, Nos. 517, 112, 106, 113, 114, 517.
7 Ibid., Nos. 2, 107, 82, 114, 214; *Tatler*, 196.
8 *Spectator*, Nos. 2, 69.
9 Ibid., Nos. 200, 232, 346.
10 Ibid., No. 549; *Guardian*, No. 6.
11 *Guardian*, No. 9.
12 Ibid., No. 76; *Freethinker*, Nos. 22, 44, 47.
13 *Spectator*, No. 328.
14 L. Davidoff and C. Hall, *Family Fortunes*, London, 1987, p. 20; Martin J. Wiener, *English Culture and the Decline of the Industrial Spirit, 1850–1980*, Cambridge, 1981; W.D. Rubinstein, *Capitalism, Culture and Decline in Britain, 1750–1990*, London, 1993 disputes Wiener's thesis.

Chapter 5

1 Ernest C. Mossner, *The Life of David Hume*, London, 1954; David Hume, *Writings in Economics*, ed. and intro. Eugene Rotwein, London, 1955.
2 D. Hume, *A Treatise of Human Nature*, ed. L.A.

Selby-Bigge, Oxford, 1888 and 1978, pp. 69–179 (hereafter *Treatise*).

3 D. Hume, 'Of the Rise and Progress of the Arts and Sciences', *Essays and Treatises*, London, 1767, I, p. 123.

4 Mossner, op. cit., pp. 257 ff; N. Phillipson, 'Adam Smith as Civic Moralist' in I. Hont and M. Ignatieff, *Wealth and Virtue: the Shaping of Political Economy in The Scottish Enlightenment*, Cambridge, 1983, pp. 179–80, 188–90, 198–9.

5 D. Hume, 'Of Refinement in the Arts', *Essays and Treatises*, I, p. 302.

6 D. Hume, *Enquiries Concerning Human Understanding and Concerning the Principles of Morals*, ed. L.A. Selby-Bigge, Oxford, 1893 and 1975, pp. 80–94 and 298.

7 Ibid., pp. 250, 298 and Appendix II.

8 Hume, 'Of Commerce', *Essays and Treatises*, p. 291.

9 Hume, *Treatise*, II, vi, vii, viii; 'Of Refinement in the Arts', p. 300.

10 Hume, 'Of the Rise and Progress', p. 130.

11 Hume, *Treatise*, II, x, pp. 448–54.

12 Hume, 'Of the Rise and Progress', pp. 127–32.

13 Hume, 'Of Commerce', pp. 293–6.

14 Ibid., p. 293.

15 Hume, 'Of Refinement', p. 297; Phillipson, op. cit., p. 189. In 1752 the essay was entitled 'Of Luxury' and this was changed in 1760, J. Sekora, *Luxury: the Concept in Western Thought*, Baltimore, 1977, p. 110.

16 D. Hume, 'Of the Balance of Trade', *Essays and Treatises*, p. 357; 'On the Jealousy of Trade', p. 363; Hugo Grotius, *The Freedom of the Seas*, tr. R. v. D. Magoffin, ed. J.B. Scott, New York, 1916, p. 7.

17 Hume, 'On the Jealousy of Trade', pp. 361–2.

18 D. Hume, 'On the Standard of Taste', *Essays and Treatises*, pp. 265–7.

19 Hume, 'Of Commerce', pp. 283–4.

20 Hume, 'Of Refinement', pp. 305–6.

21 Ibid., p. 300.

Chapter 6

1 Adam Smith, *The Theory of Moral Sentiments*, ed. D.D. Raphael and A.L. Macfie, Oxford, 1976, pp. 14 and 180 n. 2. For 'The Adam Smith Problem' see W. Letwin's review of J.Z. Muller, *Adam Smith in His Time and Ours*, New York, 1992 in *Times Literary Supplement*, 26 Feb. 1993, p. 9; I. Hont and M. Ignatieff, 'Needs and Justice in *The Wealth of Nations*', in Hont and Ignatieff, *Wealth and Virtue*, Cambridge, 1983, p. 44.

2 Smith, *Theory of Moral Sentiments*, p. 187, and for references to Hume see, p. 179 n. 1.

3 Ibid., p. 180.

4 Ibid., pp. 181 ff; Hont and Ignatieff, op. cit.,

p. 10 argue that the Rousseau of the *Second Dijon Discourse* on 'The Origin of Ineqality' was Smith's imaginary interlocutor on this issue.

5 Adam Smith, *Lectures on Justice, Police, Revenue and Arms . . . Reported by a student in 1763*, ed. E. Canaan, Oxford, 1896 and reprinted New York, 1964, pp. 158–9.

6 A. Gerard, *Essay on Taste*, London, 1759 reprinted London, 1971, pp. 31 and 38. See Part IV Ch. 3 below for Hogarth.

7 Smith, *Lectures on Justice*, pp. 157–60.

8 Adam Smith, *The Wealth of Nations*, Everyman ed., 1964, I, p. 306 and II, p. 168.

9 Smith, *Lecture on Justice*, p. 160.

10 Smith, *Theory of Moral Sentiments*, p. 183.

11 Smith, *Lectures on Justice*, p. 160.

12 Smith, *Wealth of Nations*, I, p. 248.

13 Ibid., I, pp. 149–50.

14 D.D. Raphael, *Adam Smith*, Oxford, 1985, pp. 4 and 84.

15 Ibid., p. 2 and Smith, *Theory of Moral Sentiments*, pp. 233–4.

16 Smith, *Wealth of Nations*, I, p. 412.

17 *Theory of Moral Sentiments*, pp. 182–3; *Wealth of Nations*, II, p. 264, I, p. 312.

18 R.L. Heilbroner, 'The Paradox of Progress: Decline and Decay in *The Wealth of Nations*' in A.S. Skinner and T. Wilson (eds.) *Essays on Adam Smith*, Oxford, 1975, pp. 524–39, partic. p. 524.

19 *Wealth of Nations*, II, p. 266.

20 A.E. Wrigley, *People, Cities and Wealth, The Transformation of Traditional Society*, Oxford 1987 and review by Ernest Gellner, *Times Literary Supplement*, 11 Sept. 1987, pp. 980–2. Wrigley claims, and Gellner agrees with him, that Adam Smith argued for the existence of limits to the growth of income per head as a result of the iron law of wages, the finite supply of raw materials and diminishing returns on capital. But Smith in his treatment of wages and population growth (*Wealth of Nations*, I, pp. 60–75) gives six grounds for believing high wages to be bene-ficial, both to poor and rich and to the economy as a whole. More to the point Smith notes that as wealth increases so fertility drops (I, p. 70) so that population growth levels off without a fall in the growth of real wages. Smith also has answers (I, pp. 147, 151–2, 200–1, 83–5, 103, 116) to the other 'limitations' attributed to him by Wrigley. While Smith accepted that a stationary state *might* theor-etically occur he specifically argues that he did not believe it would do so as a result of the factors attributed to him by Wrigley but only, as in the case of China, as a result of bad 'laws and institutions' (I, p. 85) which could be repealed and reformed.

21 Smith, *Wealth of Nations*, I, pp. 15–17, pp. 133–4.

22 Ibid., I, pp. 4–9.

23 Ibid., I, pp. 65, 69, 225; see too *Considerations on the East India Trade*, London, 1701, McCulloch, *Early English Tracts on Commerce*, Cambridge, 1952, pp. 541 ff.

24 *Wealth of Nations*, I, p. 11.

25 Ibid., I, p. 304; Appleby, *Economic Thought and Ideology*, Princeton, 1978, pp. 272–3; T. Hutchison, *Before Adam Smith*, Oxford, 1988, pp. 366 ff. claims that only Turgot in Section 10 of his *Reflections on the Formation and the Distribution of Riches* anticipated him here.

26 *Wealth of Nations*, I, pp. 302, 4, 5.

27 Ibid., I, pp. 302, 5, 162–3; D. Hume, 'The Epicurean' and 'The Stoic', *Essays and Treatises*, London, 1767, I, pp. 155–74, both dating from 1742.

28 *Wealth of Nations*, I, p. 305.

29 *Theory of Moral Sentiments*, pp. 5–10.

30 *Wealth of Nations*, I, p. 306.

31 Ibid., II, p. 168.

32 Ibid., II, p. 324.

33 Ibid., I, p. 305; Hont and Ignatieff, op. cit., pp. 10–12.

34 *Theory of Moral Sentiments*, p. 62.

35 *Wealth of Nations*, I, pp. 294–5.

36 Ibid., I, p. 310.

37 Loc. cit. and p. 311.

38 See above Part II, Ch. 2 (iii), and note 83; T. Fuller, *The Worthies of England*, London, 1952, 'Design of the Ensuing Work', pp. 1 ff. See also *Tudor Economic Documents*, III, p. 7.

39 *Wealth of Nations*, I, p. 305.

40 This notion of the compatibility of wealth and morality, aesthetics, religion, is also to be found in Sir William Petty's writings, where after describing the economic and political benefits of increased productivity he asks: 'What then should we busie our selves about?' His answer is: 'In Ratiocinations upon the Works and Will of God.' See *The Economic Writings of Sir William Petty*, 2 vols, Cambridge, 1899, I, pp. 118–19.

41 L. Davidoff and C. Hall, *Family Fortunes*, London, 1987.

42 *Wealth of Nations*, I, pp. 360–1, 340.

43 Ibid., I, pp. 107–30, 117, 84–5.

44 Ibid., I, pp. 341–2, 352.

45 Ibid., I, pp. 363–4; J. Lubbock, 'Walter Pater's *Marius the Epicurean* – the Imaginary Portrait as Cultural History', *Journal of the Warburg & Courtauld Institutes*, XLVI, 1983, pp.174–5.

46 *Wealth of Nations*, I, p. 297.

47 Ibid., I, pp. 343–5.

48 Ibid., II, p. 63; I, p. 345.

49 Ibid., I, pp. 346–7.

50 Ibid., I, pp. 354–5.

51 Ibid., I, pp. 367–9.

52 R.H. Tawney, 'The Rise of the Gentry, 1558–1640', *Essays in Economic History*, ed. E.M. Carus-Wilson, London, 1954, pp. 173–214, partic. pp. 197–8, 185–6.

53 *Wealth of Nations*, p. 371. D.C. Coleman argues that Adam Smith had a poor opinion of businessmen, with their tendency to conspire to create monopolies, and looked to a largely landed legislature to create the conditions for economic growth. But Smith's attitudes towards both groups was more complicated and self-contradictory. See 'Adam Smith, businessmen and the mercantile system in England', *History of European Ideas*, IX, 1988, pp. 161–70.

Part Four

Preface

1 Bram Kempers, *Painting, Power and Patronage: the Rise of the Professional Artist in the Italian Renaissance*, London, 1992; M. Crinson and J. Lubbock, *Architecture-Art or Profession? Three Hundred Years of Architectural Education in Britain*, Manchester, 1994

Part Four

Chapter 1

1 G.R. Hibbard, 'The Country House Poem of the Seventeenth Century', *Journal of the Warburg and Courtauld Institutes*, XIX, 1956, pp. 159–74, partic. pp. 159–61; Raymond Williams, *The Country and the City*, London, 1973; Howard Erskine-Hill, *The Social Milieu of Alexander Pope*, London, 1975, pp. 283 ff; Virginia Kenny, *The Country House Ethos in English Literature, 1688–1750*, Brighton, 1984, p. 7.

2 *James I Poems*, ed. J. Craigie, 2 vols, Edinburgh, 1955–8, II, p. 178; *The Political Works of James I*, Cambridge Mass., 1918, p. 343; David Riggs, *Ben Jonson*, Cambridge Mass., 1989; Virginia Kenny, op. cit., p. 3; Isabel Rivers, *The Poetry of Conservatism*, Cambridge, 1973, pp. ix–xiii.

3 W.K. Jordan, *Philanthropy in England, 1480–1660*, London, p. 94.

4 B. Jonson, *The Complete Poetry*, Garden City N.Y., pp. 81 ff.

5 Ibid., pp. 77 ff.

6 *Political Works of James I*, p. 343.

7 *Le Prince d'Amour*, London, 1660.

8 Joseph Hall, 'Virgidemiarum', 1598, Book V, section 2, in *The English Poets*, ed. T.H. Ward, London, 1895, I, p. 543.

9 R. Greene, *A Quippe for an Upstart Courtier*, 1592, in *Works* (ed. Grosart), X, p. 272, quoted in L.C. Knights, *Drama and Society in the Age of Jonson*, London, 1935 and 1957, p. 115 n.

10 Robert Herrick, 'A Panegyrick to Sir Lewis Pemberton', *Hesperides*, 2 vols, London, n.d. (*c.* 1900), I, pp. 204–8.

11 Andrew Marvell, 'Upon Appleton House, to my Lord Fairfax', *Poems*, London, 1952, pp. 79–107.

12 John Hutchins, *History and Antiquities of the County of Dorset*, 3rd ed., IV, London, 1873, pp. 5–7.

13 A. Oswald, *Country Houses of Dorset*, London, 1935.

14 M. Howard, *The Early Tudor Country House: Architecture and Politics, 1490–1550*, London, 1987, pp. 195, 198, drawn to my attention by G. Roberts for whose review see *Art History*, II, 1988, pp. 463–6. For the Common Weal see above note 52 to Part II, Ch. 2.

15 L. Humphrey, *The Nobles, or of Nobilitye . . .*, London, 1563, quoted in Howard, op. cit., p. 198.

16 F. Heal, 'The Ideal of Hospitality in Early Modern England', *Past and Present*, 102, 1984, pp. 87–8.

17 J. Summerson, *Georgian London*, Harmondsworth, 1962, pp. 27–8 and *Architecture in Britain 1530–1850*, Harmondsworth, 1955, pp. 61–2.

18 J.F. Larkin and P.L. Hughes, *Stuart Royal Proclamations, King James I*, Oxford, 1973, p. 346.

19 Ibid., p. 400.

20 Ibid., p. 267.

21 Sir Henry Wotton, *The Elements of Architecture*, London, 1624, p. 82.

22 Ibid., pp. 66 and 71.

23 *Patriarcha and Other Political Works of Sir Robert Filmer*, ed. Peter Laslett, Oxford, 1949, p. 28: 'If . . . Patriarcha implies a great deal more power in the hands of Elizabethan fathers than we know . . . they actually possessed, it is because he saw in himself and his fellows the Roman paterfamilias.' Kevin Sharpe in his *Criticism and Compliment*, Cambridge, 1987, pp. 5–21, also challenges the identity of classicism with a cosmopolitan court and traditional social and artistic values with the country party. See also his *Personal Rule Charles I*, New Haven and London, 1992, pp. 212, 222–3.

24 Graham Parry, *The Golden Age Restor'd: the Culture of the Stuart Court, 1603–42*, Manchester, 1981, p. 16; C.H.V. Sutherland, *English Coin-age, 600–1900*, London, 1973, pp.159–63; J.G. Milne, C.H.V. Sutherland and J.D.A. Thompson, *Coin Collecting*, 1950, pp. 92 and 99, Plates XXV and XXXII. For the whole period see Joseph Rykwert, *The First Moderns*, Cambridge Mass., 1980.

25 Stuart Piggott, *Ruins in a Landscape*, Edinburgh, 1976, pp. 33–53; William Camden, *Britain*, London, 1610, 'The Author to the Reader', unnumbered p. 1; Parry, op. cit., p. 8, the first arch of James I's triumphal entry into London in March 1604, represented London and referred to the Brutus legend. It was devised by Ben Jonson.

26 Camden, op. cit., pp. 9–10, 34–88, 110–29; Piggott, op. cit., pp. 55–76.

27 Camden, op. cit., p. 133.

28 Ibid., pp. 138–43.

29 Ibid., pp. 114 and 154.

30 Ibid., pp. 63–5, 67, 74, 87–8; Tacitus, *On Britain and Germany*, Harmondsworth, 1951, p. 72.

31 Inigo Jones, *The Most Notable Antiquity of Great Britain, vulgarly called Stone-Heng, on Salisbury Plain, Restored*, London, 1785, p. 1 (hereafter *Stone-Heng*); John Bold, *John Webb: Architectural Theory and Practice in the 17th century*, Oxford, 1989, pp. 47–50.

32 *Stone-Heng*, pp. 3–10.

33 Ibid., p. 27.

34 Ibid., pp. 67–70.

35 Ibid., pp. 44–8; perhaps Sir William Petty's remark about building pyramids on Salisbury Plain or moving Stonehenge to Tower Hill as a means of creating employment derives from this book, published in 1655 – see J. Appleby, *Economic Thought and Ideology*, Princeton, 1978, p. 144.

36 *Stone-Heng*, p. 71.

37 Roy Strong, *Henry, Prince of Wales and England's Lost Renaissance*, London, 1986, pp. 88–106.

38 Summerson, 1955, p. 67.

39 *Stone-Heng*, p. 28.

40 D. Howarth, *Lord Arundel and his Circle*, New Haven and London, 1985, pp.18–19.

41 H.A. Mason, *Humanism and Poetry in the Early Tudor Period*, London, 1959, pp. 266 ff.

42 Howarth, op. cit., p. 149.

43 Ibid., p. 43.

44 Ibid., Ch. 2 and p. 116.

45 Larkin and Hughes, 1973, pp. 399–400.

46 N.G. Brett-James, *The Growth of Stuart London*, London, 1935, pp. 152 ff.

47 Howarth, op. cit., pp. 30, 37, 116.

48 Ibid., pp. 79–81.

49 L.B. Alberti, *Ten Books on Architecture*, tr. J. Leoni, ed. J. Rykwert, London, 1965, Book IX, iv, Book VI, ii. (New translation by J. Rykwert, N. Leach and R. Tavernor, Cambridge Mass., 1988.)

50 J. Evelyn, *Tyrranus*, London, 1661, reprinted and ed. J.L. Nevinson, Oxford, 1951, pp. 3–5, 8, 11–12, 17–18, 20, 23–9.

51 Beverly Lemire, *Fashion's Favourite, The Cotton Trade and the Consumer in Britain, 1660–1800*, Oxford, 1991, pp. 10–12.

52 *The Diary of John Evelyn*, ed. E.S. de Beer, London, 1959, 4 Oct. 1683, pp. 756–7, 15 July 1683, p. 750; P. Thornton, *Seventeenth Century Interior Decoration*, 1978, New Haven and London, 1978.

53 *Mundus Muliebris*, London, 1690 in *Miscellaneous Writings of John Evelyn*, ed. W. Upcott, London, 1825, pp. 700–1.

54 *Parentalia or Memoirs of the Family of Wrens*, London, 1750, p. 261.

55 Ibid., p. 351, 'Of Architecture Tract I'; J. Evelyn, *An Account of Architects and Architecture* in R. Fréart, *Parallel of the Antient Architecture with the Modern*, tr. J. Evelyn, London, 1723, pp. 10 and 16.

56 J. Evelyn, *Epistle Dedicatory to Fréart*, in *Parallel of the Antient Architecture*, pages unnumbered.

57 Evelyn, *An Account*, pp. 9–10.

58 John Bowle, *John Evelyn and his World*, London, 1981; *Miscellaneous Writings of John Evelyn*, op. cit., pp. 39–95, 141–67, 92–3, 150–1.

59 Ibid., pp. 156–7.

60 J. Evelyn, *Fumifugium*, London, 1661, re-printed 1961, pp. 13, 15, 19; Vitruvius, Book I, Ch. iv; P. Brimblecombe, *The Big Smoke: a history of air pollution in London*, London, 1987, pp. 40–90.

61 *Fumifugium*, pp. 29, 30, 32–3, 37–8.

62 Ibid., p. 39, and Brett-James, *op. cit.*, p. 296.

63 Evelyn, *Epistle Dedicatory to Freart*.

64 Ibid., pp. 4, 6–7; *Miscellaneous Writings of J.E.*, p. 317; N. Pevsner, *Academies of Art*, Cambridge, 1940, pp. 82–105; see also M. Crinson and J. Lubbock, *Architecture-Art or Profession? Three Hundred Years of Architectural Education in Britain*, Manchester, 1994, Ch. 1.

65 *Parentalia*, op. cit., pp. 261–2; B. Hanson, *Mind and Hand in Architecture*, unpub. Ph.D., University of Essex, 1987.

66 *The Diary of John Evelyn*, 13 March 1661.

67 Ibid., 20 Nov. 1661.

68 Keith Thomas, *Man and the Natural World*, London, 1983, p. 198; Bowle, op. cit., p. 113; d'Israeli reference from Andrew Saint.

69 E. Panofsky, 'The First page of Giorgio Vasari's "Libro"', *Meaning in the Visual Arts*, Garden City, New York, 1955, pp. 169–225.

Chapter 2

1 Daniel Defoe, *Roxana*, ed. J. Jack, Oxford, 1964, p. 213.

2 Julian Hoppit, 'The Luxury Debate in Britain, 1660–1790', Victoria and Albert Museum Workshop on Luxury, Oct. 1987.

3 *Tatler*, 162.

4 *Tatler*, 143 and 144; *Spectator*, 34.

5 *Tatler*, 124.

6 *Spectator*, 98.

7 *The Lover*, 10; Proverb VII *Spectator*, 410.

8 *Spectator*, 328.

9 Ibid., 73.

10 Loc. cit.

11 *Tatler*, 143 and 148.

12 *Spectator*, 69.

13 Ibid., 15 and 81; *Tatler*, 168.

14 *Spectator*, 37.

15 Ibid., 414 and 583.

16 Ibid., 415.

17 Ibid., 412 and 413.

18 Ibid., 418.

19 Ibid., 419.

20 Ibid., 414.

21 *The Guardian*, 49.

22 Ibid., 173.

23 Fourth Moral Essay in *The Poems of Alexander Pope*, Twickenham Edition, III, ii, *Epistles to Several Persons (Moral Essays)*, London, 1951; Appendix C, 'A Master Key to Popery', pp. 175–88, partic. p. 185.

Chapter 3

1 *Guardian*, 49.

2 *Spectator*, 412.

3 William Hogarth, *The Analysis of Beauty*, London, 1753, p. 13; also ed. J. Burke, Oxford, 1955, pp. xxiv–xxiv, 169–75.

4 British Library, Add. Mss. 27992, fol. 20v.

5 *A Supplement to Hogarth Illustrated*, ed. J. Ireland, London, 1798, pp. 112–13.

6 British Library, Eg. Ms. 3011 (Farn. b) fol. 18v.

7 Add. Mss. 27992, fol. 20v, 33–5; Eg. Ms. 3011, fol. 24r; *Analysis of Beauty*, 1753, pp. 70–1.

8 Ibid., pp. 13–4 and 69.

9 E. Burke, *A Philosophical Inquiry into the Origin of our Ideas of the Sublime and Beautiful*, London, 1801, p. 157.

10 D. Hume, *Enquiries Concerning Human Understanding and Concerning the Principles of Morals*, ed. L.A. Selby-Bigge, 3rd ed., Oxford, 1975, pp. 212–13.

11 *Analysis of Beauty*, pp. 70–1.

12 Ibid., pp. 14 and 71.

13 Ibid., p. 45.

14 Ibid., p. 20.

15 Ibid., pp. 18 and 21.

16 Ibid., pp. 16, 25–7.

17 Ibid., pp. 17, 23, 28, 38–9.

18 Ibid., pp. 34–6.

19 Ibid., pp. 41–2.

20 Ibid., p. 45.

21 British Library, Eg. Ms. 3013, fol. 72v.

22 William T. Whitley, *Artists and Their Friends in England, 1700–1799*, London, 1928, p. 156.

23 M. Girouard, 'English Art and the Rococo', *Country Life*, 20 and 27 Jan. and 3 Feb. 1966.

24 Simon Schama, *The Embarrassment of Riches*, London, 1987, pp. 350–66; Wilfrid Blunt, *Tulipomania*, Harmondsworth, 1950.

25 *Analysis of Beauty*, p. 18.

26 Ibid., p. 24.

27 Hume, *A Treatise of Human Nature*, pp. 448–54; Hume, *Writings on Economics*, pp. xxxvi–xliv.

28 *Analysis of Beauty*, pp. 24–5.

29 Ibid, pp. 125–7, 131; R. Porter, 'Making Faces: Physiognomy and Fashion in 18th

Century England', *Etudes Anglaises*, XXXVIII Année, 4, 1985, pp. 385–96.

30 *Analysis of Beauty*, pp. 141–3.

31 Ibid., pp. 146–7.

Part Five

Chapter 1

1 D.C. Coleman, 'Politics and Economics in the Age of Anne: the Case of the Anglo-French Trade Treaty of 1713' in *Trade, Government and Economy in Pre-Industrial England*, eds. D.C. Coleman and E.H. John, London, 1976, pp. 187–211; J. Appleby, *Economic Thought and Ideology*, 1978, pp. 249 ff; D.C. Coleman (ed.), *Revisions in Mercantilism*, London, 1969, Introduction by Coleman and A. V. Judges 'The Idea of a Mercantile State', pp. 35–60; Ralph Davis, 'The Rise of Protection in England, 1689–1786', *Econ. H.R.*, 2nd ser., xix, pp. 306–17. For the older view of Mercantilism: Friedrich List, *Das Nationale System der Politischen Okonomie*, 1841; W. Cunningham, *Growth of English Industry and Commerce*, Cambridge, 1882 and later editions; E.F. Heckscher, *Mercantilism* (1st ed. 1931) Eng. tr., London, 1935; C. Gide and C. Rist, *A History of Economic Doctrines*, tr., London, 1915. Most recently D.C. Coleman, 'Adam Smith', *History of European Ideas*, IX, 1988, pp. 164–5.

2 Adam Smith, *Wealth of Nations*, Everyman Edition, I, p. 397 and pp. 375–97.

3 D.C. Coleman, 'Protected English Textiles and Competitive Indian Imports, 1660–1800', lecture to the *Textile Society*, Victoria and Albert Museum, 10 Dec. 1983.

4 F. Warner, *The Silk Industry of the UK*, London, 1921; J.H. Clapham, 'The Spitalfields Acts, 1773–1824', *Economic Journal*, XXVI, 1916, pp. 459–71; M. White, *London Treasures*, London, n.d. (*c.* 1950), p. 30; G.R. Porter, *Treatise on the Origin, Progressive Improvement and Present State of the Silk Manufacture*, London, 1831, pp. 59 ff; P. Earle, *The Making of the English Middle Class, 1660–1730*, London, 1989, p. 261.

5 W. Cobbett, *Parliamentary History of England*, VIII, London, 1811, pp. 924–9; D. Defoe, *A Tour through the whole Island of Great Britain*, London, 1742, III, p. 67; A.E. Musson and E. Robinson, *Science and Technology in the Industrial Revolution*, Manchester, 1969.

6 Porter, pp. 74 ff.

7 C.E.C. Tattersall, *A History of British Carpets*, Rev'd. S. Reed, Leigh-on-Sea, 1966; Victoria County History, *Wiltshire*, VI, London, 1962, p. 26; IV, pp. 181–2.

8 F.S. MacKenna, *Chelsea Porcelain*, Leigh-on-Sea, 1951, p. 2; W. Chaffers, *Marks and Monograms*, London, 1912, pp. 937–8; A. Lane, *English Porcelain Figures of the Eighteenth Century*, London, 1961, p. 3; Laura Weatherill, *The Growth of the Pottery Industry in England, 1660–1815*, New York, 1986 is now the most thorough study, for Fawkener see p. 214.

9 Lane, op. cit., pp. 56 ff, pp. 4–5 quoting Horace Walpole, *The World*, 8 Feb. 1753.

10 L. Jewitt, *The Ceramic Art of Great Britain*, New York, 1883, pp. 112–14.

11 Lane, op. cit., pp. 64 ff, p. 25; McKenna, op. cit., pp. 21–2.

12 Coleman, 'Protected English Textiles'; G.W. Daniels, *The Early English Cotton Industry*, Manchester, 1920; R.S. Fitton and A.P. Wadsworth, *The Strutts and the Arkwrights 1758–1830, a Study of the Early Factory System*, Manchester, 1958; S.D. Chapman, *The Cotton Industry in the Industrial Revolution*, Basingstoke, 1987; Beverly Lemire, *Fashion's Favourite*, Oxford, 1991.

13 M. Crinson and J. Lubbock, *Architecture-Art or Profession? Three Hundred Years of Architectural Education in Britain*, Manchester, 1994, Chap. 1.

14 J.P. Malcolm, *Anecdotes of the Manners and Customs of London during the 18th Century*, London, 1808, pp. 62–8; D.G.C. Allan, *William Shipley, Founder of the Royal Society of Arts*, London, 1968, pp. 6–16; Daniel Defoe, *Essays upon Several Projects . . .*, London, 1702, pp. 8–30.

15 3rd Earl of Shaftesbury, 'A Letter Concerning the Art or Science of Design', written from Italy, . . . 6 March 1712, *Characteristicks*, London, 1749, III, pp. 269–79.

16 Samuel Humphreys, *Cannons, A Poem*, London, 1728, p.10; *The Apparition: A Poem*, 2nd ed., London, 1718; C.H. Collins Baker and M.I. Baker, *The Life of the First Duke of Chandos, Patron of the Liberal Arts*, Oxford, 1949, pp. 114 ff.

17 W. Coxe, *Life of Walpole*, 4 vols, London, 1816, IV, pp. 318 ff, 370–7; J.H. Plumb, *Sir Robert Walpole*, II, London, 1972, pp. 81–91; J.H. Plumb, 'The Walpoles: Father and Son', *Studies in Social History*, London, 1955, pp. 182–92.

18 *Lord Hervey and His Friends*, 1950, pp. 70–2; H. Array Tipping, 'Houghton Hall', *Country Life*, Jan. 1921, pp. 14–22, 40–8, 64–73, 68–107; Horace Walpole, *Aedes Walpolianae*, in *Works*, II, 1798, pp. 249, 252–62, 266.

19 *Aedes Walpolianae*, 2nd ed., London, 1752, pp. 113–14, 139–40.

20 Bernard de Mandeville, *A Letter to Dion*, London, 1732, Augustan Reprint Society, Los Angeles, 1953, pp. 36–7.

21 Plumb, *Sir Robert Walpole*, I, p. 367, II, pp. 236 and 9.

22 H. Colvin, *A Biographical Dictionary of British Architects, 1600–1840*, London, 1978.

23 Mark Girouard, 'English Art and the Rococo',

Country Life, 20, 27 Jan. and 3 Feb., 1966; R. Paulson, *Hogarth*, 2 vols, New Haven, 1971, I, p. 93, 369–71; *Anecdotes of William Hogarth Written by Himself*, London, 1833, pp. 24–38; J. Nichols and G. Stevens, *The Genuine Works of William Hogarth*, London, 1808, I, pp. 35, 38–42, 244–55; William T. Whitley, *Artists and Their Friends in England, 1700–1799*, London, 1928, pp. 7–27, 94, 157–70; E. Hardcastle, *Wine and Walnuts*, 2nd ed., London, 1824, pp. 108–17, 175–80; W. Hogarth, *Analysis of Beauty*, ed. J. Burke, Oxford, 1955, pp. xix–xxii; Walter Sandby, *The History of the Royal Academy of Arts*, 2 vols, London, 1862, I, pp.18–29.

24 8 George II Cap 13; *The Case of Designers, Engravers, Etchers etc. Stated in a Letter to a Member of Parliament*, c. 1734.

25 Joshua Kirby, *Dr Brook Taylor's Perspective*, London, 1754.

26 Terence de Vere White, *The Story of the Royal Dublin Society*, Tralee, 1955, pp. 2–44; Allen, *William Shipley*, pp. 47–8.

27 H. Hayward, *Thomas Johnson and English Rococo*, London, 1964, pp. 23–5; *Gentleman's Magazine*, Nov. 1751, p. 520, August 1752, p. 381, Nov. 1752, p. 534, April–Nov. 1753, pp. 199, 245, 389, 490, 537, Jan. 1754, p. 44, 1757, pp. 91, 183, 184, 238, 427; Sir Henry Trueman, *A History of the Royal Society of Arts*, London, 1913, p. 4.

28 Trueman, op. cit., pp. 11 ff; Allan, *William Shipley*, pp. 42–6.

29 *Gentleman's Magazine*, Feb. 1756.

30 E. Meteyard, *The Life of Josiah Wedgwood*, 2 vols, London, 1865–6; Neil McKendrick, 'Josiah Wedgwood: an Eighteenth Century Entrepreneur in Salesmanship and Marketing Techniques', E.M. Carus Wilson (ed.) *Essays in Economic History*, III, London, 1962, pp. 353–79; N. McKendrick, 'Wedgwood and the Commercialisation of the Potteries' in N. McKendrick, J. Brewer and J.H. Plumb, *The Birth of a Consumer Society*, London, 1982, pp. 100–45; for a critique of McKendrick see Laura Weatherill, 1986, pp. 209–14. R. Reilly, *Josiah Wedgwood*, Basingstoke, 1992, is a recent biography.

31 F. Hannah, 'To What Extent was Josiah Wedgwood a Mandevillean?', unpublished seminar paper, University of Essex.

32 A. Finer and G. Savage, *The Selected Letters of Josiah Wedgwood*, London, 1965, pp. 58–9.

33 Ibid., p. 34.

34 Ibid., pp. 100–1; McKendrick, 1982, p. 115.

35 Finer and Savage, op. cit., pp. 235–6.

36 Ibid., pp. 45–7.

37 Ibid., pp. 44, 55, 70, 98–9, 149, 74–5, 295, 307, 313, 317, 323.

38 Ibid., pp. 30 ff, 130 ff, 208, 220–1, 286, 300–1.

39 Ibid., pp. 49–50, 81–2; for 'fribling' see

Richard Garrick, 'The Fribbleriad', 1761, in *The Poetical Works*, 2 vols, London, 1785.

40 Finer and Savage, op. cit., pp. 115, 225, 236.

41 Ibid., p. 239.

42 D. Bindman, 'John Flaxman: Art and Commerce', *John Flaxman R.A.*, Exhib. Cat., Royal Academy, London, 1979, p. 25. 'Etruria' by Benjamin West may be associated with decorations for Queen's Lodge, Windsor.

43 Finer and Savage, op. cit., pp. 71, 324, 276.

44 Ibid., pp. 107–8, 122–3, 164.

Chapter 2

1 D. Hume, 'Of Refinement in the Arts', *Essays and Treatises*, London, 1767, I, p. 302.

2 B.R. Mitchell and P. Deane, *Abstract of British Historical Statistics*, Cambridge, 1962, p. 5.

3 Ibid., pp. 24–7; R. Finlay, *Population and Metropolis*, Cambridge, 1981, Table 3.1.

4 Mitchell and Deane, op. cit., pp. 239, 235; P. Deane and W.A. Cole, *British Economic Growth, 1686–1959*, 2nd ed., Cambridge, 1967, Table 52, pp. 212, 216, 223, 231–22; P. Deane, *The First Industrial Revolution*, Cambridge, 1965, pp. 85 and 93.

5 Flora Tristan, *The London Journal of Flora Tristan*, ed. J. Hawkes, London, 1982, pp. 8 and 17; B. Lemire, *Fashion's Favourite*, Oxford, 1991, p. 183.

6 Dorothy George, *London Life inthe XVIIIth Century*, London, 1930; W. Hutton, *History of Derby*, 1817 quoted in Humphrey Jennings, *Pandaemonium, 1660–1886*, London, 1985, pp. 47–8.

7 F. Engels, *The Condition of the Working Class in England*, Oxford, 1958, p. 55 (1st ed. 1845).

8 K. Marx, *Capital*, Everyman Ed., London, 1942, I, p. 164.

9 Tristan, op. cit., pp. 22, 69; Walter Allan (ed.) *Transatlantic Crossing*, London, 1971, p. 78; H. Taine, *Notes on England*, London, 1957, p. 221.

10 Tristan, op. cit., p. 65; Taine, op. cit., pp. 219, 225–6.

11 For this debate see P. Deane, *The First Industrial Revolution*, Cambridge, 1965, Ch. 15.

12 P. Lewis, 'William Lee's Stocking Frame', *Textile History*, XVII, 1986, pp. 129–48; S.D. Chapman, *The Cotton Industry in the Industrial Revolution*, Basingstoke, 1987, pp. 13–14.

13 E.P. Thompson, *The Making of the English Working Class*, Harmondsworth, 1968, pp. 379–91; 'Luddites in the Period, 1779–1830', *The Luddites*, ed. L.M. Munby, London, 1971, pp. 38–9.

14 Thompson, op. cit., p. 581.

15 Asa Briggs, *The Age of Improvement*, London, 1960, p. 209; Eric Hopkins, *A Social History of the English Working Classes*, London, 1979, p. 34.

16 Briggs, op. cit., Ch. 5; Alexander Somerville, *The Autobiography of a Working Man*, London, 1848, pp. 244–5.

17 Briggs, op. cit., p. 280; Hopkins, op. cit., pp. 85–97; Sir James Kay-Shuttleworth, 'The Moral and Physical Conditions of the Working Classes in Manchester in 1832' in *Four Periods of Public Education*, London, 1862, p. 24.

18 J.L. and B. Hammond, *Lord Shaftesbury*, Harmondsworth, 1939, Ch. 3, pp. 41 ff; Hopkins, op. cit., pp. 54–62.

19 S.J. Curtis, *History of Education in Great Britain*, London, 1967, pp. 223, 230–1; Kay-Shuttleworth, op. cit., pp. 7 and 201.

20 W.F. Moneypenny and G.E. Buckle, *The Life of Disraeli*, London, 1912, II, pp. 82–3; J.L. and B. Hammond, *The Bleak Age*, Harmondsworth, 1947, pp. 180–1; E. Halévy, *The Triumph of Reform, 1830–41*, London, 1961, pp. 311–28; Dorothy Thompson, *The Chartists*, Hounslow, 1984 is the standard work.

21 Thomas Carlyle, 'Essay on Chartism', *English and Critical Essays*, Everyman ed., pp. 165–238.

Chapter 3

1 N. Pevsner, *Pioneers of Modern Design*, Harmondsworth, 1960, p. 47; A.W.N. Pugin, *True Principles of Pointed Architecture*, London, 1853, pp. 1–2; D. Watkin, *Morality and Architecture*, Oxford, 1977; L. Durning, *The Architecture of Humanism: an historical and critical Analysis of Geoffrey Scott's Architectural Theory*, unpub. Ph.D., University of Essex, 1990. For Pugin in general P. Atterbury and Clive Wainwright (eds.), *Pugin, a Gothic Passion*, New Haven and London, 1994.

2 M. Girouard, *The Victorian Country House*, Oxford, 1971, pp. 60–4; Rachel Hasted, *Scarisbrick Hall: A Guide*, 1987.

3 C. Wainwright, *The Romantic Interior*, New Haven and London, 1989, p. 25; C.L. Eastlake, *A History of the Gothic Revival*, London, 1872, Ch. 5.

4 Girouard, op. cit., Pl. 69.

5 B. Ferrey, *Recollections of A.W.N. Pugin* (1st ed. 1861), ed. C. and J. Wainwright, London, 1978, p. 120.

6 Pugin, *The True Principles*, pp. 69–70; see Phoebe Stanton, 'The Sources of Pugin's *Contrasts*' in *Concerning Architecture* (ed. J. Summerson), London, 1968, pp. 120–39 for the influence of Stow and Dugdale.

7 W.F. Moneypenny and G.E. Buckle, *Life of Disraeli*, London, 1912, II, Ch. 6; R. Blake, *Disraeli*, London, 1969, p. 171; Ch. 8; S. Farmer, *Benjamin Disraeli and the European Bildungsroman*, unpub. Ph.D., King's College,

University of London, Chs. 2 and 3; R. Faber, *Young England*, London, 1987.

8 B. Disraeli, *Coningsby*, London, 1844, Bk. III, Ch. 4, Bk. IX, Ch. 1.

9 Pugin, *True Principles*, pp. 50–3.

10 Ibid., pp. 61, 63.

11 A.W.N. Pugin, *Contrasts*, London, 1836, pp. 30–1.

12 Pugin, *Contrasts*, 1841, p. 2; A.W.N. Pugin, *An Apology for The Revival of Christian Architecture in England*, London, 1843, p. 37; *True Principles*, p. 2.

13 Pugin, *Contrasts*, pp. 3–5.

14 Pugin, *True Principles*, pp. 22, 25.

15 Ibid., pp. 27, 29–30.

16 Ibid., p. 34.

17 Pugin, *Apology*, pp. 39–40.

18 Pugin, *Contrasts*, 1836, p. 35.

19 Ibid., pp. 32–3; *Apology*, p. 1.

20 G.R. Owst, *Literature and the Pulpit in Mediaeval England*, Oxford, 1961, pp. 363, 347.

21 Brian Hanson, *Mind and Hand in Architecture: Ideas of the Artisan in English Architecture from William Chambers to John Ruskin*, unpub. Ph.D., University of Essex, 1986, pp. 56, 71; R.W. Postgate, *The Builders History*, London, 1923, Chs. 4–6 and p. 90.

22 Hanson, op. cit., pp. 108–30; N. Pevsner, *Some Architectural Writers of the 19th Century*, Oxford, 1972, pp. 86–94; A. Bartholomew, *Specifications for Practical Architecture*, 2nd ed., London, 1846, Preface XVI and XXVI; Hanson, op. cit., pp. 123 ff. Crinson and Lubbock, *Architecture-Art or Profession?*, pp. 50–3 and Chap. 3.

23 M. Trappes-Lomax, *Pugin*, London, 1932, p. 259.

Chapter 4

1 Quentin Bell, *The Schools of Design*, London, 1963; C. Frayling, *The Royal College of Art*, London, 1987.

2 Henry Cole, *Fifty Years of Public Work*, 2 vols, London, 1884. Unfortunately there is as yet no modern biography of Cole; we await Mrs Bonithon's major work.

3 Bell, op. cit., Ch. 3; J. Steegman, *Consort of Taste*, London, 1950, pp. 138–42; Frayling, op. cit., p. 13; E. Bulwer Lytton, *England and the English*, 1833, pp. 389 ff. dismisses demands for state-financed design schools on the grounds that Wedgwood had succeeded without any.

4 B. Lemire, *Fashion's Favourite*, Oxford, 1991, pp. 35–9; W. de Archenholtz, *A Picture of England*, London, 1797, p. 92; John Gwynn, *An Essay on Design*, London, 1749, pp. 70–1; R. Altick, *The Shows of London*, Cambridge, Mass., 1974, p. 334.

5 *Report From the Select Committee of the House of*

Commons on Arts and Manufactures, London, 1835; T. Kusamitsu, 'British Industrialisation and Design before the Great Exhibition', *Textile History*, 12, 1981, pp. 77–95.

6 *Report*, 1835, pp. 52–4.

7 Ibid., pp. 119–26; S.D. Chapman, *The Cotton Industry in the Industrial Revolution*, Basingstoke, 1987, p. 60 and S.D. Chapman, 'Quality versus Quantity', *Northern History*, XXI, 1985, pp. 175–92; H. Clark, 'The Design . . . of Printed Calicoes', *Textile History*, XV, 1984, pp. 101–18.

8 *Report of a Special Committee of the Council of the Government School of Design presented to both Houses of Parliament*, London, 1847, p. 65; W. Paley, *Natural Theology* (1st pub. 1802), with notes by Lord Brougham and Sir Charles Bell, London, 1836.

9 *Journal of Design and Manufactures*, I, p. 148.

10 *Report*, 1847, pp. 63, 36.

11 *Journal of Design*, I, p. 182.

12 Ibid., III, pp. 97 ff.

13 Cole, op. cit., I, pp. 101–9, II, pp. 178–94; N. Pevsner, 'High Victorian Design' in *Studies in Art Architecture and Design*, II, 1968, pp. 38–95; Asa Briggs, *Victorian Things*, London, 1988, Ch. 2.

14 *Journal of Design*, VI, p. 136.

15 Ibid., I, pp. 9, 11, 33, 37, 144.

16 E.W. Bovill, *English Country Life, 1780–1850*, Oxford, 1962, p. 16 quotes an example reported in the *Chelmsford Gazette* for 12 Sept. 1823; see too Lemire, op. cit., pp. 96–9 for 18th-century instances.

17 *Journal of Design*, I, p. 155.

18 Ibid., II, p. 158; IV, p. 1.

19 Ibid., V, p. 138.

20 Ibid., V, p. 158; VI, p. 22.

21 W. Dyce, *Introduction to the Drawing-Book of the School of Design*, London, 1854, pp. ix ff. For Dyce's career as a painter, Marcia Pointon, *William Dyce, 1806–1864*, Oxford, 1979.

22 *Journal of Design*, I, pp. 92 ff; see also VI, pp. 1 ff, 131 ff.

23 Dyce, op. cit., pp. xii–iii.

24 C. Wainwright, 'Pugin och Arts & Crafts – Rorelsen', *British Design Konstindustri och Design, 1851–1987*, Cat. Exh. Nationalmuseum, Stockholm, 1987.

25 A. Wedgwood, *A.W.N. Pugin*, London, 1985, pp. 78, 81, 85; B. Hanson, *Mind and Hand in Architecture*, unpub. Ph.D., University of Essex, 1986, pp. 13–5; Bell, op. cit., pp. 267–9; Crinson and Lubbock, *Architecture-Art or Profession?*, pp. 50–6..

26 *Journal of Design*, III, p. 87.

27 Yvonne ffrench, *The Great Exhibition 1851*, London, 1950, p. 284; Wedgwood, op. cit., pp. 98–9.

28 ffrench, op. cit., pp. 234–5.

29 *The Illustrated Exhibitor*, London, 1851, p. 91.

30 H. Mayhew, *1851*, London, 1851, pp. 124, 131, 155, 158.

31 Royal Commission for the Exhibition of 1851, *Reports by the Juries*, London, 1852, pp. 718, 709.

32 *Journal of Design*, V, pp. 89–93; Owen Jones, *The Grammar of Ornament*, London, 1856, reprinted New York, 1972, pp. 5–8, 77 ff.

33 *Grammar of Ornament*, op. cit., pp. 44 ff.

34 Ibid., pp. 22 ff.

35 Ibid., pp. 66 ff.

36 The best available book on Dresser's designs is Widar Halen, *Christopher Dresser*, Oxford, 1990; see also Pamela Wolchover, *Christopher Dresser's Contribution to Victorian Conventionalism*, unpub. M.A., Univ. of Essex, 1980; *Art Journal*, 1857, pp. 53–4, 57, 87; 1858, p. 239.

37 Ibid., 1858, pp. 293, 333.

38 C. Dresser, *Principles of Decorative Design*, London, 1873, p. 59.

39 Ibid., pp. 64–5; for punishment chairs see the account of the beds and chairs in the Burne-Jones's household by his granddaughter, Angela Thirkell in *Three Houses*, Oxford, 1931.

40 Dresser, op. cit., pp. 140–1.

41 Ibid., p. 25.

42 Ibid., pp. 67 and 62.

Chapter 5

1 Q. Bell, *The Schools of Design*, London, 1963, pp. 232–3, 248–9; *Report of the Department of Science and Art*, London, 1853, p. 78.

2 *Survey of London*, London, 1975, XXXVIII, pp. 50–1; John Physick, *The Victoria and Albert Museum*, London, 1982, p. 16.

3 R. Altick, *The Shows of London*, Cambridge Mass., 1974, pp. 335, 499–502; I owe the reference to 'Gremlin Grange' to Andrew Saint.

4 Department of Science and Art, *Catalogue of the Museum of Ornamental Art*, 5th ed., London, 1853, pp. 13 ff.

5 *Household Words*, 4 Dec. 1852, pp. 265–70; abridged reprint, *Architectural Review*, Feb. 1979, pp. 119–20; Asa Briggs, *Victorian Things*, London, 1988, Ch. 6.

6 'Argus' (F.J. Prouting), *A Mild Remonstrance against the Taste Censorship at Marlborough House*, London, 1853, II, p. 33. I am indebted to Sir Ernst Gombrich for this reference. Wolchover, see n. 36, Pt V, Ch. 4, claims Prouting was a novelist. For a thorough and profound treatment of these controversies see E.H. Gombrich, *The Sense of Order, a study in the Psychology of Decorative Art*, Oxford, 1979.

7 Ibid., I, pp. 6–8, 23–7.

8 Ibid., II, pp. 11, 15–18, 25–6; II, pp. 9–11.

9 Ibid., III, pp. 23–4, 34.

10 *Letters of Charles Dickens*, London, 1880, I, pp. 255, 350, 371.

11 Ibid., I, pp. 349–50.

12 Charles Dickens, *Hard Times*, London, 1854, Ch. I.

Chapter 6

1 J. Ruskin, 'Unto this Last', I, *Cornhill Magazine*, II, Aug. 1860, p. 159.

2 *Journal of Design*, II, p. 72; Henry Cole, *Fifty Years of Public Life*, London, 1884, II, Misc. VII.

3 J. Ruskin, *Seven Lamps of Architecture*, London, 1849, pp. 43–4.

4 Asa Briggs, *The Age of Improvement*, London, 1960, p. 473.

5 *The Works of John Ruskin*, Library Edition, ed. E.T. Cook and A. Weddderburn, London, 1903–12, XVI, p. 427–8; Ibid, p. xviii for a chronology of Ruskin's contributions to the design reform debate between 1856 and 1860.

6 Ibid., p. xxix.

7 Ibid., p. lv; J. Ruskin, *Two Paths*, London, 1858, p. 10; J.J. Rouseau, 'A Discourse on the Arts and Sciences', (1750) *The Social Contract and Discourses*, Everyman Ed., London, 1968, pp. 132–3, 137; M. Hardman, *Ruskin and Bradford*, Manchester, 1986, Ch. 5.

8 *Two Paths*, p. 11.

9 Ibid., pp. 35–6, 50.

10 Ibid., pp. 94–5.

11 Ibid., pp. 96–100.

12 Ibid., pp. 110–14.

13 N. Pevsner, *Pioneers of Modern Design*, Harmondsworth, 1960, p. 19.

14 J. Ruskin, *Lectures on Architecture and Painting*, London, 1854, pp. 109–14.

15 John Ruskin, *Modern Painters*, II, London, 1846, p. 54.

16 Ruskin, *Lectures*, 1854, loc. cit.

17 Ruskin, *Seven Lamps*, pp. 29, 32.

18 F. Schiller, *On the Aesthetic Education of Man*, ed. and tr. E.M. Wilkinson and L.A. Willoughby, Oxford, 1967, p. 193; Ruskin, *Seven Lamps*, p. 30.

19 Peter Fuller, *Theoria*, London, 1988, Chs. 3–5.

20 Ruskin, *Seven Lamps*, pp. 32–3, 52; *Aratra Pentelici*, London, 1872, Library Edition, XX, pp. 216–7.

21 Ruskin, *Modern Painters*, II, p. 54.

22 *Seven Lamps*, p. 94; *Stones of Venice*, London, 1851, I, pp. 205, 14 ff; J. Ruskin, 'Traffic', 1864, *Library Edition*, XVIII, pp. 450–1.

23 *Seven Lamps*, pp. 95–7.

24 *Modern Painters*, II, p. 43.

25 *Seven Lamps*, pp. 145, 148.

26 *Stones of Venice*, 1853, II, p. 174; *Modern Painters*, II, p. 50.

27 Fuller, op. cit., p. 46, 32; Ruskin, *Library Edition*, III, p. 254; *Modern Painters*, II, pp. 37–

28 ...; Robert Brownell, *John Ruskin's The Seven Lamps of Architecture and The Stones of Venice*, unpublished Ph.D., University of Essex, 1988.

28 Ruskin derived this idea from E. L. Garbett, *Rudimentary Treatise on the Principles of Design in Architecture*, London, 1850, pp. 5–11 and 15.

29 John Ruskin, *The King of the Golden River*, 4th ed., London, 1859.

30 Adam Smith, *The Wealth of Nations*, Everyman edition, II, pp. 263–4.

31 *Seven Lamps*, pp. 156–7.

32 B. Hanson, *Mind and Hand in Architecture*, unpub. Ph.D. University of Essex, 1986; *The Stones of Venice*, II, London, 1853, p. 162.

33 Ibid., p. 165.

34 Ibid., p. 172.

35 Ruskin, 'Unto This Last', pp. 278, 284.

36 See John. Ruskin, *The Political Economy of Art* (1st ed. 1857), *Library Edition*, XVI, pp. 54–6 for Ruskin's analysis of the Lorenzetti fresco.

37 'Unto This Last', op. cit., p. 417.

38 J.S. Mill, *Principles of Political Economy*, London, 1848, Bk. I, Ch. iii, 3; see also T.R. Malthus, *Principles of Political Economy*, London, 1827, Ch. 1, sect. i.

39 'Unto This Last', pp. 543 ff.

40 Mill, *Principles*, Bk. III, Ch. i, 2.

41 'Unto This Last', pp. 547, 554.

42 John Ruskin, *A Joy For Ever*, Library Edition, XVI, pp. 45–6, (originally delivered as lectures in 1857 and published as *The Political Economy of Art*, London, 1857).

Part Six

Preface

1 Anthony Bertram, *Design*, Harmondsworth, 1932, p. 32.

Chapter 1

1 A. Bertram, *Design*, Harmondsworth, 1932, p. 16.

2 L. Münz and G. Künstler, *Adolf Loos, Pioneer of Modern Architecture* (Intro. N. Pevsner), London, 1966; Adolf Loos, *Spoken into the Void, Collected Essays, 1897–1900*, Cambridge Mass., 1982; J. Lubbock, 'Adolf Loos and the English Dandy', *Architectural Review*, CLXXIV, Aug. 1983, pp. 43–9.

3 Münz and Kunstler, op. cit., p. 226.

4 A. Loos (ed. F. Gluck), *Samtliche Schriften*, Vienna, 1962, p.162.

5 Herbert Spencer, *Ceremonial Institutions*, London, 1876, pp. 36–51, 180–8, 203–10.

6 Loos, *Spoken into the Void*, pp. 10–11.

7 Lubbock, 'Adolf Loos'.

8 Loos, *Spoken into the Void*, p. 56.

9 Ibid, 'The Plumbers', p. 49.

10 Ibid, 'Furniture for Sitting', p. 33, also p. 49; Loos, *Samtliche Schriften*, p. 75.

11 *Samtliche Schriften*, p. 21.

12 G.R. Searle, *Eugenics and Politics in Britain, 1900–14*, Leyden, 1976.

13 Münz and Kunstler, op. cit., pp. 230–1.

14 Ibid., p. 229.

15 Loos, *Spoken into the Void*, pp. 23–4.

16 Münz and Kunstler, op. cit., pp. 223–5.

17 *Samtliche Schriften*, 'Ornament und Erziehung', (1924), pp. 396–7. Tr. E.H. Gombrich.

18 'Interview with Raymond Erith', in J. Gowan (ed.), *A Continuing Experiment*, London, 1975, p. 71.

19 Le Corbusier, *The Decorative Art of Today*, tr. and intro. J. Dunnett, London, 1987, p. 134.

20 Ibid., pp. xiv, 186.

21 Le Corbusier, *Précisions* (1st pub. 1930), tr. E.S. Aujame, Cambridge Mass., 1991. There is no definitive biography of Le Corbusier, but see W. Curtis, *Le Corbusier: Ideas and Forms*, Oxford, 1986 for an excellent account of his early life and influences.

22 Le Corbusier, *The Decorative Art of Today*, pp. 87, 27, 62.

23 Ibid., pp. 15–22.

24 Ibid., pp. 85, 89, 189.

25 Ibid., pp. 92, 131–3, 135.

26 Ibid., pp. 83, 85, 134, 42.

27 Ibid., p. 79.

28 Ibid., p. 112; *Machine Art*, Museum of Modern Art, New York, 1934, intro. by Philip Johnson (unpaginated).

29 *The Decorative Art of Today*, p. 190.

30 Ibid., p. 188.

31 Ibid., pp. 6–7, 120, 124–5.

32 Ibid., pp. 194 ff, 126.

33 Ibid., pp. 72, 86, 117 ff.

34 Ibid., pp. 30–1.

35 Ibid., p. 96.

36 Ibid., pp. 192, 213.

37 Ibid., p. 98; Curtis, op. cit., pp. 16–18 on Corbusier's Huguenot antecedents. In many ways the targets of Le Corbusier's critique- jazz, café society, cosmopolitanism – were the same as those of the right-wing forerunners of Vichy and its National Revolution, for which see Robert Paxton, *Vichy France*, London, 1972, pp. 22–4.

38 J.-R., Bernard, *Le Systeme 'Untility'*, Paris, 1953, Preface.

39 Council for Art and Industry (Board of Trade), *The Working Class Home. Its Furnishing and Equipment*, London, 1937.

40 *Art and Industry, Report of the Gorell Committee*, London, 1932; J. Burnett, *A Social History of Housing, 1815–1985*, London, 1986, pp. 240–8; M.J. Daunton, *Councillors and Tenants: Local Authority Housing and English Cities, 1919–1939*, Leicester, 1984; M. Swenarton, *Homes for Heroes*, London, 1981.

41 Tom Johnston, 'Destroying the Slums', *The Listener*, 17 Dec. 1930, p. 1004; H. Marshall, 'The Huge Problem of the Glasgow Slums', *The Listener*, 15 Mar. 1933, p. 408; *The Working Class Home*, pp. 11–12.

42 *The Working Class Home*, pp. 9, 12–13.

43 N. Pevsner, *Enquiry into Industrial Art in England*, Cambridge, 1937, p. 17; J. Gloag, *Industrial Art Explained*, London, 1934, p. 42. Diane Meek suggested the idea of the captive market.

44 'Is the Englishman's Home his Castle?', *The Listener*, 15 Dec. 1937, p. 1305.

45 *The Working Class Home*, p. 42.

46 Ibid., pp. 22–3.

47 Ibid., pp. 28–30.

48 Mary McLeod, '"Architecture or Revolution": Taylorism, Technology and Social Change', *Art Journal*, Summer 1983, pp. 132–47, partic. pp. 138–40; Le Corbusier, *Towards a New Architecture*, tr. F. Etchells, London, 1965, pp. 114–5, 229–31; see Adrian Forty, *Objects of Desire: Design and Society, 1750–1980*, London, 1986, Chs. 7–9 for a full treatment of this subject.

49 E. Denby, 'Design in the Kitchen', in J. Gloag (ed.), *Design in Modern Life*, London, 1934, p. 62; E. Denby, *Europe Rehoused*, London, 1938, p. 266.

50 *The Working Class Home*, p. 29.

51 Asa Briggs, *Seebohm Rowntree*, London, 1961.

52 Ibid, pp. 33–4, 86–111; for New Earswick, M. Miller, *Raymond Unwin: Garden Cities and Town Planning*, Leicester, 1992, Ch. 3.

53 Seebohm Rowntree, *Poverty and Progress*, London, 1941, pp. 451–4.

54 Ibid., p. 476.

55 Ibid., p. 477.

56 Ibid., p. 329.

57 Ibid., pp. 353 ff, 370–3 ff, 469.

58 Ibid., pp. 357–9, 445, 447–8, 471.

59 Ibid., p. 47.

60 Ibid., pp. 471–2, 408, 447.

61 Ibid., p. 477.

62 T. Sharpe, *English Panorama*, London, 1938, p. 98; N. Pevsner, *Pioneers of the Modern Movement from William Morris to Walter Gropius*, London, 1936, p. 21.

63 Pevsner, *An Enquiry into Industrial Art*, p. 11; F.R. Leavis and D. Thompson, *Culture and En-vironment*, London, 1933, p. 100; Clement Greenberg, 'Avant-Garde and Kitsch', *Art and Culture*, Boston, 1961, pp. 3–21 (1st pub. in *Partisan Review*, 1939).

64 José Harris, *William Beveridge*, Oxford, 1977, Chs. 16 and 17; P. Addison, *The Road to 1945*, London, 1975, pp. 217–28 on the wary response to the 1942 Report by the War Cabinet.

65 J. Stevenson and C. Cook, *The Slump: Society and Politics during the Depression*, London, 1977, Chs. 1 and 2; S. Constantine, *Unemployment in Britain between the Wars*, London, 1980; H.W. Richardson, *Economic Recovery in Britain*,

1932–9, London, 1967 argues that personal consumption played a crucial role in the English recovery from the slump in the 1930s.

66 W. Beveridge, *Full Employment in a Free Society*, London, 1944, pp. 20–1.
67 Ibid., p. 24.
68 Ibid., pp. 25, 29–30, 166–70.
69 Ibid., pp. 30, 184–7.
70 Ibid., p. 185.
71 Ibid., p. 186.
72 ILEA, *Utility Furniture and Fashion, 1941–51*, Exhib. Cat., London, 1974; Bernard, op. cit.

Chapter 2

1 Le Corbusier, *Towards a New Architecture*, London, 1965, pp. 166–7.
2 F.R.S. Yorke, *The Modern House* (1st ed. London, 1934), 1948, p. 1. Hence the famous Parker-Morris standards for the internal spcifications of *public* housing became the *only* standard to govern the design of a house, but they were standards for the interior in the absence of all statutory controls on the exterior.
3 Le Corbusier, *Towards a New Architecture*, pp. 114–15.
4 Yorke, op. cit., pp. 30–6; A. Bertram, *Design*, Harmondsworth, 1932, pp. 71–3.
5 Yorke, op. cit., p. 55.
6 Le Corbusier, *L'Oeuvre, 1929–34* quoted in R. McGrath et al. *Glass in Architecture and Decoration*, London, 1937, p. 149.
7 Joint Report of Medical Research Council and Building Research Station, London, 1930; D. Albrecht, *Designing Dreams; Modern Architecture and the Movies*, London, 1987; Andrew Saint, *Towards a Social Architecture*, New Haven and London, 1987, p. 37; Yorke, op. cit., pp. 43–4; McGrath, op. cit., p. 454.
8 McGrath, op. cit., pp. 103, 155, 147, 146.
9 Ibid, pp. 156, 449, 165, 452–4; 'Sick Building Syndrome', *The Economist*, 13 May 1989, pp. 121–2.
10 Post-War Building Studies, No. 30, *The Lighting of Office Buildings*, London, 1952, pp. 17–18; reported by William Allen to author.
11 Jack Pritchard, *View from a Long Chair*, London, 1984; *Modern Architecture in England*, Museum of Modern Art, New York, 1937.
12 Pritchard, op. cit., p. 80.
13 Ibid., p. 79.
14 Ibid., p. 132.
15 Mass Observation, *People's Homes*, London, 1943, p. 219; N. Bullock, 'Plans for Post-War Housing in the UK: the Case for Mixed Development and the Flat', *Planning Perspectives*, II, 1987, pp. 71–98, explains why in spite of surveys like Mass Observation's showing people wanted cottage-type houses the requirements of high density to prevent further

sprawl led to the adoption of mixed development with flats to avoid the mistakes of the 1930s, rather than an ideological commitment to Corbusian Modernism. However, Corbusier himself was opposed to high buildings for residential purposes.

Chapter 3

1 Le Corbusier, *Précisions*, Cambridge Mass., 1991, p. 169.
2 Le Corbusier, *Towards a New Architecture*, London, 1965, pp. 267–8.
3 Ibid., pp. 55, 59–61.
4 Lionel Esher, *A Broken Wave*, London, 1981, p. 44; F.R.S. Yorke, *The Modern House in England*, London, 1937, pp. 14–18; T. Sharp, *English Panorama*, London, 1936, pp. 68, 75.
5 P. Abercrombie, *Town and Country Planning* (1st ed. 1933), London, 1943, p. 27.
6 Le Corbusier, *The City of Tomorrow*, London, 1929, (and later editions), pp. 5 and 302.
7 Ibid., pp. 96–100, 202–6, 277 ff.
8 J. Gloag, *Industrial Art Explained*, London, 1934, p. 177.
9 W.A. Robson, *The War and the Planning Outlook*, Rebuilding Britain Series, No. 4., London, 1941, p. 9; J.M. Richards and J. Summerson, *The Bombed Buildings of Britain*, Cheam, 1942, p. 2.
10 Le Corbusier, *Précisions*, pp. 182–8; *City of Tomorrow*, pp. 294–7.
11 D.H. Pinkney, *Napoleon III and the Rebuilding of Paris*, Princeton, 1958, pp. 174 ff.
12 Gareth Stedman Jones, *Outcast London*, Harmondsworth, 1976, Part II, pp. 159–235; Ebenezer Howard, *Garden Cities of To-Morrow*, London, 1946 (1st pub. as *Tomorrow* in 1898); C.B. Purdom, *The Building of Satellite Towns*, London, 1948; M.J. Elson, *Green Belts*, London, 1986, pp. 3–24; J.H. Forshaw and P. Abercrombie, *County of London Plan*, London, 1943; P. Abercrombie, *Greater London Plan 1944*, London, 1945; Donald L. Foley, *Controlling London's Growth: Planning the Great Wen, 1940–60*, Berkeley and Los Angeles, 1963; A. Saint, '"Spread the People": the LCC's Dispersal Policy 1889–1965' in A. Saint (ed.) *Politics and the People of London – the LCC. 1889–1965*, London, 1989, pp. 215–35; Robert Thorne, 'London Transport and the Meaning of London', *London Transport Symposium*, Royal College of Art, 20 Oct. 1993, unpub.
13 *The Royal Commission on the Distribution of the Industrial Population*, HMSO, London, 1940, pp. 3–5.
14 *Royal Commission*, 1940, pp. 43, 50, 204–7.
15 Ibid., p. 105.
16 Ibid., pp. 106–8.
17 Ibid., pp. 230–1.

18 *Public Health Act*, 1875, 38 and 39 Vict., Ch. 55, pp. 155–65; M. Swenarton, *Homes for Heroes*, London, 1981, pp. 12 ff; M. Miller, *Raymond Unwin*, Leicester, 1992, p. 127; Raymond Unwin, *Nothing Gained by Overcrowding*, London, 1912.

19 W. Ashworth, *The Genesis of Modern British Town Planning*, London, 1954, pp. 193–4; see also *Journal of the R.I.B.A.*, 3rd Ser., XVIII, p. 162 quoted in Ashworth, loc. cit.

20 Ashworth, op. cit., p. 195; Miller, op. cit., p. 149.

21 R. Unwin, *Town Planning in Practice*, London, 1909, pp. 3–4.

22 Ibid., pp. 388–9.

23 Ibid., pp. 386–7.

24 Ibid., p. 388.

25 Ibid., pp. 387–8.

26 *Hampstead Garden Suburb Act*, 6 Edw. 7, Ch. 192; *Town Planning In Practice*, pp. 383 ff; Mervyn Miller and A. Stuart Gray, *Hampstead Garden Suburb*, Chichester, 1992.

27 Walter L. Creese, *The Search for Environment*, Baltimore, 1966, p. 240; Ashworth, op. cit., p. 161; F. Jackson, *Sir Raymond Unwin*, London, 1985, p. 89; S. Muthesius, *The English Terraced House*, New Haven and London, 1982.

28 Ashworth, op. cit., p. 192; Sir G. Gibbon and R.W. Bell, *History of the London County Council, 1889–1939*, London, 1939, p. 530.

29 *Housing and Town and Country Planning, 1934–5*, HMSO, London, 1935, pp. 34–5, Sect. 16.

30 Ministry of Health, *Model Clauses for Use in the Preparation of Schemes*, HMSO, London, Feb. 1923 onwards, Part II.

31 Ministry of Health, *Model Bye-Laws IV. New Streets and Buildings*, HMSO, London, 1924 onwards.

32 John Punter, 'A History of Aesthetic Control: Part I, 1909–1953', *Town Planning Review*, 57(4), 1986, pp. 351–81.

33 10 and 11, Geo. 6, Ch. 51, Sect. 5(1).

34 Ibid., sect. 12, 14 [author's italics]; R.E. Megarry, *Lectures on the Town and Country Planning Act, 1947*, London, 1947, pp. 8–9.

35 10 and 11, Geo. 6. Ch. 51, Sect. 5(3), 26.

36 J.B. Cullingworth, Environmental Planning 1939–69, I, *Reconstruction and Land Use Planning*, HMSO, London, 1975, pp. 4, 5, 67; J.C.W. Reith, *Into the Wind*, London, 1949, p. 442; S.V. Ward, 'Planning Politics and Social Change 1939–1945', *Polytechnic of the South Bank Dept. of Town Planning*, London, 1975.

37 Gordon Cherry and L. Penny, *Holford*, London, 1986, pp. 89–112; J. Huxley, *T.V.A.*, Cheam, 1943, p. 137.

38 Cullingworth, op. cit., pp. 83, 96.

39 Ibid., p. 95.

40 D. Lilienthal, *T.V.A., Democracy on the March*, Harmondsworth, 1944, p. 170; *The Times*, 21 and 22 May 1935; *The Listener*, 20 Nov. 1935.

41 Cullingworth, op. cit., p. 97, minute of 15 Sept. 1943; on some of the legal issues involved in planning and on public inquiries see Lord Denning, 'The Planners and the Planned, Equity and the Citizen', *Journal of the Town Planning Institute*, XL, 1954, pp. 82–6.

Chapter 4

1 G. Stephenson, 'Town Planning', *Town Planning Review*, July 1949, pp. 125 ff.

2 *Architectural Review*, Mar. 1957, pp. 158–76.

3 M. Foot, *Aneurin Bevan*, II, London, 1973; A. Jackson, *The Politics of Architecture*, London, 1970.

4 Florence Nightingale, *Notes on Hospitals*, London, 1859, pp. 99–100; Adrian Forty, 'The Modern Hospital in England and France', in Anthony D. King (ed.) *Buildings and Society*, London, 1980, pp. 61–93.

5 Trystan Edwards, *Architect and Building News*, CXVII, 18 Feb. 1927, pp. 318–19; Manning Robertson, 'Bye-Laws and a Proposal', *Everyday Architecture*, London, 1924, pp. 109–19; M. Swenarton, Homes for Heraes, London, 1981, p. 20 and R. Unwin, *Cottage Plans and Common Sense*, London, 1902.

6 W. Gropius, 'Rationelle Bebaungsweise', *3rd Int. Congress for Modern Buildings Brussels, Nov. 1930*, Stuttgart, 1931 and *The New Architecture of the Bauhaus*, London, 1935, pp. 103–8; R. Isaacs, *Gropius*, Boston, 1991, pp. 159–60; G. Fehl, 'From the Berlin Building Block to the Frankfurt Terrace and Back', *Planning Perspectives*, II, 1987, pp. 194–210.

7 Much of this information is based upon personal discussions with Mr Allen himself in Jan. 1986 and April 1989.

8 W. Allen, 'Daylighting of Buildings in Urban Districts', paper delivered to RIBA, 23 Jan. 1943, pub. in *Journal of RIBA*, Feb. 1943, pp. 85–7.

9 T. Smith and E.D. Brown (National Physical Laboratory), *The Natural Lighting of Houses and Flats*, (DSIR), HMSO, London, 1944; *The Lighting of Office Buildings*, London, 1944, pp. 14, 10.

10 *Report on the Preliminary Draft Proposals for Post-War Reconstruction in the City of London*, London, 1944, p. 12; J. Summerson, 'Rebuilding the City', *The Listener*, 24 Aug. 1944, p. 6; Mason and Tiratsoo, n. 21 below, pp. 97–8 for the battle between City Architect and City Engineer on this issue in Coventry in 1940.

11 D.H. Crompton, 'The Daylight Code', *Town Planning Review*, XXV, 1955–6, pp. 155–64; G. Cherry and L. Penny, *Holford*, op. cit., pp. 116–17; J. Lubbock, 'Ugly Offices', *Catalyst*, II, No. 2, Summer 1986, pp. 19–27.

12 Allen, *Journal of RIBA*, Feb. 1943.

13 *The Redevelopment of Central Areas*, HMSO, London, 1947, pp. 80–4.

14 C.H. Holden and W.G. Holford, *The City of London: a Record of Destruction and Survival*, London, 1951, p. 276.

15 Oliver Marriott, *The Property Boom* (1st ed. 1967), London, 1989, pp. 74–9.

16 J. Gloag, *Industrial Art Explained*, London, 1934, p. 175.

17 N. Pevsner, *An Enquiry into Industrial Art* in England, Cambridge, 1937, pp. 199, 16.

18 J. Summerson, *Georgian London*, Harmondsworth, 1962, pp. 28, 292, 295.

19 The rise of the architectural profession and of the architect-planner is discussed in M. Crinson and J. Lubbock, *Architecture-Art or Profession?, Three Hundred Tears of Architectural Education in Britain*, Manchester, 1994, partic. Ch. 3.

20 J. Summerson, 'New Groundwork of Architecture', in J.R.M. Brunwell (ed.) *This Changing World*, London, 1944, pp. 182–93.

21 A. Saint, *Towards a Social Architcture*, New Haven and London, 1987, p. 243; G. Lewison and R. Billingham, *Coventry New Architecture*, Warwick, 1969; L. Esher, op. cit., pp. 49–51; T. Mason and N. Tiratsoo, 'People, Politics and Planning: the Reconstruction of Coventry's City Centre 1940–53', in J.M. Diefendorf, *Rebuilding Britain's Bombed Cities*,

Basingstoke, 1990, pp. 94–113. See also (sadly too late to influence my conclusions) J. Hasegawa, *Replanning the blitzed city centre, Bristol, Coventry and Southampton, 1941–1950*, Buckingham, 1992.

22 L. Esher, *A Broken Wave*, London, 1981, pp. 103 ff.; J.M. Richards, *Memoirs of an Unjust Fella*, London, 1980, p. 195.

23 Esher, op. cit., pp. 104, 177; Administrative County of London, *Development Plan 1951: Analysis*, London, 1951, pp. 245–97.

24 Esher, op. cit., pp. 228, 288–9; J.Q. Hughes, *Liverpool*, London, 1969, p. 122.

25 On the issue of responsibility for high flats see P. Dunleavy, *The Politics of Mass Housing in Britain*, Oxford, 1981; Miles Horsey, 'Multi-Storey Council Housing in Britain: Introduction and Spread', *Planning Perspectives*, III, 1988, pp. 167–96; 'RIBA Symposium on High Flats', *Journal of RIBA*, 1955, pp. 195–212, 251–61.

26 Saint, op. cit.

27 Crinson and Lubbock, op. cit., Ch. 3; A. Jackson, *The Politics of Architecture*, pp. 198–200.

28 Esher, op. cit., pp. 62–4; Arts Council and RIBA, *Architecture Today*, London, 1961; W. Allen, 'Policies for Architectural Education', *Arena*, 1966, p. 223.

INDEX

399

PHOTOGRAPHIC CREDITS

The author and publisher are grateful to the following people and institutions for their help in providing photographs:

Archivi Alinari, Florence 88
Ashmolean Museum, Oxford 89
The Bodleian Library, Oxford 21
Greater London Photograph Library, 37
The Guidhall Library and Art Gallery, London 3
The Houses of Parliament, London 74
The National Gallery, London 52
The National Monuments Record Centre, Swindon 4, 24, 25, 26, 32, 43
The National Portrait Gallery, London 34, 44, 46
The National Museums of Scotland, Edinburgh 22, 35
The Religious Society of Friends, London 49
The Scottish National Portrait Gallery, Edinburgh 36
Olive Smith (for E. Smith), Edinburgh 19, 20, 59, 61
The Victoria and Albert Museum, London 30, 31, 46, 82
The Trustees of the Wedgewood Museum, Barlaston, Staffs., 7, 63
The Dean and Chapter of Westminster, Westminster Abbey 45

Other photographs belong to the author.